The Peloponnesian War

The Peloponnesian War

Thucydides

The Complete Hobbes Translation

WITH NOTES AND
A NEW INTRODUCTION BY

David Grene

The University of Chicago Press

Chicago & London

The University of Chicago Press, Chicago 60637
The University of Chicago Press, Ltd., London

98 97 96 95 94 93 92 91 90   5 4 3 2

The text of Hobbes's translation, with David Grene's notes, is
reproduced from the University of Michigan edition, first published in
1959.

Maps on pages vi, 442, and 500 are reprinted from the Loeb Classical
Library edition of *The Peloponnesian War*, with permission from Harvard
University Press.

Library of Congress Cataloging in Publication Data

Thucydides.
  [History of the Peloponnesian War. English]
  The Peloponnesian war / Thucydides : the complete Hobbes
translation, with notes and new introduction by David Grene.
      p.   cm.
  The text of Hobbes's translation, with David Grene's notes,
is reproduced from the Univ. of Michigan edition, first published in
1959.
  1. Greece—History—Peloponnesian War, 431–404 B.C.
I. Hobbes, Thomas, 1588-1679.   II. Grene, David.
III. Title.
DF229.T5H6   1989   89-14647
938'.05—dc20   CIP
ISBN 0-226-80106-3

CONTENTS

CENTRAL GREECE
AND
PELOPONNESUS

English Miles

0   50   100

Stadia

0   100   200   300   400   500   600

INTRODUCTION

It is neither for its rarity, nor, at least chiefly, for its contribution to Hobbesian studies that I would like to offer this book to the general reader, but because it is, by long odds, the greatest translation of Thucydides in English—and Thucydides and his predecessor Herodotus are arguably the two greatest historians in our Western tradition.

It is true that most translations must be made anew in each generation. As the words of the translator's language live on and change, those he has employed in his translation express less adequately, or misleadingly, the ideas of the original. There are, however, a few translations which seem to have leaped across the boundaries of time and have rendered in a new language the movement and truth of the original in the same way in which the translated author created both. In such cases, the translation has a timelessness like that of the work which it translates. It is easy to describe such versions as attaining not only the meaning, but the spirit of the original. This is only a dead phrase, and if taken as a prescription will usually ensure a translation which is both a dishonest rendering and in itself worthless. But it *is* true to say of a great translation that, if one knows both original and translation, one is conscious of them as two independent creations. Of course the originality is not to be interpreted in exactly the same way. Thucydides is naturally original in a sense in which Hobbes's translation is not. But there is the same feeling of independence and freedom in both. As far as English renderings of classical works go, I would be inclined to include in this list only Chapman's Homer and Hobbes's Thucydides.

It is perhaps not accidental that such great translations possess an exceedingly individual idiom, rooted in the personality of the translator or the style of the period. Hobbes makes of Thucydides a seventeenth-century Englishman, but he does not falsify him in doing so. He renders Thucydides as the latter would have spoken had he lived in the time of the early Stuarts. There is here, seemingly, some strange affinity between a living man and one long dead that encourages his translator to forget his sense of history's pastness, and his own self-consciousness in the face of it, and by some direct confrontation of minds to reproduce the life of the dead man's words. For Hobbes, apart from his enormous gifts and his particular understanding of Thucydides, the task of rendering Thucydides was easier, in that the seventeenth century, especially the earlier part of it, was ready to reformulate the past in the words and sentiments of its own present. As a result the wings of Hobbes's stylistic greatness are not clipped by self-consciousness or by the desire to attain a historicity perhaps unattainable.

That this is, in some aspects, a very seventeenth-century work is made clear, rather amusingly, in Hobbes's dedication to the memory of the late Earl of Devonshire and to the attention of the present Earl. Hobbes ostensibly hesitates before deciding whether to offer the book to the young Earl as the composition of a man "who had the blood of kings in his veins," or for its own sake as history. He goes on, having made up his mind to give Thucydides as history, to say: "In history actions of honor and dishonor do appear, plainly and distinctly, which is which; but in the present age they are so disguised that few there be, and those very careful, that be not grossly deceived by them." This is part of the flattery and moral claptrap associated with such formal addresses to noble patrons. It has nothing to do with what Hobbes found important in Thucydides and what he makes us see.

It is, indeed, the seventeenth-century speech of Hobbes that has made the definitive grandeur of this translation. If it is possible to isolate its two most remarkable qualities, they are eloquence and directness, and it is easy in comparing Hobbes with a typical nineteenth-century version such as that of Crawley to see how feeble and complicated Thucydides has become in the latter. The following passage is from the Funeral Speech of Pericles; it has been so well known that one would think it impossible to give any phrase of it a twist that would save it from its hackneyed flavor for us. And see the freshness and power of Hobbes' version: "And for you that remain . . . you ought not to be less venturously minded against the enemy; not weighing the profit by oration only . . . but contemplating the power of the city in the actions of the same from day to day performed, and thereby becoming enamoured of it. And when this power of the city shall seem great to you, consider then, that the same was purchased by valiant men, and by men that knew their duty, and by men that were sensible to dishonour when they were in fight; and by such men, as though they failed of their attempt, yet would not be wanting to the city with their virtue, but made unto it a most honourable contribution. For having every one given his body to the commonwealth, they receive in place thereof an undecaying commendation and a most remarkable sepulchre; not wherein they are buried so much as wherein their glory is laid up, upon all occasions both of speech and action to be remembered for ever. For to famous men all the earth is a sepulchre: and their virtues shall be testified, not only by the inscription in stone at home, but by an unwritten record of the mind, which more than any monument will remain with every one for ever."

Now let us look at Crawley (Thuc II. 43): ". . . you must yourselves realize the power of Athens, and feed your eyes on her from day to day, till love of her fills your hearts; and then when all her greatness shall break upon you, you must reflect that it was by courage, sense of duty, and a keen feeling of honor in action that men were enabled to win all this and that no personal honor in an enterprise would make them consent to deprive their country of their valor, but they laid it at her feet as the most glorious contribution they could offer. For this offering of their lives, made in common by them all, each of them individually received that renown which never grows old, and, for a sepulchre, not so much that in which their bones have been deposited, but that noblest of shrines, wherein their glory is laid up to be eternally remembered on every occasion on which deed or story shall fall for its commemoration. For heroes have the whole earth for their tomb; and in lands far from their own, where the column with its epitaph declares it, there is enshrined in every breast a record unwritten with no tables to preserve it, except that of the heart."

Translations of great works from the past appear when there is a demand for them. This demand seems to spring from some sort of understanding between the two ages, however distant. We are very near to the world of fifth-century Greece, in spite of the tiny dimensions of their political organizations, of their armies or their wars. For, strangely enough, they faced something like our problem of the mass society—a society without respect for traditional standards of birth or conduct, with few restraints in religion or morality, with war past or war impending the most dynamic force in political life. Add to this a universal Greek rationalism—that is, the Greek's belief that he could solve the problems of the cosmos and the problems of political life by applying his brains to them, and that when one solution proved a failure another had to be sought instantly. This way of thinking and acting consequentially was a uniform force throughout the Greek world in the fifth century. We recognize it as a familiar attitude of our own in dealing with both national and international events. At the conference in Sparta at the beginning of the war the Corinthians blame the Spartans for their failure to understand this, the significant rational element of modernity. Throughout the history, both in Thucydides' own comments and in those of many speakers on both sides, it is emphasized that all situations are controlled by ultimate rational factors and that the shrewd man and the shrewd state think only in such terms. The Spartan soldier's supposed invincibility is a myth; it is only a question of how much pressure is applied to him. The Spartan's standard of simplicity, austerity and honesty is a myth; it is only a question of how much temptation he is subjected to. Let him take over the Athenian empire and he will prove, if anything, worse than his predecessors. The sea and land, says Pericles, are elements of power. The struggle between states and the lawless individuals within the same state are alike due to the permanent inner will to power inherent in all, according to Diodotus' speech in Book III. Laws must be framed with only this in mind: how effectively this impulse can be checked and held in balance.

This is the world of which Thucydides wrote, with an analysis of surpassing clarity and penetration. The paradoxical thing is that its very self is expressed for us by a man of the seventeenth century, a century which would appear even farther from the Greeks than our own.

This version of Thucydides and his introductory and dedicatory essays present an interesting contribution to the study of Hobbes himself. The translation was issued in 1628, when Hobbes was forty. He tells us that he had it by him for some time before he gave it to the press, so we are not exactly certain when it was written—presumably when he was between thirty and forty. It thus comes at a time well before he had committed any of his thoughts on political philosophy to paper. It is very probable that the intense study of the Greek historian which this translation necessitated had great influence on Hobbes's later political speculations. Certainly it is tempting to link much in the *Leviathan* with Thucydides' discussion of the nature of civil strife (*stasis*) in Book III, the arguments of Diodotus on the inevitable and invincible appetite of individual and state for power, and the indentification of the basic drives to empire as fear, honor, and gain.

It would clearly be wrong to make this comparison without allowing for the tremendous effect of the Civil War on Hobbes, coming as it did between the writing of the translation and the later works. But is is a suggestive combination—the history of Thucydides studied as deeply as the translation of it demanded, and contemporary historical events as factors in the formulation of Hobbes's political ideas. However, it seems doubtful that many of Hobbes's ideas in the *Leviathan* are *derived* from Thucydides. Hobbes is not asking the same questions about the nature of man and his dealings with social organization as are implicit in Thucydides. Nor is the scope of inquiry in both the same. Thucydides is a historian, pure and simple, though of course he confessedly writes, for the instruction of future ages, of the recurrence of these happenings in the same or somewhat similar forms. But he is the historian of *this* war, a war the uniqueness of which he emphasizes because of its size, and no one reading the first book of Thucydides can fail to notice his stress on maximization—bigness involves a difference in quality, not simply in quantity. He is the historian of this war. But he is also deeply concerned with the general nature of war, as his discussion of the effect of the war on the internal split in the states proves. Thucydides raises fundamental questions to which I believe he simply invites the reader, on the strength of his scrupulous record of the truth of these particular events, to come to his own conclusion. Is war the inevitable climax of the struggle for power, between the power's present possessor and his rival and successor, with exactly the same appetites, only casually and hypocritically veiling them in moral issues? Or is it a natural and terrifying moment of explosion desired by neither rival, in which all the elements of power become critically volatile? Thucydides with his quiet confidence in his exactness in recording actions and words still invites our notice of his ironic comment, which he attributes to Pericles, "Sometimes events come out as stupidly as mens' plans" (I.40). The

Peloponnesian war is Thucydides' chief concern—how far was Pericles' planning adequate, in fact; could it have worked successfully; is the defective nature of the politicians who take over the leadership in Athens another example of "chance," or something more inevitable? On the other hand, can one account for the incredible resilience of Athens even after the Sicilian defeat? The truth of the record, as far as anyone human can ensure it, leaves the historian still, I believe, with some lingering doubt as to whether "chance" would have it so. Cornford, in *Thucydides Mythohistoricus*, is wrong to see the history as controlled so entirely by the dimensions and impetus of Greek tragedy. But we should remember Thucydides' account of the violence of natural phenomena, of earthquakes and storms, as immense and unusual as the size of the war and the plague. Somewhere Thucydides responded hesitantly, but in depth, to the *possibility* of a structure of events such that chance is not as chancy as we think. The agony of the Athenians both fighting and watching in Sicily and the even greater agony at the fall of Athens, which Thucydides knew of but did not live to treat (and of which we can read in Xenophon's *Hellenica*) leave any reader uncertain whether Thucydides has a clear theory of history and politics which leads to *sure* conclusions—whether in fact he is not rather the inspired observer and true narrator of an objective and mysterious tragedy.

Hobbes is certainly, as he tells us, a twin born with fear, from his birth in 1588, the Armada year. The war of all against all is what man's social organizations must be geared to prevent. For Hobbes perhaps history and above all Thucydides' history is the illumination of his theme: Corcyra and *stasis* show the breakdown of civilized man and the return of the war of all against all. But Thucydides' history is for Hobbes an illustration, and the theory that it validated was his Hobbes's own; I doubt whether much of it came from Thucydides. Thucydides is for Hobbes the intensely careful and truthful and sympathetic observer of the actions of his time, of immense value for contemporary England and therefore translated by Hobbes. But Hobbes's particular purposefulness and certainty in the exposition of the geometry of politics is a world apart from the inspired account of the complexity and mysteriousness of the outcome in this, the greatest war, as Thucydides saw it, that had yet taken place. It is the edginess between the two, the historian and the philosopher who translated him, that gives this extraordinary version much of its special significance. The seventeenth-century Englishman sees his author so clearly and pushes him over to his own side completely. But he is also too good a scholar and too sensitive not to respond, in all the brilliance of his rendering, to the challenge of the history that did not *quite* illustrate Hobbes's conclusions.

My aim in this edition has been in the main to let the Hobbesian Thucydides speak for himself. The Molesworth edition has a large variety of notes, archeological or linguistic, but usually not worth reproducing. Hobbes himself includes very few notes which, I think, I have invariably left as he wrote them. My own comments fall roughly into three classes. There are those concerned with passages in which Hobbes has mistranslated the Greek; they are rare but they do occur. For instance, when Pericles, speaking of the Athenians as posterity will see them, says, "they have established eternal memorials of good and bad everywhere" (*Thuc.* II.64.3–4), it is impossible to leave Hobbes unannotated when he translates, "and set up eternal monuments on all sides both of the evil we have done to our enemies and the good we have done to our friends." Here Hobbes is clearly drawing on the discussion of justice in the first book of the *Republic*. The mistranslation comes from Hobbes's decision that Thucydides means something which he didn't say and which Hobbes says for him. There are also instances scattered through the history where Hobbes condenses a passage slightly, and through impatience or forgetfulness he omits a name on a list or a detail such as "and they camped on the shore." These are unimportant and I have only commented on them where it appeared to me that the reader's understanding of the passage was seriously diminished by the missing detail.

The second sort of note deals with passages where Hobbes's seventeenth-century English might mislead a modern reader unacquainted with the Greek. The well-known passage in the Funeral Speech means, "We are lovers of beauty but with cheapness." Hobbes renders, "For we also give ourselves to bravery, and yet with thrift." Many readers today would misunderstand this.

Lastly, I have written a few elementary notes on political and historical matters, for the benefit of those readers who know little of the life of the Greek states in the fifth century B.C.

Dᴀᴠɪᴅ Gʀᴇɴᴇ, 1989

The MAPP of Antient Greece Expressing especially the Places mentioned in THVCYDIDES. by THO: HOBBES

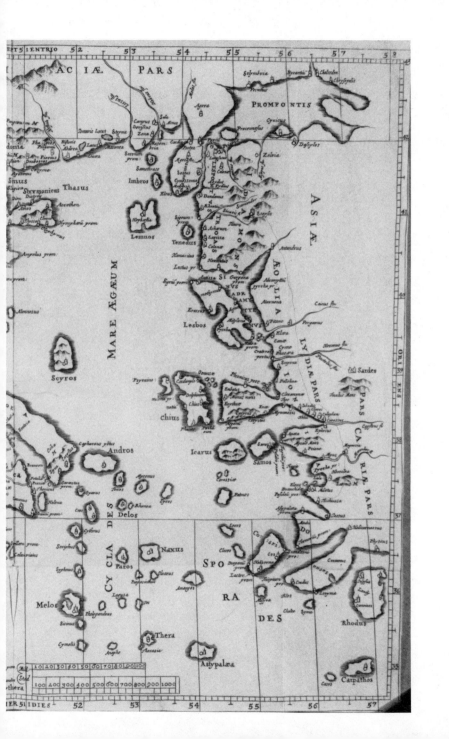

TO THE RIGHT HONOURABLE
SIR WILLIAM CAVENDISH
KNIGHT OF THE BATH, BARON OF HARDWICK, AND EARL OF DEVONSHIRE

Right Honourable, I take confidence from your Lordship's goodness in the very entrance of this Epistle, to profess, with simplicity and according to the faith I owe my master now in heaven, that it is not unto yourself, but to your Lordship's father that I dedicate this my labour, such as it is. For neither am I at liberty to make choice of one to whom I may present it as a voluntary oblation; being bound in duty to bring it in as an account to him, by whose indulgence I had both the time and ammunition to perform it. Nor if such obligation were removed, know I any to whom I ought to dedicate it rather. For by the experience of many years I had the honour to serve him, I know this: there was not any, who more really, and less for glory's sake favoured those that studied the liberal arts liberally, than my Lord your father did; nor in whose house a man should less need the university than in his. For his own study, it was bestowed, for the most part, in that kind of learning which best deserveth the pains and hours of great persons, history and civil knowledge: and directed not to the ostentation of his reading, but to the government of his life and the public good. For he read, so that the learning he took in by study, by judgment he digested, and converted into wisdom and ability to benefit his country: to which also he applied himself with zeal, but such as took no fire either from faction or ambition. And as he was a most able man, for soundness of advice and clear expression of himself, in matters of difficulty and consequence, both in public and private: so also was he one whom no man was able either to draw or justle out of the straight path of justice. Of which virtue, I know not whether he deserved more by his severity in imposing it (as he did to his last breath) on himself, or by his magnanimity in not exacting it to himself from others. No man better discerned of men: and therefore was he constant in his friendships, because he regarded not the *fortune* nor *adherence*, but the *men;* with whom also he conversed with an openness of heart that had no other guard than his own integrity and that NIL CONSCIRE. To his equals he carried himself equally, and to his inferiors familiarly; but maintaining his respect fully, and only with the native splendour of his worth. In sum, he was one in whom might plainly be perceived, that *honour* and *honesty* are but the same thing in the different degrees of persons. To him therefore, and to the memory of his worth, be consecrated this, though unworthy, offering.

And now, imitating in this *civil* worship the *religious* worship of the gentiles; who, when they dedicated any thing to their gods, brought and presented the same to their images: I bring and present this gift of mine, THE HISTORY OF THUCYDIDES, translated into English with much more diligence than elegance, to your Lordship; who are the image of your father, (for never was a man more exactly copied out than he in you), and who have in you the seeds of his virtues already springing up: humbly intreating your Lordship to esteem it amongst the goods that descend upon you, and in your due time to read it. I could recommend the author unto you, not impertinently, for that he had in his veins the blood of kings; but I choose rather to recommend him for his writings, as having in them profitable instruction for noblemen, and such as may come to have the managing of great and weighty actions. For I may confidently say, that notwithstanding the excellent both examples and precepts of heroic virtue you have at home, this book will confer not a little to your institution; especially when you come to the years to frame your life by your own observation. For in history, actions of *honour* and *dishonour* do appear plainly and distinctly, which are which; but in the present age they are so disguised, that few there be, and those very careful, that be not grossly mistaken in them. But this, I doubt not, is superfluously spoken by me to your Lordship. Therefore I end with this prayer: that it will please God to give you virtues suitable to the fair dwelling he hath prepared for them, and the happiness that such virtues lead unto both in and after this world.

Your Lordship's most humble servant,
THO: HOBBES

TO THE READERS

Though this translation have already past the censure of some, whose judgments I very much esteem: yet because there is something, I know not what, in the censure of a multitude, more terrible than any single judgment, how severe or exact soever, I have thought it discretion in all men, that have to do with so many, and to me, in my want of perfection, necessary, to bespeak your candour. Which that I may upon the better reason hope for, I am willing to acquaint you briefly, upon what grounds I undertook this work at first; and have since, by publishing it, put myself upon the hazard of your censure, with so small hope of glory as from a thing of this nature can be expected. For I know, that mere translations have in them this property: that they may much disgrace, if not well done; but if well, not much commend the doer.

It hath been noted by divers, that Homer in poesy, Aristotle in philosophy, Demosthenes in eloquence, and others of the ancients in other knowledge, do still maintain their primacy: none of them exceeded, some not approached, by any in these later ages. And in the number of these is justly ranked also our Thucydides; a workman no less perfect in his work, than any of the former; and in whom (I believe with many others) the faculty of writing history is at the highest. For the principal and proper work of history being to instruct and enable men, by the knowledge of actions past, to bear themselves prudently in the present and providently towards the future: there is not extant any other (merely human) that doth more naturally and fully perform it, than this of my author. It is true, that there be many excellent and profitable histories written since: and in some of them there be inserted very wise discourses, both of manners and policy. But being discourses inserted, and not of the contexture of the narration, they indeed commend the knowledge of the writer, but not the history itself: the nature whereof is

merely narrative. In others, there be subtle conjectures at the secret
aims and inward cogitations of such as fall under their pen; which
is also none of the least virtues in a history, where conjecture is
thoroughly grounded, not forced to serve the purpose of the writer
in adorning his style, or manifesting his subtlety in conjecturing.
But these conjectures cannot often be certain, unless withal so
evident, that the narration itself may be sufficient to suggest the
same also to the reader. But Thucydides is one, who, though he
never digress to read a lecture, moral or political, upon his own
text, nor enter into men's hearts further than the acts themselves
evidently guide him: is yet accounted the most politic historiographer that ever writ. The reason whereof I take to be this. He
filleth his narrations with that choice of matter, and ordereth them
with that judgment, and with such perspicuity and efficacy ex-
presseth himself, that, as Plutarch saith, he maketh his auditor a
spectator. For he setteth his reader in the assemblies of the people
and in the senate, at their debating; in the streets, at their seditions;
and in the field, at their battles. So that look how much a man of
understanding might have added to his experience, if he had then
lived a beholder of their proceedings, and familiar with the men
and business of the time: so much almost may he profit now, by
attentive reading of the same here written. He may from the narrations draw out lessons to himself, and of himself be able to trace
the drifts and counsels of the actors to their seat.

These virtues of my author did so take my affection, that they
begat in me a desire to communicate him further: which was the
first occasion that moved me to translate him. For it is an error we
easily fall into, to believe that whatsoever pleaseth us, will be in
like manner and degree acceptable to all: and to esteem of one
another's judgment, as we agree in the liking or dislike of the same
things. And in this error peradventure was I, when I thought, that
as many of the more judicious as I should communicate him to,
would affect him as much as I myself did. I considered also, that
he was exceedingly esteemed of the Italians and French in their
own tongues: notwithstanding that he be not very much beholden
for it to his interpreters. Of whom (to speak no more than becomes
a candidate of your good opinion in the same kind) I may say this:
that whereas the author himself so carrieth with him his own light
throughout, that the reader may continually see his way before
him, and by that which goeth before expect what is to follow; I

found it not so in them. The cause whereof, and their excuse, may be this: they followed the Latin of Laurentius Valla, which was not without some errors; and he a Greek copy not so correct as now is extant. Out of French he was done into English (for I need not dissemble to have seen him in English) in the time of King Edward the Sixth: but so, as by multiplication of error he became at length traduced, rather than translated into our language. Hereupon I resolved to take him immediately from the Greek, according to the edition of Æmilius Porta: not refusing or neglecting any version, comment, or other help I could come by. Knowing that when with diligence and leisure I should have done it, though some error might remain, yet they would be errors but of one descent; of which nevertheless I can discover none, and hope they be not many. After I had finished it, it lay long by me: and other reasons taking place, my desire to communicate it ceased.

For I saw that, for the greatest part, men came to the reading of history with an affection much like that of the people in Rome: who came to the spectacle of the gladiators with more delight to behold their blood, than their skill in fencing. For they be far more in number, that love to read of great armies, bloody battles, and many thousands slain at once, than that mind the art by which the affairs both of armies and cities be conducted to their ends. I observed likewise, that there were not many whose ears were well accustomed to the names of the places they shall meet with in this history; without the knowledge whereof it can neither patiently be read over, perfectly understood, nor easily remembered: especially being many, as here it falleth out. Because in that age almost every city both in Greece and Sicily, the two main scenes of this war, was a distinct commonwealth by itself, and a party in the quarrel.

Nevertheless I have thought since, that the former of these considerations ought not to be of any weight at all, to him that can content himself with the few and better sort of readers: who, as they only judge, so is their approbation only considerable. And for the difficulty arising from the ignorance of places, I thought it not so insuperable, but that with convenient pictures of the countries it might be removed. To which purpose, I saw there would be necessary especially two: a general map of Greece, and a general map of Sicily. The latter of these I found already extant, exactly done by Philip Cluverius; which I have caused to be cut, and you have it at the beginning of the sixth book. But for maps of Greece,

sufficient for this purpose, I could light on none. For neither are
the tables of Ptolomy, and descriptions of those that follow him,
accommodate to the time of Thucydides; and therefore few of the
places by him mentioned, therein described: nor are those that be,
agreeing always with the truth of history. Wherefore I was constrained to draw one as well as I could myself. Which to do, I was
to rely for the main figure of the country on the modern description
now in reputation: and in that, to set down those places especially
(as many as the volume was capable of) which occur in the reading
of this author, and to assign them that situation, which, by travel
in Strabo, Pausanias, Herodotus, and some other good authors, I
saw belonged unto them. And to shew you that I have not played
the mountebank in it, putting down exactly some few of the principal, and the rest at adventure, without care and without reason,
I have joined with the map an index, that pointeth to the authors
which will justify me where I differ from others. With these maps,
and those few brief notes in the margin upon such passages as I
thought most required them, I supposed the history might be read
with very much benefit by all men of good judgment and education,
(for whom also it was intended from the beginning by Thucydides),
and have therefore at length made my labour public, not without
hope to have it accepted. Which if I obtain, though no otherwise
than in virtue of the author's excellent matter, it is sufficient.

THE FIRST BOOK

1. Thucydides, an Athenian, wrote the war of the Peloponnesians and the Athenians as they warred against each other, beginning to write as soon as the war was on foot, with expectation it should prove a great one and most worthy the relation of all that had been before it; conjecturing so much both from this, that they flourished on both sides in all manner of provision, and also because he saw the rest of Greece siding with the one or the other faction, some then presently and some intending so to do. For this was certainly the greatest commotion that ever happened among the Grecians, reaching also to part of the barbarians and, as a man may say, to most nations. For the actions that preceded this and those again that are yet more ancient, though the truth of them through length of time cannot by any means clearly be discovered, yet for any argument that, looking into times far past, I have yet light on to persuade me, I

1

do not think they have been very great, either for matter of war or otherwise.

2. For it is evident that that which now is called Hellas was not of old constantly inhabited; but that at first there were often removals, everyone easily leaving the place of his abode to the violence always of some greater number. For whilst traffic was not, nor mutual intercourse, but with fear, neither by sea nor land, and every man so husbanded the ground as but barely to live upon it without any stock of riches and planted nothing (because it was uncertain when another should invade them and carry all away, especially not having the defence of walls), but made account to be masters, in any place, of such necessary sustenance as might serve them from day to day, they made little difficulty to change their habitations. And for this cause they were of no ability at all, either for greatness of cities or other provision. But the fattest soils were always the most subject to these changes of inhabitants, as that which is now called Thessalia, and Boeotia, and the greatest part of Peloponnesus, except Arcadia, and of the rest of Greece, whatsoever was most fertile. For the goodness of the land increasing the power of some particular men both caused seditions, whereby they were ruined at home, and withal made them more obnoxious to the insidiation of strangers.* From hence it is that Attica, from great antiquity for the sterility of the soil free from seditions, hath been inhabited ever by the same people. And it is none of the least evidences of what I have said that Greece, by reason of sundry transplantations, hath not in other parts received the like augmentation. For such as by war or sedition were driven out of other places, the most potent of them, as to a place of stability, retired themselves to Athens; where receiving the freedom of the city, they long since so increased the same in number of people, as, Attica being incapable of them itself, they sent out colonies into Ionia.

3. And to me the imbecility of ancient times is not a little demonstrated also by this [that followeth]. For before the Trojan war nothing appeareth to have been done by Greece in

---

* Perhaps a modern reader would understand this more easily if it were literally rendered from the Greek "and moreover they were plotted against by foreigners."

common; nor indeed was it, as I think, called all by that one name of Hellas; nor before the time of Hellen, the son of Deucalion, was there any such name at all. But Pelasgicum (which was the farthest extended) and the other parts, by regions, received their names from their own inhabitants. But Hellen and his sons being strong in Phthiotis and called in for their aid into other cities, these cities, because of their conversing with them, began more particularly to be called Hellenes; and yet could not that name of a long time after prevail upon them all. This is conjectured principally out of Homer. For though born long after the Trojan war, yet he gives them not anywhere that name in general, nor indeed to any but those that with Achilles came out of Phthiotis and were the first so called; but in his poems he mentioneth Danaans, Argives, and Achaeans. Nor doth he likewise use the word barbarians; because the Grecians, as it seemeth unto me, were not yet distinguished by one common name of Hellenes, oppositely answerable unto them. The Grecians then, neither as they had that name in particular by mutual intercourse, nor after, universally so termed, did ever before the Trojan war, for want of strength and correspondence, enter into any action with their forces joined. And to that expedition they came together by the means of navigation, which the most part of Greece had now received.*

4. For Minos was the most ancient of all that by report we know to have built a navy. And he made himself master of the now Grecian Sea, and both commanded the isles called Cyclades and also was the first that sent colonies into most of the same, expelling thence the Carians and constituting his own sons there for governors; and also freed the seas of pirates as much as he could, for the better coming in, as is likely, of his own revenue.

5. For the Grecians in old time, and such barbarians as in the continent lived near unto the sea or else inhabited the islands after once they began to cross over † one to another in ships, became thieves and went abroad under the conduct of their most puissant men, both to enrich themselves and to fetch

---

* The Greek says "But on that expedition they came together inasmuch as now they used the sea more."

† The Greek adds "began *more often* to cross over."

in maintenance for the weak, and falling upon towns unfortified and scatteringly inhabited,* rifled them and made this the best means of their living, being a matter at that time nowhere in disgrace but rather carrying with it something of glory. This is manifest by some that dwell on the continent, amongst whom, so it be performed nobly, it is still esteemed as an ornament. The same also is proved by some of the ancient poets, who introduce men questioning of such as sail by, on all coasts alike, whether they be thieves or not, as a thing neither scorned by such as were asked nor upbraided by those that were desirous to know. They also robbed one another within the mainland. And much of Greece useth that old custom, as the Locrians called *Ozolae*, the Acarnanians, and those of the continent in that quarter, unto this day. Moreover, the fashion of wearing iron remaineth yet with the people of that continent from their old trade of thieving.

6. For once they were wont throughout all Greece to go armed because their houses were unfenced and travelling was unsafe, and accustomed themselves, like the barbarians, to the ordinary wearing of their armour. And the nations of Greece that live so yet, do testify that the same manner of life was anciently universal to all the rest. Amongst whom the Athenians were the first that laid by their armour and growing civil, passed into a more tender kind of life. And such of the rich as were anything stepped into years laid away upon the same delicacy, not long after, the fashion of wearing linen coats and golden grasshoppers, which they were wont to bind up in the locks of their hair. From whence also the same fashion, by reason of their affinity, remained a long time in use amongst the ancient Ionians. But the moderate kind of garment, and conformable to the wearing of these times, was first taken up

---

* The phrase is hardly fitly rendered "scatteringly." It means literally "lived in by villages." This is the phrase Thucydides applies to Sparta (I, 10) when he wants to differentiate its appearance from that of Athens. It means that instead of all the inhabitants living in a large city, usually ringed by walls, they lived in a collection of villages, each just separated from the other physically, and often distinguished by being inhabited by different tribes or clans. When Thucydides says that this was the fashion of life in Greece in the old times, he means before the population had settled into large cities.

by the Lacedaemonians, amongst whom also, both in other things and especially in the culture of their bodies, the nobility observed the most equality with the commons. The same were also the first that when they were to contend in the Olympic games stripped themselves naked and anointed their bodies with ointment; whereas in ancient times the champions did also in the Olympic games use breeches, nor is it many years since this custom ceased. Also there are to this day amongst the barbarians, especially those of Asia, prizes propounded of fighting with fists and of wrestling, and the combatants about their privy parts wear breeches in the exercise. It may likewise by many other things be demonstrated that the old Greeks used the same form of life that is now in force amongst the barbarians of the present age.

7. As for cities, such as are of late foundation and since the increase of navigation, inasmuch as they have had since more plenty of riches, have been walled about and built upon the shore, and have taken up isthmi [that is to say, necks of land between sea and sea] both for merchandise and for the better strength against confiners. But the old cities, men having been in those times for the most part infested by thieves, are built farther up, as well in the islands as in the continent. For others also that dwelt on the seaside, though not seamen, yet they molested one another with robberies. And even to these times those people are planted up high in the country.

8. But these robberies were the exercise especially of the islanders, namely, the Carians and the Phoenicians. For by them were the greatest part of the islands inhabited, a testimony whereof is this. The Athenians when in this present war they hallowed the isle of Delos and had digged up the sepulchres of the dead found that more than half of them were Carians, known so to be both by the armour buried with them and also by their manner of burial at this day. And when Minos his navy was once afloat, navigators had the sea more free. For he expelled the malefactors out of the islands and in the most of them planted colonies of his own. By which means they who inhabited the sea-coasts, becoming more addicted to riches, grew more constant to their dwellings, of whom some, grown now rich, compassed their towns about with walls. For out of de-

sire of gain, the meaner sort underwent servitude with the mighty; and the mighty with their wealth brought the lesser cities into subjection. And so it came to pass that rising to power they proceeded afterward to the war against Troy.

9. And to me it seemeth that Agamemnon got together that fleet, not so much for that he had with him the suitors of Helen bound thereto by oath to Tindareus as for this, that he exceeded the rest in power. For they that by tradition of their ancestors know the most certainty of the acts of the Peloponnesians say that first Pelops, by the abundance of his wealth which he brought with him out of Asia to men in want, obtained such power amongst them, as, though he were a stranger, yet the country was called after his name; and that this power was also increased by his posterity. For Eurystheus being slain in Attica by the Heracleidae, Atreus, that was his uncle by the mother, and was then abiding with him as an exiled person for fear of his father for the death of Chrysippus, and to whom Eurystheus, when he undertook the expedition, had committed Mycenae and the government thereof, for that he was his kinsman; when as Eurystheus came not back (the Mycenians being willing to it for fear of the Heracleidae, and because he was an able man and made much of the common people), obtained the kingdom of Mycenae, and of whatsoever else was under Eurystheus, for himself; and the power of the Pelopides became greater than that of the Perseides. To which greatness Agamemnon succeeding, and also far excelling the rest in shipping, took that war in hand, as I conceive it, and assembled the said forces, not so much upon favour as by fear. For it is clear that he himself both conferred most ships to that action and that some also he lent to the Arcadians. And this is likewise declared by Homer (if any think his testimony sufficient), who, at the delivery of the scepter unto him, calleth him, "of many isles and of all Argos king." Now he could not, living in the continent, have been lord of the islands, other than such as were adjacent which cannot be many, unless he had also had a navy. And by this expedition we are to estimate what were those of the ages before it.

10. Now seeing Mycenae was but a small city, or if any other of that age seem but of light regard, let not any man

for that cause, on so weak an argument, think that fleet to have been less than the poets have said and fame reported it to be. For if the city of Lacedaemon were now desolate and nothing of it left but the temples and floors of the buildings, I think it would breed much unbelief in posterity long hence of their power in comparison of the fame. For although of five parts of Peloponnesus it possess two and hath the leading of the rest and also of many confederates without, yet the city being not close built and the temples and other edifices not costly, and because it is but scatteringly inhabited * after the ancient manner of Greece, their power would seem inferior to the report. Again, the same things happening to Athens, one would conjecture by the sight of their city that their power were double to what it is. We ought not therefore to be incredulous [concerning the forces that went to Troy] nor have in regard so much the external show of a city as the power; but we are to think that that expedition was indeed greater than those that went before it but yet inferior to those of the present age, if in this also we may credit the poetry of Homer, who being a poet was like to set it forth to the utmost. And yet even thus it cometh short. For he maketh it to consist of twelve hundred vessels, those that were of Boeotians carrying one hundred and twenty men apiece, and those which came with Philoctetes fifty: setting forth, as I suppose, both the greatest sort and the least; and therefore of the bigness of any of the rest he maketh in his catalogue no mention at all, but declareth that they who were in the vessels of Philoctetes served both as mariners and soldiers; for he writes that they who were at the oar were all of them archers. And for such as wrought not, it is not likely that many went along except kings and such as were in chief authority; especially being to pass the sea with munition of war, and in bottoms without decks, built after the old and piratical fashion. So then, if by the greatest and least one estimate the mean of their shipping, it will appear that the whole number of men considered as sent jointly from all Greece were not very many.

11. And the cause hereof was not so much want of men as

* See note on page 4.

of wealth. For, for want of victual they carried the lesser army, and no greater than they hoped might both follow the war and also maintain itself. When upon their arrival they had gotten the upper hand in fight (which is manifest, for else they could not have fortified their camp), it appears that from that time forward they employed not there their whole power, but that for want of victual they betook themselves, part of them to the tillage of Chersonesus and part to fetch in booties; whereby divided, the Trojans the more easily made that ten years resistance, as being ever a match for so many as remained at the siege. Whereas, if they had gone furnished with store of provision and with all their forces, eased of booty-haling and tillage, since they were masters of the field, they had also easily taken the city. But they strove not with their whole power but only with such a portion of their army as at the several occasions chanced to be present; when as, if they had pressed the siege, they had won the place both in less time and with less labour. But through want of money not only they were weak matters, all that preceded this enterprise, but also this, which is of greater name than any before it, appeareth to be in fact beneath the fame and report which, by means of the poets, now goeth of it.

12. For also after the Trojan war the Grecians continued still their shiftings and transplantations; insomuch as never resting, they improved not their power. For the late return of the Greeks from Ilium caused not a little innovation; and in most of the cities there arose seditions, and those which were driven out built cities for themselves in other places. For those that are now called Boeotians in the sixtieth year after the taking of Troy expelled Arne by the Thessalians, seated themselves in that country which, now Boeotia, was then called Cadmeis. (But there was in the same country a certain portion of that nation before, of whom also were they that went to the warfare of Troy.) And in the eightieth year the Dorians together with the Heracleidae seized on Peloponnesus. And with much ado, after long time, Greece had constant rest and, shifting their seats no longer, at length sent colonies abroad. And the Athenians planted Ionia and most of the islands, and the Peloponnesians most of Italy and Sicily and also certain parts of the

rest of Greece. But these colonies were all planted after the Trojan war.

13. But when the power of Greece was now improved, and the desire of money withal, their revenues being enlarged, in most of the cities there were erected tyrannies (for before that time kingdoms with honours limited were hereditary); and the Grecians built navies and became more seriously addicted to the affairs of the sea. The Corinthians are said to have been the first that changed the form of shipping into the nearest to that which is now in use, and at Corinth are reported to have been made the first galleys of all Greece. Now it is well known that Aminocles, the shipwright of Corinth, built four ships at Samos; and from the time that Aminocles went to Samos until the end of this present war are at the most but three hundred years. And the most ancient naval battle that we know of was fought between the Corinthians and the Corcyraeans, and from that battle to the same time are but two hundred and sixty years. For Corinth, seated on an isthmus, had been always a place of traffic (because the Grecians of old, from within and without Peloponnesus, trading by land more than by sea, had no other intercourse one to another but through the Corinthians' territory), and was also wealthy in money, as appears by the poets, who have surnamed this town the rich. And after the Grecians had commerce also by sea, then likewise having furnished themselves with a navy, they scoured the sea of pirates and, affording traffic both by sea and land, mightily increased their city in revenue of money. After this, the Ionians, in the times of Cyrus, first king of the Persians, and of his son Cambyses, got together a great navy, and making war on Cyrus, obtained for a time the dominion of that part of the sea that lieth on their own coast. Also Polycrates, who in the time of Cambyses tyrannised in Samos, had a strong navy wherewith he subdued divers of the islands; and amongst the rest having won Rhenea, he consecrated the same to Apollo of Delos. The Phocaeans likewise, when they were building the city of Marseilles, overcame the Carthaginians in a fight at sea.

14. These were the greatest navies extant. And yet even these, though many ages after the time of Troy, consisted, as

it seems, but of a few galleys, and were made up with vessels of fifty oars and with long boats, as well as those of former times. And it was but a little before the Medan war and death of Darius, successor of Cambyses in the kingdom of Persia, that the tyrants of Sicily and the Corcyraeans had of galleys any number. For these last were the only navies worth speaking of in all Greece before the invasion of the Medes. And the people of Aegina and the Athenians had but small ones, and the most of them consisting but of fifty oars apiece; and that so lately as but from the time that the Athenians making war on Aegina, and withal expecting the coming of the barbarian, at the persuasion of Themistocles built those ships which they used in that war. And these also not all had decks.

15. Such were then the navies of the Greeks, both ancient and modern. Nevertheless, such as applied themselves to naval business gained by them no small power, both in revenue of money and in dominion over other people. For with their navies (especially those men that had not sufficient land, where they inhabited, to maintain themselves) they subdued the islands. But as for war by land, such as any state might acquire power by, there was none at all; and such as were, were only between borderer and borderer. For the Grecians had never yet gone out with any army to conquer any nation far from home, because the lesser cities neither brought in their forces to the great ones as subjects nor concurred as equals in any common enterprise; but such as were neighbours warred against each other hand to hand. For the war of old between the Chalcideans and the Eretrians was it wherein the rest of Greece was most divided and in league with either party.

16. As others by other means were kept back from growing great, so also the Ionians by this: that the Persian affairs prospering, Cyrus and the Persian kingdom after the defeat of Croesus made war upon all that lieth from the river Halys to the seaside and so subdued all the cities which they possessed in the continent; and Darius afterward, when he had overcome the Phoenician fleet, did the like unto them in the islands.

17. And as for the tyrants that were in the Grecian cities, who forecasted only for themselves how with as much safety as was possible to look to their own persons and their own

families, they resided for the most part in the cities and did no action worthy of memory, unless it were against their neighbours. For as for the tyrants of Sicily, they were already arrived at greater power. Thus was Greece for a long time hindered, that neither jointly it could do anything remarkable nor the cities singly be adventurous.

18. But after that the tyrants, both of Athens and of the rest of Greece where tyrannies were, were the most and last of them, excepting those of Sicily, put down by the Lacedaemonians (for Lacedaemon, after that it was built by the Dorians that inhabited the same, though it hath been longer troubled with seditions than any other city we know, yet hath it had for the longest time good laws, and been also always free from tyrants; for it is unto the end of this war four hundred years and something more that the Lacedaemonians have used one and the same government, and thereby being of power themselves, they also ordered the affairs in the other cities); I say, after the dissolution of tyrannies in Greece, it was not long before the battle was fought by the Medes against the Athenians in the fields of Marathon. And in the tenth year again after that came the barbarian with the great fleet into Greece to subdue it. And Greece being now in great danger, the leading of the Grecians that leagued in that war was given to the Lacedaemonians, as to the most potent state. And the Athenians, who had purposed so much before and already stowed their necessaries, at the coming in of the Medes went a ship-board and became seamen. When they had jointly beaten back the barbarian, then did the Grecians, both such as were revolted from the king and such as had in common made war upon him, not long after divide themselves into leagues, one part with the Athenians and the other with the Lacedaemonians, these two cities appearing to be the mightiest, for this had the power by land and the other by sea. But this confederation lasted but awhile; for afterwards the Lacedaemonians and the Athenians, being at variance, warred each on other together with their several confederates. And the rest of Greece, where any discord chanced to arise, had recourse presently to one of these. In so much that from the war of the Medes to this present war being continually [exercised] sometimes in peace some-

times in war, either one against the other or against revolted
confederates, they arrived at this war, both well furnished with
military provisions and also expert because their practice was
with danger.

19. The Lacedaemonians governed not their confederates so
as to make them tributaries but only drew them by fair means
to embrace the oligarchy convenient to their own policy.* But
the Athenians, having with time taken into their hands the
galleys of all those that stood out (except the Chians and
Lesbians), reigned over them and ordained every of them to
pay a certain tribute of money. By which means their own
particular provision was greater in the beginning of this war
than when, in their flourishing time the league between them
and the rest of Greece remaining whole, it was at the most.

20. Such then I find to have been the state of things past,
hard to be believed, though one produce proof for every particular thereof. For men receive the report of things, though
of their own country if done before their own time, all alike,
from one as from another, without examination.

For the vulgar sort of Athenians think that Hipparchus was
the tyrant, and slain by Harmodius and Aristogeiton, and know
not that Hippias had the government, as being the eldest son
of Pisistratus, and that Hipparchus and Thessalus were his
brethren; and that Harmodius and Aristogeiton, suspecting
that some of their accomplices had that day and at that instant
discovered unto Hippias somewhat of their treason, did forbear
Hippias as a man forewarned; and desirous to effect somewhat,
though with danger, before they should be apprehended, lighting on Hipparchus slew him near the temple called Leocorium,
whilst he was setting forth the Panathenaical show. And likewise divers other things now extant, and which time hath not
yet involved in oblivion, have been conceived amiss by other
Grecians, as that the kings of Lacedaemon, in giving their
suffrages, had not single but double votes, and that Pitanate
was a band of soldiers so called there, whereas there was never

* Hobbes' rendering hardly seems accurate. The literal meaning of
the Greek gives no ground for the "fair means" of the translation. It
is "taking heedful care only that their constitutions should be oligarchic
to suit themselves" (i.e., the Lacedaemonians).

any such. So impatient of labour are the most men in search of truth, and embrace soonest the things that are next to hand.

21. Now he that by the arguments here adduced shall frame a judgment of the things past and not believe rather that they were such as the poets have sung or prose-writers have composed, more delightfully to the ear than conformably to the truth, as being things not to be disproved and by length of time turned for the most part into the nature of fables without credit, but shall think them here searched out by the most evident signs that can be, and sufficiently too, considering their antiquity: he, I say, shall not err. And though men always judge the present war wherein they live to be greatest, and when it is past, admire more those that were before it, yet if they consider of this war by the acts done in the same, it will manifest itself to be greater than any of those before mentioned.

22. What particular persons have spoken when they were about to enter into the war or when they were in it were hard for me to remember exactly, whether they were speeches which I have heard myself or have received at the second hand. But as any man seemed to me that knew what was nearest to the sum of the truth of all that had been uttered to speak most agreeably to the matter still in hand, so I have made it spoken here.* But of the acts themselves done in the war, I thought not fit to write all that I heard from all authors nor such as I myself did but think to be true, but only those whereat I was myself present and those of which with all diligence I had made particular inquiry. And yet even of those things it was hard to know the certainty, because such as were present at every action spake not all after the same manner, but as they were affected to the parts or as they could remember.

* This sentence appears quite misconstrued. It is a very important statement of Thucydides' practice in regard to the speeches, and the meaning is "As each speaker appeared to me to say roughly what was required about the particular circumstance in which he was involved . . . this is how I have set it down, sticking as closely as I could to the entire content of what was actually said." Hobbes' version is wrong because he missed the usage of the middle voice of the verb *echein*, which means "clinging to" not "possessing" or "knowing," which is how he took it.

To hear this history rehearsed, for that there be inserted in it no fables, shall be perhaps not delightful. But he that desires to look into the truth of things done and which (according to the condition of humanity) may be done again, or at least their like, he shall find enough herein to make him think it profitable.* And it is compiled rather for an everlasting possession than to be rehearsed for a prize.

23. The greatest action before this was that against the Medes; and yet that, by two battles by sea and as many by land, was soon decided. But as for this war, it both lasted long and the harm it did to Greece was such as the like in the like space had never been seen before. For neither had there ever been so many cities expugned and made desolate, what by the barbarians and what by the Greeks warring on one another (and some cities there were that when they were taken changed their inhabitants), nor so much banishing and slaughter, some by the war some by sedition, as was in this. And those things which concerning former time there went a fame of, but in fact rarely confirmed, were now made credible: as earthquakes, general to the greatest part of the world and most violent withal; eclipses of the sun oftener than is reported of any former time; great droughts in some places, and thereby famine; and that which did none of the least hurt but destroyed also its part, the plague. All these evils entered together with this war, which began from the time that the Athenians and Peloponnesians brake the league which immediately after the conquest of Euboea had been concluded between them for thirty years. The causes why they brake the same and their quarrels I have therefore set down first, because no man should be to seek from what ground so great a war amongst the Grecians could arise. And the truest quarrel,† though least in

---

* The Greek means, impersonally, "it shall be sufficient." It is more likely, in my opinion, that Thucydides meant "it shall be sufficient *for me*" than "it shall be sufficient for the man who desires to know." Thus the meaning would be "I shall be satisfied if . . ." and goes on, plausibly enough, "It has been composed as a possession forever rather than . . ."

† Hobbes' translation of this is hardly satisfactory. Thucydides is contrasting the *causes* which lie deepest, which were also least put forward at the time, and the alleged causes. The expression "truest

speech, I conceive to be the growth of the Athenian power, which putting the Lacedaemonians into fear necessitated the war. But the causes of the breach of the league publicly voiced were these.

24. Epidamnus is a city situated on the right hand to such as enter into the Ionian Gulf. Bordering upon it are the Taulantii, barbarians, a people of Illyris. This was planted by the Corcyraeans; but the captain of the colony was one Phalius, the son of Heratoclidas, a Corinthian of the lineage of Hercules, and, according to an ancient custom, called to this charge out of the metropolitan city. Besides that, the colony itself consisted in part of Corinthians and others of the Doric nation. In process of time the city of Epidamnus became great and populous; and having for many years together been annoyed with sedition, was by a war, as is reported, made upon them by the confining barbarians brought low and deprived of the greatest part of their power. But that which was the last accident before this war was that the nobility, forced by the commons to fly the city, went and joined with the barbarians and both by land and sea robbed those that remained within. The Epidamnians that were in the town, oppressed in this manner, sent their ambassadors to Corcyra, as being their mother city, praying the Corcyraeans not to see them perish but to reconcile unto them those whom they had driven forth and to put an end to the barbarian war. And this they entreated in the form of suppliants, sitting down in the temple of Juno. But the Corcyraeans, not admitting their supplication, sent them away again without effect.

25. The Epidamnians, now despairing of relief from the Corcyraeans and at a stand how to proceed in their present affairs, sending to Delphi enquired at the oracle whether it were not best to deliver up their city into the hands of the Corinthians as of their founders and make trial what aid they should obtain from thence. And when the oracle had answered that they should deliver it and take the Corinthians for their leaders, they went to Corinth and according to the advice of the oracle gave their city to them, and declared how

---

quarrel" would be to modern ears better rendered "truest occasion" or "cause."

the first founder of it was a Corinthian, and what answer the oracle had given them, entreating their help and that they would not stand by beholding their destruction. And the Corinthians undertook their defence not only for the equity of the cause, as thinking them no less their own than the Corcyraeans' colony, but also for hatred of the Corcyraeans, who being their colony yet contemned them and allowed them not their due honour in public meetings nor in the distribution of the sacrifice began at a Corinthian, as was the custom of other colonies; but being equal to the richest Grecians of their time for store of money and strongly furnished with ammunition of war, had them in contempt. Also they sticked not sometimes to boast how much they excelled in shipping, and that Corcyra had been once inhabited by the Phaeaces who flourished in glory of naval affairs, which was also the cause why they the rather provided themselves of a navy. And they were indeed not without power that way; for when they began this war, they had one hundred and twenty galleys.

26. The Corinthians therefore, having all these criminations against them, relieved Epidamnus willingly, not only giving leave to whosoever would to go and dwell there but also sent thither a garrison of Ambraciots, Leucadians, and of their own citizens. Which succours, for fear the Corcyraeans should have hindered their passage by sea, marched by land to Apollonia. The Corcyraeans, understanding that new inhabitants and a garrison were gone to Epidamnus and that the colony was delivered to the Corinthians, were vexed extremely at the same, and sailing presently thither with twenty-five galleys, and afterwards with another fleet, in an insolent manner commanded them both to recall those whom they had banished (for these banished men of Epidamnus had been now at Corcyra and, pointing to the sepulchres of their ancestors and claiming kindred, had entreated the Corcyraeans to restore them) and to send away the garrison and inhabitants sent thither by the Corinthians. But the Epidamnians gave no ear to their commandments. Whereupon the Corcyraeans with forty galleys, together with the banished men (whom they pretended to reduce) and with the Illyrians, whom they had

joined to their part, warred upon them, and having laid siege to the city, made proclamation that such of the Epidamnians as would, and all strangers, might depart safely, or otherwise were to be proceeded against as enemies. But when this prevailed not, the place being an isthmus, they enclosed the city in on every side.

27. The Corinthians, when news was brought from Epidamnus how it was besieged, presently made ready their army, and at the same time caused a proclamation to be made for the sending thither of a colony, and that such as would go should have equal and like privileges with those that were there before, and that such as desired to be sharers in the same, and yet were unwilling to go along in person at that present, if they would contribute fifty Corinthian drachmas, might stay behind. And they were very many, both that went and that laid down their silver. Moreover they sent to the Megareans, for fear of being stopped in their passage by the Corcyraeans, to aid them with some galleys, who accordingly furnished out eight; the citizens of Pale in Cephalonia, four. They also required galleys of the Epidaurians, who sent them five; the citizens of Hermione, one; the Troezenians, two; the Leucadians, ten; the Ambraciots, eight. Of the Thebans and Phliasians they required money; of the Eleans, both money and empty galleys. And of the Corinthians themselves there were ready thirty galleys and three thousand men of arms.

28. The Corcyraeans, advertised of this preparation, went to Corinth in company of the ambassadors of the Lacedaemonians and of the Sicyonians whom they took with them and required the Corinthians to recall the garrison and inhabitants which they had sent to Epidamnus, as being a city, they said, wherewith they had nothing to do; or if they had anything to allege, they were content to have the cause judicially tried in such cities of Peloponnesus as they should both agree on; and they then should hold the colony to whom the same should be adjudged. They said also that they were content to refer their cause to the oracle at Delphi, that war they would make none; but if they must needs have it, they should, by the violence of them, be forced in their own defence to seek out

better friends * than those whom they already had. To this the
Corinthians answered that if they would put off with their
fleet and dismiss the barbarians from before Epidamnus, they
would then consult of the matter; for before they could not
honestly do it because whilst they should be pleading the case,
the Epidamnians should be suffering the misery of a siege.
The Corcyraeans replied to this that if they would call back
those men of theirs already in Epidamnus, that then they also
would do as the Corinthians had required them; or otherwise
they were content to let the men on both sides stay where they
were and to suspend the war till the cause should be decided.

29. The Corinthians not assenting to any of these propositions, since their galleys were manned and their confederates
present, having defied them first by a herald, put to sea with
seventy-five galleys and two thousand men of arms, and set
sail for Epidamnus against the Corcyraeans. Their fleet was
commanded by Aristeus the son of Pellicas, Callicrates the son
of Callias, and Timanor the son of Timanthes; and the land
forces by Archetimus the son of Eurytimus and Isarchidas the
son of Isarchus. After they were come as far as Actium, in the
territory of Anactorium (which is a temple of Apollo and
ground consecrated unto him) in the mouth of the Gulf of
Ambracia, the Corcyraeans sent a herald to them at Actium
to forbid their coming on, and in the meantime manned out
their fleet, and, having repaired and made fit for service their
old galleys and furnished the rest with things necessary, shipped
their munition and went aboard. The herald was no sooner returned from the Corinthians with an answer not inclining to
peace but having their galleys already manned and furnished
to the number of eighty sail (for forty attended always the
siege of Epidamnus), they put to sea and, arranging themselves,

* This, as Hobbes points out in a note, means the Athenians, of
course. The Corcyrean position was one of limited blackmail. If the
cause of dispute between themselves and the Corinthians could be
settled by a supposedly neutral international authority (the Delphic
oracle), all would be well. Otherwise there would be war, and for
that war the Corcyreans would enlist the help of the Athenians, which,
with the Corinthians and Corcyreans themselves, were the three major
naval powers. Thus Corinth would find herself facing a dangerous
combination of two great navies.

came to a battle in which the Corcyraeans were clearly victors; and on the part of the Corinthians there perished fifteen galleys. And the same day it happened likewise that they that besieged Epidamnus had the same rendered unto them, with conditions, that the strangers therein found should be ransomed and the Corinthians kept in bonds till such time as they should be otherwise disposed of.

30. The battle being ended, the Corcyraeans, after they had set up their trophy * in Leucimna, a promontory of Corcyra, slew their other prisoners but kept the Corinthians still in bonds. After this, when the Corinthians with their vanquished fleet were gone home to Corinth, the Corcyraeans, masters now of the whole sea in those parts, went first and wasted the territory of Leucas, a Corinthian colony, and then sailed to Cyllene, which is the arsenal of the Eleans, and burnt it because they had both with money and shipping given aid to the Corinthians. And they were masters of those seas and infested the confederates of Corinth for the most part of that year, till such time as in the beginning of the summer following the Corinthians sent a fleet and soldiers unto Actium, the which, for the more safe keeping of Leucas and of other cities their friends, encamped about Chimerium in Thesprotis; and the Corcyraeans, both with their fleet and land soldiers, lay over against them in Leucimna. But neither part stirred against the other; but after they had lain quietly opposite all the summer, they retired in winter both the one side and the other to their cities.

31. All this year, as well before as after the battle, the Corinthians, being vexed at the war with the Corcyraeans, applied themselves to the building of galleys and to the preparing of a fleet, the strongest they were able to make, and to procure mariners out of Peloponnesus and all other parts of Greece. The Corcyraeans, having intelligence of their preparations, began to fear and (because they had never been in league with any Grecian city, nor were in the roll of the confederates either of the Athenians or Lacedaemonians) thought it best

* Hobbes' note on this word reads: "Turning, particularly the back. Trophies, monuments in remembrance of having made the enemy turn their backs. These were usual in those times, now out of date."

now to send to Athens to see if they could procure any aid from thence. This being perceived by the Corinthians, they also sent their ambassadors to Athens, lest the addition of the Athenian navy to that of the Corcyraeans might hinder them from carrying the war as they desired. And the assembly at Athens being met, they came to plead against each other; and the Corcyraeans spake to this effect:

32. "Men of Athens, it is but justice that such as come to implore the aid of their neighbours (as now do we), and cannot pretend by any great benefit or league some precedent merit, should, before they go any farther, make it appear, principally, that what they seek conferreth profit, or if not so, yet is not prejudicial at least to those that are to grant it; and next, that they will be constantly thankful for the same; and if they cannot do this, then not to take it ill though their suit be rejected. And the Corcyraeans, being fully persuaded that they can make all this appear on their own parts, have therefore sent us hither, desiring you to ascribe them to the number of your confederates. Now so it is that we have had a custom, both unreasonable in respect of our suit to you and also for the present unprofitable to our own estate. For having ever till now been unwilling to admit others into league with us, we are now not only suitors for league to others but also left destitute by that means of friends in this our war with the Corinthians. And that which before we thought wisdom, namely, not to enter with others into league because we would not at the discretion of others enter into danger, we now find to have been our weakness and imprudence. Wherefore, though alone we repulsed the Corinthians in the late battle by sea, yet since they are set to invade us with greater preparation out of Peloponnesus and the rest of Greece, and seeing with our own single power we are not able to go through,* and since also the danger, in case they subdue us, would be very great to all Greece, it is necessary that we seek the succours both of you and of whomsoever else we can; and we are also to be pardoned, though we make bold to cross our former custom of not having to do with other men, proceeding not from malice but error of judgment.

---

* The Greek word so rendered by Hobbes is more intelligible to a modern reader if translated "to be superior," "to get the better."

33. "Now if you yield unto us in what we request, this coincidence on our part of need will on your part be honourable for many reasons. First, in this respect, that you lend your help to such as have suffered and not to such as have committed the injustice. And next, considering that you receive into league such as have at stake their whole fortune, you shall so place your benefit as to have a testimony of it, if ever any can be so, indelible. Besides this, the greatest navy but your own is ours. Consider then, what rarer hap, and of greater grief to your enemies, can befall you than that that power which you would have prized above any money or other requital should come voluntarily and without all danger or cost present itself to your hands, bringing with it reputation amongst most men, a grateful mind from those you defend, and strength to yourselves. All which have not happened at once to many. And few there be of those that sue for league that come not rather to receive strength and reputation than to confer it. If any here think that the war wherein we may do you service will not at all be, he is in an error and seeth not how the Lacedaemonians, through fear of you, are already in labour of the war; and that the Corinthians, gracious with them and enemies to you, making way for their enterprize, assault us now in the way to the invasion of you hereafter, that we may not stand amongst the rest of their common enemies, but that they may be sure beforehand either to weaken us or to strengthen their own estate. It must therefore be your part,* we offering and you accepting the league, to begin with them and to anticipate plotting rather than to counterplot against them.

34. "If they object injustice in that you receive their colony, henceforth let them learn that all colonies so long as they receive no wrong from their mother city, so long they honour her; but when they suffer injury from her, they then become alienate; for they are not sent out to be the slaves of them that stay, but to be their equals. That they have done us the injury is manifest; for when we offered them a judicial trial of the controversy touching Epidamnus, they chose to prosecute their quarrel rather by arms than judgment. Now let that which they

* This is a disputed reading. Many authorities read the Greek word for "*our* part."

have done unto us, who are their kindred, serve you for some argument not to be seduced by their demands and made their instruments before you be aware. For he lives most secure that hath fewest benefits bestowed upon him by his enemies to repent of.

35. "As for the articles between you and the Lacedaemonians, they are not broken by receiving us into your league, because we are in league with neither party. For there it is said * that whosoever is confederate of neither party may have access lawfully to either. And sure it were very unreasonable that the Corinthians should have the liberty to man their fleet out of the cities comprised in the league, and out of any other parts of Greece, and not the least out of places in your dominion, and we be denied both the league now propounded and also all other help from whencesoever. And if they impute it to you as a fault that you grant our request, we shall take it for a greater that you grant it not. For therein you shall reject us that are invaded and be none of your enemies; and them, who are your enemies and make the invasion, you shall not only not oppose but also suffer to raise unlawful forces in your dominions. Whereas you ought in truth either not to suffer them to take up mercenaries in your states, or else to send us succours also in such manner as you shall think good yourselves, but especially by taking us into your league and so aiding us. Many commodities,† as we said in the beginning, we show unto you, but this for the greatest: that whereas they are your enemies (which is manifest enough) and not weak ones but able to hurt those that stand up against them, we offer you a naval, not a terrestrial, league; and the want of one of these is not as the want of the other. Nay, rather your principal aim, if it could be done, should be to let none at all have shipping but your-

---

* What is referred to here is the agreement between Athens and Sparta called the Thirty Years' Treaty, made in 445 B.C., in which, after an inconclusive end to the fighting which had lasted for about ten years and is sometimes referred to as the First Peloponnesian War, it was laid down that neither league might gain adherents from members of the other, but that states enrolled in neither might join which they pleased.

† Seventeenth-century English for "many advantages."

selves, or at least, if that cannot be, to make such your friends as are best furnished therewith.

36. "If any man now think thus that what we have spoken is indeed profitable, but fears, if it were admitted, the league were thereby broken, let that man consider that his fear joined with strength will make his enemies fear, and his confidence, having (if he reject us) so much the less strength, will so much the less be feared. Let him also remember that he is now in consultation no less concerning Athens than Corcyra, wherein he forecasteth none of the best (considering the present state of affairs) that makes a question whether against a war at hand and only not already on foot he should join unto it or not that city which with most important advantages or disadvantages will be friend or enemy. For it lieth so conveniently for sailing into Italy and Sicily that it can both prohibit any fleet to come to Peloponnesus from thence and convoy any coming from Peloponnesus thither, and is also for divers other uses most commodious. And to comprehend all in brief, consider whether we be to be abandoned or not by this. For Greece having but three navies of any account, yours, ours, and that of Corinth, if you suffer the other two to join in one by letting the Corinthians first seize us, you shall have to fight by sea at one time both against the Corcyraeans and the Peloponnesians; whereas by making league with us, you shall, with your fleet augmented, have to deal against the Peloponnesians alone."

Thus spake the Corcyraeans, and after them the Corinthians, thus:

37. "The Corcyraeans in their oration having made mention not only of your taking them into league, but also that they are wronged and unjustly warred on, it is also necessary for us first to answer concerning both those points, and then afterwards to proceed to the rest of what we have to say: to the end you may foreknow that ours are the safest demands for you to embrace, and that you may upon reason reject the needy estate of those others. Whereas they allege in defence of their refusing to enter league with other cities that the same hath proceeded from modesty, the truth is that they took up that custom not from any virtue but mere wickedness, as being unwilling to

have any confederate for a witness of their evil actions, and to be put to blush by calling them. Besides, their city being by the situation sufficient within itself, giveth them this point, that when they do any man a wrong, they themselves are the judges of the same, and not men appointed by consent. For going seldom forth against other nations, they intercept such as by necessity are driven into their harbour. And in this consisteth their goodly pretext for not admitting confederates, not because they would not be content to accompany others in doing evil, but because they had rather do it alone; that where they were too strong, they might oppress; and when there should be none to observe them, the less of the profit might be shared from them; and that they might escape the shame when they took anything. But if they had been honest men (as they themselves say they are), by how much the less they are obnoxious to accusation, so much the more means they have, by giving and taking what is due, to make their honesty appear.

38. "But they are not such, neither towards others nor towards us. For being our colony, they have not only been ever in revolt, but now they also make war upon us and say they were not sent out to be injured by us. But we say again that we did not send them forth to be scorned by them but to have the leading of them and to be regarded by them as is fit. For our other colonies both honour and love us much: which is an argument, seeing the rest are pleased with our actions, that these have no just cause to be offended alone, and that without some manifest wrong we should not have had colour to war against them. But say we had been in an error, it had been well done in them to have given way to our passion, as it had been also dishonourable in us to have insulted over their modesty. But through pride and wealth they have done wrong, both in many other things and also in this; that Epidamnus being ours which whilst it was vexed with wars they never claimed, as soon as we came to relieve it, was forcibly seized by them, and so holden.

39. "They say now that before they took it, they offered to put the cause to trial of judgment. But you are not to think that such a one will stand to judgment as hath advantage and is sure already of what he offereth to plead for, but rather he that

before the trial will admit equality in the matter itself as well as in the pleading. Whereas contrarily, these men offered not this specious pretence of a judicial trial before they had besieged the city but after, when they saw we meant not to put it up.* And now hither they be come, not content to have been faulty in that business themselves but to get in you, into their confederacy? no, but into their conspiracy, and to receive them in this name that they are enemies to us. But they should have come to you then when they were most in safety, not now when we have the wrong and they the danger, and when you that never partaked of their power must impart unto them of your aid, and having been free from their faults, must have an equal share from us of the blame. They should communicate their power before hand that mean to make common the issue of the same, and they that share not in the crimes ought also to have no part in the sequel of them.

40. "Thus it appears that we come for our parts with arguments of equity and right, whereas the proceedings of these other are nothing else but violence and rapine. And now we shall show you likewise that you cannot receive them in point of justice. For although it be in the articles that the cities written with neither of the parties may come in to whether of them they please, yet it holds not for such as do so to the detriment of either, but only for those that, having revolted from neither part, want protection and bring not a war with them instead of peace to those (if they be wise) that receive them. For you shall not only be auxiliaries unto these but to us, instead of confederates, enemies. For if you go with them, it follows they must defend themselves not without you. You should do most uprightly to stand out of both our ways; and if not that, then to take our parts against the Corcyraeans (for between the Corinthians and you there are articles of peace, but with the Corcyraeans you never had so much as a truce) and not to constitute a new law of receiving one another's rebels. For neither did we give our votes against you when the Samians revolted, though the rest of Peloponnesus was divided in opinion, but plainly alleged that it was reason that everyone should have liberty to proceed against their own revolting confederates.

* I.e., "not to put up with it."

And if you shall once receive and aid the doers of wrong, it will be seen that they will come over as fast from you to us; and you shall set up a law not so much against us as against yourselves.

41. "These are the points of justice we had to show you conformable to the law of the Grecians. And now we come to matter of advice and claim of favour, which (being not so much your enemies as to hurt you nor such friends as to surcharge you *), we say, ought in the present occasion to be granted us by way of requital. For when you had want of long barks against the Aeginetae a little before the Medan war, you had twenty lent to you by the Corinthians; which benefit of ours, and that other against the Samians when by us it was that the Peloponnesians did not aid them, was the cause both of your victory against the Aeginetae and of the punishment of the Samians. And these things were done for you in a season when men, going to fight against their enemies, neglect all respects but of victory. For even a man's domestic affairs are ordered the worse through eagerness of present contention.

42. "Which benefits considering, and the younger sort taking notice of them from the elder, be you pleased to defend us now in the like manner. And have not this thought: that though in what we have spoken there be equity, yet, if the war should arise, the profit would be found in the contrary. For utility followeth those actions most wherein we do the least wrong; besides that the likelihood of the war, wherewith the Corcyraeans frighting you go about to draw you to injustice, is yet obscure and not worthy to move you to a manifest and present hostility with the Corinthians; but it were rather fit for you, indeed, to take away our former jealousies concerning the Megareans. For the last good turn done in season, though but small, is able to cancel an accusation of much greater moment. Neither suffer yourselves to be drawn on by the greatness of the navy which now shall be at your service by this league. For to do no injury to our equals is a firmer power than that

---

* The Greek expression is somewhat ambiguous. Its sense seems to be: "This is our request and claim, not being enemies to hurt nor yet such as you can deal with as friends."

addition of strength which, puffed up with present shows, men are to acquire with danger.

43. "And since we be come to this, which once before we said at Lacedaemon, that everyone ought to proceed as he shall think good against his own confederates, we claim that liberty now of you; and that you that have been helped by our votes will not hurt us now by yours, but render like for like; remembering that now is that occasion wherein he that aideth us is our greatest friend, and he that opposeth us our greatest enemy; and that you will not receive these Corcyraeans into league against our wills nor defend them in their injuries. These things if you grant us, you shall both do as is fit and also advise the best for the good of your own affairs."

This was the effect of what was spoken by the Corinthians.

44. Both sides having been heard and the Athenian people twice assembled, in the former assembly they approved no less of the reasons of the Corinthians than of the Corcyraeans. But in the latter they changed their minds, not so as to make a league with the Corcyraeans both offensive and defensive, that the friends and enemies of the one should be so of the other (for then, if the Corcyraeans should have required them to go against Corinth, the peace had been broken with the Peloponnesians), but made it only defensive, that if anyone should invade Corcyra or Athens, or any of their confederates, they were then mutually to assist one another. For they expected that even thus they should grow to war with the Peloponnesians and were therefore unwilling to let Corcyra, that had so great a navy, to fall into the hands of the Corinthians, but rather, as much as in them lay, desired to break them one against another; that if need required, they might have to do with the Corinthians, and others that had shipping, when they should be weakened to their hands.* And the island seemed also to lie conveniently for passing into Italy and Sicily.

45. With this mind the people of Athens received the Corcyraeans into league, and when the Corinthians were gone,

* This is something less than the meaning of the Greek, which is "that they might go to war with the Corinthians (and others . . .) if necessary when they had been made weaker."

sent ten galleys not long after to their aid. The commanders of
them were Lacedaemonius the son of Cimon, Diotimus the son
of Strombichus, and Proteas the son of Epicles, and had order
not to fight with the Corinthians unless they invaded Corcyra
or offered to land there or in some other place of theirs, which,
if they did, then with all their might to oppose them. This
they forbad, because they would not break the peace concluded
with the Peloponnesians. So these galleys arrived at Corcyra.

46. The Corinthians, when they were ready, made towards
Corcyra with one hundred and fifty sail; of the Eleans ten, of
the Megareans twelve, of the Leucadians ten, of the Ambraciots
twenty-seven, of the Anactorians one, and ninety of their own.
The commanders of these were men chosen out of the said
several cities for the several parts of the fleet which they sent
in, and over those of Corinth was Xenocleides the son of
Euthicles with four others. After they were all come together
upon the coast of the continent over against Corcyra, they
sailed from Leucas and came to Chimerium in the country of
Thesprotis. In this place is a haven, and above it, farther from
the sea, the city of Ephyra in that part of Thesprotis which is
called Elaeatis; and near unto it disbogueth into the sea the lake
Acherusia, and into that (having first passed through Thesprotis) the river Acheron from which it taketh the name. Also
the river Thyamis runneth here, which divideth Thesprotis from
Cestrine, betwixt which two rivers ariseth this promontory of
Chimerium. To this part of the continent came the Corinthians and encamped.

47. The Corcyraeans understanding that they made against
them, having ready one hundred and ten galleys under the
conduct of Miciades, Aesimides, and Eurybatus, came and encamped in one of the islands called Sybota; and the ten galleys
of Athens were also with them. But their land forces stayed in
the promontory of Leucimna, and with them one thousand men
of arms of the Zacynthians that came to aid them. The Corinthians also had in the continent the aids of many barbarians,
which in those quarters have been evermore their friends.

48. The Corinthians, after they were ready and had taken
aboard three days' provision of victual, put off by night from
Chimerium with purpose to fight, and about break of day, as

they were sailing, descried the galleys of the Corcyraeans, which were also put off from Sybota and coming on to fight with the Corinthians. As soon as they had sight one of another, they put themselves into order of battle. In the right wing of the Corcyraeans were placed the galleys of Athens, and the rest being their own were divided into three commands under the three commanders, one under one. This was the order of the Corcyraeans. The Corinthians had in their right wing the galleys of Megara and of Ambracia; in the middle, other their confederates in order; and opposite to the Athenians and right wing of the Corcyraeans they were themselves placed, with such galleys as were best of sail, in the left.

49. The standard being on either side lift up, they joined battle, having on both parts both many men of arms and many archers and slingers, but after the old fashion as yet somewhat unskilfully appointed. The battle was not so artificially as cruelly fought, near unto the manner of a fight at land.* For after they had once run their galleys up close aboard one of another, they could not for the number and throng be easily gotten asunder again, but relied for the victory especially upon their men of arms who fought where they stood whilst the galleys remained altogether without motion. Passages through each other they made none but fought it out with courage and strength rather than with skill. Insomuch as the battle was in every part not without much tumult and disorder, in which the Athenian galleys being always, where the Corcyraeans were oppressed, at hand, kept the enemies in fear, but yet began no assault because their commanders stood in awe of the prohibition of the Athenian people. The right wing of the Corinthians was in the greatest distress, for the Corcyraeans with twenty galleys had made them turn their backs and chased them dispersed to the continent; and sailing to their very camp, went aland, burnt their abandoned tents, and took away their baggage. So that in this part the Corinthians and their confederates were vanquished, and the Corcyraeans had the victory. But in the left wing where the Corinthians were them-

---

* This is Hobbes' rendering of the Greek which means "The fight was a sharp one but not as skillful as it was sharp. Indeed, it was rather like a land battle."

selves they were far superior because the Corcyraeans had
twenty galleys of their number, which was at first less than that
of the Corinthians, absent in the chase of the enemy. And the
Athenians, when they saw the Corcyraeans were in distress,
now aided them manifestly, whereas before, they had abstained from making assault upon any. But when once they
fled outright and that the Corinthians lay sore upon them, then
everyone fell to the business without making difference any
longer; and it came at last to this necessity, that they undertook
one another, Corinthians and Athenians.

50. The Corinthians, when their enemies fled, stayed not to
fasten the hulls of the galleys they had sunk unto their own
galleys that so they might tow them after, but made after the
men, rowing up and down, to kill rather than to take alive, and
through ignorance (not knowing that their right wing had
been discomfited) slew also some of their own friends. For the
galleys of either side being many and taking up a large space at
sea, after they were once in the medley they could not easily
discern who were of the victors and who of the vanquished
party. For this was the greatest naval battle for number of
ships that ever had been before of Grecians against Grecians.
When the Corinthians had chased the Corcyraeans to the shore,
they returned to take up the broken galleys and bodies of their
dead, which for the greatest part they recovered and brought
to Sybota where also lay the land forces of the barbarians that
were come to aid them. This Sybota is a desert haven of Thesprotis. When they had done, they reunited themselves and
made again to the Corcyraeans. And they likewise, with such
galleys as they had fit for the sea remaining of the former
battle together with those of Athens, put forth to meet them,
fearing lest they should attempt to land upon their territory.
By this time the day was far spent, and the song which they
used to sing when they came to charge was ended, when suddenly the Corinthians began to row astern, for they had descried twenty Athenian galleys sent from Athens to second the
former ten for fear lest the Corcyraeans (as it also fell out)
should be overcome and those ten galleys of theirs be too few
to defend them.

51. When the Corinthians therefore had sight of these gal-

leys, suspecting that they were of Athens and more in number than they were, by little and little they fell off. But the Corcyraeans (because the course of these galleys was unto them more out of sight) descried them not but wondered why the Corinthians rowed astern, till at last some that saw them said they were enemies, and then retired also the Corcyraeans. For by this time it was dark, and the Corinthians had turned about the heads of their galleys and dissolved themselves. And thus were they parted, and the battle ended in night. The Corcyraeans lying at Leucimna, these twenty Athenian galleys under the command of Glaucon the son of Leagrus and Andocides the son of Leogorus, passing through the midst of the floating carcasses and wrecks, soon after they were descried arrived at the camp of the Corcyraeans in Leucimna. The Corcyraeans at first (being night) were afraid they had been enemies, but knew them afterwards; so they anchored there.

52. The next day both the thirty galleys of Athens and as many of Corcyra as were fit for service went to the haven in Sybota, where the Corinthians lay at anchor, to see if they would fight. But the Corinthians, when they had put off from the land and arranged themselves in the wide sea, stood quiet, not meaning of their own accord to begin the battle, both for that they saw the supply of fresh galleys from Athens and for many difficulties that happened to them, both about the safe custody of their prisoners aboard and also for that being in a desert place their galleys were not yet repaired, but took thought rather how to go home for fear lest the Athenians, having the peace already broken in that they had fought against each other, should not suffer them to depart.

53. They therefore thought good to send afore unto the Athenians certain men without privilege of heralds for to sound them and to say in this manner: "Men of Athens, you do unjustly to begin the war and violate the articles; for whereas we go about to right us on our enemies, you stand in our way and bear arms against us; if therefore you be resolved to hinder our going against Corcyra or whatsoever place else we please, dissolve the peace, and laying hands first upon us that are here, use us as enemies." Thus said they; and the Corcyraeans, as many of the army as heard them, cried out immediately to take

and kill them. But the Athenians made answer thus: "Men of Peloponnesus, neither do we begin the war nor break the peace; but we bring aid to these our confederates, the Corcyraeans; if you please therefore to go any whither else, we hinder you not, but if against Corcyra, or any place belonging unto it, we will not suffer you."

54. When the Athenians had given them this answer, the Corinthians made ready to go home and set up a trophy in Sybota of the continent. And the Corcyraeans also both took up the wreck and bodies of the dead which, carried every way by the waves and the winds that arose the night before, came driving to their hands, and, as if they had had the victory, set up a trophy likewise in Sybota the island. The victory was thus challenged on both sides upon these grounds. The Corinthians did set up a trophy because in the battle they had the better all day, having gotten more of the wreck and dead bodies than the other and taken no less than a thousand prisoners and sunk about seventy of the enemies' galleys. And the Corcyraeans set up a trophy because they had sunk thirty galleys of the Corinthians and had, after the arrival of the Athenians, recovered the wreck and dead bodies that drove to them by reason of the wind; and because the day before, upon sight of the Athenians, the Corinthians had rowed astern and went away from them; and lastly, for that when they went to Sybota, the Corinthians came not out to encounter them. Thus each side claimed victory.

55. The Corinthians in their way homeward took in Anactorium, a town seated in the mouth of the Gulf of Ambracia, by deceit (this town was common to them and to the Corcyraeans), and having put into it Corinthians only, departed and went home. Of the Corcyraeans, eight hundred that were servants they sold, and kept prisoners two hundred and fifty, whom they used with very much favour that they might be a means, at their return, to bring Corcyra into the power of the Corinthians, the greatest part of these being principal men of the city. And thus was Corcyra delivered of the war of Corinth, and the Athenian galleys went from them. This was the first cause that the Corinthians had of war against the Athenians: namely, because they had taken part with the Corcyraeans in

a battle by sea against the Corinthians with whom they were comprised in the same articles of peace.

56. Presently after this, it came to pass that other differences arose between the Peloponnesians and the Athenians to induce the war. For whilst the Corinthians studied to be revenged, the Athenians, who had their hatred in jealousy,* commanded the citizens of Potidaea, a city seated in the Isthmus of Pallene, a colony of the Corinthians but confederate and tributary to the Athenians, to pull down that part of the wall of their city that stood towards Pallene, and to give them hostages, and also to send away and no more receive the Epidemiurgi (magistrates so called) which were sent unto them year by year from Corinth, fearing lest through the persuasion of Perdiccas and of the Corinthians they should revolt and draw to revolt with them their other confederates in Thrace.

57. These things against the Potidaeans, the Athenians had precontrived presently after the naval battle fought at Corcyra. For the Corinthians and they were now manifestly at difference; and Perdiccas, who before had been their confederate and friend, now warred upon them. And the cause why he did so was that when his brother Philip and Derdas joined in arms against him, the Athenians had made a league with them. And therefore being afraid, he both sent to Lacedaemon to negotiate the Peloponnesian war and also reconciled himself to the Corinthians the better to procure the revolt of Potidaea. And likewise he practised with the Chalcideans of Thrace and with the Bottiaeans to revolt with them; for if he could make these confining cities his confederates, with the help of them he thought his war would be the easier. Which the Athenians perceiving and intending to prevent the revolt of these cities, gave order to the commanders of the fleet (for they were now sending thirty galleys with a thousand men of arms under the command of Archestratus the son of Lycomedes, and ten others, into the territories of Perdiccas) both to receive hostages of the Potidaeans and to demolish their walls, and also to have an eye to the neighbouring cities that they revolted not.

58. The Potidaeans having sent ambassadors to Athens to try

* This is more easily understood in its modern version, "suspecting their hatred."

if they could persuade the people not to make any alteration amongst them, by other ambassadors, whom they sent along with the ambassadors of Corinth to Lacedaemon, dealt with the Lacedaemonians at the same time, if need required, to be ready to revenge their quarrel. When after long solicitation at Athens and no good done, the fleet was sent away against them no less than against Macedonia, and when the magistrates of Lacedaemon had promised them if the Athenians went to Potidaea, to invade Attica, then at last they revolted, and together with them the Chalcideans and Bottiaeans, all mutually sworn in the same conspiracy. For Perdiccas had also persuaded the Chalcideans to abandon and pull down their maritime towns and to go up and dwell at Olynthus and that one city to make strong, and unto those that removed gave part of his own and part of the territory of Mygdonia, about the lake Bolbe, to live on so long as the war against the Athenians should continue. So when they had demolished their cities and were gone up higher into the country, they prepared themselves to the war.

59. The Athenian galleys, when they arrived in Thrace, found Potidaea and the other cities already revolted. And the commanders of the fleet, conceiving it to be impossible, with their present forces, to make war both against Perdiccas and the towns revolted, set sail again for Macedonia, against which they had been at first sent out, and there staying, joined with Philip and the brothers of Derdas that had invaded the country from above.

60. In the meantime after Potidaea was revolted, and whilst the Athenian fleet lay on the coast of Macedonia, the Corinthians, fearing what might become of the city and making the danger their own, sent unto it, both of their own city and of other Peloponnesians which they hired, to the number of sixteen hundred men of arms and four hundred light armed. The charge of these was given to Aristeus the son of Adimantus, for whose sake most of the volunteers of Corinth went the voyage: for he had been ever a great favourer of the Potidaeans. And they arrived in Thrace after the revolt of Potidaea forty days.

61. The news of the revolt of these cities was likewise quickly brought to the Athenian people, who, hearing withal of the forces sent unto them under Aristeus, sent forth against the

places revolted two thousand men of arms and forty galleys under the conduct of Callias,* the son of Calliades. These, coming first into Macedonia, found there the former thousand, who by this time had taken Therme and were now besieging the city of Pydna; and staying, helped for a while to besiege it with the rest. But shortly after they took composition and, having made a necessary league with Perdiccas (urged thereto by the affairs of Potidaea, and the arrival there of Aristeus), departed from Macedonia. Thence coming to Berrhoea, they attempted to take it; but when they could not do it, they turned back and marched towards Potidaea by land. They were of their own number three thousand men of arms, besides many of their confederates, and of Macedonians that had served with Philip and Pausanias, six hundred horsemen. And their galleys, seventy in number, sailing by them along the coast, by moderate journeys came in three days to Gigonus and there encamped.

62. The Potidaeans and the Peloponnesians under Aristeus, in expectation of the coming of the Athenians, lay now encamped in the isthmus near unto Olynthus and had the market kept for them without the city. And the leading of the foot the confederates had assigned to Aristeus, and of the horse to Perdiccas; for he fell off again presently from the Athenians and, having left Iolaus governor in his place, took part with the Potidaeans. The purpose of Aristeus was to have the body of the army with himself within the isthmus and therewith to attend the coming on of the Athenians, and to have the Chalcideans and their confederates without the isthmus, and also the two hundred horse under Perdiccas, to stay in Olynthus, and when the Athenians were passed by, to come on their backs and to inclose the enemy betwixt them. But Callias the Athenian general, and the rest that were in commission with him, sent out before them their Macedonian horsemen and some few of their confederates to Olynthus to stop those within from making any sally from the town, and then dislodging marched on towards Potidaea. When they were come on as far as the isthmus and saw the enemy make ready to fight, they also did

---

* The Greek adds "Callias . . . *along with four others.*" Hobbes seems not to have noticed this. The Athenians very frequently put such commands into commission.

the like; and not long after they joined battle. That wing wherein was Aristeus himself with the chosen men of the Corinthians and others put to flight that part of their enemies that stood opposite unto them and followed execution a great way. But the rest of the army of the Potidaeans and Peloponnesians were by the Athenians defeated and fled into the city.

63. And Aristeus, when he came back from the execution, was in doubt what way to take, to Olynthus or to Potidaea. In the end he resolved of the shortest way, and with his soldiers about him ran as hard as he was able into Potidaea, and with much ado got in at the pier through the sea, cruelly shot at and with the loss of a few but the safety of the greatest part of his company. As soon as the battle began, they that should have seconded the Potidaeans from Olynthus (for it is at most but sixty furlongs off, and in sight) advanced a little way to have aided them; and the Macedonian horse opposed themselves likewise in order of battle to keep them back. But the Athenians having quickly gotten the victory, and the standards being taken down, they retired again, they of Olynthus into that city, and the Macedonian horsemen into the army of the Athenians. So that neither side had their cavalry at the battle. After the battle the Athenians erected a trophy and gave truce to the Potidaeans for the taking up of the bodies of their dead. Of the Potidaeans and their friends there died somewhat less than three hundred, and of the Athenians themselves one hundred and fifty, with Callias one of their commanders.

64. Presently upon this the Athenians raised a wall before the city on the part toward the isthmus which they kept with a garrison, but the part to Pallene-ward they left unwalled. For they thought themselves too small a number both to keep a guard in the isthmus and withal to go over and fortify in Pallene, fearing lest the Potidaeans and their confederates should assault them when divided. When the people of Athens understood that Potidaea was unwalled on the part toward Pallene, not long after they sent thither sixteen hundred men of arms under the conduct of Phormio the son of Asopius, who arriving in Pallene left his galleys at Aphytis, and marching easily to Potidaea wasted the territory as he passed through. And when

none came out to give him battle, he raised a wall before the city on that part also that looketh towards Pallene. Thus was Potidaea on both sides strongly besieged, and also from the sea by the Athenian galleys that came up and rode before it.

65. Aristeus, seeing the city enclosed on every side and without hope of safety save what might come from Peloponnesus or some other unexpected way, gave advice to all but five hundred, taking the opportunity of a wind, to go out by sea that the provision might the longer hold out for the rest, and of them that should remain within offered himself to be one. But when his counsel took not place, being desirous to settle their business * and make the best of their affairs abroad, he got out by sea unseen of the Athenian guard, and staying amongst the Chalcideans, amongst other actions of the war, laid an ambush before Sermylius and slew many of that city and solicited the sending of aid from Peloponnesus. And Phormio, after the siege laid to Potidaea, having with him his sixteen hundred men of arms, wasted the territory of the Chalcideans and Bottiaeans, and some small towns he took in.

66. These were the quarrels between the Peloponnesians and the Athenians. The Corinthians quarrelled the Athenians for besieging Potidaea and in it the men of Corinth and Peloponnesus. The Athenians quarrelled the Peloponnesians for causing their confederate and tributary city to revolt, and for that they had come thither and openly fought against them in the behalf of Potidaea. Nevertheless the war brake not openly forth as yet, and they yet abstained from arms; for this was but a particular action of the Corinthians.

67. But when Potidaea was once besieged, both for their men's sakes that were within and also for fear to lose the place they could no longer hold. But out of hand they procured of their confederates to go to Lacedaemon; and thither also they went themselves with clamours and accusations against the Athenians that they had broken the league and wronged the Peloponnesians. The Aeginetae, though not openly by ambassadors for fear of the Athenians, yet privily instigated them to the war as much as any, alleging that they were not per-

* The Greek means "When he failed to persuade them, wishing to do what *was next best*."

mitted to govern themselves according to their own laws, as by the articles they ought to have been. So the Lacedaemonians having called together the confederates, and whosoever else had any injustice to lay to the charge of the Athenians, in the ordinary council of their own state commanded them to speak. Then presented everyone his accusation; and amongst the rest the Megareans, besides many other their great differences, laid open this especially, that contrary to the articles they were forbidden the Athenian markets and havens. Last of all, the Corinthians, when they had suffered the Lacedaemonians to be incensed first by the rest, came in and said as followeth.

68. "Men of Lacedaemon, your own fidelity both in matter of estate and conversation * maketh you the less apt to believe us when we accuse others of the contrary. And hereby you gain indeed a reputation of equity, but you have less experience in the affairs of foreign states.† For although we have oftentimes foretold you that the Athenians would do us a mischief, yet from time to time when we told it you, you never would take information of it but have suspected rather that what we spake hath proceeded from our own private differences. And you have therefore called hither these confederates not before we had suffered but now when the evil is already upon us. Before whom our speech must be so much the longer by how much our objections are the greater in that we have both by the Athenians been injured and by you neglected. If the Athenians lurking in some obscure place had done these wrongs unto the Grecians, we should then have needed to prove the same before you as to men that knew it not. But now what cause have we to use long discourse when you see already that some are brought into servitude, and that they are contriving the like against others, and especially against our confederates, and are themselves, in case war should be made against them, long since prepared for it? For else they would never have taken

* The Greek words so rendered are better understood by us in the form "constitution and social intercourse," i.e., public and private life.

† Hobbes' translation is hardly fair. The Greek means "By this conduct you attain *sophrosune* [to be rendered variously "moderation," "temperance," "self-restraint," perhaps most commonly what in English-speaking countries is meant by "decency"], but you are the more ignorant in your conduct of foreign affairs."

Corcyra and holden it from us by force, nor have besieged
Potidaea, whereof the one was most commodious for any action
against Thrace, and the other had brought unto the Peloponnesians a most fair navy.

69. "And of all this you are yourselves the authors, in that
you suffered them upon the end of the Persian war to fortify
their city and again afterwards to raise their long walls, whereby
you have hitherto deprived of their liberty not only the states
by them already subdued but also your own confederates. For
not he that bringeth into slavery, but he that being able to
hinder it neglects the same is most truly said to do it, especially
if they assume the honour to be esteemed the deliverers of
Greece [as you do]. And for all that, we are hardly yet come
together, and indeed not yet with any certain resolution what
to do. For the question should not have been put whether or
not we have received injury, but rather in what manner we are
to repair it. For they that do the wrong, having consulted upon
it beforehand, use no delay at all but come upon them whom
they mean to oppress whilst they be yet irresolute. And we
know not only that the Athenians have incroached upon their
neighbours but also by what ways they have done it. And as
long as they think they carry it closely through your blindness,
they are the less bold; but when they shall perceive that you
see, and will not see, they will then press us strongly indeed.
For, Lacedaemonians, you are the only men of all Greece that
sitting still defend others, not with your forces but with promises; and you are also the only men that love to pull down the
power of the enemy, not when it beginneth but when it is
doubled. You have indeed a report to be sure, but yet it is
more in fame that than in fact. For we ourselves know that the
Persian came against Peloponnesus from the utmost parts of the
earth before you encountered him as became your state. And
also now you connive at the Athenians who are not as the
Medes, far off, but hard at hand, choosing rather to defend
yourselves from their invasion than to invade them, and by
having to do with them when their strength is greater, to put
yourselves upon the chance of fortune. And yet we know that
the barbarian's own error, and in our war against the Athenians
their own oversights more than your assistance, was the thing

that gave us victory. For the hope of your aid hath been the
destruction of some that, relying on you, made no preparation
for themselves by other means. Yet let not any man think that
we speak this out of malice but only by way of expostulation:
for expostulation is with friends that err, but accusation against
enemies that have done an injury.

70. "Besides, if there be any that may challenge to exprobate
his neighbour, we think ourselves may best do it, especially on
so great quarrels as these whereof you neither seem to have
any feeling nor to consider what manner of men and how different from you in every kind the Athenians be that you are
to contend withal. For they love innovation and are swift to
devise and also to execute what they resolve on. But you on
the contrary are only apt to save your own, not devise anything new, nor scarce to attain what is necessary. They again
are bold beyond their strength, adventurous above their own
reason, and in danger hope still the best. Whereas your actions
are ever beneath your power, and you distrust even what your
judgment assures, and being in a danger never think to be delivered. They are stirrers, you studiers; they love to be abroad,
and you at home the most of any. For they make account by
being abroad to add to their estate; you, if you should go forth
against the state of another, would think to impair your own.
They, when they overcome their enemies, advance the farthest
and, when they are overcome by their enemies, fall off the
least; and as for their bodies, they use them in the service of
the commonwealth as if they were none of their own; but
their minds, when they would serve the state, are right their
own. Unless they take in hand what they have once advised
on, they account so much lost of their own. And when they
take it in hand, if they obtain anything, they think lightly of
it in respect of what they look to win by their prosecution. If
they fail in any attempt, they do what is necessary for the present and enter presently into other hopes. For they alone both
have and hope for at once whatsoever they conceive through
their celerity in execution of what they once resolve on. And
in this manner they labour and toil all the days of their lives.
What they have, they have no leisure to enjoy for continual
getting of more; nor holiday esteem they any, but whereon

they effect some matter profitable; nor think they ease with nothing to do, a less torment than laborious business. So that, in a word, to say they are men born neither to rest themselves nor suffer others is to say the truth.

71. "Now notwithstanding, men of Lacedaemon, that this city, your adversary, be such as we have said, yet you still delay time, not knowing that those only are they to whom it may suffice for the most part of their time to sit still who, though they use not their power to do injustice, yet bewray a mind unlikely to swallow injuries, but placing equity belike in this, that you neither do any harm to others nor receive it in defending of yourselves. But this is a thing you hardly could attain, though the states about you were of the same condition. But, as we have before declared, your customs are in respect of theirs antiquated; and of necessity, as it happeneth in arts, the new ones will prevail. True it is that for a city living for the most part in peace, unchanged customs are the best; but for such as be constrained to undergo many matters, many devices will be needful. Which is also the reason why the Athenian customs, through much experience, are more new to you than yours are to them.* Here, therefore, give a period to your slackness and by a speedy invasion of Attica, as you promised, relieve both Potidaea and the rest, lest otherwise you betray your friends and kindred to their cruelest enemies, and lest we and others be driven through despair to seek out some other league. Which to do were no injustice neither against the Gods, judges of men's oaths, nor against men, the hearers of them. For not they break the league who being abandoned have recourse to others, but they that yield not their assistance to whom they have sworn it. But if you mean to follow the business seriously, we will stay; for else we should do irreligiously, neither should we find any other more conformable to our manners than yourselves. Therefore, deliberate well of these points, and take such a course that Peloponnesus may not by your leading fall into worse estate than it was left unto you by your progenitors."

---

* Hobbes is not right here. The Greek means "That is why—because of their greater experience—there is far more innovation in Athenian practice than in yours."

72. Thus spake the Corinthians. The Athenian ambassadors, who chanced to be residing at Lacedaemon upon their business,* when they heard of this oration thought fit to present themselves before the Lacedaemonians, not to make apology for what they were charged with by the other cities, but to show in general that it was not fit for them in this case to take any sudden resolution but farther time to consider. Also they desired to lay open the power of their city, to the elder sort, for a remembrance of what they knew already, and to the younger, for an information of what they knew not, supposing that when they should have spoken, they would incline to quietness rather than to war. And therefore they presented themselves before the Lacedaemonians saying that they also, if they might have leave, desired to speak in the assembly, who willed them to come in. And the Athenians went into the assembly and spake to this effect:

73. "Though our embassage was not to this end, that we should argue against our † confederates, but about such other affairs as the city was pleased to employ us in; yet having heard of the great exclamation against us, we came into the court not to make answer to the criminations of the cities (for to plead before you here were not to plead before the judges either of them or us) but to the end you may not be drawn away to take the worse resolution at the persuasion of the confederates in matters of so great importance, and withal, touching the sum of the oration made against us, to inform you that what we possess we have it justly, and that our city deserveth reputation. But what need we now to speak of matters long past, confirmed more by hearsay than by the eyes of those that are to hear us relate them? But our actions against the Persian, and such as you yourselves know as well as we, those, though it be tedious to hear them ever objected, we must of necessity recite. For when we did them, we hazarded ourselves for some benefit, of which, as you had your parts in the substance, so must we have ours (if that be any benefit) in the

* The Greek is actually "There happened to be an Athenian delegation already in Lacedaemon concerned with other matters."

† This is almost certainly the wrong reading. The meaning is "*your* confederates."

commemoration. And we shall make recital of them not by way of deprecation but of protestation and declaration of what a city, in case you take ill advice, you have to enter the list withal. We therefore say that we not only first and alone hazarded battle against the barbarian in the fields of Marathon, but also afterwards, when he came again, being unable to resist him by land, embarked ourselves, every man that was able to bear arms, and gave him battle amongst the rest by sea at Salamis, which was the cause that kept him back from sailing to Peloponnesus and laying it waste city after city; for against so many galleys you were not able to give each other mutual succour. And the greatest proof of this is the Persian himself, who, when his fleet was overcome and that he had no more such forces, went away in haste with the greatest part of his army.

74. "Which being so, and evident that the whole state of the Grecians was embarked in their fleet, we conferred to the same the three things of most advantage, namely, the greatest number of galleys, the most prudent commander, and the most lively courage. For of four hundred galleys in the whole, our own were few less than two-thirds; and for commander Themistocles, who was the principal cause that the battle was fought in the strait whereby he clearly saved the whole business and whom, though a stranger, you yourselves have honoured for it more than any man that came unto you. And a forwardness we showed more adventurous than any other in this, that when none of them had aided us by land before, and the rest of the cities, as far as to our own, were brought into servitude, we were nevertheless content both to quit our city and lose our goods, and even in that estate not to betray the common cause of the confederates, or divided from them to be unuseful, but to put ourselves into our navy and undergo the danger with them, and that without passion against you for not having formerly defended us in the like manner. So that we may say that we have no less conferred a benefit upon you than we received it from you. You came indeed to aid us, but it was from cities inhabited and to the end you might still keep them so, and when you were afraid not of our danger but your own. Whereas we, coming from a city no more being, and putting ourselves into danger for a city hopeless ever to

be again, saved both you in part and ourselves. But if we had
joined with the Persian, fearing (as others did) to have our
territories wasted, or afterwards, as men lost, durst not have
put ourselves into our galleys, you must not have fought with
him by sea because your fleet had been too small; but his affairs
had succeeded as he would himself.

75. "Therefore, men of Lacedaemon, we deserve not so great
envy of the Grecians, for our courage at that time and for our
prudence and for the dominion we hold, as we now undergo.
Which dominion we obtained not by violence, but because
the confederates, when yourselves would not stay out the relics
of the war against the barbarian, came in and entreated us to
take the command of their own accord. So that at first we were
forced to advance our dominion to what it is out of the nature
of the thing itself, as chiefly for fear, next for honour, and lastly
for profit. For when we had the envy of many and had recon-
quered some that had already revolted, and seeing you were
no more our friends as you had been but suspected and
quarrelled us, we held it no longer a safe course laying by our
power to put ourselves into your danger. For the revolts from
us would all have been made to you. Now it is no fault for
men in danger to order their affairs to the best.

76. "For you also, men of Lacedaemon, have command over
the cities of Peloponnesus and order them to your best advantage. And had you, when the time was, by staying it out,
been envied in your command, as we know well, you would
have been no less heavy to the confederates than we, you must
have been constrained to rule imperiously or to have fallen
into danger. So that, though overcome by three of the greatest
things, honour, fear, and profit, we have both accepted the
dominion delivered us and refuse again to surrender it, we
have therein done nothing to be wondered at nor beside the
manner of men. Nor have we been the first in this kind, but
it hath been ever a thing fixed for the weaker to be kept under
by the stronger. Besides, we took the government upon us as
esteeming ourselves worthy of the same; and of you also so
esteemed till having computed the commodity, you now fall
to allegation of equity, a thing which no man that had the
occasion to achieve anything by strength ever so far preferred

as to divert him from his profit. Those men are worthy of commendation who following the natural inclination of man in desiring rule over others are juster than for their own power they need. And therefore if another had our power, we think it would best make appear our own moderation; and yet our moderation hath undeservedly incurred contempt rather than commendation.

77. "For though in pleas of covenants with our confederates when, in our own city we have allowed them trial by laws equal both to them and us, the judgment hath been given against us, we have then nevertheless been reputed contentious. None of them considering that others, who in other places have dominion and are toward their subject states less moderate than we, yet are never upbraided for it. For they that have the power to compel need not at all to go to law. And yet these men having been used to converse with us upon equal terms, if they lose anything which they think they should not, either by sentence or by the power of our government, they are not thankful for the much they retain, but take in worse part the little they forego than if at first, laying law aside, we had openly taken their goods by violence. For in this kind also they themselves cannot deny but the weaker must give way to the stronger. And men, it seems, are more passionate for injustice than for violence. For that, coming as from an equal, seemeth rapine, and the other, because from one stronger, but necessity. Therefore, when they suffered worse things under the Medes' dominion, they bore it, but think ours to be rigorous. And good reason, for to men in subjection the present is ever the worst estate. Insomuch as you also, if you should put us down and reign yourselves, you would soon find a change of the love which they bear you now for fear of us if you should do again as you did for awhile when you were their commanders against the Medes. For not only your own institutions are different from those of others, but also when any one of you comes abroad [with charge], he neither useth those of yours nor yet those of the rest of Greece.

78. "Deliberate therefore of this a great while as of a matter of great importance, and do not upon the opinions and criminations of others procure your own trouble. Consider before you

enter how unexpected the chances of war be. For a long war for the most part endeth in calamity from which we are equally far off, and whether part it will light on is to be tried with uncertainty. And men, when they go to war, use many times to fall first to action, the which ought to come behind; and when they have taken harm, then they fall to reasoning. But since we are neither in such error ourselves, nor do find that you are, we advise you, whilst good counsel is in both our elections, not to break the peace nor violate your oaths, but according to the articles, let the controversy be decided by judgment; or else we call the gods you have sworn by to witness that if you begin the war, we will endeavour to revenge ourselves the same way that you shall walk in before us."

79. Thus spake the Athenians. After the Lacedaemonians had heard both the complaints of the confederates against the Athenians and the Athenians' answer, they put them everyone out of the court and consulted of the business among themselves. And the opinions of the greatest part concurred in this, that the Athenians had done unjustly and ought speedily to be warred on. But Archidamus their king, a man reputed both wise and temperate, spake as followeth.

80. "Men of Lacedaemon, both I myself have the experience of many wars, and I see you of the same age with me to have the like, insomuch as you cannot desire this war either through inexperience, as many do, nor yet as apprehending it to be profitable or safe. And whosoever shall temperately consider the war we now deliberate of will find it to be no small one. For though in respect of the Peloponnesians and our neighbour states we have equal strength and can quickly be upon them, yet against men whose territory is remote and are also expert seamen and with all other things excellently furnished, as money, both private and public, shipping, horses, arms, and number, more than any one part of Greece besides, and that have many confederates paying them tribute: against such, I say, why should we lightly undertake the war? And since we are unfurnished, whereon relying should we make such haste to it? On our navy? But therein we are too weak; and if we will provide and prepare against them, it will require time. On our

money? But therein also we are more too weak; for neither hath the state any, nor will private men readily contribute.

81. "But it may be some rely on this, that we exceed them in arms and multitude of soldiers so that we may waste their territories with incursions. But there is much other land under their dominion, and by sea they are able to bring in whatsoever they shall stand in need of. Again, if we essay to alienate their confederates, we must aid them with shipping because the most of them are islanders. What a war then will this of ours be? For unless we have the better of them in shipping or take from them their revenue whereby their navy is maintained, we shall do the most hurt to ourselves. And in this case to let fall the war again will be no honour for us when we are chiefly thought to have begun it. As for the hope that if we waste their country, the war will soon be at an end, let that never lift us up; for I fear we shall transmit it rather to our children. For it is likely the Athenians have the spirit not to be slaves to their earth, nor as men without experience to be astonished at the war.

82. "And yet I do not advise that we should stupidly suffer our confederates to be wronged and not apprehend the Athenians in their plots against them, but only not yet to take up arms but to send and expostulate with them, making no great show neither of war nor of sufferance; and in the meantime to make our provision and make friends both of Greeks and barbarians, such as in any place we can get of power either in shipping or money (nor are they to be blamed that being laid in wait for, as we are by the Athenians, take unto them not Grecians only but also barbarians for their safety), and withal to set forth our own. If they listen to our ambassadors, best of all; if not, then two or three years passing over our heads, being better appointed, we may war upon them if we will. And when they see our preparation and hear words that import no less, they will perhaps relent the sooner, especially having their grounds unhurt and consulting upon commodities extant and not yet spoiled. For we must think their territory to be nothing but an hostage, and so much the more by how much the better husbanded. The which we ought therefore to spare as

long as we may, lest making them desperate, we make them also the harder to expugn. For if, unfurnished as we be, at the instigation of the confederates we waste their territory, consider if in so doing we do not make the war both more dishonourable to the Peloponnesians and also more difficult. For though accusations, as well against cities as private men, may be cleared again, a war for the pleasure of some taken up by all, the success whereof cannot be foreseen, can hardly with honour be letten fall again.

83. "Now let no man think it cowardice that being many cities, we go not presently and invade that one city. For of confederates that bring them in money, they have more than we; and war is not so much war of arms as war of money by means whereof arms are useful, especially when it is a war of land men against sea men. And therefore let us first provide ourselves of money and not first raise the war upon the persuasion of the confederates. For we that must be thought the causers of all events, good or bad, have reason also to take some leisure in part to foresee them.

84. "As for the slackness and procrastination wherewith we are reproached by the confederates, be never ashamed of it; for the more haste you make to the war, you will be the longer before you end it for that you go to it unprovided. Besides, our city hath been ever free and well thought of, and this which they object is rather to be called a modesty proceeding upon judgment. For by that it is that we alone are neither arrogant upon good success nor shrink so much as others in adversity. Nor are we, when men provoke us to it with praise, through the delight thereof moved to undergo danger more than we think fit ourselves; nor when they sharpen us with reprehension doth the smart thereof a jot the more prevail upon us. And this modesty of ours maketh us both good soldiers and good counsellors: good soldiers, because shame begetteth modesty, and valour is most sensible of shame; good counsellors in this, that we are brought up more simply than to disesteem the laws and by severity more modestly than to disobey them, and also in that we do not, like men exceeding wise in things needless, find fault bravely with the preparation of the enemy and in effect not assault him accordingly, but do think our neighbour's

cogitations like our own, and that the events of fortune cannot be discerned by a speech; and do therefore always so furnish ourselves really against the enemy as against men well advised. For we are not to build our hopes upon the oversights of them but upon the safe foresight of ourselves. Nor must we think that there is much difference between man and man, but him only to be the best, that hath been brought up amongst the most difficulties.

85. "Let us not therefore cast aside the institutions of our ancestors which we have so long retained to our profit; nor let us of many men's lives, of much money, of many cities, and much honour, hastily resolve in so small a part of one day, but at leisure, the which we have better commodity than any other to do, by reason of our power. Send to the Athenians about the matter of Potidaea; send about that wherein the confederates say they are injured; and the rather because they be content to refer the cause to judgment, and one that offereth himself to judgment may not lawfully be invaded as a doer of injury before the judgment be given. And prepare withal for the war. So shall you take the most profitable counsel for yourselves, and the most formidable to the enemy."

Thus spake Archidamus. But Sthenelaidas, then one of the Ephori, stood up last of all and spake to the Lacedaemonians in this manner:

86. "For my part, I understand not the many words used by the Athenians; for though they have been much in their own praises, yet they have said nothing to the contrary but that they have done injury to our confederates and to Peloponnesus. And if they carried themselves well against the Medes, when time was, and now ill against us, they deserve a double punishment, because they are not good as they were and because they are evil as they were not. Now are we the same we were and mean not (if we be wise) either to connive at the wrongs done to our confederates or defer to repair them, for the harm they suffer is not deferred. Others have much money, many galleys, and many horses; and we have good confederates not to be betrayed to the Athenians nor to be defended with words (for they are not hurt in words), but to be aided with all our power and with speed. Let no man tell

me that after we have once received the injury we ought to
deliberate. No, it belongs rather to the doers of injury to spend
time in consultation. Wherefore, men of Lacedaemon, decree
the war, as becometh the dignity of Sparta; and let not the
Athenians grow yet greater, nor let us betray our confederates,
but in the name of the Gods proceed against the doers of injustice."

87. Having thus spoken, being himself Ephor, he put it to
the question in the assembly of the Lacedaemonians; and saying afterwards that he could not discern whether was the greater
cry (for they used there to give their votes *viva voce* and not
with balls *) and desiring that it might be evident that their
minds were inclined most to the war, he put it unto them
again and said, "to whomsoever of you it seemeth that the peace
is broken and that the Athenians have done unjustly, let him
arise and go yonder," and withal he showed them a certain
place, "and to whomsoever it seemeth otherwise, let him go to
the other side." So they arose and the room was divided, wherein
far the greater number were those that held the peace to be
broken.

Then calling in the confederates they told them that for
their own parts their sentence was that the Athenians had done
them wrong; but yet they desired to have all their confederates
called together, and then to put it to the question again that
if they would, the war might be decreed by common consent.
This done, their confederates went home; and so did also afterwards the Athenians when they had dispatched the business
they came about. This decree of the assembly that the peace
was broken was made in the fourteenth year of those thirty
years for which a peace had been formerly concluded after
the actions past in Euboea.

88. The Lacedaemonians gave sentence that the peace was
broken and that war was to be made, not so much for the words
of the confederates as for fear the Athenian greatness should

* Hobbes' note: "*Psephos:* properly lapillus, calculus; a little stone
or ball, which he that gave his voice put into a box, either on the
affirmative or negative part, as he pleased. The Athenians used beans,
white and black. The Venetians now use balls; and the distinction
is made by the box, inscribed with yea and no."

still increase. For they saw that a great part of Greece was fallen already into their hands.

89. Now the manner how the Athenians came to the administration of those affairs by which they so raised themselves was this.* After that the Medes, overcome by sea and land, were departed, and such of them as had escaped by sea to Mycale were there also utterly overthrown, Leotychides, king of the Lacedaemonians, then commander of the Grecians at Mycale, with their confederates of Peloponnesus went home. But the Athenians with their confederates of Ionia and the Hellespont, as many as were already revolted from the king, stayed behind and besieged Sestus, holden then by the Medes; and when they had lain before it all the winter, they took it abandoned by the barbarians. And after this they set sail from the Hellespont, everyone to his own city. And the body of the Athenians, as soon as their territory was clear of the barbarians, went home also and fetched thither their wives and children and such goods as they had from the places where they had been put out to keep, and went about the reparation of their city and walls. For there were yet standing some pieces of the circuit of their wall, and likewise a few houses (though the most were down) which the principal of the Persians had reserved for their own lodgings.

90. The Lacedaemonians, hearing what they went about, sent thither their ambassadors—partly because they would themselves have been glad that neither the Athenians nor any other

* The reader should notice that the following chapters, 89 to 118 inclusive, refer to the growth of the Athenian empire *before* the war, i.e., in the years 478 when the Persians left Greece and the League of Delos was formed to 432 when the new conflict broke out. The arrangement of Book I becomes clearer if one observes the following divisions: Chaps. 1–23, introduction, proving the greater size and importance of this war over the preceding. This part also contains Thucydides' discussion of his own presentation of the material, both narrative and speeches. Chaps. 24–88 treats of the *alleged* causes of the war, which are the incident of Epidamnos and the attack on Potidaea. Chaps. 89–118 deal with the underlying cause of the war, which was the growth of the Athenian Empire in the fifty years prior to the events at Epidamnos and Potidaea. Chaps. 119 to the end of the book recount the other actions, diplomatic and military, before the actual outbreak of hostilities.

had had walls, but principally as incited thereto by their confederates who feared not only the greatness of their navy,
which they had not before, but also their courage showed
against the Persians—and entreated them not to build their
walls but rather to join with them in pulling down the walls
of what cities soever without Peloponnesus had them yet standing, not discovering their meaning and the jealousy they had
of the Athenians but pretending this: that if the barbarian returned, he might find no fortified city to make the seat of his
war, as he did of Thebes, and that Peloponnesus was sufficient
for them all whereinto to retire and from whence to withstand
the war. But the Athenians, by the advice of Themistocles,
when the Lacedaemonian ambassadors had so said, dismissed
them presently with this answer, that they would presently
send ambassadors about the business they spake of to Lacedaemon. Now Themistocles willed them to send himself to
Lacedaemon for one, and that as speedily as they could; but
such as were chosen ambassadors with him not to send away
presently, but to stay them till the walls were so raised as to
fight upon them from a sufficient height; and that all the men
in the city, in the meantime, both they and their wives and
children, sparing neither private nor public edifice that might
advance the work but pulling all down whatsoever, should help
to raise it. When he had thus instructed them, adding that he
would himself do the rest at Lacedaemon, he took his journey.
And when he came to Lacedaemon, he went not to the state,
but delaying the time excused himself, and when any of those
that were in office asked him why he did not present himself
to the state, answered, "that he stayed for his fellow-ambassadors
who, upon some business that fell out, were left behind, but
he expected them very shortly and wondered they were not
come already."

91. Hearing this, they gave credit to Themistocles for the
love they bore him; but when others coming thence averred
plainly that the wall went up and that it was come to good
height already, they could not then choose but believe it.
Themistocles, when he saw this, wished them not to be led by
reports, but rather to send thither some of their own, such as
were honest men, and, having informed themselves, would re-

late the truth, which they also did. And Themistocles sendeth privily to the Athenians about the same men to take order for their stay with as little appearance of it as they could and not to dismiss them till their own ambassadors were returned (for by this time were arrived those that were joined with him, namely, Abronychus the son of Lysicles, and Aristides the son of Lysimachus, and brought him word that the wall was of a sufficient height); for he feared lest the Lacedaemonians, when they knew the truth, would refuse to let them go. The Athenians therefore kept there those ambassadors according as it was written to them to do. Themistocles, coming now to his audience before the Lacedaemonians, said plainly, "that the city of Athens was already walled, and that sufficiently for the defence of those within, and that if it shall please the Lacedaemonians upon any occasion to send ambassadors unto them, they were to send thenceforward as to men that understood what conduced both to their own and also to the common good of all Greece. For when they thought it best to quit their city and put themselves into their galleys," he said, "they were bold to do it without asking the advice of them; and in common counsel the advice of the Athenians was as good as the advice of them. And now at this time their opinion is that it will be best, both for themselves in particular and for all the confederates in common, that their city should be walled. For that in strength unequal men cannot alike and equally advise for the common benefit of Greece. Therefore," said he, "either must all the confederate cities be unwalled, or you must not think amiss of what is done by us."

92. The Lacedaemonians when they heard him, though they made no show of being angry with the Athenians (for they had not sent their ambassadors to forbid them but, by way of advice, to admonish them not to build the wall; besides, they bare them affection then for their courage shown against the Medes), yet they were inwardly offended because they missed of their will. And the ambassadors returned home of either side without complaint.

93. Thus the Athenians quickly raised their walls, the structure itself making manifest the haste used in the building. For the foundation consisteth of stones of all sorts, and those in

some places unwrought and as they were brought to the place. Many pillars also taken from sepulchres and polished stones were piled together among the rest. For the circuit of the city was set every way farther out, and therefore hastening they took alike whatsoever came next to hand. Themistocles likewise persuaded them to build up the rest of Piraeus, for it was begun in the year that himself was archon of Athens, as conceiving the place both beautiful, in that it had three natural havens, and that being now seamen, it would very much conduce to the enlargement of their power. For he was indeed the first man that dared tell them that they ought to take upon them the command of the sea, and withal presently helped them in the obtaining it. By his counsel also it was that they built the wall of that breadth about Piraeus which is now to be seen. For two carts carrying stones met and passed upon it one by another. And yet within it there was neither rubbish nor mortar [to fill it up], but it was made all of great stones cut square and bound together with iron and lead. But for height it was raised but to the half, at the most, of what he had intended. For he would have had it able to hold out the enemy both by the height and breadth, and that a few and the less serviceable men might have sufficed to defend it and the rest have served in the navy. For principally he was addicted to the sea because, as I think, he had observed that the forces of the king had easier access to invade them by sea than by land, and thought that Piraeus was more profitable than the city above. And oftentimes he would exhort the Athenians that, in case they were oppressed by land, they should go down thither and with their galleys make resistance against what enemy soever. Thus the Athenians built their walls, and fitted themselves in other kinds, immediately upon the departure of the Persians.

94. In the meantime was Pausanias, the son of Cleombrotus, sent from Lacedaemon commander of the Grecians with twenty galleys out of Peloponnesus, with which went also thirty sail of Athens, besides a multitude of other confederates, and making war on Cyprus subdued the greatest part of the same; and afterwards, under the same commander, came before Byzantium, which they besieged and won.

95. But Pausanias, being now grown insolent, both the rest of the Grecians and especially the Ionians who had newly recovered their liberty from the king, offended with him, came to the Athenians and requested them for consanguinity's sake to become their leaders and to protect them from the violence of Pausanias. The Athenians, accepting the motion, applied themselves both to the defence of these and also to the ordering of the rest of the affairs there in such sort as it should seem best to themselves. In the meantime the Lacedaemonians sent for Pausanias home to examine him of such things as they had heard against him. For great crimes had been laid to his charge by the Grecians that came from thence; and his government was rather an imitation of tyranny than a command in war. And it was his hap to be called home at the same time that the confederates, all but the soldiers of Peloponnesus, out of hatred to him had turned to the Athenians. When he came to Lacedaemon, though he were censured for some wrongs done to private men, yet of the greatest matters he was acquit, especially of Medising,* the which seemed to be the most evident of all. Him therefore they sent general no more, but Dorcis, and some others with him, with no great army, whose command the confederates refused; and they, finding that, went their ways likewise. And after that the Lacedaemonians sent no more, because they feared lest such as went out would prove the worse for the state, as they had seen by Pausanias, and also because they desired to be rid of the Persian war, conceiving the Athenians to be sufficient leaders and at that time their friends.

96. When the Athenians had thus gotten the command by the confederates' own accord for the hatred they bare to Pausanias, they then set down an order which cities should

* I.e., taking the part of the Mede or Persian. For many years after the departure of the Persians from Greece, any politician of high standing either in Athens or Sparta was apt to be accused of "Medism" if he fell from favor. Both Themistocles and Pausanias, who had jointly been commanders of the Greek army and navy against Xerxes, were later accused and condemned on this charge. Greece lived for a long time after 478 in the shadow of the fear of another invasion, and in the suspicion that her leading statesmen might be tampered with by the Persian king.

contribute money for this war against the barbarians, and which galleys. For they pretended to repair the injuries they had suffered by laying waste the territories of the king. And then first came up amongst the Athenians the office of treasurers of Greece, who were receivers of the tribute, for so they called this money contributed. And the first tribute that was taxed came to four hundred and sixty talents. The treasury was at Delos, and their meetings were kept there in the temple.

97. Now using their authority at first in such manner as that the confederates lived under their own laws and were admitted to common council, by [the] war and administration of the common affairs of Greece from the Persian war to this, what against the barbarians, what against their own innovating confederates, and what against such of the Peloponnesians as chanced always in every war to fall in, they effected those great matters following. Which also I have therefore written both because this place hath been pretermitted by all that have written before me (for they have either compiled the Grecian acts before the invasion of the Persians or that invasion only, of which number is Hellanicus, who hath also touched them in his Attic history, but briefly and without exact mention of the times), and also because they carry with them a demonstration of how the Athenian empire grew up.

98. And first, under the conduct of Cimon the son of Miltiades they took Eion upon the river Strymon from the Medes by siege and carried away the inhabitants captives. Then the isle Scyros, in the Aegean sea, inhabited by the Dolopes, the inhabitants whereof they also carried away captives and planted therein a colony of their own. Likewise they made war on the Carystians alone without the rest of the Euboeans, and those also after a time came in by composition. After this they warred on the revolted Naxians and brought them in by siege. And this was the first confederate city which contrary to the ordinance they deprived of their free estate; * though afterwards,

* What Thucydides refers to is the fact that Naxos was the first member of the Delian confederacy which tried to withdraw from the association and when subjugated was then reduced to subject status. Henceforth it contributed money, not ships, and had no further say in the policies of the confederacy.

as it came to any of their turns, they did the like by the rest.

99. Amongst other causes of revolts the principal was their failing to bring in their tribute and galleys and their refusing (when they did so) to follow the wars. For the Athenians exacted strictly and were grievous to them by imposing a necessity of toil which they were neither accustomed nor willing to undergo. They were also otherwise not so gentle in their government as they had been, nor followed the war upon equal terms, and could easily bring back to their subjection such as should revolt. And of this the confederates themselves were the causes. For through this refusal to accompany the army the most of them, to the end they might stay at home, were ordered to excuse their galleys with money, as much as it came to, by which means the navy of the Athenians was increased at the cost of their confederates, and themselves unprovided and without means to make war in case they should revolt.

100. After this it came to pass that the Athenians and their confederates fought against the Medes, both by land and by water, upon the river of Eurymedon in Pamphilia; and in one and the same day the Athenians had victory in both and took or sunk all the Phoenician fleet to the number of two hundred galleys. After this again happened the revolt of Thasos upon a difference about the places of trade and about the mines they possessed in the opposite parts of Thrace. And the Athenians, going thither with their fleet, overthrew them in a battle at sea and landed in the island. But having about the same time sent ten thousand of their own and of their confederates' people unto the river of Strymon for a colony to be planted in a place called then the Nine-ways, now Amphipolis, they won the said Nine-ways, which was held by the Eidonians; but advancing farther towards the heart of the country of Thrace, they were defeated at Drabescus, a city of the Eidonians, by the whole power of the Thracians that were enemies to this new-built town of the Nine-ways.

101. The Thasians in the meantime, being overcome in divers battles and besieged, sought aid of the Lacedaemonians and entreated them to divert the enemy by an invasion of Attica, which, unknown to the Athenians, they promised to do and also had done it, but by an earthquake that then happened,

they were hindered. In which earthquake their Helots, and of
neighbouring towns the Thuriatae and Aethaeans, revolted and
seized on Ithome. Most of these Helots were the posterity of
the ancient Messenians brought into servitude in former times,
whereby also it came to pass that they were called all Messenians. Against these had the Lacedaemonians now a war at
Ithome. The Thasians in the third year of the siege rendered
themselves to the Athenians upon condition to raze their walls,
to deliver up their galleys, to pay both the money behind and
for the future as much as they were wont, and to quit both the
mines and the continent.

102. The Lacedaemonians, when the war against those in
Ithome grew long, amongst other their confederates sent for
aid to the Athenians, who also came with no small forces under
the command of Cimon. They were sent for principally for
their reputation in mural assaults, the long continuance of the
siege seeming to require men of ability in that kind, whereby
they might perhaps have gotten the place by force. And upon
this journey grew the first manifest dissension between the
Lacedaemonians and the Athenians. For the Lacedaemonians,
when they could not take the place by assault, fearing lest the
audacious and innovating humour of the Athenians, whom withal
they esteemed of a contrary race, might, at the persuasion of
those in Ithome, cause some alteration if they stayed,* dismissed
them alone of all the confederates, not discovering their jealousy but alleging that they had no farther need of their service. But the Athenians, perceiving that they were not sent away
upon good cause but only as men suspected, made it a heinous
matter, and conceiving that they had better deserved at the
Lacedaemonians' hands, as soon as they were gone left the
league which they had made with the Lacedaemonians against
the Persian and became confederates with their enemies the
Argives; and then both Argives and Athenians took the same
oath and made the same league with the Thessalians.

103. Those in Ithome, when they could no longer hold out,

---

* A clearer and easier translation would be "fearing the audacious
and innovating temper of the Athenians . . . lest, if they stayed, they
might be convinced by the rebels in Ithome and make a revolt themselves."

in the tenth year of the siege rendered the place to the Lacedaemonians upon condition of security to depart out of Peloponnesus and that they should no more return, and whosoever should be taken returning to be the slave of him that should take him. For the Lacedaemonians had before been warned by a certain answer of the Pythian oracle to let go the suppliant of Jupiter Ithometes. So they came forth, they and their wives and their children. And the Athenians, for hatred they bore to the Lacedaemonians, received them and put them into Naupactus; which city they had lately taken from the Locrians of Ozolae. The Megareans also revolted from the Lacedaemonians and came to the league of the Athenians because they were holden down by the Corinthians with a war about the limits of their territories. Whereupon Megara and Pegae were put into the hands of the Athenians, who built for the Megareans the long walls from the city to Nisaea and maintained them with a garrison of their own. And from hence it was chiefly that the vehement hatred grew of the Corinthians against the Athenians.

104. Moreover Inarus, the son of Psammetticus, an African,* king of the Africans that confine on Egypt, making war from Mareia above Pharus, caused the greatest part of Egypt to rebel against the king Artaxerxes; and when he had taken the government of them upon himself, he brought in the Athenians to assist him, who chancing to be then warring on Cyprus with two hundred galleys, part their own and part their confederates, left Cyprus and went to him. And going from the sea up the river of Nilus after they had made themselves masters of the river and of two parts of the city of Memphis, assaulted the third part called the White Wall. Within were of the Medes and Persians, such as had escaped, and of the Egyptians, such as had not revolted amongst the rest.

105. The Athenians came also with a fleet to Halias and landing their soldiers fought by land with the Corinthians and Epidaurians, and the Corinthians had the victory. After this, the Athenians fought by sea against the fleet of the Peloponnesians at Cecryphaleia, and the Athenians had the victory.

* Hobbes always renders the Greek words *Libyan* and *Libya* by "African" and "Africa."

After this again, the war being on foot of the Athenians against the Aeginetae, a great battle was fought between them by sea upon the coast of Aegina, the confederates of both sides being at the same, in which the Athenians had the victory, and having taken seventy galleys landed their army and besieged the city under the conduct of Leocrates the son of Stroebus. After this, the Peloponnesians, desiring to aid the Aeginetae, sent over into Aegina itself three hundred men of arms of the same that had before aided the Corinthians and Epidaurians and with other forces seized on the top of Geraneia. And the Corinthians and their confederates came down from thence into the territory of Megara, supposing that the Athenians, having much of their army absent in Aegina and in Egypt, would be unable to aid the Megareans or, if they did, would be forced to rise from before Aegina. But the Athenians stirred not from Aegina; but those that remained at Athens, both young and old, under the conduct of Myronides went to Megara; and after they had fought with doubtful victory, they parted asunder again with an opinion on both sides not to have had the worse in the action. And the Athenians, who notwithstanding had rather the better, when the Corinthians were gone away erected a trophy. But the Corinthians, having been reviled at their return by the ancient men of the city, about twelve days after came again prepared and set up their trophy likewise, as if the victory had been theirs. Hereupon the Athenians sallying out of Megara with a huge shout * both slew those that were setting up the trophy and, charging the rest, got the victory.

106. The Corinthians, being overcome, went their way; but a good part of them, being hard followed and missing their way, lighted into the enclosed ground of a private man, which fenced with a great ditch had no passage through. Which the Athenians perceiving, opposed them at the place by which they entered with their men of arms and, encompassing the ground with their light armed soldiers, killed those that were entered with stones. This was a great loss to the Corinthians, but the rest of their army got home again.

* This is too literal in Hobbes. The word, which is used of a military sally, originally meant "raising the war cry." In such a passage as the present it has come to mean no more than "sallying out."

107. About this time the Athenians began the building of their long walls from the city down to the sea, the one reaching to the haven called Phaleron, the other to Piraeus. The Phoceans also making war upon Boeum, Cytinium, and Erineus, towns that belonged to the Dorians of whom the Lacedaemonians are descended, and having taken one of them, the Lacedaemonians, under the conduct of Nicomedes the son of Cleombrotus in the place of Pleistoanactes son of king Pausanias who was yet in his minority, sent unto the aid of the Dorians fifteen hundred men of arms of their own, and of their confederates ten thousand. And when they had forced the Phoceans upon composition to surrender the town they had taken, they went their ways again. Now if they would go home by sea through the Crisaean Gulf, the Athenians going about with their fleet would be ready to stop them; and to pass over Geraneia they thought unsafe because the Athenians had in their hands Megara and Pegae. For Geraneia was not only a difficult passage of itself but was also always guarded by the Athenians. They thought good, therefore, to stay amongst the Boeotians and to consider which way they might most safely go through. Whilst they were there, there wanted not some Athenians that privily solicited them to come to the city, hoping to have put the people out of government and to have demolished the long walls then building. But the Athenians, with the whole power of their city and a thousand Argives and other confederates as they could be gotten together, in all fourteen thousand men, went out to meet them; for there was suspicion that they came thither to depose the democracy. There also came to the Athenians certain horsemen out of Thessaly, which in the battle turned to the Lacedaemonians.

108. They fought at Tanagra of Boeotia, and the Lacedaemonians had the victory; but the slaughter was great on both sides. Then the Lacedaemonians, entering into the territories of Megara and cutting down the woods before them, returned home by the way of Geraneia and the Isthmus. Upon the two-and-sixtieth day after this battle the Athenians, under the conduct of Myronides, made a journey against the Boeotians and overthrew them at Oenophyta and brought the territories of Boeotia and Phocis under their obedience, and withal razed

the walls of Tanagra and took of the wealthiest of the Locrians of Opus a hundred hostages, and finished also at the same time their long walls at home. After this, Aegina also yielded to the Athenians on these conditions: that they should have their walls pulled down and should deliver up their galleys and pay their taxed tribute for the time to come. Also the Athenians made a voyage about Peloponnesus wherein they burnt the arsenal of the Lacedaemonians' navy, took Chalcis, a city of the Corinthians, and landing their forces in Sicyonia overcame in the fight those that made head against them.

109. All this while the Athenians stayed still in Egypt and saw much variety of war. First the Athenians were masters of Egypt; and the king of Persia sent one Megabazus, a Persian, with money to Lacedaemon to procure the Peloponnesians to invade Attica, and by that means to draw the Athenians out of Egypt. But when this took no effect, and money was spent to no purpose, Megabazus returned with the money he had left into Asia. And then was Megabazus the son of Zopyrus, a Persian, sent into Egypt with great forces, and coming in by land overthrew the Egyptians and their confederates in a battle, drave the Grecians out of Memphis, and finally inclosed them in the isle of Prosopis. There he besieged them a year and a half, till such time as having drained the channel and turned the water another way, he made their galleys lie aground and the island for the most part continent, and so came over and won the island with land soldiers.

110. Thus was the army of the Grecians lost after six years' war; and few of many passing through Africa saved themselves in Cyrene, but the most perished. So Egypt returned to the obedience of the king except only Amyrtaeus that reigned in the fens. For him they could not bring in, both because the fens are great, and the people of the fens of all the Egyptians the most warlike. But Inarus, king of the Africans and author of all this stir in Egypt, was taken by treason and crucified. The Athenians moreover had sent fifty galleys more into Egypt for a supply of those that were there already, which putting in at Mendesium, one of the mouths of Nilus, knew nothing of what had happened to the rest, and being assaulted from the land by the army and from the sea by the Phoenician fleet,

lost the greatest part of their galleys and escaped home again with the lesser part. Thus ended the great expedition of the Athenians and their confederates into Egypt.

111. Also Orestes the son of Echecratidas, king of the Thessalians, driven out of Thessaly, persuaded the Athenians to restore him. And the Athenians, taking with them the Boeotians and Phoceans, their confederates, made war against Pharsalus, a city of Thessaly, and were masters of the field as far as they strayed not from the army (for the Thessalian horsemen kept them from straggling) but could not win the city nor yet perform anything else of what they came for but came back again without effect and brought Orestes with them. Not long after this, a thousand Athenians went aboard the galleys that lay at Pegae (for Pegae was in the hands of the Athenians) under the command of Pericles the son of Xantippus, and sailed into Sicyonia and landing put to flight such of the Sicyonians as made head, and then presently took up forces in Achaia, and putting over made war on Oenias, a city of Acarnania, which they besieged. Nevertheless they took it not but returned home.

112. Three years after this, was a truce made between the Peloponnesians and Athenians for five years. And the Athenians gave over the Grecian war and with two hundred galleys, part their own and part confederates, under the conduct of Cimon made war on Cyprus. Of these there went sixty sail into Egypt, sent for by Amyrtaeus that reigned in the fens; and the rest lay at the siege of Citium. But Cimon there dying and a famine arising in the army, they left Citium and when they had passed Salamis in Cyprus, fought at once both by sea and land against the Phoenicians, Cyprians, and Cilicians and, having gotten victory in both, returned home, and with them the rest of their fleet, now come back from Egypt. After this, the Lacedaemonians took in hand the war called the holy war and, having won the temple at Delphi, delivered the possession thereof to the Delphians. But the Athenians afterward, when the Lacedaemonians were gone, came with their army and, regaining it, delivered the possession to the Phoceans.

113. Some space of time after this, the outlaws of Boeotia being seized of Orchomenus and Chaeroneia and certain other

places of Boeotia, the Athenians made war upon those places,
being their enemies, with a thousand men of arms of their own
and as many of their confederates as severally came in, under
the conduct of Tolmidas the son of Tolmaeus. And when they
had taken Chaeroneia, they carried away the inhabitants captives and, leaving a garrison in the city, departed. In their return, those outlaws that were in Orchomenus, together with
the Locrians of Opus and the Euboean outlaws and others of
the same faction, set upon them at Coroneia; and overcoming
the Athenians in battle, some they slew and some they took
alive. Whereupon the Athenians relinquished all Boeotia and
made peace with condition to have their prisoners released. So
the outlaws and the rest returned, and lived again under their
own laws.

114. Not long after revolted Euboea from the Athenians;
and when Pericles had already passed over into it with the
Athenian army, there was brought him news that Megara was
likewise revolted and that the Peloponnesians were about to
invade Attica, and that the Megareans had slain the Athenian
garrison, except only such as fled into Nisaea. Now the
Megareans, when they revolted, had gotten to their aid the
Corinthians, Epidaurians, and Sicyonians. Wherefore Pericles
forthwith withdrew his army from Euboea; and the Lacedaemonians afterward brake into Attica and wasted the country
about Eleusine and Thriasium under the conduct of Pleistoanax
the son of Pausanias, king of Lacedaemon, and came no farther
on, but so went away. After which the Athenians passed again
into Euboea and totally subdued it: the Hestiaeans they put
quite out, taking their territory into their own hands, but
ordered the rest of Euboea according to composition made.

115. Being returned from Euboea, within awhile after they
made a peace with the Lacedaemonians and their confederates
for thirty years and rendered Nisaea, Achaia, Pegae, and
Troezene (for these places the Athenians held of theirs) to
the Peloponnesians. In the sixth year of this peace fell out the
war between the Samians and Milesians concerning Priene; and
the Milesians, being put to the worse, came to Athens and
exclaimed against the Samians. Wherein also certain private
men of Samos itself took part with the Milesians out of desire

to alter the form of government. Whereupon the Athenians went to Samos with a fleet of forty galleys and set up the democracy there and took of the Samians fifty boys and as many men for hostages, which, when they had put into Lemnos and set a guard upon them, they came home. But certain of the Samians (for some of them not enduring the popular government were fled into the continent) entering into a league with the mightiest of them in Samos and with Pissuthnes the son of Hystaspes, who then was governor of Sardis, and levying about seven hundred auxiliary soldiers, passed over into Samos in the evening and first set upon the popular faction and brought most of them into their power; and then stealing their hostages out of Lemnos, they revolted and delivered the Athenian guard and such captains as were there into the hands of Pissuthnes, and withal prepared to make war against Miletus. With these also revolted the Byzantines.

116. The Athenians, when they heard of these things, sent to Samos sixty galleys, sixteen whereof they did not use (for some of them went into Caria to observe the fleet of the Phoenicians and some to fetch in succours from Chios and Lesbos), but with the forty-four that remained, under the command of Pericles and nine others, fought with seventy galleys of the Samians (whereof twenty were such as served for the transport of soldiers) as they were coming altogether from Miletus; and the Athenians had the victory. After this came a supply of forty galleys more from Athens, and from Chios and Lesbos twenty-five. With these having landed their men, they overthrew the Samians in battle and besieged the city, which they inclosed with a triple wall, and shut it up by sea with their galleys. But Pericles, taking with him sixty galleys out of the road, ·made haste towards Caunus and Caria upon intelligence of the coming against them of the Phoenician fleet. For Stesagoras with five galleys was already gone out of Samos and others out of other places to meet the Phoenicians.

117. In the meantime, the Samians, coming suddenly forth with their fleet and falling upon the harbour of the Athenians which was unfortified, sunk the galleys that kept watch before it and overcame the rest in fight, insomuch that they became masters of the sea near their coast for about fourteen days to-

gether, importing and exporting what they pleased. But Pericles returning shut them up again with his galleys. And after this there came to him from Athens a supply of forty sail, with Thucydides, Agnon, and Phormio; and twenty with Tlepolemus and Anticles; and from Chios and Lesbos thirty more. And though the Samians fought against these a small battle at sea, yet unable to hold out any longer, in the ninth month of the siege they rendered the city upon composition: namely, to demolish their walls, to give hostages, to deliver up their navy, and to repay the money spent by the Athenians in the war at days appointed. And the Byzantines also yielded with condition to remain subject to them in the same manner as they had been before their revolt.

118. Now not many years after this happened the matters before related, of the Corcyraeans and the Potidaeans and whatsoever other intervenient pretext of this war. These things done by the Grecians one against another or against the barbarians came to pass all within the compass of fifty years at most, from the time of the departure of Xerxes to the beginning of this present war. In which time the Athenians both assured their government over the confederates and also much enlarged their own particular wealth. This the Lacedaemonians saw and opposed not, save now and then a little, but, as men that had ever before been slow to war without necessity and also for that they were hindered sometimes with domestic war, for the most part of the time stirred not against them; till now at last, when the power of the Athenians was advanced manifestly indeed and that they had done injury to their confederates, they could forbear no longer, but thought it necessary to go in hand with the war with all diligence and to pull down, if they could, the Athenian greatness. For which purpose it was by the Lacedaemonians themselves decreed that the peace was broken and that the Athenians had done unjustly; and also having sent to Delphi and enquired of Apollo whether they should have the better in the war or not, they received, as it is reported, this answer: "That if they warred with their whole power, they should have victory and that himself would be on their side, both called and uncalled."

119. Now when they had assembled their confederates again,

they were to put it to the question amongst them, "whether they should make war or not." And the ambassadors of the several confederates coming in and the council set, as well the rest spake what they thought fit, most of them accusing the Athenians of injury and desiring the war, as also the Corinthians, who had before entreated the cities everyone severally to give their vote for the war, fearing lest Potidaea should be lost before help came, being then present spake last of all to this effect:

120. "Confederates, we can no longer accuse the Lacedaemonians, they having both decreed the war themselves and also assembled us to do the same. For it is fit for them who have the command in a common league, as they are honoured of all before the rest, so also (administering their private affairs equally with others) to consider before the rest of the common business. And though as many of us as have already had our turns with the Athenians need not be taught to beware of them, yet it were good for those that dwell up in the land, and not as we in places of traffic on the sea side, to know that unless they defend those below, they shall with a great deal the more difficulty both carry to the sea the commodities of the seasons and again more hardly receive the benefits afforded to the inland countries from the sea; and also not to mistake what is now spoken, as if it concerned them not, but to make account that if they neglect those that dwell by the sea, the calamity will also reach to themselves; and that this consultation concerneth them no less than us, and therefore not to be afraid to change their peace for war. For though it be the part of discreet men to be quiet unless they have wrong, yet it is the part of valiant men, when they receive injury, to pass from peace into war, and after success, from war to come again to composition, and neither to swell with the good success of war nor to suffer injury through pleasure taken in the ease of peace. For he whom pleasure makes a coward, if he sit still, shall quickly lose the sweetness of the ease that made him so. And he that in war is made proud by success observeth not that his pride is grounded upon unfaithful confidence. For though many things ill advised come to good effect against enemies worse advised, yet more, thought well advised, have fallen but badly out against well

advised enemies. For no man comes to execute a thing with the same confidence he premeditates it. For we deliver opinions in safety, whereas in the action itself we fail through fear.

121. "As for the war, at this time we raise it, both upon injuries done us and upon other sufficient allegations; and when we have repaired our wrongs upon the Athenians, we will also in due time lay it down. And it is for many reasons probable that we shall have the victory: first, because we exceed them in number; and next, because when we go to any action intimated, we shall be all of one fashion. And as for a navy, wherein consisteth the strength of the Athenians, we shall provide it both out of everyone's particular wealth and with the money at Delphi and Olympia. For taking this at interest, we shall be able to draw from them their foreign mariners by offer of greater wages. For the forces of the Athenians are rather mercenary than domestic; whereas our own power is less obnoxious to such accidents, consisting more in the persons of men than in money. And if we overcome them but in one battle by sea, in all probability they are totally vanquished. And if they hold out, we also shall with longer time apply ourselves to naval affairs. And when we shall once have made our skill equal to theirs, we shall surely overmatch them in courage. For the valour that we have by nature, they shall never come unto by teaching; but the experience which they exceed us in, that must we attain unto by industry. And the money wherewith to bring this to pass, it must be all our parts to contribute. For else it were a hard case that the confederates of the Athenians should not stick to contribute to their own servitude, and we should refuse to lay out our money to be revenged of our enemies and for our own preservation, and that the Athenians take not our money from us and even with that do us mischief.

122. "We have also many other ways of war, as the revolt of their confederates, which is the principal means of lessening their revenue; the building of forts in their territory; and many other things which one cannot now foresee. For the course of war is guided by nothing less than by the points of our account, but of itself contriveth most things upon the occasion. Wherein he that complies with it with most temper standeth

the firmest, and he that is most passionate oftenest miscarries. Imagine we had differences each of us about the limits of our territory with an equal adversary; we must undergo them. But now the Athenians are a match for us all at once, and one city after another too strong for us. Insomuch that unless we oppose them jointly and every nation and city set to it unanimously, they will overcome us asunder without labour. And know that to be vanquished (though it trouble you to hear it) brings with it no less than manifest servitude, which but to mention as a doubt, as if so many cities could suffer under one, were very dishonourable to Peloponnesus. For it must then be thought that we are either punished upon merit, or else that we endure it out of fear and so appear degenerate from our ancestors. For by them the liberty of all Greece hath been restored, whereas we for our part assure not so much as our own but, claiming the reputation of having deposed tyrants in the several cities, suffer a tyrant city to be established amongst us. Wherein we know not how we can avoid one of these three great faults, foolishness, cowardice, or negligence. For certainly you avoid them not by imputing it to that which hath done most men hurt, contempt of the enemy: for contempt, because it hath made too many men miscarry, hath gotten the name of foolishness.

123. "But to what end should we object matters past more than is necessary to the business in hand? We must now by helping the present labour for the future, for it is peculiar to our country to attain honour by labour. And though you be now somewhat advanced in honour and power, you must not therefore change the custom; for there is no reason that what was gotten in want should be lost by wealth. But we should confidently go in hand with the war as for many other causes so also for this, that both the God hath by his oracle advised us thereto and promised to be with us himself, and also for that the rest of Greece, some for fear and some for profit, are ready to take our parts. Nor are you they that first break the peace, which the God, inasmuch as he doth encourage us to the war, judgeth violated by them; but you fight rather in defence of the same. For not he breaketh the peace that taketh revenge, but he that is the first invader.

124. "So that seeing it will be every way good to make the war, and since in common we persuade the same, and seeing also that both to the cities and to private men it will be the most profitable course, put off no longer neither the defence of the Potidaeans, who are Dorians and besieged (which was wont to be contrary) by Ionians, nor the recovery of the liberty of the rest of the Grecians. For it is a case that admitteth not delay when they are some of them already oppressed, and others (after it shall be known we met and durst not right ourselves) shall shortly after undergo the like. But think, confederates, you are now at a necessity and that this is the best advice; and therefore give your votes for the war, not fearing the present danger but coveting the long peace proceeding from it. For though by war groweth the confirmation of peace, yet for love of ease to refuse the war doth not likewise avoid the danger. But making account that a tyrant city set up in Greece is set up alike over all and reigneth over some already and the rest in intention, we shall bring it again into order by the war and not only live for the time to come out of danger ourselves but also deliver the already enthralled Grecians out of servitude." Thus said the Corinthians.

125. The Lacedaemonians, when they had heard the opinion of them all, brought the balls to all the confederates present in order, from the greatest state to the least; and the greatest part gave their votes for the war. Now after the war was decreed, though it were impossible for them to go in hand with it presently because they were unprovided and every state thought good without delay severally to furnish themselves of what was necessary, yet there passed not fully a year in this preparation before Attica was invaded and the war openly on foot.

126. In the meantime they sent ambassadors to the Athenians with certain criminations to the end that if they would give ear to nothing, they might have all the pretext that could be for raising of the war. And first the Lacedaemonians, by their ambassadors to the Athenians, required them to banish such as were under curse of the goddess Minerva * for pollution of sanctuary. Which pollution was thus. There had been one

* Hobbes consistently Latinizes the names of the Greek gods, in the fashion of his time. Thus Minerva for Athene and Jupiter for Zeus.

Cylon an Athenian, a man that had been victor in the Olympian exercises, of much nobility and power amongst those of old time, and that had married the daughter of Theagenes, a Megarean, in those days tyrant of Megara. To this Cylon asking counsel at Delphi the God answered that on the greatest festival day he should seize the citadel of Athens. He therefore, having gotten forces of Theagenes and persuaded his friends to the enterprise, seized on the citadel at the time of the Olympic holidays in Peloponnesus with intention to take upon him the tyranny, esteeming the feast of Jupiter to be the greatest and to touch withal on his particular in that he had been victor in the Olympian exercises. But whether the feast spoken of were meant to be the greatest in Attica or in some other place, neither did he himself consider nor the oracle make manifest. For there is also amongst the Athenians the Diasia, which is called the greatest feast of Jupiter Meilichius and is celebrated without the city, wherein in the confluence of the whole people many men offered sacrifices not of living creatures but such as was the fashion of the natives of the place.* But he, supposing he had rightly understood the oracle, laid hand to the enterprise. And when the Athenians heard of it, they came with all their forces out of the fields and lying before the citadel besieged it. But the time growing long, the Athenians, wearied with the siege, went most of them away, and left both the guard of the citadel and the whole business to the nine archontes with absolute authority to order the same as to them it should seem good. For at that time, most of the affairs of the commonweal were administered by those nine archontes. Now those that were besieged with Cylon were for want of both victual and water in very evil estate, and therefore Cylon and a brother of his fled privily out; but the rest, when they were pressed and some of them dead with famine, sat down as suppliants by the altar that is in the citadel. And the Athenians, to whose charge was committed the guard of the place, raising them upon promise to do them no harm, put them all to the

---

* It appears that in some instances, where the worshippers were poor, not living animals were sacrificed, because of the expense involved, but images made of paste. Cf. Herodotus ii.47 for the same custom in Egypt.

sword. Also they had put to death some of those that had taken
sanctuary at the altars of the severe goddesses as they were going away. And from this the Athenians, both themselves and
their posterity, were called accursed and sacrilegious persons.
Hereupon the Athenians banished those that were under the
curse; and Cleomenes, a Lacedaemonian, together with the
Athenians in a sedition, banished them afterwards again, and
not only so but disinterred and cast forth the bodies of such
of them as were dead. Nevertheless there returned of them
afterwards again, and there are of their race in the city unto
this day.

127. This pollution, therefore, the Lacedaemonians required
them to purge their city of, principally, forsooth, as taking
part with the gods, but knowing withal that Pericles the son
of Xantippus was by the mother's side one of that race. For
they thought if Pericles were banished, the Athenians would
the more easily be brought to yield to their desire. Nevertheless, they hoped not so much that he should be banished as to
bring him into the envy of the city, as if the misfortune of
him were in part the cause of the war. For being the most
powerful of his time and having the sway of the state, he was
in all things opposite to the Lacedaemonians, not suffering the
Athenians to give them the least way but inciting them to the
war.

128. Contrariwise, the Athenians required the Lacedaemonians to banish such as were guilty of breach of sanctuary at
Taenarus. For the Lacedaemonians, when they had caused their
Helots, suppliants in the temple of Neptune at Taenarus, to
forsake sanctuary, slew them: for which cause they themselves
think it was that the great earthquake happened afterwards at
Sparta. Also they required them to purge their city of the
pollution of sanctuary in the temple of Pallas Chalcioeca, which
was thus. After that Pausanias the Lacedaemonian was recalled
by the Spartans from his charge in Hellespont, and having
been called in question by them was absolved though he was
no more sent abroad by the state, yet he went again into
Hellespont in a galley of Hermione as a private man, without
leave of the Lacedaemonians, to the Grecian war, as he gave
out, but in truth to negociate with the king, as he had before

begun, aspiring to the principality of Greece. Now the benefit that he had laid up with the king, and the beginning of the whole business, was at first from this. When after his return from Cyprus he had taken Byzantium when he was there the first time (which, being holden by the Medes, there were taken in it some near to the king and of his kindred), unknown to the rest of the confederates he sent unto the king those near ones of his which he had taken and gave out they were run away. This he practised with one Gongylus, an Eretrian, to whose charge he had committed both the town of Byzantium and the prisoners. Also he sent letters unto him which Gongylus carried wherein, as was afterwards known, was thus written: "Pausanias, General of the Spartans, being desirous to do thee a courtesy, sendeth back unto thee these men whom he hath by arms taken prisoners. And I have a purpose, if the same seem also good unto thee, to take thy daughter in marriage and to bring Sparta and the rest of Greece into thy subjection. These things I account myself able to bring to pass if I may communicate my counsels with thee. If, therefore, any of these things do like thee, send some trusty man to the seaside by whose mediation we may confer together."

129. These were the contents of the writing. Xerxes, being pleased with the letter, sends away Artabazus the son of Pharnaces to the seaside with commandment to take the government of the province of Dascylis and to dismiss Megabates, that was governor there before, and withal gives him a letter to Pausanias, which he commanded him to send over to him with speed to Byzantium and to show him the seal and well and faithfully to perform whatsoever in his affairs he should by Pausanias be appointed to do. Artabazus, after he arrived, having in other things done as he was commanded, sent over the letter; wherein was written this answer: "Thus saith king Xerxes to Pausanias: For the men which thou hast saved and sent over the sea unto me from Byzantium, thy benefit is laid up in our house indelibly registered forever; and I like also of what thou hast propounded. And let neither night nor day make thee remiss in the performance of what thou hast promised unto me. Neither be thou hindered by the expense of gold and silver or multitude of soldiers requisite, whithersoever it be need-

ful to have them come. But with Artabazus, a good man whom I have sent unto thee, do boldly both mine and thine own business as shall be most fit for the dignity and honour of us both."

130. Pausanias having received these letters, whereas he was before in great authority for his conduct at Plataea, became now many degrees more elevated and endured no more to live after the accustomed manner of his country but went apparelled at Byzantium after the fashion of Persia, and when he went through Thrace, had a guard of Medes and Egyptians, and his table likewise after the Persian manner. Nor was he able to conceal his purpose, but in trifles made apparent beforehand the greater matters he had conceived of the future. He became moreover difficult of access, and would be in such choleric passions toward all men indifferently that no man might endure to approach him, which was also none of the least causes why the confederates turned from him to the Athenians.

131. When the Lacedaemonians heard of it, they called him home the first time. And when being gone out the second time without their command in a galley of Hermione, it appeared that he continued still in the same practices and, after he was forced out of Byzantium by siege of the Athenians, returned not to Sparta, but news came that he had seated himself at Colonae in the country of Troy practicing still with the barbarians and making his abode there for no good purpose, then the ephori forebore no longer but sent unto him a public officer with the scytale commanding him not to depart from the officer and, in case he refused, denounced war against him. But he, desiring as much as he could to decline suspicion and believing that with money he should be able to discharge himself of his accusations, returned unto Sparta the second time. And first he was by the ephori committed to ward (for the ephori have power to do this to their king); but afterwards, procuring his enlargement, he came forth and exhibited himself to justice against such as had anything to allege against him.

132. And though the Spartans had against him no manifest proof, neither his enemies nor the whole city, whereupon to proceed to the punishment of a man both of the race of their kings and at that present in great authority (for Plistarchus the

son of Leonidas being king and as yet in minority, Pausanias, who was his cousin-german, had the tuition of him yet), by his licentious behaviour and affectation of the barbarian customs, he gave much cause of suspicion that he meant not to live in the equality of the present state. They considered also that he differed in manner of life from the discipline established: amongst other things by this, that upon the tripode at Delphi, which the Grecians had dedicated as the best of the spoil of the Medes, he had caused to be inscribed of himself in particular this elegiac verse:

> *Pausanias, Greek General,*
> *Having the Medes defeated,*
> *To Phoebus in record thereof*
> *This gift hath consecrated.*

But the Lacedaemonians then presently defaced that inscription of the tripode and engraved thereon by name all the cities that had joined in the overthrow of the Medes, and dedicated it so. This therefore was numbered amongst the offences of Pausanias and was thought to agree with his present design, so much the rather for the condition he was now in. They had information farther that he had in hand some practice with the Helots. And so he had, for he promised them not only manumission but also freedom of the city if they would rise with him and co-operate in the whole business. But neither thus upon some impeachment of the Helots would they proceed against him but kept the custom which they have in their own cases not hastily to give a peremptory sentence against a Spartan without unquestionable proof. Till at length (as it is reported) purposing to send over to Artabazus his last letters to the king, he was bewrayed unto them by a man of Argilus, in time past his minion and most faithful to him, who, being terrified with the cogitation that not any of those which had been formerly sent had ever returned, got him a seal like to the seal of Pausanias (to the end that if his jealousy were false or that he should need to alter anything in the letter, it might not be discovered) and opened the letter, wherein (as he had suspected the addition of some such clause) he found himself also written down to be murdered.

133. The ephori, when these letters were by him shown unto them, though they believed the matter much more than they did before, yet desirous to hear somewhat themselves from Pausanias his own mouth, the man being upon design gone to Taenarus into sanctuary and having there built him a little room with a partition in which he hid the ephori, and Pausanias coming to him and asking the cause of his taking sanctuary, they plainly heard the whole matter. For the man both expostulated with him for what he had written about him and from point to point discovered all the practice, saying that though he had never boasted unto him these and these services concerning the king, he must yet have the honour as well as many other of his servants to be slain. And Pausanias himself both confessed the same things and also bade the man not to be troubled at what was past and gave him assurance to leave sanctuary, intreating him to go on in his journey with all speed and not to frustrate the business in hand.

134. Now the ephori, when they had distinctly heard him, for that time went their way, and knowing now the certain truth intended to apprehend him in the city. It is said that when he was to be apprehended in the street, he perceived by the countenance of one of the ephori coming towards him what they came for; and when another of them had by a secret beck signified the matter for good will, he ran into the close of the temple of Pallas Chalcioeca and got in before they overtook him (now the temple itself was hard by) and, entering into a house belonging to the temple to avoid the injury of the open air, there stayed. They that pursued him could not then overtake him; but afterwards they took off the roof and the doors of the house and, watching a time when he was within, beset the house and mured him up and, leaving a guard there, famished him. When they perceived him about to give up the ghost, they carried him, as he was, out of the house, yet breathing; and being out he died immediately. After he was dead, they were about to throw him into the Caeada where they use to cast in malefactors; yet afterwards they thought good to bury him in some place thereabouts. But the oracle of Delphi commanded the Lacedaemonians afterward both to remove the sepulchre from the place where he died (so that he

lies now in the entry of the temple, as is evident by the inscription of the pillar) and also (as having been a pollution of the sanctuary) to render two bodies to the goddess of Chalcioeca for that one. Whereupon they set up two brazen statues and dedicated the same unto her for Pausanias.

135. Now the Athenians, the god himself having judged this a pollution of sanctuary, required the Lacedaemonians to banish out of their city such as were touched with the same.

At the same time that Pausanias came to his end, the Lacedaemonians by their ambassadors to the Athenians accused Themistocles, for that he also had Medised together with Pausanias, having discovered it by proofs against Pausanias, and desired that the same punishment might be likewise inflicted upon him. Whereunto consenting (for he was at this time in banishment by ostracism; and though his ordinary residence was at Argos, he travelled to and fro in other places of Peloponnesus), they sent certain men in company of the Lacedaemonians who were willing to pursue him with command to bring him in wheresoever they could find him.

136. But Themistocles, having had notice of it beforehand, flieth out of Peloponnesus into Corcyra to the people of which city he had formerly been beneficial. But the Corcyraeans, alleging that they durst not keep him there for fear of displeasing both the Lacedaemonians and the Athenians, convey him into the opposite continent; and being pursued by the men thereto appointed asking continually which way he went, he was compelled at a strait to turn in to Admetus, king of the Molossians, his enemy. The king himself being then from home, he became a suppliant to his wife, and by her was instructed to take their son with him and sit down at the altar of the house. When Admetus not long after returned, he made himself known to him and desired him that though he had opposed him in some suit in Athens, not to revenge it on him now in the time of his flight, saying that being now the weaker, he must needs suffer under the stronger, whereas noble revenge is of equals upon equal terms; and that he had been his adversary but in matter of profit, not of life, whereas, if he delivered him up (telling him withal for what and by whom he was followed), he deprived him of all means of saving his life. Admetus having

heard him bade him arise together with his son whom he held as he sat, which is the most submissive supplication that is.

137. Not long after came the Lacedaemonians and the Athenians; and though they alleged much to have him, yet he delivered him not but sent him away by land to Pydna upon the other sea (a city belonging to Alexander) because his purpose was to go to the king, where finding a ship bound for Ionia, he embarked and was carried by foul weather upon the fleet of the Athenians that besieged Naxos. Being afraid, he discovered to the master (for he was unknown) who he was and for what he fled, and said that unless he would save him, he meant to say that he had hired him to carry him away for money; and that to save him, there needed no more but this, to let none go out of the ship till the weather served to be gone; to which if he consented, he would not forget to requite him according to his merit. The master did so; and having lain a day and a night at sea upon the fleet of the Athenians, he arrived afterward at Ephesus. And Themistocles having liberally rewarded him with money (for he received there both what was sent him from his friends at Athens and also what he had put out at Argos), he took his journey upwards in company of a certain Persian of the low countries and sent letters to the king Artaxerxes, the son of Xerxes, newly come to the kingdom, wherein was written to this purpose: "I, Themistocles, am coming unto thee, who, of all the Grecians, as long as I was forced to resist thy father that invaded me, have done your house the maniest damages; yet the benefits I did him were more after once I with safety, he with danger, was to make retreat. And both a good turn is already due unto me," (writing here, how he had forewarned him of the Grecians' departure out of Salamis and ascribing the then not breaking of the bridge falsely unto himself) "and at this time to do thee many other good services, I present myself, persecuted by the Grecians for thy friendship's sake. But I desire to have a year's respite that I may declare unto thee the cause of my coming myself."

138. The king, as is reported, wondered what his purpose might be and commanded him to do as he had said. In this time of respite he learned as much as he could of the language and fashions of the place. And a year after coming to the court,

he was great with the king more than ever had been any Grecian before, both for his former dignity and the hope of Greece which he promised to bring into his subjection, but especially for the trial he gave of his wisdom. For Themistocles was a man in whom most truly was manifested the strength of natural judgment, wherein he had something worthy admiration different from other men. For by his natural prudence, without the help of instruction before or after, he was both of extemporary matters upon short deliberation the best discerner and also of what for the most part would be their issue the best conjecturer. What he was perfect in he was able also to explicate, and what he was unpractised in he was not to seek how to judge of conveniently. Also he foresaw, no man better, what was best or worst in any case that was doubtful. And (to say all in few words) this man, by the natural goodness of his wit and quickness of deliberation, was the ablest of all men to tell what was fit to be done upon a sudden. But falling sick he ended his life; some say he died voluntarily by poison because he thought himself unable to perform what he had promised to the king. His monument is in Magnesia in Asia, in the market place; for he had the government of that country, the king having bestowed upon him Magnesia which yielded him fifty talents by the year for his bread, and Lampsacus for his wine (for this city was in those days thought to have store of wine), and the city of Myus for his meat. His bones are said by his kindred to have been brought home by his own appointment and buried in Attica unknown to the Athenians, for it was not lawful to bury one there that had fled for treason. These were the ends of Pausanias the Lacedaemonian and Themistocles the Athenian, the most famous men of all the Grecians of their time.

139. And this is that which the Lacedaemonians did command, and were commanded, in their first embassage touching the banishment of such as were under the curse.

After this they sent ambassadors again to Athens commanding them to levy the siege from before Potidaea and to suffer Aegina to be free, but principally and most plainly telling them that the war should not be made in case they would abrogate the act concerning the Megareans, by which act they were forbidden both the fairs of Attica and all ports within the Athenian dominion. But the Athenians would not obey them, neither in the rest of their commands nor in the abrogation of that act, but recriminated the Megareans for having tilled holy ground and unset out with bounds and for receiving of their slaves that revolted. But at length, when the last ambassadors from Lacedaemon were arrived, namely, Ramphias, Melesippus, and Agesander, and spake nothing of that which formerly they were wont but only this, that "the Lacedaemonians desire that there should be peace, which may be had if you will suffer the Grecians to be governed by their own laws," the Athenians called an assembly and, propounding their opinions amongst themselves, thought good, after they had debated the matter, to give them an answer once for all. And many stood forth and delivered their minds on either side, some for the war and some that this act concerning the Megareans ought not to stand in their way to peace but to be abrogated. And Pericles the son of Xantippus, the principal man at that time of all Athens and most sufficient both for speech and action, gave his advice in such manner as followeth:

140. "Men of Athens, I am still not only of the same opinion not to give way to the Peloponnesians (notwithstanding I know that men have not the same passions in the war itself which they have when they are incited to it but change their opinions with the events), but also I see that I must now advise the same things or very near to what I have before delivered. And I require of you with whom my counsel shall take place that if we miscarry in aught, you will either make the best of it, as decreed by common consent, or if we prosper, not to attribute it to your own wisdom only. For it falleth out with the events of actions, no less than with the purposes of man, to proceed with uncertainty, which is also the cause that when anything happeneth contrary to our expectation, we use to lay the fault on fortune. That the Lacedaemonians, both formerly and especially now, take counsel how to do us mischief is a thing manifest. For whereas it is said [in the articles] that in our mutual controversies we shall give and receive trials of judgment, and in the meantime either side hold what they possess, they never yet sought any such trial themselves nor will accept of the same offered by us. They will clear them-

selves of their accusations by war rather than by words, and
come hither no more now to expostulate but to command. For
they command us to arise from before Potidaea and to restore
the Aeginetae to the liberty of their own laws and to abrogate
the act concerning the Megareans. And they that come last
command us to restore all the Grecians to their liberty. Now let
none of you conceive that we shall go to war for a trifle by not
abrogating the act concerning Megara (yet this by them is pretended most, and that for the abrogation of it war shall stay),
nor retain a scruple in your minds as if a small matter moved
you to the war. For even this small matter containeth the trial
and constancy of your resolution. Wherein if you give them
way, you shall hereafter be commanded a greater matter as
men that for fear will obey them likewise in that. But by a
stiff denial you shall teach them plainly to come to you hereafter
on terms of more equality.

141. "Resolve therefore from this occasion either to yield
them obedience before you receive damage, or if we must have
war (which for my part I think is best), be the pretence
weighty or light, not to give way nor keep what we possess in
fear. For a great and a little claim imposed by equals upon their
neighbours before judgment by way of command hath one and
the same virtue, to make subject. As for the war, how both we
and they be furnished, and why we are not like to have the
worse, by hearing the particulars you shall now understand.
The Peloponnesians are men that live by their labour * without money either in particular or in common stock. Besides, in
long wars and by sea they are without experience, for that the
wars which they have had one against another have been but
short through poverty. And such men can neither man their
fleets nor yet send out their armies by land very often, because
they must be far from their own wealth and yet by that be
maintained and be besides barred the use of the sea. It must be
a stock of money, not forced contributions, that support the

---

* Perhaps a more significant translation in view of the context is
"men that work their land with their own hands." A great many of
the Peloponnesians (except the Spartans) did most of their farm work
themselves, with a relatively small amount of hired labor. Consequently
they were unlikely to be effective soldiers at times of sowing or harvest.

wars; and such as live by their labour are more ready to serve the wars with their bodies than with their money. For they make account that their bodies will outlive the danger, but their money they think is sure to be spent, especially if the war (as it is likely) should last. So that the Peloponnesians and their confederates, though for one battle they be able to stand out against all Greece besides, yet to maintain a war against such as have their preparations of another kind, they are not able; inasmuch as not having one and the same counsel, they can speedily perform nothing upon the occasion; and having equality of vote and being of several races, everyone will press his particular interest, whereby nothing is like to be fully executed. For some will desire to take revenge on some enemy and others to have their estates least wasted. And being long before they can assemble, they take the lesser part of their time to debate the common business and the greater to dispatch their own private affairs. And everyone supposeth that his own neglect of the common estate can do little hurt and that it will be the care of somebody else to look to that for his own good, not observing how by these thoughts of everyone in several the common business is jointly ruined.

142. "But their greatest hindrance of all will be their want of money, which being raised slowly, their actions must be full of delay, which the occasions of war will not endure. As for their fortifying here and their navy, they are matters not worthy fear. For it were a hard matter for a city equal to our own in time of peace to fortify in that manner, much less in the country of an enemy, and we no less fortified against them. And if they had a garrison here, though they might, by excursions and by the receiving of our fugitives, annoy some part of our territory, yet would not that be enough both to besiege us and also to hinder us from sallying into their territories and from taking revenge with our fleet, which is the thing wherein our strength lies. For we have more experience in land service by use of the sea than they have in sea service by use of the land. Nor shall they attain the knowledge of naval affairs easily. For yourselves, though falling to it immediately upon the Persian war, yet have not attained it fully. How then should husbandmen not seamen, whom also we will not suffer to apply

themselves to it by lying continually upon them with so great fleets, perform any matter of value? Indeed, if they should be opposed but with a few ships, they might adventure, encouraging their want of knowledge with store of men; but awed by many they will not stir that way, and not applying themselves to it will be yet more unskillful and thereby more cowardly. For knowledge of naval matters is an art as well as any other and not to be attended at idle times and on the by, but requiring rather that while it is a-learning, nothing else should be done on the by.

143. "But say they should take the money at Olympia and Delphi and therewith, at greater wages, go about to draw from us the strangers employed in our fleet, this indeed, if, going aboard both ourselves and those that dwell among us, we could not match them, were a dangerous matter. But now we can both do this and (which is the principal thing) we have steersmen and other necessary men for the service of a ship both more and better of our own citizens than are in all the rest of Greece. Besides that, not any of these strangers upon trial would be found content to fly his own country and, withal upon less hope of victory, for a few days' increase of wages take part with the other side.

"In this manner, or like to this, seems to me to stand the case of the Peloponnesians; whereas ours is both free from what in theirs I have reprehended, and has many great advantages besides. If they invade our territory by land, we shall invade theirs by sea. And when we have wasted part of Peloponnesus and they all Attica, yet shall theirs be the greater loss. For they, unless by the sword, can get no other territory instead of that we shall destroy; whereas for us there is other land both in the islands and continent. For the dominion of the sea is a great matter. Consider but this. If we dwelt in the islands, whether of us then were more inexpugnable? We must therefore now, drawing as near as can be to that imagination, lay aside the care of fields and villages, and not for the loss of them, out of passion, give battle to the Peloponnesians, far more in number than ourselves. For though we give them an overthrow, we must fight again with as many more; and if we be overthrown, we shall lose the help of our confederates, which are our strength;

for when we cannot war upon them, they will revolt. Nor bewail ye the loss of fields or houses but of men's bodies; for men may acquire these, but these cannot acquire men. And if I thought I should prevail, I would advise you to go out and destroy them yourselves and show the Peloponnesians that you will never the sooner obey them for such things as these.

144. "There be many other things that give hope of victory in case you do not, whilst you are in this war, strive to enlarge your dominion and undergo other voluntary dangers (for I am afraid of our own errors more than of their designs); but they shall be spoken of at another time in prosecution of the war itself. For the present, let us send away these men with this answer: 'that the Megareans shall have the liberty of our fairs and ports if the Lacedaemonians will also make no banishment of us nor of our confederates as of strangers,' for neither our act concerning Megara nor their banishment of strangers is forbidden in the articles, 'also, that we will let the Grecian cities be free if they were so when the peace was made; and if the Lacedaemonians will also give leave unto their confederates to use their freedom not as shall serve the turn of the Lacedaemonians, but as they themselves shall every one think good; also that we will stand to judgment according to the articles and will not begin the war but be revenged on those that shall.' For this is both just and for the dignity of the city to answer. Nevertheless you must know that of necessity war there will be; and the more willingly we embrace it, the less pressing we shall have our enemies, and that out of the greatest dangers, whether to cities or private men, arise the greatest honours. For our fathers, when they undertook the Medes, did from less beginnings, nay abandoning the little they had, by wisdom rather than fortune, by courage rather than strength, both repel the barbarian and advance this state to the height it now is at. Of whom we ought not now to come short but rather to revenge us by all means upon our enemies, and do our best to deliver the state unimpaired by us to posterity."

145. Thus spake Pericles. The Athenians, liking best of his advice, decreed as he would have them, answering the Lacedaemonians according to his direction, both in particulars as he had spoken and generally, "that they would do nothing on

command, but were ready to answer their accusations upon equal terms by way of arbitrament." So the ambassadors went home, and after these there came no more.

146. These were the quarrels and differences on either side before the war, which quarrels began presently upon the business of Epidamnus and Corcyra. Nevertheless there was still commerce betwixt them, and they went to each other without any herald, though not without jealousy. For the things that had passed were but the confusion of the articles and matter of the war to follow.*

* Hobbes has not translated this passage correctly. There is no "but" in the Greek. Referring to the sentence before and its "not without jealousy," the Greek goes on, "For what had happened *was* a breaking of the truce and the occasion of the war" (i.e., and therefore they were naturally suspicious).

THE SECOND BOOK

1. The war between the Athenians and the Peloponnesians
beginneth now from the time they had no longer commerce
one with another without a herald, and that having once begun
it they warred without intermission. And it is written in order
by summers and winters according as from time to time the
several matters came to pass.

2. The peace, which after the winning of Euboea was concluded for thirty years, lasted fourteen years. But in the fifteenth year, being the forty-eighth of the priesthood of
Chrysis in Argos, Aenesias being then ephor at Sparta and
Pythadorus, archon of Athens, having then two months of his
government to come, in the sixth month after the battle at
Potidaea and in the beginning of the spring, three hundred and

odd Thebans led by Pythangelus the son of Phyleides and
Diemporus the son of Onetoridas, Boeotian rulers, about the
first watch of the night entered with their arms into Plataea, a
city of Boeotia and confederate of the Athenians. They were
brought in and the gates opened unto them by Naucleides and
his accomplices, men of Plataea that for their own private
ambition intended both the destruction of such citizens as were
their enemies and the putting of the whole city under the subjection of the Thebans. This they negotiated with one Eurymachus the son of Leontiadas, one of the most potent men of
Thebes. For the Thebans, foreseeing the war, desired to pre-
occupy Plataea, which was always at variance with them,
whilst there was yet peace and the war not openly on foot. By
which means they more easily entered undiscovered, there being
no order taken before for a watch. And making a stand in their
arms in the market place, they did not, as they that gave them
entrance would have had them, fall presently to the business
and enter the houses of their adversaries, but resolved rather to
make favourable proclamation and to induce the city to composition and friendship. And the herald proclaimed, "that if
any man, according to the ancient custom of all the Boeotians,
would enter into the same league of war with them, he should
come and bring his arms to theirs," supposing the city by this
means would easily be drawn to their side.

3. The Plataeans, when they perceived that the Thebans
were already entered and had surprised the city, through fear
and opinion that more were entered than indeed were (for
they could not see them in the night), came to composition and
accepting the condition rested quiet, and the rather, for that
they had yet done no man harm. But whilst that these things
were treating, they observed that the Thebans were not many
and thought that if they should set upon them, they might
easily have the victory. For the Plataean commons were not
willing to have revolted from the Athenians. Wherefore it
was thought fit to undertake the matter, and they united themselves by digging through the common walls between house
and house that they might not be discovered as they passed the
streets. They also placed carts in the streets without the cattle
that drew them to serve them instead of a wall, and every other

thing they put in readiness as they severally seemed necessary for the present enterprise. When all things according to their means were ready, they marched from their houses towards the enemies, taking their time whilst it was yet night and a little before the break of day because they would not have to charge them when they should be emboldened by the light and on equal terms, but when they should by night be terrified and inferior to them in knowledge of the places of the city. So they forthwith set upon them and came quickly up to hand strokes.

4. And the Thebans, seeing this and finding they were deceived, cast themselves into a round figure and beat them back in that part where the assault was made; and twice or thrice they repulsed them. But at last, when both the Plataeans themselves charged them with a great clamour, and their wives also and families shouted and screeched from the houses and withal threw stones and tiles amongst them, the night having been also very wet, they were afraid and turned their backs and fled here and there about the city, ignorant for the most part, in the dark and dirt, of the ways out by which they should have been saved (for this accident fell out upon the change of the moon) and pursued by such as were well acquainted with the ways to keep them in; insomuch as the greatest part of them perished. The gate by which they entered, and which only was left open, a certain Plataean shut up again with the head of a javelin, which he thrust into the staple instead of a bolt, so that this way also their passage was stopped. As they were chased up and down the city, some climbed the walls and cast themselves out and for the most part died. Some came to a deserted gate of the city and with a hatchet given them by a woman cut the staple and got forth unseen; but these were not many, for the thing was soon discovered. Others again were slain dispersed in several parts of the city. But the greatest part, and those especially who had cast themselves before into a ring, happened into a great edifice adjoining to the wall, the doors whereof, being open, they thought had been the gates of the city and that there had been a direct way through to the other side. The Plataeans, seeing them now pent up, consulted whether they should burn them as they were by firing the house or else

resolve of some other punishment. At length both these and all the rest of the Thebans that were straggling in the city agreed to yield themselves and their arms to the Plataeans at discretion. And this success had they that entered into Plataea.

5. But the rest of the Thebans that should with their whole power have been there before day for fear the surprise should not succeed with those that were in, came so late with their aid that they heard the news of what was done by the way. Now Plataea is from Thebes seventy furlongs, and they marched the slower for the rain which had fallen the same night. For the river Asopus was swollen so high that it was not easily passable. So that what by the foulness of the way and what by the difficulty of passing the river, they arrived not till their men were already some slain and some taken prisoners. When the Thebans understood how things had gone, they lay in wait for such of the Plataeans as were without (for there were abroad in the villages both men and household stuff, as was not unlikely, the evil happening unexpectedly and in time of peace), desiring, if they could take any prisoners, to keep them for exchange for those of theirs within, which (if any were so) were saved alive. This was the Thebans' purpose. But the Plataeans, whilst they were yet in council, suspecting that some such thing would be done and fearing their case without, sent a herald unto the Thebans whom they commanded to say that what they had already done, attempting to surprise their city in time of peace, was done wickedly, and to forbid them to do any injury to those without, and that otherwise they would kill all those men of theirs that they had alive, which, if they would withdraw their forces out of their territory, they would again restore unto them. Thus the Thebans say, and that the Plataeans did swear it. But the Plataeans confess not that they promised to deliver them presently but upon treaty if they should agree, and deny that they swore it. Upon this the Thebans went out of their territory; and the Plataeans, when they had speedily taken in whatsoever they had in the country, immediately slew their prisoners. They that were taken were one hundred and eighty; and Eurymachus, with whom the traitors had practised, was one.

6. When they had done, they sent a messenger to Athens

and gave truce to the Thebans to fetch away the bodies of their dead, and ordered the city as was thought convenient for the present occasion.

The news of what was done coming straightway to Athens, they instantly laid hands on all the Boeotians then in Attica and sent an officer to Plataea to forbid their farther proceeding with their Theban prisoners till such time as they also should have advised of the matter; for they were not yet advertised of their putting to death. For the first messenger was sent away when the Thebans first entered the town; and the second, when they were overcome and taken prisoners; but of what followed after they knew nothing. So that the Athenians, when they sent, knew not what was done; and the officer arriving found that the men were already slain. After this, the Athenians sending an army to Plataea, victualled it and left a garrison in it, and took thence both the women and children and also such men as were unserviceable for the war.

7. This action falling out at Plataea and the peace now clearly dissolved, the Athenians prepared themselves for war; so also did the Lacedaemonians and their confederates, intending on either part to send ambassadors to the king and to other barbarians, wheresoever they had hope of succours, and contracting leagues with such cities as were not under their own command. The Lacedaemonians besides those galleys which they had in Italy and Sicily, of the cities that took part with them there, were ordered to furnish, proportionably to the greatness of their several cities, so many more as the whole number might amount to five hundred sail and to provide a sum of money assessed, and in other things not to stir farther but to receive the Athenians coming but with one galley at once till such time as the same should be ready. The Athenians, on the other side, surveyed their present confederates and sent ambassadors to those places that lay about Peloponnesus, as Corcyra, Cephalonia, Acarnania, and Zacynthus, knowing that as long as these were their friends, they might with the more security make war round about upon the coast of Peloponnesus.

8. Neither side conceived small matters but put their whole strength to the war, and not without reason. For all men in the beginnings of enterprises are the most eager. Besides, there

were then in Peloponnesus many young men, and many in Athens, who for want of experience not unwillingly undertook the war. And not only the rest of Greece stood at gaze to behold the two principal states in combat, but many prophecies were told and many sung by the priests of the oracles both in the cities about to war and in others. There was also a little before this an earthquake in Delos, which in the memory of the Grecians never shook before, and was interpreted for and seemed to be a sign of what was to come afterwards to pass. And whatsoever thing then chanced of the same nature, it was all sure to be inquired after.

But men's affections for the most part went with the Lacedaemonians, and the rather, for that they gave out they would recover the Grecians' liberty. And every man, both private and public person, endeavoured as much as in them lay both in word and deed to assist them and thought the business so much hindered as himself was not present at it. In such passion were most men against the Athenians, some for desire to be delivered from under their government and others for fear of falling into it. And these were the preparations and affections brought unto the war.

9. But the confederates of either party, which they had when they began it, were these. The Lacedaemonians had all Peloponnesus within the isthmus except the Argives and Achaeans (for these were in amity with both, save that the Pellenians at first, only of all Achaia, took their part; but afterwards all the rest did so likewise); and without Peloponnesus, the Megareans, Locrians, Boeotians, Phoceans, Ambraciotes, Leucadians, and Anactorians. Of which the Corinthians, Megareans, Sicyonians, Pellenians, Eleians, Ambraciotes, and Leucadians found shipping; the Boeotians, Phoceans, and Locrians, horsemen; and the rest of the cities, footmen. And these were the confederates of the Lacedaemonians. The Athenian confederates were these: the Chians, Lesbians, Plataeans, the Messenians in Naupactus, most of the Acarnanians, Corcyraeans, Zacynthians, and other cities their tributaries among those nations; also that part of Caria which is on the seacoast and the Dorians adjoining to them; Ionia, Hellespont, the cities bordering on Thrace; all the islands from Peloponnesus to Crete on the east and all the rest

of the Cyclades except Melos and Thera. Of these the Chians, Lesbians, and Corcyraeans found galleys; the rest, footmen and money. These were their confederates and the preparation for the war on both sides.

10. The Lacedaemonians, after the business of Plataea, sent messengers presently up and down Peloponnesus and to their confederates without to have in readiness their forces and such things as should be necessary for a foreign expedition, as intending the invasion of Attica. And when they were all ready, they came to the rendezvous in the isthmus at a day appointed, two-thirds of the forces of every city. When the whole army was gotten together, Archidamus, king of the Lacedaemonians, general of the expedition, called together the commanders of the several cities and such as were in authority and most worthy to be present and spake unto them as followeth:

11. "Men of Peloponnesus and confederates, not only our fathers have had many wars, both within and without Peloponnesus, but we ourselves also, such as are anything in years, have been sufficiently acquainted therewith; yet did we never before set forth with so great a preparation as at this present. And now, not only we are a numerous and puissant army that invade, but the state also is puissant that is invaded by us. We have reason therefore to show ourselves neither worse than our fathers nor short of the opinion conceived of ourselves. For all Greece is up at this commotion observing us, and through their hatred to the Athenians do wish that we may accomplish whatsoever we intend. And therefore, though we seem to invade them with a great army and to have much assurance that they will not come out against us to battle, yet we ought not for this to march the less carefully prepared but of every city, as well the captain as the soldier, to expect always some danger or other in that part wherein he himself is placed. For the accidents of war are uncertain, and for the most part the onset begins from the lesser number and upon passion. And oftentimes the lesser number, being afraid, hath beaten back the greater with the more ease; for that through contempt they have gone unprepared. And in the land of an enemy, though the soldiers ought always to have bold hearts yet for action, they ought to make their preparations as if they were afraid.

For that will give them both more courage to go upon the enemy and more safety in fighting with him. But we invade not now a city that cannot defend itself but a city every way well appointed. So that we must by all means expect to be fought withal, though not now because we be not yet there, yet hereafter, when they shall see us in their country wasting and destroying their possessions. For all men, when in their own sight and on a sudden they receive any extraordinary hurt, fall presently into choler; and the less they consider, with the more stomach they assault. And this is likely to hold in the Athenians somewhat more than in the others, for they think themselves worthy to have the command of others and to invade and waste the territories of their neighbours rather than to see their neighbours waste theirs. Wherefore, as being to war against a great city and to procure both to your ancestors and yourselves a great fame, either good or bad as shall be the event, follow your leaders in such sort as above all things you esteem of order and watchfulness. For there is nothing in the world more comely nor more safe than when many men are seen to observe one and the same order."

12. Archidamus, having thus spoken and dismissed the council, first sent Melesippus the son of Diacritus, a man of Sparta, to Athens to try if the Athenians, seeing them now on their journey, would yet in some degree remit of their obstinacy. But the Athenians neither received him into their city nor presented him to the state; for the opinion of Pericles had already taken place, not to receive from the Lacedaemonians neither herald nor ambassador as long as their army was abroad. Therefore they sent him back without audience with commandment to be out of their borders the selfsame day, and that hereafter if they would anything with them, they should return everyone to his home and send their ambassadors from thence. They sent with him also certain persons to convoy him out of the country to the end that no man should confer with him, who, when he came to the limits and was to be dismissed, uttered these words, "This day is the beginning of much evil unto the Grecians," and so departed. When he returned to the camp, Archidamus, perceiving that they would not relent, dislodged and marched on with his army into their territory. The Boe-

otians with their appointed part and with horsemen aided the Peloponnesians, but with the rest of their forces went and wasted the territory of Plataea.

13. Whilst the Peloponnesians were coming together in the isthmus, and when they were on their march before they brake into Attica, Pericles the son of Xantippus, who with nine others was general of the Athenians, when he saw they were about to break in, suspecting that Archidamus, either of private courtesy or by command of the Lacedaemonians to bring him into jealousy (as they had before for his sake commanded the excommunication), might oftentimes leave his lands untouched, told the Athenians beforehand in an assembly, "that though Archidamus had been his guest, it was for no ill to the state; and howsoever, if the enemy did not waste his lands and houses as well as the rest, that then he gave them to the commonwealth," and therefore desired "that for this he might not be suspected." Also he advised them concerning the business in hand the same things he had done before, "that they should make preparations for the war and receive their goods into the city; that they should not go out to battle but come into the city and guard it; that they should also furnish out their navy, wherein consisted their power, and hold a careful hand over their confederates," telling them, "how that in the money that came from these lay their strength, and that the victory in war consisted wholly in counsel and store of money." Farther he bade them be confident, "in that there was yearly coming into the state from the confederates for tribute, besides other revenue, six hundred talents, and remaining yet then in the citadel six thousand talents of silver coin," (for the greatest sum there had been was ten thousand talents wanting three hundred, out of which was taken that which had been expended upon the gate-houses of the citadel and upon other buildings and for the charges of Potidaea) "besides the uncoined gold and silver of private and public offerings, and all the dedicated vessels belonging to the shows and games, and the spoils of the Persian, and other things of that nature, which amounted to no less than five hundred talents." He added farther that "much money might be had out of other temples without the city which they might use; and if they were barred the use

of all these, they might yet use the ornaments of gold about the goddess herself"; and said that "the image had about it the weight of forty talents of most pure gold and which might all be taken off; but having made use of it for their safety," he said, "they were to make restitution of the like quantity again." Thus he encouraged them touching matter of money. "Men of arms," he said, "they had thirteen thousand besides the sixteen thousand that were employed for the guard of the city and upon the walls." For so many at the first kept watch at the coming in of the enemy, young and old together and strangers that dwelt amongst them as many as could bear arms. For the length of the Phalerian wall to that part of the circumference of the wall of the city where it joined was thirty-five furlongs, and that part of the circumference which was guarded (for some of it was not kept with a watch, namely, the part between the long wall and the Phalerian) was forty-three furlongs. And the length of the long walls down to Piraeus (of which there was a watch only on the outmost) was forty furlongs. And the whole compass of Piraeus together with Munychia was sixty furlongs, whereof that part that was watched was but half. He said farther, "they had of horsemen, accounting archers on horseback, twelve hundred; and sixteen hundred archers; and of galleys fit for the sea, three hundred." All this and no less had the Athenians when the invasion of the Peloponnesians was first in hand and when the war began. These and other words spake Pericles, as he used to do, for demonstration that they were likely to outlast this war.

14. When the Athenians had heard him, they approved of his words and fetched into the city their wives and children and the furniture of their houses, pulling down the very timber of the houses themselves. Their sheep and oxen they sent over into Euboea and into the islands over against them. Nevertheless this removal, in respect they had most of them been accustomed to the country life, grieved them very much.

15. This custom was from great antiquity more familiar with the Athenians than any other of the rest of Greece. For in the time of Cecrops and the first kings down to Theseus the inhabitants of Attica had their several boroughs and therein

their common halls and their governors, and, unless they were
in fear of some danger, went not to the king for advice; but
every city administered their own affairs and deliberated by
themselves. And some of them had also their particular wars,
as the Eleusinians who joined with Eumolpus against Erectheus.
But after Theseus came to the kingdom, one who besides his
wisdom was also a man of very great power, he not only set
good order in the country in other respects but also dissolved
the councils and magistracies of the rest of the towns; and assigning them all one hall and one council-house, brought them
all to cohabit in the city that now is; and constrained them,
enjoying their own as before, to use this one for their city,
which (now when they all paid their duties to it) grew great
and was by Theseus so delivered to posterity. And from that
time to this day, the Athenians keep a holiday at the public
charge to the goddess and call it Synoecia. That which is now
the citadel, and the part which is to the south of the citadel,
was before this time the city. An argument whereof is this:
that the temples of the gods are all set either in the citadel itself or, if without, yet in that quarter, as that of Jupiter Olympius and of Apollo Pythius and of Tellus and of Bacchus in
Limnae (in honour of whom the old Bacchanals were celebrated on the twelfth day of the month Athesterion, according
as the Ionians who are derived from Athens do still observe
them), besides other ancient temples situated in the same part.
Moreover, they served themselves with water for the best
uses of the fountain which, now the Nine-pipes, built so by
the tyrants, was formerly, when the springs were open, called
Callirhoe, and was near. And from the old custom, before mar-
riages and other holy rites they ordain the use of the same
water to this day. And the citadel, from the ancient habitation
of it, is also by the Athenians still called *the city*.

16. The Athenians therefore had lived a long time governed
by laws of their own country towns and, after they were
brought into one, were nevertheless (both for the custom
which most had, as well of the ancient time as since till the
Persian war, to live in the country with their whole families;
and also especially for that since the Persian war they had already repaired their houses and furniture) unwilling to remove.

It pressed them likewise and was heavily taken besides their houses to leave the things that pertained to their religion (which, since their old form of government, were become patrial) and to change their manner of life and to be no better than banished every man his city.

17. After they came into Athens, there was habitation for a few and place of retire with some friends or kindred. But the greatest part seated themselves in the empty places of the city and in temples and in all the chapels of the heroes, saving in such as were in the citadel and the Eleusinium and other places strongly shut up. The Pelasgicum also under the citadel, though it were a thing accursed to dwell in it and forbidden by the end of a verse in a Pythian oracle in these words, "Best is the Pelasgicum empty," was nevertheless for the present necessity inhabited. And in my opinion, this prophecy now fell out contrary to what was looked for. For the unlawful dwelling there caused not the calamities that befell the city, but the war caused the necessity of dwelling there, which war the oracle, not naming, foretold only that it should one day be inhabited unfortunately.

Many also furnished the turrets of the walls and whatsoever other place they could any of them get. For when they were come in, the city had not place for them all; but afterwards they had the long walls divided amongst them and inhabited there and in most parts of Piraeus. Withal they applied themselves to the business of the war, levying their confederates and making ready a hundred galleys to send about Peloponnesus. Thus were the Athenians preparing.

18. The army of the Peloponnesians marching forward came first to Oenoe, a town of Attica, the place where they intended to break in, and encamping before it, prepared with engines and by other means to assault the wall. For Oenoe, lying on the confines between Attica and Boeotia, was walled about; and the Athenians kept a garrison in it for defence of the country when at any time there should be war. For which cause they made preparation for the assault of it, and also spent much time about it otherwise.

And Archidamus for this was not a little taxed as thought to have been both slow in gathering together the forces for the war and also to have favoured the Athenians in that he encouraged not the army to a forwardness in it. And afterwards likewise his stay in the isthmus and his slowness in the whole journey was laid to his charge, but especially his delay at Oenoe. For in this time the Athenians retired into the city: whereas it was thought that the Peloponnesians, marching speedily, might but for this delay have taken them all without. So passionate was the army of Archidamus for his stay before Oenoe. But expecting that the Athenians, whilst their territory was yet unhurt, would relent and not endure to see it wasted, for that cause (as it is reported) he held his hand.

19. But after, when they had assaulted Oenoe and tried all means but could not take it, and seeing the Athenians sent no herald to them, then at length arising from thence—about eighty days after that which happened to the Thebans that entered Plataea, the summer and corn being now at the highest—they fell into Attica, led by Archidamus the son of Zeuxidamus, king of the Lacedaemonians. And when they had pitched their camp, they fell to wasting of the country, first about Eleusis and then in the plain of Thriasia, and put to flight a few Athenian horsemen at the brooks called Rheiti. After this, leaving the Aegaleon on the right hand, they passed through Cecropia till they came unto Acharnas, which is the greatest town in all Attica of those that are called Demoi,* and pitching there, both fortified their camp and stayed a great while wasting the country thereabout.

20. Archidamus was said to have stayed so long at Acharnas with his army in battle array and not to have come down all the time of his invasion into the champaign with this intention. He hoped that the Athenians, flourishing in number of young men and better furnished for war than ever they were before, would perhaps have come forth against him and not endured to see their fields cut down and wasted; and, therefore, seeing they met him not in Thriasia, he thought good to try if they would come out against him lying now at Acharnas. Besides, the place seemed unto him commodious for the army to lie in; and it was thought also that the Acharnans, being a great

* Hobbes' note: "Burroughs." They are electoral districts of Attic territory.

piece of the city (for they were three thousand men of arms),
would not have suffered the spoiling of their lands, but rather
have urged the rest to go out and fight. And if they came not
out against him at this invasion, they might hereafter more
boldly both waste the champaign country and come down even
to the walls of the city. For the Acharnans, after they should
have lost their own, would not be so forward to hazard themselves for the goods of other men; but there would be the
thoughts of sedition in one towards another in the city. These
were the cogitations of Archidamus, whilst he lay at Acharnas.

21. The Athenians, as long as the army of the enemy lay
about Eleusis and the fields of Thrius and as long as they had
any hope it would come on no farther, remembering that also
Pleistoanax the son of Pausanias, king of Lacedaemon, when
fourteen years before this war he entered Attica with an army
of the Peloponnesians as far as Eleusis and Thriasia, retired
again and came no farther (for which he was also banished
Sparta as thought to have gone back for money), they stirred
not. But when they saw the army now at Acharnas but sixty
furlongs from the city, then they thought it no longer to be
endured; and when their fields were wasted (as it was likely)
in their sight, which the younger sort had never seen before
nor the elder but in the Persian war, it was taken for a horrible
matter and thought fit by all, especially by the youth, to go
out and not endure it any longer. And holding councils apart
one from another, they were at much contention, some to make
a sally and some to hinder it. And the priests of the oracles
giving out prophecies of all kinds, everyone made the interpretation according to the sway of his own affection. But the
Acharnians, conceiving themselves to be no small part of the
Athenians, were they that, whilst their own lands were wasting, most of all urged their going out. Insomuch as the city
was every way in tumult and in choler against Pericles, remembering nothing of what he had formerly admonished them,
but reviled him for that being their general he refused to lead
them into the field, and imputing unto him the cause of all
their evil.

22. But Pericles, seeing them in passion for their present
loss and ill advised and being confident he was in the right

touching not sallying, assembled them not nor called any council for fear lest being together they might upon passion rather than judgment commit some error, but looked to the guarding of the city and as much as he could to keep it in quiet. Nevertheless he continually sent out horsemen to keep the scouts of the army from entering upon and doing hurt to the fields near the city. And there happened at Phrygii a small skirmish between one troop of horse of the Athenians, with whom were also the Thessalians, and the horsemen of the Boeotians. Wherein the Athenians and Thessalians had not the worse till such time as the Boeotians were aided by the coming in of their men of arms; and then they were put to flight and a few of the Athenians and Thessalians slain, whose bodies, notwithstanding, they fetched off the same day without leave of the enemy. And the Peloponnesians the next day erected a trophy. This aid of the Thessalians was upon an ancient league with the Athenians and consisted of Larissaeans, Pharsalians, Parasians, Cranonians, Pyrasians, Gyrtonians, Pheraeans. The leaders of the Larissaeans were Polymedes and Aristonus, men of contrary factions in their city; of the Pharsalians, Meno; and of the rest, out of the several cities several commanders.

23. The Peloponnesians, seeing the Athenians would not come out to fight, dislodging from Acharnas wasted certain other villages between the hills Parnethus and Brelissus. Whilst these were in Attica, the Athenians sent the hundred galleys which they had provided, and in them one thousand men of arms and four hundred archers, about Peloponnesus, the commanders whereof were Charcinus the son of Xenotimus, Proteus the son of Epicles, and Socrates the son of Antigenes, who thus furnished weighed anchor and went their way. The Peloponnesians, when they had stayed in Attica as long as their provision lasted, went home through Boeotia, not the way they came in, but passing by Oropus, wasted the country called Peiraice, which is of the tillage of the Oropians, subjects to the people of Athens. And when they were come back into Peloponnesus, they disbanded and went every man to his own city.

24. When they were gone, the Athenians ordained watches both by sea and land, such as were to continue to the end of the war, and made a decree to take out a thousand talents of

the money in the citadel and set it by so as it might not be spent, but the charges of the war be borne out of other money, and made it capital for any man to move or give his vote for the stirring of this money for any other use, but only if the enemy should come with an army by sea to invade the city for necessity of that defence. Together with this money they likewise set apart one hundred galleys, and those to be every year the best and captains to be appointed over them, which were to be employed for no other use than the money was and for the same danger if need should require.

25. The Athenians that were with the hundred galleys about Peloponnesus and with them the Corcyraeans with the aid of fifty sail more and certain others of the confederates thereabout amongst other places which they infested in their course landed at Methone, a town of Laconia, and assaulted it as being but weak and few men within. But it chanced that Brasidas the son of Tellis, a Spartan, had a garrison in those parts, and hearing of it, succoured those of the town with one hundred men of arms. Wherewith running through the Athenian army, dispersed in the fields, directly towards the town, he put himself into Methone; and with the loss of few of his men in the passage he saved the place, and for this adventure was the first that was praised at Sparta in this war. The Athenians putting off from thence sailed along the coast and put in at Pheia of Elis, where they spent two days in wasting the country and in a skirmish overthrew three hundred choice men of the Lower Elis together with other Eleians thereabouts that came forth to defend it. But the wind arising and their galleys being tossed by the weather in a harbourless place, the most of them embarked and sailed about the promontory called Icthys into the haven of Pheia. But the Messenians and certain others that could not get aboard went by land to the town of Pheia and rifled it. And when they had done, the galleys that now were come about took them in and, leaving Pheia, put forth to sea again. By which time a great army of Eleians was come to succour it, but the Athenians were now gone away and wasting some other territory.

26. About the same time the Athenians sent likewise thirty galleys about Locris, which were to serve also for a watch

about Euboea. Of these Cleopompus the son of Clinias had the conduct and, landing his soldiers in divers parts, both wasted some places of the sea coast and won the town of Thronium, of which he took hostages, and overcame in fight at Alope the Locrians that came out to aid it.

27. The same summer, the Athenians put the Aeginetae, man, woman, and child, out of Aegina, laying to their charge that they were the principal cause of the present war. And it was also thought the safer course to hold Aegina, being adjacent to Peloponnesus, with a colony of their own people; and not long after they sent inhabitants into the same. When the Aeginetae were thus banished, the Lacedaemonians gave them Thyrea to dwell in and the occupation of the lands belonging unto it to live on, both upon hatred to the Athenians, and for the benefits received at the hands of the Aeginetae in the time of the earthquake and insurrection of the Helotes. This territory of Thyrea is in the border between Argolica and Laconica, and reacheth to the seaside. So some of them were placed there, and the rest dispersed into other parts of Greece.

28. Also the same summer, on the first day of the month according to the moon (at which time it seems only possible), in the afternoon happened an eclipse of the sun. The which, after it had appeared in the form of a crescent and withal some stars had been discerned, came afterwards again to the former brightness.

29. The same summer also, the Athenians made Nymphodorus the son of Pythos, of the city of Abdera (whose sister was married to Sitalces and that was of great power with him), their host, though before they took him for an enemy, and sent for him to Athens, hoping by his means to bring Sitalces the son of Teres, king of Thrace, into their league. This Teres, the father of Sitalces, was the first that advanced the kingdom of the Odrysians above the power of the rest of Thrace. For much of Thrace consisteth of free states. And Tereus that took to wife out of Athens Procne the daughter of Pandion was no kin to this Teres nor of the same part of Thrace. But that Tereus was of the city of Daulia in the country now called Phocis, then inhabited by the Thracians. And the fact of the women concerning Itys was done there; and by the poets,

where they mention the nightingale, that bird is also called Daulias. And it is more likely that Pandion matched his daughter to this man, for vicinity and mutual succour, than with the other that was so many days' journey off as Odrysae. And Teres (which is also another name) was the first that seized on the kingdom of Odrysae. Now Sitalces, this man's son, the Athenians got into their league that they might have the towns lying on Thrace and Perdiccas to be of their party. Nymphodorus, when he came to Athens, made this league between them and Sitalces and caused Sadocus the son of Sitalces to be made free of Athens and also undertook to end the war in Thrace. For he would persuade Sitalces to send unto the Athenians a Thracian army of horsemen and targeteers. He likewise reconciled Perdiccas to the Athenians, and procured of him the restitution of Therme. And Perdiccas presently aided the Athenians and Phormio in the war against the Chalcideans. Thus were Sitalces the son of Teres, king of Thrace, and Perdiccas the son of Alexander, king of Macedonia, made confederates with the Athenians.

30. The Athenians, being yet with their hundred galleys about Peloponnesus, took Solium, a town that belonged to the Corinthians, and put the Palaerenses only, of all the Acarnanians, into the possession both of the town and territory. Having also by force taken Astacus from the tyrant Euarchus, they drave him thence and joined the place to their league. From thence they sailed to Cephalonia and subdued it without battle (this Cephalonia is an island lying over against Acarnania and Leucas and hath in it these four cities, the Pallenses, Cranii, Samaei, and Pronaei) and not long after returned with their fleet to Athens.

31. About the end of the autumn of this summer the Athenians, both themselves and the strangers that dwelt amongst them, with the whole power of the city, under the conduct of Pericles the son Xantippus, invaded the territory of Megara. And those Athenians likewise that had been with the hundred galleys about Peloponnesus, in their return, being now at Aegina, hearing that the whole power of the city was gone into Megaris, went and joined them. And this was the greatest army that ever the Athenians had together in one place before,

the city being now in her strength and the plague not yet amongst them. For the Athenians themselves were no less than ten thousand men of arms, besides the three thousand at Potidaea; and the strangers that dwelt amongst them and accompanied them in this invasion were no fewer than three thousand men of arms more, besides other great numbers of light-armed soldiers. And when they had wasted the greatest part of the country, they went back to Athens. And afterwards, year after year during this war the Athenians often invaded Megaris, sometimes with their horsemen and sometimes with their whole army, until such time as they had won Nisaea.

32. Also in the end of this summer they fortified Atalante, an island lying upon the Locrians of Opus, desolate till then, for a garrison against thieves, which passing over from Opus and other parts of Locris might annoy Euboea. These were the things done this summer after the retreat of the Peloponnesians out of Attica.

33. The winter following, Euarchus of Acarnania, desirous to return to Astacus, prevaileth with the Corinthians to go thither with forty galleys and fifteen hundred men of arms to re-establish him, to which he hired also certain other mercenaries for the same purpose. The commanders of this army were Euphamidas the son of Aristonymus, Timoxenes the son of Timocrates, and Eumachus the son of Chrysis. When they had re-established him, they endeavoured to draw to their party some other places on the seacoast of Acarnania; but missing their purpose, they set sail homeward. As they passed by the coast of Cephalonia, they disbarked in the territory of the Cranii where, under colour of composition, they were deceived and lost some part of their forces. For the assault made upon them by the Cranii being unexpected, they got off with much ado and went home.

34. The same winter the Athenians, according to their ancient custom, solemnized a public funeral of the first slain in this war in this manner. Having set up a tent, they put into it * the bones of the dead three days before the funeral; and everyone bringeth whatsoever he thinks good to his own. When the day comes of carrying them to their burial, certain cypress

* Literally it is "they *expose to view* the bones."

coffins are carried along in carts, for every tribe one, in which are the bones of the men of every tribe by themselves. There is likewise borne an empty hearse covered over for such as appear not nor were found amongst the rest when they were taken up. The funeral is accompanied by any that will, whether citizen or stranger; and the women of their kindred are also by at the burial lamenting and mourning. Then they put them into a public monument which standeth in the fairest suburbs of the city, in which place they have ever interred all that died in the wars except those that were slain in the field of Marathon, who, because their virtue was thought extraordinary, were therefore buried thereright. And when the earth is thrown over them, someone thought to exceed the rest in wisdom and dignity, chosen by the city, maketh an oration wherein he giveth them such praises as are fit; which done, the company depart. And this is the form of that burial; and for the whole time of the war, whensoever there was occasion, they observed the same. For these first the man chosen to make the oration was Pericles the son of Xantippus, who, when the time served, going out of the place of burial into a high pulpit to be heard the farther off by the multitude about him, spake unto them in this manner:

35. "Though most that have spoken formerly in this place have commended the man that added this oration to the law as honourable for those that die in the wars, yet to me it seemeth sufficient that they who have showed their valour by action should also by an action have their honour, as now you see they have, in this their sepulture performed by the state, and not to have the virtue of many hazarded on one to be believed as that one shall make a good or bad oration. For to speak of men in a just measure, is a hard matter; and though one do so, yet he shall hardly get the truth firmly believed. The favourable hearer and he that knows what was done will perhaps think what is spoken short of what he would have it and what it was; and he that is ignorant will find somewhat on the other side which he will think too much extolled, especially if he hear aught above the pitch of his own nature. For to hear another man praised finds patience so long only as each man shall think he could himself have done somewhat of that he hears.

And if one exceed in their praises, the hearer presently through envy thinks it false. But since our ancestors have so thought good, I also, following the same ordinance, must endeavour to be answerable to the desires and opinions of everyone of you as far forth as I can.

36. "I will begin at our ancestors; being a thing both just and honest that to them first be given the honour of remembrance in this kind. For they, having been always the inhabitants of this region, by their valour have delivered the same to succession of posterity hitherto in the state of liberty. For which they deserve commendation, but our fathers deserve yet more; for that besides what descended on them, not without great labour of their own they have purchased this our present dominion and delivered the same over to us that now are. Which in a great part also we ourselves that are yet in the strength of our age here present have enlarged and so furnished the city with everything, both for peace and war, as it is now all-sufficient in itself. The actions of war whereby all this was attained and the deeds of arms both of ourselves and our fathers in valiant opposition to the barbarians or Grecians in their wars against us, amongst you that are well acquainted with the sum, to avoid prolixity I will pass over. But by what institutions we arrived at this, by what form of government and by what means we have advanced the state to this greatness, when I shall have laid open this, I shall then descend to these men's praises. For I think they are things both fit for the purpose in hand and profitable to the whole company, both of citizens and strangers, to hear related.

37. "We have a form of government not fetched by imitation from the laws of our neighbouring states (nay, we are rather a pattern to others, than they to us) which, because in the administration it hath respect not to a few but to the multitude, is called a democracy. Wherein, though there be an equality amongst all men in point of law for their private controversies, yet in conferring of dignities one man is preferred before another to public charge, and that according to the reputation not of his house but of his virtue, and is not put back through poverty for the obscurity of his person as long as he can do good service to the commonwealth. And we live not only free

in the administration of the state but also one with another void of jealousy touching each other's daily course of life, not offended at any man for following his own humour, nor casting on any man censorious looks, which though they be no punishment, yet they grieve. So that conversing one with another for the private without offence, we stand chiefly in fear to transgress against the public and are obedient always to those that govern and to the laws, and principally to such laws as are written for protection against injury, and such unwritten as bring undeniable shame to the transgressors.

38. "We have also found out many ways to give our minds recreation from labour by public institution of games and sacrifices for all the days of the year with a decent pomp and furniture of the same by private men, by the daily delight whereof we expel sadness. We have this farther by the greatness of our city that all things from all parts of the earth are imported hither, whereby we no less familiarly enjoy the commodities of all other nations than our own.

39. "Then in the studies of war we excel our enemies in this. We leave our city open to all men; nor was it ever seen that by banishing of strangers we denied them the learning or sight of any of those things which, if not hidden, an enemy might reap advantage by, not relying on secret preparation and deceit but upon our own courage in the action. They, in their discipline, hunt after valour presently from their youth with laborious exercise, and yet we that live remissly undertake as great dangers as they. For example, the Lacedaemonians invade not our dominion by themselves alone but with the aid of all the rest. But when we invade our neighbours, though we fight in hostile ground against such as in their own ground fight in defence of their own substance, yet for the most part we get the victory. Never enemy yet fell into the hands of our whole forces at once both because we apply ourselves much to navigation and by land also send many of our men into divers countries abroad. But when, fighting with a part of it, they chance to get the better, they boast they have beaten the whole; and when they get the worse, they say they are beaten by the whole. And yet when, from ease rather than studious labour and upon natural rather than doctrinal valour, we come to undertake

any danger, we have this odds by it that we shall not faint beforehand with the meditation of future trouble, and in the action we shall appear no less confident than they that are ever toiling,

40. procuring admiration to our city as well in this as in divers other things. For we also give ourselves to bravery, and yet with thrift; and to philosophy, and yet without mollification of the mind.* And we use riches rather for opportunities of action than for verbal ostentation, and hold it not a shame to confess poverty but not to have avoided it. Moreover there is in the same men a care both of their own and the public affairs and a sufficient knowledge of state matters even in those that labour with their hands. For we only think one that is utterly ignorant therein to be a man not that meddles with nothing but that is good for nothing. We likewise weigh what we undertake and apprehend it perfectly in our minds, not accounting words for a hindrance of action but that it is rather a hindrance to action to come to it without instruction of words before. For also in this we excel others, daring to undertake as much as any and yet examining what we undertake; whereas with other men ignorance makes them dare, and consideration dastards. And they are most rightly reputed valiant who, though they perfectly apprehend both what is dangerous and what is easy, are never the more thereby diverted from adventuring. Again, we are contrary to most men in matter of bounty. For we purchase our friends not by receiving but by bestowing benefits. And he that bestoweth a good turn is ever the most constant friend because he will not lose the thanks due unto him from him whom he bestowed it on. Whereas the friendship of him that oweth a benefit is dull and flat, as knowing his benefit not to be taken for a favour but for a debt. So that we only do good to others not upon computation of profit but freeness of trust.

41. "In sum it may be said both that the city is in general a school of the Grecians, and that the men here have everyone

---

* This is a magnificent seventeenth-century sentence, but liable to misconstruction by a modern reader. In our idiom the literal rendering is "We are lovers of beauty, but with cheapness; we are lovers of culture, but without softness."

in particular his person disposed to most diversity of actions, and yet all with grace and decency. And that this is not now rather a bravery of words upon the occasion than real truth, this power of the city, which by these institutions we have obtained, maketh evident. For it is the only power now found greater in proof than fame, and the only power, that neither grieveth the invader when he miscarries with the quality of those he was hurt by, nor giveth cause to the subjected states to murmur as being in subjection to men unworthy. For both with present and future ages we shall be in admiration for a power not without testimony but made evident by great arguments, and which needeth not either a Homer to praise it or any other such whose poems may indeed for the present bring delight, but the truth will afterwards confute the opinion conceived of the actions. For we have opened unto us by our courage all seas and lands and set up eternal monuments on all sides both of the evil we have done to our enemies and the good we have done to our friends.*

"Such is the city for which these men, thinking it no reason to lose it, valiantly fighting have died. And it is fit that every man of you that be left should be like minded to undergo any travail for the same.

42. "And I have therefore spoken so much concerning the city in general as well to show you that the stakes between us and them, whose city is not such, are not equal as also to make known by effects the worth of these men I am to speak of, the greatest part of their praises being therein already delivered. For what I have spoken of the city hath by these, and such as these, been achieved. Neither would praises and actions appear so levelly concurrent in many other of the Grecians as they do in these, the present revolution of these men's lives seeming unto me an argument of their virtues, noted in the first act thereof and in the last confirmed. For even such of them as were worse than the rest do nevertheless deserve that for their valour shown in the wars for defence of their country they should be preferred before the rest. For having by their good actions abolished the memory of their evil, they have profited

---

* Thucydides says only "Having set up everywhere eternal memorials of *both good deeds and ill*."

the state thereby more than they have hurt it by their private behaviour. Yet there was none of these that preferring the further fruition of his wealth was thereby grown cowardly, or that for hope to overcome his poverty at length and to attain to riches did for that cause withdraw himself from the danger. For their principal desire was not wealth but revenge on their enemies, which esteeming the most honourable cause of danger, they made account through it both to accomplish their revenge and to purchase wealth withal; putting the uncertainty of success to the account of their hope, but for that which was before their eyes relying upon themselves in the action, and therein choosing rather to fight and die than to shrink -and be saved, they fled from shame, but with their bodies they stood out the battle; and so in a moment whilst fortune inclineth neither way, left their lives not in fear but in opinion of victory.

43. "Such were these men, worthy of their country. And for you that remain, you may pray for a safer fortune, but you ought not to be less venturously minded against the enemy, not weighing the profit by an oration only, which any man amplifying may recount to you that know as well as he the many commodities that arise by fighting valiantly against your enemies, but contemplating the power of the city in the actions of the same from day to day performed and thereby becoming enamoured of it. And when this power of the city shall seem great to you, consider then that the same was purchased by valiant men, and by men that knew their duty, and by men that were sensible of dishonour when they were in fight, and by such men as, though they failed of their attempt, yet would not be wanting to the city with their virtue but made unto it a most honourable contribution. For having everyone given his body to the commonwealth, they receive in place thereof an undecaying commendation and a most remarkable sepulchre not wherein they are buried so much as wherein their glory is laid up upon all occasions both of speech and action to be remembered forever. For to famous men all the earth is a sepulchre; and their virtues shall be testified not only by the inscription in stone at home but by an unwritten record of the mind, which more than of any monument will remain with everyone forever. In imitation therefore of these men and plac-

ing happiness in liberty and liberty in valour, be forward to encounter the dangers of war. For the miserable and desperate men are not they that have the most reason to be prodigal of their lives, but rather such men as, if they live, may expect a change of fortune and whose losses are greatest if they miscarry in aught. For to a man of any spirit death, which is without sense, arriving whilst he is in vigour and common hope, is nothing so bitter as after a tender life to be brought into misery.

44. "Wherefore I will not so much bewail as comfort you, the parents, that are present, of these men. For you know that whilst they lived, they were obnoxious to manifold calamities. Whereas whilst you are in grief, they only are happy that die honourably as these have done, and to whom it hath been granted not only to live in prosperity but to die in it. Though it be a hard matter to dissuade you from sorrow for the loss of that which the happiness of others, wherein you also when time was rejoiced yourselves, shall so often bring into your remembrance (for sorrow is not for the want of a good never tasted but for the privation of a good we have been used to); yet such of you as are of the age to have children may bear the loss of these in the hope of more. For the later children will both draw on with some the oblivion of those that are slain and also doubly conduce to the good of the city by population and strength. For it is not likely that they should equally give good counsel to the state that have not children to be equally exposed to danger in it. As for you that are past having of children, you are to put the former and greater part of your life to the account of your gain; and supposing the remainder of it will be but short, you shall have the glory of these for a consolation of the same. For the love of honour never groweth old, nor doth that unprofitable part of our life take delight (as some have said) in gathering of wealth so much as it doth in being honoured.

45. "As for you that are the children or brethren of these men, I see you shall have a difficult task of emulation. For every man useth to praise the dead, so that with odds of virtue you will hardly get an equal reputation but still be thought a little short. For men envy their competitors in glory while they live,

but to stand out of their way is a thing honoured with an affection free from opposition. And since I must say somewhat also of feminine virtue for you that are now widows, I shall express it in this short admonition. It will be much for your honour not to recede from your sex and to give as little occasion of rumour amongst the men, whether of good or evil, as you can.

46. "Thus also have I, according to the prescript of the law, delivered in word what was expedient; and those that are here interred have in fact been already honoured; and further, their children shall be maintained till they be at man's estate at the charge of the city, which hath therein propounded both to these and them that live a profitable garland in their matches of valour. For where the rewards of virtue are greatest, there live the worthiest men. So now having lamented everyone his own, you may be gone."

47. Such was the funeral made this winter, which ending, ended the first year of this war.

In the very beginning of summer the Peloponnesians and their confederates, with two-thirds of their forces as before, invaded Attica under the conduct of Archidamus the son of Zeuxidamas, king of Lacedaemon, and after they had encamped themselves, wasted the country about them. They had not been many days in Attica when the plague first began amongst the Athenians, said also to have seized formerly on divers other parts, as about Lemnos and elsewhere; but so great a plague and mortality of men was never remembered to have happened in any place before. For at first neither were the physicians able to cure it through ignorance of what it was but died fastest themselves, as being the men that most approached the sick, nor any other art of man availed whatsoever. All supplications to the gods and enquiries of oracles and whatsoever other means they used of that kind proved all unprofitable; insomuch as subdued with the greatness of the evil, they gave them all over.

48. It began, by report, first in that part of Ethiopia that lieth upon Egypt, and thence fell down into Egypt and Africa and into the greatest part of the territories of the king. It invaded Athens on a sudden and touched first upon those that dwelt in Piraeus, insomuch as they reported that the Pelo-

ponnesians had cast poison into their wells (for springs there were not any in that place). But afterwards it came up into the high city, and then they died a great deal faster. Now let every man, physician or other, concerning the ground of this sickness, whence it sprung, and what causes he thinks able to produce so great an alteration, speak according to his own knowledge. For my own part, I will deliver but the manner of it and lay open only such things as one may take his mark by to discover the same if it come again, having been both sick of it myself and seen others sick of the same.

49. This year, by confession of all men, was of all other, for other diseases, most free and healthful. If any man were sick before, his disease turned to this; if not, yet suddenly, without any apparent cause preceding and being in perfect health, they were taken first with an extreme ache in their heads, redness and inflammation of the eyes; and then inwardly, their throats and tongues grew presently bloody and their breath noisome and unsavoury. Upon this followed a sneezing and hoarseness, and not long after the pain, together with a mighty cough, came down into the breast. And when once it was settled in the stomach, it caused vomit; and with great torment came up all manner of bilious purgation that physicians ever named. Most of them had also the hickyexe * which brought with it a strong convulsion, and in some ceased quickly but in others was long before it gave over. Their bodies outwardly to the touch were neither very hot nor pale but reddish, livid, and beflowered with little pimples and whelks, but so burned inwardly as not to endure any the lightest clothes or linen garment to be upon them nor anything but mere nakedness, but rather most willingly to have cast themselves into the cold water. And many of them that were not looked to, possessed with insatiate thirst, ran unto the wells, and to drink much or little was indifferent, being still from ease and power to sleep as far as ever. As long as the disease was at its height, their bodies wasted not but resisted the torment beyond all expectation; insomuch as the most of them either died of their inward burning in nine or

---

* Krauss's note calls it an "empty hiccough," in which vomiting spasms continue after the stomach is already empty. Perhaps the nearest modern equivalent is "the dry heaves."

seven days whilst they had yet strength, or, if they escaped that, then the disease falling down into their bellies and causing there great exulcerations and immoderate looseness, they died many of them afterwards through weakness. For the disease, which took first the head, began above and came down and passed through the whole body; and he that overcame the worst of it was yet marked with the loss of his extreme parts; for breaking out both at their privy members and at their fingers and toes, many with the loss of these escaped; there were also some that lost their eyes. And many that presently upon their recovery were taken with such an oblivion of all things whatsoever, as they neither knew themselves nor their acquaintance.

50. For this was a kind of sickness which far surmounted all expression of words and both exceeded human nature in the cruelty wherewith it handled each one and appeared also otherwise to be none of those diseases that are bred amongst us, and that especially by this. For all, both birds and beasts, that use to feed on human flesh, though many men lay abroad unburied, either came not at them or tasting perished. An argument whereof as touching the birds is the manifest defect of such fowl, which were not then seen, neither about the carcases or anywhere else. But by the dogs, because they are familiar with men, this effect was seen much clearer.

51. So that this disease (to pass over many strange particulars of the accidents that some had differently from others) was in general such as I have shown, and for other usual sicknesses at that time no man was troubled with any. Now they died some for want of attendance and some again with all the care and physic that could be used. Nor was there any to say certain medicine that applied must have helped them; for if it did good to one, it did harm to another. Nor any difference of body, for strength or weakness, that was able to resist it; but it carried all away, what physic soever was administered. But the greatest misery of all was the dejection of mind in such as found themselves beginning to be sick (for they grew presently desperate and gave themselves over without making any resistance), as also their dying thus like sheep, infected by mutual visitation, for the greatest mortality proceeded that way. For if men forebore to visit them for fear, then they died forlorn;

whereby many families became empty for want of such as should take care of them. If they forbore not, then they died themselves, and principally the honestest men. For out of shame they would not spare themselves but went in unto their friends, especially after it was come to this pass that even their domestics, wearied with the lamentations of them that died and overcome with the greatness of the calamity, were no longer moved therewith. But those that were recovered had much compassion both on them that died and on them that lay sick, as having both known the misery themselves and now no more subject to the danger. For this disease never took any man the second time so as to be mortal. And these men were both by others counted happy, and they also themselves, through excess of present joy, conceived a kind of light hope never to die of any other sickness hereafter.

52. Besides the present affliction, the reception of the country people and of their substance into the city oppressed both them and much more the people themselves that so came in. For having no houses but dwelling at that time of the year in stifling booths, the mortality was now without all form; and dying men lay tumbling one upon another in the streets, and men half-dead about every conduit through desire of water. The temples also where they dwelt in tents were all full of the dead that died within them. For oppressed with the violence of the calamity and not knowing what to do, men grew careless both of holy and profane things alike. And the laws which they formerly used touching funerals were all now broken, every one burying where he could find room. And many for want of things necessary, after so many deaths before, were forced to become impudent in the funerals of their friends. For when one had made a funeral pile, another getting before him would throw on his dead and give it fire. And when one was in burning, another would come and, having cast thereon him whom he carried, go his way again.

53. And the great licentiousness, which also in other kinds was used in the city, began at first from this disease. For that which a man before would dissemble and not acknowledge to be done for voluptuousness, he durst now do freely, seeing before his eyes such quick revolution, of the rich dying and men worth nothing inheriting their estates. Insomuch as they justified

a speedy fruition of their goods even for their pleasure, as men that thought they held their lives but by the day. As for pains, no man was forward in any action of honour to take any because they thought it uncertain whether they should die or not before they achieved it. But what any man knew to be delightful and to be profitable to pleasure, that was made both profitable and honourable. Neither the fear of the gods nor laws of men awed any man, not the former because they concluded it was alike to worship or not worship from seeing that alike they all perished, nor the latter because no man expected that lives would last till he received punishment of his crimes by judgment. But they thought there was now over their heads some far greater judgment decreed against them before which fell, they thought to enjoy some little part of their lives.

54. Such was the misery into which the Athenians being fallen were much oppressed, having not only their men killed by the disease within but the enemy also laying waste their fields and villages without. In this sickness also (as it was not unlikely they would) they called to mind this verse said also of the elder sort to have been uttered of old:

> *A Doric war shall fall,*
> *And a great plague withal.*

Now were men at variance about the word, some saying it was not *loimos* [plague], that was by the ancients mentioned in that verse, but *limos* [famine]. But upon the present occasion the word *loimos* deservedly obtained. For as men suffered, so they made the verse to say. And I think if after this there shall ever come another Doric war and with it a famine, they are like to recite the verse accordingly. There was also reported by such as knew a certain answer given by the oracle to the Lacedaemonians when they inquired whether they should make this war or not: *that if they warred with all their power, they should have the victory, and that the God himself would take their parts.* And thereupon they thought the present misery to be a fulfilling of that prophecy. The Peloponnesians were no sooner entered Attica but the sickness presently began, and never came into Peloponnesus, to speak of, but reigned principally in Athens and in such other places afterwards as were most populous. And thus much of this disease.

55. After the Peloponnesians had wasted the champaign country, they fell upon the territory called Paralos as far as to the mountain Laurius where the Athenians had silver mines, and first wasted that part of it which looketh towards Peloponnesus and then that also which lieth toward Andros and Euboea. And Pericles, who was also then general, was still of the same mind he was of in the former invasion, that the Athenians ought not to go out against them to battle.

56. Whilst they were yet in the plain and before they entered into the maritime country, he furnished a hundred galleys to go about Peloponnesus and, as soon as they were ready, put to sea. In these galleys he had four thousand men of arms, and in vessels then purposely first made to carry horses, three hundred horsemen. The Chians and Lesbians joined likewise with him with fifty galleys. This fleet of the Athenians, when it set forth, left the Peloponnesians still in Paralia; and coming before Epidaurus, a city of Peloponnesus, they wasted much of the country thereabout and assaulting the city had a hope to take it, though it succeeded not. Leaving Epidaurus, they wasted the territories about of Troezene, Halias, and Hermione, places all on the seacoast of Peloponnesus. Putting off from hence, they came to Prasiae, a small maritime city of Laconia, and both wasted the territory about it and took and razed the town itself. And having done this, came home and found the Peloponnesians not now in Attica but gone back.

57. All the while the Peloponnesians were in the territory of the Athenians and the Athenians abroad with their fleet, the sickness, both in the army and city, destroyed many, insomuch as it was said that the Peloponnesians, fearing the sickness (which they knew to be in the city both by fugitives and by seeing the Athenians burying their dead), went the sooner away out of the country. And yet they stayed there longer in this invasion than they had done anytime before and wasted even the whole territory, for they continued in Attica almost forty days.

58. The same summer Agnon the son of Nicias and Cleopompus the son of Clinias, who were joint commanders with Pericles with that army which he had employed before, went presently and made war upon the Chalcideans of Thrace and

against Potidaea which was yet besieged. Arriving, they presently applied engines and tried all means possible to take it, but neither the taking of the city nor anything else succeeded worthy so great preparation. For the sickness coming amongst them afflicted them mightily indeed and even devoured the army. And the Athenian soldiers which were there before and in health catched the sickness from those that came with Agnon. As for Phormio and his sixteen hundred, they were not now amongst the Chalcideans. And Agnon therefore came back with his fleet, having of four thousand men in less than forty days lost one thousand and fifty of the plague. But the soldiers that were there before stayed upon the place and continued the siege of Potidaea.

59. After the second invasion of the Peloponnesians the Athenians, having their fields now the second time wasted and both the sickness and war falling upon them at once, changed their minds and accused Pericles, as if by his means they had been brought into these calamities, and desired earnestly to compound with the Lacedaemonians, to whom also they sent certain ambassadors, but they returned without effect. And being then at their wits' end, they kept a stir at Pericles. And he, seeing them vexed with their present calamity and doing all those things which he had before expected, called an assembly (for he was yet general) with intention to put them again into heart and, assuaging their passion, to reduce their minds to a more calm and less dismayed temper. And standing forth, he spake unto them in this manner:

60. "Your anger towards me cometh not unlooked for, for the cause of it I know. And I have called this assembly, therefore, to remember you and reprehend you for those things wherein you have either been angry with me or given way to your adversity without reason. For I am of this opinion, that the public prosperity of the city is better for private men than if the private men themselves were in prosperity and the public wealth in decay. For a private man, though in good estate, if his country come to ruin, must of necessity be ruined with it; whereas he that miscarrieth in a flourishing commonwealth shall much more easily be preserved. Since then the commonwealth is able to bear the calamities of private men, and every-

one cannot support the calamities of the commonwealth, why should not everyone strive to defend it and not, as you now, astonished with domestic misfortune, forsake the common safety and fall a-censuring both me that counselled the war and yourselves that decreed the same as well as I? And it is I you are angry withal, one, as I think myself, inferior to none either in knowing what is requisite or in expressing what I know, and a lover of my country and superior to money. For he that hath good thoughts and cannot clearly express them were as good to have thought nothing at all. He that can do both and is ill affected to his country will likewise not give it faithful counsel. And he that will do that too yet if he be superable by money will for that alone set all the rest to sale. Now if you followed my advice in making this war, as esteeming these virtues to be in me somewhat above the rest, there is sure no reason that I should now be accused of doing you wrong.

61. "For though to such as have it in their own election (being otherwise in good estate), it were madness to make choice of war; yet when we must of necessity either give way, and so without more ado be subject to our neighbours, or else save ourselves from it by danger, he is more to be condemned that declineth the danger than he that standeth to it. For mine own part I am the man I was and of the mind I was; but you are changed, won to the war when you were entire but repenting it upon the damage and condemning my counsel in the weakness of your own judgment. The reason of this is because you feel already everyone in particular that which afflicts you, but the evidence of the profit to accrue to the city in general you see not yet. And your minds, dejected with the great and sudden alteration, cannot constantly maintain what you have before resolved. For that which is sudden and unexpected and contrary to what one hath deliberated enslaveth the spirit, which by this disease principally, in the neck of the other incommodities, is now come to pass in you. But you that are born in a great city and with education suitable, how great soever the affliction be, ought not to shrink at it and eclipse your reputation (for men do no less condemn those that through cowardice lose the glory they have than hate those that through impudence arrogate the glory they have not) but to set aside

the grief of your private losses and lay your hands to the common safety.

62. "As for the toil of the war, that it may perhaps be long and we in the end never the nearer to victory, though that may suffice which I have demonstrated at other times touching your causeless suspicion that way, yet this I will tell you, moreover, touching the greatness of your means for dominion, which neither you yourselves seem ever to have thought on nor I touched in my former orations, nor would I also have spoken it now * but that I see your minds dejected more than there is cause for. That though you take your dominion to extend only to your confederates, I affirm that of the two parts of the world of manifest use, the land and the sea, you are of one of them entire masters, both of as much of it as you make use of and also of as much more as you shall think fit yourselves. Neither is there any king or nation whatsoever † of those that now are that can impeach your navigation with the fleet and strength you now go. So that you must not put the use of houses and lands wherein now you think yourselves deprived of a mighty matter into the balance with such a power as this nor take the loss of these things heavily in respect of it, but rather set little by them as but a light ornament and embellishment of wealth, and think that our liberty as long as we hold fast that will easily recover unto us these things again; whereas subjected once to others, even that which we possess besides will be diminished. Show not yourselves both ways inferior to your ancestors, who not only held this (gotten by their own labours not left them) but have also preserved and delivered the same unto us (for it is more dishonour to lose what one possesseth than to miscarry in the acquisition of it), and encounter the enemy not only with magnanimity but also with disdain. For a coward may have a high mind upon a prosperous ignorance; but he that is confident upon judgment to be superior to his enemy doth also disdain him, which is now our case. And courage in

---

* Hobbes unaccountably has left out a clause in the Greek; the full statement runs "nor would I have employed it (the argument) now as it has somewhat too much the appearance of boasting."

† This is more imposing than the exact meaning of the Greek, which is specific: "Neither the King (of Persia) nor any other nation."

equal fortune is the safer for our disdain of the enemy where
a man knows what he doth; for he trusteth less to hope, which
is of force only in uncertainties, and more to judgment upon
certainties, wherein there is a more sure foresight.

63. "You have reason besides to maintain the dignity the city
hath gotten for her dominion in which you all triumph, and
either not decline the pains or not also pursue the honour. And
you must not think the question is now of your liberty and
servitude only. Besides the loss of your rule over others, you
must stand the danger you have contracted by offence given in
the administration of it. Nor can you now give it over (if any
fearing at this present that that may come to pass, encourage
himself with the intention of not to meddle hereafter *), for
already your government is in the nature of a tyranny, which
is both unjust for you to take up and unsafe to lay down. And
such men as these, if they could persuade others to it or lived in
a free city by themselves, would quickly overthrow it. For the
quiet life can never be preserved if it be not ranged with the
active life, nor is it a life conducible to a city that reigneth but
to a subject city that it may safely serve.

64. "Be not therefore seduced by this sort of men nor angry
with me, together with whom yourselves did decree this war,
because the enemy invading you hath done what was likely he
would if you obeyed him not. And as for the sickness, the
only thing that exceeded the imagination of all men, it was
unlooked for; and I know you hate me somewhat the more for
that, but unjustly, unless when anything falleth out above your
expectation fortunate, you will also dedicate unto me that.
Evils that come from heaven you must bear necessarily, and
such as proceed from your enemies, valiantly; for so it hath
been the custom of this city to do heretofore, which custom
let it not be your part to reverse. Knowing that this city hath a
great name amongst all people for not yielding to adversity and
for the mighty power it yet hath after the expense of so many
lives and so much labour in the war, the memory whereof,
though we should now at length miscarry (for all things are

---

* This is not quite the full implication of the Greek, which means
"In case anyone at the present fearing this very thing wants to *play
the honest man* and avoid involvement."

made with this law, to decay again), will remain with posterity
forever. How that being Grecians, most of the Grecians were
our subjects; that we have abided the greatest wars against
them, both universally and singly, and have inhabited the
greatest and wealthiest city. Now this he with the quiet life
will condemn, the active man will emulate, and they that have
not attained to the like will envy. But to be hated and to dis-
please is a thing that happeneth for the time to whosoever he
be that hath the command of others; and he does well, that
undergoeth hatred for matters of great consequence. For the
hatred lasteth not and is recompensed both with a present
splendour and an immortal glory hereafter. Seeing then you
foresee both what is honourable for the future and not dishonourable for the present procure both the one and the other
by your courage now. Send no more heralds to the Lacedaemonians, nor let them know the evil present does anyway afflict
you; for they whose minds least feel and whose actions most
oppose a calamity both among states and private persons are
the best."

65. In this speech did Pericles endeavour to appease the anger
of the Athenians towards himself and withal to withdraw their
thoughts from the present affliction. But they, though for the
state in general they were won and sent to the Lacedaemonians
no more but rather inclined to the war, yet they were everyone
in particular grieved for their several losses: the poor because
entering the war with little, they lost that little; and the rich
because they had lost fair possessions, together with goodly
houses and costly furniture in them, in the country; but the
greatest matter of all was that they had war instead of peace.
And altogether, they deposed not their anger till they had first
fined him in a sum of money. Nevertheless, not long after (as
is the fashion of the multitude) they made him general again
and committed the whole state to his administration. For the
sense of their domestic losses was now dulled, and for the
need of the commonwealth they prized him more than any
other whatsoever. For as long as he was in authority in the
city in time of peace, he governed the same with moderation
and was a faithful watchman of it; and in his time it was at the
greatest. And after the war was on foot, it is manifest that he

therein also foresaw what it could do. He lived after the war began two years and six months. And his foresight in the war was best known after his death. For he told them that if they would be quiet and look to their navy, and during this war seek no further dominion nor hazard the city itself, they should then have the upper hand. But they did contrary in all, and in such other things besides as seemed not to concern the war managed the state, according to their private ambition and covetousness, perniciously both for themselves and their confederates. What succeeded well the honour and profit of it came most to private men, and what miscarried was to the city's detriment in the war. The reason whereof was this: that being a man of great power both for his dignity and wisdom, and for bribes manifestly the most incorrupt, he freely controlled the multitude and was not so much led by them as he led them. Because, having gotten his power by no evil arts, he would not humour them in his speeches but out of his authority durst anger them with contradiction. Therefore, whensoever he saw them out of season insolently bold, he would with his orations put them into a fear; and again, when they were afraid without reason, he would likewise erect their spirits and embolden them. It was in name a state democratical, but in fact a government of the principal man. But they that came after, being more equal amongst themselves and affecting everyone to be the chief, applied themselves to the people and let go the care of the commonwealth. From whence amongst many other errors, as was likely in a great and dominant city, proceeded also the voyage into Sicily, which was not so much upon mistaking those whom they went against as for want of knowledge in the senders of what was necessary for those that went the voyage. For through private quarrels about who should bear the greatest sway with the people they both abated the vigour of the army and then also first troubled the state at home with division. Being overthrown in Sicily and having lost, besides other ammunition, the greatest part of their navy, and the city being then in sedition, yet they held out three years *

---

* This is a very vexed reading in Thucydides. The fact is that if he meant three years after the Sicilian expedition (i.e., 415 to 412) the passage cannot be correct. Athens did not fall till 404 B.C. Many editors have tried to read "eight" or "ten" instead of three.

both against their first enemies and the Sicilians with them and against most of their revolted confederates besides, and also afterwards against Cyrus the king's son, who took part with and sent money to the Peloponnesians to maintain their fleet and never shrunk till they had overthrown themselves with private dissensions. So much was in Pericles above other men at that time that he could foresee by what means the city might easily have outlasted the Peloponnesians in this war.

66. The Lacedaemonians and their confederates made war the same summer with one hundred galleys against Zacynthus, an island lying over against Elis. The inhabitants whereof were a colony of Achaeans of Peloponnesus but confederates of the people of Athens. There went in this fleet a thousand men of arms and Cnemus a Spartan for admiral, who, landing, wasted the greatest part of the territory. But they of the island not yielding, they put off again and went home.

67. In the end of the same summer, Aristeus of Corinth and Aneristus, Nicolaus, Stratodemus, and Timagorus of Tegea, ambassadors of the Lacedaemonians, and Pollis of Argos, a private man, as they were travelling into Asia to the king to get money of him and to draw him into their league, took Thrace in their way and came unto Sitalces the son of Teres with a desire to get him also, if they could, to forsake the league with Athens and to send his forces to Potidaea, which the Athenian army now besieged, and not to aid the Athenians any longer, and withal to get leave to pass through his country to the other side of the Hellespont to go, as they intended, to Pharnabazus the son of Pharnaces, who would convoy them to the king. But the ambassadors of Athens, Learchus the son of Callimachus and Ameiniades the son of Philemon, then resident with Sitalces, persuaded Sadocus the son of Sitalces, who was now a citizen of Athens, to put them into their hands that they might not go to the king and do hurt to the city whereof he himself was now a member. Whereunto condescending, as they journeyed through Thrace to take ship to cross the Hellespont, he apprehended them before they got to the ship by such others as he sent along with Learchus and Ameiniades with command to deliver them into their hands. And they, when they had them, sent them away to Athens. When they came thither, the Athenians, fearing Aristeus, lest

escaping he should do them further mischief (for he was manifestly the author of all the business of Potidaea and about Thrace), the same day put them all to death, unjudged and desirous to have spoken, and threw them into the pits, thinking it but just to take revenge of the Lacedaemonians that began it and had slain and thrown into pits the merchants of the Athenians and their confederates whom they took sailing in merchant ships about the coast of Peloponnesus. For in the beginning of the war, the Lacedaemonians slew as enemies whomsoever they took at sea, whether confederates of the Athenians or neutral, all alike.

68. About the same time, in the end of summer, the Ambraciotes, both they themselves and divers barbarian nations by them raised, made war against Argos of Amphilochia and against the rest of that territory. The quarrel between them and the Argives arose first from hence. This Argos and the rest of Amphilochia was planted by Amphilochus the son of Amphiaraus after the Trojan war, who, at his return, misliking the then state of Argos, built this city in the Gulf of Ambracia and called it Argos after the name of his own country. And it was the greatest city and had the most wealthy inhabitants of all Amphilochia. But many generations after, being fallen into misery, they communicated their city with the Ambraciotes, bordering upon Amphilochia; and then they first learned the Greek language now used from the Ambraciotes that lived among them. For the rest of the Amphilochians were barbarians. Now the Ambraciotes in process of time drave out the Argives and held the city by themselves. Whereupon the Amphilochians submitted themselves to the Acarnanians, and both together called in the Athenians who sent thirty galleys to their aid and Phormio for general. Phormio, being arrived, took Argos by assault and, making slaves of the Ambraciotes, put the town into the joint possessions of the Amphilochians and Acarnanians. And this was the beginning of the league between the Athenians and Acarnanians. The Ambraciotes therefore, deriving their hatred to the Argives from this their captivity, came in with an army partly of their own and partly raised amongst the Chaonians and other neighbouring barbarians now in this war. And coming to Argos, were masters of the field; but when they

could not take the city by assault, they returned and disbanding went every nation to his own. These were the acts of the summer.

69. In the beginning of the winter the Athenians sent twenty galleys about Peloponnesus under the command of Phormio, who, coming to lie at Naupactus, guarded the passage that none might go in or out from Corinth and the Crisaean gulf. And other six galleys under the conduct of Melesander they sent into Caria and Lycia, as well to gather tribute in those parts as also to hinder the Peloponnesian pirates lying on those coasts from molesting the navigation of such merchant ships as they expected to come to them from Phaselis, Phoenicia, and that part of the continent. But Melesander, landing in Lycia with such forces of the Athenians and their confederates as he had aboard, was overcome in battle and slain with the loss of a part of his army.

70. The same winter, the Potidaeans, unable any longer to endure the siege, seeing the invasion of Attica by the Peloponnesians could not make them rise and seeing their victual failed and that they were forced, amongst divers other things done by them for necessity of food, to eat one another, propounded at length to Xenophon the son of Euripides, Hestiodorus the son of Aristocleidas, and Phanomachus the son of Callimachus, the Athenian commanders that lay before the city, to give the same into their hands. And they, seeing both that the army was already afflicted by lying in that cold place and that the state had already spent two thousand talents upon the siege, accepted of it. The conditions agreed on were these: "to depart, they and their wives and children and their auxiliary soldiers, every man with one suit of clothes and every woman with two,* and to take with them everyone a certain sum of money for his charges by the way." Hereupon a truce was granted them to depart; and they went, some to the Chalcideans and others to other places as they could get to. But the people of Athens called the

---

* This is an amusing rendering of the Greek, which says "every man with one garment and every woman with two." The garment referred to was a *chlaina*, worn both by men and, in some cases, by women. It was a long, enveloping cloaklike garment and singularly ill-translated as "suit of clothes."

commanders in question for compounding without them, conceiving that they might have gotten the city to discretion, and sent afterwards a colony to Potidaea of their own citizens. These were the things done in this winter. And so ended the second year of this war, written by Thucydides.

71. The next summer, the Peloponnesians and their confederates came not into Attica but turned their arms against Plataea, led by Archidamus the son of Zeuxidamus, king of the Lacedaemonians, who, having pitched his camp, was about to waste the territory thereof. But the Plataeans sent ambassadors presently unto him with words to this effect: "Archidamus, and you Lacedaemonians, you do neither justly nor worthy yourselves and ancestors in making war upon Plataea. For Pausanias of Lacedaemon, the son of Cleombrotus, having, together with such Grecians as were content to undergo the danger of the battle that was fought in this our territory, delivered all Greece from the slavery of the Persians, when he offered sacrifice in the market-place of Plataea to Jupiter the deliverer, called together all the confederates and granted to the Plataeans this privilege: *that their city and territory should be free; that none should make any unjust war against them nor go about to subject them; and if any did, the confederates then present should to their utmost ability revenge their quarrel.* These privileges your fathers granted us for our valour and zeal in those dangers. But now do you the clean contrary; for you join with our greatest enemies, the Thebans, to bring us into subjection. Therefore calling to witness the gods then sworn by and the gods both of your and our country, we require you that you do no damage to the territory of Plataea nor violate those oaths, but that you suffer us to enjoy our liberty in such sort as was allowed us by Pausanias."

72. The Plataeans having thus said, Archidamus replied and said thus: "Men of Plataea, if you would do as ye say, you say what is just. For as Pausanias hath granted to you, so also be you free and help to set free the rest, who, having been partakers of the same dangers then and being comprised in the same oath with yourselves, are now brought into subjection by the Athenians. And this so great preparation and war is only for the deliverance of them and others, of which if you will espe-

cially participate, keep your oaths; at least (as we have also advised you formerly) be quiet and enjoy your own in neutrality, receiving both sides in the way of friendship, neither side in the way of faction." * Thus said Archidamus. And the ambassadors of Plataea, when they had heard him, returned to the city, and having communicated his answer to the people, brought word again to Archidamus: "that what he had advised was impossible for them to perform without leave of the Athenians in whose keeping were their wives and children; and that they feared also for the whole city lest when the Lacedaemonians were gone, the Athenians should come and take the custody of it out of their hands; or that the Thebans, comprehended in the oath of receiving both sides, should again attempt to surprise it." But Archidamus, to encourage them, made this answer: "Deliver you unto us Lacedaemonians your city and your houses, show us the bounds of your territory, give us your trees by tale, and whatsoever else can be numbered; and depart yourselves whither you shall think good as long as the war lasteth: and when it shall be ended, we will deliver it all unto you again. In the meantime we will keep them as deposited and will cultivate your ground and pay you rent for it, as much as shall suffice for your maintenance."

73. Hereupon the ambassadors went again into the city and, having consulted with the people, made answer "that they would first acquaint the Athenians with it, and if they would consent, they would then accept the conditions; till then, they desired a suspension of arms and not to have their territory wasted." Upon this he granted them so many days truce, as was requisite for their return, and for so long forebore to waste their territory. When the Plataean ambassadors were arrived at Athens and had advised on the matter with the Athenians, they returned to the city with this answer: "The Athenians say thus: that neither in former times, since we were their confederates, did they ever abandon us to the injuries of any, nor will they now neglect us but give us their utmost assistance. And they conjure us by the oath of our fathers not to make any alienation touching the league."

74. When the ambassadors had made this report, the Plataeans

* Hobbes omits the following sentence: "And this will content us."

resolved in their councils not to betray the Athenians but
rather to endure, if it must be, the wasting of their territory
before their eyes and to suffer whatsoever misery could befall
them, and no more to go forth but from the walls to make this
answer: "that it was impossible for them to do as the Lacedaemonians had required." When they had answered so, Archidamus, the king, first made a protestation to the gods and
heros of the country, saying thus: "All ye Gods and Heros,
protectors of Plataeis, be witnesses that we neither invade this
territory (wherein our fathers after their vows unto you overcame the Medes, and which you made propitious for the
Grecians to fight in) unjustly now in the beginning because
they have first broken the league they had sworn, nor what we
shall further do will be any injury because, though we have
offered many and reasonable conditions, they have yet been all
refused; assent ye also to the punishment of the beginners of
injury and to the revenge of those that bear lawful arms."

75. Having made this protestation to the gods, he made ready
his army for the war.

And first having felled trees, he therewith made a palisade
about the town that none might go out. That done, he raised a
mount against the wall, hoping with so great an army all at
work at once, to have quickly taken it. And having cut down
wood in the hill Cithaeron, they built a frame of timber and
wattled it about on either side to serve instead of walls to keep
the earth from falling too much away and cast into it stones and
earth and whatsoever else would serve to fill it up. Seventy
days and nights continually they poured on, dividing the work
between them for rest in such manner as some might be carrying, whilst others took their sleep and food. And they were
urged to labour by the Lacedaemonians that commanded the
mercenaries of the several cities and had the charge of the
work. The Plataeans, seeing the mount to rise, made the frame
of a wall with wood which, having placed on the wall of the
city in the place where the mount touched, they built it within
full of bricks taken from the adjoining houses for that purpose
demolished, the timber serving to bind them together that the
building might not be weakened by the height. The same was
also covered with hides and quilts both to keep the timber from

shot of wildfire and those that wrought from danger. So that the height of the wall was great on one side, and the mount went up as fast on the other. The Plataeans used also this device: they brake a hole in their own wall where the mount joined and drew the earth from it into the city.

76. But the Peloponnesians, when they found it out, took clay and therewith daubing hurdles of reeds cast the same into the chink, which mouldering not, as did the earth, they could not draw it away. The Plataeans, excluded here, gave over that plot, and digging a secret mine, which they carried under the mount from within the city by conjecture, fetched away the earth again and were a long time undiscovered; so that still casting on, the mount grew still less, the earth being drawn away below and settling over the part where it was voided. The Plataeans, nevertheless, fearing that they should not be able even thus to hold out, being few against many, devised this further. They gave over working at the high wall against the mount and, beginning at both ends of it where the wall was low, built another wall in form of a crescent, inward to the city; that if the great wall were taken, this might resist and put the enemy to make another mount, and by coming further in to be at double pains and withal more encompassable with shot. The Peloponnesians, together with the rising of their mount, brought to the city their engines of battery. One of which, by the help of the mount, they applied to the high wall, wherewith they much shook it and put the Plataeans into great fear. And others to other parts of the wall, which the Plataeans partly turned aside by casting ropes about them and partly with great beams, which, being hung in long iron chains by either end upon two other great beams jetting over and inclining from above the wall like two horns, they drew up to them athwart; and where the engine was about to light, slacking the chains and letting their hands go, they let fall with violence to break the beak of it.

77. After this the Peloponnesians, seeing their engines availed not and thinking it hard to take the city by any present violence, prepared themselves to besiege it. But first they thought fit to attempt it by fire, being no great city, and when the wind should rise, if they could, to burn it; for there was no

way they did not think on to have gained it without expense
and long siege. Having therefore brought faggots, they cast
them from the mount into the space between it and their new
wall, which by so many hands was quickly filled, and then into
as much of the rest of the city as at that distance they could
reach and, throwing amongst them fire, together with brimstone and pitch, kindled the wood and raised such a flame, as
the like was never seen before made by the hand of man. For
as for the woods in the mountains, the trees have indeed taken
fire; but it hath been by mutual attrition and have flamed out of
their own accord. But this fire was a great one, and the
Plataeans that had escaped other mischiefs wanted little of
being consumed by this. For near the wall they could not get by
a great way; and if the wind had been with it (as the enemy
hoped it might), they could never have escaped. It is also reported that there fell much rain then with great thunder and
that the flame was extinguished and the danger ceased by that.

78. The Peloponnesians, when they failed likewise of this,
retaining a part of their army and dismissing the rest, enclosed
the city about with a wall, dividing the circumference thereof
to the charge of the several cities. There was a ditch both
within and without it out of which they made their bricks; and
after it was finished, which was about the rising of Arcturus,
they left a guard for one half of the wall (for the other was
guarded by the Boeotians) and departed with the rest of their
army and were dissolved according to their cities. The Plataeans had before this sent their wives and children and all their
unserviceable men to Athens. The rest were besieged, being in
number of the Plataeans themselves four hundred, of Athenians eighty, and a hundred and ten women to dress their
meat.* These were all when the siege was first laid and not one
more, neither free nor bond, in the city. In this manner was
the city besieged.

79. The same summer at the same time that this journey was

---

* The Greek word actually means "to make their bread," which more
accurately indicates what the Greek women would have done in
this case. The Plataeans would have lived mostly on ground wheat,
baked as bread and eaten as porridge, and the preparation of this,
grinding and cooking, would be the task of the women of the garrison.

made against Plataea, the Athenians with two thousand men of arms of their own city and two hundred horsemen made war upon the Chalcideans of Thrace and the Bottiaeans, when the corn was at the highest, under the conduct of Xenophon the son of Euripides and two others. These coming before Spartolus in Bottiaea destroyed the corn and expected that the town should have been rendered by the practice of some within. But such as would not have it so having sent for aid to Olynthus before, there came into the city for safeguard thereof a supply both of men of arms and other soldiers from thence. And these issuing forth of Spartolus, the Athenians put themselves into order of battle under the town itself. The men of arms of the Chalcideans and certain auxiliaries with them were overcome by the Athenians and retired within Spartolus. And the horsemen of the Chalcideans and their light-armed soldiers overcame the horsemen and light-armed of the Athenians, but they had some few targeteers besides of the territory called Crusis. When the battle was now begun, came a supply of other targeteers from Olynthus. Which the light-armed soldiers of Spartolus perceiving, emboldened both by this addition of strength and also as having had the better before, with the Chalcidean horse and this new supply charged the Athenians afresh. The Athenians hereupon retired to two companies they had left with the carriages.* And as oft as the Athenians charged, the Chalcideans retired; and when the Athenians retired, the Chalcideans charged them with their shot. Especially the Chalcidean horsemen rode up and, charging them where they thought fit, forced the Athenians in extreme affright to turn their backs and chased them a great way. The Athenians fled to Potidaea and, having afterwards fetched away the bodies of their dead upon truce, returned with the remainder of their army to Athens. Four hundred and thirty men they lost and their chief commanders all three. And the Chalcideans and Bottiaeans, when they had set up a trophy and taken up their dead bodies, disbanded and went everyone to his city.

80. Not long after this, the same summer, the Ambraciotes and Chaonians, desiring to subdue all Acarnania and to make it revolt from the Athenians, persuaded the Lacedaemonians to

* The Greek means "in charge of the baggage."

make ready a fleet out of the confederate cities and to send a
thousand men of arms into Acarnania, saying that if they aided
them both with a fleet and a land army at once, the Acarnanians
of the seacoast being thereby disabled to assist the rest, having
easily gained Acarnania they might be masters afterward both
of Zacynthus and Cephalonia and the Athenians hereafter less
able to make their voyages about Peloponnesus, and that there
was a hope beside to take Naupactus. The Peloponnesians assenting sent thither Cnemus, who was yet admiral, with his
men of arms in a few galleys immediately, and withal sent word
to the cities about, as soon as their galleys were ready, to sail
with all speed to Leucas. Now the Corinthians were very
zealous in the behalf of the Ambraciotes, as being their own
colony. And the galleys which were to go from Corinth,
Sicyonia, and that part of the coast were now making ready;
and those of the Leucadians, Anactorians, and Ambraciotes
were arrived before and stayed at Leucas for their coming.
Cnemus and his thousand men of arms, when they had crossed
the sea undescried of Phormio, who commanded the twenty
Athenian galleys that kept watch at Naupactus, presently prepared for the war by land. He had in his army of Grecians, the
Ambraciotes, Leucadians, Anactorians, and the thousand Peloponnesians he brought with him; and of barbarians, a thousand
Chaonians, who have no king but were led by Photius and
Nicanor, which two being of the families eligible had now the
annual government. With the Chaonians came also the Thes-
protians, they also without a king. The Molossians and Atin-
tanians were led by Sabylinthus, protector of Tharups their
king, who was yet in minority. The Parauaeans were led by
their king Oroedus; and under Oroedus served likewise, by permission of Antiochus their king, a thousand Orestians. Also
Perdiccas sent thither, unknown to the Athenians, a thousand
Macedonians; but these last were not yet arrived. With this
army began Cnemus to march without staying for the fleet
from Corinth. And passing through Argeia, they destroyed
Limnaea, a town unwalled. From thence they marched towards
Stratus, the greatest city of Acarnania, conceiving that if they
could take this first, the rest would come easily in.

81. The Acarnanians seeing a great army by land was entered

their country already and expecting the enemy also by sea, joined not to succour Stratus but guarded everyone his own and sent for aid to Phormio. But he answered them that since there was a fleet to be set forth from Corinth, he could not leave Naupactus without a guard. The Peloponnesians and their confederates, with their army divided into three, marched on towards the city of the Stratians to the end that, being encamped near it, if they yielded not on parley, they might presently assault the walls. So they went on, the Chaonians and other barbarians in the middle, the Leucadians and Anactorians and such others as were with these on the right hand, and Cnemus with the Peloponnesians and Ambraciotes on the left, each army at great distance and sometimes out of sight of one another. The Grecians in their march kept their order and went warily on till they had gotten a convenient place to encamp in. But the Chaonians, confident of themselves and by the inhabitants of that continent accounted most warlike, had not the patience to take in any ground for a camp but carried furiously on together with the rest of the barbarians, thought to have taken the town by their clamour and to have the action ascribed only to themselves. But they of Stratus, aware of this whilst they were yet in their way and imagining if they could overcome these thus divided from the other two armies, that the Grecians also would be the less forward to come on, placed divers ambushes not far from the city and, when the enemies approached, fell upon them both from the city and from the ambushes at once and, putting them into affright, slew many of the Chaonians upon the place; and the rest of the barbarians, seeing these to shrink, stayed no longer but fled outright. Neither of the Grecian armies had knowledge of this skirmish because they were gone so far before to choose (as they then thought) a commodious place to pitch in. But when the barbarians came back upon them running, they received them and joining both camps together stirred no more for that day. And the Stratians assaulted them not, for want of the aid of the rest of the Acarnanians, but used their slings against them and troubled them much that way (for without their men of arms there was no stirring for them); and in this kind the Acarnanians are held excellent.

82. When night came, Cnemus withdrew his army to the river Anapus, from Stratus eighty furlongs, and fetched off the dead bodies upon truce the next day. And whereas the city Oeniadae was come in of itself, he made his retreat thither before the Acarnanians should assemble with their succours; and from thence went everyone home. And the Stratians set up a trophy of the skirmish against the barbarians.

83. In the meantime the fleet of Corinth and the other confederates that was to set out from the Crisaean gulf and to join with Cnemus to hinder the lower Acarnanians from aiding the upper came not at all but were compelled to fight with Phormio and those twenty Athenian galleys that kept watch at Naupactus, about the same time that the skirmish was at Stratus. For as they sailed along the shore, Phormio waited on them till they were out of the strait, intending to set upon them in the open sea. And the Corinthians and their confederates went not as to fight by sea but furnished rather for the land service in Acarnania and never thought that the Athenians with their twenty galleys durst fight with theirs that were seven-and-forty. Nevertheless, when they saw that the Athenians as themselves sailed by one shore kept over against them on the other, and that now when they went off from Patrae in Achaia to go over to Acarnania in the opposite continent, the Athenians came towards them from Chalcis and the river Evenus and also knew that they had come to anchor there the night before, they found they were then to fight of necessity directly against the mouth of the strait. The commanders of the fleet were such as the cities that set it forth had severally appointed, but of the Corinthians, these: Machon, Isocrates, and Agatharchidas. The Peloponnesians ordered their fleet in such manner as they made thereof a circle as great as, without leaving the spaces so wide as for the Athenians to pass through, they were possibly able with the stems of their galleys outward and sterns inward, and into the midst thereof received such small vessels as came with them and also five of their swiftest galleys, the which were at narrow passages to come forth in whatsoever part the enemy should charge.

84. But the Athenians with their galleys ordered one after one in file went round them and shrunk them up together by

wiping them ever as they past and putting them in expectation of present fight. But Phormio had before forbidden them to fight till he himself had given them the signal. For he hoped that this order of theirs would not last long, as in an army on land, but that the galleys would fall foul of one another and be troubled also with the smaller vessels in the midst. And if the wind should also blow out of the gulf, in expectation whereof he so went round them, and which usually blew there every morning, he made account they would then instantly be disordered. As for giving the onset, because his galleys were more agile than the galleys of the enemy, he thought it was in his own election and would be most opportune on that occasion. When this wind was up and the galleys of the Peloponnesians, being already contracted into a narrow compass, were both ways troubled, by the wind and withal by their own lesser vessels that encumbered them, and when one galley fell foul of another and the mariners laboured to set them clear with their poles and, through the noise they made keeping off and reviling each other, heard nothing neither of their charge nor of the galleys' direction, and through want of skill unable to keep up their oars in a troubled sea, rendered the galley untractable to him that sat at the helm, then and with this opportunity he gave the signal. And the Athenians, charging, drowned first one of the admiral galleys and divers others after it in the several parts they assaulted and brought them to that pass at length that not one applying himself to the fight they fled all towards Patrae and Dyme, cities of Achaia. The Athenians, after they had chased them and taken twelve galleys and slain most of the men that were in them, fell off and went to Molycreium; and when they had there set up a trophy and consecrated one galley to Neptune, they returned with the rest to Naupactus. The Peloponnesians with the remainder of their fleet went presently along the coast of Cyllene, the arsenal of the Eleians; and thither, after the battle at Stratus, came also Cnemus from Leucas and with him those galleys that were there and with which this other fleet should have been joined.

85. After this the Lacedaemonians sent unto Cnemus to the fleet Timocrates, Brasidas, and Lycophron to be of his council with command to prepare for another better fight and not to

suffer a few galleys to deprive them of the use of the sea. For they thought this accident (especially being their first proof by sea) very much against reason, and that it was not so much a defect of the fleet as of their courage, never comparing the long practice of the Athenians with their own short study in these businesses. And therefore they sent these men thither in passion. Who, being arrived with Cnemus, intimated to the cities about to provide their galleys and caused those they had before to be repaired. Phormio likewise sent to Athens to make known both the enemy's preparation and his own former victory and withal to will them to send speedily unto him as many galleys as they could make ready because they were every day in expectation of a new fight. Hereupon they sent him twenty galleys but commanded him that had the charge of them to go first into Crete. For Nicias, a Cretan of Gortyna, the public host of the Athenians, had persuaded them to a voyage against Cydonia, telling them they might take it in, being now their enemy, which he did to gratify the Polichnitae that bordered upon the Cydonians. Therefore with these galleys he sailed into Crete and together with the Polichnitae wasted the territory of the Cydonians, where also, by reason of the winds and weather unfit to take sea in, he wasted not a little of his time.

86. In the meantime, whilst these Athenians were wind-bound in Crete, the Peloponnesians that were in Cyllene in order of battle sailed along the coast of Panormus of Achaia, to which also were their land forces come to aid them. Phormio likewise sailed by the shore to Rhium Molycricum and anchored without it with twenty galleys, the same he had used in the former battle. Now this Rhium was of the Athenians' side, and the other Rhium in Peloponnesus lies on the opposite shore, distant from it at the most but seven furlongs of sea; and these two make the mouth of the Crisaean gulf. The Peloponnesians therefore came to an anchor at Rhium of Achaia with seventy-seven galleys, not far from Panormus where they left their land forces. After they saw the Athenians and had lain six or seven days one against the other meditating and providing for the battle, the Peloponnesians not intending to put off without Rhium into the wide sea for fear of what they had suffered by it before, nor the other to enter the strait because to fight within they thought

to be the enemy's advantage. At last Cnemus, Brasidas, and the other commanders of the Peloponnesians, desiring to fight speedily before a new supply should arrive from Athens, called the soldiers together and, seeing the most of them to be fearful through their former defeat and not forward to fight again, encouraged them first with words to this effect:

87. "Men of Peloponnesus, if any of you be afraid of the battle at hand for the success of the battle past, his fear is without ground. For you know we were inferior to them then in preparation and set not forth as to a fight at sea but rather to an expedition by land. Fortune likewise crossed us in many things, and somewhat we miscarried by unskilfulness.* So as the loss can no way be ascribed to cowardice, nor is it just, so long as we were not overcome by mere force but have somewhat to allege in our excuse, that the mind should be dejected for the calamity of the event; but we must think that though fortune may fail men, yet the courage of a valiant man can never fail, and not that we may justify cowardice in anything by pretending want of skill, and yet be truly valiant. And yet you are not so much short of their skill as you exceed them in valour. And though this knowledge of theirs, which you so much fear, joined with courage will not be without a memory also to put what they know in execution; yet without courage no art in the world is of any force in the time of danger. For fear confoundeth the memory, and skill without courage availeth nothing. To their odds therefore of skill oppose your odds of valour, and to the fear caused by your overthrow oppose your being then unprovided. You have further now a greater fleet and to fight on your own shore with your aids at hand of men of arms; and, for the most part, the greatest number and best provided get the victory. So that we can neither see any one cause in particular why we should miscarry; and whatsoever were our wants in the former battle, supplied in this will now turn to our instruction. With courage therefore, both masters and mariners, follow every man in his order, not forsaking the place assigned him. And for us, we shall order the battle as well as the former commanders and leave no

* Hobbes does not add, as the Greek does, "as it was our first sea fight."

excuse to any man of his cowardice. And if any will needs be a coward, he shall receive condign punishment; and the valiant shall be rewarded according to their merit."

88. Thus did the commanders encourage the Peloponnesians. And Phormio, he likewise doubting that his soldiers were but fainthearted and observing they had consultations apart and were afraid of the multitude of the enemy's galleys, thought good, having called them together, to encourage and admonish them upon the present occasion. For though he had always before told them and predisposed their minds to an opinion that there was no number of galleys so great which setting upon them they ought not to undertake, and [also] most of the soldiers had of long time assumed a conceit of themselves that being Athenians they ought not to decline any number of galleys whatsoever of the Peloponnesians, yet when he saw that the sight of the enemy present had dejected them, he thought fit to revive their courage and, having assembled the Athenians, said thus:

89. "Soldiers, having observed your fear of the enemy's number, I have called you together, not enduring to see you terrified with things that are not terrible. For first, they have prepared this great number and odds of galleys for that they were overcome before and because they are even in their own opinions too weak for us. And next, their present boldness proceeds only from their knowledge in land service, in confidence whereof (as if to be valiant were peculiar unto them) they are now come up, wherein having for the most part prospered, they think to do the same in service by sea. But in reason the odds must be ours in this as well as it is theirs in the other kind. For in courage they exceed us not; and as touching the advantage of either side, we may better be bold now than they. And the Lacedaemonians, who are the leaders of the confederates, bring them to fight for the greatest part (in respect of the opinion they have of us) against their wills. For else they would never have undertaken a new battle after they were once so clearly overthrown. Fear not therefore any great boldness on their part. But the fear which they have of you is far both greater and more certain, not only for that you have overcome them before, but also for this, that they would never

believe you would go about to resist unless you had some notable thing to put in practice upon them. For when the enemy is the greater number, as these are now, they invade chiefly upon confidence of their strength; but they that are much the fewer must have some great and sure design when they dare fight unconstrained. Wherewith these men now amazed fear us more for our unlikely preparation than they would if it were more proportionable. Besides, many great armies have been overcome by the lesser through unskilfulness and some also by timorousness, both which we ourselves are free from. As for the battle, I will not willingly fight it in the gulf nor go in thither, seeing that to a few galleys with nimbleness and art against many without art, straitness of room is disadvantage. For neither can one charge with the beak of the galley as is fit unless he have sight of the enemy afar off, or if he be himself over-pressed, again get clear. Nor is there any getting through them or turning to and fro at one's pleasure, which are all the works of such galleys as have their advantage in agility; but the sea fight would of necessity be the same with a battle by land wherein the greater number must have the better. But of this I shall myself take the best care I am able. In the meantime, keep you your order well in the galleys, and every man receive his charge readily; and the rather because the enemy is at anchor so near us. In the fight have in great estimation order and silence as things of great force in most military actions, especially in a fight by sea; and charge these your enemies according to the worth of your former acts. You are to fight for a great wager, either to destroy the hope of the Peloponnesian navies or to bring the fear of the sea nearer home to the Athenians. Again, let me tell you, you have beaten them once already; and men once overcome will not come again to the danger so well resolved as before."

90. Thus did Phormio also encourage his soldiers. The Peloponnesians, when they saw the Athenians would not enter the gulf and strait, desiring to draw them in against their wills, weighed anchor and betime in the morning, having arranged their galleys by four and four in a rank, sailed along their own coast within the gulf, leading the way in the same order as they had lain at anchor, with their right wing. In this wing they

had placed twenty of their swiftest galleys to the end that if Phormio, thinking them going to Naupactus, should for safeguard of the town sail along his own coast likewise within the strait, the Athenians might not be able to get beyond that wing of theirs and avoid the impression but be inclosed by their galleys on both sides. Phormio, fearing (as they expected) what might become of the town now without guard, as soon as he saw them from anchor, against his will and in extreme haste went aboard and sailed along the shore with the land forces of the Messenians marching by to aid him. The Peloponnesians, when they saw them sail in one long file, galley after galley, and that they were now in the gulf and by the shore (which they most desired), upon one sign given turned suddenly everyone as fast as he could upon the Athenians, hoping to have intercepted them every galley. But of those the eleven foremost, avoiding that wing and the turn made by the Peloponnesians, got out into the open sea. The rest they intercepted and, driving them to the shore, sunk them. The men, as many as swam not out, they slew; and the galleys some they tied to their own and towed them away empty, and one with the men and all in her they had already taken. But the Messenian succours on land, entering the sea with their arms, got aboard of some of them and fighting from the decks recovered them again after they were already towing away.

91. And in this part the Peloponnesians had the victory and overcame the galleys of the Athenians. Now the twenty galleys that were their right wing gave chase to those eleven Athenian galleys which had avoided them when they turned and were gotten into the open sea. These flying toward Naupactus arrived there before the enemies, all save one, and when they came under the temple of Apollo, turned their beakheads and put themselves in readiness for defence in case the enemy should follow them to the land. But the Peloponnesians, as they came after, were paeanising as if they had already had the victory; and one galley which was of Leucas, being far before the rest, gave chase to one Athenian galley that was behind the rest of the Athenians. Now it chanced that there lay out into the sea a certain ship at anchor to which the Athenian galley first coming fetched a compass about her and came back full butt

against the Leucadian galley that gave her chase and sunk her. Upon this unexpected and unlikely accident they began to fear; and having also followed the chase, as being victors, disorderly, some of them let down their oars into the water and hindered the way of their galleys (a matter of very ill consequence, seeing the enemy was so near) and stayed for more company; and some of them, through ignorance of the coast, ran upon the shelves.

92. The Athenians seeing this took heart again and together with one clamour set upon them who resisted not long, because of their present errors committed and their disarray, but turned and fled to Panormus from whence at first they set forth. The Athenians followed and took from them six galleys that were hindmost and recovered their own which the Peloponnesians had sunk by the shore and tied astern of theirs. Of the men some they slew and some also they took alive. In the Leucadian galley that was sunk near the ship was Timocrates, a Lacedaemonian, who, when the galley was lost, ran himself through with his sword; and his body drave into the haven of Naupactus. The Athenians, falling off, erected a trophy in the place from whence they set forth to this victory and took up their dead and the wreck, as much as was on their own shore, and gave truce to the enemy to do the like. The Peloponnesians also set up a trophy, as if they also had had the victory, in respect of the flight of those galleys which they sunk by the shore; and the galley which they had taken they consecrated to Neptune in Rhium of Achaia, hard by their trophy. After this, fearing the supply which was expected from Athens, they sailed by night into the Crisaean gulf and to Corinth, all but the Leucadians. And those Athenians with twenty galleys out of Crete, that should have been with Phormio before the battle, not long after the going away of the galleys of Peloponnesus arrived at Naupactus. And the summer ended.

93. But before the fleet, gone into the Crisaean gulf and to Corinth, was dispersed, Cnemus and Brasidas and the rest of the commanders of the Peloponnesians in the beginning of winter instructed by the Megareans thought good to make an attempt upon Peiraeus, the haven of the Athenians. Now it was without guard or bar, and that upon very good cause, con-

sidering how much they exceeded others in the power of their navy. And it was resolved that every mariner with his oar, his cushion, and one thong for his oar to turn in should take his way by land from Corinth to the other sea that lieth to Athens and, going with all speed to Megara, launch forty galleys out of Nisaea, the arsenal of the Megareans, which then were there, and sail presently into Peiraeus. For at that time there neither stood any galleys for a watch before it, nor was there any imagination that the enemies would on such a sudden come upon them; for they durst not have attempted it openly, though with leisure; nor if they had had any such intention, could it but have been discovered. As soon as it was resolved on, they set presently forward and, arriving by night, launched the said galleys of Nisaea and set sail, not now towards Peiraeus, as they intended, fearing the danger (and a wind was also said to have risen that hindered them), but toward a promontory of Salamis lying out towards Megara. Now there was in it a little fort, and underneath in the sea lay three galleys that kept watch to hinder the importation and exportation of anything to or from the Megareans. This fort they assaulted, and the galleys they towed empty away after them and, being come upon the Salaminians unawares, wasted also other parts of the island.

94. By this time the fires signifying the coming of enemies were lifted up towards Athens and affrighted them more than anything that had happened in all this war. For they in the city thought the enemies had been already in Peiraeus, and they in Peiraeus thought the city of the Salaminians had been already taken and that the enemy would instantly come into Peiraeus, which, had they not been afraid nor been hindered by the wind, they might also easily have done. But the Athenians, as soon as it was day, came with the whole strength of the city into Peiraeus and launched their galleys and embarking in haste and tumult set sail toward Salamis, leaving for the guard of Peiraeus an army of foot. The Peloponnesians upon notice of these succours, having now overrun most of Salamis and taken many prisoners and much other booty besides the three galleys from the fort of Budorus, went back in all haste to Nisaea. And somewhat they feared the more for that their galleys had

lain long in the water and were subject to leaking. And when they came to Megara, they went thence to Corinth again by land. The Athenians likewise, when they found not the enemy at Salamis, went home and from that time forward looked better to Peiraeus both for the shutting of the ports and for their diligence otherwise.

95. About the same time in the beginning of the same winter, Sitalces an Odrysian, the son of Teres, king of Thrace, made war upon Perdiccas the son of Alexander, king of Macedonia, and upon the Chalcideans bordering on Thrace upon two promises, one of which he required to be performed to him, and the other he was to perform himself. For Perdiccas had promised somewhat unto him for reconciling him to the Athenians, who had formerly oppressed him with war, and for not restoring his brother Philip to the kingdom, that was his enemy, which he never paid him. And Sitalces himself had covenanted with the Athenians when he made league with them that he would end the war which they had against the Chalcideans of Thrace. For these causes therefore he made this expedition and took with him both Amyntas the son of Philip (with purpose to make him king of Macedonia) and also the Athenian ambassadors then with him for that business and Agnon the Athenian commander. For the Athenians ought also to have joined with him against the Chalcideans both with a fleet and with as great land forces as they could provide.

96. Beginning therefore with the Odrysians, he levied first those Thracians that inhabit on this side the mountains Haemus and Rhodope, as many as were of his own dominion, down to the shore of the Euxine Sea and the Hellespont. Then beyond Haemus he levied the Getes and all the nations between Ister and the Euxine Sea. The Getes and the people of those parts are borderers upon the Scythians and furnished as the Scythians are, all archers on horseback. He also drew forth many of those Scythians that inhabit the mountains and are free states, all swordsmen, and are called Dii, the greatest part of which are on the mountain Rhodope; whereof some he hired, and some went as voluntaries. He levied also the Agrianes and Laeaeans and all other the nations of Paeonia in his own dominion. These are the utmost bounds of his dominion, extending to the

Graaeans and Laeaeans, nations of Paeonia, and to the river Strymon, which, rising out of the mountain Scomius, passeth through the territories of the Graaeans and Laeaeans, who make the bounds of his kingdom toward Paeonia and are subject only to their own laws. But on the part that lieth to the Triballians, who are also a free people, the Treres make the bound of his dominion, and the Tilataeans. These dwell on the north side of the mountain Scomius and reach westward as far as to the river Oscius, which cometh out of the same hill Nestus and Hebrus doth; a great and desert hill adjoining to Rhodope.

97. The dimensions of the dominion of the Odrysians by the seaside is from the city of the Abderites to the mouth of Ister in the Euxine Sea; and is, the nearest way, four days' and as many nights' sail for a round ship, with a continual fore wind. By land likewise the nearest way, it is from the city Abdera to the mouth of Ister eleven days' journey for an expedite footman. Thus it lay in respect of the sea. Now for the continent: from Byzantium to the Laeaeans and to the river Strymon (for it reacheth this way farthest into the main land) it is for the like footman thirteen days' journey. The tribute they received from all the barbarian nations and from the cities of Greece, in the reign of Seuthes (who reigned after Sitalces and made the most of it), was in gold and silver, by estimation, four hundred talents by year. And presents of gold and silver came to as much more, besides vestures, both wrought and plain, and other furniture presented not only to him but also to all the men of authority and Odrysian nobility about him. For they had a custom, which also was general to all Thrace contrary to that of the kingdom of Persia, to receive rather than to give; and it was there a greater shame to be asked and deny than to ask and go without. Nevertheless they held this custom long by reason of their power, for without gifts there was nothing to be gotten done amongst them. So that this kingdom arrived thereby to great power. For of all the nations of Europe that lie between the Ionian Gulf and the Euxine Sea, it was, for revenue of money and other wealth, the mightiest; though indeed for strength of an army and multitudes of soldiers, the same be far short of the Scythians. For there is no nation, not to say of Europe but neither of Asia, that are

comparable to this, or that as long as they agree, are able, one nation to one, to stand against the Scythians. And yet in matter of counsel and wisdom in the present occasions of life, they are not like to other men.

98. Sitalces therefore, king of this great country, prepared his army and, when all was ready, set forward and marched towards Macedonia: first, through his own dominion; then, over Cercine, a desert mountain dividing the Sintians from the Paeonians, over which he marched the same way himself had formerly made with timber when he made war against the Paeonians. Passing this mountain out of the country of the Odrysians, they had on their right hand the Paeonians and on the left the Sintians and Medes; and beyond it they came to the city of Doberus in Paeonia. His army, as he marched, diminished not any way, except by sickness, but increased by the accession of many free nations of Thrace that came in uncalled in hope of booty. Insomuch as the whole number is said to have amounted to no less than a hundred and fifty thousand men, whereof the most were foot, the horse being a third part or thereabouts. And of the horse, the greatest part were the Odrysians themselves and the next most, the Getes. And of the foot, those swordsmen, a free nation that came down to him out of the mountain Rhodope, were the most warlike. The rest of the promiscuous multitude were formidable only for their number.

99. Being all together at Doberus, they made ready to fall in from the hill's side into the lower Macedonia, the dominion of Perdiccas. For there are in Macedonia the Lyncestians and the Elimeiotae and other highland nations, who, though they be confederates and in subjection to the other, yet have their several kingdoms by themselves. But of that part of the now Macedonia which lieth toward the sea, Alexander, the father of this Perdiccas, and his ancestors the Temenidae, who came out of Argos, were the first possessors and reigned in the same, having first driven out of Pieria the Pierians, which afterwards seated themselves in Phagres and other towns beyond Strymon at the foot of Pangaeum (from which cause that country is called the Gulf of Pieria to this day which lieth at the foot of Pangaeum and bendeth toward the sea), and out of that which

is called Bottia, the Bottiaeans, that now border upon the Chalcideans. They possessed besides a certain narrow portion of
Paeonia near unto the river Axius reaching from above down
to Pella and to the sea. Beyond Axius they possess the country
called Mygdonia as far as to Strymon, from whence they have
driven out the Edonians. Furthermore, they drave the Eordians
out of the territory now called Eordia (of whom the greatest
part perished, but there dwell a few of them yet about Physca)
and the Almopians out of Almopia. The same Macedonians
subdued also other nations and hold them yet, as Anthemus,
Crestonia, and Bisaltia, and a great part of the Macedonians
themselves. But the whole is called Macedonia and was the
kingdom of Perdiccas the son of Alexander when Sitalces came
to invade it.

100. The Macedonians, unable to stand in the field against
so huge an army, retired all within their strongholds and walled
towns, as many as the country afforded, which were not many
then, but were built afterwards by Archelaus the son of Perdiccas when he came to the kingdom, who then also laid out
the highways straight and took order both for matter of war,
as horses and arms and for other provision, better than all the
other eight kings that were before him. The Thracian army,
arising from Doberus, invaded that territory first which had
been the principality of Philip and took Eidomene by force;
but Gortynia, Atalanta, and some other towns he had yielded
to him for the love of Amyntas the son of Philip, who was
then in the army. They also assaulted Europus but could not
take it. Then they went on further into Macedonia on the part
that lies on the right hand of Pella and Cyrrhus; but within
these into Bottiaea and Pieria they entered not but wasted
Mygdonia, Crestonia, and Anthemus. Now the Macedonians
had never any intention to make head against them with their
foot; but sending out their horsemen, which they had procured
from their allies of the higher Macedonia, they assaulted the
Thracian army in such places where, few against many, they
thought they might do it with most convenience. And where
they charged, none was able to resist them, being both good
horsemen and well armed with breastplates; but enclosed by
the multitude of the enemies, they fought against manifest odds

of number so that in the end they gave it over, esteeming themselves too weak to hazard battle against so many.

101. After this Sitalces gave way to a conference with Perdiccas touching the motives of this war. And forasmuch as the Athenians were not arrived with their fleet (for they thought not that Sitalces would have made the journey, but had sent ambassadors to him with presents), he sent a part of his army against the Chalcideans and Bottiaeans, wherewith, having compelled them within their walled towns, he wasted and destroyed their territory. Whilst he stayed in these parts, the Thessalians southward, and the Magnetians, and the rest of the nations subject to the Thessalians, and all the Grecians as far as to Thermopylae were afraid he would have turned his forces upon them and stood upon their guard. And northward, those Thracians that inhabit the champaign country beyond Strymon, namely the Panaeans, Odomantians, Droans, and Dersaeans, all of them free states, were afraid of the same. He gave occasion also to a rumour that he meant to lead his army against all those Grecians that were enemies to the Athenians, as called in by them to that purpose by virtue of their league. But whilst he stayed, he wasted the Chalcidean, Bottiaean, and Macedonian territories; and when he could not effect what he came for and his army both wanted victual and was afflicted with the coldness of the season, Seuthes the son of Spardocus, his cousin-german and of greatest authority next himself, persuaded him to make haste away. Now Perdiccas had dealt secretly with Seuthes and promised him his sister in marriage and money with her; and Sitalces at the persuasion of him after the stay of full thirty days, whereof he spent eight in Chalcidea, retired with his army with all speed into his own kingdom. And Perdiccas shortly after gave to Seuthes his sister Stratonica in marriage, as he had promised. This was the issue of this expedition of Sitalces.

102. The same winter, after the fleet of the Peloponnesians was dissolved, the Athenians that were at Naupactus under the conduct of Phormio sailed along the coast to Astacus and, disbarking, marched into the inner parts of Acarnania. He had in his army four hundred men of arms that he brought with him in his galleys and four hundred more Messenians. With these

he put out of Stratus, Coronta, and other places all those whose fidelity he thought doubtful. And when he had restored Cynes the son of Theolytus to Coronta, they returned again to their galleys. For they thought they should not be able to make war against the Oeniades (who only of all Acarnania are the Athenians' enemies) in respect of the winter. For the river Achelöus, springing out of the mountain Pindus and running through Dolopia, and through the territories of the Agraeans and the Amphilochians, and through most part of the champaign of Acarnania, passing above by the city of Stratus, and falling into the sea by the city of the Oeniades, which also it moateth about with fens, by the abundance of water maketh it hard lying there for an army in time of winter. Also most of the islands Echinades lie just over against Oenia, hard by the mouth of Achelöus. And the river, being a great one, continually heapeth together the gravel, insomuch that some of those islands are become continent already; and the like in short time is expected by the rest. For not only the stream of the river is swift, broad, and turbidous, but also the islands themselves stand thick, and, because the gravel cannot pass, are joined one to another, lying in and out, not in a direct line nor so much as to give the water his course directly forward into the sea. These islands are all desert and but small ones. It is reported that Apollo by his oracle did assign this place for an habitation to Alcmaeon the son of Amphiareus, at such time as he wandered up and down for the killing of his mother, telling him "that he should never be free from the terrors that haunted him till he had found out and seated himself in such a land as when he slew his mother, the sun had never seen nor was then land because all other lands were polluted by him." Hereupon being at a nonplus, as they say, with much ado he observed this ground congested by the river Achelöus and thought there was enough cast up to serve his turn already since the time of the slaughter of his mother, after which it was now a long time that he had been a wanderer. Therefore, seating himself in the places about the Oeniades, he reigned there and named the country after the name of his son Acarnas. Thus goes the report, as we have heard it concerning Alcmaeon.

103. But Phormio and the Athenians, leaving Acarnania and

returning to Naupactus, in the very beginning of the spring came back to Athens and brought with them such galleys as they had taken and the freemen they had taken prisoners in their fights at sea, who were again set at liberty by exchange of man for man. So ended that winter, and the third year of the war written by Thucydides.

THE THIRD BOOK

1. The summer following, the Peloponnesians and their confederates, at the time when corn was at the highest, entered
with their army into Attica under the conduct of Archidamus,
the son of Zeuxidamus, king of the Lacedaemonians, and there
set them down and wasted the territory about. And the Athenian horsemen, as they were wont, fell upon the enemy where
they thought fit and kept back the multitude of light-armed
soldiers from going out before the men of arms and infesting
the places near the city. And when they had stayed as long
as their victual lasted, they returned and were dissolved according to their cities.

2. After the Peloponnesians were entered Attica, Lesbos immediately, all but Methymne, revolted from the Athenians,

157

which though they would have done before the war and the
Lacedaemonians would not then receive them, yet even now
they were forced to revolt sooner than they had intended to
do. For they stayed to have first straitened the mouth of their
haven with dams of earth, to have finished their walls and their
galleys then in building, and to have gotten in all that was to
come out of Pontus, as archers, and victual, and whatsoever
else they had sent for. But the Tenedians, with whom they were
at odds, and the Methymnaeans, and of the Mytilenaeans themselves certain particular men upon faction, being hosts to the
Athenians, made known unto them that the Lesbians were
forced to go all into Mytilene; that by the help of the Lacedaemonians and their kindred, the Boeotians, they hastened all
manner of provision necessary for a revolt; and that unless it
were presently prevented, all Lesbos would be lost.

3. The Athenians, afflicted with the disease, and with the
war now on foot and at the hottest, thought it a dangerous
matter that Lesbos, which had a navy and was of strength entire, should thus be added to the rest of their enemies, and at
first received not the accusations, holding them therefore the
rather feigned because they would not have them true. But
after, when they had sent ambassadors to Mytilene and could
not persuade them to dissolve themselves and undo their preparation, they then feared the worst and would have prevented
them, and to that purpose suddenly sent out the forty galleys
made ready for Peloponnesus with Cleïppedes and two other
commanders. For they had been advertised that there was a
holiday of Apollo Maloeis to be kept without the city and
that to the celebration thereof the Mytilenaeans were accustomed
to come all out of the town; and they hoped, making haste, to
take them there unawares. And if the attempt succeeded, it
was well; if not, they might command the Mytilenaeans to deliver up their galleys and to demolish their walls; or they might
make war against them if they refused. So these galleys went
their way. And ten galleys of Mytilene which then chanced
to be at Athens, by virtue of their league to aid them, the
Athenians stayed and cast into prison the men that were in
them. In the meantime a certain man went from Athens into
Euboea by sea and then by land to Geraestus and, finding there

a ship ready to put off, having the wind favourable, arrived in Mytilene three days after he set forth from Athens and gave them notice of the coming of the fleet. Hereupon they not only went not out to Maloeis, as was expected, but also stopped the gaps of their walls and ports where they were left unfinished and placed guards to defend them.

4. When the Athenians not long after arrived and saw this, the commanders of the fleet delivered to the Mytilenaeans what they had in charge, which not hearkened unto, they presently fell to the war. The Mytilenaeans, unprovided and compelled to a war on such a sudden, put out some few galleys before the haven to fight; but being driven in again by the galleys of Athens, they called to the Athenian commanders to parley, desiring, if they could upon reasonable conditions, to get the galleys for the present sent away. And the Athenian commander allowed the conditions, he also fearing they should be too weak to make war against the whole island.

When a cessation of arms was granted, the Mytilenaeans amongst others sent to Athens one of those that had given intelligence there of their design, and had repented him after of the same, to try if they could persuade them to withdraw their fleet from them as not intending any innovation. Withal they sent ambassadors at the same time to Lacedaemon, undiscovered of the fleet of the Athenians which was riding at anchor in Malea to the north of the city, being without any confidence of their success at Athens. And these men, after an ill voyage through the wide sea, arriving at Lacedaemon, negotiated the sending of aid from thence.

5. But when their ambassadors were come back from Athens without effect, the Mytilenaeans and the rest of Lesbos, save only Methymne (for these, together with the Imbrians, Lemnians, and some few other their confederates, aided the Athenians), prepared themselves for the war. And the Mytilenaeans with the whole strength of the city made a sally upon the Athenian camp and came to a battle; wherein, though the Mytilenaeans had not the worse, yet they lay not that night without the walls nor durst trust to their strength but retiring into the town, lay quiet there, expecting to try their fortune with the accession of such forces as (if any came) they were to have

from Peloponnesus. For there were now come into the city one Meleas a Laconian and Hermiondas a Theban, who, having been sent out before the revolt but unable to arrive before the coming of the Athenian fleet, secretly after the end of the battle entered the haven in a galley and persuaded them to send another galley along with them with other ambassadors to Sparta, which they did.

6. But the Athenians, much confirmed by this the Mytilenaeans' cessation, called in their confederates (who, because they saw no assurance on the part of the Lesbians, came much sooner in than was thought they would have done) and, riding at anchor to the south of the city, fortified two camps, on either side one, and brought their galleys before both the ports and so quite excluded the Mytilenaeans from the use of the sea. As for the land, the Athenians held so much only as lay near their camps, which was not much; and the Mytilenaeans and other Lesbians, that were now come to aid them, were masters of the rest. For Malea served the Athenians for a station only for their galleys and to keep their market in. And thus proceeded the war before Mytilene.

7. About the same time of the same summer, the Athenians sent likewise thirty galleys into Peloponnesus under the conduct of Asopius the son of Phormio. For the Acarnanians had desired them to send some son or kinsman of Phormio for general into those parts. These, as they sailed by, wasted the maritime country of Laconia; and then sending back the greatest part of his fleet to Athens, Asopius himself with twelve galleys went on to Naupactus. And afterwards, having raised the whole power of Acarnania, he made war upon the Oeniades and both entered with his galleys into the river of Achelöus and with his land forces wasted the territory. But when the Oeniades would not yield, he disbanded his land forces and sailed with his galleys to Leucas and landed his soldiers on the territory of Neritum, but in going off was by those of the country that came out to defend it and by some few of the garrison soldiers there both himself and part of his company slain. And having upon truce received from the Leucadians their dead bodies, they went their ways.

8. Now the ambassadors of the Mytilenaeans that went out

in the first galley, having been referred by the Lacedaemonians to the general meeting of the Grecians at Olympia to the end they might determine of them together with the rest of the confederates, went to Olympia accordingly. It was that Olympiad wherein Dorieus of Rhodes was the second time victor. And when after the solemnity they were set in council, the ambassadors spake unto them in this manner:

9. "Men of Lacedaemon and confederates, we know the received custom of the Grecians. For they that take into league such as revolt in the wars and relinquish a former league, though they like them as long as they have profit by them, yet accounting them but traitors to their former friends, they esteem the worse of them in their judgment. And to say the truth, this judgment is not without good reason when they that revolt and they from whom the revolt is made are mutually like minded and affected, and equal in provision and strength, and no just cause of their revolt given. But now between us and the Athenians it is not so. Nor let any man think the worse of us for that having been honoured by them in time of peace, we have now revolted in time of danger.

10. "For the first point of our speech, especially now we seek to come into league with you, shall be to make good the justice and honesty of our revolt. For we know there can be neither firm friendship between man and man nor any communion between city and city to any purpose whatsoever without a mutual opinion of each other's honesty, and also a similitude of customs otherwise; for in the difference of minds is grounded the diversity of actions.

"As for our league with the Athenians, it was first made when you gave over the Medan war, and they remained to prosecute the relics of that business. Yet we entered not such a league as to be their helpers in bringing the Grecians into the servitude of the Athenians but to set free the Grecians from the servitude of the Medes. And as long as they led us as equals, we followed them with much zeal: but when we saw they remitted their enmity against the Medes and led us to the subjugation of the confederates, we could not then but be afraid. And the confederates, through the multitude of distinct counsels unable to unite themselves for resistance, fell all but ourselves and the

Chians into their subjection. And we, having still our own laws and being in name a free state, followed them to the wars; but so, as by the examples of their former actions, we held them not any longer for faithful leaders. For it was not probable when they had subdued those whom together with us they took into league but that, when they should be able, they would do the like also by the rest.

11. "It is true that if we were now in liberty all, we might be the better assured that they would forbear to innovate; but since they have under them the greatest part already, in all likelihood they will take it ill to deal on equal terms with us alone and, the rest yielding, to let us only stand up as their equals. Especially when by how much they are become stronger by the subjection of their confederates, by so much the more are we become desolate. But the equality of mutual fear is the only band of faith in leagues. For he that hath the will to transgress, yet when he hath not the odds of strength, will abstain from coming on. Now the reason why they have left us yet free is no other but that they may have a fair colour to lay upon their domination over the rest and because it hath seemed unto them more expedient to take us in by policy than by force. For therein they made use of us for an argument that having equal vote with them we would never have followed them to the wars if those against whom they led us had not done the injury: and thereby also they brought the stronger against the weaker and, reserving the strongest to the last, made them the weaker by removing the rest. Whereas if they had begun with us, when the confederates had had both their own strength and a side to adhere to, they had never subdued them so easily. Likewise our navy kept them in some fear, lest united and added to yours or to any other, it might have created them some danger. Partly also we escaped by our observance toward their commons and most eminent men from time to time. But yet we still thought we could not do so long, considering the examples they have showed us in the rest, if this war should not have fallen out.

12. "What friendship then or assurance of liberty was this when we received each other with alienated affections: when

whilst they had wars, they for fear courted us; and when they had peace, we for fear courted them: and whereas in others good will assureth loyalty, in us it was the effect of fear? So it was more for fear than love that we remained their confederates; and whomsoever security should first embolden, he was first likely by one means or other to break the league. Now if any man think we did unjustly to revolt upon the expectation of evil intended without staying to be certain whether they would do it or not, he weigheth not the matter aright. For if we were as able to contrive evil against them and again to defer it, as they can against us, being thus equal, what needed us to be at their discretion? But seeing it is in their hands to invade at pleasure, it ought to be in ours to anticipate.

13. "Upon these pretensions, therefore, and causes, men of Lacedaemon and confederates, we have revolted, the which are both clear enough for the hearers to judge upon, that we had reason for it, and weighty enough to affright, and compel us to take some course for our own safety, which we would have done before, when before the war we sent ambassadors to you about our revolt, but could not because you would not then admit us into your league. And now when the Boeotians invited us to it, we presently obeyed. Wherein we thought we made a double revolt, one from the Grecians, in ceasing to do them mischief with the Athenians and helping to set them free, and another from the Athenians, in breaking first and not staying to be destroyed by them hereafter. But this revolt of ours hath been sooner than was fit and before we were provided for it. For which cause also the confederates ought so much the sooner to admit us into the league and send us the speedier aid, thereby the better at once both to defend those you ought to defend and to annoy your enemies. Whereof there was never better opportunity than at present. For the Athenians being both with the sickness and their great expenses consumed and their navy divided, part upon your own coasts and part upon ours, it is not likely they should have many galleys to spare in case you again this summer invade them both by sea and land, but that they should either be unable to resist the invasion of your fleet or be forced to come off from both our coasts. And

let not any man conceive that you shall herein at your own danger defend the territory of another. For though Lesbos seem remote, the profit of it will be near you. For the war will not be, as a man would think, in Attica but there from whence cometh the profit to Attica. This profit is the revenue they have from the confederates, which, if they subdue us, will still be greater. For neither will any other revolt; and all that is ours will accrue unto them, and we shall be worse handled besides than those that were under them before. But aiding us with diligence, you shall both add to your league a city that hath a great navy, the thing you most stand in need of, and also easily overthrow the Athenians by subduction of their confederates because everyone will then be more confident to come in, and you shall avoid the imputation of not assisting such as revolt unto you. And if it appear that your endeavour is to make them free, your strength in this war will be much the more confirmed.

14. "In reverence therefore of the hopes which the Grecians have reposed in you and of the presence of Jupiter Olympius, in whose temple here we are in a manner suppliants to you, receive the Mytilenaeans into league and aid us. And do not cast us off, who (though, as to the exposing of our persons, the danger be our own) shall bring a common profit to all Greece if we prosper and a more common detriment to all the Grecians if, through your inflexibleness, we miscarry. Be you therefore men such as the Grecians esteem you and our fears require you to be."

15. In this manner spake the Mytilenaeans. And the Lacedaemonians and their confederates, when they had heard and allowed their reasons, decreed not only a league with the Lesbians but also again to make an invasion into Attica. And to that purpose the Lacedaemonians appointed their confederates there present to make as much speed as they could with two parts of their forces into the isthmus; and they themselves being first there prepared engines in the isthmus for the drawing up of galleys, with intention to carry the navy from Corinth to the other sea that lieth towards Athens, and to set upon them both by sea and land. And these things diligently did they. But the rest of the confederates assembled but slowly,

being busied in the gathering in of their fruits and weary of warfare.

16. The Athenians, perceiving all this preparation to be made upon an opinion of their weakness and desirous to let them see they were deceived as being able, without stirring the fleet at Lesbos, easily to master the fleet that should come against them out of Peloponnesus, manned out a hundred galleys and embarked therein generally, both citizens (except those of the degree of Pentacosiomedimni and Horsemen *) and also strangers that dwelt amongst them, and sailing to the isthmus made a show of their strength and landed their soldiers in such parts of Peloponnesus as they thought fit. When the Lacedaemonians saw things so contrary to their expectation, they thought it false which was spoken by the Lesbian ambassadors, and esteeming the action difficult, seeing their confederates were not arrived and that news was brought of the wasting of the territory near their city by the thirty galleys formerly sent about Peloponnesus by the Athenians, went home again, and afterwards prepared to send a fleet to Lesbos, and intimated to the cities rateably to furnish forty galleys, and appointed Alcidas, who was to go thither with them, for admiral. And the Athenians, when they saw the Peloponnesians gone, went likewise home with their hundred galleys.

17. About the time that this fleet was out, they had surely the most galleys (besides the beauty of them) together in action in these employments; yet in the beginning of the war they had both as good and more in number. For a hundred attended the guard of Attica, Euboea, and Salamis; and another hundred were about Peloponnesus, besides those that were at Potidaea and other places, so that in one summer they had in all two hundred and fifty sail. And this, together with Potidaea, was it that most exhausted their treasure. For the men of arms that besieged the city had each of them two drachmes a day, one for himself and another for his man, and were three thousand in number that were sent thither at first and remained to the end of the siege, besides sixteen hundred more that went with Phormio and came away before the town was won. And

* This refers to the two highest classifications among the Athenian citizenry.

the galleys had all the same pay. In this manner was their money consumed and so many galleys employed, the most indeed that ever they had manned at once.

18. About the same time that the Lacedaemonians were in the isthmus, the Mytilenaeans marched by land, both they and their auxiliaries, against Methymne in hope to have had it betrayed unto them and, having assaulted the city, when it succeeded not the way they looked for, they went thence to Antissa, Pyrrha, and Eressus; and after they had settled the affairs of those places and made strong their walls returned speedily home. When these were gone, the Methymnaeans likewise made war upon Antissa; but beaten by the Antisaeans and some auxiliaries that were with them, they made haste again to Methymne with the loss of many of their soldiers. But the Athenians being advertised hereof and understanding that the Mytilenaeans were masters of the land and that their own soldiers there were not enough to keep them in, sent thither, about the beginning of autumn, Paches, the son of Epicurus, with a thousand men of arms of their own city, who, supplying the place of rowers themselves, arrived at Mytilene and ingirt it with a single wall, save that in some places, stronger by nature than the rest, they only built turrets and placed guards in them. So that the city was every way strongly besieged, both by sea and land, and the winter began.

19. The Athenians, standing in need of money for the siege, both contributed themselves and sent thither two hundred talents of this their first contribution, and also dispatched Lysicles and four others with twelve galleys to levy money amongst the confederates.* But Lysicles, after he had been to and fro and gathered money in divers places, as he was going up from Myus through the plains of Maeander in Caria as far

---

* What Thucydides means here—which does not become entirely clear in Hobbes' version—is "Being in need of money the Athenians now for the first time levied a special tax on their own citizens and also sent special commissions to collect taxes among the allies." Normally there was no *eisphora*, or general tax, paid by Athenian citizens, and the allies made their regular contributions themselves at fixed times of year through their representatives instead of, as in this instance, being dunned by special Athenian collection agents.

as to the hill Sandius, was set upon there by the Carians and Anaeitans and himself with a great part of his soldiers slain.

20. The same winter the Plataeans (for they were besieged by the Peloponnesians and Boeotians), pressed now with want of victual and hopeless of relief from Athens, and no other means of safety appearing, took counsel, both they and the Athenians that were besieged with them, at first all to go out and, if they could, to pass over the wall of the enemy by force. The authors of this attempt, were Theaenetus the son of Tolmidas, a soothsayer, and Eupompidas the son of Daïmachus, one of their commanders. But half of them afterwards, by one means or other, for the greatness of the danger shrunk from it again; but two hundred and twenty or thereabouts voluntarily persisted to go out in this manner. They made them ladders fit for the height of the enemy's wall; the wall they measured by the lays of bricks on the part toward the town where it was not plastered over; and divers men at once numbered the lays of bricks, whereof, though some missed, yet the greatest part took the reckoning just, especially numbering them so often and at no great distance but where they might easily see the part to which their ladders were to be applied, and so by guess of the thickness of one brick took the measure of their ladders.

21. As for the wall of the Peloponnesians, it was thus built. It consisted of a double circle, one towards Plataea and another outward in case of an assault from Athens. These two walls were distant one from the other about sixteen foot; and that sixteen foot of space which was betwixt them was disposed and built into cabins for the watchmen, which was so joined and continued one to another that the whole appeared to be one thick wall with battlements on either side. At every ten battlements stood a great tower of a just breadth to comprehend both walls and reach from the outmost to the inmost front of the whole, so that there was no passage by the side of a tower but through the midst of it. And such nights as there happened any storm of rain, they used to quit the battlements of the wall and to watch under the towers, as being not far asunder and covered beside overhead. Such was the form of the wall wherein the Peloponnesians kept their watch.

22. The Plataeans, after they were ready and had attended a tempestuous night,* and withal moonless, went out of the city and were conducted by the same men that were the authors of the attempt. And first they passed the ditch that was about the town and then came up close to the wall of the enemy, who, because it was dark, could not see them coming; and the noise they made as they went could not be heard for the blustering of the wind. And they came on besides at a good distance one from the other, that they might not be betrayed by the clashing of their arms, and were but lightly armed and not shod but on the left foot for the more steadiness in the wet. They came thus to the battlements in one of the spaces between tower and tower, knowing that there was now no watch kept there. And first came they that carried the ladders and placed them to the wall: then twelve lightly armed, only with a dagger and a breastplate, went up, led by Ammeas the son of Coroebus, who was the first that mounted; and they that followed him went up into either tower six. To these succeeded others lightly armed that carried the darts for whom they that came after carried targets at their backs that they might be the more expedite to get up, which targets they were to deliver to them when they came to the enemy. At length, when most of them were ascended, they were heard by the watchmen that were in the towers. For one of the Plataeans taking hold of the battlements threw down a tile which made a noise in the fall. And presently there was an alarm, and the army ran to the wall. For in the dark and stormy night they knew not what the danger was, and the Plataeans that were left in the city came forth withal and assaulted the wall of the Peloponnesians on the opposite side to that where their men went over. So that though they were all in a tumult in their several places, yet not any of them that watched durst stir to the aid of the rest nor were able to conjecture what had happened. But those three hundred that were appointed to assist the watch upon all occasions of need went without the wall and made towards the place of the clamour. They also held up the fires, by which they used to make known the approach of enemies, towards Thebes. But then the Plataeans likewise held out many other

* The Greek actually says "a stormy night with rain and wind."

fires from the wall of the city, which for that purpose they had before prepared, to render the fires of the enemy insignificant, and that the Thebans, apprehending the matter otherwise than it was, might forbear to send help till their men were over and had recovered some place of safety.

23. In the meantime those Plataeans, which having scaled the wall first and slain the watch were now masters of both the towers, not only guarded the passages by standing themselves in the entries but also, applying ladders from the wall to the towers and conveying many men to the top, kept the enemies off with shot both from above and below. In the mean space, the greatest number of them having reared to the wall many ladders at once and beaten down the battlements passed quite over between the towers. And ever as any of them got to the other side, they stood still upon the brink of the ditch without and with arrows and darts kept off those that came by the outside of the wall to hinder their passage. And when the rest were over, then last of all, and with much ado, came they also down to the ditch which were in the two towers. And by this time the three hundred that were to assist the watch came and set upon them and had lights with them, by which means the Plataeans that were on the further brink of the ditch discerned them the better from out of the dark and aimed their arrows and darts at their most disarmed parts; for standing in the dark, the lights of the enemy made the Plataeans the less discernible, insomuch as these last passed the ditch, though with difficulty and force. For the water in it was frozen over, though not so hard as to bear, but watery, and such as when the wind is at east rather than at north. And the snow which fell that night, together with so great a wind as that was, had very much increased the water, which they waded through with scarce their heads above. But yet the greatness of the storm was the principal means of their escape.

24. From the ditch the Plataeans in troop took the way towards Thebes, leaving on the left hand the temple of Juno built by Androcrates, both for that they supposed they would least suspect the way that led to their enemies, and also because they saw the Peloponnesians with their lights pursue that way, which by Mount Cithaeron and the Oak-heads led to Athens.

The Plataeans, when they had gone six or seven furlongs, forsook the Theban way and turned into that which led towards the mountain to Erythrae and Hysiae and, having gotten the hills, escaped through to Athens, being two hundred and twelve persons of a greater number. For some of them returned into the city before the rest went over, and one of their archers was taken upon the ditch without. And so the Peloponnesians gave over the pursuit and returned to their places. But the Plataeans that were within the city, knowing nothing of the event * and those that turned back having told them that not a man escaped, as soon as it was day sent a herald to entreat a truce for the taking up of their dead bodies; but when they knew the truth, they gave it over. And thus these men of Plataea passed through the fortification of their enemies and were saved.

25. About the end of the same winter Salaethus, a Lacedaemonian, was sent in a galley to Mytilene and, coming first to Pyrrha and thence going to Mytilene by land, entered the city by the dry channel of a certain torrent, which had a passage through the wall of the Athenians, undiscovered. And he told the magistrates that Attica should again be invaded and that the forty galleys which were to aid them were coming, and that himself was sent afore both to let them know it and withal to give order in the rest of their affairs. Hereupon the Mytilenaeans grew confident and hearkened less to composition with the Athenians. And the winter ended, and the fourth year of this war written by Thucydides.

26. In the beginning of the summer after they had sent Alcidas away with the forty-two galleys, whereof he was admiral, unto Mytilene, both they and their confederates invaded Attica to the end that the Athenians, troubled on both sides, might the less send supply against the fleet now gone to Mytilene. In this expedition Cleomenes was general instead of Pausanias, the son of Pleistoanax, who being king was yet in minority; and Cleomenes was his uncle by the father. And they now cut down both what they had before wasted and began to grow again, and also whatsoever else they had before pretermitted: and this was the sharpest invasion of all but the sec-

---

* I.e., the outcome.

ond. For whilst they stayed to hear news from their fleet at Lesbos, which by this time they supposed to have been arrived, they went abroad and destroyed most part of the country. But when nothing succeeded according to their hopes and seeing their corn failed,* they retired again and were dissolved according to their cities.

27. The Mytilenaeans, in the meantime, seeing the fleet came not from Peloponnesus but delayed the time and their victuals failed, were constrained to make their composition with the Athenians upon this occasion. Salaethus, when he also expected these galleys no longer, armed the commons of the city, who were before unarmed, with intention to have made a sally upon the Athenians. But they, as soon as they had gotten arms, no longer obeyed the magistrates but, holding assemblies by themselves, required the rich men either to bring their corn to light and divide it amongst them all, or else, they said, they would make their composition by delivering up the city to the Athenians.

28. Those that managed the state perceiving this and unable to hinder it, knowing also their own danger in case they were excluded out of the composition, they all jointly agreed to yield the city to Paches and his army with these conditions: "to be proceeded withal at the pleasure of the people of Athens and to receive the army into the city; and that the Mytilenaeans should send ambassadors to Athens about their own business; and that Paches, till their return, should neither put in bonds, nor make slave of, nor slay any Mytilenaean." This was the effect of that composition. But such of the Mytilenaeans as had principally practised with the Lacedaemonians, being afraid of themselves, when the army was entered the city durst not trust to the conditions agreed on but took sanctuary at the altars. But Paches, having raised them upon promise to do them no injury, sent them to Tenedos to be in custody there till the people of Athens should have resolved what to do. After this he sent some galleys to Antissa and took in that town and ordered the affairs of his army as he thought convenient.

29. In the meantime those forty galleys of Peloponnesus

* I.e., not the corn they were burning, but the grain they carried with them for provisioning themselves.

which should have made all possible haste trifled away the time about Peloponnesus and, making small speed in the rest of their navigation, arrived at Delos unknown to the Athenians at Athens. From thence sailing to Icarus and Myconus, they got first intelligence of the loss of Mytilene. But to know the truth more certainly, they went thence to Embatus in Erythraea. It was about the seventh day after the taking of Mytilene that they arrived at Embatus where, understanding the certainty, they went to council about what they were to do upon the present occasion; and Teutiaplus, an Eleian, delivered his opinion to this effect:

30. "Alcidas, and the rest that have command of the Peloponnesians in this army, it were not amiss, in my opinion, to go to Mytilene as we are before advice be given of our arrival. For in all probability we shall find the city, in respect they have but lately won it, very weakly guarded and to the sea (where they expect no enemy, and we are chiefly strong) not guarded at all. It is also likely that their land soldiers are dispersed, some in one house and some in another, carelessly as victors. Therefore if we fall upon them suddenly and by night, I think, with the help of those within, if any be left there that will take our part, we may be able to possess ourselves of the city. And we shall never fear the danger if we but think this: that all stratagems of war * whatsoever are no more but such occasions as this, which, if a commander avoid in himself and take the advantage of them in the enemy, he shall for the most part have good success."

31. Thus said he, but prevailed not with Alcidas. And some others, fugitives of Ionia and those Lesbians that were with him in the fleet, gave him counsel that, seeing he feared the danger of this, he should seize some city of Ionia or Cume in Aeolia, that having some town for the seat of the war, they might from thence force Ionia to revolt, whereof there was hope because the Ionians would not be unwilling to see him there; and if they could withdraw from the Athenians this their great revenue and withal put them to maintain a fleet against

* The reading of the Greek here is doubtful. The most likely version is the word *kainon,* which means "the novelty," i.e., "the surprises of war."

them, it would be a great exhausting of their treasure. They said besides that they thought they should be able to get Pissuthnes to join with them in the war. But Alcidas rejected this advice likewise, inclining rather to this opinion that since they were come too late to Mytilene, they were best to return speedily into Peloponnesus.

32. Whereupon putting off from Embatus, he sailed by the shore to Myonnesus of the Teians and there slew most of the prisoners he had taken by the way. After this he put in at Ephesus; and thither came ambassadors to him from the Samians of Anaea and told him that it was but an ill manner of setting the Grecians at liberty to kill such as had not lift up their hands against him nor were indeed enemies to the Peloponnesians but confederates to the Athenians by constraint, and that, unless he gave over that course, he would make few of the enemies his friends but many now friends to become his enemies. Wherefore upon these words of the ambassadors he set the Chians and some others, all that he had left alive, at liberty. For when men saw their fleet, they never fled from it but came unto them as to Athenians, little imagining that the Athenians being masters of the sea, the Peloponnesians durst have put over to Ionia.

33. From Ephesus Alcidas went away in haste, indeed fled; for he had been descried by the Salaminia and the Paralus * (which by chance were then in their course for Athens) whilst he lay at anchor about Claros and, fearing to be chased, kept the wide sea, meaning by his good will to touch no land till he came into Peloponnesus. But the news of them came to Paches from divers places, especially from Erythraea. For the cities of Ionia being unwalled were afraid extremely lest the Peloponnesians, sailing by without intention to stay, should have pillaged them as they passed. But the Salaminia and the Paralus, having seen him at Claros, brought the news themselves. And Paches thereupon made great haste after and followed him as far as Latmos the island. But when he saw he could not reach him, he came back again and thought he had a good turn, see-ing he could not overtake those galleys upon the wide sea that the same were not compelled, by being taken in some place

* These were the two state ships of Athens, used principally for sending embassies to Delphi, carrying envoys, collecting tribute, etc.

near land, to fortify themselves and so to give him occasion with guards and galleys to attend them.

34. As he came by in his return, he put in at Notium, a city of the Colophonians, into which the Colophonians came and inhabited after the town above, through their own sedition, was taken by Itamanes and the barbarians. (This town was taken at the time when Attica was the second time invaded by the Peloponnesians.) They then that came down and dwelt in Notium, falling again into sedition, the one part having procured some forces, Arcadians and barbarians, of Pissuthnes, kept them in a part of the town which they had severed from the rest with a wall; and there, with such of the Colophonians of the high town as being of the Medan faction entered with them, they governed the city at their pleasure; and the other part, which went out from these and were the fugitives, brought in Paches. He, when he had called out Hippias, captain of the Arcadians that were within the said wall, with promise, if they should not agree, to set him safe and sound within the wall again, and Hippias was thereupon come to him, committed him to custody, but without bonds, and withal, assaulting the wall on a sudden when they expected not, took it and slew as many of the Arcadians and barbarians as were within; and when he had done, brought Hippias in again, according as he had promised, but, after he had him there, laid hold on him and caused him to be shot to death and restored Notium to the Colophonians, excluding only such as had medized. Afterwards the Athenians sent governors to Notium of their own and, having gathered together the Colophonians out of all cities whatsoever, seated them there under the law of the Athenians.

35. Paches, when he came back to Mytilene, took in Pyrrha and Eressus and, having found Salaethus the Lacedaemonian hidden in Mytilene, apprehended him and sent him, together with those men he had put in custody at Tenedos and whomsoever else he thought author of the revolt, to Athens. He likewise sent away the greatest part of his army and with the rest stayed and settled the state of Mytilene and the rest of Lesbos as he thought convenient.

36. These men, and Salaethus with them, being arrived at Athens, the Athenians slew Salaethus presently, though he made

them many offers, and amongst other to get the army of the Peloponnesians to rise from before Plataea, for it was yet besieged. But upon the rest they went to council and in their passion decreed to put them to death, not only those men there present but also all the men of Mytilene that were of age, and to make slaves of the women and children, laying to their charge the revolt itself in that they revolted not being in subjection as others were; and withal the Peloponnesian fleet, which durst enter into Ionia to their aid, had not a little aggravated that commotion. For by that it seemed that the revolt was not made without much premeditation. They therefore sent a galley to inform Paches of their decree with command to put the Mytilenaeans presently to death. But the next day they felt a kind of repentance in themselves and began to consider what a great and cruel decree it was that not the authors only but the whole city should be destroyed. Which when the ambassadors of the Mytilenaeans that were there present and such Athenians as favoured them understood, they wrought with those that bare office to bring the matter again into debate, wherein they easily prevailed, forasmuch as to them also it was well known that the most of the city were desirous to have means to consult of the same anew. The assembly being presently met, among the opinions of divers others Cleon also, the son of Cleaenetus, who in the former assembly had won to have them killed, being of all the citizens most violent and with the people at that time far the most powerful, stood forth and said in this manner:

37. "I have often on other occasions thought a democracy incapable of dominion over others, but most of all now for this your repentance concerning the Mytilenaeans. For through your own mutual security and openness, you imagine the same also in your confederates and consider not that when at their persuasion you commit an error or relent upon compassion, you are softened thus to the danger of the commonwealth not to the winning of the affections of your confederates; nor do you consider that your government is a tyranny and those that be subject to it are against their wills so and are plotting continually against you, and obey you not for any good turn, which to your own detriment you shall do them, but only for that you exceed them in strength, and for no good will. But the

worst mischief of all is this, that nothing we decree shall stand
firm and that we will not know that a city with the worse laws,
if immoveable, is better than one with good laws when they
be not binding, and that a plain wit accompanied with modesty
is more profitable to the state than dexterity with arrogance,
and that the more ignorant sort of men do, for the most part,
better regulate a commonwealth than they that are wiser. For
these love to appear wiser than the laws and in all public debatings to carry the victory as the worthiest things wherein to
show their wisdom, from whence most commonly proceeds
the ruin of the states they live in. Whereas the other sort, mistrusting their own wits, are content to be esteemed not so
wise as the laws and not able to carp at what is well spoken
by another, and so, making themselves equal judges rather than
contenders for mastery, govern a state for the most part well.
We therefore should do the like and not be carried away with
combats of eloquence and wit to give such counsel to your
multitude as in our own judgments we think not good.

38. "For my own part, I am of the opinion I was before; and
I wonder at these men that have brought this matter of the
Mytilenaeans in question again and thereby caused delay, which
is the advantage only of them that do the injury. For the sufferer
by this means comes upon the doer with his anger dulled;
whereas revenge, the opposite of injury, is then greatest when
it follows presently. I do wonder also what he is that shall
stand up now to contradict me and shall think to prove that
the injuries done us by the Mytilenaeans are good for us or
that our calamities are any damage to our confederates. For certainly he must either trust in his eloquence to make you believe
that that which was decreed was not decreed or, moved with
lucre, must with some elaborate speech endeavour to seduce
you. Now of such matches [of eloquence] as these, the city
giveth the prizes to others; but the danger that hence proceedeth, she herself sustaineth. And of all this you yourselves
are the cause, by the evil institution of these matches, in that
you use to be spectators of words and hearers of actions, beholding future actions in the words of them that speak well as
possible to come to pass and actions already past in the orations
of such as make the most of them, and that with such as-

surance, as if what you saw with your eyes were not more certain than what you hear related. You are excellent men for one to deceive with a speech of a new strain but backward to follow any tried advice, slaves to strange things, contemners of things usual. You would everyone chiefly give the best advice; but if you cannot, then you will contradict those that do. You would not be thought to come after with your opinion but rather, if anything be acutely spoken, to applaud it first and to appear ready apprehenders of what is spoken even before it be out, but slow to preconceive the sequel of the same. You would hear, as one may say, somewhat else than what our life is conversant in; and yet you sufficiently understand not that that is before your eyes. And to speak plainly, overcome with the delight of the ear, you are rather like unto spectators sitting to hear the contentions of sophisters than to men that deliberate of the state of a commonwealth.

39. "To put you out of this humour, I say unto you that the Mytilenaeans have done us more injury than ever did any one city. For those that have revolted through the over-hard pressure of our government or that have been compelled to it by the enemy, I pardon them. But they that were islanders and had their city walled so as they needed not fear our enemies but only by sea, in which case also they were armed for them with sufficient provision of galleys, and they that were permitted to have their own laws and whom we principally honoured, and yet have done thus, what have they done but conspired against us and rather warred upon us than revolted from us (for a revolt is only of such as suffer violence) and joined with our bitterest enemies to destroy us? This is far worse than if they had warred against us for increasing of their own power.* But these men would neither take example by their neighbour's calamity, who are, all that revolted, already subdued by us; nor could their own present felicity make them afraid of changing it into misery, but being bold against future events and aiming at matters above their strength though below their desires, have taken arms against us and preferred force before justice. For no sooner they thought they might get the

* The Greek says actually "than if gathering a power on their own they had warred against us."

victory but immediately, though without injury done them, they rose against us. But with cities that come to great and unexpected prosperity, it is usual to turn insolent; whereas most commonly that prosperity which is attained according to the course of reason is more firm than that which cometh unhoped for; and such cities, as one may say, do more easily keep off an adverse, than maintain a happy, fortune. Indeed we should not formerly have done any honour more to the Mytilenaeans than to the rest of our confederates, for then they had never come to this degree of insolence. For it is natural to men to contemn those that observe them and to have in admiration such as will not give them way. Now therefore let them be punished according to their wicked dealing, and let not the fault be laid upon a few and the people be absolved. For they have all alike taken arms against us; and the commons, if they had been constrained to it, might have fled hither and have recovered their city afterwards again. But they, esteeming it the safer adventure to join with the few, are alike with them culpable of the revolt. Have also in consideration your confederates; and if you inflict the same punishment on them that revolt upon compulsion of the enemy that you do on them that revolt of their own accord, who, think you, will not revolt, though on light pretence, seeing that speeding they win their liberty and failing their case is not incurable? Besides, that against every city we must be at a new hazard, both of our persons and fortunes. Wherein with the best success we recover but an exhausted city and lose that wherein our strength lieth, the revenue of it; but miscarrying, we add these enemies to our former and must spend that time in warring against our own confederates, which we needed to employ against the enemies we have already.

40. "We must not therefore give our confederates hope of pardon, either impetrable * by words or purchasable by money, as if their errors were but such as are commonly incident to humanity. For these did us not an injury unwillingly but wittingly conspired against us; whereas it ought to be involuntary whatsoever is pardonable. Therefore both then at first, and now again, I maintain that you ought not to alter your former

* I.e., obtainable.

decree nor to offend in any of these three most disadvantageous things to empire, pity, delight in plausible speeches, and lenity. As for pity, it is just to show it on them that are like us and will have pity again but not upon such as not only would not have had pity upon us but must also of necessity have been our enemies forever hereafter. And for the rhetoricians that delight you with their orations, let them play their prizes in matters of less weight and not in such wherein the city for a little pleasure must suffer a great damage, but they for their well speaking must well have. Lastly for lenity, it is to be used towards those that will be our friends hereafter rather than towards such as being suffered to live will still be as they are, not a jot the less our enemies. In sum I say only this, that if you follow my advice, you shall do that which is both just in respect of the Mytilenaeans and profitable for yourselves; whereas if you decree otherwise, you do not gratify them but condemn yourselves. For if these have justly revolted, you must unjustly have had dominion over them. Nay though your dominion be against reason, yet if you resolve to hold it, you must also, as a matter conducing thereunto, against reason punish them; or else you must give your dominion over, that you may be good without danger.* But if you consider what was likely they would have done to you if they had prevailed, you cannot but think them worthy the same punishment nor be less sensible, you that have escaped, than they that have conspired, especially they having done the injury first. For such as do an injury without precedent cause persecute most, and even to the death, him they have done it to, as jealous of the danger his remaining enemy may create him; for he that is wronged without cause and escapeth will commonly be more cruel than if it were against any enemy on equal quarrel. Let us not therefore betray ourselves, but in contemplation of what you were near suffering and how you once prized above all things else to have them in your power, requite them now accordingly. Be not softened at the sight of their present estate, nor forget the danger that hung over our own heads so lately. Give not only unto these their deserved punishment but also unto the rest of our confederates

---

* A more literal translation brings out the force of the sentiment better: "and be honest men from a position of no danger."

a clear example that death is their sentence whensoever they shall rebel. Which when they know, you shall the less often have occasion to neglect your enemies and fight against your own confederates."

41. To this purpose spake Cleon. After him Diodotus the son of Eucrates, who also in the former assembly opposed most the putting of the Mytilenaeans to death, stood forth and spake as followeth.

42. "I will neither blame those who have propounded the business of the Mytilenaeans to be again debated nor commend those that find fault with often consulting in affairs of great importance. But I am of opinion that nothing is so contrary to good counsel as these two, haste and anger, whereof the one is ever accompanied with madness and the other with want of judgment.* And whosoever maintaineth that words are not instructors to deeds, either he is not wise or doth it upon some private interest of his own. Not wise, if he think that future and not apparent things may be demonstrated otherwise than by words; interested, if desiring to carry an ill matter and knowing that a bad cause will not bear a good speech, he go about to deter his opposers and hearers by a good calumniation. But they of all others are most intolerable that when men give public advice will accuse them also of bribery. For if they charged a man with no more but ignorance when he had spoken in vain, he might yet depart with the opinion of a fool. But when they impute corruption also, if his counsel take place, he is still suspected; and if it do not take place, he shall be held not only a fool but also void of honesty. The commonwealth gets no good by such courses for through fear hereof it will want counsellors. And the state would do their business for the most part well if this kind of citizens were they that had least ability in speaking, for they should then persuade the city to the fewer errors. For a good statesman should not go about to terrify those that contradict him but rather to make good his counsel upon liberty of speech. And a wise state ought not either to add unto, or, on the other side, to derogate from, the honour of him that giveth good advice, nor yet punish, nay,

* The Greek literally taken is "the other with want of education and narrowness of judgment."

nor disgrace, the man whose counsel they receive not. And then, neither would he that lighteth on good advice deliver anything against his own conscience, out of ambition of further honour and to please the auditory, nor he that doth not, covet thereupon by gratifying the people some way or other that he also may endear them.

43. "But we do here the contrary; and besides, if any man be suspected of corruption, though he give the best counsel that can be given, yet through envy for this uncertain opinion of his gain, we lose a certain benefit to the commonwealth. And our custom is to hold good counsel given suddenly no less suspect then bad, by which means as he that gives the most dangerous counsel must get the same received by fraud, so also he that gives the most sound advice is forced by lying to get himself believed. So that the commonwealth is it alone which, by reason of these suspicious imaginations, no man can possibly benefit by the plain and open way without artifice. For if any man shall do a manifest good unto the commonwealth, he shall presently be suspected of some secret gain unto himself in particular. We, therefore, that in the most important affairs and amidst these jealousies do give our advice have need to foresee further than you that look not far, and the rather because we stand accountable for our counsel, and you are to render no account of your hearing it. For if the persuader and the persuaded had equal harm, you would be the more moderate judges. But now, according to the passion that takes you when at any time your affairs miscarry, you punish the sentence of that one only that gave the counsel, not the many sentences of your own that were in fault as well as his.

44. "For my own part, I stood not forth with any purpose of contradiction in the business of the Mytilenaeans nor to accuse any man. For we contend not now, if we be wise, about the injury done by them but about the wisest counsel for ourselves. For how great soever be their fault, yet I would never advise to have them put to death unless it be for our profit, [nor yet would I pardon them,] though they were pardonable, unless it be good for the commonwealth. And in my opinion, our deliberation now is of the future rather than of the present. And whereas Cleon contendeth that it will be profitable for the

future to put them to death in that it will keep the rest from rebelling, I, contending likewise for the future, affirm the contrary. And I desire you not to reject the profit of my advice for the fair pretexts of his, which agreeing more with your present anger against the Mytilenaeans may quickly perhaps win your consent. We plead not judicially with the Mytilenaeans so as to need arguments of equity, but we consult of them which way we may serve ourselves of them to our most advantage hereafter.

45. "I say, therefore, that death hath been in states ordained for a punishment of many offences, and those not so great but far less than this. Yet encouraged by hope, men hazard themselves; nor did any man ever yet enter into a practice which he knew he could not go through with.* And a city when it revolteth, supposeth itself to be better furnished, either of themselves or by their confederates, than it is, or else it would never take the enterprise in hand. They have it by nature, both men and cities, to commit offences; nor is there any law that can prevent it. For men have gone over all degrees of punishment, augmenting them still, in hope to be less annoyed by malefactors. And it is likely that gentler punishments were inflicted of old even upon the most heinous crimes; but that in tract of time, men continuing to transgress, they were extended afterwards to the taking away of life; and yet they still transgress. And therefore, either some greater terror than death must be devised, or death will not be enough for coercion. For poverty will always add boldness to necessity; and wealth, covetousness to pride and contempt. And the other [middle] fortunes, they also through human passion, according as they are severally subject to some insuperable one or other, impel men to danger. But hope and desire work this effect in all estates. And this as the leader, that as the companion; this contriving the enterprize, that suggesting the success are the cause of most crimes that are committed, and being least discerned, are more mischievous than evils seen. Besides these

---

* Hobbes' translation is misleading here. The Greek is "Yet exalted by hope they take the risk and no one yet has ever condemned in advance his success in the design and therefore has not gone to meet terror."

two, fortune also puts men forward as much as anything else. For presenting herself sometimes unlooked for, she provoketh some to adventure, though not provided as they ought for the purpose, and especially cities because they venture for the greatest matters, as liberty and dominion over others; and amongst a generality, everyone, though without reason, somewhat the more magnifies himself in particular. In a word, it is a thing impossible and of great simplicity to believe when human nature is earnestly bent to do a thing that by force of law or any other danger it can be diverted.

46. "We must not, therefore, relying on the security of capital punishment, decree the worst against them nor make them desperate, as if there were no place to repent and, as soon as they can, to cancel their offence. For observe: if a city revolted should know it could not hold out, it would now compound whilst it were able both to pay us our charges for the present and our tribute for the time to come. But the way that Cleon prescribeth, what city, think you, would not provide itself better than this did and endure the siege to the very last if to compound late and soon be all one? And how can it be but detriment to us to be at charge of long sieges through their obstinacy and, when we have taken a city to find it exhausted and to lose the revenue of it for the future? And this revenue is the only strength we have against our enemies. We are not then to be exact judges in the punition of offenders but to look rather how by their moderate punishment we may have our confederate cities, such as they may be able to pay us tribute; and not think to keep them in awe by the rigour of laws but by the providence of our own actions. But we to the contrary, when we recover a city which, having been free and held under our obedience by force hath revolted justly, think now that we ought to inflict some cruel punishment upon them. Whereas we ought rather not mightily to punish a free city revolted but mightily to look to it before it revolt and to prevent the intention of it, but when we have overcome them, to lay the fault upon as few as we can.

47. "Consider also, if you follow the advice of Cleon, how much you shall offend likewise in this other point. For in all your cities the commonalty are now your friends and either

revolt not with the few, or, if they be compelled to it by force, they presently turn enemies to them that caused the revolt; whereby when you go to war, you have the commons of the adverse city on your side. But if you shall destroy the commonalty of the Mytilenaeans, which did neither partake of the revolt and as soon as they were armed presently delivered the city into your hands, you shall first do unjustly to kill such as have done you service, and you shall effect a work besides which the great men do everywhere most desire. For when they have made a city to revolt, they shall have the people presently on their side, you having foreshown them by the example that both the guilty and not guilty must undergo the same punishment. Whereas indeed, though they were guilty, yet we ought to dissemble it, to the end that the only party now our friend may not become our enemy. And for the assuring of our dominion, I think it far more profitable voluntarily to put up an injury than justly to destroy such as we should not. And that same both justice and profit of revenge, alleged by Cleon, can never possibly be found together in the same thing.

48. "You, therefore, upon knowledge that this is the best course, not upon compassion or lenity (for neither would I have you won by that) but upon consideration of what hath been advised, be ruled by me, and proceed to judgment at your own leisure against those whom Paches hath sent hither as guilty, and suffer the rest to enjoy their city. For that will be both good for the future and also of present terror to the enemy. For he that consulteth wisely is a sorer enemy than he that assaulteth with the strength of action unadvisedly."

49. Thus spake Diodotus. After these two opinions were delivered, the one most opposite to the other, the Athenians were at contention which they should decree; and at the holding up of hands they were both sides almost equal, but yet the sentence of Diodotus prevailed. Whereupon they presently in haste sent away another galley, lest not arriving before the former they should find the city already destroyed. The first galley set forth before the second a day and a night. But the Mytilenaean ambassadors having furnished this latter with wine and barley cakes and promised them great rewards if they over-

took the other galley, they rowed diligently, at one and the same time both plying their oars and taking their refection of the said barley cakes steeped in wine and oil; and by turns part of them slept, and the other part rowed. It happened also that there blew no wind against them; and the former galley making no great haste, as going on so sad an errand, whereas the former proceeded in the manner before mentioned, arrived indeed first, but only so much as Paches had read the sentence and prepared to execute what they had decreed. But presently after came in the other galley and saved the city from being destroyed. So near were the Mytilenaeans to the danger.

50. But those whom Paches had sent home as most culpable of the revolt, the Athenians, as Cleon had advised, put to death, being in number somewhat above a thousand. They also razed the walls of Mytilene and took from them all their galleys. After which they imposed on the Lesbians no more tribute; but having divided their land (all but that of the Methymnaeans) into three thousand parts, three hundred of those parts [of the choicest land] they consecrated to the gods.* And for the rest, they sent men by lot out of their own city to possess it of whom the Lesbians, at the rent of two minae of silver yearly upon a lot, had the land again to be husbanded by themselves. The Athenians took in all such towns also as the Mytilenaeans were masters of in the continent, which were afterwards made subjects to the people of Athens. Thus ended the business touching Lesbos.

51. The same summer, after the recovery of Lesbos the Athenians, under the conduct of Nicias the son of Niceratus, made war on Minoa, an island adjacent to Megara. For the Megareans had built a tower in it and served themselves of

---

* All that this means was that these three hundred lots became the national property of the Athenian state, which usually let it to individual citizens subject to the payment of dues to the god concerned. What the passage seems to mean, in general, is that Athenian citizens, chosen by lot, were given possession of these lands in Lesbos. They did not work them themelves but made arrangements with the former owners to work them as tenants for a rent. The procedure would thus be roughly similar to many of the land grants made to Englishmen in Ireland in the seventeenth century.

the island for a place of garrison. But Nicias desired that the
Athenians might keep their watch upon Megara in that island
as being nearer and no more at Budorum and Salamis, to the
end that the Peloponnesians might not go out thence with their
galleys undescried nor send out pirates as they had formerly
done, and to prohibit the importation of all things to the
Megareans by sea. Wherefore, when he had first taken two
towers that stood out from Nisaea, with engines applied from
the sea, and so made a free entrance for his galleys between the
island and the firm land, he took it in with a wall also from the
continent in that part where it might receive aid by a bridge
over the marshes; for it was not far distant from the main land.
And, that being in few days finished, he built a fort in the
island itself and, leaving there a garrison, carried the rest of his
army back.

52. It happened also about the same time of this summer,
that the Plataeans, having spent their victual and being unable
longer to hold out, yielded their city in this manner to the
Peloponnesians. The Peloponnesians assaulted the walls, but
they within were unable to fight. Whereupon the Lacedaemonian commander, perceiving their weakness, would not take
the place by force (for he had command to that purpose from
Lacedaemon, to the end that if they should ever make peace
with the Athenians with conditions of mutual restitution of
such cities as on either side had been taken by war, Plataea, as
having come in of its own accord, might not be thereby re-
coverable) but sent a herald to them who demanded whether
or no they would give up their city voluntarily into the hands
of the Lacedaemonians and take them for their judges with
power to punish the offenders, but none without form of justice. So said the herald, and they (for they were now at the
weakest) delivered up the city accordingly. So the Peloponnesians gave the Plataeans food for certain days till the judges,
which were five, should arrive from Lacedaemon. And when
they were come, no accusation was exhibited; but calling them
man by man, they asked of everyone only this question:
whether they had done to the Lacedaemonians and their confederates in this war any good service. But the Plataeans, having sued to make their answer more at large and having ap-

pointed Astymachus the son of Asopolaus and Lacon the son of Aeimnestus (who had been heretofore the host * of the Lacedaemonians) for their speakers, said as followeth:

53. "Men of Lacedaemon, relying upon you we yielded up our city, not expecting to undergo this but some more legal manner of proceeding; and we agreed not to stand to the judgment of others (as now we do) but of yourselves only,† conceiving we should so obtain the better justice. But now we fear we have been deceived in both. For we have reason to suspect both that the trial is capital, and you, the judges, partial, gathering so much both from that, that there hath not been presented any accusation to which we might answer, and also from this, that the interrogatory is short and such, as if we answer to it with truth, we shall speak against ourselves and be easily convinced ‡ if we lie. But since we are on all hands in a strait, we are forced (and it seems our safest way) to try what we can obtain by pleading. For, for men in our case the speech not spoken may give occasion to some to think, that spoken it had preserved us. But besides other inconveniences, the means also of persuasion go ill on our side. For if we had not known one another, we might have helped ourselves by producing testimony in things you knew not. Whereas now, all that we shall say will be before men that know already what it is. And we fear not that you mean, because you know us inferior in virtue to yourselves, to make that a crime, but lest you bring us to a judgment already judged to gratify somebody else.

54. "Nevertheless, we will produce our reasons of equity

* The Greek word is *proxenus*, one who stands for a foreigner. This was apparently a semiofficial position of a Plataean, in this case, appointed to act in Plataea for such Spartans temporarily resident in Plataea as had business with the Plataean state. It might be very roughly equated with the modern position of consul, with the difference that the proxenus was a citizen of the state in which the foreigner found himself. Thucydides explains later that one of Alcibiades' reasons for hating the Spartans was that they had not granted him the position of Spartan proxenus in Athens, which had been held by his grandfather.

† This glances at the presence of the Thebans, bitterest enemies of Plataea, among those who attended the "court."

‡ We would say "easily convicted."

against the quarrel of the Thebans and withal make mention of our services done both to you and to the rest of Greece, and make trial if by any means we can persuade you. As to that short interrogatory, whether we have any way done good in this present war to the Lacedaemonians and their confederates, or not, if you ask us as enemies, we say that, if we have done them no good, we have also done them no wrong; if you ask us as friends, then we say that they rather have done us the injury in that they made war upon us. But in the time of the peace and in the war against the Medes we behaved ourselves well; for the one we brake not first, and in the other we were the only Boeotians that joined with you for the delivery of Greece. For though we dwell up in the land, yet we fought by sea at Artemisium; and in the battle fought in this our own territory, we were with you; and whatsoever dangers the Grecians in those times underwent, we were partakers of all, even beyond our strength. And unto you, Lacedaemonians, in particular, when Sparta was in greatest affright after the earthquake, upon the rebellion of the Helotes and seizing of Ithome,* we sent the third part of our power to assist you, which you have no reason to forget.

55. "Such then we showed ourselves in those ancient and most important affairs. It is true, we have been your enemies since; but for that you are to blame yourselves. For when oppressed by the Thebans we sought league of you, you rejected us and bade us go to the Athenians that were nearer hand, yourselves being far off. Nevertheless, you neither have in this war nor were to have suffered at our hands anything that misbecame us. And if we denied to revolt from the Athenians when you bade us, we did you no injury in it. For they both aided us against the Thebans when you shrunk from us, and it was now no more any honesty to betray them, especially having been well used by them, and we ourselves having sought their league and being made denizens also of their city.† Nay, we

---

* The battle of Ithome, 464 B.C.

† This refers to a kind of honorary Athenian citizenship earlier conferred on the Plataeans for their good service at the time of the Persian Wars. We are not exactly clear as to the nature of the rights associated with this citizenship.

ought rather to have followed them in all their commands with alacrity. When you or the Athenians have the leading of the confederates, if evil be done, not they that follow are culpable but you that lead to the evil.

56. "The Thebans have done us many other injuries; but this last, which is the cause of what we now suffer, you yourselves know what it was. For we avenged us but justly of those that in time of peace, and upon the day of our novilunial sacrifice, had surprised our city; and by the law of all nations it is lawful to repel an assailing enemy, and therefore there is no reason you should punish us now for them. For if you shall measure justice by your and their present benefit in the war, it will manifestly appear that you are not judges of the truth but respecters only of your profit. And yet if the Thebans seem profitable to you now, we and the rest of the Grecians were more profitable to you then when you were in greater danger. For though the Thebans are now on your side when you invade others; yet at that time when the barbarian came in to impose servitude on all, they were on his. It is but justice that with our present offence (if we have committed any) you compare our forwardness then which you will find both greater than our fault and augmented also by the circumstance of such a season when it was rare to find any Grecian that durst oppose his valour to Xerxes' power, and when they were most commended not that with safety helped to further his invasion but that adventured to do what was most honest, though with danger. But we being of that number and honoured for it amongst the first are afraid lest the same shall be now a cause of our destruction, as having chosen rather to follow the Athenians justly than you profitably. But you should ever have the same opinion in the same case and think this only to be profitable that doing what is useful for the present occasion, you reserve withal a constant acknowledgment of the virtue of your good confederates.

57. "Consider also that you are an example of honest dealing to the most of the Grecians. Now if you shall decree otherwise than is just (for this judgment of yours is conspicuous, you that be praised against us that be not blamed), take heed that they do not dislike that good men should undergo an unjust

sentence, though at the hands of better men, or that the spoil of us that have done the Grecians service should be dedicated in their temples. For it will be thought a horrible matter that Plataea should be destroyed by Lacedaemonians and that you, whereas your fathers in honour of our valour inscribed the name of our city on the tripod at Delphi, should now blot it out of all Greece to gratify the Thebans. For we have proceeded to such a degree of calamity that if the Medes had prevailed, we must have perished then; and now the Thebans have overcome us again in you, who were before our greatest friends, and have put us to two great hazards, one before of famishing if we yielded not, and another now of a capital sentence. And we Plataeans, who even beyond our strength have been zealous in the defence of the Grecians, are now abandoned and left unrelieved by them all.

58. "But we beseech you for those gods' sakes, in whose names once we made mutual league, and for our valour's sake shown in the behalf of the Grecians, to be moved towards us and, if at the persuasion of the Thebans you have determined aught against us, to change your minds and reciprocally to require at the hands of the Thebans this courtesy, that whom you ought to spare, they would be contented not to kill and so receive an honest benefit in recompense of a wicked one, and not to bestow pleasure upon others and receive wickedness upon yourselves in exchange. For though to take away our lives be a matter quickly done, yet to make the infamy of it cease will be work enough. For being none of your enemies but well-willers and such as have entered into the war upon constraint, you cannot put us to death with justice. Therefore, if you will judge uncorruptly, you ought to secure our persons and to remember that you received us by our own voluntary submission and with hands upheld (and it is the law among Grecians not to put such to death), besides that we have from time to time been beneficial to you. For look upon the sepulchres of your fathers whom, slain by the Medes and buried in this territory of ours, we have yearly honoured at the public charge both with vestments and other rites; and of such things as our land hath produced, we have offered unto them the first fruits of it all, as friends in an amicable land and confederates use to do to

those that have formerly been their fellows in arms. But now by a wrong sentence you shall do the contrary of this. For consider this. Pausanias, as he thought, interred these men in amicable ground and amongst their friends. But you, if you slay us, and of Plataeis make Thebais, what do you but leave your fathers and kindred, deprived of the honours they now have, in an hostile territory and amongst the very men that slew them? And moreover, put into servitude that soil whereon the Grecians were put into liberty? And make desolate the temples wherein they prayed when they prevailed against the Medes? And destroy the patrial sacrifices which were instituted by the builders and founders of the same?

59. "These things are not for your glory, men of Lacedaemon, nor to violate the common institutions of Greece and wrong your progenitors, nor to destroy us that have done you service for the hatred of another when you have received no injury from us yourselves, but to spare our lives, to relent, to have a moderate compassion in contemplation not only of the greatness of the punishment but also of who we are that must suffer and of the uncertainty where calamity may light, and that undeservedly. Which we, as becometh us and our need compelleth us to do, cry aloud unto the common gods of Greece * to persuade you unto producing the oath sworn by your fathers to put you in mind; and also we become here sanctuary men at the sepulchres of your fathers, crying out upon the dead not to suffer themselves to be in the power of the Thebans nor to let their greatest friends be betrayed into the hands of their greatest enemies, remembering them of that day upon which, though we have done glorious acts in their company, yet we are in danger at this day of most miserable suffering. But to make an end of speaking (which is as necessary so most bitter to men in our case because the hazard of our lives cometh so soon after), for a conclusion we say that it was not to the Thebans

* The Greek means "Gods common to the Greeks and gods whose altars are common to the Greeks," i.e., gods worshipped at Delphi and Olympia. This appeal is meant to be, for instance, to Zeus and Apollo, as they were worshipped at altars common to all of Greece. They are to be distinguished from the same gods in the local habitat where, perhaps, they were really felt as almost different deities protecting peculiarly the community in which they lived.

that we rendered our city (for we would rather have died of famine, the most base perdition of all other), but we came out on trust in you. And it is but justice that if we cannot persuade you, you should set us again in the estate we were in and let us undergo the danger at our own election. Also we require you, men of Lacedaemon, not only not to deliver us Plataeans, who have been most zealous in the service of the Grecians especially being sanctuary men,* out of your own hands and your own trust into the hands of our most mortal enemies the Thebans but also to be our saviours and not to destroy us utterly, you that set at liberty all other Grecians."

60. Thus spake the Plataeans. But the Thebans, fearing lest the Lacedaemonians might relent at their oration, stood forth and said that since the Plataeans had had the liberty of a longer speech (which they thought they should not) than for answer to the question was necessary, they also desired to speak, and being commanded to say on, spake to this effect:

61. "If these men had answered briefly to the question and not both turned against us with an accusation and also out of the purpose and wherein they were not charged made much apology and commendation of themselves in things unquestioned, we had never asked leave to speak. But as it is, we are to the one point to answer and to confute the other, that neither the fault of us nor their own reputation may do them good, but your sentence may be guided by hearing of the truth of both. The quarrel between us and them arose at first from this, that when we had built Plataea last of all the cities of Boeotia, together with some other places which, having driven out the promiscuous nations, we had then in our dominion, they would not (as was ordained at first) allow us to be their leaders; but being the only men of all the Boeotians that transgressed the common ordinance of the country when they should have been compelled to their duty, they turned unto the Athenians and together with them did us many evils, for which they likewise suffered as many from us.

62. "But when the barbarian invaded Greece, then, say they, that they of all the Boeotians only also Medized not. And this

* More comprehensible would be the literal rendering of the Greek "being your suppliants."

is the thing wherein they both glory most themselves and most detract from us. Now we confess they Medized not because also the Athenians did not. Nevertheless, when the Athenians afterwards invaded the rest of the Grecians, in the same kind then of all the Boeotians they only Atticized. But take now into your consideration withal what form of government we were in both the one and the other when we did this. For then had we our city governed neither by an oligarchy with laws common to all nor by a democracy; but the state was managed by a few with authority absolute, than which there is nothing more contrary to laws and moderation nor more approaching unto tyranny. And these few, hoping yet further, if the Medes prevailed, to increase their own power, kept the people under and furthered the coming in of the barbarian. And so did the whole city, but it was not then master of itself nor doth it deserve to be upbraided with what it did when they had no laws [but were at the will of others]. But when the Medes were gone and our city had laws, consider now, when the Athenians attempted to subdue all Greece and this territory of ours with the rest wherein through sedition they had gotten many places already, whether by giving them battle at Coroneia and defeating them, we delivered not Boeotia from servitude then, and do not also now with much zeal assist you in the asserting of the rest, and find not more horses and more provision of war than any of the confederates besides. And so much be spoken by way of apology to our Medizing.

63. "And we will endeavour to prove now that the Grecians have been rather wronged by you and that you are more worthy of all manner of punishment. You became, you say, confederates and denizens of Athens for to be righted against us. Against us then only the Athenians should have come with you and not you with them have gone to the invasion of the rest, especially when if the Athenians would have led you whither you would not, you had the league of the Lacedaemonians made with you against the Medes, which you so often object, to have resorted unto, which was sufficient not only to have protected you from us but, which is the main matter, to have secured you to take what course you had pleased. But voluntarily and without constraint you rather chose to follow the Athenians. And

you say it had been a dishonest thing to have betrayed your benefactors. But it is more dishonest and more unjust by far to betray the Grecians universally, to whom you have sworn, than to betray the Athenians alone, especially when these go about to deliver Greece from subjection and the other to subdue it. Besides, the requital you make the Athenians is not proportionable nor free from dishonesty. For you, as you say yourselves, brought in the Athenians to right you against injuries; and you co-operate with them in injuring others. And howsoever, it is not so dishonest to leave a benefit unrequited as to make such a requital, as though justly due cannot be justly done.

64. "But you have made it apparent that even then it was not for the Grecians' sake that you alone of all the Boeotians Medized not but because the Athenians did not; yet now you that would do as the Athenians did, and contrary to what the Grecians did, claim favour of these for what you did for the others' sake. But there is no reason for that; but as you have chosen the Athenians, so let them help you in this trial. And produce not the oath of the former league as if that should save you now. For you have relinquished it and, contrary to the same, have rather helped the Athenians to subdue the Aeginetae and others than hindered them from it. And this you not only did voluntarily and having laws the same you have now, and none forcing you to it as there did us, but also rejected our last invitation, a little before the shutting up of your city, to quietness and neutrality. Who can therefore more deservedly be hated of the Grecians in general than you that pretend honesty to their ruin? And those acts wherein formerly, as you say, you have been beneficial to the Grecians, you have now made apparent to be none of yours and made true proof of what your own nature inclines you to. For with Athenians you have walked in the way of injustice. And thus much we have laid open touching our involuntary Medizing and your voluntary Atticizing.

65. "And for this last injury you charge us with, namely, the unlawful invading of your city in time of peace and of your new-moon sacrifice, we do not think, no not in this action, that we have offended so much as you yourselves. For though we

had done unjustly if we had assaulted your city or wasted your territory as enemies of our own accord; yet when the prime men of your own city, both for wealth and nobility, willing to discharge you of foreign league and conform you to the common institutions of all Boeotia, did of their own accord call us in, wherein lieth the injury then? For they that lead transgress rather than they that follow. But as we conceive, neither they nor we have transgressed at all. But being citizens as well as you and having more to hazard, they opened their own gates and took us into the city as friends not as enemies with intention to keep the ill-affected from being worse and to do right to the good, taking upon them to be moderators of your councils and not to deprive the city of your persons but to reduce you into one body with the rest of your kindred, and not to engage you in hostility with any but to settle you in peace with all.

66. "And for an argument that we did not this as enemies, we did harm to no man but proclaimed that if any man were willing to have the city governed after the common form of all Boeotia, he should come to us. And you came willingly at first and were quiet. But afterwards, when you knew we were but few, though we might seem to have done somewhat more than was fit to do without the consent of your multitude, you did not by us as we did by you, first innovate nothing in fact and then with words persuade us to go forth again, but contrary to the composition assaulted us. And for those men you slew in the affray, we grieve not so much; for they suffered by a kind of law. But to kill those that held up their hands for mercy, whom taken alive you afterwards had promised to spare, was not this a horrible cruelty? You committed in this business three crimes, one in the neck of another; first, the breach of the composition; then, the death that followed of our men; and thirdly, the falsifying of your promise to save them if we did no hurt to anything of yours in the fields. And yet you say that we are the transgressors and that you for your parts deserve not to undergo a judgment. But it is otherwise. And if these men judge aright, you shall be punished now for all your crimes at once.

67. "We have herein, men of Lacedaemon, been thus large both for your sakes and ours: for yours, to let you see that if

you condemn them, it will be no injustice; for ours, that the equity of our revenge may the better appear. Be not moved with the recital of their virtues of old, if any they had, which, though they ought to help the wronged, should double the punishment of such as commit wickedness because their offence doth not become them. Nor let them fare ever the better for their lamentation or your compassion when they cry out upon your fathers' sepulchres and their own want of friends. For we on the other side affirm that the youth of our city suffered harder measure from them; and their fathers, partly slain at Coroneia in bringing Boeotia to your confederation and partly alive and now old and deprived of their children, make far juster supplication to you for revenge. And pity belongeth to such as suffer undeservedly; but, on the contrary, when men are worthily punished, as these are, it is to be rejoiced at. And for their present want of friends they may thank themselves. For of their own accord they rejected the better confederates. And the law hath been broken by them, without precedent wrong from us, in that they condemned our men spitefully rather than judicially, in which point we shall now come short of requiting them; for they shall suffer legally and not, as they say they do, with hands upheld from battle but as men that have put themselves upon trial by consent. Maintain therefore, ye Lacedaemonians, the law of the Grecians against these men that have transgressed it, and give unto us that have suffered contrary to the law the just recompense of our alacrity in your service. And let not the words of these give us a repulse from you; but set up an example to the Grecians by presenting [unto these men] a trial not of words but of facts, which, if they be good, a short narration of them will serve the turn; if ill, compt orations do but veil them. But if such as have the authority, as you have now, would collect the matter to a head and, according as any man should make answer thereunto, so proceed to sentence, men would be less in the search of fair speeches wherewith to excuse the foulness of their actions."

68. Thus spake the Thebans. And the Lacedaemonian judges, conceiving their interrogatory to stand well, namely, whether they had received any benefit by them or not in this present war, for they had indeed intreated them both at other times,

according to the ancient league of Pausanias after the Medan war, to stand neutral, and also a little before the siege the Plataeans had rejected their proposition of being common friends to both sides according to the same league, taking themselves, in respect of these their just offers, to be now discharged of the league and to have received evil at their hands, caused them one by one to be brought forth and, having asked them again the same question, whether they had any way benefited the Lacedaemonians and their confederates in this present war or not, as they answered not led them aside and slew them, not exempting any. Of the Plataeans themselves they slew no less than two hundred; of the Athenians who were besieged with them, twenty-five. The women they made slaves; and the Thebans assigned the city for a year, or thereabouts, for a habitation to such Megareans as in sedition had been driven from their own and to all those Plataeans which, living, were of the Theban faction. But afterwards, pulling it all down to the very foundation, they built a hospital * in the place near the temple of Juno of two hundred foot diameter with chambers on every side in circle both above and below, using therein the roofs and doors of the Plataeans' buildings. And of the rest of the stuff that was in the city wall, as brass and iron, they made bedsteads and dedicated them to Juno, to whom also they built a stone chapel of a hundred foot over. The land they confiscated and set it to farm afterwards for ten years to the Thebans. So far were the Lacedaemonians alienated from the Plataeans, especially, or rather altogether, for the Thebans' sake, whom they thought useful to them in the war now on foot. So ended the business at Plataea in the fourscore and thirteenth year after their league made with the Athenians.

69. The forty galleys of Peloponnesus, which having been sent to aid the Lesbians fled, as hath been related, through the wide sea chased by the Athenians and tossed by storms on the coast of Crete, came thence dispersed into Peloponnesus and found thirteen galleys, Leucadians and Ambraciotes, in the haven of Cyllene with Brasidas the son of Tellis come hither to

---

* This is not what we would mean by hospital. It was a kind of large inn for the reception of visitors who came to worship at the temple of Hera.

be of council with Alcidas. For the Lacedaemonians, seeing
they failed of Lesbos, determined with their fleet augmented
to sail to Corcyra, which was in sedition (there being but
twelve Athenian galleys about Naupactus), to the end they
might be there before the supply of a greater fleet should come
from Athens. So Brasidas and Alcidas employed themselves in
that.

70. The sedition in Corcyra began upon the coming home of
those captives which were taken in the battles by sea at Epidamnus and released afterwards by the Corinthians at the
ransom, as was voiced, of eighty talents for which they had
given security to their hosts,* but in fact for that they had persuaded the Corinthians that they would put Corcyra into their
power. These men going from man to man solicited the city
to revolt from the Athenians. And two galleys being now come
in, one of Athens, another of Corinth, with ambassadors from
both those states, the Corcyraeans upon audience of them both
decreed to hold the Athenians for their confederates on articles
agreed on but withal to remain friends to the Peloponnesians
as they had formerly been. There was one Peithias, voluntary
host † of the Athenians and that had been principal magistrate
of the people. Him these men called into judgment and laid
to his charge a practice to bring the city into the servitude of
the Athenians. He again, being acquit, called in question five of
the wealthiest of the same men saying they had cut certain
stakes ‡ in the ground belonging to the temples both of Jupiter

* The Greek word is *proxenus*. See note, p. 187 above.
† See last note. Apparently in some states there were in addition
to, or as a substitute for, the official consuls unofficial or voluntary
consuls. It is not clear under what circumstances they were so chosen
or what their privileges were.
‡ Actually, vine-poles. In all probability these men either rented
from the state this land which was dedicated to Zeus, or it abutted
on their property. The so-called *temenos*, or sanctuary, in Greece,
when dedicated to the god, was usually not railed off in any way.
Inadvertent or conscious infringement of some of the sacred rights
of the *temenos* was a constant charge. It was particularly useful
against public or private enemies because it was comparatively easy
to find, as in this instance, that vine-poles had been cut without au-
thorization or that some other minor infraction of the law had been
committed. If proved, this could expose the persons guilty to exceed-

and of Alcinus, upon every of which there lay a penalty of a stater. And the cause going against them, they took sanctuary in the temples to the end, the sum being great, they might pay it by portions [as they should be taxed]. But Peithias (for he was also of the senate) obtained that the law should proceed. These five being by the law excluded the senate and understanding that Peithias, as long as he was a senator, would cause the people to hold for friends and foes the same that were so to the Athenians, conspired with the rest and, armed with daggers, suddenly brake into the senate-house and slew both Peithias and others, as well private men as senators, to the number of about sixty persons; only a few of those of Peithias his faction escaped in the Athenian galley that lay yet in the harbour.

71. When they had done this and called the Corcyraeans to an assembly, they told them that what they had done was for the best and that they should not be now in bondage to the Athenians; and for the future they advised them to be in quiet and to receive neither party with more than one galley at once and to take them for enemies if they were more. And when they had spoken, forced them to decree it accordingly. They also presently sent ambassadors to Athens both to show that it was fit for them to do what they had done and also to dissuade such Corcyraeans as were fled thither of the other faction from doing anything to their prejudice for fear the matter should fall into a relapse.

72. When these arrived, the Athenians apprehended both the ambassadors themselves as seditious persons and also all those Corcyraeans whom they had there prevailed with and sent them to custody in Aegina. In the meantime, upon the coming in of a galley of Corinth * with ambassadors from Lacedaemon, those that managed the state assailed the commons,† and over-

---

ingly serious penalties, since their offense was technically sacrilege. On the other hand, without some special motive for the question being raised, such practices could continue indefinitely without comment.

* Readers should notice the shift of scene here. "When these arrived, the Athenians apprehended both the ambassadors . . ." refers to Athens, but at "in the meantime . . ." we are back again in Corcyra.

† What Hobbes here and elsewhere translates "commons" and "nobility" would more accurately be rendered "the democratic" and "the oligarchic parties." In Greek the words used are usually "the people"

came them in fight. And night coming on, the commons fled into the citadel and the higher parts of the city where they rallied themselves and encamped and made themselves masters of the haven called the Hillaique haven. But the nobility seized on the market place (where also the most of them dwelt) and on the haven on the side toward the continent.

73. The next day they skirmished a little with shot, and both parts sent abroad into the villages to solicit the slaves with promise of liberty to take their parts. And the greatest part of the slaves took part with the commons, and the other side had an aid of eight hundred men from the continent.

74. The next day but one they fought again; and the people had the victory, having the odds both in strength of places and in number of men. And the women also manfully assisted them, throwing tiles from the houses and enduring the tumult even beyond the condition of their sex. The few began to fly about twilight and fearing lest the people should even with their shout take the arsenal and so come on and put them to the sword, to stop their passage set fire on the houses in circle about the market place and upon others near it. Much goods of merchants was hereby burnt, and the whole city, if the wind had risen and carried the flame that way, had been in danger to have been destroyed. When the people had gotten the victory, the

---

(*demos*) and "the few" (*oligoi*). Naturally, the division was roughly according to wealth or the want of it, and Aristotle in the Constitution of Athens refers to the factions indifferently as "the few and the many," "the best and the demos," "the rich and the poor." Plato speaks of the condition of all large Greek cities of his time as in fact each containing another within it, one city of the rich and one of the poor. In Athens, at least, the interests of the two factions crystallized around certain constitutional issues, such as the unlimited versus the limited franchise, the arming of the forces by state expense as against a system of volunteers with their own arms, the question of the public law courts, etc. Moreover, from early in this war Athenian conservatives (oligarchs or a conservative section of the democratic party) were for peace with Sparta, while the democratic party as a whole, or certainly the larger part of it, was for the prosecution of the war. In view of the political issues, long and short term, thus divided between the many and the few, I do not think it misleading to speak of two political parties with many of the present-day implications of the word. There was, of course, very little party organization comparable with that of a modern democratic state.

Corinthian galley stole away; and most of the auxiliaries got over privily into the continent.

75. The next day Nicostratus, the son of Diitrephes, an Athenian commander, came in with twelve galleys and five hundred Messenian men of arms from Naupactus; and both negociated a reconciliation and induced them (to the end they might agree) to condemn ten of the principal authors of the sedition (who presently fled) and to let the rest alone, with articles both between themselves and with the Athenians to esteem friends and enemies the same the Athenians did. When he had done this, he would have been gone; but the people persuaded him before he went to leave behind him five of his galleys, the better to keep their adversaries from stirring, and to take as many of theirs, which they would man with Corcyraeans and send with him. To this he agreed; and they made a list of those that should embark, consisting altogether of their enemies. But these, fearing to be sent to Athens, took sanctuary in the temple of Castor and Pollux. But Nicostratus endeavoured to raise them and spake to them to put them into courage. But when he could not prevail, the people, arming themselves on pretence that their diffidence to go along with Nicostratus proceeded from some evil intention, took away their arms out of their houses and would also have killed some of them such as they chanced on if Nicostratus had not hindered them. Others also when they saw this took sanctuary in the temple of Juno, and they were in all above four hundred. But the people fearing some innovation got them by persuasion to rise and, conveying them into the island that lieth over against the temple of Juno, sent them their necessaries thither.

76. The sedition standing in these terms, the fourth or fifth day after the putting over of these men into the island arrived the Peloponnesian fleet from Cyllene, where since their voyage of Ionia they had lain at anchor, to the number of three and fifty sail. Alcidas had the command of these as before, and Brasidas came with him as a counsellor. And having first put in at Sybota, a haven of the continent, they came on the next morning by break of day toward Corcyra.

77. The Corcyraeans, being in great tumult and fear both of the seditious within and of the invasion without, made ready

threescore galleys, and still as any of them were manned sent them out against the enemy; whereas the Athenians had advised them to give leave to them to go forth first and then the Corcyraeans to follow after with the whole fleet together. When their galleys came forth thus thin, two of them presently turned to the enemy; and in others they that were aboard were together by the ears amongst themselves, and nothing was done in due order. The Peloponnesians, seeing their confusion, opposed themselves to the Corcyraeans with twenty galleys only; the rest they set in array against the twelve galleys of Athens, whereof the Salaminia and the Paralus were two.

78. The Corcyraeans having come disorderly up, and by few at once, were on their part in much distress; but the Athenians, fearing the enemy's number and doubting to be environed, would never come up to charge the enemy where they stood thick nor would set upon the galleys that were placed in the midst but charged one end of them and drowned one of their galleys. And when the Peloponnesians afterwards had put their fleet into a circular figure, they then went about and about it endeavouring to put them into disorder. Which they that were fighting against the Corcyraeans perceiving and fearing such another chance as befell them formerly at Naupactus, went to their aid and, uniting themselves, came upon the Athenians all together. But they retiring rowed astern, intending that the Corcyraeans should take that time to escape in, they themselves in the meantime going as leisurely back as was possible and keeping the enemy still ahead. Such was this battle, and it ended about sunset.

79. The Corcyraeans, fearing lest the enemy in pursuit of their victory should have come directly against the city or take aboard the men which they had put over into the island or do them some other mischief, fetched back the men into the temple of Juno again and guarded the city. But the Peloponnesians, though they had won the battle, yet durst not invade the city but, having taken thirteen of the Corcyraean galleys, went back into the continent from whence they had set forth. The next day they came not unto the city no more than before, although it was in great tumult and affright and though also Brasidas (as it is reported) advised Alcidas to it but had not equal authority,

but only landed soldiers at the promontory of Leucimna and wasted their territory.

80. In the meantime the people of Corcyra, fearing extremely lest those galleys should come against the city, not only conferred with those in sanctuary and with the rest about how the city might be preserved but also induced some of them to go aboard. For notwithstanding the sedition they manned thirty galleys in expectation that the fleet of the enemy should have entered. But the Peloponnesians, having been wasting of their fields till it was about noon, went their ways again. Within night the Corcyraeans had notice by fires of three-score Athenian galleys coming toward them from Leucas, which the Athenians, upon intelligence of the sedition and of the fleet to go to Corcyra under Alcidas, had sent to aid them under the conduct of Eurymedon the son of Thucles.

81. The Peloponnesians therefore, as soon as night came, sailed speedily home, keeping still the shore and causing their galleys to be carried over at the isthmus of Leucas that they might not come in sight as they went about. But the people of Corcyra, hearing of the Attic galleys coming in and the going off of the Peloponnesians, brought into the city those Messenians which before were without and appointing the galleys which they had furnished to come about into the Hillaique haven, whilst accordingly they went about, slew all the contrary faction they could lay hands on, and also afterwards threw overboard out of the same galleys * all those they had before persuaded to embark, and so went thence. And coming to the temple of Juno, they persuaded fifty of those that had taken sanctuary to refer themselves to a legal trial, all which they condemned to die. But the most of the sanctuary men, that is, all those that were not induced to stand to trial by law, when they saw what was done, killed one another there right in the temple; some hanged themselves on trees; everyone as he had

---

* The Greek is not quite so picturesque. It says only "Taking out of the galleys the men they had persuaded to go on board them, they liquidated them." The Greek word literally means "used them up"; it is one of the unpleasantly neutral words in Thucydides for such executions and corresponds to the modern use of "liquidate" in a similar connection.

means made himself away. And for seven days together that Eurymedon stayed there with his sixty galleys, the Corcyraeans did nothing but kill such of their city as they took to be their enemies, laying to their charge a practice to have everted the popular government. Amongst whom some were slain upon private hatred and some by their debtors for the money which they had lent them. All forms of death were then seen; and (as in such cases it usually falls out) whatsoever had happened at any time happened also then, and more. For the father slew his son; men were dragged out of the temples and then slain hard by; and some immured in the temple of Bacchus died within it. So cruel was this sedition and seemed so the more because it was of these the first.

82. For afterwards all Greece, as a man may say, was in commotion; and quarrels arose everywhere between the patrons of the commons, that sought to bring in the Athenians, and the few, that desired to bring in the Lacedaemonians. Now in time of peace they could have had no pretence nor would have been so forward to call them in; but being war and confederates to be had for either party, both to hurt their enemies and strengthen themselves, such as desired alteration easily got them to come in. And many and heinous things happened in the cities through this sedition, which though they have been before and shall be ever as long as human nature is the same, yet they are more calm and of different kinds according to the several conjunctures. For in peace and prosperity as well cities as private men are better minded because they be not plunged into necessity of doing anything against their will. But war, taking away the affluence of daily necessaries, is a most violent master and conformeth most men's passions to the present occasion. The cities therefore being now in sedition and those that fell into it later having heard what had been done in the former, they far exceeded the same in newness of conceit, both for the art of assailing and for the strangeness of their revenges. The received value of names imposed for signification of things was changed into arbitrary. For inconsiderate boldness was counted true-hearted manliness; provident deliberation, a handsome fear; modesty, the cloak of cowardice; to be wise in everything, to be lazy in everything. A furious suddenness was reputed a

point of valour. To re-advise for the better security was held for a fair pretext of tergiversation. He that was fierce was always trusty, and he that contraried such a one was suspected. He that did insidiate, if it took, was a wise man; but he that could smell out a trap laid, a more dangerous man than he. But he that had been so provident as not to need to do the one or the other was said to be a dissolver of society and one that stood in fear of his adversary. In brief, he that could outstrip another in the doing of an evil act or that could persuade another thereto that never meant it was commended. To be kin to another was not to be so near as to be of his society because these were ready to undertake anything and not to dispute it. For these societies were not made upon prescribed laws of profit but for rapine, contrary to the laws established. And as for mutual trust amongst them, it was confirmed not so much by divine law as by the communication of guilt. And what was well advised of their adversaries, they received with an eye to their actions to see whether they were too strong for them or not, and not ingenuously. To be revenged was in more request than never to have received injury. And for oaths (when any were) of reconcilement, being administered in the present for necessity, were of force to such as had otherwise no power; but upon opportunity, he that first durst thought his revenge sweeter by the trust than if he had taken the open way. For they did not only put to account the safeness of that course but, having circumvented their adversary by fraud, assumed to themselves withal a mastery in point of wit. And dishonest men for the most part are sooner called able than simple men honest, and men are ashamed of this title but take a pride in the other.

The cause of all this is desire of rule out of avarice and ambition, and the zeal of contention from those two proceeding. For such as were of authority in the cities, both of the one and the other faction, preferring under decent titles, one, *the political equality of the multitude*, the other, *the moderate aristocracy*, though in words they seemed to be servants of the public, they made it in effect but the prize of their contention; and striving by whatsoever means to overcome both ventured on most horrible outrages and prosecuted their revenges still farther without any regard of justice or the public good, but limiting them, each faction, by their own appetite, and stood ready, whether by unjust sentence or with their own hands, when they should get power, to satisfy their present spite. So that neither side made account to have anything the sooner done for religion [of an oath], but he was most commended that could pass a business against the hair with a fair oration. The neutrals of the city were destroyed by both factions, partly because they would not side with them and partly for envy that they should so escape.

83. Thus was wickedness on foot in every kind throughout all Greece by the occasion of their sedition. Sincerity (whereof there is much in a generous nature) was laughed down; and it was far the best course to stand diffidently against each other with their thoughts in battle array, which no speech was so powerful nor oath terrible enough to disband. And being all of them the more they considered the more desperate of assurance, they rather contrived how to avoid a mischief than were able to rely on any man's faith. And for the most part, such as had the least wit had the best success; for both their own defect and the subtlety of their adversaries putting them into a great fear to be overcome in words, or at least in pre-insidiation, by their enemies' great craft, they therefore went roundly to work with them with deeds. Whereas the other, not caring though they were perceived and thinking they needed not to take by force what they might do by plot, were thereby unprovided and so the more easily slain.

84. In Corcyra then were these evils for the most part committed first; and so were all other, which either such men as have been governed with pride rather than modesty by those on whom they take revenge were like to commit in taking it; or which such men as stand upon their delivery from long poverty out of covetousness, chiefly to have their neighbours' goods would contrary to justice give their voices to; or which men, not for covetousness but assailing each other on equal terms, carried away with the unruliness of their anger would cruelly and inexorably execute. And the common course of life being at that time confounded in the city, the nature of man, which is wont even against law to do evil, gotten now above

the law, showed itself with delight to be too weak for passion, too strong for justice, and enemy to all superiority. Else they would never have preferred revenge before innocence nor lucre (whensoever the envy of it was without power to do them hurt) before justice. And for the laws common to all men in such cases (which, as long as they be in force, give hope to all that suffer injury), men desire not to leave them standing against the need a man in danger may have of them but by their revenges on others to be beforehand in subverting them.

85. Such were the passions of the Corcyraeans, first of all other Grecians, towards one another in the city; and Eurymedon and the Athenians departed with their galleys. Afterwards, such of the Corcyraeans as had fled (for there escaped about five hundred of them), having seized on the forts in the continent, impatronized themselves of their own territory on the other side and from thence came over and robbed the islanders and did them much hurt; and there grew a great famine in the city. They likewise sent ambassadors to Lacedaemon and Corinth concerning their reduction; and when they could get nothing done, having gotten boats and some auxiliary soldiers, they passed, awhile after, to the number of about six hundred into the island. Where, when they had set fire on their boats that they might trust to nothing but to make themselves masters of the field, they went up into the hill Istone and, having there fortified themselves with a wall, infested those within and were masters of the territory.

86. In the end of the same summer the Athenians sent twenty galleys into Sicily under the command of Laches the son of Melanopus and Charoeadas the son of Euphiletus, for the Syracusians and the Leontines were now warring against each other. The confederates of the Syracusians were all the Doric cities except the Camarinaeans, which also in the beginning of this war were reckoned in the league of the Lacedaemonians but had not yet aided them in the war. The confederates of the Leontines were the Chalcidique cities together with Camarina. And in Italy the Locrians were with the Syracusians; but the Rhegians, according to their consanguinity, took part with the Leontines. Now the confederates of the Leontines, in respect of their ancient alliance with the Athenians as also for

that they were Ionians, obtained of the Athenians to send them galleys, for that the Leontines were deprived by the Syracusians of the use both of the land and sea. And so the people of Athens sent aid unto them, pretending propinquity but intending both to hinder the transportation of corn from thence into Peloponnesus and also to test the possibility of taking the states of Sicily into their own hands. These arriving at Rhegium in Italy joined with the confederates and began the war. And so ended this summer.

87. The next winter, the sickness fell upon the Athenians again (having indeed never totally left the city, though there was some intermission) and continued above a year after; but the former lasted two years, insomuch as nothing afflicted the Athenians or impaired their strength more than it. For the number that died of it of men of arms enrolled were no less than four thousand four hundred; and horsemen, three hundred; of the other multitude, innumerable. There happened also at the same time many earthquakes both in Athens and Euboea and also amongst the Boeotians, and in Boeotia chiefly at Orchomenus.

88. The Athenians and Rhegians that were now in Sicily made war the same winter on the islands called the islands of Aeolus with thirty galleys. For in summer it was impossible to war upon them for the shallowness of the water. These islands are inhabited by the Liparaeans who are a colony of the Cnidians and dwell in one of the same islands, no great one, called Lipara; and thence they go forth and husband the rest which are Didyme, Strongyle, and Hiera. The inhabitants of those places have an opinion that in Hiera Vulcan exerciseth the craft of a smith. For it is seen to send forth abundance of fire in the daytime and of smoke in the night. These islands are adjacent to the territory of the Siculi and Messanians but were confederates of the Syracusians. When the Athenians had wasted their fields and saw they would not come in, they put off again and went to Rhegium. And so ended this winter and the fifth year of this war written by Thucydides.

89. The next summer the Peloponnesians and their confederates came as far as the isthmus under the conduct of Agis the son of Archidamus, intending to have invaded Attica; but

by reason of the many earthquakes that then happened, they turned back, and the invasion proceeded not. About the same time (Euboea being then troubled with earthquakes), the sea came in at Orobiae on the part which then was land and, being impetuous withal, overflowed most part of the city, whereof part it covered and part it washed down and made lower in the return so that it is now sea which before was land. And the people, as many as could not prevent it by running up into the higher ground, perished. Another inundation like unto this happened in the isle of Atalanta, on the coast of Locris of the Opuntians, and carried away part of the Athenians' fort there; and of two galleys that lay on dry land, it brake one in pieces. Also there happened at Peparethus a certain rising of the water, but it brake not in; and a part of the wall, the town-house, and some few houses besides were overthrown by the earthquakes. The cause of such inundation, for my part, I take to be this: that the earthquake, where it was very great, did there send off the sea; and the sea returning on a sudden, caused the water to come on with greater violence. And it seemeth unto me that without an earthquake such an accident could never happen.

90. The same summer divers others, as they had several occasions, made war in Sicily; so also did the Sicilians amongst themselves and the Athenians with their confederates. But I will make mention only of such most memorable things as were done either by the confederates there with the Athenians or against the Athenians by the enemy.

Charoeades the Athenian general being slain by the Syracusians, Laches, who was now sole commander of the fleet, together with the confederates made war on Mylae, a town belonging to Messana. There were in Mylae two companies of Messanians in garrison, the which also laid a certain ambush for those that came up from the fleet. But the Athenians and their confederates both put to flight those that were in ambush with the slaughter of the most of them and also, assaulting their fortification, forced them on composition both to render the citadel and to go along with them against Messana. After this, upon the approach of the Athenians and their confederates, the Messanians compounded likewise and gave them hostages and such other security as was requisite.

91. The same summer the Athenians sent thirty galleys about Peloponnesus under the command of Demosthenes the son of Alkisthenes and Proclus the son of Theodorus and sixty galleys more with two thousand men of arms, commanded by Nicias the son of Niceratus, into Melos. For the Athenians, in respect that the Melians were islanders and yet would neither be their subjects nor of their league, intended to subdue them. But when upon the wasting of their fields they still stood out, they departed from Melos and sailed to Oropus in the opposite continent. Being there arrived within night, the men of arms left the galleys and marched presently by land to Tanagra in Boeotia. To which place, upon a sign given, the Athenians that were in the city of Athens came also forth with their whole forces, led by Hipponnicus the son of Callias and Eurymedon the son of Thucles, and joined with them and, pitching their camp, spent the day in wasting the territory of Tanagra and lay there the night following. The next day, they defeated in battle such of the Tanagrians as came out against them and also certain succours sent them from Thebes; and when they had taken up the arms of those that were slain and erected a trophy, they returned back, the one part to Athens, the other to their fleet. And Nicias with his sixty galleys, having first sailed along the coast of Locris and wasted it, came home likewise.

92. About the same time the Peloponnesians erected the colony of Heracleia in Trachinia with this intention. The Melians in the whole contain these three parts: Paralians, Hierans, and Trachinians. Of these the Trachinians, being afflicted with war from the Oetaeans their borderers, thought at first to have joined themselves to the Athenians; but fearing that they would not be faithful to them, they sent to Lacedaemon, choosing for their ambassador Tisamenus. And the Dorians, who are the mother nation to the Lacedaemonians, sent their ambassadors likewise with him with the same requests; for they also were infested with war from the same Oetaeans. Upon audience of these ambassadors the Lacedaemonians concluded to send out a colony, both intending the reparation of the injuries done to the Trachinians and to the Dorians and conceiving withal that the town would stand very commodiously for their war with the Athenians, inasmuch as

they might thereby have a navy ready, where the passage was but short, against Euboea; and it would much further their conveyance of soldiers into Thrace. And they had their mind wholly bent to the building of the place.

First, therefore, they asked counsel of the oracle in Delphi. And the oracle having bidden them do it, they sent inhabitants thither, both of their own people and of the neighbours about them, and gave leave also to any that would to go thither out of the rest of Greece, save only to the Ionians, Achaeans, and some few other nations. The conductors of the colony were three Lacedaemonians, Leon, Alcidas, and Damagon. Who, taking it in hand, built the city which is now called Heracleia from the very foundation, being distant from Thermopylae forty furlongs and from the sea twenty. Also they made houses for galleys to lie under, beginning close to Thermopylae against the very strait, to the end to have them the more defensible.

93. The Athenians, when this city was peopled, were at first afraid and thought it to be set up especially against Euboea; because from thence to Cenaeum, a promontory of Euboea, the passage is but short. But it fell out afterwards otherwise than they imagined; for they had no great harm by it, the reason whereof was this. That the Thessalians, who had the towns of those parts in their power and upon whose ground it was built, afflicted these new planters with a continual war till they had worn them out, though they were many indeed in the beginning. For being the foundation of the Lacedaemonians, everyone went thither boldly, conceiving the city to be an assured one. And chiefly the governors themselves, sent hither from Lacedaemon, undid the business and dispeopled the city by frighting most men away, for that they governed severely and sometimes also unjustly, by which means their neighbours more easily prevailed against them.

94. The same summer, and about the same time that the Athenians stayed in Melos, those other Athenians that were in the thirty galleys about Peloponnesus slew first certain garrison soldiers in Ellomenus, a place of Leucadia, by ambush. But afterwards with a greater fleet and with the whole power of the Acarnanians, who followed the army, all (but the Oeniades) that could bear arms, and with the Zacynthians and

Cephalonians and fifteen galleys of the Corcyraeans, made war against the city itself of Leucas. The Leucadians, though they saw their territory wasted by them both without the isthmus and within where the city of Leucas standeth and the temple of Apollo, yet they durst not stir because the number of the enemy was so great. And the Acarnanians entreated Demosthenes, the Athenian general, to wall them up, conceiving that they might easily be expugned by a siege and desiring to be rid of a city their continual enemy. But Demosthenes was persuaded at the same time by the Messenians that, seeing so great an army was together, it would be honourable for him to invade the Aetolians, principally as being enemies to Naupactus; and that if these were subdued, the rest of the continent thereabouts would easily be added to the Athenian dominion. For they alleged that though the nation of the Aetolians were great and warlike, yet their habitation was in villages unwalled and those at great distances, and were but light-armed and might, therefore, with no great difficulty be all subdued before they could unite themselves for defense. And they advised him to take in hand first the Apodotians, next the Ophionians, and after them the Eurytanians (which are the greatest part of Aetolia, of a most strange language, and that are reported to eat raw flesh); for these being subdued, the rest would easily follow.

95. But he, induced by the Messenians whom he favoured, but especially because he thought without the forces of the people of Athens with the confederates only of the continent and with the Aetolians to invade Boeotia by land, going first through the Locri Ozolae and so to Cytinium of Doris, having Parnassus on the right hand till the descent thereof into the territory of the Phoceans, which people, for the friendship they ever bore to the Athenians, would, he thought, be willing to follow his army, and if not, might be forced; and upon the Phoceans bordereth Boeotia; putting off therefore with his whole army, against the minds of the Acarnanians, from Leucas, he sailed unto Solium by the shore. And there, having communicated his conceit with the Acarnanians, when they would not approve of it because of his refusal to besiege Leucas, he himself with the rest of his army, Cephalonians, Zacynthians,

and three hundred Athenians, the soldiers of his own fleet (for the fifteen galleys of Corcyra were now gone away), warred on the Aetolians, having Oeneon, a city of Locris, for the seat of his war. Now these Locrians called Ozolae were confederates of the Athenians and were to meet them with their whole power in the heart of the country. For being confiners on the Aetolians and using the same manner of arming, it was thought it would be a matter of great utility in the war to have them in their army for that they knew their manner of fight and were acquainted with the country.

96. Having lain the night with his whole army in the temple of Jupiter Nemeius (wherein the poet Hesiodus is reported by them that dwell thereabout to have died, foretold by an oracle that he should die in Nemea), in the morning betimes he dislodged and marched into Aetolia. The first day he took Potidania; the second day, Crocyleium; the third, Teichium. There he stayed and sent the booty he had gotten to Eupalium in Locris. For he purposed, when he had subdued the rest, to invade the Ophionians afterwards (if they submitted not) in his return to Naupactus. But the Aetolians knew of this preparation when it was first resolved on. And afterwards, when the army was entered, they were united into a mighty army to make head, insomuch as that the farthest off of the Ophionians that reach out to the Melian Gulf, the Bomians and Callians, came in with their aids.

97. The Messenians gave the same advice to Demosthenes that they had done before and, alleging that the conquest of the Aetolians would be but easy, willed him to march with all speed against them, village after village, and not to stay till they were all united and in order of battle against him but to attempt always the place which was next to hand. He, persuaded by them and confident of his fortune because nothing had crossed him hitherto, without tarrying for the Locrians that should have come in with their aids (for his greatest want was of darters light-armed), marched to Aegitium, which approaching he won by force, the men having fled secretly out and encamped themselves on the hills above it; for it stood in a mountainous place and about eighty furlongs from the sea. But the Aetolians (for by this time they were come with their

forces to Aegitium) charged the Athenians and their confederates and, running down upon them, some one way and some another, from the hills, plied them with their darts. And when the army of the Athenians assaulted them, they retired; and when it retired, they assaulted. So that the fight for a good while was nothing but alternate chase and retreat, and the Athenians had the worst in both.

98. Nevertheless, as long as their archers had arrows and were able to use them (for the Aetolians, by reason they were not armed, were put back still with the shot), they held out. But when upon the death of their captain the archers were dispersed and the rest were also wearied, having a long time continued the said labour of pursuing and retiring, and the Aetolians continually afflicting them with their darts, they were forced at length to fly and, lighting into hollows without issue and into places they were not acquainted withal, were destroyed. For Chromon a Messenian, who was their guide for the ways, was slain. And the Aetolians, pursuing them still with darts, slew many of them quickly whilst they fled, being swift of foot and without armour. But the most of them missing their way and entering into a wood which had no passage through, the Aetolians set it on fire and burnt it about them. All kinds of shifts to fly and all kinds of destruction were that day in the army of the Athenians. Such as remained with much ado got to the sea and to Oeneon, a city of Locris, from whence they first set forth. There died very many of the confederates and a hundred and twenty men of arms of the Athenians; that was their number, and all of them able men; these men of the very best died in this war. Procles also was there slain, one of the generals. When they had received the bodies of their dead from the Aetolians under truce and were gotten again to Naupactus, they returned with the fleet to Athens. But they left Demosthenes about Naupactus and those parts because he was afraid of the Athenian people for the loss that had happened.

99. About the same time the Athenians that were on the coast of Sicily sailed unto Locris and, landing, overcame such as made head and took in Peripolium, situated on the river Halex.

100. The same summer, the Aetolians, having sent their am-

bassadors, Tolophus, an Ophionian, Boryades, an Eurytanian, and Tisander, an Apodotian, to Corinth and Lacedaemon, persuaded them to send an army against Naupactus for that it harboured the Athenians against them. And the Lacedaemonians, towards the end of autumn, sent them three thousand men of arms of their confederates of which five hundred were of Heracleia, the new-built city of Trachinia. The general of the army was Eurylochus, a Spartan, with whom Macarius and Menedaeus went also along, Spartans likewise.

101. When the army was assembled at Delphi, Eurylochus sent a herald to the Locrians of Ozolae both because their way lay through them to Naupactus, and also because he desired to make them revolt from the Athenians. Of all the Locrians the Amphissians co-operated with him most, as standing most in fear for the enmity of the Phoceans. And they first giving hostages induced others who likewise were afraid of the coming in of the army to do the like: the Myoneans first, being their neighbours, for this way is Locris of most difficult access; then the Ipneans, Messapians, Tritaeans, Chalaeans, Tolophonians, Hessians, and the Oeantheans. All these went with them to the war. The Olpaeans gave them hostages but followed not the army. But the Hyaeans would give them no hostages till they had taken a village of theirs called Polis.

102. When everything was ready and he had sent the hostages away to Cytinium in Doris, he marched with his army towards Naupactus through the territory of the Locrians. And as he marched, he took Oeneon, a town of theirs, and Eupalium because they refused to yield unto him. When they were come into the territory of Naupactus, the Aetolians being there already to join with them, they wasted the fields about and took the suburbs of the city, being unfortified. Then they went to Molycreium, a colony of the Corinthians but subject to the people of Athens, and took that. Now Demosthenes, the Athenian (for ever since the Aetolian business he abode about Naupactus), having been pre-advertised of this army and being afraid to lose the city, went amongst the Acarnanians and with much ado, because of his departure from before Leucas, persuaded them to relieve Naupactus; and they sent along with him in his galleys a thousand men of arms. Which entering

were the preservation of the city; for there was danger, the walls being of a great compass and the defendants few, that else they should not have been able to make them good. Eurylochus and those that were with him, when they perceived that those forces were entered and that it was impossible to take the city by assault, departed thence not into Peloponnesus but to Aeolis, now called Calydon, and to Pleuron and other places thereabouts, and also to Proschion in Aetolia. For the Ambraciotes coming to them persuaded them to undertake, together with themselves, the enterprise against Argos and the rest of Amphilochia, and Acarnania, saying withal that if they could overcome these, the rest of that continent would enter into the league of the Lacedaemonians. Whereunto Eurylochus assented and, dismissing the Aetolians, lay quiet in those parts with his army till such time as the Ambraciotes being come with their forces before Argos he should have need to aid them. And so this summer ended.

103. The Athenians that were in Sicily in the beginning of winter, together with the Grecians of their league and as many of the Siculi as having obeyed the Syracusans by force, or being their confederates before, had now revolted, warred jointly against Nessa, a town of Sicily, the citadel whereof was in the hands of the Syracusans. And they assaulted the same; but when they could not win it, they retired. In the retreat, the Syracusans that were in the citadel sallied out upon the confederates that retired later than the Athenians, and charging, put a part of the army to flight and killed not a few. After this, Laches and the Athenians landed some time at Locris and overcame in battle by the river Caicinus about three hundred Locrians, who with Proxenus, the son of Capaton, came out to make resistance; and when they had stripped them of their arms, departed.

104. The same winter also the Athenians hallowed the isle of Delos, by the admonition indeed of a certain oracle. For Pisistratus also, the tyrant, hallowed the same before; not all, but only so much as was within the prospect of the temple. But now they hallowed it all over in this manner. They took away all sepulchres whatsoever of such as had died there before, and for the future made an edict that none should be suffered to die nor any woman to bring forth child in the is-

land; but [when they were near the time, either of the one or
the other] they should be carried over into Rheneia. This
Rheneia is so little a way distant from Delos that Polycrates,
the tyrant of Samos, who was once of great power by sea and
had the dominion of the other islands, when he won Rheneia
dedicated the same to Apollo of Delos, tying it unto Delos with
a chain. And now after the hallowing of it, the Athenians instituted the keeping, every fifth year, of the Delian games.

There had also in old time been great concourse in Delos,
both of Ionians and of the islanders round about. For they then
came to see the games, with their wives and children, as the
Ionians do now the games at Ephesus. There were likewise
matches set of bodily exercise and of music; and the cities did
severally set forth dances. Which things to have been so, is
principally declared by Homer in these verses of his hymn to
Apollo:

> *But thou, Apollo, takest most delight*
> *In Delos. There assemble in thy sight*
> *The long-coat Ions, with their children dear*
> *And venerable bedfellows; and there*
> *In matches set of buffets, song, and dance,*
> *Both show thee pastime and thy name advance.*

That there were also matches of music and that men resorted
thither to contend therein he again maketh manifest in these
verses of the same hymn. For after he hath spoken of the Delian
dance of the women, he endeth their praise with these verses,
wherein also he maketh mention of himself:

> *But well: let Phoebus and Diana be*
> *Propitious; and farewell you, each one.*
> *But yet remember me when I am gone:*
> *And if of earthly men you chance to see*
> *Any toil'd pilgrim, that shall ask you, Who,*
> *O damsels, is the man that living here*
> *Was sweet'st in song, and that most had your ear?*
> *Then all, with a joint murmur, thereunto*
>   *Make answer thus: A man deprived of seeing;*
>   *In the isle of sandy Chios is his being.*

So much hath Homer witnessed touching the great meeting and solemnity celebrated of old in the isle of Delos. And the islanders and the Athenians, since that time, have continued still to send dancers along with their sacrificers; but the games and things of that kind were worn out, as is likely, by adversity till now that the Athenians restored the games and added the horse race, which was not before.

105. The same winter the Ambraciotes, according to their promise made to Eurylochus when they retained his army, made war upon Argos in Amphilochia with three thousand men of arms, and invading Argeia, they took Olpae, a strong fort on a hill by the sea-side, which the Acarnanians had forti- fied and used for the place of their common meetings for mat- ters of justice, and is distant from the city of Argos, which stands also on the sea-side, about twenty-five furlongs. The Acarnanians, with part of their forces, came to relieve Argos; and with the rest they encamped in that part of Amphilochia which is called Crenae to watch the Peloponnesians that were with Eurylochus that they might not pass through to the Ambraciotes without their knowledge; and sent to Demosthe- nes, who had been leader of the Athenians in the expedition against the Aetolians, to come to them and be their general. They sent also to the twenty Athenian galleys that chanced to be then on the coast of Peloponnesus under the conduct of Aristoteles, the son of Timocrates, and Hierophon, the son of Antimnestus. In like manner the Ambraciotes that were at Olpae sent a messenger to the city of Ambracia, willing them to come to their aid with their whole power, as fearing that those with Eurylochus would not be able to pass by the Acar- nanians, and so they should be either forced to fight alone or else have an unsafe retreat.

106. But the Peloponnesians that were with Eurylochus, as soon as they understood that the Ambraciotes were come to Olpae, dislodging from Proschion went with all speed to assist them; and passing over the river Achelöus, marched through Acarnania, which, by reason of the aids sent to Argos, was now disfurnished. On their right hand they had the city of Stratus and that garrison; on the left, the rest of Acarnania. Having passed the territory of the Stratians, they marched through

Phytia, and again by the utmost limits of Medeon; then through Limnaea; then they went into the territory of the Agraeans, which are out of Acarnania, and their friends: and getting to the hill Thiamus, which is a desert hill, they marched over it and came down into Argeia when it was now night; and passing between the city of the Argives and the Arcarnanians that kept watch at [the] Wells, came unseen and joined with the Ambraciotes at Olpae.

107. When they were all together, they sat down about break of day at a place called Metropolis and there encamped. And the Athenians not long after with their twenty galleys arrived in the Ambracian gulf to the aid of the Argives, to whom also came Demosthenes with two hundred Messenian men of arms and threescore Athenian archers. The galleys lay at sea before the hill upon which the fort of Olpae standeth. But the Acarnanians, and those few Amphilochians (for the greatest part of them the Ambraciotes kept back by force) that were come already together at Argos, prepared themselves to give the enemy battle, and chose Demosthenes, with their own commanders, for general of the whole league. He, when he had brought them up near unto Olpae, there encamped. There was between them a great hollow. And for five days together they stirred not; but the sixth day both sides put themselves into array for the battle. The army of the Peloponnesians reached a great way beyond the other, for indeed it was much greater; but Demosthenes, fearing to be encompassed, placed an ambush in a certain hollow way and fit for such a purpose, of armed and unarmed soldiers, in all to the number of four hundred; which, in that part where the number of the enemies overreached, should in the heat of the battle rise out of ambush and charge them on their backs. When the battles were in order on either side, they came to blows. Demosthenes, with the Messenians and those few Athenians that were there, stood in the right wing; and the Acarnanians (as they could one after another be put in order) and those Amphilochian darters which were present, made up the other. The Peloponnesians and Ambraciotes were ranged promiscuously, except only the Mantineans, who stood together most of them in the left wing, but not in the utmost part of it; for Eurylochus and those that

were with him made the extremity of the left wing, against Demosthenes and the Messenians.

108. When they were in fight, and that the Peloponnesians with that wing overreached and had encircled the right wing of their enemies, those Acarnanians that lay in ambush, coming in at their backs, charged them and put them to flight in such sort as they endured not the first brunt, and besides, caused the greatest part of the army through affright to run away. For when they saw that part of it defeated which was with Eurylochus, which was the best of their army, they were a great deal the more afraid. And the Messenians that were in that part of the army with Demosthenes, pursuing them, dispatched the greatest part of the execution. But the Ambraciotes that were in the right wing, on that part had the victory, and chased the enemy unto the city of Argos. But in their retreat, when they saw that the greatest part of the army was vanquished, the rest of the Acarnanians setting upon them, they had much ado to recover Olpae in safety. And many of them were slain, whilst they ran into it out of array and in disorder, save only the Mantineans, for these made a more orderly retreat than any part of the army. And so this battle ended, having lasted till the evening.

109. The next day, Menedaius (Eurylochus and Macarius being now slain), taking the command upon him and not finding how, if he stayed, he should be able to sustain a siege, wherein he should both be shut up by land and also with those Attic galleys by sea, or if he should depart, how he might do it safely, had speech with Demosthenes and the Acarnanian captains, both about a truce for his departure and for the receiving of the bodies of the slain. And they delivered unto them their dead, and having erected a trophy took up their own dead, which were about three hundred. But for their departure they would make no truce openly [nor] to all; but secretly Demosthenes with his Acarnanian fellow-commanders made a truce with the Mantineans, and with Menedaius and the rest of the Peloponnesian captains and men of most worth, to be gone as speedily as they could, with purpose to disguard the Ambraciotes and multitude of mercenary strangers, and withal to use this as a means to bring the Peloponnesians into hatred

with the Grecians of those parts as men that had treacherously advanced their particular interest. Accordingly they took up their dead, and buried them as fast as they could; and such as had leave consulted secretly touching how to be gone.

110. Demosthenes and the Acarnanians had now intelligence that the Ambraciotes from the city of Ambracia, according to the message sent to them before from Olpae [which was that they should bring their whole power through Amphilochia to their aid], were already on their march (ignorant of what had passed here) to join with those at Olpae. And hereupon he sent a part of his army presently forth to beset the ways with ambushment and to pre-occupy all places of strength, and prepared withal to encounter with the rest of his army.

111. In the meantime, the Mantineans and such as had part in the truce, going out on pretence to gather potherbs and firewood, stole away by small numbers, and as they went, did indeed gather such things as they pretended to go forth for; but when they were gotten far from Olpae, they went faster away. But the Ambraciotes and others that came forth in the same manner, but in greater troops, seeing the others go quite away, were eager to be gone likewise, and ran outright, as desiring to overtake those that were gone before. The Acarnanians at first thought they had gone all without a truce alike and pursued the Peloponnesians and threw darts at their own captains for forbidding them and for saying that they went away under truce, as thinking themselves betrayed. But at last they let go the Mantineans and Peloponnesians, and slew the Ambraciotes only. And there was much contention and ignorance of which was an Ambraciote and which a Peloponnesian. So they slew about two hundred of them, and the rest escaped into Agraïs, a bordering territory, where Salynthius, king of the Agraeans and their friend, received them.

112. The Ambraciotes out of the city of Ambracia were come as far as Idomene. Idomene are two high hills, to the greater whereof came first undiscovered that night they whom Demosthenes had sent afore from the camp and seized it; but the Ambraciotes got first to the lesser and there encamped the same night. Demosthenes, after supper, in the twilight, marched forward with the rest of the army, one half whereof

himself took with him for the assault of the camp, and the other half he sent about through the mountains of Amphilochia. And the next morning before day, he invaded the Ambraciotes whilst they were yet in their lodgings and knew not what was the matter, but thought rather that they had been some of their own company. For Demosthenes had placed the Messenians on purpose in the foremost ranks, and commanded them to speak unto them as they went in the Doric dialect and to make the sentinels secure, especially seeing their faces could not be discerned, for it was yet night. Wherefore they put the army of the Ambraciotes to flight at the first onset and slew many upon the place; the rest fled as fast as they could towards the mountains. But the ways being beset and the Amphilochians being well acquainted with their own territory and armed but lightly against men in armour unacquainted and utterly ignorant which way to take, they lit into hollow ways and to the places forelaid with ambushes and perished. And having been put to all manner of shifts for their lives, some fled towards the sea; and when they saw the galleys of Athens sailing by the shore (this accident concurring with their defeat), swam to them, and chose rather in their present fear to be killed of those in the galleys than by the barbarians and their most mortal enemies the Amphilochians. The Ambraciotes with this loss came home, a few of many, in safety to their city. And the Acarnanians, having taken the spoil of the dead and erected their trophies, returned unto Argos.

113. The next day there came a herald from those Ambraciotes which fled from Olpae into Agraïs to demand leave to carry away the bodies of those dead which were slain after the first battle, when without truce they went away together with the Mantineans and with those that had truce. But when the herald saw the armours of those Ambraciotes that came from the city, he wondered at the number, for he knew nothing of this last blow but thought they had been armours of those with them. Then one asked him what he wondered at and how many he thought were slain; for he that asked him the question thought, on the other side, that he had been a herald sent from those at Idomene. And he answered, about two hundred.

Then he that asked replied and said: "Then these are not the armours of them, but of above a thousand."

"Then," said he again, "they belong not to them that were in battle with us." The other answered: "Yes, if you fought yesterday in Idomene."

"But we fought not yesterday at all, but the other day in our retreat."

"But we yet fought yesterday with those Ambraciotes that came from the city to aid the rest."

When the herald heard that and knew that the aid from the city was defeated, he burst out into Aimees, and astonished with the greatness of the present loss, forthwith went his way without his errand and required the dead bodies no farther. For this loss was greater than, in the like number of days, happened to any one city of Greece in all this war. I have not written the number of the slain because it was said to be such as is incredible for the quantity of the city. But this I know: that if the Acarnanians and Amphilochians, as Demosthenes and the Athenians would have had them, would have subdued Ambracia, they might have done it even with the shout of their voices. But they feared now that if the Athenians possessed it, they would prove more troublesome neighbours unto them than the other.

114. After this, having bestowed the third part of the spoils upon the Athenians, they distributed the other two parts according to the cities. The Athenians' part was lost by sea. For those three hundred complete armours which are dedicated in the temples in Attica, were picked out for Demosthenes [himself], and he brought them away with him. His return was withal the safer for this action, after his defeat in Aetolia. And the Athenians that were in the twenty galleys returned to Naupactus.

The Acarnanians and Amphilochians, when the Athenians and Demosthenes were gone, granted truce at the city of the Oeniades to those Ambraciotes and Peloponnesians that were fled to Salynthius and the Agraeans to retire, the Oeniades being gone over to Salynthius and the Agraeans likewise. And for the future, the Acarnanians and Amphilochians made a

league with the Ambraciotes for a hundred years, upon these
conditions: "That neither the Ambraciotes with the Acarnanians should make war against the Peloponnesians, nor the Acarnanians with the Ambraciotes against the Athenians; that they
should give mutual aid to one another's country; that the
Ambraciotes should restore whatsoever towns or bordering
fields they held of the Amphilochians; and that they should
at no time aid Anactorium, which was in hostility with the
Acarnanians." And upon this composition the war ended. After
this, the Corinthians sent a garrison of about three hundred
men of arms of their own city to Ambracia under the conduct
of Xenocleides, the son of Euthycles, who, with much difficulty
passing through Epirus, at length arrived. Thus passed the business in Ambracia.

115. The same winter the Athenians that were in Sicily invaded Himeraea by sea, aided by the Sicilians that invaded the
skirts of the same by land. They sailed also to the islands of
Aeolus. Returning afterwards to Rhegium, they found there
Pythodorus, the son of Isolochus, [with certain galleys], come
to receive charge of the fleet commanded by Laches. For the
Sicilian confederates had sent to Athens and persuaded the
people to assist them with a greater fleet. For though the
Syracusans were masters by land, yet seeing they hindered
them but with few galleys from the liberty of the sea, they
made preparation, and were gathering together a fleet with intention to resist them. And the Athenians furnished out forty
galleys to send into Sicily, conceiving that the war there would
the sooner be at an end and desiring withal to train their men
in naval exercise. Therefore Pythodorus, one of the commanders, they sent presently away with a few of those galleys, and
intended to send Sophocles, the son of Sostratides, and Eurymedon, the son of Thucles, with the greatest number afterwards. But Pythodorus, having now the command of Laches'
fleet, sailed in the end of winter unto a certain garrison of the
Locrians which Laches had formerly taken, and overthrown
in a battle there by the Locrians, retired.

116. The same spring, there issued a great stream of fire out
of the mountain Aetna, as it had also done in former times,
and burned part of the territory of the Catanaeans, that dwell

at the foot of Aetna, which is the highest mountain of all Sicily. From the last time that the fire brake out before to this time, it is said to be fifty years. And it hath now broken out thrice in all since Sicily was inhabited by the Grecians. These were the things that came to pass this winter. And so ended the sixth year of this war written by Thucydides.

THE FOURTH BOOK

1. The spring following, when corn began to be in the ear,
ten galleys of Syracuse and as many of Locris went to Messana
in Sicily, called in by the citizens themselves, and took it; and
Messana revolted from the Athenians. This was done by the
practice chiefly of the Syracusans, that saw the place to be
commodious for invasion of Sicily, and feared lest the Athenians, some time or other hereafter making it the seat of their
war, might come with greater forces into Sicily and invade
them from thence; but partly also of the Locrians, as being
in hostility with the Rhegians and desirous to make war upon
them on both sides. The Locrians had now also entered the

229

lands of the Rhegians with their whole power, both because they would hinder them from assisting the Messanians and because they were solicited thereunto by the banished men of Rhegium that were with them. For they of Rhegium had been long in sedition and were unable for the present to give them battle, for which cause they the rather also now invaded them. And after they had wasted the country, the Locrians withdrew their land-forces; but their galleys lay still at the guard of Messana, and more were setting forth, to lie in the same harbour, to make the war on that side.

2. About the same time of the spring, and before corn was at full growth, the Peloponnesians and their confederates, under the conduct of Agis, the son of Archidamus, king of the Lacedaemonians, invaded Attica, and there lay and wasted the country about. And the Athenians sent forty galleys into Sicily, the same which they had provided before for that purpose, and with them the other two generals, Eurymedon and Sophocles. For Pythodorus, who was the third in that commission, was arrived in Sicily before. To these they gave commandment also to take order, as they went by, for the state of those Corcyraeans that were in the city and were pillaged by the outlaws in the mountain; and threescore galleys of the Peloponnesians were gone out to take part with those in the mountain, who, because there was a great famine in the city, thought they might easily be masters of that state. To Demosthenes also, who ever since his return out of Acarnania had lived privately, they gave authority, at his own request, to make use of the same galleys, if he thought good so to do, about Peloponnesus.

3. As they sailed by the coast of Laconia and had intelligence that the Peloponnesian fleet was at Corcyra already, Eurymedon and Sophocles hasted to * Corcyra; but Demosthenes willed them to put in first at Pylus, and when they had done what was requisite there, then to proceed in their voyage. But whilst they denied to do it, the fleet was driven into Pylus by a tempest that then arose by chance. And presently Demosthenes required them to fortify the place, alleging that he came with them for no other purpose, and showing how there was great

* The Greek means "were for hastening on to Corcyra."

store of timber and stone and that the place itself was naturally strong and desert, both it and a great deal of the country about. For it lieth from Sparta about four hundred furlongs in the territory that, belonging once to the Messenians, is called by the Lacedaemonians Coryphasion. But they answered him that there were many desert promontories in Peloponnesus, if they were minded to put the city to charges in taking them in. But there appeared unto Demosthenes a great difference between this place and other places, because there was here a haven, and the Messenians, the ancient inhabitants thereof, speaking the same language the Lacedaemonians did, would both be able to annoy them much by excursions thence and be also faithful guardians of the place.

4. When he could not prevail, neither with the generals nor with the soldiers, having also at last communicated the same to the captains of companies, he gave it over, till at last, the weather not serving to be gone, there came upon the soldiers lying idle a desire, occasioned by dissension, to wall in the place of their own accord. And falling in hand with the work, they performed it, not with iron tools to hew stone, but picked out such stones as they thought good and afterwards placed them as they would severally fit. And for mortar, where it was needed, for want of vessels they carried it on their backs, with their bodies inclining forward so as it might best lie, and their hands clasped behind to stay it from falling, making all possible haste to prevent the Lacedaemonians and to finish the most assailable parts before they came to succour it. For the greatest part of the place was strong by nature and needed no fortifying at all.

5. The Lacedaemonians were [that day] celebrating a certain holiday, and when they heard the news did set lightly by it, conceiving that whensoever it should please them to go thither, they should find them either already gone or easily take the place by force. Somewhat also they were retarded by reason that their army was in Attica. The Athenians, having in six days finished the wall to the land and in the places where was most need, left Demosthenes with five galleys to defend it and with the rest hastened on in their course for Corcyra and Sicily.

6. The Peloponnesians that were in Attica, when they were

advertised of the taking of Pylus, returned speedily home; for the Lacedaemonians and Agis, their king, took this accident of Pylus to concern their own particular. And the invasion was withal so early, corn being yet green, that the most of them were scanted with victual. The army was also much troubled with the weather, which was colder than for the season. So as for many reasons it fell out that they returned sooner now than at other times they had done, and this invasion was the shortest, for they continued in Attica in all but fifteen days.

7. About the same time, Simonides, an Athenian commander, having drawn a few Athenians together out of the garrisons and a number of the confederates of those parts, took the city of Eion in Thrace, a colony of the Mendaeans, that was their enemy, by treason, but was presently again driven out by the Chalcideans and Bottiaeans that came to succour it, and lost many of his soldiers.

8. When the Peloponnesians were returned out of Attica, they of the city of Sparta and of other the neighbouring towns went presently to the aid of Pylus; but [the rest of] the Lacedaemonians came slowlier on, as being newly come from the former expedition. Nevertheless they sent about to the cities of the Peloponnesus to require their assistance with all speed at Pylus, and also to their threescore galleys that were at Corcyra, which, transported over the isthmus of Leucas, arrived at Pylus unseen of the Athenian galleys lying at Zacynthus. And by this time their army of foot was also there. Whilst the Peloponnesian galleys were coming toward Pylus, Demosthenes sent two galleys secretly to Eurymedon and the Athenian fleet at Zacynthus, in all haste, to tell them that they must come presently to him for as much as the place was in danger to be lost. And according as Demosthenes' message imported, so the fleet made haste. The Lacedaemonians in the meantime prepared themselves to assault the fort both by sea and land, hoping easily to win it, being a thing built in haste and not many men within it. And because they expected the coming of the Athenian fleet from Zacynthus, they had a purpose, if they took not the fort before, to bar up the entries of the harbour. For the island called Sphacteria, lying just before and very near to the place, maketh the haven safe and the entries straight, one of them,

nearest to Pylus and to the Athenian fortification, admitting passage for no more but two galleys in front; and the other, which lieth against the other part of the continent, for not above eight or nine. The island, by being desert, was all wood and untrodden, in bigness, about fifteen furlongs over. Therefore they determined with their galleys thick set, and with the beak-heads outward, to stop up the entries of the haven. And because they feared the island, lest the Athenians [putting men into it] should make war upon them from thence, they carried over men of arms into the same and placed others likewise along the shore of the continent. For by this means the Athenians at their coming should find the island their enemy, and no means of landing in the continent. For the coast of Pylus itself without these two entries, being to the sea harbourless, would afford them no place from whence to set forth to the aid of their fellows; and they in all probability might by siege, without battle by sea or other danger, win the place, seeing there was no provision of victual within it and that the enemy took it but on short preparation. Having thus resolved, they put over into the island their men of arms out of every band by lot. Some also had been sent over before by turns; but they which went over now last and were left there, were four hundred and twenty, besides the Helotes that were with them. And their captain was Epitadas, the son of Molobrus.

9. Demosthenes, when he saw the Lacedaemonians bent to assault him both from their galleys and with their army by land, prepared also to defend the place. And when he had drawn up his galleys, all that were left him, to the land, he placed them athwart the fort and armed the mariners that belonged to them with bucklers, though bad ones, and for the greatest part made of osiers. For they had no means in a desert place to provide themselves of arms. Those they had they took out of a piratical boat of thirty oars and a light-horseman * of the Messenians, which came by chance. And the men of arms of the Messenians were about forty, which he made use of amongst the rest. The greatest part therefore, both of armed and unarmed, he placed on the parts of the wall toward the

* Not, of course, literally a light-horseman. This was the name of a special kind of light boat.

land which were of most strength and commanded them to make good the place against the land-forces if they assaulted it. And he himself, with sixty men of arms chosen out of the whole number and a few archers, came forth from the fort to the sea-side in that part where he most expected their landing, which part was of troublesome access and stony and lay to the wide sea. But because their wall was there the weakest, he thought they would be drawn to adventure for that. For neither did the Athenians think they should ever have been mastered with galleys, which caused them to make the place [to the seaward] the less strong; and if the Peloponnesians should by force come to land, they made no other account but the place would be lost. Coming therefore in this part to the very brink of the sea, he put in order his men of arms and encouraged them with words to this effect:

10. "You that participate with me in the present danger, let not any of you in this extremity go about to seem wise and reckon every peril that now besetteth us, but let him rather come up to the enemy with little circumspection and much hope and look for his safety by that. For things that are come once to a pinch, as these are, admit not debate, but a speedy hazard. And [yet] if we stand it out, and betray not our advantages with fear of the number of the enemy, I see well enough that most things are with us. For I make account, the difficulty of their landing makes for us, which, as long as we abide ourselves, will help us; but if we retire, though the place be difficult, yet when there is none to impeach them they will land well enough. For whilst they are in their galleys, they are most easy to be fought withal; and in their disbarking, being but on equal terms, their number is not greatly to be feared; for though they be many, yet they must fight but by few for want of room to fight in. And for an army to have odds by land is another matter than when they are to fight from galleys, where they stand in need of so many accidents to fall out opportunely from the sea. So that I think their great difficulties do but set them even with our small number. And for you, that be Athenians and by experience of disbarking against others know that if a man stand it out and do not fear of the sowsing of a wave or the menacing approach of a galley give back of

himself, he can never be put back by violence; I expect that you should keep your ground and by fighting it out upon the very edge of the water preserve both yourselves and the fort."

11. Upon this exhortation of Demosthenes the Athenians took better heart and went down and arranged themselves close by the sea. And the Lacedaemonians came and assaulted the fort, both with their army by land and with their fleet, consisting of three-and-forty galleys, in which was admiral Thrasymelidas, the son of Cratesicles, a Spartan. And he made his approach where Demosthenes had before expected him. So the Athenians were assaulted on both sides, both by sea and by land. The Peloponnesians, dividing their galleys into small numbers because they could not come near with many at once and resting between, assailed them by turns, using all possible valour and mutual encouragement to put the Athenians back and gain the fort. Most eminent of all the rest was Brasidas. For having the command of a galley and seeing other captains of galleys and steersmen (the place being hard of access), when there appeared sometimes possibility of putting ashore, to be afraid and tender of breaking their galleys, he would cry out unto them, saying, "They did not well for sparing of wood to let the enemy fortify in their country." And [to the Lacedaemonians] he gave advice to force landing with the breaking of their galleys and prayed the confederates that in requital of many benefits they would not stick to bestow their galleys at this time upon the Lacedaemonians and, running them ashore, to use any means whatsoever to land and to get into their hands both the men [in the isle] and the fort.

12. Thus he urged others; and having compelled the steersman of his own galley to run her ashore, he came to the ladders, but attempting to get down was by the Athenians put back, and after he had received many wounds, swooned; and falling upon the ledges of the galley, his buckler tumbled over into the sea. Which brought to land, the Athenians took up, and used afterwards in the trophy which they set up for this assault. Also the rest endeavoured with much courage to come aland; but the place being ill to land in, and the Athenians not budging, they could not do it. So that at this time fortune came so much about, that the Athenians fought from the land, Laconique

land, against the Lacedaemonians in galleys; and the Lacedaemonians from their galleys fought against the Athenians, to get landing in their own now hostile territory. For at that time there was an opinion far spread, that these were rather landmen and expert in a battle of foot, and that in maritime and naval actions the other excelled.

13. This day then and a part of the next, they made sundry assaults and after that gave over. And the third day they sent out some galleys to Asine for timber wherewith to make engines, hoping with engines to take that part of the wall that looketh into the haven, which, though it were higher, yet the landing to it was easier. In the meantime arrive the forty Athenian galleys from Zacynthus; for there were joined with them certain galleys of the garrison of Naupactus and four of Chios. And when they saw both the continent and the island full of men of arms and that the galleys that were in the haven would not come forth, not knowing where to cast anchor they sailed for the present to the isle Prote, being near and desert, and there lay for that night. The next day, after they had put themselves in order, they put to sea again with purpose to offer them battle if the other would come forth into the wide sea against them; if not, to enter the haven upon them. But the Peloponnesians neither came out against them nor had stopped up the entries of the haven, as they had before determined, but lying still on the shore manned out their galleys and prepared to fight, if any entered, in the haven itself, which was no small one.

14. The Athenians, understanding this, came in violently upon them at both the mouths of the haven, and most of the Lacedaemonian galleys, which were already set out and opposed them, they charged and put to flight; and in following the chase, which was but short, they brake many of them and took five, whereof one with all her men in her; and they fell in also with them that fled to the shore. And the galleys which were but in manning out were torn and rent before they could put off from the land. Others they tied to their own galleys and towed them away empty. Which the Lacedaemonians perceiving, and extremely grieved with the loss, because their fellows were hereby intercepted in the island, came in with

their aid [from the land], and entering armed into the sea took hold of the galleys with their hands to have pulled them back again, every one conceiving the business to proceed the worse wherein himself was not present. So there arose a great affray about the galleys, and such as was contrary to the manner of them both. For the Lacedaemonians, out of eagerness and out of fear, did (as one may say) nothing else but make a sea-fight from the land; and the Athenians, who had the victory and desired to extend their present fortune to the utmost, made a land-fight from their galleys. But at length, having wearied and wounded each other, they fell asunder; and the Lacedaemonians recovered all their galleys,* save only those which were taken at the first onset. When they were on both sides retired to their camps, the Athenians erected a trophy, delivered to the enemy their dead, and possessed the wreck, and immediately went round the island with their galleys, keeping watch upon it as having intercepted the men within it. The Peloponnesians, in the meantime, that were in the continent and were by this time assembled there with their succours from all parts of Peloponnesus, remained upon the place at Pylus.

15. As soon as the news of what had passed was related at Sparta, they thought fit, in respect the loss was great, to send the magistrates down to the camp to determine, upon view of the state of their present affairs there, what they thought requisite to be done. These, when they saw there was no possibility to relieve their men and were not willing to put them to the danger either of suffering by famine or of being forced by multitude, concluded amongst themselves to take truce with the Athenian commanders, as far as concerned the particulars of Pylus, if they also would be content, and to send ambassadors to Athens about agreement, and to endeavour to fetch off their men as soon as they could.

16. The Athenian commanders accepting the proposition, the truce was made in this manner:

That the Lacedaemonians should deliver up not only those galleys wherein they fought but also bring to Pylus and put into the Athenians' hands whatsoever vessels of the long form of building were anywhere else in Laconia; that they should

* The Greek says "their *empty* galleys."

not make any assault upon the fort, neither by sea nor land.—
That the Athenians should permit the Lacedaemonians that
were in the continent to send over to those in the island a
portion of ground corn agreed on, to wit, to every one two
Attic choenickes of meal and two cotyles of wine and a piece
of flesh, and to every of their servants half that quantity; that
they should send this the Athenians looking on, and not send
over any vessel by stealth.—That the Athenians should nevertheless continue guarding of the island, provided that they
landed not in it, and should not invade the Peloponnesian army
neither by land nor sea.—That if either side transgressed in any
part thereof, the truce was then immediately to be void, otherwise to hold good till the return of the Lacedaemonian ambassadors from Athens.—That the Athenians should convoy them
in a galley unto Athens and back.—That at their return the
truce should end, and the Athenians should restore them their
galleys in as good estate as they had received them.

Thus was the truce made, and the galleys were delivered to
the Athenians, to the number of about three score; and the
ambassadors were sent away, who, arriving at Athens, said as
followeth:

17. "Men of Athens, the Lacedaemonians have sent us hither
concerning our men in the island, to see if we can persuade
you to such a course, as being most profitable for you, may, in
this misfortune, be the most honourable for us that our present
condition is capable of. We will not be longer in discourse than
standeth with our custom, being the fashion with us, where
few words suffice there indeed not to use many; but yet to use
more when the occasion requireth that by words we should
make plain that which is to be done in actions of importance.
But the words we shall use we pray you to receive not with the
mind of an enemy nor as if we went about to instruct you as
men ignorant, but for a remembrance to you of what you know
that you may deliberate wisely therein. It is now in your
power to assure your present good fortune with reputation,
holding what you have, with the addition of honour and glory
besides, and to avoid that which befalleth men upon extraordinary success, who through hope aspire to greater fortune because the fortune they have already came unhoped for. Whereas

they that have felt many changes of both fortunes ought indeed to be most suspicious of the good. So ought your city, and ours especially, upon experience in all reason to be.

18. "Know it, by seeing this present misfortune fallen on us, who, being of greatest dignity of all the Grecians, come to you to ask that which before we thought chiefly in our own hands to give. And yet we are not brought to this through weakness nor through insolence upon addition of strength, but because it succeeded not with the power we had as we thought it should, which may as well happen to any other as to ourselves. So that you have no reason to conceive that for your power and purchases fortune also must be therefore always yours. Such wise men as safely reckon their prosperity in the account of things doubtful do most wisely also address themselves towards adversity and not think that war will so far follow and no further as one shall please more or less to take it in hand, but rather so far as fortune shall lead it. Such men also, seldom miscarrying because they be not puffed up with the confidence of success, choose then principally to give over when they are in their better fortune. And so it will be good for you, men of Athens, to do with us, and not, if rejecting our advice you chance to miscarry (as many ways you may), to have it thought hereafter that all your present successes were but mere fortune; whereas, on the contrary, it is in your hands without danger to leave a reputation to posterity both of strength and wisdom.

19. "The Lacedaemonians call you to a peace and end of the war, giving you peace and alliance and much other friendship and mutual familiarity, requiring for the same [only] those their men that are in the island, though also we think it better for both sides not to try the chance of war, whether it fall out that by some occasion of safety offered they escape by force, or being expugned by siege should be more in your power than they be. For we are of this mind, that great hatred is most safely cancelled not when one that having beaten his enemy and gotten much the better in the war brings him through necessity to take an oath and to make peace on unequal terms, but when having it in his power lawfully so to do if he please, he overcome him likewise in goodness, and, contrary to what he expects, be reconciled to him on moderate conditions. For in this

case, his enemy being obliged not to seek revenge as one that had been forced, but to requite his goodness, will, for shame, be the more inclined to the conditions agreed on. And, naturally, to those that relent of their own accord men give way reciprocally with content; but against the arrogant they will hazard all, even when in their own judgments they be too weak.

20. "But for us both, if ever it were good to agree, it is surely so at this present and before any irreparable accident be interposed. Whereby we should be compelled, besides the common, to bear you a particular eternal hatred, and you be deprived of the commodities we now offer you. Let us be reconciled while matters stand undecided, and whilst you have gained reputation and our friendship, and we not suffered dishonour and but indifferent loss. And we shall not only ourselves prefer peace before war, but also give a cessation of their miseries to all the rest of the Grecians, who will acknowledge it rather from you than us. For they make war not knowing whether side begun; but if an end be made, which is now for the most part in your own hands, the thanks will be yours. And by decreeing the peace, you may make the Lacedaemonians your sure friends, inasmuch as they call you to it and are therein not forced but gratified. Wherein consider how many commodities are like to ensue. For if we and you go one way, you know the rest of Greece, being inferior to us, will honour us in the highest degree."

21. Thus spake the Lacedaemonians, thinking that in times past the Athenians had coveted peace and been hindered of it by them, and that being now offered, they would gladly accept of it. But they, having these men intercepted in the island, thought they might compound at pleasure and aspired to greater matters. To this they were set on for the most part by Cleon, the son of Cleaenetus, a popular man at that time and of greatest sway with the multitude. He persuaded them to give this answer: "That they in the island ought first to deliver up their arms, and come themselves to Athens; and when they should be there, if the Lacedaemonians would make restitution of Nisaea and Pegae and Troezen and Achaia"—the which they had not won in war but had received by former treaty when the Athenians, being in distress and at that time in more need

of peace than now, [yielded them up into their hands]—"then they should have their men again, and peace should be made for as long as they both should think good."

22. To this answer they replied nothing, but desired that commissioners might be chosen to treat with them, who, by alternate speaking and hearing, might quietly make such an agreement as they could persuade each other unto. But then Cleon came mightily upon them saying he knew before that they had no honest purpose and that the same was now manifest in that they refused to speak before the people but sought to sit in consultation only with a few, and willed them, if they had aught to say that was real, to speak it before them all. But the Lacedaemonians finding that, although they had a mind to make peace with them upon this occasion of adversity, yet it would not be fit to speak in it before the multitude, lest speaking and not obtaining they should incur calumny with their confederates; and seeing withal that the Athenians would not grant what they sued for upon reasonable conditions, they went back again without effect.

23. Upon their return, presently the truce at Pylus was at an end; and the Lacedaemonians, according to agreement, demanded restitution of their galleys. But the Athenians, laying to their charge an assault made upon the fort, contrary to the articles, and other matters of no great importance, refused to render them, standing upon this, that it was said that the accord should be void upon whatsoever the least transgression of the same. But the Lacedaemonians, denying it and protesting this detention of their galleys for an injury, went their ways and betook themselves to the war. So the war at Pylus was on both sides renewed with all their power; the Athenians went every day about the island with two galleys, one going one way, another another way, and lay at anchor about it every night with their whole fleet, except on that part which lieth to the open sea; and that only when it was windy. (From Athens also there came a supply of thirty galleys more, to guard the island, so that they were in the whole threescore and ten.) And the Lacedaemonians made assaults upon the fort,*

* The Greek adds "The Lacedaemonians, *being encamped upon the mainland*, made assault."

and watched every opportunity that should present itself to save their men in the island.

24. Whilst these things passed, the Syracusians and their confederates in Sicily, adding to those galleys that lay in garrison at Messana the rest of the fleet which they had prepared, made war out of Messana, instigated thereto chiefly by the Locrians, as enemies to the Rhegians, whose territory they had also invaded with their whole forces by land; and seeing the Athenians had but a few galleys present and hearing that the greater number which were to come to them were employed in the siege of the island, desired to try with them a battle by sea. For if they could get the better with their navy, they hoped, lying before Rhegium, both with their land-forces on the field side and with their fleet by sea, easily to take it into their hands and thereby strengthen their affairs. For Rhegium, a promontory of Italy, and Messana in Sicily lying near together, they might both hinder the Athenians from lying at anchor there against them and make themselves masters of the strait. This strait is the sea between Rhegium and Messana where Sicily is nearest to the continent, and is that which is called Charybdis, where Ulysses is said to have passed through. Which, for that it is very narrow, and because the sea falleth in there from two great mains, the Tyrrhene and Sicilian, and is rough, hath therefore not without good cause been esteemed dangerous.

25. In this strait then the Syracusians and their confederates, with somewhat more than thirty galleys, were constrained in the latter end of the day to come to a sea-fight, having been drawn forth about the passage of a certain boat to undertake sixteen galleys of Athens and eight of Rhegium, and being overcome by the Athenians, fell off with the loss of one galley and went speedily each [side] to their own camp at Messana and Rhegium; and the night overtook them in the action. After this the Locrians departed out of the territory of the Rhegians, and the fleet of the Syracusians and their confederates came together to an anchor at Peloris and had their land-forces by them. But the Athenians and Rhegians came up to them and, finding their galleys empty of men, fell in amongst them; and by means of a grapnel cast into one of their galleys they lost that galley, but the men swam out. Upon this the Syracusians

went aboard, and whilst they were towed along the shore towards Messana the Athenians came up to them again; and the
Syracusians, opening themselves, charged first and sunk another of their galleys. So the Syracusians passed on to the port
of Messana, having had the better in their passage by the shore
and in the sea-fight, which were both together in such manner as
is declared.

The Athenians, upon news that Camarina should by Archias
and his complices be betrayed to the Syracusians, went thither.
In the meantime the Messanians, with their whole power by
land and also with their fleet, warred on Naxos, a Chalcidique
city and their borderer. The first day, having forced the
Naxians to retire within their walls, they spoiled their fields;
the next day they sent their fleet about into the river Acesine,
which spoiled the country [as it went up the river], and with
their land-forces assaulted the city. In the meantime many of the
Siculi, mountaineers, came down to their assistance against the
Messanians, which when they of Naxos perceived, they took
heart and, encouraging themselves with an opinion that the
Leontines and all the rest of the Grecians their confederates
had come to succour them, sallied suddenly out of the city and
charged upon the Messanians and put them to flight with the
slaughter of a thousand of their soldiers, and the rest hardly
escaping home. For the barbarians fell upon them and slew
the most part of them in the highways. And the galleys that lay
at Messana not long after divided themselves and went to their
several homes. Hereupon the Leontines and their confederates,
together with the Athenians, marched presently against Messana, as being now weakened, and assaulted it, the Athenians
with their fleet by the haven and the land-forces at the wall
to the field. But the Messanians and certain Locrians with
Demoteles, who after this loss had been left there in garrison,
issuing forth and falling suddenly upon them, put a great part
of the Leontines' army to flight and slew many. But the Athenians, seeing that, disbarked and relieved them and, coming
upon the Messanians now in disorder, chased them again into
the city. Then they erected a trophy and put over to Rhegium.
After this, the Grecians of Sicily warred one upon another
without the Athenians.

26. All this while the Athenians at Pylus besieged the Lace-daemonians in the island; and the army of the Peloponnesians in the continent remained still upon the place. This keeping of watch was exceedingly painful to the Athenians in respect of the want they had both of corn and water, for there was no well but one and that was in the fort itself of Pylus and no great one. And the greatest number turned up the gravel and drank such water as they were like to find there. They were also scanted of room for their camp, and their galleys not having place to ride in, they were forced by turns some to stay ashore and others to take their victual and lie off at anchor. But their greatest discouragement was the time which they had stayed there longer than they had thought to have done, for they thought to have famished them out in a few days, being in a desert island and having nothing to drink but salt water. The cause hereof were the Lacedaemonians, who had proclaimed that any man that would should carry in meal, wine, cheese, and all other esculents necessary for a siege into the island, appointing for the same a great reward of silver; and if any Helot should carry in any thing, they promised him liberty. Hereupon divers with much danger imported victual, but especially the Helotes, who, putting off from all parts of Peloponnesus, wheresoever they chanced to be, came in at the parts of the island that lay to the wide sea. But they had a care above all to take such a time as to be brought in with the wind. For when it blew from the sea, they could escape the watch of the galleys easily; for they could not then lie round about the island at anchor. And the Helotes were nothing tender in putting ashore, for they ran their galleys on ground, valued at a price in money; and the men of arms also watched at all the landing places of the island. But as many as made attempt when the weather was calm were intercepted. There were also such as could dive, that swam over into the island through the haven, drawing after them in a string bottles filled with poppy tempered with honey, and pounded linseed; whereof some at the first passed unseen, but were afterwards watched. So that on either part they used all possible art, one side to send over food, the other to apprehend those that carried it.

27. The people of Athens being advertised of the state of

their army, how it was in distress, and that victual was transported into the island, knew not what they should do to it and
feared lest winter should overtake them in their siege, fearing
not only that to provide them of necessaries about Peloponnesus, and in a desert place withal, would be a thing impossible,
but also that they should be unable to send forth so many
things as were requisite, though it were summer; and again,
that the parts thereabout being without harbour, there would be
no place to lie anchor in against them, but that the watch there
ceasing of itself, the men would by that means escape or in
some foul weather be carried away in the same boats that
brought them meat. But that which they feared most was that
the Lacedaemonians seemed to have some assurance of them already, because they sent no more to negotiate about them. And
they repented now that they had not accepted of the peace.
But Cleon, knowing himself to be the man suspected for
hindering the agreement, said that they who brought the news
reported not the truth. Whereupon, they that came thence
advising them, if they would not believe it, to send to view the
estate of the army, he and Theogenes were chosen by the
Athenians to view it. But when he saw that he must of force
either say as they said whom he before calumniated or, saying
the contrary, be proved a liar, he advised the Athenians, seeing
them inclined of themselves to send thither greater forces than
they had before thought to do, that it was not fit to send to
view the place nor to lose their opportunity by delay; but if the
report seemed unto them to be true, they should make a voyage
against those men; and glanced at Nicias, the son of Niceratus,
then general, upon malice and with language of reproach, saying
it was easy, if the leaders were men, to go and take them there
in the island; and that himself, if he had the command, would
do it.

28. But Nicias, seeing the Athenians to be in a kind of
tumult against Cleon, for that when he thought it so easy a
matter he did not presently put it in practice, and seeing also
he had upbraided him, willed him to take what strength he
would that they could give him and undertake it. Cleon, supposing at first that he gave him this leave but in words, was
ready to accept it; but when he knew he would give him the

authority in good earnest, then he shrunk back and said that not
he but Nicias was general, being now indeed afraid and hoping
that he durst not have given over the office to him. But then
Nicias again bade him do it and gave over his command [to
him] for so much as concerned Pylus and called the Athenians to witness it. They (as is the fashion of the multitude),
the more Cleon declined the voyage and went back from his
word, pressed Nicias so much the more to resign his power to
him and cried out upon Cleon to go. Insomuch as not knowing
how to disengage himself of his word, he undertook the voyage,
and stood forth saying that he feared not the Lacedaemonians
and that he would not carry any man with him out of the city
but only the Lemnians and Imbrians that then were present
and those targettiers that were come to them from Aenus and
four hundred archers out of other places; and with these, he
said, added to the soldiers that were at Pylus already, he would
within twenty days either fetch away the Lacedaemonians alive
or kill them upon the place. This vain speech moved amongst
the Athenians some laughter, and was heard with great content
of the wiser sort. For of two benefits, the one must needs fall
out: either to be rid of Cleon (which was their greatest hope)
or, if they were deceived in that, then to get those Lacedaemonians into their hands.

29. Now when he had dispatched with the assembly and the
Athenians had by their voices decreed him the voyage, he
joined unto himself Demosthenes, one of the commanders at
Pylus, and presently put to sea. He made choice of Demosthenes for his companion because he heard that he also of himself had a purpose to set his soldiers aland in the isle. For the
army, having suffered much by the straitness of the place and
being rather the besieged than the besieger, had a great desire
to put the matter to the hazard of a battle; confirmed therein
the more for that the island had been burnt. For having been
for the most part wood and (by reason it had lain ever desert)
without path, they were before [the more] afraid and thought
it the advantage of the enemy; for assaulting them out of sight,
they might annoy a very great army that should offer to come
aland. For their errors being in the wood and their preparation
could not so well have been discerned, whereas all the faults

of their own army should have been in sight, so that the enemy might have set upon them suddenly in what part soever they had pleased, because the onset had been in their own election. Again, if they should by force come up to fight with the Lacedaemonians at hand in the thick woods, the fewer and skilful of the ways, he thought, would be too hard for the many and unskilful. Besides, their own army being great it might receive an overthrow before they could know of it, because they could not see where it was needful to relieve one another.

30. These things came into his head especially from the loss he received in Aetolia; which in part also happened by occasion of the woods. But the soldiers, for want of room, having been forced to put in at the outside of the island to dress their dinners with a watch before them, and one of them having set fire on the wood, [it burnt on by little and little], and the wind afterwards rising, the most of it was burnt before they were aware. By this accident, Demosthenes, the better discerning that the Lacedaemonians were more than he had imagined, having before, by victual sent unto them, thought them not so many, did now prepare himself for the enterprise as a matter deserving the Athenians' utmost care and as having better commodity of landing in the island than before he had, and both sent for the forces of such confederates as were near and put in readiness every other needful thing. And Cleon, who had sent a messenger before to signify his coming, came himself also, with those forces which he had required, unto Pylus.

When they were both together, first they sent a herald to the camp in the continent to know if they would command those in the island to deliver up themselves and their arms without battle, to be held with easy imprisonment till some agreement were made touching the main war.

31. Which when they refused, the Athenians for one day held their hands; but the next day, having put aboard upon a few galleys all their men of arms, they put off in the night and landed a little before day on both sides of the island, both from the main and from the haven, to the number of about eight hundred men of arms, and marched upon high speed towards the foremost watch of the island. For thus the Lacedaemonians lay quartered. In this foremost watch were about thirty men

of arms; the middest and evenest part of the island and about
the water was kept by Epitadas, their captain, with the greatest
part of the whole number; and another part of them, which
were not many, kept the last guard towards Pylus, which place
to the seaward was on a cliff and least assailable by land. For
there was also a certain fort which was old and made of chosen
[not of hewn] stones, which they thought would stand them in
stead in case of violent retreat. Thus they were quartered.

32. Now the Athenians presently killed those of the foremost guard, which they so ran to, in their cabins and as they
were taking arms. For they knew not of their landing but
thought those galleys had come thither to anchor in the night
according to custom, as they had been wont to do. As soon as
it was morning, the rest of the army also landed, out of somewhat more than seventy galleys, every one with such arms as
he had, being all [that rowed] except only the Thalamii: eight
hundred archers, targetiers as many, all the Messenians that
came to aid them, and as many of them besides as held any place
about Pylus, except only the garrison of the fort itself. Demosthenes then, disposing his army by two hundred and more in
a company, and in some less, [at certain distances], seized on all
the higher grounds to the end that the enemies, compassed
about on every side, might the less know what to do or against
what part to set themselves in battle and be subject to the shot
of the multitude from every part; and when they should make
head against those that fronted them, be charged behind; and
when they should turn to those that were opposed to their
flanks, be charged at once both behind and before. And which
way soever they marched, the light-armed and such as were
meanliest provided of arms followed them at the back with
arrows, darts, stones, and slings, who have courage enough afar
off, and could not be charged, but would overcome flying, and
also press the enemies when they should retire. With this
design Demosthenes both intended his landing at first and
afterwards ordered his forces accordingly in the action.

33. Those that were about Epitadas, who were the greatest
part of those in the island, when they saw that the foremost
guard was slain and that the army marched towards them, put
themselves in array and went towards the men of arms of the

Athenians with intent to charge them; for these were opposed
to them in front, and the light-armed soldiers on their flanks
and at their backs. But they could neither come to join with
them nor any way make use of their skill. For both the light-
armed soldiers kept them off with shot from either side, and
the men of arms advanced not. Where the light-armed soldiers
approached nearest, they were driven back; but returning, they
charged them afresh, being men armed lightly, and that easily
got out of their reach by running, especially the ground being
uneasy and rough by having been formerly desert, so that the
Lacedaemonians in their armour could not follow them.

34. Thus for a little while they skirmished one against another afar off. But when the Lacedaemonians were no longer
able to run out after them where they charged, these light-
armed soldiers, seeing them less earnest in chasing them and
taking courage chiefly from their sight, as being many times
their number, and having also been used to them so much as
not to think them now so dangerous as they had done, for that
they had not received so much hurt at their hands as their subdued minds, because they were to fight against the Lacedaemonians, had at their first landing prejudged, contemned them;
and with a great cry ran all at once upon them, casting stones,
arrows, and darts, as to every man came next to hand. Upon
this cry and assault they were much terrified, as not accustomed
to such kind of fight; and withal a great dust of the woods
lately burnt mounted into the air, so that by reason of the arrows and stones, that together with the dust flew from such a
multitude of men, they could hardly see before them. Then
the battle grew sore on the Lacedaemonians' side, for their jacks
now gave way to the arrows, and the darts that were thrown
stuck broken in them, so as they could not handle themselves,
as neither seeing before them, nor hearing any direction given
them for the greater noise of the enemy, but danger being on
all sides, were hopeless to save themselves upon any side by
fighting.

35. In the end, many of them being now wounded, for that
they could not shift their ground, they made their retreat in
close order to the last guard of the island and to the watch that
was there. When they once gave ground, then were the light-

armed soldiers much more confident than before and pressed
upon them with a mighty noise; and as many of the Lacedaemonians as they could intercept in their retreat they slew; but
the most of them recovered the fort and together with the
watch of the same put themselves in order to defend it in all
parts that were subject to assault. The Athenians following
could not now encompass and hem them in, for the strong
situation of the place, but, assaulting them in the face, sought
only how to put them from the wall. And thus they held out
a long time, the better part of a day, either side tired with the
fight and with thirst and with the sun, one endeavouring to
drive the enemy from the top, the other to keep their ground.
And the Lacedaemonians defended themselves easilier now than
before because they were not now encompassed upon their
flanks.

36. When there was no end of the business, the captain of
the Messenians said unto Cleon and Demosthenes that they
spent their labour there in vain and that if they would deliver
unto him a part of the archers and light-armed soldiers to get
up by such a way as he himself should find out and come behind upon their backs, he thought the entrance might be forced.
And having received the forces he asked, he took his way from
a place out of sight to the Lacedaemonians that he might not
be discovered making his approach under the cliffs of the island
where they were continual in which part, trusting to the natural strength thereof, they kept no watch, and with much
labour and hardly unseen, came behind them, and appearing
suddenly from above at their backs, both terrified the enemies
with the sight of what they expected not and much confirmed
the Athenians with the sight of what they expected. And the
Lacedaemonians, being now charged with their shot both before and behind, were in the same case (to compare small matters with great) that they were in at Thermopylae. For then
they were slain by the Persians, shut up on both sides in a narrow path; and these now, being charged on both sides, could
make good the place no longer, but fighting few against many
and being weak withal for want of food, were at last forced to
give ground; and the Athenians by this time were also masters
of all the entrances.

37. But Cleon and Demosthenes, knowing that the more they gave back the faster they would be killed by their army, stayed the fight and held in the soldiers, with desire to carry them alive to Athens in case their spirits were so much broken and their courage abated by this misery as upon proclamation made they would be content to deliver up their arms. So they proclaimed that they should deliver up their arms and themselves to the Athenians to be disposed of as to them should seem good.

38. Upon hearing hereof the most of them threw down their bucklers and shook their hands above their heads, signifying their acceptation of what was proclaimed. Whereupon a truce was made and they came to treat, Cleon and Demosthenes of one side, and Styphon, the son of Pharax, on the other side. For of them that had command there, Epitadas, who was the first, was slain; and Hippagretes, who was chosen to succeed him, lay amongst the dead, though yet alive; and this man was the third to succeed in the command by the law in case the others should miscarry. Styphon and those that were with him said they would send over to the Lacedaemonians in the continent to know what they there would advise them to. But the Athenians, letting none go thence, called for heralds out of the continent; and the question having been twice or thrice asked, the last of the Lacedaemonians that came over from the continent brought them this answer: "The Lacedaemonians bid you take advice touching yourselves such as you shall think good, provided you do nothing dishonourably." Whereupon, having consulted, they yielded up themselves and their arms. And the Athenians attended them that day and the night following with a watch; but the next day, after they had set up their trophy in the island, they prepared to be gone and committed the prisoners to the custody of the captains of the galleys. And the Lacedaemonians sent over a herald and took up the bodies of their dead. The number of them that were slain and taken alive in the island was thus: There went over into the island in all four hundred and twenty men of arms; of these were sent away alive three hundred wanting eight; and the rest slain. Of those that lived, there were of the city itself of Sparta one hundred and twenty. Of the Athenians there died not many, for it was no standing fight.

39. The whole time of the siege of these men in the island, from the fight of the galleys to the fight in the island, was seventy-two days, of which for twenty days victual was allowed to be carried to them, that is to say, in the time that the ambassadors were away that went about the peace; in the rest, they were fed by such only as put in thither by stealth; and yet there was both corn and other food left in the island. For their captain Epitadas had distributed it more sparingly than he needed to have done. So the Athenians and the Peloponnesians departed from Pylus, and went home both of them with their armies. And the promise of Cleon, as senseless as is was, took effect; for within twenty days he brought home the men as he had undertaken.

40. Of all the accidents of this war, this same fell out the most contrary to the opinion of the Grecians. For they expected that the Lacedaemonians should never, neither by famine nor whatsoever other necessity, have been constrained to deliver up their arms, but have died with them in their hands, fighting as long as they had been able, and would not believe that those that yielded were like to those that were slain. And when one afterwards of the Athenian confederates asked one of the prisoners, by way of insulting, if they which were slain were valiant men, he answered that a spindle (meaning an arrow) deserved to be valued at a high rate if it could know what was a good man, signifying that the slain were such as the stones and arrows chanced to light on.

41. After the arrival of the men, the Athenians ordered that they should be kept in bonds till there should be made some agreement; and if before that the Peloponnesians should invade their territory, then to bring them forth and kill them. They took order also [in the same assembly] for the settling of the garrison at Pylus. And the Messenians of Naupactus, having sent thither such men of their own as were fittest for the purpose, as to their native country (for Pylus is in that country which belonged once to the Messenians), infested Laconia with robberies and did them much other mischief, as being of the same language. The Lacedaemonians, not having in times past been acquainted with robberies and such war as that, and because their Helotes ran over to the enemy, fearing also some

greater innovation in the country, took the matter much to heart; and though they would not be known of it to the Athenians, yet they sent ambassadors and endeavoured to get the restitution both of the fort of Pylus and of their men. But the Athenians aspired to greater matters; and the ambassadors, though they came often about it, yet were always sent away without effect. These were the proceedings at Pylus.

42. Presently after this, the same summer, the Athenians, with eighty galleys, two thousand men of arms of their own city, and two hundred horse in boats built for transportation of horses, made war upon the territory of Corinth. There went also with them Milesians, Andrians, and Carystians, of their confederates. The general of the whole army was Nicias, the son of Niceratus, with two others in commission with him. Betimes in a morning they put in at a place between Chersonesus and Rheitus on that shore above which standeth the hill Solygeius, whereon the Dorians in old time sat down to make war on the Corinthians in the city of Corinth, that were then Aeolians, and upon which there standeth now a village, called also Solygeia. From the shore where the galleys came in, this village is distant twenty furlongs, and the city of Corinth sixty, and the isthmus twenty. The Corinthians, having long before from Argos had intelligence that an army of the Athenians was coming against them, came all of them with their forces to the isthmus, save only such as dwelt without the isthmus and five hundred garrison soldiers absent in Ambracia and Leucadia; all the rest of military age came forth to attend the Athenians where they should put in. But when the Athenians had put to shore in the night unseen and that advertisement thereof was given them by signs put up into the air, they left the one half of their forces in Cenchreia lest the Athenians should go against Crommyon: and with the other half made haste to meet them.

43. Battus, one of their commanders (for there were two of them present at the battle), with one squadron went toward the village of Solygeia, being an open one, to defend it; and Lycophron with the rest charged the enemy. And first they gave the onset on the right wing of the Athenians, which was but newly landed before Chersonesus; and afterwards they

charged likewise the rest of the army. The battle was hot and at hand-strokes. And the right wing of the Athenians and Carystians (for of these consisted their utmost files) sustained the charge of the Corinthians; and with much ado drave them back. But as they retired they came up (for the place was all rising ground) to a dry wall, and from thence, being on the upper ground, threw down stones at them; and after having sung the Paean, came again close to them, whom when the Athenians abode, the battle was again at hand-strokes. But a certain band of Corinthians that came in to the aid of their own left wing put the right wing of the Athenians to flight and chased them to the sea-side; but then from their galleys they turned head again, both the Athenians and the Carystians. The other part of their army continued fighting on both sides, especially the right wing of the Corinthians, where Lycophron fought against the left wing of the Athenians; for they expected that the Athenians would attempt to go to Solygeia.

44. So they held each other to it a long time, neither side giving ground. But in the end (for that the Athenians had horsemen, which did them great service, seeing the other had none) the Corinthians were put to flight and retired to the hill, where they laid down their arms and descended no more, but there rested. In this retreat, the greatest part of their right wing was slain, and amongst others Lycophron, one of the generals. But the rest of the army being in this manner neither much urged, nor retiring in much haste, when they could do no other, made their retreat up the hill and there sat down. The Athenians, seeing them come no more down to battle, rifled the dead bodies of the enemy and took up their own and presently erected a trophy on the place. That half of the Corinthians that lay at Cenchreia to watch the Athenians, that they went not against Crommyon, saw not this battle for the hill Oneius; but when they saw the dust and so knew what was in hand, they went presently to their aid. So did also the old men of Corinth from the city when they understood how the matter had succeeded. The Athenians, when all these were coming upon them together, imagining them to have been the succours of the neighbouring cities of Peloponnesus, retired speedily to their galleys, carrying with them the booty and

the bodies of their dead, all save two, which, not finding, they left. Being aboard, they crossed over to the islands on the other side, and from thence sent a herald and fetched away those two dead bodies which they left behind. There were slain in this battle Corinthians, two hundred and twelve, and Athenians, somewhat under fifty.

45. The Athenians, putting off from the islands, sailed the same day to Crommyon in the territory of Corinth, distant from the city a hundred and twenty furlongs; where anchoring, they wasted the fields and stayed all that night. The next day they sailed along the shore, first to the territory of Epidaurus, whereinto they made some little incursion from their galleys, and then went to Methone, between Epidaurus and Troezen, and there took in the isthmus of Chersonesus with a wall, and placed a garrison in it, which afterwards exercised robberies in the territories of Troezen, Halias, and Epidaurus. And when they had fortified this place, they returned home with their fleet.

46. About the same time that these things were in doing, Eurymedon and Sophocles, after their departure from Pylus with the Athenian fleet towards Sicily, arriving at Corcyra, joined with those of the city, and made war upon those Corcyraeans which lay encamped upon the hill Istone, and which after the sedition had come over, and both made themselves masters of the field and much annoyed the city, and having assaulted their fortification, took it. But the men all in one troop escaped to a certain high ground and thence made their composition, which was this: that they should deliver up the strangers that aided them; and that they themselves, having rendered their arms, should stand to the judgment of the people of Athens. Hereupon the generals granted them truce and transported them to the island of Ptychia to be there in custody till the Athenians should send for them; with this condition, that if any one of them should be taken running away, then the truce to be broken for them all. But the patrons of the commons of Corcyra, fearing lest the Athenians would not kill them when they came thither, devise against them this plot. To some few of those in the island they secretly send their friends and instruct them to say, as if forsooth it were for good will, that it was their best course with all speed to get away;

and withal, to offer to provide them of a boat; for that the Athenian commanders intended verily to deliver them to the Corcyraean people.

47. When they were persuaded to do so and that a boat was treacherously prepared, as they rowed away they were taken; and the truce being now broken, were all given up into the hands of the Corcyraeans. It did much further this plot, that to make the pretext seem more serious and the agents in it less fearful, the Athenian generals gave out that they were nothing pleased that the men should be carried home by others, whilst they themselves were to go into Sicily, and the honour of it be ascribed to those that should convoy them. The Corcyraeans, having received them into their hands, imprisoned them in a certain edifice, from whence afterwards they took them out by twenty at a time and made them pass through a lane of men of arms, bound together and receiving strokes and thrusts from those on either side, according as any one espied his enemy. And to hasten the pace of those that went slowliest on, others were set to follow them with whips.

48. They had taken out of the room in this manner and slain to the number of threescore before they that remained knew it, who thought they were but removed and carried to some other place. But when they knew the truth, some or other having told them, they then cried out to the Athenians and said that if they would themselves kill them they should do it, and refused any more to go out of the room; nor would suffer, they said, as long as they were able, any man to come in. But neither had the Corcyraeans any purpose to force entrance by the door; but getting up to the top of the house, uncovered the roof and threw tiles and shot arrows at them. They in prison defended themselves as well as they could, but many also slew themselves with the arrows shot by the enemy, by thrusting them into their throats, and strangled themselves with the cords of certain beds that were in the room and with ropes made of their own garments rent in pieces. And having continued most part of the night (for night overtook them in the action) partly strangling themselves by all such means as they found, and partly shot at from above, they [all] perished. When day came, the Corcyraeans laid them one

across another in carts and carried them out of the city. And of their wives, as many as were taken in the fortification, they made bondwomen. In this manner were the Corcyraeans that kept the hill brought to destruction by the commons. And thus ended this far-spread sedition for so much as concerned this present war; for of other seditions there remained nothing worth the relation. And the Athenians being arrived in Sicily, whither they were at first bound, prosecuted the war there together with the rest of their confederates of those parts.

49. In the end of this summer, the Athenians that lay at Naupactus went forth with an army and took the city of Anactorium, belonging to the Corinthians and lying at the mouth of the Ambracian gulf, by treason. And when they had put forth the Corinthians, the Acarnanians held it with a colony sent thither from all parts of their own nation. And so this summer ended.

50. The next winter, Aristides, the son of Archippus, one of the commanders of a fleet which the Athenians had sent out to gather tribute from their confederates, apprehended Artaphernes, a Persian, in the town of Eion upon the river Strymon, going from the king to Lacedaemon. When he was brought to Athens, the Athenians translated his letters out of the Assyrian language * into Greek and read them; wherein, amongst many other things that were written to the Lacedaemonians, the principal was this: that he knew not what they meant, for many ambassadors came, but they spake not the same thing; if therefore they had any thing to say certain, they should send somebody to him with this Persian. But Artaphernes they send afterwards away in a galley, with ambassadors of their own, to Ephesus. And there encountering the news that king Artaxerxes, the son of Xerxes, was lately dead (for about that time he died), they returned home.

51. The same winter also, the Chians demolished their new

---

* What the Greek says is "Assyrian *letters*," and this would seem to be right. Apparently the Persians used Assyrian characters for their language. Herodotus (iv.87) records that Darius erected two pillars on the Bosporus and wrote on them, one in Greek and the other in Assyrian characters, the names of the tribes that had accompanied him to Scythia.

wall by command of the Athenians, upon suspicion that they intended some innovation, notwithstanding they had given the Athenians their faith and the best security they could to the intent they should let them be as they were. Thus ended this winter, and the seventh year of this war written by Thucydides.

52. The next summer, in the very beginning, at a change in the moon the sun was eclipsed in part; and in the beginning of the same month happened an earthquake.

At this time the Mytilenaean and other Lesbian outlaws, most of them residing in the continent, with mercenary forces out of Peloponnesus and some which they levied where they were, seize on Rhoeteium, and for two thousand Phocaean staters render it again without doing them other harm. After this they came with their forces to Antander and took that city also by treason. They had likewise a design to set free the rest of the cities called Actaeae, which were in the occupation formerly of the Mytilenaeans, but subject to the Athenians; but above all the rest Antander, which when they had once gotten (for there they might easily build galleys, because there was store of timber, and Mount Ida was above their heads), they might issue from thence with other their preparation and infest Lesbos, which was near, and bring into their power the Aeolic towns in the continent. And this were those men preparing.

53. The Athenians the same summer, with sixty galleys, two thousand men of arms, and a few horsemen, taking with them also the Milesians and some other of their confederates, made war upon Cythera, under the conduct of Nicias, the son of Niceratus, Nicostratus, the son of Diotrephes, and Autocles, the son of Tolmaeus. This Cythera is an island upon the coast of Laconia, over against Malea. The inhabitants be Lacedaemonians, of the same that dwell about them. And every year there goeth over unto them from Sparta a magistrate called *Cytherodikes*. They likewise sent over men of arms from time to time to lie in the garrison there, and took much care of the place. For it was the place where their ships used to put in from Egypt and Libya, and by which Laconia was the less infested by thieves from the sea, being that way only subject to that mis-

chief. For the island lieth wholly out into the Sicilian and Cretic seas.

54. The Athenians, arriving with their army, with ten of their galleys and two thousand men of arms of the Milesians, took a town lying to the sea, called Scandeia; and with the rest of their forces, having landed in the parts of the island towards Malea, marched into the city itself of the Cythereans, lying likewise to the sea. The Cythereans they found standing all in arms prepared for them. And after the battle began, the Cythereans for a little while made resistance, but soon after turned their backs and fled into the higher part of the city, and afterwards compounded with Nicias and his fellow-commanders that the Athenians should determine of them whatsoever they thought good but death. Nicias had had some conference with certain of the Cythereans before, which was also a cause that those things which concerned the accord both now and afterwards were both the sooner and with the more favour dispatched. For the Athenians did but remove the Cythereans, and that also because they were Lacedaemonians, and because the island lay in that manner upon the coast of Laconia. After this composition, having as they went by received Scandeia, a town lying upon the haven, and put a guard upon the Cythereans, they sailed to Asine and most of the towns upon the sea-side. And going sometimes aland, and staying where they saw cause, wasted the country for about seven days together.

55. The Lacedaemonians, though they saw the Athenians had Cythera and expected withal that they would come to land in the same manner in their own territory, yet came not forth with their united forces to resist them; but distributed a number of men of arms into sundry parts of their territory to guard it wheresoever there was need; and were otherwise also exceedingly watchful, fearing lest some innovation should happen in the state, as having received a very great and unexpected loss in the island, and the Athenians having gotten Pylus and Cythera, and as being on all sides encompassed with a busy and unavoidable war. In so much that contrary to their custom they ordained four hundred horsemen, and some archers. And

if ever they were fearful in matter of war, they were so now, because it was contrary to their own way to contend in a naval war, and against Athenians, who thought they lost whatsoever they not attempted. Withal, their so many misfortunes in so short a time, falling out so contrary to their own expectation, exceedingly affrighted them. And fearing lest some such calamity should again happen as they had received in the island, they durst the less to hazard battle, and thought that whatsoever they should go about would miscarry, because their minds, not used formerly to losses, could now warrant them nothing.

56. As the Athenians therefore wasted the maritime parts of the country and disbarked near any garrison, those of the garrison for the most part stirred not, both as knowing themselves singly to be too small a number, and as being in that manner dejected. Yet one garrison fought about Cortyta and Aphrodisia and frighted in the straggling rabble of light-armed soldiers; but when the men of arms had received them, it retired again with the loss of a few, whom they also rifled of their arms; and the Athenians, after they had erected a trophy, put off again and went to Cythera. From thence they sailed about to Epidaurus, called Limera, and having wasted some part of that territory, came to Thyrea, which is of the territory called Cynuria, but is nevertheless the middle border between Argeia and Laconia. The Lacedaemonians, possessing this city, gave the same for an habitation to the Aeginetae, after they were driven out of Aegina, both for the benefit they had received from them about the time of the earthquake and of the insurrection of the Helotes, and also for that, being subject to the Athenians, they had nevertheless gone ever the same way with the Lacedaemonians.

57. When the Athenians were coming towards them, the Aeginetae left the wall which they happened to be then building toward the sea-side and retired up into the city above where they dwelt, and which was not above ten furlongs from the sea. There was also with them one of those garrisons which the Lacedaemonians had distributed into the several parts of the country; and these, though they helped them to build the fort below, yet would not now enter with them into the town, though the Aeginetae entreated them, apprehending danger in

being cooped up within the walls; and therefore retiring into the highest ground, lay still there, as finding themselves too weak to give them battle. In the meantime the Athenians came in, and marching up presently with their whole army, won Thyrea, and burnt it, and destroyed whatsoever was in it. The Aeginetae, as many as were not slain in the affray, they carried prisoners to Athens, amongst whom Tantalus also, the son of Patroclus, captain of such Lacedaemonians as were amongst them, was wounded and taken alive. They carried likewise with them some few men of Cythera, whom for safety's sake they thought good to remove into some other place. These therefore, the Athenians decreed, should be placed in the islands; and that the rest of the Cythereans at the tribute of four talents should inhabit their own territory; that the Aeginetae, as many as they had taken (out of former inveterate hatred), should be put to death; and that Tantalus should be put in bonds amongst those Lacedaemonians that were taken in the island.

58. In Sicily the same summer was concluded a cessation of arms, first between the Camarinaeans and the Geloans; but afterwards the rest of the Sicilians, assembling by their ambassadors out of every city at Gela, held a conference amongst themselves for making of a peace. Wherein, after many opinions delivered by men disagreeing and requiring satisfaction, every one as he thought himself prejudiced, Hermocrates, the son of Hermon, a Syracusian, who also prevailed with them the most, spake unto the assembly to this effect:

59. "Men of Sicily, I am neither of the least city nor of the most afflicted with war that am now to speak and to deliver the opinion which I take to conduce most to the common benefit of all Sicily. Touching war, how calamitous a thing it is, to what end should a man, particularising the evils thereof, make a long speech before men that already know it? For neither doth the not knowing of them necessitate any man to enter into war, nor the fear of them divert any man from it, when he thinks it will turn to his advantage. But rather it so falls out that the one thinks the gain greater than the danger; and the other prefers danger before present loss. But lest they should both the one and the other do it unseasonably, exhortations unto peace are profitable, and will be very much worth to us

if we will follow them at this present. For it was out of a desire that every city had to assure their own, both that we fell ourselves into the war, and also that we endeavour now, by reasoning the matter, to return to mutual amity. Which if it succeed not so well that we may depart satisfied every man with reason, we will be at wars again.

60. "Nevertheless you must know that this assembly, if we be wise, ought not to be only for the commodity of the cities in particular, but how to preserve Sicily in general, now sought to be subdued (at least in my opinion) by the Athenians. And you ought to think, that the Athenians are more urgent persuaders of the peace than any words of mine; who, having of all the Grecians the greatest power, lie here with a few galleys to observe our errors, and by a lawful title of alliance, handsomely to accommodate their natural hostility to their best advantage. For if we enter into a war and call in these men, who are apt enough to bring their army in uncalled, and if we weaken ourselves at our own charges and withal cut out for them the dominion here, it is likely, when they shall see us spent, they will sometime hereafter come upon us with a greater fleet and attempt to bring all these states into their subjection.

61. "Now, if we were wise, we ought rather to call in confederates and undergo dangers for the winning of somewhat that is none of ours than for the impairing of what we already have; and to believe that nothing so much destroys a city as sedition, and that Sicily, though we the inhabitants thereof be insidiated by the Athenians as one body, is nevertheless city against city in sedition within itself. In contemplation whereof, we ought, man with man and city with city, to return again into amity; and with one consent to endeavour the safety of all Sicily: and not to have this conceit, that though the Dorians be the Athenians' enemies, yet the Chalcideans are safe, as being of the race of the Ionians. For they invade not these divided races upon hatred of a side, but upon a covetous desire of those necessaries which we enjoy in common. And this they have proved themselves in their coming hither to aid the Chalcideans. For though they never received any aid by virtue of their league from the Chalcideans, yet have they on their part been more forward to help them than by the league they were bound

unto. Indeed, the Athenians, that covet and meditate these things, are to be pardoned. I blame not those that are willing to reign, but those that are most willing to be subject; for it is the nature of man everywhere to command such as give way and to be shy of such as assail. We are to blame that know this and do not provide accordingly and make it our first care of all to take good order against the common fear. Of which we should soon be delivered, if we would agree amongst ourselves (for the Athenians come not amongst us out of their own country, but from theirs here that have called them in); and so, not war by war, but all our quarrels shall be ended by peace without trouble; and those that have been called in, as they came with fair pretence to injure us, so shall they with fair reason be dismissed by us without their errand.

62. "And thus much for the profit that will be found by advising wisely concerning the Athenians. But when peace is confessed by all men to be the best of things, why should we not make it also in respect of ourselves? Or do you think, perhaps, if any of you possess a good thing or be pressed with an evil, that peace is not better than war, to remove the latter or preserve the former, to both; or that it hath not honours and eminence more free from danger, or whatsoever else one might discourse at large concerning war? Which things considered, you ought not to make light of my advice, but rather make use of it, every one to provide for his own safety. Now if some man be strongly conceited to go through with some design of his, be it by right or by violence, let him take heed that he fail not, so much the more to his grief as it is contrary to his hope, knowing that many men ere now, hunting after revenge on such as had done them injury, and others trusting, by some strength they have had, to take away another's right, have, the first sort, instead of being revenged been destroyed, and the other, instead of winning from others, left behind them what they had of their own. For revenge succeeds not according to justice, as that because an injury hath been done it should therefore prosper; nor is strength therefore sure because hopeful. It is the instability of fortune that is most predominant in things to come, which, though it be the most deceivable of all things, yet appears to be the most profitable.

For whilst every one fear it alike, we proceed against each other with the greater providence.

63. "Now therefore terrified doubly, both with the implicit fear of the uncertainty of events, and with the terror of the Athenians present, and taking these for hindrances sufficient to have made us come short of what we had severally conceived to effect, let us send away our enemies that hover over us and make an eternal peace amongst overselves, or if not that, then a truce at least for as long as may be, and put off our private quarrels to some other time. In sum, let us know this: that following my counsel, we shall every of us have our cities free; whereby being masters of ourselves, we shall be able to remunerate according to their merit such as do us good or harm; whereas rejecting it and following the counsel of others, our contention shall no more be how to be revenged, or at the best, [if it be], we must be forced to become friends to our greatest enemies and enemies to such as we ought not.

64. "For my part, as I said in the beginning, I bring to this the greatest city, and which is rather an assailant than assailed; and yet foreseeing these things, I hold it fit to come to an agreement, and not so to hurt our enemies as to hurt ourselves more. Nor yet through foolish spite will I look to be followed as absolute in my will and master of fortune, which I cannot command; but I will also give way where it is reason. And so I look the rest should do as well as I; and that of yourselves, and not forced to it by the enemy. For it is no dishonour to be overcome kinsmen of kinsmen, one Dorian of another Dorian, and one Chalcidean of another of his own race, or in sum, any one by another of us, being neighbours and cohabiters of the same region, encompassed by the sea, and all called by one name, Sicilians. Who, as I conceive, will both war when it happens, and again by common conferences make peace by our own selves. But when foreigners invade us, we shall, if wise, unite all of us to encounter them, inasmuch as being weakened singly, we are in danger universally. As for confederates, let us never hereafter call in any, nor arbitrators. For so shall Sicily attain these two benefits, to be rid of the Athenians and of domestic war for the present, and to be inhabited by our-

selves with liberty and less insidiated by others for the time to come."

65. Hermocrates having thus spoken, the Sicilians followed his advice and agreed amongst themselves that the war should cease, every one retaining what they then presently enjoyed; and that the Camarinaeans should have Morgantina, paying for the same unto the Syracusians a certain sum of money then assessed. They that were confederates with the Athenians, calling such of the Athenians unto them as were in authority, told them that they also were willing to compound and be comprehended in the same peace. And the Athenians approving it, they did so; and hereupon the Athenians departed out of Sicily. The people of Athens, when their generals came home, banished two, namely Pythodorus and Sophocles, and laid a fine upon the third, which was Eurymedon, as men that might have subdued the estates of Sicily, but had been bribed to return. So great was their fortune at that time that they thought nothing could cross them, but that they might have achieved both easy and hard enterprises with great and slender forces alike. The cause whereof was the unreasonable prosperity of most of their designs, subministering strength unto their hope.

66. The same summer the Megareans in the city of Megara, pinched both by the war of the Athenians, who invaded their territory with their whole forces every year twice, and by their own outlaws from Pegae, who in a sedition driven out by the commons grievously afflicted them with robberies, began to talk one to another how it was fit to call them home again and not to let their city by both these means to be ruined. The friends of those without, perceiving the rumour, they also, more openly now than before, required to have it brought to council. But the patrons of the commons, fearing that they with the commons, by reason of the miseries they were in, should not be able to carry it against the other side, made an offer to Hippocrates, the son of Ariphon, and Demosthenes, the son of Alcisthenes, commanders of the Athenian army, to deliver them the city, as esteeming that course less dangerous for themselves than the reduction of those whom they had before driven out. And they agreed that first the Athenians should possess

themselves of the long-walls (these were about eight furlongs in length, and reached from the city to Nisaea their haven), thereby to cut off the aid of the Peloponnesians in Nisaea, in which (the better to assure Megara to their side) there lay no other soldiers in garrison but they; and then afterwards, that these men would attempt to deliver them the city above, which would the more easily succeed if that were effected first.

67. The Athenians therefore, after all was done and said on both sides and everything ready, sailed away by night to Minoa, an island of the Megareans, with six hundred men of arms led by Hippocrates, and sat down in a certain pit, out of which bricks had been made for the walls, and which was not far off. But they that were with the other commander, Demosthenes, light-armed Plataeans and others called peripoli, lay in ambush at the temple of Mars, not so far off as the former. And none of the city perceived any thing of this, but only such as had peculiar care to know the passages of this same night. When it was almost day, the Megarean traitors did thus: They had been accustomed long, as men that went out for booty with leave of the magistrates, of whom they had obtained by good offices the opening of the gates, to carry out a little boat, such as wherein the watermen used an oar in either hand, and to convey it by night down the ditch to the sea-side in a cart, and in a cart to bring it back again and set it within the gates, to the end that the Athenians which lay in Minoa might not know where to watch for them, no boat being to be seen in the haven. At this time was that cart at the gates, which were opened according to custom as for the boat. And the Athenians seeing it (for so it was agreed on), arose from their ambush and ran with all speed to get in before the gates should be shut again, and to be there whilst the cart was yet in the gates and kept them open. And first those Plataeans and peripoli that were with Demosthenes ran in, in that same place where the trophy is now extant, and fighting presently within the gates (for those Peloponnesians that were nearest heard the stir), the Plataeans overcame those that resisted and made good the gates for the Athenian men of arms that were coming after.

68. After this the Athenian soldiers, as they entered, went up every one to the wall. And a few of the Peloponnesians

that were of the garrison, made head at first and fought and were some of them slain; but the most of them took their heels, fearing in the night both the enemy that charged them and also the traitors of the Megareans that fought against them, apprehending that all the Megareans in general had betrayed them. It chanced also that the Athenian herald of his own discretion made proclamation that if any Megarean would take part with the Athenians, he should come and lay down his arms. When the Peloponnesians heard this, they stayed no longer, but seriously believing that they jointly warred upon them, fled into Nisaea. As soon as it was day, the walls being now taken and the Megareans being in a tumult within the city, they that had treated with the Athenians, and with them the rest, as many as were conscious, said it was fit to have the gates opened and to go out and give the enemy battle. Now it was agreed on between them that when the gates were open, the Athenians should rush in, and that themselves would be easily known from the rest, to the end they might have no harm done them, for that they would besmear themselves with some ointment. And the opening of the gates would be for their greater safety, for the four thousand men of arms of Athens and six hundred horsemen, which according to the appointment were to come to them, having marched all night, were already arrived. When they had besmeared themselves and were now about the gates, one of those who were privy discovered the conspiracy to the rest that were not. These joining their strength came all together to the gates, denying that it was fit to go out to fight, for that neither in former times when they were stronger than now, durst they do so, or to put the city into so manifest danger, and said, that if they would not be satisfied, the battle should be thereright. Yet they discovered not that they knew of the practice, but only, as having given good advice, meant to maintain it. And they stayed at the gates, insomuch as the traitors could not perform what they intended.

69. The Athenian commanders, knowing some cross accident had happened and that they could not take the city by assault, fell to enclosing of Nisaea with a wall, which if they could take before aid came, they thought Megara would the sooner yield. Iron was quickly brought unto them from Athens, and masons,

and whatsoever else was necessary. And beginning at the wall they had won, when they had built cross over to the other side, from thence both ways they drew it on to the sea on either side Nisaea; and having distributed the work amongst the army, as well the wall as the ditch, they served themselves of the stones and bricks of the suburbs, and having felled trees and timber, they supplied what was defective with a strong palisade. The houses also themselves of the suburbs, when they had put on battlements, served them for a fortification. All that day they wrought; the next day about evening they had within very little finished. But then they that were in Nisaea, seeing themselves to want victual (for they had none but what came day by day from the city above), and without hope that the Peloponnesians could quickly come to relieve them, conceiving also that the Megareans were their enemies, compounded with the Athenians on these terms: to be dismissed every one at a certain ransom in money; to deliver up their arms; and the Lacedaemonians, both the captain and whosoever of them else was within, to be at discretion of the Athenians. Having thus agreed, they went out. And the Athenians, when they had broken off the long walls from the city of Megara and taken in Nisaea, prepared for what was further to be done.

70. Brasidas, the son of Tellus, a Lacedaemonian, happened at this time to be about Sicyon and Corinth, preparing of an army to go into Thrace. And when he heard of the taking of the long walls, fearing what might become of the Peloponnesians in Nisaea, and lest Megara should be won, sent unto the Boeotians, willing them to meet him speedily with their forces at Tripodiscus, a village of Megaris so called at the foot of the hill Geraneia; and he marched presently himself with two thousand seven hundred men of arms of Corinth, four hundred of Phlius, six hundred of Sicyon, and those of his own all that he had yet levied, thinking to have found Nisaea yet untaken. When he heard the contrary (for he set forth towards Tripodiscus in the night), with three hundred men chosen out of the whole army, before news should arrive of his coming, he came unseen of the Athenians that lay by the sea-side to the city of Megara, pretending in word, and intending also in good earnest if he could have done it, to attempt upon Nisaea,

but desiring to get into Megara to confirm it; and required to be let in, for that he was, he said, in hope to recover Nisaea.

71. But the Megarean factions, being afraid, one, lest he should bring in the outlaws and cast out them, the other, lest the commons out of this very fear should assault them, whereby the city, being at battle within itself and the Athenians lying in wait so near, would be lost, received him not, but resolved on both sides to sit still and attend the success. For both the one faction and the other expected that the Athenians and these that came to succour the city would join battle; and then they might with more safety, such as were the favoured side, turn unto them that had the victory. And Brasidas, not prevailing, went back to the rest of the army.

72. Betimes in the morning arrived the Boeotians, having also intended to come to the aid of Megara before Brasidas sent, as esteeming the danger to concern themselves, and were then with their whole forces come forward as far as Plataea. But when they had received also this message, they were a great deal the more encouraged and sent two thousand two hundred men of arms and two hundred horse to Brasidas, but went back with the greater part of their army. The whole army being now together of no less than six thousand men of arms, and the Athenian men of arms lying indeed in good order about Nisaea and the sea-side, but the light-armed straggling in the plains, the Boeotian horsemen came unexpectedly upon the light-armed soldiers, and drove them towards the sea; for in all this time till now, there had come no aid at all to the Megareans from any place. But when the Athenian horse went likewise out to encounter them, they fought, and there was a battle between the horsemen of either side that held long, wherein both sides claimed the victory. For the Athenians slew the general of the Boeotian horse and some few others and rifled them, having themselves been first chased by them to Nisaea; and having these dead bodies in their power they restored them upon truce and erected a trophy. Nevertheless, in respect of the whole action, neither side went off with assurance; but parting asunder, the Boeotians went to the army, and the Athenians to Nisaea.

73. After this, Brasidas with his army came down nearer to the sea and to the city of Megara, and having seized on a place

of advantage, set his army in battle array and stood still. For they thought the Athenians would be assailants, and knew the Megareans stood observing whether side should have the victory, and that it must needs fall out well for them both ways; first, because they should not be the assailant and voluntarily begin the battle and danger, since having showed themselves ready to fight, the victory must also justly be attributed to them without their labour; and next, it must fall out well in respect of the Megareans, for if they should not have come in sight, the matter had not been any longer in the power of fortune, but they had without all doubt been presently deprived of the city as men conquered; whereas now, if haply the Athenians declined battle likewise, they should obtain what they came for without stroke stricken; which also indeed came to pass. For the Megareans—when the Athenians went out and ordered their army without the long walls, but yet, because the enemy charged not, stood also still, their commanders likewise considering, that if they should begin the battle against a number greater than their own, after the greatest part of their enterprise was already achieved, the danger would be unequal; for if they should overcome, they could win but Megara, and if they were vanquished, must lose the best part of their men of arms; whereas the enemy, who out of the whole power and number that was present in the field did adventure but every one a part, would in all likelihood put it to the hazard; and so for a while affronted each other, and, neither doing any thing, withdrew again, the Athenians first into Nisaea, and afterwards the Peloponnesians to the place from whence they had set forth—then, I say, the Megareans, such as were the friends of the outlaws, taking heart because they saw the Athenians were unwilling to fight, set open the gates to Brasidas as victor, and to the rest of the captains of the several cities; and when they were in (those that had practised with the Athenians being all the while in a great fear), they went to council.

74. Afterwards Brasidas, having dismissed his confederates to their several cities, went himself to Corinth in pursuit of his former purpose to levy an army for Thrace. Now the Megareans that were in the city (when the Athenians also were gone home), all that had chief hand in the practice with

the Athenians, knowing themselves discovered, presently slipt away; but the rest, after they had conferred with the friends of the outlaws, recalled them from Pegae, upon great oaths administered unto them no more to remember former quarrels, but to give the city their best advice. These, when they came into office, took a view of the arms, and disposing bands of soldiers in divers quarters of the city, picked out of their enemies and of those that seemed most to have co-operated in the treason with the Athenians, about a hundred persons; and having constrained the people to give their sentence upon them openly, when they were condemned slew them, and established in the city the estate almost of an oligarchy. And this change of government, made by a few upon sedition, did nevertheless continue for a long time after.

75. The same summer, when Antandros was to be furnished by the Mytilenaeans as they intended, Demodicus and Aristides, captains of certain galleys set forth by the Athenians to fetch in tribute, being then about Hellespont (for Lamachus that was the third in that commission, was gone with ten galleys into Pontus), having notice of the preparation made in that place, and thinking it would be dangerous to have it happen there as it had done in Anaea over against Samos, in which the Samian outlaws having settled themselves, aided the Peloponnesians in matters of the sea by sending them steersmen, and both bred trouble within the city and entertained such as fled out of it, levied an army amongst the confederates, and marched to it; and having overcome in fight those that came out of Antandros against them, recovered the place again. And not long after, Lamachus that was gone into Pontus, as he lay at anchor in the river Calex in the territory of Heracleia, much rain having fallen above in the country and the stream of a land flood coming suddenly down, lost all his galleys and came himself and his army through the territory of the Bithynians (who are Thracians dwelling in Asia on the other side) to Chalcedon, a colony of the Megareans in the mouth of Pontus Euxinus, by land.

76. The same summer likewise Demosthenes, general of the Athenians, with forty galleys, presently after his departure out of Megaris, sailed to Naupactus. For certain men in the cities

thereabouts, desiring to change the form of the Boeotian government and to turn it into a democracy according to the government of Athens, practised with him and Hippocrates to betray unto him the estates of Boeotia, induced thereunto principally by Ptoeodorus, a Theban outlaw; and they ordered the design thus: Some had undertaken to deliver up Siphae (Siphae is a city of the territory of Thespiae, standing upon the seaside in the Crissaean gulf); and Chaeroneia, which was a town that paid duties to Orchomenus (called heretofore Orchomenus in Minyeia, but now Orchomenus in Boeotia), some others of Orchomenus were to surrender into their hands. And the Orchomenian outlaws had a principal hand in this and were hiring soldiers to that end out of Peloponnesus. This Chaeroneia is the utmost town of Boeotia towards Phanotis in the country of Phocis; and some Phoceans also dwelt in it. [On the other side], the Athenians were to seize on Delium, a place consecrated to Apollo in the territory of Tanagra, on the part toward Euboea. All this ought to have been done together upon a day appointed, to the end that the Boeotians might not oppose them with their forces united, but might be troubled every one to defend his own. And if the attempt succeeded, and that they once fortified Delium, they easily hoped, though no change followed in the state of the Boeotians for the present, yet being possessed of those places, and by that means continually fetching in prey out of the country, because there was for every one a place at hand to retire unto, that it could not stand long at a stay; but that the Athenians joining with such of them as rebelled, and the Boeotians not having their forces united, they might in time order the state to their own liking. Thus was the plot laid.

77. And Hippocrates himself, with the forces of the city, was ready when time should serve to march; but sent Demosthenes before with forty galleys to Naupactus, to the end that he should levy an army of Acarnanians and other their confederates in these quarters, and sail to Siphae to receive it by treason. And a day was set down betwixt them on which these things should have been done together. Demosthenes, when he arrived and found the Oeniades by compulsion of the rest of Acarnania entered into the Athenian confederation and had

himself raised all the confederates thereabouts, made war first upon Salynthius and the Agraeans, and having taken in other places thereabouts, stood ready, when the time should require, to go to Siphae.

78. About the same time of this summer, Brasidas, marching towards the cities upon Thrace with seventeen hundred men of arms, when he came to Heracleia in Trachinia, sent a messenger before him to his friends at Pharsalus, requiring them to be guides unto him and to his army. And when there were come unto him Panaerus and Dorus and Hippolochidas and Torylaus and Strophacus, who was the public host of the Chalcideans, all which met him at Melitia, a town of Achaia, he marched on. There were other of the Thessalians also that convoyed him; and from Larissa he was convoyed by Niconidas, a friend of Perdiccas. For it had been hard to pass Thessaly without a guide howsoever, but especially with an army. And to pass through a neighbour territory without leave is a thing that all Grecians alike are jealous of. Besides, that the people of Thessaly had ever borne good affection to the Athenians. Insomuch, as if by custom the government of that country had not been lordly rather than a commonwealth, he could never have gone on. For also now as he marched forward, there met him at the river Enipeus others, of a contrary mind to the former, that forbade him and told him that he did unjustly to go on without the common consent of all. But those that convoyed him answered that they would not bring him through against their wills, but that coming to them on a sudden, they conducted him as friends. And Brasidas himself said he came thither a friend both to the country and to them; and that he bore arms, not against them, but against the Athenians their enemies; and that he never knew of any enmity between the Thessalians and Lacedaemonians whereby they might not use one another's ground; and that even now he would not go on without their consent; for neither could he, but [only] entreated them not to stop him. When they heard this, they went their ways. And he, by the advice of his guides, before any greater number should unite to hinder him, marched on with all possible speed, staying nowhere by the way. And the same day he set forth from Melitia he reached Pharsalus and en-

camped by the river Apidanus; from thence he went to Phacium; from thence into Peraebia.* The Peraebians, though subject to the Thessalians, set him at Dion in the dominion of Perdiccas, a little city of the Macedonians situate at the foot of Olympus on the side towards Thessaly.

79. In this manner Brasidas ran through Thessaly before any there could put in readiness to stop him and came into the territory of the Chalcideans † and to Perdiccas. For Perdiccas and the Chalcideans, all that had revolted from the Athenians, when they saw the affairs of the Athenians prosper, had drawn this army out of Peloponnesus for fear; the Chalcideans, because they thought the Athenians would make war on them first, as having been also incited thereto by those cities amongst them that had not revolted; and Perdiccas, not that he was their open enemy, but because he feared the Athenians for ancient quarrels, but principally because he desired to subdue Arrhibaeus, king of the Lyncesteans. And the ill success which the Lacedaemonians in these times had was a cause that they obtained an army from them the more easily.

80. For the Athenians vexing Peloponnesus, and their particular territory Laconia most of all, they thought the best way to divert them was to send an army to the confederates of the Athenians, so to vex them again. And the rather because Perdiccas and the Chalcideans were content to maintain the army, having called it thither to help the Chalcideans in their revolt. And because also they desired a pretence to send away part of their Helotes,‡ for fear they should take the oppor-

* Hobbes for some reason omits the following sentence: "And there his Thessalian guides left him."

† This is what the Greeks called Chalcidice. It denotes the peninsula in the Aegean which had been originally colonized from Chalcis in Euboea. It is sometimes also called in Thucydides "the parts Thracewards," and Hobbes sometimes renders it "Thrace" though in fact the territory is not Thrace at all.

‡ *Helot* is the general name applied to the people who cultivated the ground for the Spartans. As the latter lived entirely in barracks till the age of thirty and even after that were closely attached to the army, the farming of their estates had to be done by others. These farm workers were serfs, but not slaves. They were bound to the land but could not be sold, and they were paid a proportion of produce from the land they worked. They were of various races, being

tunity of the present state of their affairs, the enemies lying now in Pylus, to innovate. For they did also this further, fearing the youth and multitude of their Helotes, for the Lacedaemonians had ever many ordinances concerning how to look to themselves against the Helotes. They caused proclamation to be made that as many of them as claimed the estimation to have done the Lacedaemonians best service in their wars should be made free; * feeling them in this manner and conceiving that, as they should every one out of pride deem himself worthy to be first made free, so they would soonest also rebel against them. And when they had thus preferred about two thousand, which also with crowns on their heads went in procession about the temples as to receive their liberty, they not long after made them away; and no man knew how they perished. And now at this time, with all their hearts, they sent away seven hundred men of arms more of the same men along with Brasidas. The rest of the army were mercenaries, hired by Brasidas out of Peloponnesus. [But] Brasidas himself the Lacedaemonians sent out, chiefly because it was his own desire;

81. notwithstanding the Chalcideans also longed to have him, as one esteemed also in Sparta every way an active man. And when he was out, he did the Lacedaemonians very great service. For by showing himself at that present just and moderate towards the cities, he caused the most of them to revolt; and some of them he also took by treason. Whereby it came to pass that if the Lacedaemonians pleased to come to composition (as also they did), they might have towns to render and receive reciprocally.† And also long after, after the Sicilian war, the virtue and wisdom which Brasidas showed now, to some known by experience, by others believed upon from report, was the principal cause that made the Athenian confederates affect the Lacedaemonians. For being the first that went out, and esteemed in all points for a worthy man, he left behind him an assured hope that the rest also were like him.

82. Being now come into Thrace, the Athenians upon notice

---

composed of the people who had owned the land when the Spartans conquered it.

* The Greek adds "should *separate themselves out* to be made free."

† The Greek adds "and also a relief for the Peloponnese from war."

thereof declared Perdiccas an enemy, as imputing to him this expedition, and reinforced the garrisons in the parts thereabouts.

83. Perdiccas with Brasidas and his army, together with his own forces, marched presently against Arrhibaeus, the son of Bromerus, king of the Lyncesteans, a people of Macedonia, confining on Perdiccas his dominion, both for a quarrel they had against him and also as desiring to subdue him. When he came with his army, and Brasidas with him, to the place where they were to have fallen in, Brasidas told him that he desired, before he made war, to draw Arrhibaeus by parley, if he could, to a league with the Lacedaemonians. For Arrhibaeus had also made some proffer by a herald to commit the matter to Brasidas' arbitrement. And the Chalcidean ambassadors, being present, gave him likewise advice not to thrust himself into danger in favour of Perdiccas,* to the end they might have him more prompt in their own affairs. Besides, the ministers of Perdiccas, when they were at Lacedaemon, had spoken there as if they had meant to bring [as] many of the places about him [as they could] into the Lacedaemonian league. So that Brasidas favoured Arrhibaeus for the public good of their own state. But Perdiccas said that he brought not Brasidas thither to be a judge of his controversies, but to destroy those enemies which he should show him; and that it will be an injury, seeing he pays the half of his army, for Brasidas to parley with Arrhibaeus. Nevertheless Brasidas, whether Perdiccas would or not, and though it made a quarrel, had conference with Arrhibaeus, by whom also he was induced to withdraw his army. But from that time forward Perdiccas, instead of half, paid but a third part of his army, as conceiving himself to have been injured.

84. The same summer, a little before the vintage, Brasidas, having joined to his own the forces of the Chalcideans, marched to Acanthus, a colony of the Andrians. And there arose sedition about receiving him between such as had joined with the Chalcideans in calling him thither and the common people. Nevertheless, for fear of their fruits, which were not yet gotten

---

* More literally the Greek is "not to remove all danger for Perdiccas."

in, the multitude was won by Brasidas to let him enter alone, and then, after he had said his mind, to advise what to do amongst themselves. And presenting himself before the multitude (for he was not uneloquent, though a Lacedaemonian), he spake to this effect:

85. "Men of Acanthus, the reason why the Lacedaemonians have sent me and this army abroad is to make good what we gave out in the beginning for the cause of our war against the Athenians, which was that we meant to make a war for the liberties of Greece. But if we be come late, as deceived by the war there in the opinion we had that we ourselves should soon have pulled the Athenians down without any danger of yours, no man hath reason therefore to blame us. For we are come as soon as occasion served, and with your help will do our best to bring them under. But I wonder why you shut me forth of your gates, and why I was not welcome. For we Lacedaemonians have undergone this great danger of passing many days' journey through the territory of strangers, and showed all possible zeal, because we imagined that we went to such confederates as before we came had us present in their hearts and were desirous of our coming. And therefore it were hard that you should now be otherwise minded and withstand your own and the rest of the Grecians' liberty, not only in that yourselves resist us, but also because others whom I go to will be the less willing to come in, making difficulty because you to whom I came first, having a flourishing city and being esteemed wise, have refused us. For which I shall have no sufficient excuse to plead, but must be thought either to pretend to set up liberty unjustly, or to come weak and without power to maintain you against the Athenians. And yet against this same army I now have, when I went to encounter the Athenians at Nisaea, though more in number they durst not hazard battle. Nor is it likely that the Athenians will send forth so great a number against you as they had in their fleet there at Nisaea.

86. "I come not hither to hurt, but to set free the Grecians; and I have the Lacedaemonian magistrates bound unto me by great oaths that whatsoever confederates shall be added to their side, at least by me, shall still enjoy their own laws; and that we shall not hold you as confederates to us brought in either by

force or fraud, but on the contrary, be confederates to you that are kept in servitude by the Athenians. And therefore I claim not only that you be not jealous of me (especially having given you so good assurance), or think me unable to defend you, but also that you declare yourselves boldly with me. And if any man be unwilling so to do through fear of some particular man, apprehending that I would put the city into the hands of a few, let him cast away that fear; for I came not to side, nor do I think I should bring you an assured liberty, if neglecting the ancient use here I should enthral either the multitude to the few, or the few to the multitude. For to be governed so were worse than the domination of a foreigner; and there would result from it to us Lacedaemonians not thanks for our labours, but instead of honour and glory, an imputation of those crimes for which we make war amongst the Athenians, and which would be more odious in us than in them that never pretended the virtue. For it is more dishonourable, at least to men in dignity, to amplify their estate by specious fraud than by open violence. For the latter assaileth with a certain right of power given us by fortune, but the other with the treachery of a wicked conscience.

87. "But besides the oath which they have sworn already, the greatest further assurance you can have is this: that our actions weighed with our words, you must needs believe that it is to our profit to do as I have told you. But if after these promises of mine you shall say you cannot, and yet, forasmuch as your affection is with us, will claim impunity for rejecting us, or shall say that this liberty I offer you seems to be accompanied with danger, and that it were well done to offer it to such as can receive it, but not to force it upon any, then will I call to witness the gods and heroes of this place that my counsel which you refuse was for your good, and will endeavour, by wasting of your territory, to compel you to it. Nor shall I think I do you therein any wrong, but have reason for it for two necessities: one, of the Lacedaemonians, lest whilst they have your affections and not your society, they should receive hurt from your contributions of money to the Athenians; another, of the Grecians, lest they should be hindered of their liberty by your example. For otherwise indeed we could not

justly do it; nor ought we Lacedaemonians to set any at liberty against their wills if it were not for some common good. We covet not dominion [over you]; but seeing we haste to make others lay down the same, we should do injury to the greater part, if bringing liberty to the other states in general we should tolerate you to cross us. Deliberate well of these things; strive to be the beginners of liberty in Greece, to get yourselves eternal glory, to preserve every man his private estate from damage, and to invest the whole city with a most honourable title."

88. Thus spake Brasidas. The Acanthians, after much said on either side, partly for that which Brasidas had effectually spoken and partly for fear of their fruits abroad, the most of them decreed to revolt from the Athenians, having given their votes in secret. And when they had made him take the same oath which the Lacedaemonian magistrates took when they sent him out, namely, that what confederates soever he should join to the Lacedaemonians should enjoy their own laws, they received his army into the city. And not long after revolted Stageirus, another colony of the Andrians. And these were the acts of this summer.

89. In the very beginning of the next winter, when the Boeotian cities should have been delivered to Hippocrates and Demosthenes, generals of the Athenians, and Demosthenes should have gone to Siphae, and Hippocrates to Delium; having mistaken the days on which they should have both set forward, Demosthenes went to Siphae first, and having with him the Acarnans and many confederates of those parts in his fleet, [yet] lost his labour. For the treason was detected by one Nicomachus, a Phocean of the town of Phanotis, who told it unto the Lacedaemonians, and they again unto the Boeotians. Whereby the Boeotians, concurring universally to relieve those places (for Hippocrates was not yet gone to trouble them in their own several territories), preoccupied both Siphae and Chaeroneia. And the conspirators, knowing the error, attempted in those cities no further.

90. But Hippocrates, having raised the whole power of the city of Athens, both citizens and others that dwelt amongst them and all strangers that were then there, arrived afterwards at Delium when the Boeotians were now returned from Siphae;

and there stayed and took, in Delium, a temple of Apollo, with a wall, in this manner: Round about the temple and the whole consecrated ground they drew a ditch; and out of the ditch, instead of a wall they cast up the earth; and having driven down piles on either side, they cast thereinto the matter of the vineyard about the temple, which to that purpose they cut down, together with the stones and bricks of the ruined buildings; and by all means heightened the fortification, and in such places as would give leave, erected turrets of wood upon the same. There was no edifice of the temple standing, for the cloister that had been was fallen down. They began the work the third day after they set forth from Athens and wrought all the same day and all the fourth and the fifth day till dinner. And then being most part of it finished, the camp came back from Delium about ten furlongs homewards. And the light-armed soldiers went most of them presently away; but the men of arms laid down their arms there and rested. Hippocrates stayed yet behind and took order about the garrison and about the finishing of the remainder of the fortification.

91. The Boeotians took the same time to assemble at Tanagra; and when all the forces were come in that from every city were expected, and when they understood that the Athenians drew homewards, though the rest of the Boeotian commanders, which were eleven, approved not giving battle, because they were not now in Boeotia (for the Athenians, when they laid down their arms,* were in the confines of Oropia); yet Pagondas, the son of Aioladas, being the Boeotian commander for Thebes, whose turn it was to have the leading of the army, was, together with Arianthidas, the son of Lysimachidas, of opinion to fight, and held it the best course to try the fortune of a battle; wherefore calling them unto him every company by itself, that they might not be all at once from their arms, he exhorted the Boeotians to march against the Athenians and to hazard battle, speaking in this manner:

92. "Men of Boeotia, it ought never to have so much as entered into the thought of any of us the commanders that, because we find not the Athenians now in Boeotia, it should therefore be unfit to give them battle. For they out of a border-

* This only means "when they encamped."

ing country have entered Boeotia and fortified in it with intent to waste it, and are indeed enemies in whatsoever ground we find them, or whencesoever they come doing the acts of hostility. But now if any man think it also unsafe, let him henceforth be of another opinion. For providence, in them that are invaded, endureth not such deliberation concerning their own as may be used by them who, retaining their own, out of desire to enlarge, voluntarily invade the estate of another. And it is the custom of this country of yours, when a foreign enemy comes against you, to fight with him both on your own and on your neighbour's ground alike; but much more you ought to do it against the Athenians when they be borderers. For liberty with all men is nothing else but to be a match for the cities that are their neighbours. With these, then, that attempt the subjugation not only of their neighbours, but of estates far from them, why should we not try the utmost of our fortune? We have for example the estate that the Euboeans over against us, and also the greatest part of the rest of Greece, do live in under them. And you must know that though others fight with their neighbours about the bounds of their territories, we, if we be vanquished, shall have but one bound amongst us all, so that we shall no more quarrel about limits. For if they enter, they will take all our several states into their own possession by force. So much more dangerous is the neighbourhood of the Athenians than of other people. And such as upon confidence in their strength invade their neighbours, as the Athenians now do, use to be bold in warring on those that sit still, defending themselves only in their own territories; whereas they be less urgent to those that are ready to meet them without their own limits, or [also] to begin the war when opportunity serveth. We have experience hereof in these same men. For after we had overcome them at Coroneia, at what time through our own sedition they held our country in subjection, we established a great security in Boeotia, which lasted till this present. Remembering which, we ought now, the elder sort to imitate our former acts there, and the younger sort, who are the children of those valiant fathers, to endeavour not to disgrace the virtue of their houses; but rather with confidence that the god, whose temple fortified they unlawfully dwell in, will be with us, the sacrifices we offered him appearing fair, to march against them, and let them see that though they may gain what they covet when they invade such as will not fight, yet men that have the generosity to hold their own in liberty by battle, and not invade the state of another unjustly, will never let them go away unfoughten."

93. Pagondas with this exhortation persuaded the Boeotians to march against the Athenians, and making them rise led them speedily on, for it was drawing towards night. And when he was near to their army, in a place from whence by the interposition of a hill they saw not each other, making a stand he put his army into order and prepared to give battle. When it was told Hippocrates, who was then at Delium, that the Boeotians were marching after them, he sends presently to the army, commanding them to be put in array. And not long after he came himself, having left some three hundred horse about Delium, both for a guard to the place if it should be assaulted, and withal to watch an opportunity to come upon the Boeotians when they were in fight. But for these, the Boeotians appointed some forces purposely to attend them. And when all was as it should be, they showed themselves from the top of the hill, where they sat down with their arms in the same order they were to fight in, being about seven thousand men of arms, of light-armed soldiers above ten thousand, a thousand horsemen, and five hundred targetiers. Their right wing consisting of the Thebans, and their partakers; * in the middle battle were the Haliartians, Coronaeans, Copaeans, and the rest that dwell about the lake; in the left were the Thespians, Tanagraeans, and Orchomenians. The horsemen and light-armed soldiers were placed on either wing. The Thebans were ordered by twenty-five in file; but the rest, every one as it fell out. This was the preparation and order of the Boeotians.

94. The Athenian men of arms, in number no fewer than the enemy, were ordered by eight in file throughout; their horse they placed on either wing. But for light-armed soldiers, armed as was fit, there were none; nor was there any in the city. Those that went out followed the camp for the most part without

* The Greek word is *symmoroi,* and the people designated are allies that stood in a certain constitutional relation to the Theban state.

arms, as being a general expedition both of citizens and strangers; and after they once began to make homeward, there stayed
few behind. When they were now in their order and ready to
join battle, Hippocrates, the general, came into the army of the
Athenians and encouraged them, speaking to this effect:

95. "Men of Athens, my exhortation shall be short, but with
valiant men it hath as much force as a longer, and is for a
remembrance rather than a command. Let no man think, because it is in the territory of another, that we therefore
precipitate ourselves into a great danger that did not concern
us. For in the territory of these men, you fight for your own.
If we get the victory, the Peloponnesians will never invade our
territories again, for want of the Boeotian horsemen. So that in
one battle you shall both gain this territory and free your own.
Therefore march on against the enemy, every one as becometh
the dignity both of his natural city, which he glorieth to be
chief of all Greece, and of his ancestors, who having overcome
these men at Oenophyta under the conduct of Myronides, were
in times past masters of all Boeotia."

96. Whiles Hippocrates was making this exhortation, and
had gone with it over half the army,* but [could proceed] no

---

* From this and certain other passages it is clear that the Greek
generals would deliver orations personally and frequently to their
armies and obviously when numbers such as the present were involved the speech would have to be made more than once so that all
soldiers should hear it. This detail is one of the many points which
indicate that Thucydides is not inventing speeches for dramatic purposes, unless we conclude that he is designedly deceiving us in his
record. Undoubtedly, however, in many if not all cases it was impossible for him to record the actual words of the speakers, which is what
he tells us himself in Book i, Chapter 22. But he almost certainly in
every case possessed notes or a few sentences reported to him which
carried the gist of the speaker's oration. This he would expand and
put into as forceful rhetorical periods as he could write. I take this
to be the meaning of i.22: "I have set it down as each of them [the
speakers] seemed to me to have spoken, saying the things that were
required by their several circumstances, sticking as closely as possible to the whole tenor of what was actually said." It is quite certain
on the basis of this passage and such passages as that commented on
in this note that Thucydides cannot record speeches where none were
made unless by such details as here mentioned he deliberately wished
to mislead us.

further, the Boeotians (for Pagondas likewise made but a short exhortation and had there sung the Paean) came down upon them from the hill. And the Athenians likewise went forward to meet them, [so fast that] they met together running. The utmost parts of both the armies never came to join, hindered both by one and the same cause; for certain currents of water kept them asunder. But the rest made sharp battle, standing close, and striving to put by each others' bucklers. The left wing of the Boeotians, to the very middle of the army, were overthrown by the Athenians, who in this part had to deal, amongst others, principally with the Thespians. For whilst they that were placed within the same wing gave back and were circled in by the Athenians in a narrow compass, those Thespians that were slain were hewed down in the very fight. Some also of the Athenians themselves, troubled with inclosing them, through ignorance slew one another. So that the Boeotians were overcome in this part and fled to the other part where they were yet in fight. But the right wing, wherein the Thebans stood, had the better of the Athenians, and by little and little forced them to give ground and followed upon them from the very first. It happened also that Pagondas, while the left wing of his army was in distress, sent two companies of horse secretly about the hill, whereby that wing of the Athenians which was victorious, apprehending upon their sudden appearing that they had been a fresh army, was put into affright; and the whole army of the Athenians, now doubly terrified by this accident and by the Thebans that continually won ground and brake their ranks, betook themselves to flight. Some fled toward Delium and the sea, and some towards Oropus; others toward the mountain Parnethus, and others other ways, as to each appeared hope of safety. The Boeotians, especially their horse and those Locrians that came in after the enemy was already defeated, followed killing them. But night surprising them, the multitude of them that fled was the easier saved. The next day those that were gotten to Oropus and Delium went thence by sea to Athens, having left a garrison in Delium, which place, notwithstanding this defeat, they yet retained.

97. The Boeotians, when they had erected their trophy, taken away their own dead, rifled those of the enemy, and left a

guard upon the place, returned back to Tanagra and there
entered into consultation for an assault to be made on Delium.
In the meantime, a herald sent from the Athenians to require
the bodies met with a herald by the way sent by the Boeotians,
which turned him back by telling him he could get nothing
done till himself was returned from the Athenians. This herald,
when he came before the Athenians, delivered unto them what
the Boeotians had given him in charge, namely, that they had
done unjustly to transgress the universal law of the Grecians,
being a constitution received by them all; that the invader of
another's country should abstain from all holy places in the
same; that the Athenians had fortified Delium and dwelt in it,
and done whatsoever else men use to do in places profane, and
had drawn that water to the common use, which was unlawful
for themselves to have touched, save only to wash their hands
for the sacrifice; that therefore the Boeotians, both in the behalf of the god and of themselves, invoking Apollo and all the
interested spirits, did warn them to be gone and to remove
their stuff out of the temple.

98. After the herald had said this, the Athenians sent a herald
of their own to the Boeotians, denying that either they had
done any wrong to the holy place already or would willingly
do any hurt to it hereafter; for neither did they at first enter
into it to such intent, but to requite the greater injuries which
had been done unto them; as for the law which the Grecians
have, it is no other but that they which have the dominion of
any territory, great or small, have ever the temples also, and
besides the accustomed rites, may superinduce what other they
can: for also the Boeotians, and most men else, all that having
driven out another nation possess their territory, did at first invade the temples of others and make them their own; that therefore, if they could win from them more of their land, they
would keep it, and for the part they were now in, they were in
it with a good will and would not out of it, as being their own;
that for the water, they meddled with it upon necessity; which
was not to be ascribed to insolence, but to this, that fighting
against the Boeotians that had invaded their territory first,
they were forced to use it; for whatsoever is forced by war or
danger hath in reason a kind of pardon even with the god

himself; for the altars, in cases of involuntary offences, are a
refuge, and they are said to violate laws that are evil without
constraint, not they that are a little bold upon occasion of distress; that the Boeotians themselves, who require restitution
of the holy places for a redemption of the dead, are more
irreligious by far than they, who, rather than let their temples
go, are content to go without that which were fit for them to
receive; and they bade him say plainly that they would not
depart out of the Boeotian territory, for that they were not now
in it, but in a territory which they had made their own by the
sword; and nevertheless, required truce, according to the ordinances of the country, for the fetching away of the dead.

99. To this the Boeotians answered that if the dead were in
Boeotia, they should quit the ground and take with them
whatsoever was theirs; but if the dead were in their own territory, the Athenians themselves knew best what to do. For
they thought that though Oropia, wherein the dead lay (for
the battle was fought in the border between Attica and Boeotia),
by subjection belonged to the Athenians, yet they could not
fetch them off by force; and for truce that the Athenians might
come safely on Athenian ground, they would give none, but
conceived it was a handsome answer to say that if they would
quit the ground, they should obtain whatsoever they required.
Which when the Athenian herald heard, he went his way without effect.

100. The Boeotians presently sent for darters and slingers
from [the towns on] the Melian gulf; and with these, and with
two thousand men of arms of Corinth, and with the Peloponnesian garrison that was put out of Nisaea, and with the
Megareans, all which arrived after the battle, they marched
forthwith to Delium and assaulted the wall. And when they had
attempted the same many other ways, at length they brought
to it an engine, wherewith they also took it, made in this
manner: Having slit in two a great mast, they made hollow
both the sides, and curiously set them together again in the
form of a pipe. At the end of it in chains they hung a cauldron;
and into the cauldron from the end of the mast they conveyed
a snout of iron, having with iron also armed a great part of the
rest of the wood. They carried it to the wall, being far off, in

carts, to that part where it was most made up with the matter of the vineyard and with wood. And when it was to, they applied a pair of great bellows to the end next themselves, and blew. The blast, passing narrowly through into the cauldron, in which were coals of fire, brimstone, and pitch, raised an exceeding great flame, and set the wall on fire, so that no man being able to stand any longer on it, but abandoning the same and betaking themselves to flight, the wall was by that means taken. Of the defendants, some were slain and two hundred taken prisoners; the rest of the number recovered their galleys and got home.

101. Delium thus taken on the seventeenth day after the battle, and the herald, which not long after was sent again about the fetching away of the dead, not knowing it, the Boeotians let him have them, and answered no more as they had formerly done. In the battle there died Boeotians few less than five hundred; the Athenians few less than a thousand, with Hippocrates the general; but of light-armed soldiers and such as carried the provisions of the army, a great number.

Not long after this battle, Demosthenes, that had been with his army at Siphae, seeing the treason succeeded not, having aboard his galleys his army of Acarnanians and Agraeans and four hundred men of arms of Athens, landed in Sicyonia. But before all his galleys came to shore, the Sicyonians, who went out to defend their territory, put to flight such as were already landed and chased them back to their galleys, having also slain some and taken some alive. And when they had erected a trophy, they gave truce to the Athenians for the fetching away of their dead. About the time that these things passed at Delium, died Sitalces, king of the Odrysians, overcome in battle in an expedition against the Triballians. And Seuthes, the son of Spardocus, his brother's son, succeeded him in the kingdom, both of the Odrysians and of the rest of Thrace as much as was before subject to Sitalces.

102. The same winter, Brasidas with the confederates in Thrace made war upon Amphipolis, a colony of the Athenians, situated on the river Strymon. The place whereon the city now standeth, Aristagoras of Miletus had formerly attempted to inhabit when he fled from king Darius, but was beaten away

by the Edonians. Two-and-thirty years after this, the Athenians assayed the same, and sent thither ten thousand of their own city, and of others as many as would go; and these were destroyed all by the Thracians at Drabescus. In the twenty-ninth year after, conducted by Agnon, the son of Nicias, the Athenians came again, and having driven out the Edonians, became founders of this place, formerly called the Nine-ways. His army lay then at Eion, a town of traffic by the seaside subject to the Athenians, at the mouth of the river Strymon, five-and-twenty furlongs from the city. Agnon named this city Amphipolis because it was surrounded by the river Strymon, that runs on either side it. When he had taken it in with a long wall from river to river, he put inhabitants into the place, being conspicuous round about both to the sea and land.

103. Against this city marched Brasidas with his army, dislodging from Arnae in Chalcidea. Being about twilight come as far as Aulon and Bromiscus, where the lake Bolbe entereth into the sea, he caused his army to sup, and then marched forward by night. The weather was foul, and a little it snowed, which also made him to march the rather, as desiring that none of Amphipolis, but only the traitors, should be aware of his coming. For there were both Argilians that dwelt in the same city (now Argilus is a colony of the Andrians), and others, that contrived this, induced thereunto some by Perdiccas and some by the Chalcideans. But above all the Argilians, being of a city near unto it, and ever suspected by the Athenians, and secret enemies to the place, as soon as opportunity was offered and Brasidas arrived (who had also long before dealt underhand with as many of them as dwelt in Amphipolis to betray it), both received him into their own city, and revolting from the Athenians, brought the army forward the same night as far as to the bridge of the river. The town stood not close to the river, nor was there a fort at the bridge then as there is now; but they kept it only with a small guard of soldiers. Having easily forced this guard, both in respect of the treason and of the weather, and of his own unexpected approach, he passed the bridge and was presently master of whatsoever the Amphipolitans had that dwelt without.

104. Having thus suddenly passed the bridge, and many of

those without being slain, and some fled into the city, the
Amphipolitans were in very great confusion at it; and the rather
because they were jealous one of another. And it is said that if
Brasidas had not sent out his army to take booty, but had
marched presently to the city, he had in all likelihood taken
it then. But so it was that he pitched there and fell upon those
without; and seeing nothing succeeded by those within, lay still
upon the place. But the contrary faction to the traitors being
superior in number, whereby the gates were not opened presently, both they and Eucles the general, who was then there for
the Athenians to keep the town, sent unto the other general,
Thucydides, the son of Olorus, the writer of this history, who
had charge in Thrace, and was now about Thasos (which is an
island and a colony of the Parians, distant from Amphipolis
about half a day's sail), requiring him to come and relieve
them. When he heard the news, he went thitherwards in all
haste with seven galleys, which chanced to be with him at that
time. His purpose principally was to prevent the yielding up of
Amphipolis; but if he should fail of that, then to possess himself of Eion [before Brasidas' coming].

105. Brasidas, in the meantime, fearing the aid of the galleys
to come from Thasos, and having also been informed that
Thucydides possessed mines of gold in the parts of Thrace
thereabouts, and was thereby of ability amongst the principal
men of the continent, hasted by all means to get Amphipolis
before he should arrive, lest otherwise at his coming the commons of Amphipolis, expecting that he would levy confederates
both from the sea-side and in Thrace, and relieve them, should
thereupon refuse to yield. And to that end offered them a
moderate composition, causing to be proclaimed that whosoever, Amphipolitan or Athenian, would, might continue to
dwell there and enjoy his own, with equal and like form of
government; and that he that would not, should have five days'
respite to be gone and carry away his goods.

106. When the commons heard this, their minds were turned;
and the rather, because the Athenians amongst them were but
few, and the most were a promiscuous multitude; and the kinsmen of those that were taken without flocked together within.
And in respect of their fear, they all thought the proclamation

reasonable; the Athenians thought it so because they were willing to go out, as apprehending their own danger to be greater than that of the rest, and withal, not expecting aid in haste; and the rest of the multitude, as being thereby both delivered of the danger, and withal to retain their city with the equal form of government. Insomuch that they which conspired with Brasidas now openly justified the offer to be reasonable; and seeing the minds of the commons were now turned and that they gave ear no more to the words of the Athenian general, they compounded, and upon the conditions proclaimed received him. Thus did these men deliver up the city. Thucydides with his galleys arrived in the evening of the same day at Eion.* Brasidas had already gotten Amphipolis, and wanted but a night of taking Eion also; for if these galleys had not come speedily to relieve it, by next morning it had been had.

107. After this Thucydides assured Eion, so as it should be safe both for the present, though Brasidas should assault it, and for the future; and took into it such as, according to the proclamation made, came down from Amphipolis. Brasidas with many boats came suddenly down the river to Eion and attempted to seize on the point of the ground lying out from the wall into the sea, and thereby to command the mouth of the river; he assayed also the same at the same time by land, and was in both beaten off; but Amphipolis he furnished with all things necessary. Then revolted to him Myrcinus, a city of the Edonians, Pittacus, the king of the Edonians, being slain by the sons of Goaxis and by Braures his own wife. And not long after Gapselus also, and Oesyme, colonies of the Thasians. Perdiccas also, after the taking of these places, came to him and helped him in assuring of the same.

108. After Amphipolis was taken, the Athenians were brought into great fear, especially for that it was a city that yielded them much profit, both in timber which is sent them for the building of galleys and in revenue of money, and because also, though the Lacedaemonians had a passage open to come against

* This is a very impersonal statement of Thucydides' great failure as a military commander. As he records later, he was disgraced for his failure to save Amphipolis and was banished from Athens.

their confederates, the Thessalians convoying them, as far as to Strymon, yet if they had not gotten that bridge, the river being upwards nothing but a vast fen, and towards Eion well guarded with their galleys, they could have gone no further; which now they thought they might easily do, and therefore feared lest their confederates should revolt. For Brasidas both showed himself otherwise very moderate, and also gave out in speech that he was sent forth to recover the liberty of Greece. And the cities which were subject to the Athenians, hearing of the taking of Amphipolis, and what assurance he brought with him, and of his gentleness besides, were extremely desirous of innovation, and sent messengers privily to bid him draw near, every one striving who should first revolt. For they thought they might do it boldly, falsely estimating the power of the Athenians to be less than afterwards it appeared, and making a judgment of it according to [blind] wilfulness rather than safe forecast; it being the fashion of men, what they wish to be true to admit even upon an ungrounded hope, and what they wish not, with a magistral kind of arguing to reject. Withal, because the Athenians had lately received a blow from the Boeotians, and because Brasidas had said (not as was the truth, but as served best to allure them) that when he was at Nisaea the Athenians durst not fight with those forces of his alone, they grew confident thereon, and believed not that any man would come against them. But the greatest cause of all was that for the delight they took at this time to innovate, and for that they were to make trial of the Lacedaemonians, not till now angry, they were content by any means to put it to the hazard. Which being perceived, the Athenians sent garrison soldiers into those cities, as many as the shortness of the time and the season of winter would permit. And Brasidas sent unto Lacedaemon to demand greater forces, and in the meantime prepared to build galleys on the river Strymon. But the Lacedaemonians, partly through envy of the principal men, and partly because they more affected the redemption of their men taken in the island and the ending of the war, refused to furnish him.

109. The same winter the Megareans, having recovered their long walls holden by the Athenians, razed them to the very ground.

Brasidas, after the taking of Amphipolis, having with him the confederates, marched with his army into the territory called Acte. This Acte is that prominent territory which is disjoined from the continent by a ditch made by the king; and Athos, a high mountain in the same, determineth at the Aegean sea. Of the cities it hath, one is Sane, a colony of the Andrians, by the side of the said ditch on the part which looketh to the sea towards Euboea; the rest are Thyssus, Cleone, Acrothoi, Olophyxus, and Dion, and are inhabited by promiscuous barbarians of two languages. Some few there are also of the Chalcidean nation; but the most are Pelasgic, of those Tyrrhene nations that once inhabited Athens and Lemnos, and of the Bisaltic and Chrestonic nations, and Edonians, and dwell in small cities. The most of which yielded to Brasidas; but Sane and Dion held out, for which cause he stayed with his army and wasted their territories.

110. But seeing they would not hearken unto him, he led his army presently against Torone of Chalcidea, held by the Athenians. He was called in by the few, who were ready withal to deliver him the city; and arriving there a little before break of day, he sat down with his army at the temple of Castor and Pollux, distant about three furlongs from the city. So that to the rest of the city and to the Athenian garrison in it, his coming was unperceived. But the traitors, knowing he was to come (some few of them being also privily gone to him), attended his approach; and when they perceived he was come, they took in unto them seven men armed only with daggers (for of twenty appointed at first to that service, seven only had the courage to go in; and were led by Lysistratus of Olynthus); which, getting over the wall towards the main sea unseen, went up (for the town standeth on a hill's side) to the watch that kept the upper end of the town, and having slain the watchmen brake open the postern gate towards Canastraea.

111. Brasidas this while with the rest of his army lay still, and then coming a little forward, sent a hundred targetiers before, who, when the gates should be opened and sign agreed on be set up, should run in first. These men, expecting long and wondering at the matter, by little and little were at length come up close to the city. Those Toronaeans within, which

helped the men that entered to perform the enterprise, when the postern gate was broken open, and the gate leading to the market-place opened likewise by cutting asunder the bar, went first and fetched some of them about to the postern, to the end that they might suddenly affright such of the town as knew not the matter, both behind and on either side; and then they put up the sign appointed, which was fire, and received the rest of the targetiers by the gate that leadeth to the market-place.

112. Brasidas, when he saw the sign, made his army rise, and with a huge cry of all at once, to the great terror of those within, entered into the city running. Some went directly in by the gate, and some by certain squared timber-trees, which lay at the wall (which having been lately down was now again in building) for the drawing up of stone. Brasidas, therefore, with the greatest number, betook himself to the highest places of the city to make sure the winning of it by possessing the places of advantage. But the rest of the rabble ran dispersed here and there without difference.

113. When the town was taken, the most of the Toronaeans were much troubled, because they were not acquainted with the matter; but the conspirators, and such as were pleased with it, joined themselves presently with those that entered. The Athenians (of which there were about fifty men of arms asleep in the market-place), when they knew what had happened, fled all, except some few that were slain upon the place, some by land, some by water in two galleys that kept watch there, and saved themselves in Lecythus, which was a fort which they themselves held, cut off from the rest of the city to the seaward in a narrow isthmus. And thither also fled all such Toronaeans as were affected to them.

114. Being now day, and the city strongly possessed, Brasidas caused a proclamation to be made that those Toronaeans which were fled with the Athenians might come back, as many as would, to their own and inhabit there in security. To the Athenians he sent a herald, bidding them depart out of Lecythus under truce with all that they had, as a place that belonged to the Chalcideans. The Athenians denied to quit the place, but the truce they desired for one day for the taking up of their dead. And Brasidas granted it for two, in which two days he fortified

the buildings near; and so also did the Athenians theirs. He also called an assembly of the Toronaeans and spake unto them as he had done before to the Acanthians, adding that there was no just cause why either they that had practised to put the city into his hands should be the worse thought of or accounted traitors for it, seeing that they did it with no intent to bring the city into servitude, nor were hired thereunto with money, but for the benefit and liberty of the city; or that they which were not made acquainted with it should think that themselves were not to reap as much good by it as the others; for he came not to destroy either city or man, but had therefore made that proclamation touching those that fled with the Athenians because he thought them never the worse for that friendship, and made account when they had made trial of the Lacedaemonians, they would show as much good will also unto them, or rather more, inasmuch as they would behave themselves with more equity; and that their present fear was only upon want of trial. Withal he wished them to prepare themselves to be true confederates for the future, and from henceforward, to look to have their faults imputed; for, for what was past, he thought they had not done any wrong, but suffered it rather from other men that were too strong for them, and therefore were to be pardoned if they had in aught been against him.

115. When he had thus said and put them again into heart, the truce being expired, he made divers assaults upon Lecythus. The Athenians fought against them from the wall, though a bad one, and from the houses such as had battlements, and for the first day kept them off. But the next day, when the enemies were to bring to the wall a great engine, out of which they intended to cast fire upon their wooden fences, and that the army was now coming up to the place where they thought they might best apply the engine, and which was easiest to be assaulted, the Athenians, having upon the top of the building erected a turret of wood, and carried up many buckets of water, and many men being also gone up into it, the building overcharged with weight fell suddenly to the ground, and that with so huge a noise that though those which were near and saw it were grieved more than afraid, yet such as stood further off, especially the furthest of all, supposing the place to be in that

part already taken, fled as fast as they could towards the sea and went aboard their galleys.

116. Brasidas, when he perceived the battlements to be abandoned and saw what had happened, came on with his army and presently got the fort and slew all that he found within it. But the rest of the Athenians, which before abandoned the place, with their boats and galleys put themselves into Pallene.

There was in Lecythus a temple of Minerva. And when Brasidas was about to give the assault, he had made proclamation that whosoever first scaled the wall should have thirty minae of silver for a reward. Brasidas now, conceiving that the place was won by means not human, gave those thirty minae to the goddess to the use of the temple. And then pulling down Lecythus, he built it anew and consecrated unto her the whole place.

The rest of this winter he spent in assuring the places he had already gotten and in contriving the conquest of more. Which winter ending, ended the eighth year of this war.

117. The Lacedaemonians and Athenians, in the spring of the summer following, made a cessation of arms presently for a year, having reputed with themselves, the Athenians, that Brasidas should by this means cause no more of their cities to revolt, but that by this leisure they might prepare to secure them; and that if this suspension liked them, they might afterwards make some agreement for a longer time; the Lacedaemonians, that the Athenians fearing what they feared, would, upon the taste of this intermission of their miseries and weary life, be the willinger to compound, and with the restitution of their men to conclude a peace for a longer time. For they would fain have recovered their men while Brasidas' good fortune continued; and whilst, if they could not recover them, they might yet (Brasidas prospering and setting them equal with the Athenians) try it out upon even terms and get the victory. Whereupon a suspension of arms was concluded, comprehending both themselves and their confederates, in these words:

118. "Concerning the temple and oracle of Apollo Pythius, it seemeth good unto us that whosoever will may without fraud and without fear ask counsel thereat, according to the laws of

his country. The same also seemeth good to the Lacedaemonians and their confederates here present; and they promise moreover to send ambassadors to the Boeotians and Phoceans, and do their best to persuade them to the same. That concerning the treasure belonging to the god, we shall take care to find out those that have offended therein, both we and you, proceeding with right and equity, according to the laws of our several states; and that whosoever else will may do the same every one according to the law of his own country.

"If the Athenians will accord that each side shall keep within their own bounds, retaining what they now possess, the Lacedaemonians and the rest of the confederates touching the same think good thus:

"That the Lacedaemonians in Coryphasium stay within the mountains of Buphras and Tomeus, and the Athenians in Cythera without joining together in any league, either we with them or they with us. That those in Nisaea and Minoa pass not the highway, which from the gate of Megara near the temple of Nisus leadeth to the temple of Neptune, and so straightforward to the bridge that lies over into Minoa; that the Megareans pass not the same highway, nor into the island which the Athenians have taken, neither having commerce with other. That the Megareans keep what they now possess in Troezen and what they had before by agreement with the Athenians, and have free navigation, both upon the coasts of their own territories and their confederates.

"That the Lacedaemonians and their confederates shall pass the seas not in a long ship, but in any other boat rowed with oars of burden not exceeding five hundred talents.

"That the heralds and ambassadors that shall pass between both sides for the ending of the war or for trials of judgment may go and come without impeachment, with as many followers as they shall think good, both by sea and land.

"That during this time of truce, neither we nor you receive one another's fugitives, free nor bond.

"That you to us and we to you shall afford law according to the use of our several states, to the end our controversies may be decided judicially without war.

"This is thought good by the Lacedaemonians and their

confederates. But if you shall conceive any other articles more fair or of more equity than these, then shall you go and declare the same at Lacedaemon. For neither shall the Lacedaemonians nor their confederates refuse anything that you shall make appear to be just. But let those that go, go with full authority, even as you do now require it of us.—That this truce shall be for a year.

"The people decreed it. Acamantis was president of the assembly. Phaenippus the scribe. Niciades overseer, and Laches pronounced these words: 'With good fortune to the people of Athens, a suspension of arms is concluded, according as the Lacedaemonians and their confederates have agreed.' And they consented before the people that the suspension should continue for a year, beginning that same day, being the fourteenth of the month Elaphebolion, in which time the ambassadors and heralds, going from one side to the other, should treat about a final end of the wars; and that the commanders of the army and the presidents of the city calling an assembly, the Athenians should hold a council, touching the manner of embassage for ending of the war first; and the ambassadors there present should now immediately swear this truce for a year."

119. The same articles the Lacedaemonians propounded and the confederates agreed unto with the Athenians and their confederates in Lacedaemon on the twelfth day of the month Gerastion. The men that agreed upon these articles, and sacrificed, were these, viz.: Of the Lacedaemonians, Taurus, the son of Echetimidas, Athenaeus, the son of Pericleidas, and Philocharidas, the son of Eryxidaidas; of the Corinthians, Aeneas, the son of Ocytes, and Euphamidas, the son of Aristonymus; of the Sicyonians, Damotimos, the son of Naucrates, and Onasimus, the son of Megacles; of the Megareans, Nicasus, the son of Cecalus, and Menecrates, the son of Amphidorus; of the Epidaurians, Amphias the son of Eupaidas; of the Athenians, the generals [themselves], Nicostratus, the son of Diotrephes, Nicias, the son of Niceratus, and Autocles the son of Tolmaeus. This was the truce; and during the same they were continually in treaty about a longer peace.

120. About the same time, whilst they were going to and fro, Scione, a city in Pallene, revolted from the Athenians to

Brasidas. The Scionaeans say that they be Pallenians descended of those of Peloponnesus, and that their ancestors, passing the seas from Troy, were driven in by a tempest, which tossed the Achaeans up and down, and planted themselves in the place they now dwell in. Brasidas, upon their revolt, went over into Scione by night; and though he had a galley with him that went before, yet he himself followed aloof in a light-horseman. His reason was this: that if his light-horseman should be assaulted by some greater vessel, the galley would defend it; but if he met with a galley equal to his own, he made account that such a one would not assault his boat, but rather the galley, whereby he might in the meantime go through in safety. When he was over and had called the Scionaeans to assemble, he spake unto them as he had done before to them of Acanthus and Torone, adding that they of all the rest were most worthy to be commended, inasmuch as Pallene, being cut off in the isthmus by the Athenians that possess Potidaea, and being no other than islanders, did yet of their own accord come forth to meet their liberty, and stayed not through cowardliness till they must of necessity have been compelled to their own manifest good; which was an argument that they would valiantly undergo any other great matter to have their state ordered to their minds; and that he would verily hold them for most faithful friends to the Lacedaemonians, and also otherwise do them honour.

121. The Scionaens were erected with these words of his; and now every one alike encouraged, as well they that liked not what was done as those that liked it, entertained a purpose stoutly to undergo the war; and received Brasidas both otherwise honourably and crowned him with a crown of gold, in the name of the city, as the deliverer of Greece. And private persons honoured him with garlands and came to him as they use to do to a champion that hath won a prize. But he leaving there a small garrison for the present, came back, and not long after carried over a greater army, with design by the help of those of Scione to make an attempt upon Mende and Potidaea. For he thought the Athenians would send succours to the place, as to an island, and desired to prevent them. Withal, he had

in hand a practice with some within to have those cities be-trayed. So he attended, ready to undertake that enterprise.

122. But in the meantime came unto him in a galley Aris-tonymus for the Athenians and Athenaeus for the Lacedaemon-ians, that carried about the news of the truce. Whereupon he sent away his army again to Torone: and these men related unto Brasidas the articles of the agreement. The confederates of the Lacedaemonians in Thrace approved of what was done; and Aristonymus had in all other things satisfaction. But for the Scionaeans, whose revolt by computation of the days he had found to be after the making of the truce, he denied that they were comprehended therein. Brasidas said much in con-tradiction of this, and that the city revolted before the truce, and refused to render it. But when Aristonymus had sent to Athens to inform them of the matter, the Athenians were ready presently to have sent an army against Scione. The Lacedae-monians in the meantime sent ambassadors to the Athenians to tell them that they could not send an army against it with-out breach of the truce, and, upon Brasidas' word, challenged the city to belong unto them, offering themselves to the deci-sion of law. But the Athenians would by no means put the matter to judgment, but meant with all the speed they could make to send an army against it, being angry at the heart that it should come to this pass, that even islanders durst revolt and trust to the unprofitable help of the strength of the Lacedae-monians by land. Besides, touching [the time of] the revolt, the Athenians had more truth on their side than themselves alleged; for the revolt of the Scionaeans was after the truce two days. Whereupon, by the advice of Cleon, they made a decree to take them by force and to put them all to the sword. And, forbearing war in all places else, they prepared themselves only for that.

123. In the meantime revolted also Mende in Pallene, a colony of the Eretrians. These also Brasidas received into protection, holding it for no wrong, because they came in openly in time of truce; and somewhat there was also which he charged the Athenians with, about breach of the truce. For which cause the Mendaeans had also been the bolder, as sure of the inten-

tion of Brasidas, which they might guess at by Scione, inasmuch as he could not be gotten to deliver it. Withal, the few were they which had practised the revolt, who, being once about it, would by no means give it over, but, fearing lest they should be discovered, forced the multitude contrary to their own inclination to the same. The Athenians being hereof presently advertised, and much more angry now than before, made preparation to war upon both; and Brasidas expecting that they would send a fleet against them, received the women and children of the Scionaeans and Mendaeans into Olynthus in Chalcidea, and sent over thither five hundred Peloponnesian men of arms and three hundred Chalcidean targetiers, and for commander of them all Polydamidas. And those that were left in Scione and Mende joined in the administration of their affairs, as expecting to have the Athenian fleet immediately with them.

124. In the meantime Brasidas and Perdiccas, with joint forces, march into Lyncus against Arrhibaeus the second time. Perdiccas led with him the power of the Macedonians, his subjects, and such Grecian men of arms as dwelt among them. Brasidas, besides the Peloponnesians that were left him, led with him the Chalcideans, Acanthians, and the rest, according to the forces they could severally make. The whole number of the Grecian men of arms were about three thousand. The horsemen, both Macedonians and Chalcideans, somewhat less than a thousand; but the other rabble of barbarians was great. Being entered the territory of Arrhibaeus, and finding the Lyncesteans encamped in the field, they also sat down opposite to their camp. And the foot of each side being lodged upon a hill, and a plain lying betwixt them both, the horsemen ran down into the same, and a skirmish followed, first between the horse only of them both. But afterwards, the men of arms of the Lyncesteans coming down to aid their horse from the hill, and offering battle first, Brasidas and Perdiccas drew down their army likewise, and charging, put the Lyncesteans to flight; many of which being slain, the rest retired to the hill-top and lay still. After this they erected a trophy and stayed two or three days, expecting the Illyrians who were coming to Perdiccas upon hire; and Perdiccas meant afterwards to have gone on against the villages of Arrhibaeus one after another, and

to have sitten still there no longer. But Brasidas, having his thoughts on Mende, lest if the Athenians came thither before his return it should receive some blow, seeing withal that the Illyrians came not, had no liking to do so, but rather to retire.

125. Whilst they thus varied, word was brought that the Illyrians had betrayed Perdiccas and joined themselves with Arrhibaeus. So that now it was thought good to retire by them both, for fear of these who were a warlike people; but yet for the time when to march, there was nothing concluded, by reason of their variance. The next night, the Macedonians and multitude of barbarians (as it is usual with great armies to be terrified upon causes unknown) being suddenly affrighted, and supposing them to be many more in number than they were, and even now upon them, betook themselves to present flight and went home. And Perdiccas, who at first knew not of it, they constrained when he knew, before he had spoken with Brasidas (their camps being far asunder), to be gone also. Brasidas betimes in the morning, when he understood that the Macedonians were gone away without him, and that the Illyrians and Arrhibaeans were coming upon him, putting his men of arms into a square form and receiving the multitude of his light-armed into the middle, intended to retire likewise. The youngest men of his soldiers he appointed to run out upon the enemy when they charged the army anywhere [with shot]; and he himself, with three hundred chosen men marching in the rear, intended, as he retired, to sustain the foremost of the enemy, fighting if they came close up. But before the enemy approached, he encouraged his soldiers, as the shortness of time gave him leave, with words to this effect:

126. "Men of Peloponnesus, if I did not mistrust, in respect you are thus abandoned by the Macedonians and that the barbarians which come upon you are many, that you were afraid, I should not [at this time] instruct you and encourage you as I do. But now, against this desertion of your companions and the multitude of your enemies, I will endeavour with a short instruction and hortative to give you encouragement to the full. For to be good soldiers is unto you natural, not by the presence of any confederates, but by your own valour; and not to fear others for the number, seeing you are not come from a city

where the many bear rule over the few, but the few over the many; and have gotten this for power by no other means than by overcoming in fight. And as to these barbarians, whom through ignorance you fear, you may take notice, both by the former battles fought by us against them before, in favour of the Macedonians, and also by what I myself conjecture and have heard by others, that they have no great danger in them. For when any enemy whatsoever maketh show of strength, being indeed weak, the truth once known doth rather serve to embolden the other side; whereas, against such as have valour indeed, a man will be the boldest when he knoweth the least. These men here, to such as have not tried them, do indeed make terrible offers; for the sight of their number is fearful, the greatness of their cry intolerable, and the vain shaking of their weapons on high is not without signification of menacing. But they are not answerable to this when with such as stand them they come to blows. For fighting without order they will quit their place without shame if they be once pressed; and seeing it is with them honourable alike to fight or run away, their valours are never called in question; and a battle wherein every one may do as he lists, affords them a more handsome excuse to save themselves. But they trust rather in their standing out of danger and terrifying us afar off than in coming to hands with us; for else they would rather have taken that course than this. And you see manifestly that all that was before terrible in them is in effect little, and serves only to urge you to be going with their show and noise. Which if you sustain at their first coming on, and again withdraw yourselves still, as you shall have leisure, in your order and places, you shall not only come the sooner to a place of safety, but shall learn also against hereafter that such a rabble as this, to men prepared to endure their first charge, do but make a flourish of valour with threats from afar before the battle; but to such as give them ground, they are eager enough to seem courageous where they may do it safely."

127. When Brasidas had made his exhortation, he led away his army. And the barbarians, seeing it, pressed after them with great cries and tumult, as supposing he fled. But seeing that those who were appointed to run out upon them [did so, and]

met them which way soever they came on, and that Brasidas himself, with his chosen band, sustained them where they charged close and endured the first brunt beyond their expectation, and seeing also that afterwards continually when they charged, the other received them and fought, and when they ceased the other retired, then at length the greatest part of the barbarians forbore the Grecians that with Brasidas were in the open field, and leaving a part to follow them with shot, the rest ran with all speed after the Macedonians which were fled, of whom as many as they overtook they slew; and withal prepossessed the passage, which is a narrow one between two hills, giving entrance into the country of Arrhibaeus, knowing that there was no other passage by which Brasidas could get away. And when he was come to the very strait, they were going about him to have cut him off.

128. He, when he saw this, commanded the three hundred that were with him to run every man as fast as he could to one of the tops, which of them they could easliest get up to, and try if they could drive down those barbarians that were now going up to the same, before any greater number was above to hem them in. These accordingly fought with and overcame those barbarians upon the hill, and thereby the rest of the army marched the more easily to the top. For this beating of them from the vantage of the hill made the barbarians also afraid, so that they followed them no further, conceiving withal that they were now at the confines and already escaped through. Brasidas, having now gotten the hills and marching with more safety, came first the same day to Arnissa, of the dominion of Perdiccas. And the soldiers of themselves, being angry with the Macedonians for leaving them behind, whatsoever teams of oxen or fardles fallen from any man (as was likely to happen in a retreat made in fear and in the night) they lighted on by the way, the oxen they cut in pieces and took the fardles to themselves. And from this time did Perdiccas first esteem Brasidas as his enemy, and afterwards hated the Peloponnesians, not with ordinary hatred for the Athenians' sake, but being utterly fallen out with him about his own particular interest, sought means as soon as he could to compound with these and be disleagued from the other.

129. Brasidas, at his return out of Macedonia to Torone, found that the Athenians had already taken Mende; and therefore staying there (for he thought it impossible to pass over into Pallene and to recover Mende), he kept good watch upon Torone. For about the time that these things passed amongst the Lyncesteans, the Athenians, after all was in readiness, set sail for Mende and Scione with fifty galleys (whereof ten were of Chios) and a thousand men of arms of their own city, six hundred archers, a thousand Thracian mercenaries, and other targetiers of their own confederates thereabouts, under the conduct of Nicias, the son of Niceratus, and Nicostratus, the son of Diotrephes. These, launching from Potidaea with their galleys and putting in at the temple of Neptune, marched presently against the Mendaeans. The Mendaeans with their own forces, three hundred of Scione that came to aid them, and the aids of the Peloponnesians, in all seven hundred men of arms, and Polydamidas their commander, were encamped upon a strong hill without the city. Nicias, with a hundred and twenty light-armed soldiers of Methone and sixty chosen men of arms of Athens and all his archers, attempting to get up by a path that was in the hill's side, was wounded in the attempt and could not make his way by force. And Nicostratus, with all the rest of the army, going another way further about, as he climbed the hill, being hard of access, was quite disordered; and the whole army wanted little of being utterly discomfited. So for this day, seeing the Mendaeans and their confederates stood to it, the Athenians retired and pitched their camp; and at night the Mendaeans retired into the city.

130. The next day the Athenians, sailing about unto that part of the city which is towards Scione, seized on the suburbs, and all that day wasted their fields, no man coming forth to oppose them (for there was also sedition in the city); and the three hundred Scionaeans the night following went home again. The next day Nicias, with the one half of the army, marched to the confines and wasted the territory of the Scionaeans; and Nicostratus at the same time, with the other half, sat down against the city before the higher gates towards Potidaea. Polydamidas (for it fell out that the Mendaeans and their aids had their arms lying within the wall in this part) set his

men in order for the battle and encouraged the Mendaeans to
make a sally. But when one of the faction of the commons in
sedition said, to the contrary, that they would not go out and
that it was not necessary to fight, and was upon this contradiction by Polydamidas pulled and molested, the commons in passion presently took up their arms and made towards the Peloponnesians and such other with them as were of the contrary
faction; and falling upon them put them to flight, partly with
the suddenness of the charge and partly through the fear they
were in of the Athenians, to whom the gates were at the same
time opened. For they imagined that this insurrection was by
some appointment made between them. So they fled into the
citadel, as many as were not presently slain, which was also
in their own hands before. But the Athenians (for now was
Nicias also come back, and at the town-side) rushed into the
city with the whole army and rifled it, not as opened to them by
agreement, but as taken by force; and the captains had much
ado to keep them that they also killed not the men. After this,
they bade the Mendaeans use the same form of government
they had done before, and to give judgment upon those they
thought the principal authors of the revolt amongst themselves.
Those that were in the citadel they shut up with a wall reaching on both sides to the sea, and left a guard to defend it. And
having thus gotten Mende, they led their army against Scione.

131. The Scionaeans and the Peloponnesians, coming out
against them, possessed themselves of a strong hill before the
city, which if the enemy did not win, he should not be able
to enclose the city with a wall. The Athenians, having strongly
charged them [with shot] and beaten the defendants from it,
encamped upon the hill, and after they had set up their trophy,
prepared to build their wall about the city. Not long after,
whilst the Athenians were at work about this, those aids that
were besieged in the citadel of Mende, forcing the watch by
the sea-side, came by night, and escaping most of them through
the camp before Scione, put themselves into that city.

132. As they were enclosing of Scione, Perdiccas sent a herald
to the Athenian commanders and concluded a peace with the
Athenians, upon hatred to Brasidas about the retreat made out
of Lyncus, having then immediately begun to treat of the same.

For it happened also at this time that Ischagoras, a Lacedaemonian, was leading an army of foot unto Brasidas. And Perdiccas, partly because Nicias advised him, seeing the peace was made, to give some clear token that he would be firm, and partly because he himself desired not that the Peloponnesians should come any more into his territories, wrought with his hosts in Thessaly, having in that kind ever used the prime men, and so stopped the army and munition as they would not so much as try the Thessalians [whether they would let them pass or not]. Nevertheless Ischagoras and Ameinias and Aristeus themselves went on to Brasidas, as sent by the Lacedaemonians to view the state of affairs there, and also took with them from Sparta, contrary to the law, such men as were but in the beginning of their youth to make them governors of cities rather than commit the cities to the care of such as were there before. And Clearidas, the son of Cleonymus, they made governor of Amphipolis; and Epitelidas the son of Hegesander, governor of Torone.

133. The same summer, the Thebans demolished the walls of the Thespians, laying Atticism to their charge. And though they had ever meant to do it, yet now it was easier, because the flower of their youth was slain in the battle against the Athenians. The temple of Juno in Argos was also burnt down the same summer, by the negligence of Chrysis the priest, who, having set a burning torch by the garlands, fell asleep, insomuch as all was on fire and flamed out before she knew. Chrysis, the same night, for fear of the Argives, fled presently to Phlius; and they, according to the law formerly used, chose another priest in her room, called Phaeinis. Now, when Chrysis fled, was the eighth year of this war ended, and half of the ninth. Scione, in the very end of this summer, was quite enclosed; and the Athenians, having left a guard there, went home with the rest of their army.

134. The winter following nothing was done between the Athenians and Lacedaemonians because of the truce. But the Mantineans and the Tegeatae, with the confederates of both, fought a battle at Laodicium, in the territory of Orestis, wherein the victory was doubtful; for either side put to flight one wing of their enemies, both sides set up trophies, and both sides sent

of their spoils unto Delphi. Nevertheless, after many slain on either side, and equal battle which ended by the coming of night, the Tegeatae lodged all night in the place and erected their trophy then presently; whereas the Mantineans turned to Bucolion and set up their trophy afterwards.

135. The same winter ending and the spring now approaching, Brasidas made an attempt upon Potidaea. For coming by night, he applied his ladders and was thitherto undiscerned. He took the time to apply his ladders when the bell passed by, and before he that carried it to the next returned. Nevertheless, being discovered, he scaled not the wall, but presently again withdrew his army with speed, not staying till it was day. So ended this winter, and the ninth year of this war written by Thucydides.

THE FIFTH BOOK

1. The summer following, the truce for a year, which was
to last till the Pythian holidays,* expired. During this truce,
the Athenians removed the Delians out of Delos, because
[though they were consecrated, yet] for a certain crime committed of old they esteemed them polluted persons; because
also they thought there wanted this part to make perfect the
purgation of the island, in the purging whereof, as I declared
before, they thought they did well to take up the sepulchres

* Exercises dedicated to Apollo, and celebrated at Delphi (Hobbes).

311

of the dead. These Delians seated themselves afterwards, every
one as he came, in Adramyttium in Asia, a town given unto
them by Pharnaces.

2. After the truce was expired, Cleon prevailed with the
Athenians to be sent out with a fleet against the cities lying
upon Thrace. He had with him of Athenians twelve hundred
men of arms and three hundred horsemen, of confederates
more, and thirty galleys. And first arriving at Scione, which
was yet besieged, he took aboard some men of arms of those
that kept the siege and sailed into the haven of the Colophonians, not far distant from the city of Torone. And there, having heard by fugitives that Brasidas was not in Torone nor
those within sufficient to give him battle, he marched with
his army to the city and sent ten of his galleys about into the
haven. And first he came to the new wall, which Brasidas had
raised about the city to take in the suburbs, making a breach
in the old wall that the whole might be one city.

3. And Pasitelidas, a Lacedaemonian, captain of the town,
with the garrison there present came to the defence and fought
with the Athenians that assaulted it. But being oppressed, and
the galleys which were before sent about being by this time
come into the haven, Pasitelidas was afraid lest those galleys
should take the town, unfurnished of defendants, before he
could get back, and that the Athenians on the other side should
win the wall and he be intercepted between them both; and
thereupon abandoned the wall and ran back into the city. But
the Athenians that were in the galleys, having taken the town
before he came, and the land-army following in after him without resistance and entering the city by the breach of the old
wall, slew some of the Peloponnesians and Toronaeans on the
place; and some others, amongst whom was the captain Pasitelidas, they took alive. Brasidas was now coming with aid
towards Torone, but, advertised by the way that it was already
lost, went back again, being about forty furlongs short of preventing it. Cleon and the Athenians erected two trophies, one
at the haven, another at the wall. The women and children of
the Toronaeans they made slaves; but the men of Torone and
the Peloponnesians and such Chalcideans as were amongst them,
in all about seven hundred, they sent away prisoners to Athens.

The Peloponnesians were afterwards at the making of the peace dismissed; the rest were redeemed by the Olynthians by exchange of man for man.

About the same time the Boeotians took Panactum, a fort of the Athenians standing in their confines, by treason.

Cleon, after he had settled the garrison in Torone, went thence by sea about the mountain Athos [to make war] against Amphipolis.

4. About the same time Phaeax the son of Erasistratus, who with two others was sent ambassador into Italy and Sicily, departed from Athens with two galleys. For the Leontines, after the Athenians upon the making of the peace were gone out of Sicily, received many strangers into the freedom of their city; and the commons had a purpose also to have made division of the land. But the great men, perceiving it, called in the Syracusians and drave the commons out; and they wandered up and down, every one as he chanced; and the great men, upon conditions agreed on with the Syracusians, abandoning and deserting that city, went to dwell with the privilege of free citizens in Syracuse. After this again, some of them upon dislike relinquished Syracuse and seized on Phoceae, a certain part of the city of the Leontines, and upon Bricinniae, a castle in the Leontine territory. Thither also came unto them most of the commons that had before been driven out, and settling themselves, made war from those places of strength. Upon intelligence hereof the Athenians sent Phaeax thither to persuade their confederates there and, if they could, all the Sicilians jointly to make war upon the Syracusians, that were now beginning to grow great, to try if they might thereby preserve the common people of the Leontines. Phaeax arriving prevailed with the Camarinaeans and Agrigentines; but the business finding a stop at Gela, he went unto no more, as conceiving he should not be able to persuade them. So he returned through the cities of the Siculi unto Catana, having been at Bricinniae by the way and there encouraged them to hold out; and from Catana he set sail and departed.

5. In his voyage to Sicily, both going and coming, he dealt as he went by with sundry cities also of Italy to enter into friendship with the Athenians. He also lighted on those Locrians

which having dwelt once in Messana were afterwards driven
out again, being the same men which, after the peace in Sicily,
upon a sedition in Messana, wherein one of the factions called
in the Locrians, had been then sent to inhabit there, [and now
were sent away again]; for the Locrians held Messana for a
while. Phaeax, therefore, chancing to meet with these as they
were going to their own city, did them no hurt, because the
Locrians had been in speech with him about an agreement with
the Athenians. For when the Sicilians made a general peace,
these only of all the confederates refused to make any peace
at all with the Athenians. Nor indeed would they have done
it now but that they were constrained thereunto by the war
they had with the Itoneans and Melaeans, their own colonies
and borderers. And Phaeax after this returned to Athens.

6. Cleon, who was now gone from Torone and come about
to Amphipolis, making Eion the seat of the war, assaulted the
city of Stageirus, a colony of the Andrians, but could not take
it; but Galepsus, a colony of the Thasians, he took by assault.
And having sent ambassadors to Perdiccas to will him to come
to him with his forces, according to the league, and other ambassadors into Thrace unto Polles, king of the Odomantians,
to take up as many mercenary Thracians as he could, he lay
still in Eion to expect their coming. Brasidas upon notice hereof,
sat down over against him at Cerdylium. This is a place belonging to the Argilians, standing high and beyond the river, not
far from Amphipolis, and from whence he might discern all
that was about him. So that Cleon could not but be seen if he
should rise with his army to go against Amphipolis, which he
expected he would do, and that in contempt of his small number he would go up with the forces he had then present. Withal
he furnished himself with fifteen hundred mercenary Thracians,
and took unto him all his Edonians, both horsemen and targetiers. He had also of Myrcinians and Chalcideans a thousand
targetiers, besides them in Amphipolis. But for men of arms,
his whole number was at the most two thousand, and of Grecian
horsemen three hundred. With fifteen hundred of these came
Brasidas and sat down at Cerdylium; the rest stood ready ordered with Clearidas, their captain, within Amphipolis.

7. Cleon for a while lay still, but was afterwards forced

to do as was expected by Brasidas. For the soldiers being angry
with their stay there, and recounting with themselves what a
command his would be, and with what ignorance and cowardice against what skill and boldness of the other, and how
they came forth with him against their wills, he perceived their
muttering, and being unwilling to offend them with so long
a stay in one place, dislodged and led them forward. And he
took the same course there, which having succeeded well before at Pylus gave him cause to think himself to have some
judgment. For he thought not that any body would come forth
to give him battle, and gave out he went up principally to see
the place, and stayed for greater forces, not to secure him in
case he should be compelled to fight, but that he might therewith environ the city on all sides at once, and in that manner
take it by force. So he went up and set his army down on a
strong hill before Amphipolis, standing himself to view the fens
of the river Strymon and the situation of the city towards
Thrace; and thought he could have retired again at his pleasure,
without battle. For neither did any man appear upon the walls
nor come out of the gates, which were all fast shut. Insomuch
as he thought he had committed an error in coming without
engines, because he thought he might by such means have won
the city, as being without defendants.

8. Brasidas, as soon as he saw the Athenians remove, came
down also from Cerdylium and put himself into Amphipolis.
He would not suffer them to make any sally nor to face the
Athenians in order of battle, mistrusting his own forces, which
he thought inferior, not in number (for they were in a manner
equal) but in worth (for such Athenians as were there were
pure,* and the Lemnians and Imbrians which were amongst
them were of the very ablest); but prepared to set upon them
by a wile. For if he should have showed to the enemy both
his number and their armour, such as for the present they were
forced to use, he thought that thereby he should not so soon
get the victory as by keeping them out of sight and out of their
contempt till the very point. Wherefore choosing to himself a
hundred and fifty men of arms and committing the charge of
the rest to Clearidas, he resolved to set suddenly upon them

* I.e., were citizens.

before they should retire, as not expecting to take them so alone another time if their succours chanced to arrive. And when he had called his soldiers together to encourage them and to make known unto them his design, he said as followeth:

9. "Men of Peloponnesus, as for your country, how by valour it hath ever retained her liberty, and that being Dorians you are now to fight against Ionians, of whom you were ever wont to get the victory, let it suffice that I have touched it thus briefly. But in what manner I intend to charge, that I am now to inform you of, lest the venturing by few at once, and not all together, should seem to proceed from weakness and so dishearten you. I do conjecture that it was in contempt of us, and as not expecting to be fought withal, that the enemy both came up to this place, and that they have now betaken themselves carelessly and out of order to view the country. But he that best observing such errors in his enemies shall also to his strength give the onset, not always openly and in ranged battle, but as is best for his present advantage, shall for the most part attain his purpose. And these wiles carry with them the greatest glory of all, by which, deceiving most the enemy, a man doth most benefit his friends. Therefore whilst they are secure without preparation, and intend, for aught I see, to steal away rather than to stay, I say, in this their looseness of resolution, and before they put their minds in order, I for my part with those I have chosen will, if I can, before they get away fall in upon the midst of their army running. And you, Clearidas, afterwards, as soon as you shall see me to have charged and, as it is probable, to have put them into affright, take those that are with you, both Amphipolitans and all the rest of the confederates, and setting open the gates run out upon them, and with all possible speed come up to stroke of hand. For there is great hope this way to terrify them, seeing they which come after are ever of more terror to the enemy than those that are already present and in fight. And be valiant, as is likely you should that are a Spartan; and you, confederates, follow manfully, and believe that the parts of a good soldier are willingness, sense of shame, and obedience to his leaders; and that this day you shall either gain yourselves liberty by your valour, and to be called confederates of the Lacedaemon-

ians, or else not only to serve the Athenians yourselves, and at the best, if you be not led captives nor put to death, to be in greater servitude than before, but also to be the hinderers of the liberty of the rest of the Grecians. But be not you cowards, seeing how great a matter is at stake; and I, for my part, will make it appear that I am not more ready to persuade another than to put myself into action."

10. When Brasidas had thus said, he both prepared to go out himself, and also placed the rest that were with Clearidas before the gates called the Thracian gates to issue forth afterwards as was appointed. Now Brasidas having been in sight when he came down from Cerdylium and again when he sacrificed in the city by the temple of Pallas, which place might be seen from without, it was told Cleon [whilst Brasidas was ordering of his men] (for he was at this time gone off a little to look about him) that the whole army of the enemies was plainly to be discerned within the town, and that the feet of many men and horses, ready to come forth, might be discerned from under the gate. Hearing this, he came to the place; and when he saw it was true, being not minded to fight until his aids arrived, and yet making no other account but that his retreat would be discovered, he commanded at once to give the signal of retreat, and that as they went the left wing should march foremost, which was the only means they had to withdraw towards Eion. But when he thought they were long about it, causing the right wing to wheel about and lay open their disarmed parts to the enemy, he led away the army himself. Brasidas at the same time, having spied his opportunity and that the army of the Athenians removed, said to those about him and the rest: "These men stay not for us; it is apparent by the wagging of their spears and of their heads; for where such motion is, they use not to stay for the charge of the enemy; therefore open me some body the gates appointed and let us boldly and speedily sally forth upon them." Then he went out himself at the gate towards the trench, and which was the first gate of the long wall, which then was standing; and at high speed took the straight way, in which, as one passeth by the strongest part of the town, there standeth now a trophy, and charging upon the midst of the Athenian army, which was terrified both with their own dis-

array and the valour of the man, forced them to fly. And Clearidas, as was appointed, having issued out by the Thracian gates, was withal coming upon them. And it fell out that the Athenians, by this unexpected and sudden attempt, were on both sides in confusion; and the left wing which was next to Eion, and which indeed was marching away before, was immediately broken off from the rest of the army and fled. When that was gone, Brasidas coming up to the right wing, was there wounded. The Athenians saw not when he fell; and they that were near took him up and carried him off. The right wing stood longer to it: and though Cleon himself presently fled (as at first he intended not to stay) and was intercepted by a Myrcinian targetier and slain, yet his men of arms, casting themselves into a circle on the [top of a little] hill, twice or thrice resisted the charge of Clearidas and shrunk not at all, till begirt with the Myrcinian and Chalcidean horse and with the targetiers, they were put to flight by their darts. Thus the whole army of the Athenians, getting away with much ado over the hills and by several ways, all that were not slain upon the place or by the Chalcidean horse and targetiers, recovered Eion. The other side taking up Brasidas out of the battle, and having so long kept him alive, brought him yet breathing into the city; and he knew that his side had gotten the victory, but expired shortly after. When Clearidas with the rest of the army were returned from pursuit of the enemy, they rifled those that were slain and erected a trophy.

11. After this the confederates, following the corpse of Brasidas, all of them in their arms, buried him in the city, at the public charge, in the entrance of that which is now the market place. And the Amphipolitans afterwards, having taken in his monument with a wall, killed unto him as to a hero, honoured him with games and anniversary sacrifice, and attributed their colony unto him as to the founder, pulling down the edifices of Agnon, and defacing whatsoever monument might maintain the memory of his foundation. This they did both for that they esteemed Brasidas for their preserver and also because at this time, through fear of the Athenians, they courted the Lacedaemonians for a league. As for Agnon, because of their hostility with the Athenians, they thought it neither expedient for

them to give him honours, nor that they would be acceptable unto him if they did. The dead bodies they rendered to the Athenians, of whom there were slain about six hundred, and but seven of the other side, by reason that it was no set battle, but fought upon such an occasion and precedent affright. After the dead were taken up, the Athenians went home by sea; and Clearidas and those with him stayed to settle the estate of Amphipolis.

12. About the same time of the summer now ending, Ramphias, Autocharidas, and Epicydidas, Lacedaemonians, were leading a supply towards the parts upon Thrace of nine hundred men of arms; and when they were come to Heracleia in Trachinia, they stayed there to amend such things as they thought amiss. Whilst they stayed, this battle was fought; and the summer ended.

13. The next winter, they that were with Ramphias went presently forward as far as [the hill] Pierium in Thessaly. But the Thessalians forbidding them to go on, and Brasidas, to whom they were carrying this army, being dead, they returned homewards, conceiving that the opportunity now served not, both because the Athenians were upon this overthrow gone away and for that they themselves were unable to perform any of those designs which the other had intended. But the principal cause of their return was this: that they knew at their coming forth that the Lacedaemonians had their minds more set upon a peace than war.

14. Presently after the battle of Amphipolis and return of Ramphias out of Thessaly, it fell out that neither side did any act of war but were inclined rather to a peace; the Athenians for the blow they had received at Delium, and this other a little after at Amphipolis, and because they had no longer that confident hope in their strength on which they relied when formerly they refused the peace, as having conceived upon their present success that they should have had the upper hand; also they stood in fear of their own confederates, lest emboldened by these losses of theirs they should more and more revolt; and repented that they made not the peace after their happy success at Pylus, when occasion was offered to have done it honourably; and the Lacedaemonians on the other side did

desire peace because the war had not proceeded as they expected; for they had thought they should in a few years have warred down the power of Athens by wasting their territory; and because they were fallen into that calamity in the island, the like whereof had never happened unto Sparta before; because also their country was continually ravaged by those of Pylus and Cythera, and their Helotes continually fled to the enemy; and because they feared lest those which remained, trusting in them that were run away, should in this estate of theirs raise some innovation, as at other times before they had done. Withal it happened that the thirty years' peace with the Argives was now upon the point of expiring; and the Argives would not renew it without restitution made them of Cynuria; so that to war against the Argives and the Athenians, both at once, seemed impossible. They suspected also that some of the cities of Peloponnesus would revolt to the Argives, as indeed it came afterwards to pass.

15. These things considered, it was by both parts thought good to conclude a peace, but especially by the Lacedaemonians for the desire they had to recover their men taken in the island. For the Spartans that were amongst them were both of the prime men of the city and their kinsmen. And therefore they began to treat presently after they were taken; but the Athenians, by reason of their prosperity, would not lay down the war at that time on equal terms. But after their defeat at Delium, the Lacedaemonians, knowing they would be apter now to accept it, made that truce for a year, during which they were to meet and consult about a longer time.

16. But when also this other overthrow happened to the Athenians at Amphipolis, and that both Cleon and Brasidas were slain, the which on either side were most opposite to the peace, the one for that he had good success and honour in the war, the other because in quiet times his evil actions would more appear and his calumniations be the less believed, those two that in the two states aspired most to be chief, Pleistoanax, the son of Pausanias, and Nicias, the son of Niceratus, who in military charges had been the most fortunate of his time, did most of all other desire to have the peace go forward. Nicias because he was desirous, having hitherto never been overthrown, to

carry his good fortune through and to give both himself and the city rest from their troubles for the present, and for the future to leave a name that in all his time he had never made the commonwealth miscarry; which he thought might be done by standing out of danger and by putting himself as little as he might into the hands of fortune; and to stand out of danger is the benefit of peace. Pleistoanax had the same desire because of the imputation laid upon him about his return from exile by his enemies, that suggested unto the Lacedaemonians upon every loss they received that the same befell them for having, contrary to the law, repealed his banishment. For they charged him further that he and his brother Aristocles had suborned the prophetess of Delphi to answer the deputies of the Lacedaemonians, when they came thither, most commonly with this: that they should bring back the seed of the semigod, the son of Jupiter, out of a strange country into his own; and that if they did not, they should plough their land with a silver plough; * and so at length to have made the Lacedaemonians, nineteen years after, with such dances and sacrifices as they who were the first founders of Lacedaemon had ordained to be used at the enthroning of their kings, to fetch him home again; who lived in the meantime in exile in the mountain Lycaeum, in a house whereof the one half was part of the temple of Jupiter, for fear of the Lacedaemonians, as being suspected to have taken a bribe to withdraw his army out of Attica.

17. Being troubled with these imputations and considering with himself, there being no occasion of calamity in time of peace and the Lacedaemonians thereby recovering their men, that he also should cease to be obnoxious to the calumniations of his enemies whereas, in war, such as had charge could not but be quarrelled upon their losses—he was therefore forward to have the peace concluded.

And this winter they fell to treaty, and withal the Lacedaemonians braved them with a preparation already making against the spring, sending to the cities about for that purpose, as if they meant to fortify in Attica, to the end that the Athenians might give them the better ear. When after many meetings

* A proverbial expression for a time of farming when the crops were worth so much that the farmer "ploughed with a silver plough."

and many demands on either side, it was at last agreed that peace should be concluded, each part rendering what they had taken in the war, save that the Athenians should hold Nisaea (for when they [likewise] demanded Plataea and the Thebans answered that it was neither taken by force nor by treason, but rendered voluntarily, the Athenians said that they also had Nisaea in the same manner), the Lacedaemonians calling together their confederates, and all but the Boeotians, Corinthians, Eleians, and Megareans, (for these disliked it) giving their votes for the ending of the war, they concluded the peace, and confirmed it to the Athenians with sacrifice, and swore it, and the Athenians again unto them, upon these articles:

18. "The Athenians and Lacedaemonians and their confederates have made peace and sworn it, city by city, as followeth:

"Touching the public temples, it shall be lawful to whomsoever will to sacrifice in them and to have access unto them and to ask counsel of the oracles in the same and to send their deputies unto them, according to the custom of his country, securely both by sea and land.

"The whole place consecrate and temple of Apollo in Delphi, and Delphi itself, shall be governed by their own law, taxed by their own state, and judged by their own judges, both city and territory, according to the institution of the place.

"The peace shall endure between the Athenians with their confederates and the Lacedaemonians with their confederates for fifty years, both by sea and land, without fraud and without harm-doing.

"It shall not be lawful to bear arms with intention of hurt, neither for the Lacedaemonians and their confederates against the Athenians nor for the Athenians and their confederates against the Lacedaemonians by any art or machination whatsoever; if any controversy shall arise between them, the same shall be decided by law and by oath, in such manner as they shall agree on.

"The Lacedaemonians and their confederates shall render Amphipolis to the Athenians; the inhabitants of whatsoever city the Lacedaemonians shall render unto the Athenians shall be at liberty to go forth whither they will with bag and baggage.

"Those cities which paid the tribute taxed in the time of Aristides, continuing to pay it, shall be governed by their own laws. And now that the peace is concluded, it shall be unlawful for the Athenians or their confederates to bear arms against them or to do them any hurt as long as they shall pay the said tribute; the cities are these: Argilus, Stageirus, Acanthus, Scolus, Olynthus, Spartolus; and they shall be confederates of neither side, neither of the Lacedaemonians nor of the Athenians; but if the Athenians can persuade these cities unto it, then it shall be lawful for the Athenians to have them for confederates, having gotten their consent.

"The Mecybernaeans, Sanaeans, and Singaeans shall inhabit their own cities on the same conditions with the Olynthians and Acanthians.

"The Lacedaemonians and their confederates shall render Panactum unto the Athenians.

"And the Athenians shall render to the Lacedaemonians Coryphasium, Cythera, Methone, Pteleum, and Atalante; they shall likewise deliver whatsoever Lacedaemonians are in the prison of Athens or in any prison of what place soever in the Athenian dominion, and dismiss all the Peloponnesians besieged in Scione and all that Brasidas did there put in, and whatsoever confederates of the Lacedaemonians are in prison, either at Athens or in the Athenian state.

"And the Lacedaemonians and their confederates shall deliver whomsoever they have in their hands of the Athenians or their confederates in the same manner.

"Touching the Scionaeans, Toronaeans, and Sermylians, and whatsoever other city belonging to the Athenians, the Athenians shall do with them what they think fit.

"The Athenians shall take an oath to the Lacedaemonians and their confederates, city by city; and that oath shall be the greatest that in each city is in use. The thing that they shall swear shall be this: 'I stand to these articles and to this peace, truly and sincerely.' And the Lacedaemonians and their confederates shall take the same oath to the Athenians. This oath they shall on both sides every year renew and shall erect pillars [inscribed with this peace] at Olympia, Pythia, and in the Isthmus; at Athens, within the citadel; and at Lacedaemon, in the Amyclaeum.

"And if anything be on either side forgotten, or shall be thought fit upon good deliberation to be changed, it shall be lawful for them to do it, in such manner as the Lacedaemonians and Athenians shall think fit, jointly.

19. "This peace shall take beginning from the 24th of the month Artemisium, Pleistolas being ephore at Sparta, and the 15th of Elaphebolium, after the account of Athens, Alcaeus being archon.

"They that took the oath and sacrificed, were these. Of the Lacedaemonians: Pleistolas, Damagetus, Chionis, Metagenes, Acanthus, Daidus, Ischagoras, Philocaridas, Zeuxidas, Anthippus, Tellis, Alcinidas, Empedias, Menas, Laphilus. Of the Athenians these: Lampon, Isthmionicus, Nicias, Laches, Euthydemus, Procles, Pythodorus, Hagnon, Myrtilus, Thrasycles, Theagenes, Aristocrates, Iolcius, Timocrates, Leon, Lamachus, Demosthenes."

20. This peace was made in the very end of winter and the spring then beginning presently after the City Bacchanals and [full] ten years and some few days over after the first invasion of Attica and the beginning of this war. But now for the certainty hereof, let a man consider the times themselves and not trust to the account of the names of such as in the several places bare chief offices or for some honour to themselves had their names ascribed for marks to the actions foregoing. For it is not exactly known who was in the beginning of his office, or who in the midst, or how he was, when anything fell out. But if one reckon the same by summers and winters, according as they are written, he shall find by the two half years which make the whole, that this first war was of ten summers and as many winters continuance.

21. The Lacedaemonians (for it fell unto them by lot to begin the restitution) both dismissed presently those prisoners they had then in their hands and also sent ambassadors, Ischagoras, Menas, and Philocaridas, into the parts upon Thrace with command to Clearidas to deliver up Amphipolis to the Athe-

nians, and requiring the rest of their confederates there to accept of the peace in such manner as was for every of them accorded. But they would not do it because they thought it was not for their advantage; and Clearidas also, to gratify the Chalcideans, surrendered not the city, alleging that he could not do it whether they would or not. And coming away soon after with those ambassadors to Lacedaemon, both to purge himself, if he should be accused by those with Ischagoras for disobeying the state's command, and also to try if the peace might by any means be shaken; when he found it firm, he himself, being sent back by the Lacedaemonians with command principally to surrender the place, and if he could not do that, then to draw thence all the Peloponnesians that were in it, immediately took his journey.

22. But the confederates chanced to be present themselves in Lacedaemon; and the Lacedaemonians required such of them as formerly refused that they would accept the peace. But they, upon the same pretence on which they had rejected it before, said that unless it were more reasonable they would not accept it. And the Lacedaemonians, seeing they refused, dismissed them and by themselves entered with the Athenians into a league, because they imagined that the Argives would not renew their peace (because they had refused it before when Ampelidas and Lichas went to Argos, and held them for no dangerous enemies without the Athenians); and also conceived that by this means the rest of Peloponnesus would not stir; for if they could, they would turn to the Athenians. Wherefore the ambassadors of Athens being then present, and conference had, they agreed; and the oath and league was concluded on in the terms following:

23. "The Lacedaemonians shall be confederates with the Athenians for fifty years.

"If any enemy invade the territory of the Lacedaemonians and do the Lacedaemonians any harm, the Athenians shall aid the Lacedaemonians against them in the strongest manner they can possibly; but if the enemy, after he hath spoiled the country, shall be gone away, then that city shall be held as enemy both to the Lacedaemonians and to the Athenians and shall be warred upon by them both; and both cities shall again lay down the war jointly; and this is to be done justly, readily, and sincerely.

"And if any enemy shall invade the territories of the Athenians and do the Athenians any harm, then the Lacedaemonians shall aid the Athenians against them in the strongest manner they can possibly; but if the enemy, after he hath spoiled the country, shall be gone away, then shall that city be held for enemy both to the Lacedaemonians and to the Athenians and shall be warred upon by both; and both the cities shall again lay down the war together; and this to be done justly, readily, and sincerely.

"If their slaves shall rebel, the Athenians shall assist the Lacedaemonians with all their strength possible.

"These things shall be sworn unto by the same men on either side that swore the peace and shall be every year renewed by the Lacedaemonians [at their] coming to the Bacchanals at Athens and by the Athenians [at their] going to the Hyacinthian feast at Lacedaemon; and either side shall erect a pillar [inscribed with this league], one at Lacedaemon, near unto Apollo in the Amyclaeum, another at Athens, near Minerva in the citadel.

"If it shall seem good to the Lacedaemonians and Athenians to add or take away anything touching the league, it shall be lawful for them to do it jointly.

24. "Of the Lacedaemonians, took the oath these: Pleistoanax, Agis, Pleistolas, Damagetus, Chionis, Metagenes, Acanthus, Daidus, Ischagoras, Philocharidas, Zeuxidas, Anthippus, Alcinadas, Tellis, Empedias, Menas, Laphilus. Of the Athenians: Lampon, Isthmionicus, Laches, Nicias, Euthydemus, Procles, Pythodorus, Hagnon, Myrtilus, Thrasycles, Theagenes, Aristocrates, Iolcius, Timocrates, Leon, Lamachus, and Demosthenes."

This league was made not long after the peace; and the Athenians delivered to the Lacedaemonians the men they had taken in the island; and by this time began the summer of the eleventh year. And hitherto hath been written these ten years, which this first war continued without intermission.

25. After the peace and league made between the Lacedaemonians and Athenians after the ten years' war, Pleistolas being

ephore at Lacedaemon and Alcaeus archon of Athens, though there were peace to those that had accepted it, yet the Corinthians and some cities of Peloponnesus endeavoured to overthrow what was done, and presently arose another stir by the confederates against Lacedaemon. And the Lacedaemonians also after a while became suspect unto the Athenians for not performing somewhat agreed on in the articles. And for six years and ten months they abstained from entering into each other's territories with their arms; but the peace being weak, they did each other abroad what harm they could, and in the end were forced to dissolve the peace made after those ten years, and fell again into open war.

26. This also hath the same Thucydides of Athens written from point to point, by summers and winters, as everything came to pass, until such time as the Lacedaemonians and their confederates had made an end of the Athenian dominion and had taken their long walls and Pieraeus. To which time, from the beginning of the war, it is in all twenty-seven years.* As for the composition between, if any man shall think it not to be accounted with the war, he shall think amiss. For let him look into the actions that passed as they are distinctly set down and he shall find that that deserveth not to be taken for a peace, in which they neither rendered all nor accepted all, according to the articles. Besides, in the Mantinean and Epidaurian wars and in other actions, it was on both sides infringed; moreover, the confederates on the borders of Thrace continued in hostility as before; and the Boeotians had but a truce from one ten days to another. So that with the first ten years' war, and with this doubtful cessation, and the war that followed after it, a man shall find, counting by the times, that it came to just so many

* This indicates that Thucydides lived to the end of the war. We do not know how much longer he lived after. There is a story that he was executed by the Thirty Tyrants, the oligarchic government installed by the Lacedaemonians in Athens in 404–403. The History breaks off in Book viii, when dealing with the events following 411. Thucydides may have had notes for the progress of the war from then till the capture of Athens, but being busy with the revision and final draft of the rest of the work, and particularly Books i–iv, he was unable to give final shape to the last part and so did not leave it in form for publication.

years and some few days, and that those who built upon the prediction of the oracles have this number only to agree. And I remember yet that from the very beginning of this war and so on till the end it was uttered by many that it should be of thrice nine years' continuance. And for the time thereof I lived in my strength and applied my mind to gain an accurate knowledge of the same. It happened also that I was banished my country for twenty years, after my charge at Amphipolis; whereby being present at the affairs of both, and especially of the Lacedaemonians by reason of my exile, I could at leisure the better learn the truth of all that passed. The quarrels, therefore, and perturbations of the peace, after those ten years, and that which followed, according as from time to time the war was carried, I will now pursue.

27. After the concluding of the fifty years' peace and the league which followed, and when those ambassadors which were sent for out of the rest of Peloponnesus to accept the said peace were departed from Lacedaemon, the Corinthians (the rest going all to their own cities), turning first to Argos, entered into treaty with some of the Argive magistrates to this purpose: that the Lacedaemonians having made a peace and league with the Athenians, their hitherto mortal enemies, tending not to the benefit, but to the enslaving of Peloponnesus, it behoved them to consider of a course for the safety of the same, and to make a decree that any city of the Grecians that would, and were a free city, and admitted the like and equal trials of judgment with theirs, might make a league with the Argives for the one mutually to aid the other; and to assign them a few men, with absolute authority from the state, to treat with; and that it should not be motioned to the people, to the end that, if the multitude would not agree to it, it might be unknown that ever they had made such a motion; affirming that many would come into this confederacy upon hatred to the Lacedaemonians. And the Corinthians, when they had made this overture, went home.

28. These men of Argos having heard them and reported their proposition both to the magistrates and to the people, the Argives ordered the same accordingly and elected twelve men with whom it should be lawful for any Grecian to make the league that would, except the Lacedaemonians and Athe-

nians, with neither of which they were to enter into any league without the consent of the Argive people. And this the Argives did the more willingly admit, as well for that they saw the Lacedaemonians would make war upon them (for the truce between them was now upon expiring), as also because they hoped to have the principality of Peloponnesus.* For about this time Lacedaemon had but a bad report and was in contempt for the losses it had received. And the Argives in all points were in good estate, as not having concurred in the Attic war, but rather been at peace with both, and thereby gotten in their revenue. Thus the Argives received into league all such Grecians as came unto them.

29. First of all, therefore, came in the Mantineans and their confederates, which they did for fear of the Lacedaemonians. For a part of Arcadia, during the war of Athens, was come under the obedience of the Mantineans, over which they thought the Lacedaemonians, now they were at rest, would not permit them any longer to command; and therefore they willingly joined with the Argives, as being, they thought, a great city, ever enemy to the Lacedaemonians, and governed as their own by democracy. When the Mantineans had revolted, the rest of Peloponnesus began also to mutter amongst themselves that it was fit for them to do the like; conceiving that there was somewhat in it more than they knew that made the Mantineans to turn; and were also angry with the Lacedaemonians, amongst many other causes, for that it was written in

* I.e., to obtain the leadership (hegemony) of all the various states in the Peloponnese. The Spartans were at the head of the Peloponnesian confederacy and therefore held at this time the hegemonia. The confederation was loosely organized; Sparta had no right to interfere in the internal affairs of the several states, but there was a kind of gentleman's agreement that external (i.e., outside the Peloponnese) affairs should only be settled by consultation with Sparta. In addition it seems as though, in fact, the Spartans did apply pressure unofficially to secure that only oligarchic governments friendly to Sparta held power in the Peloponnesian states. The confederacy was certainly never as tightly organized as that of Delos with Athens at its head, nor did the Lacedaemonians exact any official yearly tributes. But the bitter words of the Athenian envoys at Sparta at the beginning of the war comparing the two as actual and potential empires would seem to have been justified.

the articles of the Attic peace that it should be lawful to add unto or take away from the same, whatsoever should seem good to the two cities of the Lacedaemonians and the Athenians. For this was the article that the most troubled the Peloponnesians and put them into a jealousy that the Lacedaemonians might have a purpose, joining with the Athenians, to bring them into subjection; for in justice, the power of changing the articles ought to have been ascribed to all the confederates in general. Whereupon, many, fearing such an intention, applied themselves to the Argives, every one severally striving to come into their league.

30. The Lacedaemonians, perceiving this stir to begin in Peloponnesus, and that the Corinthians were both the contrivers of it and entered themselves also into the league with Argos, sent ambassadors unto Corinth with intention to prevent the sequel of it: and accused them both for the whole design and for their own revolt in particular, which they intended to make from them to the league of the Argives, saying that they should therein infringe their oath and that they had already done unjustly to refuse the peace made with the Athenians; forasmuch as it is an article of their league * that what the major part of the confederates should conclude, unless it were hindered by some god or hero, the same was to stand good. But the Corinthians, those confederates which had refused the peace as well as they being now at Corinth (for they had sent for them before), in their answer to the Lacedaemonians did not openly allege the wrongs they had received; as that the Athenians had not restored Solium nor Anactorium nor anything else they had in this war lost; but pretended not to betray those of Thrace, for that they had in particular taken an oath to them, both when together with Potidaea they first revolted and also another afterwards. And therefore, they said, they did not break the oath of their league by rejecting the peace with Athens. For having sworn unto them by the gods, they should in betraying them offend the gods. And whereas it is said "unless some god or hero hinder it," this appeareth to be a divine hindrance. Thus they answered for their old oath. Then, for their league with the Argives, they gave this answer: that when they had

---

* I.e., the Peloponnesian League.

advised with their friends, they would do afterwards what should be just. And so the ambassadors of Lacedaemon went home. At the same time were present also in Corinth the ambassadors of Argos to invite the Corinthians to their league, and that without delay. But the Corinthians appointed them to come again at their next sitting.

31. Presently after this came unto them an ambassage also from Eleians; and first they made a league with the Corinthians, and going thence to Argos, made a league with the Argives, according to the declaration before mentioned. The Eleians had a quarrel with the Lacedaemonians concerning Lepreum. For the Lepreates having heretofore warred on certain of the Arcadians, and for their aid called the Eleians into their confederacy with condition to give the moiety of the land [to be won from them], when the war was ended, the Eleians gave unto the Lepreates the whole land to be enjoyed by themselves, with an imposition thereon of a talent to be paid to Jupiter Olympian, which they continued to pay till the beginning of the Athenian war. But afterwards upon pretense of that war giving over the payment, the Eleians would have forced them to it again. The Lepreates for help having recourse to the Lacedaemonians, and the cause being referred to their decision, the Eleians afterwards, upon suspicion that the Lacedaemonians would not do them right, renounced the reference and wasted the territory of the Lepreates. The Lacedaemonians nevertheless gave sentence that the Lepreates should be at liberty to pay it or not, and that the Eleians did the injury; and because the Eleians had not stood to the reference, the Lacedaemonians put into Lepreum a garrison of men at arms. The Eleians, taking this as if the Lacedaemonians had received their revolted city, and producing the article of their league "that what every one possessed when they entered into the Attic war, the same they should possess when they gave it over," revolted to the Argives as wronged and entered league with them as is before related. After these came presently into the Argive league the Corinthians and the Chalcideans upon Thrace. The Boeotians also and Megareans threatened as much; but because they thought the Argive democracy would not be so commodious for them, who were governed according to the govern-

ment of the Lacedaemonians, by oligarchy, they stirred no further in it.

32. About the same time of this summer the Athenians expugned Scione, slew all that were within it at man's estate, made slaves of the women and children, and gave their territory to the Plataeans. They also replanted the Delians in Delos, both in consideration of the defeats they had received after their expulsion, and also because the oracle at Delphi had commanded it. The Phoceans and Locrians also began a war at that time against each other.

And the Corinthians and Argives, being now leagued, went to Tegea to cause it to revolt from the Lacedaemonians, conceiving it to be an important piece [of Peloponnesus], and making account, if they gained it to their side, they should easily obtain the whole. But when the Tegeates refused to become enemies to the Lacedaemonians, the Corinthians, who till then had been very forward, grew less violent and were afraid that no more of the rest would come in. Nevertheless they went to the Boeotians, and solicited them to enter into league with them and the Argives and to do as they did. And the Corinthians further desired the Boeotians to go along with them to Athens and to procure for them the like ten days' truce to that which was made between the Athenians and Boeotians presently after the making of the fifty years' peace, on the same terms as the Boeotians had it; and if the Athenians refused, then to renounce theirs and make no more truces hereafter without the Corinthians. The Corinthians having made this request, the Boeotians willed them, touching the league with the Argives, to stay a while longer, and went with them to Athens, but obtained not the ten days' truce; the Athenians answering that if the Corinthians were confederates with the Lacedaemonians, they had a peace already. Nevertheless the Boeotians would not relinquish their ten days' truce, though the Corinthians both required the same and affirmed that it was so before agreed on. Yet the Athenians granted the Corinthians a cessation of arms, but without solemn ratification.

33. The same summer the Lacedaemonians with their whole power, under the conduct of Pleistonanax, the son of Pausanias, king of the Lacedaemonians, made war upon the Parrhasians

of Arcadia, subjects of the Mantineans, partly as called in by occasion of sedition and partly because they intended, if they could, to demolish a fortification which the Mantineans had built and kept with a garrison in Cypsela, in the territory of the Parrhasians towards Sciritis of Laconia. The Lacedaemonians therefore wasted the territory of the Parrhasians. And the Mantineans, leaving their own city to the custody of the Argives, came forth to aid the Parrhasians their confederates; but being unable to defend both the fort of Cypsela and the cities of the Parrhasians too, they went home again. And the Lacedaemonians, when they had set the Parrhasians at liberty and demolished the fortification, went home likewise.

34. The same summer, when those soldiers which went out with Brasidas and of which Clearidas after the making of the peace had the charge were returned from the parts upon Thrace, the Lacedaemonians made a decree that those Helotes which had fought under Brasidas should receive their liberty and inhabit where they thought good. But not long after they placed them, together with such others as had been newly enfranchised, in Lepreum, a city standing in the confines between Laconia and the Eleians, with whom they were now at variance. Fearing also lest those citizens of their own, which had been taken in the island and had delivered up their arms to the Athenians, should upon apprehension of disgrace for that calamity, if they remained capable of honours, make some innovation in the state, they disabled them [though] some of them were in office already. And their disablement was this: that they should neither bear office, nor be capable to buy and sell. Yet in time they were again restored to their former honours.

35. The same summer also the Dictideans * took Thyssus, a town in Mount Athos, and confederate of the Athenians. This whole summer there was continual commerce between the Athenians and the Peloponnesians; nevertheless they began, both the Athenians and the Lacedaemonians, to have each other in suspicion immediately after the peace, in respect of the places not yet mutually surrendered. For the Lacedaemonians, to whose lot it fell to make restitution first, had not rendered

---

* The Greek word is actually the *Dians*, i.e., the inhabitants of Dium in the Athos peninsula.

Amphipolis and the other cities, nor had caused the peace to be accepted by the confederates upon Thrace, nor by the Boeotians nor Corinthians, though they had ever professed that in case they refused they would join with the Athenians to bring them to it by force, and had prefixed a time (though not by writing) within the which such as entered not into this peace were to be held as enemies unto both. The Athenians, therefore, when they saw none of this really performed, suspected that they had no sincere intention, and thereupon refused to render Pylus when they required it; nay, they repented that they had delivered up the prisoners they took in the island; and detained the rest of the towns they then held till the Lacedaemonians should have performed the conditions on their part also. The Lacedaemonians to this alleged that they had done what they were able to do, for they had delivered the Athenian prisoners that were in their hands and had withdrawn their soldiers from the parts upon Thrace, and whatsoever else was in their own power to perform; but Amphipolis, they said, was not in their power to surrender; that they would endeavour to bring the Boeotians and Corinthians to accept the peace, and to get Panactum restored, and all the Athenian prisoners in Boeotia to be sent home; and therefore desired them to make restitution of Pylus, or, if not so, at least to draw out of it the Messenians and Helotes, as they for their part had drawn their garrisons out of the towns upon Thrace; and if they thought good, to keep it with a garrison of Athenians. After divers and long conferences had this summer, they so far prevailed with the Athenians at the last as they drew thence all the Messenians and Helotes and all other Laconian fugitives and placed them in Cranii, a city of Cephallenia. So for this summer there was peace and free passage from one to another.

36. In the beginning of winter (for now there were other ephores in office; not those in whose time the peace was made, but some of them that opposed it), ambassadors being come from the confederates, and the Athenian, Boeotian, and Corinthian ambassadors being [already] there, and having had much conference together but concluded nothing, Cleobulus and Xenares, ephores that most desired the dissolution of the peace, when the rest of the ambassadors were gone home, entered into

private conference with the Boeotians and Corinthians, exhorting them to run both the same course; and advised the Boeotians to endeavour first to make a league themselves with the Argives and then to get the Argives together with themselves into a league with the Lacedaemonians, for that they might by this means avoid the necessity of accepting the peace with Athens; for the Lacedaemonians would more regard the friendship and league of the Argives than the enmity and dissolution of the peace with the Athenians; for they knew the Lacedaemonians had ever desired to have Argos their friend upon any reasonable conditions, because they knew that their war without Peloponnesus would thereby be a great deal the easier. Wherefore they entreated the Boeotians to put Panactum into the hands of the Lacedaemonians, to the end that, if they could get Pylus for it in exchange, they might make war against the Athenians the more commodiously.

37. The Boeotians and Corinthians, being dismissed by Xenares and Cleobulus, and all the other Lacedaemonians of that faction, with these points to be delivered to their commonwealths, went to their several cities. And two men of Argos, of principal authority in that city, having waited for and met with them by the way, entered into a treaty with them about a league between the Argives and the Boeotians as there was between them and the Corinthians and the Eleians and Mantineans already; for they thought, if it succeeded, they might [the more] easily have either war or peace (forasmuch as the cause would now be common), either with the Lacedaemonians or whomsoever else it should be needful. When the Boeotian ambassadors heard this, they were well pleased. For as it chanced, the Argives requested the same things of them, that they by their friends in Lacedaemon had been sent to procure of the Argives. These men therefore of Argos, when they saw that the Boeotians accepted of the motion, promised to send ambassadors to the Boeotians about it, and so departed. When the Boeotians were come home, they related there what they had heard both at Lacedaemon and by the way from the Argives. The governors of Boeotia were glad thereof, and much more forward in it now than formerly they had been, seeing that not only their friends in Lacedaemon desired, but the Ar-

gives themselves hastened to have done the self-same thing. Not long after this the ambassadors came to them from Argos to solicit the dispatch of the business before propounded; but the governors of Boeotia commended [only] the proposition and dismissed them with promise to send ambassadors about the league to Argos.

38. In the meantime the governors of Boeotia thought fit that an oath should first be taken by themselves and by the ambassadors from Corinth, Megara, and the confederates upon Thrace to give mutual assistance upon any occasion to them that should require it and neither to make war nor peace without the common consent; and next that the Boeotians and Megareans (for these two ran the same course) should make a league with the Argives. But before this oath was [to be] taken, the governors of Boeotia communicated the business to the four Boeotian councils, in the which the whole authority of the state consisteth, and withal presented their advice that any city that would might join with them in the like oath for mutual assistance. But they that were of these councils approved not the proposition, because they feared to offend the Lacedaemonians in being sworn to the Corinthians that had revolted from their confederacy. For the governors of Boeotia had not reported unto them what had passed at Lacedaemon, how Cleobulus and Xenares, the ephores, and their friends there had advised them to enter first into league with the Argives and Corinthians and then afterwards to make the same league with the Lacedaemonians; for they thought that the councils, though this had never been told them, would have decreed it no otherwise than they upon premeditation should advise. So the business was checked and the ambassadors from Corinth and from the cities upon Thrace departed without effect. And the governors of Boeotia, that were before minded, if they had gotten this done, to have leagued themselves also with the Argives, made no mention of the Argives in the councils at all nor sent the ambassadors to Argos, as they had before promised; but a kind of carelessness and delay possessed the whole business.

39. The same winter the Olynthians took Mecyberne, held with a garrison of the Athenians, by assault.

After this the Lacedaemonians (for the conferences between

the Athenians and Lacedaemonians about reciprocal restitution continued still), hoping that if the Athenians should obtain from the Boeotians Panactum, that then they also should recover Pylus, sent ambassadors to the Boeotians with request that Panactum and the Athenian prisoners might be put into the hands of the Lacedaemonians, that they might get Pylus restored in exchange. But the Boeotians answered that unless the Lacedaemonians would make a particular league with them as they had done with the Athenians, they would not do it. The Lacedaemonians, though they knew they should therein wrong the Athenians, for that it was said in the articles that neither party should make either league or war without the other's consent, yet such was their desire to get Panactum to exchange it for Pylus, and withal they that longed to break the peace with Athens were so eager in it, that at last they concluded a league with the Boeotians, winter then ending and the spring approaching; and Panactum was presently pulled down to the ground. So ended the eleventh year of this war.

40. In the spring following, the Argives, when they saw that the ambassadors which the Boeotians promised to send unto them came not, and that Panactum was razed, and that also there was a private league made between the Boeotians and the Lacedaemonians, were afraid lest they should on all hands be abandoned, and that the confederates would all go to the Lacedaemonians. For they apprehended that the Boeotians had been induced both to raze Panactum and also to enter into the Athenian peace by the Lacedaemonians; and that the Athenians were privy to the same, so that now they had no means to make league with the Athenians neither; whereas before they made account that if their truce with the Lacedaemonians continued not, they might upon these differences have joined themselves to the Athenians. The Argives being therefore at a stand and fearing to have war all at once with the Lacedaemonians, Tegeats, Boeotians, and Athenians, [as] having formerly refused the truce with the Lacedaemonians and imagined to themselves the principality of all Peloponnesus, they sent ambassadors with as much speed as might be, Eustrophus and Aeson, persons as they thought most acceptable unto them, with this cogitation, that by compounding with the Lacedaemonians as well as for

their present estate they might, howsoever the world went, they should at least live at quiet.

41. When these ambassadors were there, they fell to treat of the articles upon which the agreement should be made. And at first the Argives desired to have the matter referred, either to some private man or to some city, concerning the territory of Cynuria, about which they have always differed, as lying on the borders of them both (it containeth the cities of Thyrea and Anthena, and is possessed by the Lacedaemonians). But afterwards, the Lacedaemonians not suffering mention to be made of that, but that if they would have the truce go on as it did before, they might, the Argive ambassadors got them to yield to this: that for the present an accord should be made for fifty years; but withal, that it should be lawful nevertheless, if one challenged the other thereunto, both for Lacedaemon and Argos to try their titles to this territory by battle, so that there were in neither city a plague nor a war to excuse them (as once before they had done, when, as both sides thought, they had the victory); and that it should not be lawful for one part to follow the chase of the other further than to the bounds either of Lacedaemon or Argos. And though this seemed to the Lacedaemonians at first to be but a foolish proposition, yet afterwards, because they desired by all means to have friendship with the Argives, they agreed unto it and put into writing what they required. Howsoever, before the Lacedaemonians would make any full conclusion of the same, they willed them to return first to Argos and to make the people acquainted with it, and then, if it were accepted, to return at the Hyacinthian feast and swear it. So these departed.

42. Whilst the Argives were treating about this, the Lacedaemonian ambassadors, Andromedes and Phaedimus and Antimenidas, commissioners for receiving of Panactum and the prisoners from the Boeotians to render them to the Athenians, found that Panactum was demolished, and that their pretext was this: that there had been anciently an oath, by occasion of difference between the Athenians and them, that neither part should inhabit the place solely, but jointly both. But for the Athenian prisoners, as many as the Boeotians had, they that were with Andromedes received, convoyed, and delivered them unto

the Athenians, and withal told them of the razing of Panactum, alleging it as rendered in that no enemy of Athens should dwell in it hereafter. But when this was told them, the Athenians made it a heinous matter, for that they conceived that the Lacedaemonians had done them wrong, both in the matter of Panactum, which was pulled down and should have been rendered standing, and because also they had heard of the private league made with the Boeotians, whereas they had promised to join with the Athenians in compelling such to accept of the peace as had refused it. Withal they weighed whatsoever other points the Lacedaemonians had been short in, touching the performance of the articles, and thought themselves abused; so that they answered the Lacedaemonian ambassadors roughly and dismissed them.

43. This difference arising between the Lacedaemonians and the Athenians, it was presently wrought upon by such also of Athens as desired to have the peace dissolved. Amongst the rest was Alcibiades, the son of Clinias, a man, though young in years,* yet in the dignity of his ancestors honoured as much as any man of what city soever. Who was of opinion that it was better to join with the Argives, not only for the matter itself, but also out of stomach labouring to cross the Lacedaemonians, because they had made the peace, by the means of Nicias and Laches, without him, whom for his youth they had neglected and not honoured as for the ancient hospitality between his house and them had been requisite; which his father had indeed renounced,† but he himself, by good offices done to those prisoners which were brought from the island, had a purpose to have renewed. But supposing himself on all hands disparaged, he both opposed the peace at first, alleging that the Lacedaemonians would not be constant and that they had made the peace only to get the Argives by that means away from them and afterwards to invade the Athenians again when they should be destitute of their friends; and also, as soon as this difference was on foot, he sent presently to Argos of himself, willing them

* The Greek adds "though still young *by the standards of any other state.*"

† According to the Greek it was his grandfather who had renounced it, and the hospitality was the office of proxenus or consul.

with all speed to come to Athens, as being thereunto invited, and to bring with them the Eleians and Mantineans to enter with the Athenians into a league, the opportunity now serving, and promising that he would help them all he could.

44. The Argives, having heard the message, and knowing that the Athenians had made no league with the Boeotians, and that they were at great quarrel with the Lacedaemonians, neglected the ambassadors they had then in Lacedaemon, whom they had sent about the truce, and applied themselves to the Athenians, with this thought: that if they should have war, they should by this means be backed with a city that had been their ancient friend, governed like their own by democracy, and of greatest power by sea. Whereupon they presently sent ambassadors to Athens to make a league; and together with theirs went also the ambassadors of the Eleians and Mantineans. Thither also with all speed came the Lacedaemonian ambassadors, Philocharidas, Leon, and Endius, persons accounted most gracious with the Athenians, for fear, lest in their passion they should make a league with the Argives, and withal to require the restitution of Pylus for Panactum, and to excuse themselves concerning their league with the Boeotians, as not made for any harm intended to the Athenians.

45. Now speaking of these things before the council, and how that they were come thither with full power to make agreement concerning all controversies betwixt them, they put Alcibiades into fear, lest, if they should say the same before the people, the multitude would be drawn unto their side, and so the Argive league fall off. But Alcibiades deviseth against them this plot. He persuaded the Lacedaemonians not to confess their plenary power before the people, and giveth them his faith that then Pylus should be rendered (for he said he would persuade the Athenians to it as much as he now opposed it), and that the rest of their differences should be compounded. This he did to alienate them from Nicias; and that by accusing them before the people as men that had no true meaning nor ever spake one and the same thing, he might bring on the league with the Argives, Eleians, and Mantineans. And it came to pass accordingly. For when they came before the people, and to the ques-

tion whether they had full power of concluding, had, contrary to what they had said in council, answered *No*, the Athenians would no longer endure them, but gave ear to Alcibiades, that exclaimed against the Lacedaemonians far more now than ever; and were ready then presently to have the Argives and those others with them brought in, and to make the league; but an earthquake happening before anything was concluded, the assembly was adjourned.

46. In the next day's meeting, Nicias, though the Lacedaemonians had been abused, and he himself also deceived touching their coming with full power to conclude, yet he persisted to affirm that it was their best course to be friends with the Lacedaemonians and to defer the Argives' business till they had sent to the Lacedaemonians again to be assured of their intention, saying that it was honour unto themselves and dishonour to the Lacedaemonians to have the war put off. For, for themselves, being in estate of prosperity, it was best to preserve their good fortune as long as they might; whereas to the other side, who were in evil estate, it should be in place of gain to put things as soon as they could to the hazard. So he persuaded them to send ambassadors, whereof himself was one, to require the Lacedaemonians, if they meant sincerely, to render Panactum standing, and also Amphipolis; and if the Boeotians would not accept of the peace, then to undo their league with them, according to the article that the one should not make league with any without the consent of the other. They willed him to say further that they themselves also, if they had had the will to do wrong, had ere this made a league with the Argives, who were present then at Athens for the same purpose. And whatsoever they had to accuse the Lacedaemonians of besides, they instructed Nicias in it and sent him and the other his fellow-ambassadors away. When they were arrived and had delivered what they had in charge, and this last of all, that the Athenians would make league with the Argives unless the Lacedaemonians would renounce their league with the Boeotians if the Boeotians accepted not the peace, the Lacedaemonians denied to renounce their league with the Boeotians; for Xenares, the ephore, and the rest of that faction carried it; but at the request of Nicias

they renewed their former oath. For Nicias was afraid he should return with nothing done and be carped at (as after also it fell out) as author of the Lacedaemonian peace.

At his return, when the Athenians understood that nothing was effected at Lacedaemon, they grew presently into choler; and apprehending injury (the Argives and their confederates being there present, brought in by Alcibiades), they made a peace and a league with them in these words:

47. "The Athenians and Argives and Mantineans and Eleians, for themselves and for the confederates commanded by every of them, have made an accord for one hundred years, without fraud or damage, both by sea and land. It shall not be lawful for the Argives nor Eleians nor Mantineans nor their confederates to bear arms against the Athenians or the confederates under the command of the Athenians or their confederates by any fraud or machination whatsoever.

"And the Athenians, Argives, and Mantineans have made league with each other for one hundred years on these terms:

"If any enemy shall invade the territory of the Athenians, then the Argives, Eleians, and Mantineans shall go unto Athens to assist them, according as the Athenians shall send them word to do, in the best manner they possibly can. But if the enemy, after he have spoiled the territory, shall be gone back, then their city shall be held as an enemy to the Argives, Eleians, Mantineans, and Athenians, and war shall be made against it by all those cities; and it shall not be lawful for any of those cities to give over the war without the consent of all the rest.

"And if an enemy shall invade the territory, either of the Argives or of the Eleians or of the Mantineans, then the Athenians shall come unto Argos, Elis, and Mantineia to assist them, in such sort as those cities shall send them word to do, in the best manner they possibly can. But if the enemy, after he hath wasted their territory, shall be gone back, then their city shall be held as an enemy both to the Athenians and also to the Argives, Eleians, and Mantineans, and war shall be made against it by all those cities; and it shall not be lawful for any of them to give over the war against that city without the consent of all the rest.

"There shall no armed men be suffered to pass through the

dominions either of themselves or of any the confederates under their several commands to make war in any place whatsoever, unless by the suffrage of all the cities, Athens, Argos, Elis, and Mantineia, their passage be allowed.

"To such as come to assist any of the other cities, that city which sendeth them shall give maintenance for thirty days after they shall arrive in the city that sent for them; and the like at their going away; but if they will use the army for a longer time, then the city that sent for them shall find them maintenance, at the rate of three oboles of Aegina a day for a man of arms, and of a drachma of Aegina for a horseman.

"The city which sendeth for the aids shall have the leading and command of them whilst the war is in their own territory; but if it shall seem good unto these cities to make a war in common, then all the cities shall equally participate of the command.

"The Athenians shall swear unto the articles both for themselves and for their confederates; and the Argives, Eleians, and Mantineans, and the confederates of these shall every one swear unto them city by city. And their oath shall be the greatest that by custom of the several cities is used, and with most perfect hosts,* and in these words: 'I will stand to this league, according to the articles thereof, justly, innocently, and sincerely, and not transgress the same by any art or machination whatsoever.'

"This oath shall be taken at Athens by the senate and the officers of the commons, and administered by the Prytanes. At Argos it shall be taken by the senate and the council of eighty and by the Artynae, and administered by the council of eighty. At Mantineia it shall be taken by the procurators of the people and by the senate and by the rest of the magistrates, and administered by the theori and by the tribunes of the soldiers. At Elis it shall be taken by the procurators of the people and by the officers of the treasury and by the council of six hundred, and administered by the procurators of the people and by the keepers of the law.

"This oath shall be renewed by the Athenians, who shall go to Elis and to Mantineia and to Argos thirty days before the

---

* I.e., with full-grown sacrificial victims.

Olympian games; and by the Argives, Eleians, and Mantineans, who shall come to Athens ten days before the Panathenaean holidays.

"The articles of this league and peace and the oath shall be inscribed in a pillar of stone by the Athenians in the citadel; by the Argives in their market place within the precincts of the temple of Apollo; and by the Mantineans in their market place within the precinct of the temple of Jupiter. And at the Olympian games now at hand, there shall jointly erected by them all a brazen pillar in Olympia [with the same inscription].

"If it shall seem good to any of these cities to add anything to these articles, whatsoever shall be determined by them all in common council, the same shall stand good."

48. Thus was the league and the peace concluded; and that which was made before between the Lacedaemonians and the Athenians was, notwithstanding, by neither side renounced. But the Corinthians, although they were the confederates of the Argives, yet would they not enter into this league; nay, though there were made a league before this between [them and] the Argives, Eleians, and Mantineans that where one there all should have war or peace, yet they refused to swear to it, but said that their league defensive was enough, whereby they were bound to defend each other but not to take part one with another in invading. So the Corinthians fell off from their confederates and inclined again to the Lacedaemonians.

49. This summer were celebrated the Olympian games, in which Androsthenes, an Arcadian, was the first victor in the exercise called Pancratium.* And the Lacedaemonians were by the Eleians prohibited the temple there, so as they might neither sacrifice nor contend for the prizes amongst the rest; for that they had not paid the fine set upon them, according to an Olympic law, by the Eleians, that laid to their charge that they had put soldiers into the fort of Phyrcon and into Lepreum in the time of the Olympic truce. The fine amounted unto two thousand minae, which was two minae for every man of arms, according to the law. But the Lacedaemonians, by their ambassadors which they sent thither, made answer that they had been

* I.e., wrestling and boxing.

unjustly condemned, alleging that the truce was not published in Lacedaemon when their soldiers were sent out. To this the Eleians said again that the truce was already begun amongst themselves, who used to publish it first in their own dominion; and thereupon, whilst they lay still and expected no such matter, as in time of truce, the Lacedaemonians did them the injury unawares. The Lacedaemonians hereunto replied that it was not necessary to proceed to the publishing of the truce in Lacedaemon at all if they thought themselves wronged already; but rather, if they thought themselves not wronged yet, then to do it by way of prevention, that they should not arm against them afterwards. The Eleians stood stiffly in their first argument, that they would never be persuaded but injury had been done them, but were nevertheless contented if they would render Lepreum, both to remit their own part of the money and also to pay that part for them which was due unto the god.

50. When this would not be agreed unto, they then required this: not that they should render Lepreum, unless they would, but that then they should come to the altar of Jupiter Olympian, seeing they desired to have free use of the temple, and there before the Grecians to take an oath to pay the fine at least hereafter. But when the Lacedaemonians refused that also, they were excluded the temple, the sacrifices, and the games, and sacrificed at home; but the rest of the Grecians, except the Lepreates, were all admitted to be spectators. Nevertheless, the Eleians, fearing lest they would come and sacrifice there by force, kept a guard there of their youngest men in arms, to whom were added Argives and Mantineans, of either city one thousand, and certain Athenian horsemen, who were then at Argos waiting the celebration of the feast. For a great fear possessed all the assembly lest the Lacedaemonians should come upon them with an army; and the rather because Lichas, the son of Arcesilaus, a Lacedaemonian, had been whipped by the serjeants upon the race; for that when his chariot had gotten the prize, after proclamation made that the chariot of the Boeotian state had won it (because he himself was not admitted to run), he came forth into the race and crowned his charioteer, to make it known that the chariot was his own. This added much

unto their fear, and they verily expected some accident to follow. Nevertheless the Lacedaemonians stirred not; and the feast passed over.

After the Olympian games, the Argives and their confederates went to Corinth to get the Corinthians into their league. And the Lacedaemonian ambassadors chanced to be there also; and after much conference and nothing concluded, upon occasion of an earthquake they brake off the conference and returned every one to his own city. And so this summer ended.

51. The next winter, the men of Heracleia in Trachinia fought a battle against the Aenianians, Dolopians, Melians, and certain Thessalians. For the neighbour cities were enemies to this city, as built to the prejudice only of them; and both opposed the same from the time it was first founded, annoying it what they could; and also in this battle overcame them and slew Xenares, a Lacedaemonian, their commander, with some others, Heracleots. Thus ended this winter, and the twelfth year of this war.

52. In the very beginning of the next summer, the Boeotians took Heracleia, miserably afflicted, into their own hands, and put Hegesippidas, a Lacedaemonian, out of it for his evil government. They took it because they feared lest, whilst the Lacedaemonians were troubled about Peloponnesus, it should have been taken in by the Athenians. Nevertheless the Lacedaemonians were offended with them for doing it. The same summer Alcibiades, the son of Clinias, being general of the Athenians, by the practice of the Argives and their confederates, went into Peloponnesus, and having with him a few men at arms and archers of Athens and some of the confederates which he took up there as he passed through the country with his army, both ordered such affairs by the way concerning the league as was fit; and coming to the Patreans, persuaded them to build their walls down to the seaside, and purposed to raise another wall himself towards Rhium in Achaia. But the Corinthians, Sicyonians, and such others as this wall would have prejudiced came forth and hindered him.

53. The same summer fell out a war between the Epidaurians and the Argives; the pretext thereof was about a beast for sacrifice, which the Epidaurians ought to have sent in con-

sideration of their pastures to Apollo Pythius, and had not done it, the Argives being the principal owners of the temple. But Alcibiades and the Argives had indeed determined to take in the city, though without pretence at all, both that the Corinthians might not stir and also that they might bring the Athenian succours from Aegina into those parts, a nearer way than by compassing the promontory of Scyllaeum. And therefore the Argives prepared, as of themselves, to exact the sacrifice by invasion.

54. About the same time also the Lacedaemonians, with their whole forces, came forth as far as Leuctra, in the confines of their own territory towards Lycaeum, under the conduct of Agis, the son of Archidamus, their king. No man knew against what place they intended the war; no, not the cities themselves out of which they were levied. But when in the sacrifices which they made for their passage the tokens observed were unlucky, they went home again and sent word about to their confederates (being now the month Carneius) to prepare themselves, after the next feast of the new moon (kept by the Dorians), to be again upon their march. The Argives, who set forth the twenty-sixth day of the month before Carneius, though they celebrated the same day, yet all the time they continued invading and wasting Epidauria. And the Epidaurians called in their confederates to help them, whereof some excused themselves upon the quality of the month; and others came but to the confines of Epidauria and there stayed.

55. Whilst the Argives were in Epidauria, the ambassadors of divers cities, solicited by the Athenians, met together at Mantineia, where in a conference amongst them Euphamidas of Corinth said that their actions agreed not with their words; forasmuch as whilst they were sitting there to treat of a peace, the Epidaurians with their confederates and the Argives stood armed, in the meantime, against each other in order of battle; that it was therefore fit that somebody should go first unto the armies from either side and dissolve them, and then come again and dispute of peace. This advice being approved, they departed, and withdrew the Argives from Epidauria. And meeting afterwards again in the same place, they could not for all that agree; and the Argives again invaded and wasted Epidauria.

The Lacedaemonians also drew forth their army against Caryae; but then again, their sacrifice for passage being not to their mind, they returned. And the Argives, when they had spoiled about the third part of Epidauria, went home likewise. They had the assistance of one thousand men of arms of Athens, and Alcibiades their commander; but these hearing that the Lacedaemonians were in the field, and seeing now there was no longer need of them, departed. And so ended this summer.

56. The next winter the Lacedaemonians, unknown to the Athenians, put three hundred garrison soldiers under the command of Agesippidas into Epidaurus by sea. For which cause the Argives came and expostulated with the Athenians that whereas it was written in the articles of the league that no enemy should be suffered to pass through either of their dominions, yet had they suffered the Lacedaemonians to pass by sea; and said they had wrong, unless the Athenians would again put the Messenians and Helotes into Pylus against the Lacedaemonians. Hereupon the Athenians, at the persuasion of Alcibiades, wrote upon the Laconian pillar, [under the inscription of the peace], that the Lacedaemonians had violated their oath; and they drew the Helotes out of Cranii and put them again into Pylus to infest the territory with driving off booties; but did no more.

All this winter, though there was war between the Argives and Epidaurians, yet was there no set battle, but only ambushes and skirmishes, wherein were slain on both sides such as it chanced. But in the end of winter, and the spring now at hand, the Argives came to Epidaurus with ladders, as destitute of men by reason of the war, thinking to have won it by assault, but returned again with their labour lost. And so ended this winter, and the thirteenth year of this war.

57. In the middle of the next summer, the Lacedaemonians, seeing that the Epidaurians their confederates were tired and that of the rest of the cities of Peloponnesus some had already revolted and others were but in evil terms, and apprehending that if they presented it not the mischief would spread still further, put themselves into the field with all their own forces, both of themselves and their Helotes, to make war against Argos, under the conduct of Agis, the son of Archidamus, their king. The Tegeats went also with them, and of the rest of Arcadia

all that were in the Lacedaemonian league. But the rest of their confederates, both within Peloponnesus and without, were to meet together at Phlius; that is to say, of the Boeotians five thousand men of arms and as many light-armed, five hundred horse, and to every horseman another man on foot, of Corinthians two thousand men of arms, and of the rest more or less as they were; but the Phliasians, because the army was assembled in their own territory, put forth their whole power.

58. The Argives, having had notice both formerly of the preparation of the Lacedaemonians and afterward of their marching on to join with the rest at Phlius, brought their army likewise into the field. They had with them the aids of the Mantineans and their confederates and three thousand men of arms of the Eleians; and marching forward, met the Lacedaemonians at Methydrium, a town of Arcadia, each side seizing on a hill. And the Argives prepared to give battle to the Lacedaemonians whilst they were single. But Agis, dislodging his army by night, marched on to Phlius to the rest of the confederates, unseen. Upon knowledge hereof, the Argives betimes in the morning retired first to Argos and afterwards to the forest of Nemea, by which they thought the Lacedaemonians and their confederates would fall in. But Agis came not the way which they expected, but with the Lacedaemonians, Arcadians, and Epidaurians, whom he acquainted with his purpose, took another more difficult way to pass and came down into the Argive plains. The Corinthians also, and Pellenians and Phliasians, marched another troublesome way. [Only] the Boeotians, Megareans, and Sicyonians were appointed to come down by the way of the forest of Nemea, in which the Argives were encamped, to the end that if the Argives should turn head against the Lacedaemonians, these might set upon them at the back with their horse. Thus ordered, Agis entered into the plains and spoiled Saminthus and some other towns thereabouts.

59. Which when the Argives understood, they came out of the forest somewhat after break of day to oppose them, and lighting among the Phliasians and Corinthians, slew some few of the Phliasians, but had more slain of their own by the Corinthians, though not many. The Boeotians, Megareans, and Sicyonians marched forward towards Nemea and found that the

Argives were departed; for when they came down and saw their country wasted, they put themselves into order of battle. And the Lacedaemonians on the other side did the same; and the Argives stood intercepted in the midst of their enemies. For in the plain between them and the city stood the Lacedaemonians and those with them; above them were the Corinthians, Phliasians, and Pellenians; and towards Nemea were the Boeotians, Sicyonians, and Megareans. And horsemen they had none; for the Athenians alone of all their confederates were not yet come.

Now the generality of the army of the Argives and their confederates did not think the danger present so great as indeed it was, but rather that the advantage in the battle would be their own; and that the Lacedaemonians were intercepted, not only in the Argives territory, but also hard by the city. But two men of Argos, Thrasyllus, one of the five commanders of the army, and Alciphron, entertainer * of the Lacedaemonians, when the armies were even ready to join, went unto Agis and dealt with him to have the battle put off, forasmuch as the Argives were content and ready both to propound and accept of equal arbitrators in whatsoever the Lacedaemonians should charge them withal, and in the meantime to have peace with them solemnly confirmed.

60. This these Argives said of themselves, without the command of the generality. And Agis, of himself likewise, accepting their proposition without deliberation, had with the major part, and having communicated it only to some one or more of those that had charge in the army, made truce with them for four months, in which space they were to perform the things agreed upon betwixt them; and then presently he withdrew his army without giving account to any of the rest of the league why he did so. The Lacedaemonians and the confederates followed Agis, according to the law, as being their general, but among themselves taxed him exceedingly; for that having a very fair occasion of battle, the Argives being inclosed on all sides both by their horse and foot, he yet went his way doing nothing worthy the great preparation they had made. For this was, in very truth, the fairest army that ever the Grecians had in the

* Again, proxenus.

field unto this day. But it was most to be seen when they were all together in the forest of Nemea, where the Lacedaemonians were with their whole forces, besides the Arcadians, Boeotians, Corinthians, Sicyonians, Pellenians, Phliasians, and Megareans; and these all chosen men of their several cities and such as were thought a match not only for the league of the Argives but for such another added to it. The army, thus offended with Agis, departed, and were dissolved every man to his home.

The Argives were much more offended with those of their city, which without the consent of the multitude had made the truce, they also supposing that the Lacedaemonians had escaped their hands in such an advantage as they never had the like before, in that the battle was to have been fought under the city walls and with the assistance of many and good confederates. And in their return they began to stone Thrasyllus at the Charadrum, the place where the soldiers, before they enter into the city from warfare, use to have their military causes heard. But he, flying to the altar, saved himself; nevertheless they confiscated his goods.

61. After this, the Athenians coming in with the aid of one thousand men of arms and three hundred horse under the conduct of Laches and Nicostratus, the Argives (for they were afraid for all this to break the truce with the Lacedaemonians) willed them to be gone again; and when they desired to treat, would not present them to the people till such time as the Mantineans and Eleians, who were not yet gone, forced them unto it by their importunity. Then the Athenians, in the presence of Alcibiades, that was ambassador there, spake unto the Argives and their confederates, saying that the truce was unduly made without the assent of the rest of their confederates, and that now (for they were come time enough) they ought to fall again to the war; and did by their words so prevail with the confederates that they all, save the Argives, presently marched against Orchomenus of Arcadia. And these, though satisfied, stayed behind at first, but afterwards they also went, and sitting down before Orchomenus, jointly besieged and assaulted the same, desiring to take it in as well for other causes as chiefly for that the hostages which the Arcadians had given to the Lacedaemonians were there in custody. The Orcho-

menians, fearing the weakness of their walls, and the greatness of the army, and lest they should perish before any relief could arrive, yielded up the town on conditions to be received into the league, give hostages for themselves, and to surrender the hostages held there by the Lacedaemonians into the hands of the Mantineans.

62. The confederates after this, having gotten Orchomenus, sat in council about what town they should proceed against next. The Eleians gave advice to go against Lepreum, but the Mantineans against Tegea. And the Argives and Athenians concurred in opinion with the Mantineans. But the Eleians, taking it in evil part that they did not decree to go against Lepreum, went home. But the rest prepared themselves at Mantineia to go against Tegea, which also some within had a purpose to put into their hands.

63. The Lacedaemonians, after their return from Argos with their four months' truce, severely questioned Agis for that, upon so fair an opportunity as they never had before, he subdued not Argos to the state; for so many and so good confederates would hardly be gotten together again at one time. But when also the news came of the taking of Orchomenus, then was their indignation much greater; and they presently resolved, contrary to their own custom, in their passion, to raze his house, and fine him in the sum of ten thousand drachmes.* But he besought them that they would do neither of these things yet, and promised that, leading out the army again, he would by some valiant action cancel those accusations; or, if not, they might proceed afterwards to do with him whatsoever they thought good. So they forbore both the fine and the razing of his house, but made a decree for that present, such as had never been before, that ten Spartans should be elected and

---

* The Greek says a *hundred* thousand drachmae. It is nearly impossible to give any statement as to the actual value of money in fifth-century Greece. The most useful indication of the comparative significance of sums of money in their coinage and ours is perhaps given by the pay of soldiers. Double pay for tasks of extreme difficulty or hardship was one drachma a man a day. Some authorities have considered that this sum represents enough to support the man and his family in food for one day.

joined with him as councillors, without whom it should not be lawful for him to lead the army into the field.

64. In the meantime came news from their side in Tegea that, unless they came presently with aid, the Tegeans would revolt to the Argives and their confederates, and that they wanted little of being revolted already. Upon this, the Lacedaemonians with speed levied all their forces, both of themselves and their Helotes, in such number as they had never done before, and marched unto Oresteium in Maenalia, and appointed the Arcadians, such as were of their league, to assemble and follow them at the heels to Tegea. The Lacedaemonians, being come entire to Oresteium, from thence sent back the sixth part of their army, in which they put both the youngest and the eldest sort, for the custody of the city, and with the rest marched on to Tegea; and not long after arrived also their confederates of Arcadia. They also sent to Corinth, and to the Boeotians, Phoceans, and Locrians to come with their aids with all speed to Mantineia. But these had too short a warning; nor was it easy for them, unless they came all together and stayed for one another, to come through the enemy's country, which lay between and barred them of passage. Nevertheless, they made what haste they could. And the Lacedaemonians, taking with them their Arcadian confederates present, entered into the territory of Mantineia, and pitching their camp by the temple of Hercules, wasted the territory about.

65. The Argives and their confederates, as soon as they came in sight, seized on a certain place fortified by nature and of hard access and put themselves into battle array. And the Lacedaemonians marched presently towards them and came up within a stone or a dart's cast. But then one of the ancient men of the army cried out unto Agis (seeing him to go on against a place of that strength) that he went about to amend one fault with another, signifying that he intended to make amends for his former retreat from Argos, which he was questioned for, with his now unseasonable forwardness. But he, whether it were upon that increpation or some other sudden apprehension of his own, presently withdrew his army before the fight began, and marching unto the territory of Tegea, turned

the course of the water into the territory of Mantineia; touching which water, because into what part soever it had his course it did much harm to the country, the Mantineans and Tegeans were at wars. Now his drift was, by the turning of that water to provoke those Argives and their confederates which kept the hill, when they should hear of it, to come down and oppose them, that so they might fight with them in the plain. And by that time he had stayed about the water a day, he had diverted the stream. The Argives and their confederates were at first amazed at this their sudden retreat from so near them and knew not what to make of it. But when after the retreat they returned no more in sight, and that they themselves, lying still on the place, did not pursue them, then began they anew to accuse their commanders, both for suffering the Lacedaemonians to depart formerly, when they had them inclosed at so fair an advantage before Argos, and now again for not pursuing them when they ran away, but giving them leave to save themselves, and betraying the army. The commanders for the present were much troubled hereat; but afterwards they drew down the army from the hill, and coming forth into the plain, encamped as to go against the enemy.

66. The next day, the Argives and their confederates put themselves into such order as, if occasion served, they meant to fight in; and the Lacedaemonians returning from the water to the temple of Hercules, the same place where they had formerly encamped, perceived the enemies to be all of them in order of battle hard by them, come down already from the hill. Certainly the Lacedaemonians were more affrighted at this time than ever they had been to their remembrance before. For the time they had to prepare themselves was exceedingly short; and such was their diligence that every man fell immediately into his own rank, Agis, the king, commanding all according to the law. For whilst the king hath the army in the field, all things are commanded by him; and he signifieth what is to be done to the polemarchi, they to the lochagi, these to the pentecontateres, and these again to the enomotarchi, who lastly make it known, every one to his own enomotia. In this manner, when they would have anything to be done, their commands pass through the army and are quickly executed. For almost all the

Lacedaemonian army, save a very few, are captains of captains; and the care of what is to be put in execution lieth upon many.

67. Now their left wing consisted of the Sciritae, which amongst the Lacedaemonians have ever alone that place. Next to these were placed the Brasideian soldiers lately come out of Thrace, and with them those that had been newly made free. After them in order the rest of the Lacedaemonians, band after band; and by them Arcadians, first the Heraeans, after these the Maenalians. In the right wing were the Tegeats, and a few Lacedaemonians in the point of the same wing. And upon the outside of either wing, the horsemen. So stood the Lacedaemonians. Opposite to them, in the right wing, stood the Mantineans, because it was upon their own territory; and with them such Arcadians as were of their league. Then the thousand chosen Argives, which the city had for a long time caused to be trained for the wars at the public charge, and next to them the rest of the Argives. After these, the Cleonaeans and Orneates, their confederates. And lastly, the Athenians, with the horsemen (which were also theirs) had the left wing.

68. This was the order and preparation of both the armies. The army of the Lacedaemonians appeared to be the greater. But what the number was, either of the particulars of either side or in general, I could not exactly write. For the number of the Lacedaemonians, agreeable to the secrecy of that state, was unknown; and of the other side, for the ostentation usual with all men touching the number of themselves, was unbelieved. Nevertheless, the number of the Lacedaemonians may be attained by computing thus. Besides the Sciritae, which were six hundred, there fought in all seven regiments; in every regiment were four companies, in each company were four enomotiae, and of every enomotia there stood in front four; but they were not ranged all alike in file, but as the captains of bands thought it necessary; but the army in general was so ordered as to be eight men in depth. And the first rank of the whole, besides the Sciritae, consisted of four hundred and forty-eight soldiers.

69. Now when they were ready to join, the commanders made their hortatives, every one to those that were under his own command. To the Mantineans it was said that they were

to fight for their territory, and concerning their liberty and servitude; that the former might not be taken from them, and that they might not again taste of the latter. The Argives were admonished that whereas anciently they had the leading of Peloponnesus, and in it an equal share, they should not now suffer themselves to be deprived of it for ever; and that withal, they should now revenge the many injuries of a city, their neighbour and enemy. To the Athenians, it was remembered how honourable a thing it would be for them, in company of so many and good confederates, to be inferior to none of them; and that if they had once vanquished the Lacedaemonians in Peloponnesus, their own dominion would become both the more assured and the larger by it; and that no other would invade their territory hereafter. Thus much was said to the Argives and their confederates. But the Lacedaemonians encouraged one another both of themselves and also by the manner of their discipline in the war, taking encouragement, being valiant men, by the commemoration of what they already knew; as being well acquainted that a long actual experience conferred more to their safety than any short verbal exhortation, though never so well delivered.

70. After this followed the battle. The Argives and their confederates marched to the charge with great violence and fury. But the Lacedaemonians slowly and with many flutes, according to their military discipline, not as a point of religion, but that, marching evenly and by measure, their ranks might not be distracted, as the greatest armies, when they march in the face of the enemy, use to be.

71. Whilst they were yet marching up, Agis, the king thought of this course. All armies do thus. In the conflict they extend their right wing so as it cometh in upon the flank of the left wing of the enemy: and this happeneth for that every one, through fear, seeketh all he can to cover his unarmed side with the shield of him that standeth next to him on his right hand, conceiving that to be so locked together is their best defence. The beginning hereof is in the leader of the first file on the right hand, who ever striving to shift his unarmed side from the enemy, the rest upon like fear follow after. And at this time, the Mantineans in the right wing had far encompassed

the Sciritae; and the Lacedaemonians on the other side, and the Tegeats, were come in yet further upon the flank of the Athenians, by as much as they had the greater army. Wherefore Agis, fearing lest his left wing should be encompassed, and supposing the Mantineans to be come in far, signified unto the Sciritae and Brasideians to draw out part of their bands, and therewith to equalise their left wing to the right wing of the Mantineans; and into the void space he commanded to come up Hipponoidas and Aristocles, two colonels, with their bands out of the right wing, and to fall in there and make up the breach, conceiving that more than enough would still be remaining in their right wing, and that the left wing opposed to the Mantineans would be the stronger.

72. But it happened (for he commanded it in the very onset and on the sudden) both that Aristocles and Hipponoidas refused to go to the place commanded (for which they were afterwards banished Sparta, as thought to have disobeyed out of cowardice), and that the enemy had in the meantime also charged; and when those which he commanded to go to the place of the Sciritae went not, they could no more reunite themselves nor close again the empty space. But the Lacedaemonians, though they had the worst at this time in every point for skill, yet in valour they manifestly showed themselves superior. For after the fight was once begun, notwithstanding that the right wing of the Mantineans did put to flight the Sciritae and Brasideians, and that the Mantineans together with their confederates and those thousand chosen men of Argos, falling upon them in flank by the breach not yet closed up, killed many of the Lacedaemonians, and put to flight and chased them to their carriages, slaying also certain of the elder sort left there for a guard, so as in this part the Lacedaemonians were overcome, yet with the rest of the army, and especially the middle battle where Agis was himself, and those which are called "the three hundred horsemen" about him, they charged upon the eldest of the Argives, and upon those which are named "the five cohorts," and upon the Cleonaeans and Orneates, and certain Athenians arranged amongst them, and put them all to flight; in such sort as many of them never struck stroke, but as soon as the Lacedaemonians charged gave ground presently,

and some for fear to be overtaken were trodden under foot.

73. As soon as the army of the Argives and their confederates had in this part given ground, they began also to break on either side. The right wing of the Lacedaemonians and Tegeats had now with their surplusage of number hemmed the Athenians in, so as they had the danger on all hands, being within the circle, pent up, and without it, already vanquished. And they had been the most distressed part of all the army had not their horsemen come in to help them. Withal it fell out that Agis, when he perceived the left wing of his own army to labour, namely, that which was opposed to the Mantineans and to those thousand Argives, commanded the whole army to go and relieve the part overcome. By which means the Athenians and such of the Argives as, together with them, were overlaid, whilst the army passed by and declined them, saved themselves at leisure. And the Mantineans with their confederates and those chosen Argives had no more mind now of pressing upon their enemies, but seeing their side was overcome and the Lacedaemonians approaching them, presently turned their backs. Of the Mantineans the greatest part were slain; but of those chosen Argives the most were saved; by reason the flight and going off was neither hasty nor long. For the Lacedaemonians fight long and constantly, till they have made the enemy to turn his back; but that done, they follow him not far.

74. Thus, or near thus, went the battle, the greatest that had been of a long time between Grecians and Grecians, and of two the most famous cities. The Lacedaemonians, laying together the arms of their slain enemies, presently erected a trophy and rifled their dead bodies. Their own dead they took up and carried them to Tegea, where they were also buried, and delivered to the enemy theirs under truce. Of the Argives, and Orneates, and Cleonaeans were slain seven hundred; of the Mantineans, two hundred; and of the Athenians with the Aeginetae, likewise two hundred, and both the captains. The confederates of the Lacedaemonians were never pressed, and therefore their loss was not worth mentioning; and of the Lacedaemonians themselves, it is hard to know the certainty; but it is said there were slain three hundred.

75. When it was certain they would fight, Pleistoanax, the

other king of the Lacedaemonians, and with him both old and young, came out of the city to have aided the army, and came forth as far as Tegea, but being advertised of the victory, they returned. And the Lacedaemonians sent out to turn back also those confederates of theirs which were coming to them from Corinth and from without the isthmus. And then they also went home themselves, and having dismissed their confederates (for now were the Carneian holidays), celebrated that feast. Thus in this one battle they wiped off their disgrace with the Grecians; for they had been taxed both with cowardice for the blow they received in the island and with imprudence and slackness on other occasions. But after this, their miscarriage was imputed to fortune, and for their minds they were esteemed to have been ever the same they had been.

The day before this battle it chanced also that the Epidaurians with their whole power invaded the territory of Argos, as being emptied much of men, and whilst the Argives were abroad, killed many of those that were left behind to defend it. Also three thousand men of Elis and a thousand Athenians, besides those which had been sent before, being come after the battle to aid the Mantineans, marched presently all to Epidaurus and lay before it all the while the Lacedaemonians were celebrating the Carneian holidays; and assigning to every one his part, began to take in the city with a wall. But the rest gave over; only the Athenians quickly finished a fortification (which was their task), wherein stood the temple of Juno. In it amongst them all they left a garrison, and went home every one to his own city. And so this summer ended.

76. In the beginning of the winter following, the Lacedaemonians, presently after the end of the Carneian holidays, drew out their army into the field, and being come to Tegea, sent certain propositions of agreement before to Argos. There were, before this time, many citizens in Argos well affected to the Lacedaemonians and that desired the deposing of the Argive people; and now after the battle they were better able by much to persuade the people to composition than they formerly were. And their design was, first, to get a peace made with the Lacedaemonians, and after that a league, and then at last to set upon the commons.

There went thither Lichas the son of Archesilaus, entertainer
of the Argives in Lacedaemon, and brought to Argos two propositions: one of war, if the war were to proceed; another of
peace, if they were to have peace. And after much contradiction (for Alcibiades was also there), the Lacedaemonian faction, that boldly now discovered themselves, prevailed with
the Argives to accept the proposition of peace, which was this:

77. "It seemeth good to the council of the Lacedaemonians
to accord with the Argives on these articles:

"The Argives shall redeliver unto the Orchomenians their
children, and unto the Maenalians their men, and unto the Lacedaemonians those men that are at Mantineia; they shall withdraw their soldiers from Epidaurus and raze the fortification
there.

"And if the Athenians depart not from Epidaurus [likewise],
they shall be held as enemies both to the Argives and to the
Lacedaemonians and also to the confederates of them both.

"If the Lacedaemonians have any men of theirs in custody,
they shall deliver them every one to his own city.

"And for so much as concerneth the god, the Argives shall
accept composition with the Epidaurians, upon an oath which
they shall swear, touching that controversy; and the Argives
shall give the form of that oath.

"All the cities of Peloponnesus, both small and great, shall
be free according to their patrial laws.

"If any without Peloponnesus shall enter into it to do it harm,
the Argives shall come forth to defend the same, in such sort
as in a common council shall by the Peloponnesians be thought
reasonable.

"The confederates of the Lacedaemonians without Peloponnesus shall have the same conditions which the confederates of the Argives and of the Lacedaemonians have, every one
holding his own.

"This composition is to hold from the time that they shall
both parts have showed the same to their confederates and obtained their consent.

"And if it shall seem good to either part to add or alter
anything, their confederates shall be sent unto and made acquainted therewith."

78. These propositions the Argives accepted at first; and the army of the Lacedaemonians returned from Tegea to their own city. But shortly after, when they had commerce together, the same men went further, and so wrought that the Argives, renouncing their league with the Mantineans, Eleians, and Athenians, made league and alliance with the Lacedaemonians in this form.

79. "It seemeth good to the Lacedaemonians and Argives to make league and alliance for fifty years on these articles:

"That either side shall allow unto the other equal and like trials of judgment, after the form used in their cities.

"That the rest of the cities of Peloponnesus (this league and alliance comprehending also them) shall be free both from the laws and payments of any other city than their own, holding what they have and affording equal and like trials of judgment according to the form used in their several cities.

"That every of the cities confederate with the Lacedaemonians, without Peloponnesus, shall be in the same condition with the Lacedaemonians; and the confederates of the Argives in the same with the Argives, every one holding his own.

"That if at any time there shall need an expedition to be taken in common, the Lacedaemonians and the Argives shall consult thereof and decree as shall stand most with equity towards the confederates. And that if any controversy arise between any of the cities, either within or without Peloponnesus, about limits or other matter, they also shall decide it.

"That if any confederate city be at contention with another, it shall have recourse to that city which they both shall think most indifferent; but the particular men of any one city shall be judged according to the law of the same."

80. Thus was the peace and league concluded; and whatsoever one had taken from the other in the war, or whatsoever one had against another otherwise, was all acquitted. Now, when they were together settling their business, they ordered that the Argives should neither admit herald nor ambassage from the Athenians till they were gone out of Peloponnesus and had quit the fortification, nor should make peace or war with any without consent of the rest. And amongst other things which they did in this heat, they sent ambassadors from both

their cities to the towns lying upon Thrace and unto Perdiccas, whom they also persuaded to swear himself of the same league. Yet he revolted not from the Athenians presently, but intended it, because he saw the Argives had done so, and was himself also anciently descended out of Argos. They likewise renewed their old oath with the Chalcideans and took another besides it. The Argives sent ambassadors also to Athens, requiring them to abandon the fortification they had made against Epidaurus. And the Athenians, considering that the soldiers they had in it were few in respect to the many others that were with them in the same, sent Demosthenes to fetch them away. He, when he was come and had exhibited for a pretence a certain exercise of naked men without the fort, when the rest of the garrison were gone forth to see it, made fast the gates; and afterwards having renewed the league with the Epidaurians, the Athenians by themselves put the fort into their hands.

81. After the revolt of the Argives from the league, the Mantineans also, though they withstood it at first, yet being too weak without the Argives, made their peace with the Lacedaemonians and laid down their command over the other cities. And the Lacedaemonians and Argives with a thousand men of either city having joined their arms, the Lacedaemonians first, with their single power, reduced the government of Sicyon to a smaller number; and then they both together dissolved the democracy at Argos. And the oligarchy was established conformable to the state of Lacedaemon.

These things passed in the end of winter and near the spring. And so ended the fourteenth year of this war.

82. The next summer the Dictidears seated in Mount Athos revolted from the Athenians to the Chalcideans.

And the Lacedaemonians ordered the state of Achaia after their own form, which before was otherwise. But the Argives, after they had by little and little assembled themselves and recovered heart, taking the time when the Lacedaemonians were celebrating their exercises of the naked youth, assaulted the few; and in a battle fought within the city, the commons had the victory; and some they slew, others they drave into exile. The Lacedaemonians, though those of their faction in Argos sent for them, went not a long time after; yet at last they ad-

journed the exercises and came forth with intention of giving
them aid. But hearing by the way at Tegea that the few were
overcome, they could not be entreated by such as had escaped
thence to go on, but returning, went on with the celebration
of their exercises. But afterwards, when there came ambassadors
unto them, both from the Argives in the city, and from them
that were driven out, there being present also their confederates, and much alleged on either side, they concluded at last
that those in the city had done the wrong and decreed to go
against Argos with their army; but many delays passed, and
much time was spent between. In the meantime the common
people of Argos, fearing the Lacedaemonians and regaining the
league with Athens, as conceiving the same would turn to their
very great advantage, raised long walls from their city down
to the sea-shore, to the end that if they were shut up by land,
they might yet with the help of the Athenians bring things
necessary into the city by sea. And with this their building
some other cities of Peloponnesus were also acquainted. And
the Argives universally, themselves and wives and servants,
wrought at the wall, and had workmen and hewers of sto..
from Athens. So this summer ended.

83. The next winter the Lacedaemonians, understanding that
they were fortifying, came to Argos with their army, they
and their confederates all but the Corinthians; and some practice they had beside within the city itself of Argos. The army
was commanded by Agis, the son of Archidamus, king of the
Lacedaemonians. But those things which were practising in
Argos and supposed to have been already mature did not then
succeed. Nevertheless they took the walls that were then in
building and razed them to the ground; and then, after they
had taken Hysiae, a town in the Argive territory, and slain
all the freemen in it, they went home and were dissolved every
one to his own city. After this, the Argives went with an army
into Phliasia, which when they had wasted, they went back.
They did it because the men of Phlius had received their outlaws; for there the greatest part of them dwelt.

The same winter the Athenians shut up Perdiccas in Macedonia [from the use of the sea], objecting that he had sworn
the league of the Argives and Lacedaemonians; and that when

they had prepared an army, under the command of Nicias, the son of Niceratus, to go against the Chalcideans upon Thrace and against Amphipolis, he had broken the league made betwixt them and him, and by his departure was the principal cause of the dissolution of that army, and was therefore an enemy. And so this winter ended, and the fifteenth year of this war.

84. The next summer went Alcibiades to Argos with twenty galleys and took thence the suspected Argives and such as seemed to savour of the Lacedaemonian faction, to the number of three hundred, and put them into the nearest of the islands subject to the Athenian state.

The Athenians made war also against the isle of Melos, with thirty galleys of their own, six of Chios, and two of Lesbos. Wherein were of their own twelve hundred men of arms, three hundred archers, and twenty archers on horseback; and of their confederates and islanders, about fifteen hundred men of arms. The Melians are a colony of the Lacedaemonians, and therefore refused to be subject, as the rest of the islands were, unto the Athenians, but rested at the first neutral; and afterwards, when the Athenians put them to it by wasting of their land, they entered into open war.

Now the Athenian commanders, Cleomedes, the son of Lycomedes, and Tisias, the son of Tisimachus, being encamped upon their land with these forces, before they would hurt the same sent ambassadors to deal with them first by way of conference. These ambassadors the Melians refused to bring before the multitude, but commanded them to deliver their message before the magistrates and the few; and they accordingly said as followeth:

85. *Athenians.* "Since we may not speak to the multitude, for fear lest when they hear our persuasive and unanswerable arguments all at once in a continued oration, they should chance to be seduced (for we know that this is the scope of your bringing us to audience before the few), make surer yet that point, you that sit here; answer you also to every particular, not in a set speech, but presently interrupting us whensoever anything shall be said by us which shall seem unto you to be otherwise. And first answer us whether you like this motion or not?"

86. Whereunto the council of the Melians answered: "The

equity of a leisurely debate is not to be found fault withal; but this preparation of war, not future but already here present, seemeth not to agree with the same. For we see that you are come to be judges of the conference, and that the issue of it, if we be superior in argument and therefore yield not, is likely to bring us war, and if we yield, servitude."

87. *Ath.* "Nay, if you be come together to reckon up suspicions of what may be, or to any other purpose than to take advice upon what is present and before your eyes, how to save your city from destruction, let us give over. But if this be the point, let us speak to it."

88. *Mel.* "It is reason, and pardonable for men in our cases, to turn both their words and thoughts upon divers things. Howsoever, this consultation being held only upon the point of our safety, we are content, if you think good, to go on with the course you have propounded."

89. *Ath.* "As we therefore will not, for our parts, with fair pretences, as, that having defeated the Medes, our reign is therefore lawful, or that we come against you for injury done, make a long discourse without being believed; so would we have you also not expect to prevail by saying either that you therefore took not our parts because you were a colony of the Lacedaemonians or that you have done us no injury. But out of those things which we both of us do really think, let us go through with that which is feasible, both you and we knowing that in human disputation justice is then only agreed on when the necessity is equal; whereas they that have odds of power exact as much as they can, and the weak yield to such conditions as they can get."

90. *Mel.* "Well then (seeing you put the point of profit in the place of justice), we hold it profitable for ourselves not to overthrow a general profit to all men, which is this: that men in danger, if they plead reason and equity, nay, though somewhat without the strict compass of justice, yet it ought ever to do them good. And the same most of all concerneth you, forasmuch as you shall else give an example unto others of the greatest revenge that can be taken if you chance to miscarry."

91. *Ath.* "As for us, though our dominion should cease, yet

we fear not the sequel. For not they that command, as do the Lacedaemonians, are cruel to those that are vanquished by them (yet we have nothing to do now with the Lacedaemonians), but such as having been in subjection have assaulted those that commanded them and gotten the victory. But let the danger of that be to ourselves. In the meantime we tell you this: that we are here now both to enlarge our own dominion and also to confer about the saving of your city. For we would have dominion over you without oppressing you, and preserve you to the profit of us both."

92. *Mel.* "But how can it be profitable for us to serve, though it be so for you to command?"

93. *Ath.* "Because you, by obeying, shall save yourselves from extremity; and we, not destroying you, shall reap profit by you."

94. *Mel.* "But will you not accept that we remain quiet and be your friends (whereas before we were your enemies), and take part with neither?"

95. *Ath.* "No. For your enmity doth not so much hurt us as your friendship will be an argument of our weakness and your hatred of our power amongst those we have rule over."

96. *Mel.* "Why? Do your subjects measure equity so, as to put those that never had to do with you, and themselves, who for the most part have been your own colonies, and some of them after revolt conquered, into one and the same consideration?"

97. *Ath.* "Why not? For they think they have reason on their side, both the one sort and the other, and that such as are subdued are subdued by force, and such as are forborne are so through our fear. So that by subduing you, besides the extending of our dominion over so many more subjects, we shall assure it the more over those we had before, especially being masters of the sea, and you islanders, and weaker (except you can get the victory) than others whom we have subdued already."

98. *Mel.* "Do you think then, that there is no assurance in that which we propounded? For here again (since driving us from the plea of equity you persuade us to submit to your profit), when we have shewed you what is good for us, we

must endeavour to draw you to the same, as far forth as it shall be good for you also. As many therefore as now are neutral, what do you but make them your enemies, when, beholding these your proceedings, they look that hereafter you will also turn your arms upon them? And what is this, but to make greater the enemies you have already, and to make others your enemies, each against their wills, that would not else have been so?"

99. *Ath.* "We do not think that they shall be ever the more our enemies, who inhabiting anywhere in the continent, will be long ere they so much as keep guard upon their liberty against us. But islanders unsubdued, as you be, or islanders offended with the necessity of subjection which they are already in, these may indeed, by unadvised courses, put both themselves and us into apparent danger."

100. *Mel.* "If you then to retain your command, and your vassals to get loose from you, will undergo the utmost of danger, would it not in us, that be already free, be great baseness and cowardice if we should not encounter anything whatsoever rather than suffer ourselves to be brought into bondage?"

101. *Ath.* "No, if you advise rightly. For you have not in hand a match of valour upon equal terms, wherein to forfeit your honour, but rather a consultation upon your safety that you resist not such as be so far your overmatches."

102. *Mel.* "But we know that, in matter of war, the event is sometimes otherwise than according to the difference of number in sides; and that if we yield presently, all our hope is lost; whereas if we hold out, we have yet a hope to keep ourselves up."

103. *Ath.* "Hope, the comfort of danger, when such use it as have to spare, though it hurt them, yet it destroys them not. But to such as set their rest upon it (for it is a thing by nature prodigal), it at once by failing maketh itself known; and known, leaveth no place for future caution.* Which let not be your

---

* The Greek here is exceedingly difficult, but Hobbes has at best expressed only the gist of this sentence. It means "But for those who are making a cast for their all (and hope is naturally prodigal), it (hope) is only known for what it is at the moment of failure, and even in a case where a man knows it so and guards against it,

own case, you that are but weak and have no more but this one stake. Nor be you like unto many men, who, though they may presently save themselves by human means, will yet, when upon pressure of the enemy their most apparent hopes fail them, betake themselves to blind ones, as divination, oracles, and other such things which with hopes destroy men."

104. *Mel.* "We think it, you well know, a hard matter for us to combat your power and fortune, unless we might do it on equal terms. Nevertheless we believe that, for fortune, we shall be nothing inferior, as having the gods on our side, because we stand innocent against men unjust; and for power, what is wanting in us will be supplied by our league with the Lacedaemonians, who are of necessity obliged, if for no other cause, yet for consanguinity's sake and for their own honour, to defend us. So that we are confident, not altogether so much without reason as you think."

105. *Ath.* "As for the favour of the gods, we expect to have it as well as you; for we neither do nor require anything contrary to what mankind hath decreed, either concerning the worship of the gods or concerning themselves.* For of the gods we think according to the common opinion; and of men, that for certain by necessity of nature they will everywhere reign over such as they be too strong for. Neither did we make this law nor are we the first that use it made; but as we found it, and shall leave it to posterity for ever, so also we use it, knowing that you likewise, and others that should have the same power which we have, would do the same. So that forasmuch as toucheth the favour of the gods, we have in reason no fear of being inferior. And as for the opinion you have of the Lacedaemonians, in that you believe they will help you for their own honour, we bless your innocent minds, but affect not your folly. For the Lacedaemonians, though in respect of themselves

---

it still plagues him" (literally, "does not desert him"). The following passage explains a lot. Men in a dangerous situation might save themselves by human means. Instead, they trust to open or reasonable hope, and when these fail have recourse to the blind expectation of oracles, divination, etc.

* A closer translation would be something like this: "Neither in what we claim nor what we do are we outside of what man thinks about the gods and what he wishes for himself."

and the constitutions of their own country they are wont for the most part to be generous; yet in respect of others, though much might be alleged, yet the shortest way one might say it all thus: that most apparently of all men, they hold for honourable that which pleaseth, and for just that which profiteth. And such an opinion maketh nothing for your now absurd means of safety."

106. *Mel.* "Nay, for this same opinion of theirs, we now the rather believe that they will not betray their own colony, the Melians, and thereby become perfidious to such of the Grecians as be their friends and beneficial to such as be their enemies."

107. *Ath.* "You think not, then, that what is profitable must be also safe, and that which is just and honourable must be performed with danger, which commonly the Lacedaemonians are least willing of all men to undergo [for others]."

108. *Mel.* "But we suppose that they will undertake danger for us rather than for any other; and that they think that we will be more assured unto them than unto any other, because for action, we lie near to Peloponnesus, and for affection, are more faithful than others for our nearness of kin."

109. *Ath.* "The security of such as are at wars consisteth not in the good will of those that are called to their aid, but in the power of those means they excel in. And this the Lacedaemonians themselves use to consider more than any; and therefore, out of diffidence in their own forces, they take many of their confederates with them, though to an expedition but against their neighbours. Wherefore it is not likely, we being masters of the sea, that they will ever pass over into an island."

110. *Mel.* "Yea, but they may have others to send; and the Cretic sea is wide, wherein to take another is harder for him that is master of it than it is for him that will steal by to save himself. And if this course fail, they may turn their arms against your own territory or those of your confederates not invaded by Brasidas. And then you shall have to trouble yourselves no more about a territory that you have nothing to do withal, but about your own and your confederates."

111. *Ath.* "Let them take which course of these they will that you also may find by experience and not be ignorant that the Athenians never yet gave over siege for fear of any diver-

sion upon others. But we observe that, whereas you said you would consult of your safety, you have not yet in all this discourse said anything which a man relying on could hope to be preserved by; the strongest arguments you use are but future hopes; and your present power is too short to defend you against the forces already arranged against you. You shall therefore take very absurd counsel, unless, excluding us, you make amongst yourselves some more discreet conclusion; for [when you are by yourselves], you will no more set your thoughts upon shame, which, when dishonour and danger stand before men's eyes, for the most part undoeth them. For many, when they have foreseen into what dangers they were entering, have nevertheless been so overcome by that forcible word dishonour that that which is but called dishonour hath caused them to fall willingly into immedicable calamities, and so to draw upon themselves really, by their own madness, a greater dishonour than could have befallen them by fortune. Which you, if you deliberate wisely, will take heed of, and not think shame to submit to a most potent city, and that upon so reasonable conditions as of league and of enjoying your own under tribute; and seeing choice is given you of war or safety, do not out of peevishness take the worse. For such do take the best course who, though they give no way to their equals, yet do fairly accommodate to their superiors, and towards their inferiors use moderation. Consider of it, therefore, whilst we stand off; and have often in your mind that you deliberate of your country, which is to be happy or miserable in and by this one consultation."

112. So the Athenians went aside from the conference; and the Melians, after they had decreed the very same things which before they had spoken, made answer unto them in this manner: "Men of Athens, our resolution is no other than what you have heard before; nor will we, in a small portion of time, overthrow that liberty in which our city hath remained for the space of seven hundred years since it was first founded. But trusting to the fortune by which the gods have preserved it hitherto and unto the help of men, that is, of the Lacedaemonians, we will do our best to maintain the same. But this we offer: to be your

friends, enemies to neither side, and you to depart out of our land, after agreement such as we shall both think fit."

113. Thus the Melians answered. To which the Athenians, the conference being already broken off, replied thus: "You are the only men, as it seemeth to us, by this consultation, that think future things more certain than things seen, and behold things doubtful, through desire to have them true, as if they were already come to pass. As you attribute and trust the most unto the Lacedaemonians, and to fortune and hopes, so will you be the most deceived."

114. This said, the Athenian ambassadors departed to their camp. And the commanders, seeing that the Melians stood out, fell presently to the war, and dividing the work among the several cities, encompassed the city of the Melians with a wall. The Athenians afterwards left some forces of their own and of their confederates for a guard both by sea and land, and with the greatest part of their army went home. The rest that were left besieged the place.

115. About the same time the Argives, making a road into Phliasia, lost about eighty of their men by ambush laid for them by the men of Phlius and the outlaws of their own city. And the Athenians that lay in Pylus fetched in thither a great booty from the Lacedaemonians. Notwithstanding which, the Lacedaemonians did not war upon them [as] renouncing the peace, but gave leave by edict only to any of their people that would to take booties reciprocally in the territory of the Athenians. The Corinthians also made war upon the Athenians; but it was for certain controversies of their own, and the rest of Peloponnesus stirred not.

The Melians also took that part of the wall of the Athenians, by an assault in the night, which looked towards the market place, and having slain the men that guarded it, brought into the town both corn and other provision, whatsoever they could buy for money, and so returned and lay still. And the Athenians from thenceforth kept a better watch. And so this summer ended.

116. The winter following, the Lacedaemonians being about to enter with their army into the territory of the Argives, when

they perceived that the sacrifices which they made on the border for their passage were not acceptable, returned. And the Argives, having some of their own city in suspicion in regard of this design of the Lacedaemonians, apprehended some of them, and some escaped.

About the same time the Melians took another part of the wall of the Athenians, they that kept the siege being then not many. But this done, there came afterwards some fresh forces from Athens, under the conduct of Philocrates, the son of Demeas. And the town being now strongly besieged, there being also within some that practised to have it given up, they yielded themselves to the discretion of the Athenians, who slew all the men of military age, made slaves of the women and children, and inhabited the place with a colony sent thither afterwards of five hundred men of their own.

THE SIXTH BOOK

1. The same winter the Athenians, with greater forces than
they had before sent out with Laches and Eurymedon, resolved
to go again into Sicily, and, if they could, wholly to subdue
it, being for the most part ignorant both of the greatness of
the island, and of the multitude of people, as well Greeks as
barbarians, that inhabited the same, and that they undertook
a war not much less than the war against the Peloponnesians.
For the compass of Sicily is little less than eight days' sail for
a ship; and though so great, is yet divided with no more than
twenty furlongs, sea measure, from the continent.

2. It was inhabited in old time thus, and these were the nations that held it: The most ancient inhabitants in a part thereof are said to have been the Cyclopes and Laestrigones, of whose stock and whence they came or to what place they removed I have nothing to say. Let that suffice which the poets have spoken and which every particular man hath learned of them. After them, the first that appear to have dwelt therein are the Sicanians, as they say themselves, nay, before the other, as being the natural breed of the island. But the truth is, they were Iberians, and driven away by the Ligyans from the banks of Sicanus, a river on which they were seated in Iberia. And the island from them came to be called Sicania, which was before Trinacria. And these [two] inhabit yet in the western parts of Sicily. After the taking of Illium, certain Trojans, escaping the hands of the Grecians, landed with small boats in Sicily; and having planted themselves on the borders of the Sicanians, both the nations in one were called Elymi; and their cities were Eryx and Egesta. Hard by these came and dwelled also certain Phoceans, who, coming from Troy, were by tempest carried first into Africa and thence into Sicily. But the Siculi passed out of Italy (for there they inhabited), flying from the Opici, having, as is most likely and as it is reported, observed the strait, and with a fore wind gotten over in boats which they made suddenly on the occasion, or perhaps by some other means.

There is at this day a people in Italy called Siculi. And Italy itself got that name after the same manner from a king of Arcadia called Italus. Of these a great army crossing into Sicily overthrew the Sicanians in battle and drave them into the south and west parts of the same; and instead of Sicania, caused the island to be called Sicilia; and held and inhabited the best of the land for near three hundred years after their going over, and before any of the Grecians came thither. And till now they possess the midland and north parts of the island.

Also the Phoenicians inhabited the coast of Sicily on all sides, having taken possession of certain promontories and little islands adjacent, for trade's sake with the Sicilians. But after that many Grecians were come in by sea, the Phoenicians abandoned most of their former habitations, and uniting themselves, dwelt in Motya and Soloeis and Panormus, upon the borders of the Elymi, as relying upon their league with the Elymi, and because also from thence lay the shortest cut over unto Carthage. These were the barbarians, and thus they inhabited Sicily.

3. Now for Grecians, first a colony of Chalcideans, under Thucles, their conductor, going from Euboea, built Naxos and the altar of Apollo Archegetes, now standing without the city, upon which the ambassadors employed to the oracles, as often as they launch from Sicily, are accustomed to offer their first sacrifice. The next year Archias, a man of the Herculean family, carried a colony from Corinth and became founder of Syracuse, where first he drave the Siculi out of that island in which the inner part of the city now standeth, not now environed wholly with the sea as it was then. And in process of time, when the city also that is without was taken in with a wall, it became a populous city. In the fifth year after the building of Syracuse, Thucles and the Chalcideans, going from Naxos, built Leontium, expelling thence the Siculi, and after that Catana; but they that went to Catana chose Euarchus for their founder.

4. About the same time in Sicily arrived also Lamis, with a colony from Megara, and first built a certain town called Trotilus, upon the river Pantacius, where for a while after he governed the estate of his colony in common with the Chalcideans of Leontium. But afterwards, when he was by them thrust out, and had builded Thapsus, he died; and the rest going from Thapsus, under the conduct of Hyblon, a king of the Siculi, built Megara, called Megara-Hyblaea. And after they had there inhabited two hundred and forty-five years, they were by Gelon, a tyrant of Syracuse, put out both of the city and territory. But before they were driven thence, namely one hundred years after they had built it, they sent out Pammilus and built the city of Selinus. This Pammilus came to them from Megara, their own metropolitan city, and so together with them founded Selinus. Gela was built in the forty-fifth year after Syracuse, by Antiphemus, that brought a colony out of Rhodes, and by Entymus, that did the like out of Crete, jointly. This city was named after the name of the river Gela; and the place where now the city standeth, and which at first they walled

in, was called Lindii. And the laws which they established were
the Doric. About one hundred and eight years after their own
foundation, they of Gela built the city of Acragante, calling
the city after the name of the river; and for their conductors
chose Aristonous and Pystilus, and gave unto them the laws
of Gela. Zancle was first built by pirates that came from Cume,
a Chalcidean city in Opicia; but afterwards there came a multitude, and helped to people it, out of Chalcis and the rest of
Euboea; and their conductors were Perieres and Crataemenes,
one of Cume, the other of Chalcis. And the name of the city
was at first Zancle, so named by the Sicilians because it hath
the form of a sickle, and the Sicilians call a sickle *zanclon*. But
these inhabitants were afterwards chased thence by the Samians
and other people of Ionia that in their flight from the Medes
fell upon Sicily. After this, Anaxilas, tyrant of Rhegium, drave
out the Samians, and peopling the city with a mixed people
of them and his own, instead of Zancle called the place by the
name of his own country from whence he was anciently descended, Messana.

5. After Zancle was built Himera, by Eucleides, Simus, and
Sacon, the most of which colony were Chalcideans; but there
were also amongst them certain outlaws of Syracuse, the vanquished part of a sedition, called the Myletidae. Their language
grew to a mean between the Chalcidean and Doric; but the laws
of the Chalcidean prevailed. Acrae and Casmenae were built by
the Syracusians, Acrae twenty years after Syracuse, and Casmenae almost twenty after Acrae. Camarina was at first built by
the Syracusians, very near the hundred and thirty-fifth year of
their own city, Dascon and Menecolus being the conductors.
But the Camarinaeans having been by the Syracusians driven
from their seat by war for revolt, Hippocrates, tyrant of Gela,
in process of time, taking of the Syracusians that territory for
ransom of certain Syracusian prisoners, became their founder,
and placed them in Camarina again. After this again, having
been driven thence by Gelon, they were planted the third time
in the same city.

6. These were the nations, Greeks and barbarians, that inhabited Sicily. And though it were thus great, yet the Athenians longed very much to send an army against it, out of a

desire to bring it all under their subjection, which was the true motive, but as having withal this fair pretext of aiding their kindred and new confederates. But principally they were instigated to it by the ambassadors of Egesta, who were at Athens and earnestly pressed them thereto. For bordering on the territory of the Selinuntians, they had begun a war about certain things concerning marriage and about a piece of ground that lay doubtfully between them. And the Selinuntians, having leagued themselves with the Syracusians, infested them with war both by sea and by land. Insomuch as the Egestaeans, putting the Athenians in mind of their former league with the Leontines made by Laches, prayed them to send a fleet thither in their aid, alleging, amongst many other things, this as principal: that if the Syracusians, who had driven the Leontines from their seat, should pass without revenge taken on them, and so proceed, by consuming the rest of the allies of the Athenians there, to get the whole power of Sicily into their hands, it would be dangerous lest hereafter some time or other, being Dorians, they should with great forces aid the Dorians for affinity, and being a colony of the Peloponnesians join with the Peloponnesians that sent them out, to pull down the Athenian empire; that it were wisdom, therefore, with those confederates they yet retain, to make head against the Syracusians; and the rather, because for the defraying of the war the Egestaeans would furnish money sufficient of themselves. Which things when the Athenians had often heard in their assemblies from the mouths of the Egestaean ambassadors and of their advocates and patrons, they decreed to send ambassadors to Egesta to see, first, whether there were in their treasury and temples so much wealth as they said there was, and to bring word in what terms the war stood between that city and the Selinuntians. And ambassadors were sent into Sicily accordingly.

7. The same winter the Lacedaemonians and their confederates, all but the Corinthians, having drawn out their forces into the territory of the Argives, wasted a small part of their fields and carried away certain cart-loads of their corn. Thence they went to Orneae, and having placed there the Argive outlaws, left with them a few others of the rest of the army; and then making a composition for a certain time, that they of

Orneae and those Argives should not wrong each other, they carried their army home. But the Athenians arriving not long after with thirty galleys and six hundred men of arms, the people of Argos came also forth with their whole power, and joining with them, sat down betimes in the morning * before Orneae. But when at night the army went somewhat far off to lodge, they within fled out; and the Argives, the next day perceiving it, pulled Orneae to the ground and went home. And so also did the Athenians not long after with their galleys. Also the Athenians transported certain horsemen by sea, part of their own and part Macedonian fugitives that lived with them, into Methone and ravaged the territory of Perdiccas. And the Lacedaemonians sent unto the Chalcideans upon Thrace, who held peace with the Athenians from ten days to ten days, appointing them to aid Perdiccas. But they refused. And so ended the winter, and the sixteenth year of this war written by Thucydides.

8. The next summer, early in the spring, the Athenian ambassadors returned from Sicily, and the ambassadors of Egesta with them, and brought in silver uncoined sixty talents, for a month's pay of sixty galleys, which they would entreat the Athenians to send thither. And the Athenians, having called an assembly and heard both from the Egestaean and their own ambassadors, amongst other persuasive but untrue allegations, touching their money, how they had great store ready both in their treasury and temples, decreed the sending of sixty galleys into Sicily, and Alcibiades, the son of Cleinias, Nicias, the son of Niceratus, and Lamachus, the son of Xenophanes, for commanders with authority absolute; the which were to aid the people of Egesta against the Selinuntians, and withal, if they had time to spare, to plant the Leontines anew in their city, and to order all other the affairs of Sicily as they should think most for the profit of the Athenians. Five days after this the people assembled again to consult of the means how most speedily to put this armada in readiness and to decree such things as the generals should further require for the expedition. But Nicias, having heard that himself was chosen for one of the generals, and conceiving that the state had not well re-

* The Greek means "for one day."

solved, but affected the conquest of all Sicily, a great matter, upon small and superficial pretences, stood forth, desiring to have altered this the Athenians' purpose, and spake as followeth:

9. "Though this assembly was called to deliberate of our preparation and of the manner how to set forth our fleet for Sicily, yet to me it seemeth that we ought rather once again to consult whether it be not better not to send it at all than, upon a short deliberation in so weighty an affair and upon the credit of strangers, to draw upon ourselves an impertinent war. For my own part, I have honour by it; and for the danger of my person, I esteem it the least of all men (not but that I think him a good member of the commonwealth * that hath regard also to his own person and estate; for such a man especially will desire the public to prosper for his own sake): but as I have never spoken heretofore, so nor now will I speak anything that is against my conscience, for gaining to myself a pre-eminence of honour: but that only which I apprehend for the best. And although I am sure that if I go about to persuade you to preserve what you already hold, and not to hazard things certain for uncertain and future, my words will be too weak to prevail against your humour; yet this I must needs let you know, that neither your haste is seasonable nor your desires easy to be achieved.

10. "For I say that going thither you leave many enemies here behind you, and more you endeavour to draw hither. You perhaps think that the league will be firm that you have made with the Lacedaemonians; which, though as long as you stir not, may continue a league in name (for so some have made it of their own side †), yet if any considerable forces of ours chance to miscarry, our enemies will soon renew the war, as having made the peace constrained by calamities, and upon terms of more dishonour and necessity than ourselves; besides, in the league itself we have many things controverted. And some there be that refuse utterly to accept it, and they none of the

---

* The Greek says "an *equally* good citizen."
† The Greek says "for that is the way some have made it both on our own side and the enemy's." What is meant is a reference to Alcibiades on the Athenian side and the Spartan ephors Cleobulus and Xenares.

weakest; whereof some are now in open war against us, and others, because the Lacedaemonians stir not, maintain only a truce with us from ten to ten days, and so are contented yet to hold their hands. But, peradventure, when they shall hear that our power is distracted, which is the thing we now hasten to do, they will be glad to join in the war with the Sicilians against us, the confederacy of whom they would heretofore have valued above many other. It behoveth us * therefore to consider of these things and not to run into new dangers when the state of our own city hangeth unsettled, nor seek a new dominion before we assure that which we already have. For the Chalcideans of Thrace, after so many years' revolt, are yet unreduced; and from others in divers parts of the continent we have but doubtful obedience. But the Egestaeans, being forsooth our confederates and wronged, they in all haste must be aided; though to right us on those by whom we have a long time ourselves been wronged, that we defer.

11. "And yet if we should reduce the Chalcideans into subjection, we could easily also keep them so; but the Sicilians, though we vanquish them, yet being many and far off, we should have much ado to hold them in obedience. Now it were madness to invade such, whom conquering you cannot keep, and failing, should lose the means for ever after to attempt the same again. As for the Sicilians, it seemeth unto me, at least as things now stand, that they shall be of less danger to us if they fall under the dominion of the Syracusians than they are now; and yet this is it that the Egestaeans would most affright us with. For now the states of Sicily, in several, may perhaps be induced, in favour of the Lacedaemonians, to take part against us; whereas then, being reduced into one, it is not likely they would hazard with us state against state. For by the same means that they, joining with the Peloponnesians, may pull down our dominion, by the same it would be likely that the Peloponnesians

---

* It is hard to be sure about the meaning of this. Where Hobbes translates "us," the Greek uses the word which means "a certain," but it also means "one," like the French *on* or German *man*. Consequently, Thucydides may be saying either "It behoves one (i.e., us) to consider," or, more directly, "It behooves someone (i.e., Alcibiades) to consider."

would subvert theirs. The Grecians there will fear us most if we go not at all; next, if we but show our forces and come quickly away. But if any misfortune befall us, they will presently despise us and join with the Grecians here to invade us. For we all know that those things are most admired which are farthest off, and which least come to give proof of the opinion conceived of them. And this, Athenians, is your own case with the Lacedaemonians and their confederates, whom because beyond your hope you have overcome in those things for which at first you feared them, you now in contempt of them turn your arms upon Sicily. But we ought not to be puffed up upon the misfortunes of our enemies, but to be confident then only when we have mastered their designs. Nor ought we to think that the Lacedaemonians set their minds on anything else but how they may yet for the late disgrace repair their reputation, if they can, by our overthrow, and the rather because they have so much and so long laboured to win an opinion in the world of their valour. The question with us therefore, if we be well advised, will not be of the Egestaeans in Sicily, but how we may speedily defend our city against the insidiation of them that favour the oligarchy.

12. "We must remember also that we have had now some short recreation from a late great plague and great war, and thereby are improved both in men and money, which it is most meet that we should spend here upon ourselves and not upon those outlaws which seek for aid, seeing it maketh for them to tell us a specious lie; who, contributing only words whilst their friends bear all the danger, if they speed well, shall be disobliged of thanks, if ill, undo their friends for company. Now if there be any man here that for ends of his own, as being glad to be general, especially being yet too young to have charge in chief, shall advise the expedition to the end he may have admiration for his expense upon horses and help from his place to defray that expense, suffer him not to purchase his private honour and splendour with the danger of the public fortune. Believe rather that such men, though they rob the public, do nevertheless consume also their private wealth. Besides, the matter itself is full of great difficulties, such as it is not fit for a young man to consult of, much less hastily to take in hand.

13. "And I, seeing those now sit by and abet the same man, am fearful of them; and I do on the other side exhort the elder sort (if any of them sit near those other) not to be ashamed to deliver their minds freely, as fearing that if they gave their voice against the war they should be esteemed cowards, nor to doat (as they do) upon things absent, knowing that by passion the fewest actions and by reason the most do prosper; but rather for the benefit of their country, which is now cast into greater danger than ever before, to hold up their hands on the other side and decree that the Sicilians, within the limits they now enjoy, not misliked by you, and with liberty to sail by the shore in the Ionian gulf, and in the main of the Sicilian sea, shall possess their own and compound their differences between themselves. And for the Egestaeans, to answer them in particular thus: that as without the Athenians they had begun the war against the Selinuntians, so they should without them likewise end it; and that we shall no more hereafter, as we have used to do, make such men our confederates, as when they do injury, we must maintain it, and when we require their assistance, cannot have it.

14. "And you, the president, if you think it your office to take care of the commonwealth and desire to be a good member of the same, put these things once more to the question, and let the Athenians speak to it again. Think (if you be afraid to infringe the orders of the assembly) * that before so many witnesses it will not be made a crime, but that you shall be rather thought a physician of your country, that hath swallowed down evil counsel. And he truly dischargeth the duty of a president who laboureth to do his country the most good, or at least will not willingly do it hurt."

15. Thus spake Nicias. But the most of the Athenians that spake after him were of opinion that the voyage ought to pro-

---

* Plainly, the putting of the question the second time, that is, asking for a second vote on a matter already determined by this same assembly, could be construed as a fundamental questioning of the will of the people and, presumably, as punishable on somewhat the same grounds as treason is. Certainly it is hard to get the president and the presiding tribe to do it. Notice, for instance, the same difficulty in regard to the second debate on the fate of the people of Mitylene in Book iii.

ceed, the decree already made not to be reversed; yet some there were that said to the contrary. But the expedition was most of all pressed by Alcibiades, the son of Cleinias, both out of desire he had to cross Nicias, with whom he was likewise at odds in other points of state, and also for that he had glanced at him invidiously in his oration, but principally for that he affected to have charge, hoping that himself should be the man to subdue both Sicily and Carthage to the state of Athens, and withal, if it succeeded, to increase his own private wealth and glory. For being in great estimation with the citizens, his desires were more vast than for the proportion of his estate, both in maintaining of horses and other his expenses, was meet; which proved afterwards none of the least causes of the subversion of the Athenian commonwealth. For most men fearing him, both for his excess in things that concerned his person and form of life and for the greatness of his spirit in every particular action he undertook, as one that aspired to the tyranny, they became his enemy. And although for the public he excellently managed the war, yet every man, privately displeased with his course of life, gave the charge of the wars to others, and thereby not long after overthrew the state. Alcibiades at this time stood forth and spake to this effect:

16. "Men of Athens, it both belongeth unto me more than to any other to have this charge; and withal I think myself (for I must needs begin with this, as having been touched by Nicias) to be worthy of the same. For those things for which I am so much spoken of do indeed purchase glory to my progenitors and myself; but to the commonwealth they confer both glory and profit. For the Grecians have thought our city a mighty one, even above the truth, by reason of my brave appearance at the Olympic games, whereas before they thought easily to have warred it down. For I brought thither seven chariots * and not only won the first, second, and fourth prize, but carried also in all other things a magnificence worthy the honour of the victory. And in such things as these, as there is honour to

---

* The Greek adds "which no private person had ever done before," distinguishing between the chariots equipped by private persons and the national teams, publicly financed, sent by the several states. At the Olympic races the national and private chariots ran together.

be supposed according to the law, so is there also a power conceived upon sight of the thing done. As for my expenses in the
city upon setting forth of shows,* or whatsoever else is remarkable in me, though naturally it procure envy in other
citizens, yet to strangers this also is an argument of our greatness. Now, it is no unprofitable course of life when a man shall
at his private cost not only benefit himself but also the commonwealth. Nor doth he that beareth himself high upon his
own worth and refuseth to make himself fellow with the rest
wrong the rest; for if he were in distress, he should not find any
man that would share with him in his calamity. Therefore, as
we are not so much as saluted when we be in misery, so let
them likewise be content to be contemned of us when we
flourish; or if they require equality, let them also give it. I know
that such men, or any man else that excelleth in the glory of
anything whatsoever, shall as long as he liveth be envied, principally of his equals, and then also of others amongst whom he
converseth; but with posterity they shall have kindred claimed
of them, though there be none; and his country will boast of
him, not as of a stranger or one that had been a man of lewd
life, but as their own citizen and one that had achieved worthy
and laudable acts. This being the thing I aim at and for which
I am renowned, consider now whether I administer the public
the worse for it or not. For having reconciled unto you the
most potent states of Peloponnesus without much either danger
or cost, I compelled the Lacedaemonians to stake all that ever
they had upon the fortune of one day of Mantineia.†

17. And this hath my youth and madness, supposed to have
been very madness, with familiar and fit words wrought upon
the power of the Peloponnesians, and shewing reason for my
passion, made my madness now no longer to be feared.‡ But as

* In Athens the expenses incurred in the putting on of plays were all
discharged by rich men who paid them as part of their tax obligations.

† The Greek adds "From this battle it is true they escaped, but
even now they have not recovered their confidence."

‡ This does not seem the correct sense. The literal translation would
be something like this: "This is what my youth (and what appears to
be my unnatural folly) achieved in its dealing with the power of the
Peloponnesians by the use of appropriate speeches, and by its very
passion carried conviction."

long as I flourish with it, and Nicias is esteemed fortunate, make you use of both our services. And abrogate not your decree touching the voyage into Sicily, as though the power were great you are to encounter withal. For the number wherewith their cities are populous is but of promiscuous nations, easily shifting and easily admitting new comers, and consequently not sufficiently armed, any of them, for the defence of their bodies, nor furnished, as the custom of the place appointeth, to fight for their country. But what any of them thinks he may get by fair speech or snatch from the public by sedition, that only he looks after, with purpose, if he fail, to run the country.* And it is not likely that such a rabble should either with one consent give ear to what is told them or unite themselves for the administration of their affairs in common; but if they hear of fair offers, they will one after one be easily induced to come in, especially if there be seditions amongst them, as we hear there are. And the truth is, there are neither so many men of arms as they boast of, nor doth it appear that there are so many Grecians there in all as the several cities have every one reckoned for their own number. Nay, even Greece hath much belied itself, and was scarce sufficiently armed in all this war past. So that the business there, for all that I can by fame understand, is even as I have told you, and will yet be easier. For we shall have many of the barbarians, upon hatred of the Syracusians, to take our parts against them there; and if we consider the case aright, there will be nothing to hinder us at home. For our ancestors, having the same enemies which they say we leave behind us now in our voyage to Sicily, and the Persian besides, did nevertheless erect the empire we now have by our only odds of strength at sea. And the hope of the Peloponnesians against us was never less than now it is, though their power were also as great as ever; for they would be able to invade our land, though we went not into Sicily; and by sea they can do us no harm though we go, for we shall leave a navy sufficient to oppose theirs behind us.

18. "What therefore can we allege with any probability for our backwardness; or what can we pretend unto our con-

---

* Our colloquial usage may mislead us; Hobbes' meaning is "intending, if he should fail, to flee from the country."

federates for denying them assistance? Whom we ought to defend, were it but because we have sworn it to them, without objecting that they have not reciprocally aided us. For we took them not into league that they should come hither with their aids, but that by troubling our enemies there they might hinder them from coming hither against us. And the way whereby we, and whosoever else hath dominion hath gotten it, hath ever been the cheerful succouring of their associates that required it, whether they were Greeks or barbarians. For if we should all sit still, or stand to make choice which were fit to be assisted and which not, we should have little under our government of the estates of other men, but rather hazard our own. For when one is grown mightier than the rest, men use not only to defend themselves against him when he shall invade, but to anticipate him, that he invade not at all. Nor is it in our power to be our own carvers how much we will have subject to us; but considering the case we are in, it is as necessary for us to seek to subdue those that are not under our dominion, as to keep so those that are; lest if others be not subject to us, we fall in danger of being subjected unto them. Nor are we to weigh quietness in the same balance that others do, unless also the institution of this state were like unto that of other states. Let us rather make reckoning by enterprising abroad to increase our power at home, and proceed on our voyage that we may cast down the haughty conceit of the Peloponnesians and show them the contempt and slight account we make of our present ease by undertaking this our expedition into Sicily. Whereby, either conquering those states we shall become masters of all Greece, or weaken the Syracusians, to the benefit of ourselves and our confederates. And for our security to stay, if any city shall come to our side, or to come away if otherwise, our galleys will afford it. For in that we shall be at our own liberty, though all the Sicilians together were against it.

"Let not the speech of Nicias, tending only to laziness and to the stirring of debate between the young men and the old, avert you from it; but with the same decency wherewith your ancestors, consulting young and old together, have brought our dominion to the present height, endeavour you likewise to enlarge the same. And think not that youth or age, one without the other, is of any effect, but that the simplest, the middle sort, and the exactest judgments tempered together is it that doth the greatest good; and that a state as well as any other thing will, if it rest, wear out of itself, and all men's knowledge decay; whereas by the exercise of war experience will continually increase, and the city will get a habit of resisting the enemy, not with words, but action. In sum, this is my opinion: that a state accustomed to be active, if it once grow idle, will quickly be subjected by the change; and that they of all men are most surely planted that with most unity observe the present laws and customs, though not always of the best."

19. Thus spake Alcibiades. The Athenians, when they had heard him, together with the Egestaeans and Leontine outlaws, who being then present entreated, and objecting to them their oath, begged their help in form of suppliants, were far more earnestly bent upon the journey than they were before. But Nicias, when he saw he could not alter their resolution with his oration, but thought he might perhaps put them from it by the greatness of the provision, if he should require it with the most, stood forth again and said in this manner.

20. "Men of Athens, forasmuch as I see you violently bent on this expedition, such effect may it take as is desired. Nevertheless I shall now deliver my opinion upon the matter as it yet standeth. As far as we understand by report, we set out against great cities, not subject one to another, nor needing innovation, whereby they should be glad, out of hard servitude, to admit of easier masters, nor such as are likely to prefer our government before their own liberty; but many (as for one island), and those Greek cities. For besides Naxos and Catana (which too I hope will join with us for their affinity with the Leontines), there are other seven, furnished in all respects after the manner of our own army, and especially those two against which we bend our forces most, Selinus and Syracuse. For there are in them many men of arms, many archers, many darters, besides many galleys and a multitude of men to man them. They have also store of money, both amongst private men and in their temples. This have the Selinuntians. The Syracusians have a tribute beside, coming in from some of the barbarians. But that wherein they exceed us most is this: that they abound in

horses, and have corn of their own, not fetched in from other places.

21. "Against such a power we shall therefore need not a fleet only, and with it a small army, but there must great forces go along of land soldiers, if we mean to do anything worthy of our design and not to be kept by their many horsemen from landing; especially if the cities there, terrified by us, should now hold all together, and none but the Egestaeans prove our friends and furnish us with a cavalry to resist them. And it would be a shame either to come back with a repulse or to send for a new supply afterwards, as if we had not wisely considered our enterprise at first. Therefore we must go sufficiently provided from hence, as knowing that we go far from home and are to make war in a place of disadvantage, and not as when we went as confederates to aid some of our subjects here at home, where we had easy bringing in of necessaries to the camp from the territories of friends. But we go far off, and into a country of none but strangers, and from whence in winter there can hardly come a messenger unto us in so little as four months.

22. "Wherefore I am of opinion that we ought to take with us many men of arms of our own, of our confederates, and of our subjects; and also out of Peloponnesus as many as we can get, either for love or money; and also many archers and slingers, whereby to resist their cavalry; and much spare shipping, for the more easy bringing in of provision. Also our corn, I mean wheat and barley parched, we must carry with us from hence in ships; and bakers from the mills, hired and made to work by turns, that the army, if it chance to be weatherbound, may not be in want of victual. For being so great, it will not be for every city to receive it. And so for all things else, we must as much as we can provide them ourselves and not rely on others. Above all, we must take hence as much money as we can; for as for that which is said to be ready at Egesta, think it ready in words, but not in deeds.

23. "For although we go thither with an army not only equal unto theirs, but also (excepting their men of arms for battle) in everything exceeding it, yet so shall we scarce be able both to overcome them and withal to preserve our own. We must

also make account that we go to inhabit some city in that foreign and hostile country, and either the first day we come thither to be presently masters of the field, or failing, be assured to find all in hostility against us. Which fearing, and knowing that the business requires much good advice and more good fortune (which is a hard matter, being we are but men), I would so set forth as to commit myself to fortune as little as I may and take with me an army that in likelihood should be secure. And this I conceive to be both the surest course for the city in general and the safest for us that go the voyage. If any man be of a contrary opinion, I resign him my place."

24. Thus spake Nicias, imagining that either the Athenians would, upon the multitude of the things required, abandon the enterprise; or if he were forced to go, he might go with the more security. But the Athenians gave not over the desire they had of the voyage for the difficulty of the preparation, but were the more inflamed thereby to have it proceed; and the contrary fell out of that which he before expected. For they approved his counsel and thought now there would be no danger at all. And every one alike fell in love with the enterprise: the old men, upon hope to subdue the place they went to, or that at least so great a power could not miscarry; and the young men, upon desire to see a foreign country and to gaze, making little doubt but to return with safety. As for the common sort and the soldiers, they made account to gain by it not only their wages for the time, but also so to amplify the state in power as that their stipend should endure forever. So that through the vehement desire thereunto of the most, they also that liked it not, for fear if they held up their hands against it to be thought evil-affected to the state, were content to let it pass.

25. And in the end a certain Athenian stood up and, calling upon Nicias, said he ought not to shift off nor delay the business any longer, but to declare there before them all what forces he would have the Athenians to decree him. To which unwillingly he answered and said he would consider of it first with his fellow-commanders. Nevertheless, for so much as he could judge upon the sudden, he said there would need no less than one hundred galleys, whereof for transporting of men of arms, so many of the Athenians' own as they themselves should think

meet, and the rest to be sent for to their confederates; and that of men of arms in all, of their own and of their confederates, there would be requisite no less than five thousand, but rather more, if they could be gotten; and other provision proportionable. As for archers, both from hence and from Crete, and slingers, and whatsoever else should seem necessary, they would provide it themselves and take it with them.

26. When the Athenians had heard him, they presently decreed that the generals should have absolute authority, both touching the greatness of the preparation and the whole voyage, to do therein as should seem best unto them for the commonwealth. And after this, they went in hand with the preparation accordingly, and both sent unto the confederates and enrolled soldiers at home. The city had by this time recovered herself from the sickness and from their continual wars, both in number of men fit for the wars, grown up after the ceasing of the plague, and in store of money gathered together by means of the peace; whereby they made their provisions with much ease. And thus were they employed in preparations for the voyage.

27. In the meantime the Mercuries of stone throughout the whole city of Athens (now there were many of these of square stone set up by the law of the place, and many in the porches of private houses and in the temples) had in one night most of them their faces pared. And no man knew who had done it; and yet great rewards out of the treasury had been propounded to the discoverers, and a decree made that if any man knew of any other profanation, he might boldly declare the same, were he citizen, stranger, or bondman. And they took the fact exceedingly to heart as ominous to the expedition and done withal upon conspiracy for alteration of the state and dissolution of the democracy.

28. Hereupon, certain strangers dwelling in the city and certain serving-men revealed something, not about the Mercuries, but of the paring of the statues of some other of the gods, committed formerly through wantonness and too much wine by young men; and withal, how they had in private houses acted the mysteries of their religion in mockery; amongst whom they also accused Alcibiades. This they that most envied Alcibiades, because he stood in the way that they could not constantly

bear chief sway with the people, making account to have the primacy if they could thrust him out, took hold of and exceedingly aggravated, exclaiming that both the mockery of the mysteries and the paring of the Mercuries tended to the deposing of the people, and that nothing therein was done without him, alleging for argument his other excess in the ordinary course of his life, not convenient in a popular estate.

29. He at that present made his apology and was there ready, if he had done any such thing, to answer it before he went the voyage (for by this time all their preparation was in readiness) and to suffer justice if he were guilty and if absolved to resume his charge, protesting against all accusations to be brought against him in his absence, and pressing to be put to death then presently if he had offended, and saying that it would not be discreetly done to send away a man accused of so great crimes with the charge of such an army before his trial. But his enemies, fearing lest if he came then to his trial he should have had the favour of his army and lest the people, which loved him because the Argives and some of the Mantineans served them in this war only for his sake, should have been mollified, put the matter off and hastened his going out by setting on other orators to advise that for the present he should go, and that the setting forward of the fleet should not be retarded, and that at his return he should have a day assigned him for his trial; their purpose being, upon further accusation, which they might easily contrive in his absence, to have him sent for back to make his answer. And thus it was concluded that Alcibiades should go.

30. After this, the summer being now half spent, they put to sea for Sicily. The greatest part of the confederates and the ships that carried their corn and all the lesser vessels and the rest of the provision that went along, they before appointed to meet [upon a day set] at Corcyra, thence all together to cross over the Ionian gulf to the promontory of Iapygia. But the Athenians themselves and as many of their confederates as were at Athens, upon the day appointed, betimes in the morning came down into Peiraeus and went aboard to take sea. With them came down in a manner the whole multitude of the city, as well inhabitants as strangers, the inhabitants to

follow after such as belonged unto them, some their friends, some their kinsmen, and some their children, filled both with hope and lamentations; hope of conquering what they went for, and lamentation as being in doubt whether ever they should see each other any more, considering what a way they were to go from their own territory; (and now when they were to leave one another to danger, they apprehended the greatness of the same more than they had done before when they decreed the expedition: nevertheless their present strength, by the abundance of everything before their eyes prepared for the journey, gave them heart again in beholding it); but the strangers and other multitude came only to see the shew, as of a worthy and incredible design.

31. For this preparation, being the first Grecian power that ever went out of Greece from one only city, was the most sumptuous and the most glorious of all that ever had been sent forth before it to that day. Nevertheless, for number of galleys and men of arms, that which went forth with Pericles to Epidaurus and that which Agnon carried with him to Potidaea was not inferior to it. For there went four thousand men of arms, three hundred horse, and one hundred galleys out of Athens itself, and out of Lesbos and Chios fifty galleys, besides many confederates that accompanied him in the voyage. But they went not far and were but meanly furnished. Whereas this fleet, as being to stay long abroad, was furnished for both kinds of service, in which of them soever it should have occasion to be employed, both with shipping and land-soldiers. For the shipping, it was elaborate with a great deal of cost, both of the captains of galleys and of the city. For the state allowed a drachma a day to every mariner; the empty galleys which they sent forth, being of nimble ones sixty and of such as carried their men of arms forty more, and the captains of galleys both put into them the most able servants, and besides the wages of the state, unto the [uppermost bank of oars, called the] Thranitae, and to the servants, gave somewhat of their own, and bestowed great cost otherwise every one upon his own galley, both in the badges and other rigging, each one striving to the utmost to have his galley, both in some ornament and also in swiftness, to exceed the rest. And for the

land forces, they were levied with exceeding great choice, and every man endeavoured to excel his fellow in the bravery of his arms and utensils that belonged to his person. Insomuch as amongst themselves it begat quarrel about precedency, but amongst other Grecians, a conceit that it was an ostentation rather of their power and riches than a preparation against an enemy. For if a man enter into account of the expense, as well of the public as of private men that went the voyage, namely, of the public, what was spent already in the business, and what was to be given to the commanders to carry with them, and of private men, what every one had bestowed upon his person and every captain on his galley, besides what every one was likely, over and above his allowance from the state, to bestow on provision for so long a warfare, and what the merchant carried with him for traffic, he will find the whole sum carried out of the city to amount to a great many talents. And the fleet was no less noised amongst those against whom it was to go for the strange boldness of the attempt and gloriousness of the show than it was for the excessive report of their number, for the length of the voyage, and for that it was undertaken with so vast future hopes in respect of their present power.

32. After they were all aboard, and all things laid in that they meant to carry with them, silence was commanded by the trumpet; and after the wine had been carried about to the whole army, and all, as well the generals as the soldiers, had drunk a health to the voyage,* they made their prayers, such as by the law were appointed for before their taking sea, not in every galley apart, but all together, the herald pronouncing them. And the company from the shore, both of the city and whosoever else wished them well, prayed with them. And when they had sung the Paean and ended the health, they put forth to sea; and having at first gone out in a long file, galley after galley, they after went a vie by Aegina. Thus hasted these to

---

* A fair enough seventeenth-century rendering. What the Greeks actually did was to pour a small portion of wine out of each cup in honor of one of the gods and drink off the rest. But the ceremony was, in fact, a solemn wish for good luck for the expedition while asking the god's blessing upon it.

be at Corcyra, to which place also the other army of the confederates were assembling.

At Syracuse they had advertisement of the voyage from divers places; nevertheless it was long ere anything would be believed. Nay, an assembly being there called, orations were made, such as follow, on both parts, as well by them that believed the report touching the Athenian army to be true as by others that affirmed the contrary. And Hermocrates the son of Hermon, as one that thought he knew the certainty, stood forth and spake to this effect:

33. "Concerning the truth of this invasion, though perhaps I shall be thought, as well as other men, to deliver a thing incredible, and though I know that such as be either the authors or relaters of matter incredible shall not only not persuade, but be also accounted fools, nevertheless, I will not fear thereof hold my tongue, as long as the commonwealth is in danger, being confident that I know the truth hereof somewhat more certainly than others do. The Athenians are bent to come even against us (which you verily wonder at), and that with great forces both for the sea and land, with pretence indeed to aid their confederates the Egestaeans and replant the Leontines; but in truth they aspire to the dominion of all Sicily, and especially of this city of ours, which obtained, they make account to get the rest with ease. Seeing then they will presently be upon us, advise with your present means how you may with most honour make head against them, that you may not be taken unprovided through contempt nor be careless through incredulity, and that such as believe it may not be dismayed with their audaciousness and power. For they are not more able to do hurt unto us than we be unto them. Neither indeed is the greatness of their fleet without some advantage unto us; nay, it will be much the better for us in respect of the rest of the Sicilians. For being terrified by them, they will the rather league with us. And if we either vanquish or repulse them without obtaining what they came for (for I fear not at all the effecting of their purpose), verily it will be a great honour to us, and in my opinion not unlikely to come to pass. For in truth there have been few great fleets, whether of Grecians or barbarians, sent far from home that have not prospered ill. Neither are

these that come against us more in number than ourselves and the neighbouring cities; for surely we shall all hold together upon fear. And if for want of necessaries in a strange territory they chance to miscarry, the honour of it will be left to us against whom they bend their councils, though the greatest cause of their overthrow should consist in their own errors. Which was also the case of these very Athenians, who raised themselves by the misfortune of the Medes (though it happened for the most part contrary to reason); because in name they went only against the Athenians. And that the same shall now happen unto us is not without probability.

34. "Let us therefore with courage put in readiness our own forces; let us send to the Siculi to confirm those we have, and to make peace and league with others; and let us send ambassadors to the rest of Sicily to show them that it is a common danger, and into Italy to get them into our league, or at least that they receive not the Athenians. And in my judgment it were our best course to send also to Carthage, for even they are not without expectation of the same danger. Nay, they are in a continual fear that the Athenians will bring war upon them also, even to their city. So that upon apprehension that if they neglect us the trouble will come home to their own door, they will perhaps, either secretly or openly or some way assist us. And of all that now are, they are the best able to do it, if they please. For they have the most gold and silver, by which the wars and all things else are the best expedited. Let us also send to Lacedaemon and to Corinth, praying them not only to send their succours hither with speed, but also to set on foot the war there. But that which I think the best course of all, though through an habit of sitting still you will hardly be brought to it, I will nevertheless now tell you what it is. If the Sicilians all together, or if not all, yet if we and most of the rest, should draw together our whole navy, and with two months' provision go and meet the Athenians at Tarentum and the promontory of Iapygia, and let them see that they must fight for their passage over the Ionian gulf before they fight for Sicily, it would both terrify them the most and also put them into a consideration that we, as the watchmen of our country, come upon them out of an amicable territory (for

we shall be received at Tarentum), whereas they themselves have a great deal of sea to pass with all their preparations and cannot keep themselves in their order for the length of the voyage; and that for us it will be an easy matter to assail them, coming up slowly as they do and thin. Again, if lightening their galleys, they shall come up to us more nimbly and more close together, we shall charge upon them already wearied, or we may, if we please, retire again into Tarentum. Whereas they, if they come over but with a part of their provisions, as to fight at sea, shall be driven into want of victuals in those desert parts, and either staying be there besieged, or, attempting to go by, leave behind them the rest of their provision, and be dejected, as not assured of the cities whether they will receive them or not. I am therefore of opinion that dismayed with this reckoning they will either not put over at all from Corcyra, or whilst they spend time in deliberating and in sending out to explore how many and in what place we are, the season will be lost and winter come; or deterred with our unlooked-for opposition, they will give over the voyage. And the rather for that as I hear the man of most experience amongst their commanders hath the charge against his will and would take a light occasion to return if he saw any considerable stop made by us in the way. And I am very sure we should be voiced amongst them to the utmost. And as the reports are, so are men's minds; and they fear more such as they hear will begin with them than such as give out that they will no more but defend themselves, because then they think the danger equal. Which would be now the case of the Athenians. For they come against us with an opinion that we will not fight, deservedly contemning us because we joined not with the Lacedaemonians to pull them down. But if they should see us once bolder than they looked for, they would be terrified more with the unexpectedness than with the truth of our power itself. Be persuaded therefore, principally to dare to do this, or if not this, yet speedily to make yourselves otherwise ready for the war, and every man to remember that though to show contempt of the enemy be best in the heat of fight, yet those preparations are the surest that are made with fear and opinion of danger. As for the Athenians, they come; and I am sure are already in the way and want only that they are not now here."

35. Thus spake Hermocrates. But the people of Syracuse were at much strife amongst themselves, some contending that the Athenians would by no means come and that the reports were not true, and others that if they came they would do no more harm than they were likely again to receive. Some contemned and laughed at the matter; but some few there were that believed Hermocrates and feared the event. But Athenagoras, who was chief magistrate of the people, and at that time most powerful with the commons, spake as followeth:

36. "He is either a coward or not well affected to the state, whosoever he be, that wishes the Athenians not to be so mad as coming hither to fall into our power. As for them that report such things as these and put you into fear, though I wonder not at their boldness, yet I wonder at their folly, if they think their ends not seen. For they that are afraid of anything themselves will put the city into affright that they may shadow their own with the common fear. And this may the reports do at this time, not raised by chance, but framed on purpose by such as always trouble the state. But if you mean to deliberate wisely, make not your reckoning by the reports of these men but by that which wise men and men of great experience, such as I hold the Athenians to be, are likely to do. For it is not probable that, leaving the Peloponnesians and the war there not yet surely ended, they should willingly come hither to a new war no less the former, seeing, in my opinion, they may be glad that we invade not them, so many and so great cities as we are.

37. "And if indeed they come, as these men say they will, I think Sicily more sufficient to dispatch the war than Peloponnesus, as being in all respects better furnished, and that this our own city is much stronger than the army which they say is now coming, though it were twice as great as it is. For I know they neither bring horses with them nor can they get any here, save only a few from the Egestaeans, nor have men of arms so many as we, in that they are to bring them by sea. For it is a hard matter to come so far as this by sea, though they carried no men of arms in their galleys at all, if they carry with them all other their necessaries, which cannot be small

against so great a city. So that I am so far from the opinion of these others that I think the Athenians, though they had here another city as great as Syracuse, and confining on it, and should from thence make their war, yet should not be able to escape from being destroyed, every man of them, much less now, when all Sicily is their enemy. For in their camp, fenced with their galleys, they shall be cooped up and from their tents and forced munition never be able to stir far abroad without being cut off by our horsemen. In short, I think they shall never be able to get landing, so much above theirs do I value our own forces.

38. "But these things, as I said before, the Athenians, considering, I am very sure will look unto their own; and our men talk here of things that neither are or ever will be, who I know have desired, not only now but ever, by such reports as these or by worse, or by their actions, to put the multitude in fear that they themselves might rule the state. And I am afraid, lest attempting it often, they may one day effect it; and for us, we are too poor-spirited either to foresee it ere it be done, or foreseeing to prevent it. By this means our city is seldom quiet, but subject to sedition and contention, not so much against the enemy as within itself, and sometimes also to tyranny and usurpation. Which I will endeavour (if you will second me) so to prevent hereafter as nothing more of this kind shall befall you; which must be done, first by gaining you the multitude, and then by punishing the authors of these plots, not only when I find them in the action (for it will be hard to take them so), but also for those things which they would and cannot do. For one must not only take revenge upon an enemy for what he hath already done, but strike him first for his evil purpose; for if a man strike not first, he shall first be stricken. And as for the few, I shall in somewhat reprove them, in somewhat have an eye to them, and in somewhat advise them. For this, I think, will be the best course to avert them from their bad intentions. Tell me forsooth (I have asked this question often), you that are the younger sort, What would you have? Would you now bear office? The law allows it not; and the law was made because ye are not [now] sufficient for government, not to disgrace you when you shall be sufficient. But forsooth,

you would not be ranked with the multitude! But what justice
is it, that the same men should not have the same privileges?

39. "Some will say that the democracy is neither a well-gov-
erned nor a just state, and that the most wealthy are aptest to
make the best government. But I answer first, *democracy* is a
name of the whole, *oligarchy* but of a part. Next, though the
rich are indeed fittest to keep the treasure, yet the wise are
the best counsellors, and the multitude, upon hearing, the best
judge. Now in a democracy all these, both jointly and severally,
participate equal privileges. But in the oligarchy they allow
indeed to the multitude a participation of all dangers, but in
matters of profit, they not only encroach upon the multitude,
but take from them and keep the whole. Which is the thing
that you the rich and the younger sort affect, but in a great
city cannot possibly embrace. But yet, O ye the most unwise
of all men, unless you know that what you affect is evil, and
if you know not that, you are the most ignorant of all the
Grecians I know; or, ye most wicked of all men, if knowing
it you dare do this.

40. "Yet I say, inform yourselves better or change your purpose and help to amplify the common good of the city, making account that the good amongst you shall not only have an
equal but a greater share therein than the rest of the multitude;
whereas if you will needs have all, you shall run the hazard
of losing all. Away therefore with these rumours, as discovered
and not allowed. For this city, though the Athenians come, will
be able to defend itself with honour. And we have generals
to look to that matter. And if they come not (which I rather
believe), it will not, upon the terror of your reports, make
choice of you for commanders and cast itself into voluntary
servitude; but taking direction of itself, it both judgeth your
words virtually as facts, and will not upon words let go her
present liberty, but endeavour to preserve it by not committing
the same actually to your discretion."

41. Thus said Athenagoras. Then one of their generals, rising up, forbade any other to stand forth, and spake himself to
the matter in hand to this effect:

"It is no wisdom, neither for the speakers to utter such
calumnies one against another, nor for the hearers to receive

them. We should rather consider, in respect of these reports, how we may in the best manner, both every one in particular and the city in general, be prepared to resist them when they come. And if there be no need, yet to furnish the city with horses and arms and other habiliments of war can do us no hurt. As for the care hereof and the musters, we will look to it, and will send men abroad both to the cities and for spials, and do whatsoever else is requisite. Somewhat we have done already; and what more we shall hereafter find meet, we will from time to time report unto you."

Which when the general had said, the Syracusians dissolved the assembly.

42. The Athenians were now all in Corcyra, both they and their confederates. And first the generals took a view of the whole army and put them into the order wherein they were to anchor and make their naval camp; and having divided them into three squadrons, to each squadron they assigned a captain by lot, to the end that being at sea they might not come into want of water or harbours or any other necessaries where they chanced to stay; and that they might otherwise be the more easy to be governed when every squadron had his proper commander. After this they sent before them three galleys into Italy and Sicily to bring them word what cities in those parts would receive them, whom they appointed to come back and meet them that they might know whether they might be received or not before they put in.

43. This done, the Athenians with all their provisions put out from Corcyra towards Sicily, having with them in all one hundred and thirty-four galleys and two Rhodian long-boats of fifty oars a-piece. Of these, a hundred were of Athens itself, whereof sixty were expedite, the other forty for transportation of soldiers; the rest of the navy belonged to the Chians and other the confederates. Of men of arms they had in all five thousand one hundred. Of these, there were of the Athenians themselves fifteen hundred enrolled and seven hundred more [of the poorer sort, called] Thetes, hired for defence of the galleys. The rest were of their confederates, some of them being their subjects: of Argives there were five hundred; of Mantineans and mercenaries, two hundred and fifty. Their

archers in all, four hundred and eighty, of which eighty were Cretans. Rhodian slingers they had seven hundred. Of light-armed Megarean fugitives, one hundred and twenty; and in one vessel made for transportation of horses, thirty horsemen.

44. These were the forces that went over to the war at first. With these went also thirty ships carrying necessaries, wherein went also the bakers and masons and carpenters and all tools of use in fortification; and with these thirty ships went one hundred boats by constraint, and many other ships and boats that voluntarily followed the army for trade; which then passed all together from Corcyra over the Ionian gulf. And the whole fleet being come to the promontory of Iapygia and to Tarentum and such other places as every one could recover, they went on by the coast of Italy, neither received of the states there into any city nor allowed any market, having only the liberty of anchorage and water (and that also at Tarentum and Locri denied them), till they were at Rhegium, where they all came together again and settled their camp in the temple of Diana (for neither there were they suffered to come in) without the city, where the Rhegians allowed them a market. And when they had drawn their galleys to land, they lay still. Being here, they dealt with the Rhegians, who were Chalcideans, to aid the Leontines, Chalcideans likewise. To which was answered that they would take part with neither, but what the rest of the Italians * should conclude, that also they would do. So the Athenians lay still, meditating on their Sicilian business, how they might carry it the best, and withal expected the return from Egesta of the three galleys which they had sent before them, desiring to know if so much money were there or not, as was reported by their messengers at Athens.

45. The Syracusians in the meantime from divers parts and also from their spies had certain intelligence that the fleet was now at Rhegium: and therefore made their preparations with all diligence and were no longer incredulous, but sent unto the

---

* Hobbes' use of *Italians* is confusing. The Greek word is *Italiots*. This signifies the Greek settlers in Italy. *Italoi* (Italians) is the word used by Thucydides for the non-Greek natives. There is the same distinction between *Siciliots* (Greek settlers in Sicily) and *Siculi* (native Sicilians).

Siculi, to some cities men to keep them from revolting, to others, ambassadors, and into such places as lay upon the sea, garrisons; and examined the forces of their own city, by a view taken of the arms and horse, whether they were complete or not, and ordered all things as for a war at hand and only not already present.

46. The three galleys sent before to Egesta returned to the Athenians at Rhegium and brought word that for the rest of the money promised there was none, only there appeared thirty talents. At this the generals were presently discouraged, both because this first hope was crossed, and because also the Rhegians, whom they had already begun to persuade to their league, and whom it was most likely they should have won, as being of kin to the Leontines and always heretofore favourable to the Athenian state, now refused. And though to Nicias this news from the Egestaeans was no more than he expected, yet to the other two it was extreme strange. But the Egestaeans, when the first ambassadors from Athens went to see their treasure, had thus deceived them. They brought them into the temple of Venus in Eryx and showed them the holy treasure, goblets, flagons, censers, and other furniture, in no small quantity; which being but silver, appeared to the eye a great deal above their true value in money. Then they feasted such as came with them in their private houses, and at those feastings exhibited all the gold and silver vessels they could get together, either in the city of Egesta itself, or could borrow in other as well Phoenician as Grecian cities, for their own. So all of them in a manner making use of the same plate, and much appearing in every of those houses, it put those which came with the ambassadors into a very great admiration, insomuch as at their return to Athens they strove who should first proclaim what wealth they had seen. These men, having both been abused themselves and having abused others, when it was told that there was no such wealth in Egesta, were much taxed by the soldiers. But the generals went to counsel upon the business in hand.

47. Nicias was of this opinion: that it was best to go presently with the whole fleet to Selinus, against which they were chiefly set forth, and if the Egestaeans would furnish them with money

for the whole army, then to deliberate further upon the occasion; if not, then to require maintenance for the sixty galleys set forth at their own request, and staying with them by force or composition to bring the Selinuntians and them to a peace; and thence passing along by other of those cities, to make a show of the power of the Athenian state, and of their readiness to help their friends and confederates; and so to go home, unless they could light on some quick and unthought-of means to do some good for the Leontines, or gain some of the other cities to their own league; and not to put the commonwealth in danger at her own charges.

48. Alcibiades said it would not do well to have come out from Athens with so great a power and then dishonourably without effect to go home again; but rather to send heralds to every city but Selinus and Syracuse and assay to make the Siculi revolt from the Syracusians and others to enter league with the Athenians, that they might aid them with men and victual; and first to deal with the Messanians, as being seated in the passage and most opportune place of all Sicily for coming in, and having a port and harbour sufficient for their fleet; and when they had gained those cities, and knew what help they were to have in the war, then to take in hand Syracuse and Selinus, unless these would agree with the Egestaeans and the other suffer the Leontines to be replanted.

49. But Lamachus was of opinion that it was best to go directly to Syracuse and to fight with them as soon as they could at their city whilst they were yet unfurnished and their fear at the greatest. For that an army is always most terrible at first, but if it stay long ere it come in sight, men recollect their spirits and contemn it the more when they see it. Whereas if it come upon them suddenly while they expect it with fear, it would the more easily get the victory, and everything would affright them, as the sight of it (for then they would appear most for number) and the expectation of their sufferings, but especially the danger of a present battle. And that it was likely that many men might be cut off in the villages without, as not believing they would come; and though they should be already gotten in, yet the army, being master of the field and sitting. down before the city, could want no money; and the other

Sicilians would then neglect leaguing with the Syracusians, and
join with the Athenians, no longer standing off and spying who
should have the better. And for a place to retire unto and
anchor in, he thought Megara most fit: being desert, and not
far from Syracuse neither by sea nor land.

50. Lamachus said, but came afterwards to the opinion of
Alcibiades. After this, Alcibiades, with his own galley having
passed over to Messana, and propounded to them a league and
not prevailed, they answering that they would not let the army
in but allow them only a market without the walls, returned
back to Rhegium. And presently the generals, having out of
the whole fleet manned threescore galleys and taken provision
aboard, went along the shore to Naxos, having left the rest
of the army with one of the generals at Rhegium. The Naxians
having received them into the city, they went on by the coast
to Catana. But the Catanaeans receiving them not (for there
were some within that favoured the Syracusians), they entered
the river of Terias; and having stayed there all that night, went
the next day towards Syracuse leisurely with the rest of their
galleys; but ten they sent before into the great haven, ⌈not to
stay, but⌉ to discover if they had launched any fleet there,
and to proclaim from their galleys that the Athenians were come
to replant the Leontines on their own, according to league and
affinity, and that therefore such of the Leontines as were in
Syracuse, should without fear go forth to the Athenians as to
their friends and benefactors. And when they had thus proclaimed, and well considered the city and the havens and the
region where they were to seat themselves for the war, they
returned to Catana.

51. An assembly being called at Catana, though they refused
to receive the army they admitted the generals and willed them
to speak their minds. And whilst Alcibiades was in his oration
and the citizens at the assembly, the soldiers, having secretly
pulled down a little gate which was but weakly built, entered
the city and were walking up and down in the market. And
the Catanaeans, such as favoured the Syracusians, seeing the
army within, for fear stole presently out of the town, being
not many. The rest concluded the league with the Athenians
and willed them to fetch in the rest of the army from Rhegium.
After this, the Athenians went back to Rhegium, and rising

from thence, came to Catana with their whole army together.

52. Now they had news from Camarina that if they would come thither, the Camarinaeans would join with them, and that the Syracusians were manning their navy. Whereupon with the whole army they went along the coast, first to Syracuse, where not finding any navy manned, they went on to Camarina. And being come close up to the shore, they sent a herald unto them. But the Camarinaeans would not receive the army, alleging that they had taken an oath not to receive the Athenians with more than one galley unless they should have sent for more of their own accord. Having lost their labour, they departed, and landed in a part of the territory of Syracuse, and had gotten some booty. But the Syracusian horsemen coming out and killing some stragglers of the light-armed, they returned again to Catana.

53. Here they find the galley called Salaminia, come thither from Athens, both for Alcibiades, who was commanded to come home to purge himself of such things as were laid to his charge by the state, and also for other soldiers that were with him, whereof some were accused for profanation of the mysteries and some also for the Mercuries. For the Athenians, after the fleet was put to sea, proceeded nevertheless in the search of those that were culpable, both concerning the mysteries and the Mercuries. And making no inquiry into the persons of the informers, but through jealousy admitting of all sorts, upon the reports of evil men apprehended very good citizens and cast them into prison, choosing rather to examine the fact and find the truth by torments,* than that any man, how good soever in estimation, being once accused should escape unquestioned. For the people, having by fame understood that the tyranny of Peisistratus and his sons was heavy in the latter end, and withal, that neither themselves nor Harmodius, but the Lacedaemonians overthrew it,† were ever fearful, and apprehended every thing suspiciously.

* Hobbes is probably wrong in his interpretation here. The word used means "to sift completely," "to torture," but since the object of the verb is "the matter," it seems likely that what Thucydides means is "to sift the affair completely."

† Thucydides is referring to the dictatorship of Peisistratus and his sons which was terminated nearly one hundred years before this time. Popular legend was that two popular young Athenians, Harmodius

54. For the fact of Aristogeiton and Harmodius was undertaken upon an accident of love, which unfolding at large, I
shall make appear that neither any other, nor the Athenians
themselves, report any certainty either of their own tyrants or
of the fact. For the old Peisistratus dying in the tyranny, not
Hipparchus, as the most thing, but Hippias, who was his eldest
son, succeeded in the government. Now Harmodius, a man in
the flower of his youth, of great beauty, was in the power of
one Aristogeiton, a citizen of a middle condition that was his
lover. This Harmodius, having been solicited by Hipparchus,
the son of Peisistratus, and not yielding, discovered the same
unto Aristogeiton. He apprehending it (as lovers use) with
a great deal of anguish and fearing the power of Hipparchus,
lest he should take him away by force, fell presently, as much
as his condition would permit, to a contriving how to pull down
the tyranny. In the meantime Hipparchus, having again attempted Harmodius and not prevailed, intended, though not
to offer him violence, yet in secret, as if forsooth he did it not
for that cause, to do him some disgrace. For neither was the
government otherwise heavy till then, but carried without their
evil will. And to say the truth, these tyrants held virtue and
wisdom in great account for a long time, and taking of the
Athenians but a twentieth part of their revenues, adorned the
city, managed their wars, and administered their religion
worthily. In other points they were governed by the laws
formerly established, save that these took a care ever to prefer
to the magistracy men of their own adherence. And amongst
many that had the annual office of archon, Peisistratus also
had it, the son of Hippias, of the same name with his grandfather, who also, when he was archon, dedicated the altar of

---

and Aristogeiton, put an end to the tyranny by murdering the reigning
tyrant, one of the sons of Peisistratus. The fact, as narrated below, was
that the murdered man was the nonreigning brother of the tyrant, that
the motives were personal and discreditable, and that the deliverance
of Athens from dictatorship had to wait for the action of the Lacedaemonians. The latter were traditionally for aristocratic feudalism
if at all possible, and otherwise for an oligarchy of wealth, but opposed either to an openly exercised democratic power or a dictatorship, which in Greece was usually the outcome of a period of
democratic crisis.

the twelve gods in the market place and that other in the temple of Apollo Pythius. And though the people of Athens, amplifying afterwards that altar which was in the market place, thereby defaced the inscription; yet that upon the altar that is in the temple of Apollo Pythius is to be seen still, though in letters somewhat obscure, in these words:

> *Peisistratus the son of Hippias*
> *Erected this to stand*
> *I'th' Temple of Apollo Pythius,*
> *Witness of his command.*

55. And that Hippias, being the elder brother, had the government, I can affirm, as knowing it by a more exact relation than other men; and it may be known also by this: It appears that of all the legitimate brethren, this only had children, as is both signified by the altar and also by that pillar which for a testimony of the injustice of the tyrants was erected in the Athenian citadel. In which there is no mention of any son of Thessalus or of Hipparchus, but of five sons of Hippias, which he had by Myrrhine, the daughter of Callias, the son of Hyperechidas; for it is probable that the eldest was first married. And in the forepart of the pillar, his name after his father's was the first, not without reason, as being both next him in age and having also enjoyed the tyranny. Nor indeed could Hippias have easily taken on him the government on a sudden, if his brother had died seized of the tyranny, and he been the same day to settle it on himself. Whereas he retained the same with abundant security, both for the customary fear in the people and diligence in the guard, and was not to seek like a younger brother, to whom the government had not continually been familiar. But Hipparchus came to be named for his misfortune, and thereby grew an opinion afterwards that he was also tyrant.

56. This Harmodius therefore that denied his suit, he disgraced as he before intended. For when some had warned a sister of his, a virgin, to be present to carry a little basket in a procession, they rejected her again when she came and said that they had never warned her at all, as holding her unworthy the honour. This was taken heavily by Harmodius; but Aris-

togeiton, for his sake, was far more exasperated than he. Whereupon, with the rest of the conspirators, he made all things
ready for the execution of the design. Only they were to stay
the time of the holiday called the Great Panathenaea, upon
which day only such citizens as lead the procession might, without suspicion, be armed in good number. And they were to
begin the fact themselves; but the rest were to help them against
the halberdiers. Now the conspirators, for their better security,
were not many; for they hoped that such also as were not
privy to it, if they saw it once undertaken, being upon this occasion armed, would assist in the recovery of their own liberty.

57. When this holiday was come, Hippias was gone out of
the city into the place called Cerameicum with his guard of
halberdiers, and was ordering the procession how it was to go.
And Harmodius and Aristogeiton, with each of them a dagger,
proceeded to the fact. But when they saw one of the conspirators familiarly talking with Hippias (for Hippias was very
affable to all men), they were afraid and believed that they were
discovered and must presently have been apprehended. They
resolved therefore (if it were possible) to be revenged first upon
him that had done them the wrong, and for whose sake they
had undergone all this danger, and, furnished as they were, ran
[furiously] into the city, and finding Hipparchus at a place
called Leocorium, without all regard of themselves fell upon
him, and with all the anger in the world, one upon jealousy, the
other upon disgrace, struck and slew him. Aristogeiton, for the
present, by means of the great confluence of people, escaped
through the guard, but taken afterwards, was ungently handled;
but Harmodius was slain upon the place.

58. The news being brought to Hippias in the Cerameicum,
he went not towards the place where the fact was committed,
but presently unto those that were armed for the solemnity of
the shows and were far off, that he might be with them before
they heard of it; and composing his countenance [as well as he
could] to dissemble the calamity, pointed to a certain place
and commanded them to repair thither without their arms.
Which they did accordingly, expecting that he would have told
them somewhat. But having commanded his guard to take
those arms away, he then fell presently to picking out of such

as he meant to question and whosoever else was found amongst them with a dagger. For with shields and spears to be in [the head of] the procession was of custom.

59. Thus was the enterprise first undertaken upon quarrel of love, and then upon a sudden fear followed this unadvised adventure of Harmodius and Aristogeiton. And after this time the tyranny grew sorer to the Athenians than it had been before. And Hippias, standing more in fear, not only put many of the citizens to death, but also cast his eye on the states abroad to see if he might get any security from them in this alteration at home. He therefore afterwards (though an Athenian and to a Lampsacen) gave his daughter Archedice unto Aeantidas, the son of Hippocles, tyrant of Lampsacus, knowing that the Lampsacens were in great favour with King Darius. And her sepulchre is yet to be seen with this inscription:

> *Archedice, the daughter of King Hippias,*
> *Who in his time*
> *Of all the potentates of Greece was prime,*
> *This dust doth hide.*
> *Daughter, wife, sister, mother unto kings she was,*
> *Yet free from pride.*

And Hippias, after he had reigned three years more in Athens, and was in the fourth deposed by the Lacedaemonians and the exiled Alcmaeonides, went under truce to Sigeium, and to Aeantidas at Lampsacus, and thence to King Darius; from whence, twenty years after in his old age, he came to Marathon with the Medan army.

60. The people of Athens bearing this in mind, and remembering all they had heard concerning them, were extremely bitter and full of jealousy towards those that had been accused of the mysteries, and thought all to have been done upon some oligarchical or tyrannical conspiracy. And whilst they were passionate upon this surmise, many worthy men had already been cast in prison; and yet they were not likely so to give over, but grew daily more savage, and sought to apprehend more still. Whilst they were at this pass, a prisoner * that seemed most to be guilty was persuaded by one of his fellow prisoners to

---

* Andocides, the orator whose speech "On the Mysteries" we possess.

accuse somebody, whether it were true or not true; (for it is but conjectural on both sides; nor was there ever, then or after, any man that could say certainly who it was that did the deed); who brought him to it by telling him that though he had not done it, yet he might be sure to save his own life and should deliver the city from the present suspicion; and that he should be more certain of his own safety by a free confession than by coming to his trial if he denied it. Hereupon, he accused both himself and others for the Mercuries. The people of Athens, gladly receiving the certainty (as they thought) of the fact, and having been much vexed before to think that the conspirators should never [perhaps] be discovered to their multitude, presently set at liberty the accuser and the rest with him whom he had not appeached; but for those that were accused, they appointed judges, and all they apprehended they executed; and having condemned to die such as fled, they ordained a sum of money to be given to those that should slay them. And though it were all this while uncertain whether they suffered justly or unjustly, yet the rest of the city had a manifest ease for the present.

61. But touching Alcibiades, the Athenians took it extreme ill through the instigation of his enemies, the same that had opposed him before he went. And seeing it was certain, as they thought, for the Mercuries, the other crime also concerning the mysteries, whereof he had been accused, seemed a great deal the more to have been committed by him upon the same reason and conspiracy against the people. For it fell out withal, whilst the city was in a tumult about this, that an army of the Lacedaemonians was come as far as the isthmus upon some design against the Boeotians.* These therefore they thought were come thither not against the Boeotians, but by appointment of him, and that if they had not first apprehended the persons appeached, the city had been betrayed. And one night they watched all night long in their arms in the temple of Theseus within the city. And the friends of Alcibiades in

---

* This is a slip on the part of Hobbes. The Greek means "a small army of the Lacedaemonians came as far as the isthmus on some matter where they had an understanding with the Boeotians." Similarly in the next sentence the meaning is "not because of the Boeotians."

Argos were at the same time suspected of a purpose to set upon the people there; whereupon the Athenians also delivered unto the Argive people those hostages which they held of theirs in the islands to be slain. And there were presumptions against Alcibiades on all sides. Insomuch, as purposing by law to put him to death, they sent, as I have said, the galley called Salaminia into Sicily both for him and the rest with him that had been accused; but gave command to those that went not to apprehend him, but to bid him follow them to make his purgation, because they had a care not to give occasion of stir either amongst their own or their enemy's soldiers, but especially because they desired that the Mantineans and the Argives, who they thought followed the war by his persuasion, might not depart from the army. So he and the rest accused with him in his own galley, in company of the Salaminia, left Sicily and set sail for Athens. But being at Thurii they followed no further, but left the galley and were no more to be found, fearing indeed to appear to the accusation. They of the Salaminia made search for Alcibiades and those that were with him for a while, but not finding him, followed on their course for Athens. Alcibiades, now an outlaw, passed shortly after in a small boat from Thurii · into Peloponnesus; and the Athenians, proceeding to judgment upon his not appearing, condemned both him and them to death.

62. After this, the Athenian generals that remained in Sicily, having divided the army into two and taken each his part by lot, went with the whole towards Selinus and Egesta with intention both to see if the Egestaeans would pay them the money and withal to get knowledge of the designs of the Selinuntians and learn the state of their controversy with the Egesteans. And sailing by the coast of Sicily, having it on their left hand, on that side which lieth to the Tyrrhene gulf, they came to Himera, the only Grecian city in that part of Sicily; which not receiving them, they went on, and by the way took Hyccara, a little town of the Sicanians enemy to the Egestaeans, and a sea-town; and having made the inhabitants slaves, delivered the town to the Egestaeans, whose horse-forces were there with them. Thence the Athenians with their landsmen returned through the territory of the Siculi to Catana; and the galleys went about with the captives. Nicias going with the fleet presently from Hyccara

to Egesta, when he had dispatched with them his other business and received thirty talents of money, returned to the army. The captives they ransomed, of which they made one hundred and twenty talents more. Then they sailed about to their confederates of the Siculi, appointing them to send their forces; and with the half of their own they came before Hybla in the territory of Gela, an enemy city, but took it not. And so ended this summer.

63. The next winter the Athenians fell presently to make preparation for their journey against Syracuse; and the Syracusians, on the other side, prepared to invade the Athenians. For seeing the Athenians had not presently, upon the first fear and expectation of their coming, fallen upon them, they got every day more and more heart. And because they went far from them into those other parts of Sicily, and assaulting Hybla could not take it, they contemned them more than ever, and prayed their commanders (as is the manner of the multitude when they be in courage), seeing that the Athenians came not unto them, to conduct them to Catana. And the Syracusian horsemen, which were ever abroad for scouts, spurring up to the camp of the Athenians, amongst other scorns asked them whether they came not rather to dwell in the land of another than to restore the Leontines to their own.

64. The Athenian generals, having observed this and being desirous to draw forth the Syracusians' whole power as far as might be from the city, to be able in the meantime without impeachment, going thither in the night by sea, to seize on some convenient place to encamp in; for they knew they should not be able to do it so well in the face of an enemy prepared, nor if they were known to march by land, for that the Syracusian horsemen being many would greatly annoy the light-armed and other multitude, they themselves having no horsemen there; whereas thus they might possess themselves of a place where the horse could not do them any hurt at all to speak of (now the Syracusian outlaws that were with them had told them of a place near the temple Olympieium, which also they seized); I say, the Athenian generals, to bring this their purpose to effect contrived the matter thus: They send a man, of whose fidelity they were well assured, and in the opinion of the Syracusian

commanders no less a friend of theirs. This man was a Catanaean and said he came from Catana, from such and such, whose names they knew, and knew to be the remnant of their well-willers in that city. He told them that the Athenians lay every night within the town and far from their arms; and that if with the whole power of their city, at a day appointed betimes in a morning they would come to their camp, those friends of the Syracusians would shut the Athenians in and set on fire their galleys, by which means the Syracusians, assaulting the pallisado, might easily win the camp, and that the Catanaeans that were to help them herein were many, and those he came from already prepared for it.

65. The Syracusian commanders, having been also otherwise encouraged, and having intended a preparation to go against Catana thought this messenger had not come, did so much the more unadvisedly believe the man, and straightways being agreed of the day on which they were to be there, sent him away. These commanders (for by this time the Selinuntians and some other their confederates were come in) appointed the Syracusians universally to set forwards by a day. And when all their necessaries were in readiness and the day at hand on which they were to be there, they set forwards towards Catana and encamped the night following upon the banks of the river Simaethus in the territory of the Leontines. The Athenians, upon advertisement that they were set forth, rising with their whole army, both themselves and such of the Siculi and others as went with them, and going aboard their galleys and boats, in the beginning of the night set sail for Syracuse. In the morning betimes the Athenians disbarked over against Olympieium to make their camp. And the Syracusian horsemen, who were at Catana before the rest, finding the camp risen, came back to the foot and told them; whereupon they went all together back to the aid of the city.

66. In the meantime, the way the Syracusians had to go being long, the Athenians had pitched their camp at leisure in a place of advantage, wherein it was their own power to begin battle when they list, and where both in and before the battle the Syracusian horsemen could least annoy them. For on one side there were walls and houses and trees and a lake that kept them

off; on the other side steep rocks; and having felled trees hard by and brought them to the seaside, they made a pallisado both before their galleys and towards Dascon. And on that part that was most accessible to the enemy, they made a fort with stone (the best they could find, but unwrought) and with wood, and withal pulled down the bridge of the river Anapus. Whilst this was doing, there came none to empeach them from the city. The first that came against them were the Syracusian horsemen, and by and by after, all the foot together. And though at first they came up near unto the camp of the Athenians, yet after, seeing the Athenians came not out against them, they retired again, and crossing to the other side of the Helorine highway, stayed there that night.

67. The next day the Athenians and their confederates prepared to fight, and were ordered thus: The Argives and the Mantineans had the right wing, the Athenians were in the middle, and the rest of their confederates in the other wing. That half of the army which stood foremost was ordered by eight in file; the other half towards their tents, ordered likewise by eights, was cast into the form of a long square and commanded to observe diligently where the rest of the army was in distress and to make specially thither. And in the midst of these so arranged were received such as carried the weapons and tools of the army.

The Syracusians arranged their men of arms, who were Syracusians of all conditions and as many of their confederates as were present, by sixteen in file (they that came to aid them, were chiefly the Selinuntians, and then the horsemen of the Geloans, about two hundred, and of the Camarinaeans, about twenty horsemen and fifty archers); the cavalry they placed in the right point of the battle, being in all no less than a thousand two hundred, and with them the darters. But the Athenians intending to begin the battle, Nicias went up and down the army, from one nation to another, to whom and to all in general he spake to this effect:

68. "What need I, sirs, to make a long exhortation when this battle is the thing for which we all came hither? For in my opinion, the present preparation is more able to give you encouragement than any oration how well soever made, if with a

weak army. For where we are together, Argives, Mantineans, Athenians, and the best of the islanders, how can we choose among so many and good confederates, but conceive great hope of the victory; especially against tag and rag, and not chosen men, as we are ourselves, and against Sicilians, who though they contemn us, cannot stand against us, their skill not being answerable to their courage? It must be remembered also that we be far from our own and not near to any amicable territory but such as we shall acquire by the sword. My exhortation to you, I am certain, is contrary to that of the enemy. For they say to theirs, 'You are to fight *for* your country.' I say to you, You are to fight *out of* your country, where you must either get the victory, or not easily get away; for many horsemen will be upon us. Remember therefore every man his own worth, and charge valiantly; and think the present necessity and strait we are in to be more formidable than the enemy."

69. Nicias, having thus exhorted the army, led it presently to the charge. The Syracusians expected not to have fought at that instant; and the city being near, some of them were gone away; and some for haste came in running; and though late, yet every one, as he came, put himself in where was the greatest number. For they wanted neither willingness nor courage, either in this or any other battle, being no less valiant, so far forth as they had experience, than the Athenians; but the want of this made them, even against their wills, to abate also somewhat of their courage. Nevertheless though they thought not the Athenians would have begun the battle, and were thereby constrained to fight upon a sudden, yet they resumed their arms and came presently forward to the encounter.

And first, the casters of stones and slingers and archers of either side skirmished in the midst between the armies, mutually chasing each other, as amongst the light-armed was not unlikely. After this, the soothsayers brought forth their sacrifices according to the law of the place; and the trumpets instigated the men of arms to the battle. And they came on to fight, the Syracusians for their country and their lives for the present, and for their liberty in the future; on the other side, the Athenians to win the country of another and make it their own and not to weaken their own by being vanquished; the Argives and other free confederates, to help the Athenians to conquer the country they came against and to return to their own with victory; and their subject confederates came also on with great courage, principally for their better safety, as desperate if they overcame not, and withal upon the by, that by helping the Athenians to subdue the country of another, their own subjection might be the easier.

70. After they were come to hand-strokes, they fought long on both sides. But in the meantime there happened some claps of thunder and flashes of lightning together with a great shower of rain; insomuch as it added to the fear of the Syracusians, that were now fighting their first battle and not familiar with the wars; whereas to the other side that had more experience, the season of the year seemed to expound that accident; and their greatest fear proceeded from the so long resistance of their enemies, in that they were not all this while overcome. When the Argives first had made the left wing of the Syracusians to give ground, and after them the Athenians had also done the like to those that were arranged against them, then the rest of the Syracusian army was presently broken and put to flight. But the Athenians pursued them not far, because the Syracusian horsemen, being many and unvanquished, whensoever any men of arms advanced far from the body of the army, charged upon them and still drave them in again; but having followed as far as safely they might in great troops, they retired again and erected a trophy. The Syracusians, having rallied themselves in the Helorine way and recovered their order as well as they could for that time, sent a guard into Olympieium, lest the Athenians should take the treasure there, and returned with the rest of the army into the city.

71. The Athenians went not to assault the temple, but gathering together their dead, laid them upon the funeral fire, and stayed that night upon the place. The next day they gave truce to the Syracusians to take up their dead, of whom and of their confederates were slain about two hundred and sixty; and gathered up the bones of their own. Of the Athenians and their confederates there died about fifty. And thus, having rifled the bodies of their dead enemies, they returned to Catana. For it was now winter; and to make war there, they thought it yet

unpossible before they had sent for horsemen to Athens and levied other amongst their confederates there in Sicily, to the end they might not be altogether over-mastered in horse; and before they had also both levied money there and received more from Athens and made league with certain cities, which they hoped after this battle would the more easily hearken thereunto, and before they had likewise provided themselves of victuals and other things necessary, as intending the next spring to undertake Syracuse again.

72. With this mind they went to winter at Naxos and Catana. The Syracusians, after they had buried their dead, called an assembly; and Hermocrates, the son of Hermon, a man not otherwise second to any in wisdom, and in war both able for his experience and eminent for his valour, standing forth gave them encouragement and would not suffer them to be dismayed with that which had happened. Their courage, he said, was not overcome, though their want of order had done them hurt. And yet in that they were not so far inferior as it was likely they would have been, especially being (as one may say) home-bred artificers, against the most experienced in the war of all the Grecians. That they had also been hurt by the number of their generals and commanders—for there were fifteen that commanded in chief—and by the many supernumerary soldiers under no command at all. Whereas if they would make but a few and skilful leaders, and prepare armour this winter for such as want it, to increase as much as might be the number of their men of arms, and compel them in other things to the exercise of discipline, in all reason they were to have the better of the enemy. For valour they had already, and to keep their order would be learnt by practice; and both of these would still grow greater: skill, by practising with danger; and their courage would grow bolder of itself, upon the confidence of skill. And for their generals, they ought to choose them few and absolute, and to take an oath unto them to let them lead the army wheresoever they thought best. For by this means, both the things that require secrecy would the better be concealed and all things would be put in readiness with order and less tergiversation.

73. The Syracusians, when they had heard him, decreed all

that he advised and elected three generals, him, Heracleides, the son of Lysimachus, and Sicanus, the son of Exekestus. They sent also ambassadors to Corinth and Lacedaemon, as well to obtain a league with them as also to persuade the Lacedaemonians to make a hotter war against the Athenians and to declare themselves in the quarrel of the Syracusians, thereby either to withdraw them from Sicily or to make them the less able to send supply to their army which was there already.

74. The Athenian army at Catana sailed presently to Messana to receive it by treason of some within; but the plot came not to effect. For Alcibiades, when he was sent for from his charge, being resolved to fly and knowing what was to be done, discovered the same to the friends of the Syracusians in Messana, who with those of their faction slew such as were accused, and being armed upon occasion of the sedition, obtained to have the Athenians kept out. And the Athenians, after thirteen days' stay, troubled with tempestuous weather, provision also failing and nothing succeeding, returned again to Naxos; and having fortified their camp with a pallisado, they wintered there, and dispatched a galley to Athens for money and horsemen to be with them early in the spring.

75. The Syracusians this winter raised a wall before their city, all the length of the side towards Epipolae, including Temenites, to the end, if they chanced to be beaten, they might not be so easily enclosed as when they were in a narrower compass. And they put a guard into Megara and another into Olympieium, and made pallisadoes on the seaside at all the places of landing. And knowing that the Athenians wintered at Naxos, they marched with all the power of the city unto Catana, and after they had wasted the territory and burnt the cabins and camp where the Athenians had lodged before, returned home. And having heard that the Athenians had sent ambassadors to Camarina, according to a league made before in the time of Laches, to try if they could win them to their side, they also sent ambassadors to oppose it. For they suspected that the Camarinaeans had sent those succours in the former battle with no great good will; and that now they would take part with them no longer, seeing the Athenians had the better of the day, but would rather join with the Athenians upon the former

league. Hermocrates, therefore, and others being come to Camarina from the Syracusians, and Euphemus and others from the Athenians, when the assembly was met, Hermocrates, desiring to increase their envy to the Athenians, spake unto them to this effect:

76. "Men of Camarina, we come not hither upon fear that the forces of the Athenians here present may affright you, but lest their speeches which they are about to make may seduce you before you have also heard what may be said by us. They are come into Sicily with that pretence indeed which you hear given out, but with that intention which we all suspect; and to me they seem not to intend the replantation of the Leontines, but rather our supplantation. For surely it holdeth not in reason that they who subvert the cities yonder should come to plant any city here; nor that they should have such a care of the Leontines, because Chalcideans, for kindred's sake, when they keep in servitude the Chalcideans themselves of Euboea, of whom these here are but the colonies. But they both hold the cities there and attempt those here in one and the same kind. For when the Ionians and the rest of the confederates, their own colonies, had willingly made them their leaders in the war to avenge them of the Medes, the Athenians, laying afterwards to their charge, to some the not sending of their forces, to some their war amongst themselves, and so to the rest the most colourable criminations they could get, subdued them all to their obedience. And it was not for the liberty of the Grecians that these men, nor for the liberty of themselves that the Grecians made head against the Medes; but the Athenians did it to make them serve not the Medes but them, and the Grecians to change their master, as they did, not for one less wise, but for one worse wise.

77. "But in truth we come not to accuse the Athenian state, though it be obnoxious enough, before you that know sufficiently the injuries they have done, but far rather to accuse ourselves, who, though we have the examples before our eyes of the Grecians there brought into servitude for want of defending themselves, and though we see them now, with the same sophistry of replanting the Leontines and their kindred and aiding of their confederates the Egestaeans, prepare to do

the like unto us, do not yet unite ourselves and with better courage make them to know that we be not Ionians nor Hellespontines nor islanders, that changing serve always the Mede or some other master, but that we are Dorians and freemen, come to dwell here in Sicily out of Peloponnesus, a free country. Shall we stand still till we be taken city after city when we know that that only way we are conquerable; and when we find them wholly bent to this, that by drawing some from our alliance with their words, and causing some to wear each other out with war upon hope of their confederacy, and winning others by other fit language, they may have the power to do us hurt? But we think, though one of the same island perish, yet if he dwell far off, the danger will not come to us; and before it arrive, we count unhappy only him that suffereth before us.

78. "If any therefore be of this opinion, that it is not he but the Syracusian that is the Athenian's enemy, and thinketh it a hard matter that he should endanger himself for the territory that is mine, I would have him to consider that he is to fight not chiefly for mine, but equally for his own in mine, and with the more safety for that I am not destroyed before and he thereby destitute of my help, but stand with him in the battle. Let him also consider that the Athenians come not hither to punish the Syracusians for being enemies to you, but by pretence of me to make himself the stronger by your friendship. If any man here envieth or also feareth us (for the strongest are still liable unto both), and would therefore wish that the Syracusians might be weakened to make them more modest, but not vanquished for their own safety's sake, that man hath conceived a hope beyond the power of man. For it is not reasonable that the same man should be the disposer both of his desires and of his fortune. And if his aim should fail him, he might, deploring his own misery, peradventure wish to enjoy my prosperity again. But this will not be possible to him that shall abandon me and not undertake the same dangers, though not in title, yet in effect the same that I do. For though it be our power in title, yet in effect it is your own safety you defend. And you men of Camarina, that are borderers and likely to have the second place of danger, you should most of all have foreseen this and not have aided us so dully. You should rather have come to us; and that which, if

the Athenians had come first against Camarina, you should in your need have implored at our hands, the same you should now also have been seen equally to hearten us withal to keep us from yielding. But as yet, neither you nor any of the rest have been so forward.

79. "Perhaps, upon fear, you mean to deal evenly between us both and allege your league with the Athenians. You made no league against your friends, but against your enemies, in case any should invade you; and by it you are also tied to aid the Athenians when others wrong them; but not when, as now, they wrong their neighbour. For even the Rhegians, who are also Chalcideans, refuse to help them in replanting the Leontines, though these also be Chalcideans. And then it were a hard case if they, suspecting a bad action under a fair justification, are wise without a reason; and you, upon pretence of reason, should aid your natural enemies and help them that most hate you to destroy your more natural kindred.

"But this is no justice; to fight with them is justice, and not to stand in fear of their preparation. Which, if we hold together, is not terrible, but is, if contrarily (which they endeavour) we be disunited. For neither when they came against us, being none but ourselves, and had the upperhand in battle, could they yet effect their purpose; but quickly went their ways.

80. "There is no reason therefore we should be afraid when we are all together, but that we should have the better will to unite ourselves in a league; and the rather because we are to have aid from Peloponnesus, who every way excel these men in military sufficiency. Nor should you think that your purpose to aid neither, as being in league with both, is either just in respect of us or safe for yourselves; for it is not so just in substance as it is in the pretence. For if through want of your aid the assailed perish and the assailant become victor, what do you by your neutrality but leave the safety of the one undefended and suffer the other to do evil? Whereas it were more noble in you, by joining with the wronged and with your kindred, both to defend the common good of Sicily and keep the Athenians, as your friends, from an act of injustice. To be short, we Syracusians say that to demonstrate plainly to you or

to any other the thing you already know is no hard matter; but we pray you, and withal if you reject our words we protest, that whereas the Ionians, who have ever been our enemies, do take counsel against us, you, that are Dorians as well as we, betray us. And if they subdue us, though it be by your counsels that they do it, yet they only shall have the honour of it; and for the prize of their victory, they will have none other but even the authors of their victory; but if the victory fall unto us, even you also, the cause of this our danger, shall undergo the penalty. Consider therefore now and take your choice whether you will have the servitude without the present danger, or saving yourselves with us, both avoid the dishonour of having a master and escape our enmity, which is likely otherwise to be lasting."

81. Thus spake Hermocrates. After him Euphemus, ambassador from the Athenians, spake thus:

82. "Though our coming were to renew our former league, yet seeing we are touched by the Syracusian, it will be necessary we speak something here of the right of our dominion. And the greatest testimony of this right he hath himself given, in that he said the Ionians were ever enemies to the Dorians. And it is true. For being Ionians, we have ever endeavoured to find out some means or other how best to free ourselves from subjection to the Peloponnesians, that are Dorians, more in number than we and dwelling near us. After the Medan war, having gotten us a navy, we were delivered thereby from the command and leading of the Lacedaemonians, there being no cause why they should rather be leaders of us than we of them save only that they were then the stronger. And when we were made commanders of those Grecians which before lived under the king, we took upon us the government of them, because we thought that, having power in our hands to defend ourselves, we should thereby be the less subject to the Peloponnesians. And to say truth, we subjected the Ionians and islanders (whom the Syracusians say we brought into bondage being our kindred) not without just cause; for they came with the Medes against ours, their mother city, and for fear of losing their wealth durst not revolt, as we did, that abandoned our very city. But

as they were content to serve, so they would have imposed the same condition upon us.

83. "For these causes we took upon us our dominion over them, both as worthy of the same, in that we brought the greatest fleet and promptest courage to the service of the Grecians, whereas they, with the like promptness in favour of the Medes, did us hurt; and also as being desirous to procure ourselves a strength against the Peloponnesians. And follow any other we will not,* seeing we alone have pulled down the barbarian and therefore have right to command, or at least have put ourselves into danger more for the liberty of the Peloponnesians than of all the rest of Greece, and our own besides. Now to seek means for one's own preservation is a thing unblameable. And as it is for our own safety's cause that we are now here, so also we find that the same will be profitable for you. Which we will make plain from those very things which they accuse, and you, as most formidable, suspect us of, being assured that such as suspect with vehement fear, though they may be won for the present with the sweetness of an oration, yet when the matter comes to performance, will then do as shall be most for their turn.

"We have told you that we hold our dominion yonder upon fear; and that upon the same cause we come hither now, by the help of our friends to assure the cities here, and not to bring you into subjection but rather to keep you from it.

84. "And let no man object that we be solicitous for those that are nothing to us; for as long as you be preserved and able to make head against the Syracusians, we shall be the less annoyed by their sending of forces to the Peloponnesians. And in this point you are very much unto us. For the same reason it is meet also that we replant the Leontines; not to subject them, as their kindred in Euboea, but to make them as puissant as we can, that, being near, they may from their own territory weaken the Syracusians in our behalf. For as for our wars at home, we

---

* I believe Hobbes has taken the wrong reading here. The other reading would mean "we will not use any fine phrases to the effect that because we alone destroyed the power of the Persians we have a natural right to empire."

are a match for our enemies without their help; and the
Chalcidean (whom having made a slave yonder, the Syracusian
said, we absurdly attempt to vindicate into liberty here) is
most beneficial to us there without arms, paying money only;
but the Leontines, and our other friends here, are the most
profitable to us when they are most in liberty.

85. "Now to a tyrant or city that reigneth, nothing can be
thought absurd if profitable, nor any man a friend that may
not be trusted to. Friend or enemy he must be, according to the
several occasions. But here it is for our benefit not to weaken
our friends, but by our friends' strength to weaken our enemies.
This you must needs believe, inasmuch as yonder also we so
command over our confederates as every of them may be most
useful to us: the Chians and Methymnaeans redeem their liberty
with providing us some galleys; the most of the rest, with a
tribute of money somewhat more pressing. Some again of our
confederates are absolutely free, notwithstanding that they be
islanders and easy to be subdued; the reason whereof is this:
they are situate in places commodious about Peloponnesus. It is
probable, therefore, that here also we will so order our affairs
as shall be most for our own turn and most according to our
fear, as we told you, of the Syracusians. For they affect a
dominion over you, and having by advantage of your suspicion
of us drawn you to their side, will themselves by force, or (if
we go home without effect) by your want of friends, have the
sole command of Sicily, which, if you join with them, must of
necessity come to pass. For neither will it be easy for us to bring
so great forces again together, nor will the Syracusians want
strength to subdue you if we be absent. Him that thinketh
otherwise, the thing itself convinceth.

86. "For when you called us in to aid you at the first, the
fear you pretended was only this: that if we neglected you, the
Syracusians would subdue you, and we thereby should participate of the danger. And it were unjust that the argument
you would needs have to prevail then with us should now have
no effect with yourselves, or that you should be jealous of the
much strength we bring against the power of the Syracusians
when much rather you should give the less ear unto them. We
cannot so much as stay here without you; and if becoming

perfidious we should subdue these states, yet we are unable to hold them, both in respect of the length of the voyage and for want of means of guarding them, because they be great and provided after the manner of the continent. Whereas they, not lodged near you in a camp, but inhabiting near you in a city of greater power than this of ours,* will be always watching their advantages against you; and when an opportunity shall be offered against any of your cities, will be sure not to let it slip. This they have already made to appear, both in their proceedings against the Leontines, and also otherwise. And yet have these the face to move you against us that hinder this, and that have hitherto kept Sicily from falling into their hands. But we, on the other side, invite you to a far more real safety, and pray you not to betray that safety which we both of us hold from one another at this present, but to consider that they by their own number have way to you always, though without confederates, whereas you shall seldom have so great an aid again to resist them. Which if through your jealousy you suffer to go away without effect, or if it miscarry, you will hereafter wish for the least part of the same, when their coming can no more do you good.

87. "But, Camarinaeans, be neither you nor others moved with their calumnies. We have told you the very truth why we are suspected; and summarily we will tell it you again, claiming to prevail with you thereby. We say we command yonder lest else we should obey, and we assert into liberty the cities here lest else we should be harmed by them; many things we have to be doing, because many things we are forced to beware of; and both now and before, we came not uncalled, but called as confederates to such of you as suffer wrong. Make not yourselves judges of what we do, nor go about as censors (which were now hard to do) to divert us; but as far as this busy humour and fashion of ours may be for your own service, so far take and use it; and think not the same hurtful alike to all, but that the greatest part of the Grecians have good by it. For in all places, though we be not of any side, yet both he that looketh to be wronged and he that contriveth to do the wrong, by the obviousness of the hope that the one hath of our aid

---

* I.e., "than this *army* of ours which we have brought here."

and of the fear that the other hath of their own danger if we should come, are brought by necessity, the one to moderation against his will, the other into safety without his trouble. Refuse not therefore the security now present, common both to us that require it, and to yourselves. But do as others use to do: come with us, and instead of defending yourselves always against the Syracusians, take your turn once and put them to their guard as they have done you."

88. Thus spake Euphemus. The Camarinaeans stood thus affected: they bare good will to the Athenians, save that they thought they meant to subjugate Sicily; and were ever at strife with the Syracusians about their borders. Yet because they were afraid that the Syracusians, that were near them, might as well get the victory as the other, they had both formerly sent them some few horse, and also now resolved for the future to help the Syracusians, but underhand and as sparingly as possible; and withal that they might no less seem to favour the Athenians than the Syracusians, especially after they had won a battle, to give for the present an equal answer unto both. So after deliberation had, they answered thus: that forasmuch as they that warred were both of them their confederates, they thought it most agreeable to their oath for the present to give aid to neither. And so the ambassadors of both sides went their ways.

And the Syracusians made preparations for the war by themselves.

The Athenians, being encamped at Naxos, treated with the Siculi to procure as many of them as they might to their side. Of whom, such as inhabited the plain and were subject to the Syracusians for the most part held off; but they that dwelt in the most inland parts of the island, being a free people, and ever before dwelling in villages, presently agreed with the Athenians, and brought corn into the army, and some of them also money. To those that held off the Athenians went with their army; and some they forced to come in and others they hindered from receiving the aids and garrisons of the Syracusians. And having brought their fleet from Naxos, where it had been all the winter till now, they lay the rest of the winter at Catana and re-erected their camp formerly burnt by the Syracusians. They sent a galley also to Carthage to procure amity and what help

they could from thence; and into Hetruria,* because some cities
there had of their own accord promised to take their parts.
They sent likewise to the Siculi about them and to Egesta, appointing them to send in all the horse they could, and made
ready bricks and iron and whatsoever else was necessary for a
siege, and every other thing they needed, as intending to fall in
hand with the war early the next spring.

The ambassadors of Syracuse which were sent to Corinth and
Lacedaemon, as they sailed by, endeavoured also to move the
Italians to a regard of this action of the Athenians. Being come
to Corinth, they spake unto them and demanded aid upon the
title of consanguinity. The Corinthians, having forthwith for
their own part decreed cheerfully to aid them, sent also ambassadors from themselves along with these to Lacedaemon to
help them to persuade the Lacedaemonians both to make a more
open war against the Athenians at home and to send some
forces also into Sicily. At the same time that these ambassadors
were at Lacedaemon from Corinth, Alcibiades was also there
with his fellow fugitives, who presently upon their escape
passed over from Thurii first to Cyllene, the haven of the
Eleians, in a ship, and afterwards went thence to Lacedaemon,
sent for by the Lacedaemonians themselves, under public security. For he feared them for his doings about Mantineia. And
it fell out that in the assembly of the Lacedaemonians the Corinthians, Syracusians, and Alcibiades made all of them the same
request. Now the ephores and magistrates, though intending to
send ambassadors to Syracuse to hinder them from compounding with the Athenians, being yet not forward to send them
aid, Alcibiades stood forth and sharpened the Lacedaemonians,
inciting them with words to this effect:

89. "It will be necessary that I say something first concerning
mine own accusation, lest through jealousy of me you bring a
prejudicate ear to the common business. My ancestors having

---

* The Greek is actually *Tyrsenia,* by which is meant the whole of
western Italy. According to Herodotus, the people inhabiting this
area were Pelasgians originally. But in historical times the race that
dominated the country were Etrurians (hence Hobbes' *Hetruria*),
who are certainly of no Greek origin. The Greeks continued to speak
of them as Tyrsenians and actually to identify them with the original
Pelasgians.

on a certain quarrel renounced the office of receiving you,* I
was the man that restored the same again and showed you all
possible respect, both otherwise and in the matter of your loss
at Pylus. Whilst I persisted in my good will to you, being to
make a peace at Athens, by treating the same with my adversaries, you invested them with authority and me with disgrace. For which cause, if in applying myself afterwards to the
Mantineans and Argives, or in anything else I did you hurt, I
did it justly; and if any man here were causelessly angry with me
then when he suffered, let him be now content again when he
knows the true cause of the same. Or if any man think the worse
of me for inclining to the people, let him acknowledge that
therein also he is offended without a cause. For we have been
always enemies to tyrants; and what is contrary to a tyrant is
called the people; and from thence hath continued our adherence to the multitude.† Besides, in a city governed by democracy, it was necessary in most things to follow the present
course; nevertheless we have endeavoured to be more moderate
than suiteth with the now headstrong humour of the people.
But others there have been, both formerly and now, that have
incited the common people to worse things than I; and they
are those that have also driven out me. But as for us, when we
had the charge of the whole, we thought it reason, by what
form it was grown most great and most free and in which we
received it, in the same to preserve it. For though such of us
as have judgment do know well enough what the democracy is,
and I no less than another (insomuch as I could inveigh against
it; but of confessed madness nothing can be said that is new),
yet we thought it not safe to change it when you our enemies
were so near us.

90. "Thus stands the matter touching my own accusation.
And concerning what we are to consult of, both you and I,
if I know anything which you yourselves do not, hear it now.
We made this voyage into Sicily, first (if we could) to subdue

* This is another reference to the office of proxenus.
† The Greek is stronger than Hobbes' words. It means "our primacy
in the democratic party." Alcibiades refers to the leadership of the
democratic party which had been in the hands of the Alcmaeonidae,
his family.

the Sicilians, after them the Italians, after them, to assay the dominion of Carthage, and Carthage itself. If these or most of these enterprises succeeded, then next we should have undertaken Peloponnesus, with the accession both of the Greek forces there and with many mercenary barbarians, Iberians and others of those parts, confessed to be the most warlike of the barbarians that are now. We should also have built many galleys besides these which we have already (there being plenty of timber in Italy); with the which besieging Peloponnesus round, and also taking the cities thereof with our land forces, upon such occasions as should arise from the land, some by assault and some by siege, we hoped easily to have debelled it and afterwards to have gotten the dominion of all Greece. As for money and corn to facilitate some points of this, the places we should have conquered there, besides what here we should have found, would sufficiently have furnished us.

91. "Thus, from one that most exactly knoweth it, you have heard what is the design of the fleet now gone; and which the generals there, as far as they can, will also put in execution. Understand next that unless you aid them, they yonder cannot possibly hold out. For the Sicilians, though inexpert, if many of them unite may well subsist; but that the Syracusians alone, with their whole power already beaten and withal kept from the use of the sea, should withstand the forces of the Athenians already there is a thing impossible. And if their city should be taken, all Sicily is had, and soon after Italy also; and the danger from thence which I foretold you would not be long ere it fell upon you. Let no man therefore think that he now consulteth of Sicily only but also of Peloponnesus, unless this be done with speed. Let the army you send be of such as being aboard may row and landing presently be armed; and (which I think more profitable than the army itself) send a Spartan for commander, both to train the soldiers already there and to compel unto it such as refuse. For thus will your present friends be the more encouraged, and such as be doubtful come to you with the more assurance. It were also good to make war more openly upon them here, that the Syracusians, seeing your care, may the rather hold out, and the Athenians be less able to send supply to their army. You ought likewise to fortify Deceleia

in the territory of Athens, a thing which the Athenians themselves most fear, and reckon for the only evil they have not
yet tasted in this war. And the way to hurt an enemy most is
to know certainly what he most feareth and to bring the same
upon him. For in reason a man therefore feareth a thing most
as having the precisest knowledge of what will most hurt him.
As for the commodities which yourselves shall reap and deprive
the enemy of by so fortifying, letting much pass, I will sum
you up the principal. Whatsoever the territory is furnished
withal will come most of it unto you, partly taken and partly
of its own accord. The revenue of the silver mines in Laurium
and whatsoever other profit they have from their land or from
their courts of justice will presently be lost; and, which is worse,
their confederates will be remiss in bringing in their revenue
and will care little for the Athenians if they believe once that
you follow the war to the utmost. That any of these things
be put in act speedily and earnestly, men of Lacedaemon, it
resteth only in yourselves; for I am confident, and I think I
err not, that all these things are possible to be done.

92. "Now I must crave this: that I be neither the worse esteemed for that, having once been thought a lover of my country, I go now amongst the greatest enemies of the same against
it, nor yet mistrusted as one that speaketh with the zeal of a
fugitive. For though I fly from the malice of them that drave
me out, I shall not, if you take my counsel, fly your profit. Nor
are you enemies so much, who have hurt but your enemies, as
they are that have made enemies of friends. I love not my
country as wronged by it, but as having lived in safety in it.
Nor do I think that I do herein go against any country of mine,
but that I far rather seek to recover the country I have not.
And he is truly a lover of his country not that refuseth to invade the country he hath wrongfully lost, but that desires so
much to be in it as by any means he can he will attempt to recover it. I desire you therefore, Lacedaemonians, to make use
of my service in whatsoever danger or labour confidently, seeing you know, according to the common saying, if I did hurt
you much when I was your enemy, I can help you much when
I am your friend. And so much the more in that I know the
state of Athens and but conjectured at yours. And considering

you are now in deliberation upon a matter of so extreme importance, I pray you think not much to send an army both into Sicily and Attica, as well to preserve the great matters that are there with the presence of a small part of your force, as also to pull down the power of the Athenians both present and to come, and afterwards to dwell in safety yourselves, and to have the leading of all Greece, not forced, but voluntary and with their good affection."

93. Thus spake Alcibiades. And the Lacedaemonians, though before this they had a purpose of their own accord to send an army against Athens but had delayed and neglected it, yet when these particularly were delivered by him, they were a great deal the more confirmed in the same, conceiving that what they had heard was from one that evidently knew it. Insomuch as they had set their minds already upon the fortifying of Deceleia and upon the sending of some succours into Sicily for the present. And having assigned Gylippus, the son of Cleandridas, unto the Syracusian ambassadors for chief commander, they willed him to consider, both with them and the Corinthians, how best for their present means and with greatest speed some help might be conveyed unto them in Sicily. He thereupon appointed the Corinthians to send him two galleys presently to Asine, and to furnish the rest they meant to send, and to have them ready to sail when occasion should serve. This agreed upon, they departed from Lacedaemon.

In the meantime the galley arrived at Athens which the generals sent home for money and horsemen. And the Athenians, upon hearing, decreed to send both provision and horsemen to the army. So the winter ended, and the seventeenth year of this war written by Thucydides.

94. In the very beginning of the next spring the Athenians in Sicily departed from Catana and sailed by the coast to Megara of Sicily. The inhabitants whereof, in the time of the tyrant Gelon, the Syracusians (as I mentioned before) had driven out and now possess the territory themselves. Landing here, they wasted the fields; and having assaulted a certain small fortress of the Syracusians, not taking it, they went presently back, part by land and part by sea, unto the river Tereas. And landing again in the plain fields, wasted the same and burnt up their

corn; and lighting on some Syracusians, not many, they slew
some of them, and having set up a trophy, went all again on
board their galleys. Thence they returned to Catana and took
in victual; then with their whole army they went to Centoripa,
a small city of the Siculi, which yielding on composition, they
departed, and in their way burnt up the corn of the Inessaeans
and the Hyblaeans. Being come again to Catana, they find there
two hundred and fifty horsemen arrived from Athens, without
horses, though not without the furniture, supposing to have
horses there, and thirty archers on horseback, and three hundred talents of silver.

95. The same spring the Lacedaemonians led forth their army
against Argos and went as far as to Cleonae; but an earthquake
happening, they went home again. But the Argives invaded
the territory of Thyrea, confining on their own, and took a
great booty from the Lacedaemonians, which they sold for no
less than twenty-five talents.

Not long after, the commons of Thespiae set upon them that
had the government, but not prevailing, were part apprehended
and part escaped to Athens, the Athenians having also aided
them.

96. The Syracusians the same summer, when they heard that
the Athenians had horsemen sent to them from Athens and
that they were ready now to come against them, conceiving
that if the Athenians gat not Epipolae, a rocky ground and
lying just against the city, they would not be able, though masters of the field, to take in the city with a wall, intended therefore, lest the enemy should come secretly up, to keep the
passages by which there was access unto it with a guard. For
the rest of the place is to the outside high and steep, falling
to the city by degrees, and on the inside wholly subject to the
eye. And it is called by the Syracusians Epipolae,* because it
lieth above the level of the rest. The Syracusians, coming out
of the city with their whole power into a meadow by the side
of the river Anapus betimes in the morning (for Hermocrates
and his fellow-commanders had already received their charge),
were there taking a view of their arms; but first they had set
apart seven hundred men of arms, under the leading of Diomilus,

---

* Literally, "the city above"; cf. the English name *Overton*.

an outlaw of Andros, both to guard Epipolae and to be ready together quickly upon any other occasion wherein there might be use of their service.

97. The Athenians the day following, having been already mustered, came from Catana with their whole forces and landed their soldiers at a place called Leon, six or seven furlongs from Epipolae, unperceived, and laid their navy at anchor under Thapsus. Thapsus is almost an island, lying out into the sea and joined to the land with a narrow isthmus, not far from Syracuse, neither by sea nor land. And the naval forces of the Athenians, having made a pallisado across the said isthmus, lay there quiet. But the land soldiers marched at high speed towards Epipolae and gat up by Euryelus before the Syracusians could come to them from out of the meadow where they were mustering. Nevertheless they came on, every one with what speed he could, not only Diomilus with his seven hundred, but the rest also. They had no less to go from the meadow than twenty-five furlongs before they could reach the enemy. The Syracusians, therefore, coming up in this manner and thereby defeated in battle at Epipolae, withdrew themselves into the city. But Diomilus was slain, and three hundred of the rest. The Athenians after this erected a trophy and delivered to the Syracusians the bodies of their dead under truce, and came down the next day to the city. But when none came out to give them battle, they retired again, and built a fort upon Labdalum, in the very brink of the precipices of Epipolae, on the side that looketh towards Megara, for a place to keep their utensils and money in when they went out either to fight or to work.

98. Not long after, there came unto them from Egesta three hundred horsemen, and from the Siculi, namely the Naxians and some others, about one hundred; and the Athenians had of their own two hundred and fifty for which they had horses, part from the Egestaeans and Catanaeans, and part they bought. So that they had together in the whole, six hundred and fifty horsemen. Having put a guard into Labdalum, the Athenians went down to Syca and raised there a wall in circle very quickly, so that they struck a terror into the Syracusians with the celerity of the work. Who, therefore, coming forth, intended to have given them battle and no longer to have neglected the matter.

But when the armies were one set against the other, the Syracusian generals, perceiving their own to be in disarray and not
easily to be embattled, led them again into the city, save only
a certain part of their horsemen; which staying, kept the Athenians from carrying of stone and straggling far abroad from
their camp. But the Athenians with one squadron of men of
arms, together with their whole number of horse, charged the
horsemen of the Syracusians and put them to flight, of whom
they slew a part, and erected a trophy for this battle of horse.

99. The next day the Athenians fell to work upon their wall
to the north side of their circular wall, some building and some
fetching stone and timber, which they still laid down toward
the place called Trogilus, in the way by which the wall should
come with the shortest compass from the great haven to the
other sea. The Syracusians, by the persuasion of their generals,
and principally of Hermocrates, intended not to hazard battle
with their whole power against the Athenians any more, but
thought fit rather, in the way where the Athenians were to
bring their wall, to raise a counterwall; which, if they could
but do before the wall of the Athenians came on, it would exclude their further building; and if the Athenians should set
upon them as they were doing it, they might send part of the
army to defend it, and pre-occupy the accesses to it with a
pallisado; and if they would come with their whole army to
hinder them, then must they also be forced to let their own
work stand still. Therefore they came out, and beginning at
their own city, drew a cross-wall beneath the circular fortifications of the Athenians, and set wooden turrets upon it, made
of the olive trees which they felled in the ground belonging to
the temple. The Athenian navy was not yet come about into
the great haven from Thapsus, but the Syracusians were masters of the places near the sea; and the Athenians brought their
provision to the army from Thapsus by land.

100. The Syracusians, when they thought both their pallisado
and wall sufficient, and considering that the Athenians came
not to impeach them in the work, as they that feared to divide
their army and to be thereby the more easy to be fought withal,
and that also hasted to make an end of their own wall wherewith to encompass the city, left one squadron for a guard of

their works and retired with the rest into the city. And the Athenians cut off the pipes of their conduits, by which their water to drink was conveyed under ground into the town. And having observed also that about noon the Syracusians kept within their tents, and that some of them were also gone into the city, and that such as were remaining at the pallisado kept but negligent watch, they commanded three hundred chosen men of arms, and certain other picked out and armed from amongst the unarmed, to run suddenly to that counter-wall of the Syracusians. The rest of the army, divided in two, went one part with one of the generals to stop the succour which might be sent from the city, and the other with the other general to the pallsado next to the gate of the [counter-wall]. The three hundred assaulted and took the pallisado, the guard whereof, forsaking it, fled within the wall into the temple ground; and with them entered also their pursuers; but after they were in were beaten out again by the Syracusians and some slain, both of the Argives and Athenians, but not many. Then the whole army went back together and pulled down the wall and plucked up the pallisado, the pales whereof they carried with them to their camp and erected a trophy.

101. The next day, the Athenians, beginning at their circular wall, built onwards to that crag over the marshes, which on that part of Epipolae looketh to the great haven, and by which the way to the haven, for their wall to come through the plain and marsh, was the shortest. As this was doing, the Syracusians came out again and made another pallisado, beginning at the city, through the middle of the marsh, and a ditch at the side of it, to exclude the Athenians from bringing their wall to the sea. But the Athenians, when they had finished their work as far as to the crag, assaulted the pallisado and trench of the Syracusians again. And having commanded their galleys to be brought about from Thapsus into the great haven of Syracuse, about break of day went straight down into the plain, and passing through the marsh, where the ground was clay and firmest, [and partly] upon boards and planks, won both the trench and pallisado, all but a small part, betimes in the morning, and the rest not long after. And here also they fought, and the victory fell to the Athenians; the Syracusians, those of

the right wing, fled to the city, and they of the left, to the river. The three hundred chosen Athenians, desiring to cut off their passage, marched at high speed towards the bridge. But the Syracusians, fearing to be prevented (for most of the horsemen were in this number), set upon these three hundred, and putting them to flight, drave them upon the right wing of the Athenians, and following, affrighted also the foremost guard of the wing. Lamachus, seeing this, came to aid them with a few archers from the left wing of their own and with [all] the Argives, and passing over a certain ditch, having but few with him, was deserted and slain with some six or seven more. These the Syracusians hastily snatched up and carried into a place of safety beyond the river; and when they saw the rest of the Athenian army coming towards them, they departed.

102. In the meantime, they that fled at first to the city, seeing how things went, took heart again, and re-embattled themselves against the same Athenians that stood ranged against them before; and withal sent a certain portion of their army against the circular fortification of the Athenians upon Epipolae, supposing to find it without defendants and so to take it. And they took and demolished the outworks ten plethers in length; but the circle itself was defended by Nicias, who chanced to be left within it for infirmity. For he commanded his servants to set fire on all the engines and whatsoever wooden matter lay before the wall: knowing there was no other possible means to save themselves for want of men. And it fell out accordingly, for by reason of this fire they came no nearer, but retired. For the Athenians, having by this time beaten back the enemy below, were coming up to relieve the circle; and their galleys withal (as is before mentioned) were going about from Thapsus into the great haven. Which they above perceiving, speedily made away, they and the whole army of the Syracusians, into the city, with opinion that they could no longer hinder them, with the strength they now had, from bringing their wall through unto the sea.

103. After this the Athenians erected a trophy and delivered to the Syracusians their dead under truce; and they on the other side delivered to the Athenians the body of Lamachus and of the rest slain with him. And their whole army, both land and

sea forces, being now together, they began to enclose the Syracusians with a double wall from Epipolae and the rocks unto the seaside. The necessaries of the army were supplied from all parts of Italy. And many of the Siculi, who before stood aloof to observe the way of fortune, took part now with the Athenians, to whom came also three penteconteri, [long boats of fifty oars apiece,] from Hetruria; and divers other ways their hopes were nourished. For the Syracusians also, when there came no help from Peloponnesus, made no longer account to subsist by war; but conferred, both amongst themselves and with Nicias, of composition; for Lamachus being dead, the sole command of the army was in him. And though nothing were concluded, yet many things (as was likely with men perplexed, and now more straitly besieged than before) were propounded unto Nicias, and more amongst themselves. And the present ill success had also spread some jealousy amongst them, one of another. And they discharged the generals under whose conduct this happened, as if their harm had come either from their unluckiness or from their perfidiousness, and chose Heracleides, Eucles, and Tellias in their places.

104. Whilst this passed, Gylippus of Lacedaemon and the Corinthian galleys were already at Leucas, purposing with all speed to go over into Sicily. But when terrible reports came unto them from all hands, agreeing in an untruth, that Syracuse was already quite enclosed, Gylippus had hope of Sicily no longer; but desiring to assure Italy, he and Pythen, a Corinthian, with two Laconic and two Corinthian galleys, with all speed crossed the Ionic sea to Tarentum; and the Corinthians were to man ten galleys of their own, two of Leucas, and three of Ambracia, and come after. Gylippus went first from Tarentum to Thurii, as ambassador, by his father's right, who was free of the city of Tarentum; but not winning them to his side, he put out again, and sailed along the coast of Italy. Passing by the Terinaean gulf, he was put from the shore by a wind which in that quarter bloweth strongly against the north, and driven into the main sea; and after another extreme tempest brought in again into Tarentum, where he drew up such of his galleys as had been hurt by the weather and repaired them. Nicias, hearing that he came, contemned the small number of his gal-

leys, as also the Thurians had before, supposing them furnished as for piracy, and appointed no watch for them yet.

105. About the same time of this summer, the Lacedaemonians invaded the territory of Argos, they and their confederates, and wasted a great part of their land. And the Athenians aided the Argives with thirty galleys; which most apparently broke the peace between them and the Lacedaemonians. For before, they went out from Pylus with the Argives and Mantineans but in the nature of freebooters, and that also not into Laconia, but other parts of Peloponnesus. Nay, when the Argives have often entreated them but only to land with their arms in Laconia, and having wasted never so little of their territory to return, they would not. But now, under the conduct of Pythodorus, Laespodius, and Demaratus, they landed in the territory of Epidaurus Limera and in Prasiae, and there and in other places wasted the country, and gave unto the Lacedaemonians a most justifiable cause to fight against the Athenians. After this, the Athenians being departed from Argos with their galleys, and the Lacedaemonians gone likewise home, the Argives invaded Phliasia, and when they had wasted part of their territory, and killed some of their men, returned.

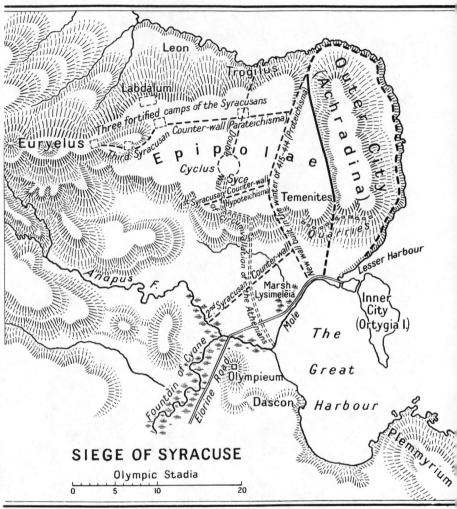

SIEGE OF SYRACUSE

Olympic Stadia

0   5   10   20

Edward Stanford Ltd., London.
DS. 1120

THE SEVENTH BOOK

1. Gylippus and Pythen, having repaired their galleys, from
Tarentum went along the coast to Locri Epizephyrii. And upon
certain intelligence now that Syracuse was not wholly enclosed,
but coming with an army there was entrance still by Epipolae,
they consulted whether it were better to take Sicily on their
right hand and adventure into the town by sea, or on the left
and so first to go to Himera, and then taking along both them
and as many other as they could get to their side, to go into it
by land. And it was resolved to go to Himera, the rather be-

cause the four Attic galleys, which Nicias, though he contemned them before, had now when he heard they were at
Locri sent to wait for them, were not arrived yet at Rhegium.
Having prevented this guard, they crossed the strait, and touching at Rhegium and Messana by the way, came to Himera. Being there, they prevailed so far with the Himeraeans that they
not only followed them to the war themselves, but also furnished
with armour such of Gylippus and Pythen's mariners as wanted;
for at Himera they had drawn their galleys to land. They likewise sent to the Selinuntians to meet them at a place assigned
with their whole army. The Geloans also, and other of the
Siculi, promised to send them forces, though not many, being
much the willinger to come to the side both for that Archonidas
was lately dead (who reigning over some of the Siculi in those
parts, and being a man of no mean power, was friend to the
Athenians), and also for that Gylippus seemed to come from
Lacedaemon with a good will to the business. Gylippus, taking
with him of his own mariners and sea-soldiers, for whom he
had gotten arms, at the most seven hundred, and Himeraeans
with armour and without in the whole one thousand, and one
hundred horse, and some light-armed Selinuntians, with some
few horse of the Geloans, and of the Siculi in all about one
thousand, marched with these towards Syracuse.

2. In the meantime, the Corinthians with the rest of their
galleys putting to sea from Leucas, made after [as they were]
every one with what speed he could; and Gongylus, one of
the Corinthian commanders, though the last that set forth,
arrived first at Syracuse with one galley, and but a little before the coming of Gylippus. And finding them ready to call
an assembly about an end of the war, he hindered them from
it and put them into heart, relating how both the rest of the
galleys were coming, and also Gylippus, the son of Cleandridas,
for general, sent unto them by the Lacedaemonians. With this
the Syracusians were re-confirmed, and went presently out with
their whole army to meet him, for they understood now that
he was near. He, having taken Iegas, a fort, in his way as he
passed through the territory of the Siculi, and embattled his
men, cometh to Epipolae, and getting up by Euryelus, where
also the Athenians had gotten up before, marched together

with the Syracusians towards the wall of the Athenians. At the time when he arrived, the Athenians had finished a double wall of seven or eight furlongs towards the great haven, save only a little next the sea, which they were yet at work on. And on the other side of their circle, towards Trogilus and the other sea, the stones were for the most part laid ready upon the place; and the work was left in some places half, and in some wholly finished. So great was the danger that Syracuse was now brought into.

3. The Athenians, at the sudden coming on of Gylippus, though somewhat troubled at first, yet put themselves in order to receive him. And he, making a stand when he came near, sent a herald to them, saying that if they would abandon Sicily within five days with bag and baggage, he was content to give them truce. Which the Athenians contemning, sent him away without any answer. After this, they were putting themselves into order of battle one against another; but Gylippus, finding the Syracusians troubled and not easily falling into their ranks, led back his army in a more open ground. Nicias led not the Athenians out against him, but lay still at his own fortification. And Gylippus, seeing he came not up, withdrew his army into the top called Temenites, where he lodged all night. The next day, he drew out the greater part of his army and embattled them before the fortification of the Athenians that they might not send succour to any other place; but a part also they sent to the fort of Labdalum, and took it, and slew all those they found within it; for the place was out of sight to the Athenians. The same day the Syracusians also took an Athenian galley as it entered into the great haven.

4. After this, the Syracusians and their confederates began a wall through Epipolae, from the city towards the single cross wall upwards, that the Athenians, unless they could hinder it, might be excluded from bringing their own wall any further on. And the Athenians by this time, having made an end of their wall to the sea, were come up again; and Gylippus (for some part of the wall was but weak), rising with his army by night, went to assault it. But the Athenians, also knowing it (for they lodged all night without the wall), went presently to relieve it; which Gylippus perceiving, again retired. And

the Athenians, when they had built it higher, kept the watch in this part themselves, and divided the rest of the wall to the charge of their confederates. Also it seemed good to Nicias to fortify the place called Plemmyrium. It is a promontory over against the city, which, shooting into the entrance of the great haven, straiteneth the mouth of the same; which fortified, he thought would facilitate the bringing in of necessaries to the army. For by this means, their galleys might ride nearer to the haven of the Syracusians, and not upon every motion of the navy of the enemies to be to come out against them, as they were before, from the bottom of the [great] haven. And he had his mind set chiefly now upon the war by sea, seeing his hopes by land diminished since the arrival of Gylippus. Having therefore drawn his army and galleys to that place, he built about it three fortifications, wherein he placed his baggage, and where now also lay at road both his great vessels of carriage and the nimblest of his galleys. Hereupon principally ensued the first occasion of the great loss of his sea soldiers. For having but little water, and that far to fetch, and his mariners going out also to fetch in wood, they were continually intercepted by the Syracusian horsemen, that were masters of the field. For the third part of the Syracusian cavalry were quartered in a little town called Olympieium to keep those in Plemmyrium from going abroad to spoil the country. Nicias was advertised moreover of the coming of the rest of the Corinthian galleys, and sent out a guard of twenty galleys with order to wait for them about Locri and Rhegium and the passage there into Sicily.

5. Gylippus in the meantime went on with the wall through Epipolae, using the stones laid ready there by the Athenians, and withal drew out the Syracusians and their confederates beyond the point of the same, and ever as he brought them forth put them into their order; and the Athenians, on the other side, embattled themselves against them. Gylippus, when he saw his time, began the battle; and being come to hands, they fought between the fortifications of them both, where the Syracusians and their confederates had no use at all of their horsemen. The Syracusians and their confederates being overcome, and the Athenians having given them truce to take up their dead and erected a trophy, Gylippus assembled the army and told them

that this was not theirs, but his own fault, who, by pitching the battle so far within the fortifications, had deprived them of the use both of their cavalry and darters; and that therefore he meant to bring them on again, and wished them to consider that for forces they were nothing inferior to the enemy; and for courage, it were a thing not to be endured that, being Peloponnesians and Dorians, they should not master and drive out of the country Ionians, islanders, and a rabble of mixed nations.

6. After this, when he saw his opportunity, he brought out the army again. Nicias and the Athenians, who thought it necessary, if not to begin the battle, yet by no means to set light by the wall in hand (for by this time it wanted but little of passing the point of theirs, and proceeding, would give the enemy advantage, both to win if he fought, and not to fight unless he listed), did therefore also set forth to meet the Syracusians. Gylippus, when he had drawn his men of arms farther without the walls than he had done before, gave the onset. His horsemen and darters he placed upon the flank of the Athenians, in ground enough, to which neither of their walls extended. And these horsemen, after the fight was begun, charging upon the left wing of the Athenians next them, put them to flight; by which means the rest of the army was by the Syracusians overcome likewise and driven headlong within their fortifications. The night following, the Syracusians brought up their wall beyond the wall of the Athenians so as they could no longer hinder them, but should be utterly unable, though masters of the field, to enclose the city.

7. After this, the other twelve galleys of the Corinthians, Ambraciotes, and Leucadians, undescried of the Athenian galleys that lay in wait for them, entered the haven, under the command of Erasinides, a Corinthian, and helped the Syracusians to finish what remained to the cross wall.

Now Gylippus went up and down Sicily, raising forces both for sea and land and soliciting to his side all such cities as formerly either had not been forward or had wholly abstained from the war. Other ambassadors also, both of the Syracusians and Corinthians, were sent to Lacedaemon and Corinth to procure new forces to be transported either in ships or boats, or how they could; because the Athenians had also sent to Athens for the like. In the meantime, the Syracusians both manned their navy and made trial of themselves, as intending to take in hand that part also, and were otherwise exceedingly encouraged.

8. Nicias perceiving this and seeing the strength of the enemy and his own necessities daily increasing, he also sent messengers to Athens, both at other times and often, upon the occasion of every action that passed, and now especially, as finding himself in danger, and that unless they quickly sent for those away that were there already, or sent a great supply unto them, there was no hope of safety. And fearing lest such as he sent, through want of utterance or judgment * or through desire to please the multitude, should deliver things otherwise than they were, he wrote unto them a letter, conceiving that thus the Athenians should best know his mind, whereof no part could now be suppressed by the messenger, and might therefore enter into deliberation upon true grounds. With these letters and other their instructions, the messengers took their journey. And Nicias, in the meantime having a care to the well guarding of his camp, was wary of entering into any voluntary dangers.

9. In the end of this summer, Euetion, general for the Athenians, with Perdiccas, together with many Thracians, warring against Amphipolis, took not the city, but bringing his galleys about into Strymon, besieged it from the river, lying at Imeraeum. And so this summer ended.

10. The next winter, the messengers from Nicias arrived at Athens, and having spoken what they had in charge, and answered to such questions as they were asked, they presented the letter; which the clerk of the city, standing forth, read unto the Athenians, containing as followeth:

11. "Athenians, you know by many other my letters what hath passed formerly; nor is it less needful for you to be informed of the state we are in, and to take counsel upon it, at this present. When we had in many battles beaten the Syracusians, against whom we were sent, and had built the walls within which we now lie, came Gylippus a Lacedaemonian, with an army out of Peloponnesus, and also out of some of the cities of

* The Greek is "want of capacity or memory."

Sicily, and in the first battle was overcome by us; but in the second, forced by his many horsemen and darters, we retired within our works. Whereupon giving over our walling up of the city for the multitude of our enemies, we now sit still. Nor can we indeed have the use of our whole army, because some part of the men of arms are employed to defend our walls. And they have built a single wall up to us, so that now we have no more means to enclose it, except one should come with a great army and win that cross wall of theirs by assault. And so it is that we who seemed to besiege others are besieged ourselves for so much as concerneth the land; for we cannot go far abroad by reason of their cavalry.

12. "They have also sent ambassadors for another army into Peloponnesus; and Gylippus is gone amongst the cities of Sicily, both to solicit such to join with him in the war as have not yet stirred, and of others to get, if he can, both more land soldiers and more munition for their navy. For they intend, as I have been informed, both to assault our wall by land with their army and to make trial what they are able to do with their navy by sea. For though our fleet (which they also have heard) were vigorous at first, both for soundness of the galleys and entireness of the men, yet our galleys are now soaked with lying so long in the water and our men consumed. For we want the means to haul a-land our galleys and trim them, because the galleys of the enemy, as good as ours and more in number, do keep us in a continual expectation of assault, which they manifestly endeavour. And seeing it is in their own choice to attempt or not, they have therefore liberty to dry their galleys at their pleasure; for they lie not, as we, in attendance upon others.

13. "Nay, we could hardly do it, though we had many galleys spare, and were not constrained, as now, to keep watch upon them with our whole number. For should we abate though but a little of our observance, we should want provision; which, as we are, being to pass so near their city, is brought in with difficulty. And hence it is that our mariners both formerly have been and are now wasted. For our mariners, fetching wood and water and foraging far off, are intercepted by the horsemen; and our slaves, now we are on equal terms, run over to

the enemy. As for strangers, some of them having come aboard by constraint, return presently to their cities; and others having been levied at first with great wages, thinking they came to enrich themselves rather than to fight, now they see the enemy make so strong resistance, both otherwise beyond their expectation and especially with their navy, partly take pretext to be gone that they may serve the enemy, and partly, Sicily being large, shift themselves away every one as he can. Some there are also, who having bought here Hyccarian slaves, have gotten the captains of galleys to accept of them in the room of themselves, and thereby destroyed the purity of our naval strength.

14. "To you I write, who know how small a time any fleet continueth in the height of vigour, and how few of the mariners are skilful both how to hasten the course of a galley and how to contain the oar. But of all, my greatest trouble is this: that being general, I can neither make them do better (for your natures are hard to be governed) nor get mariners in any other place (which the enemy can do from many places), and must of necessity have them from whence we brought both those we have and those we have lost. For our now confederate cities, Naxos and Catana, are not able to supply us. Had the enemy but that one thing more, that the towns of Italy that now send us provision, seeing what estate we are now in and you not helping us, would turn to them, the war were at an end and we expugned without another stroke.

"I could have written to you other things more pleasing than these, but not more profitable, seeing it is necessary for you to know certainly the affairs here when you go to council upon them. Withal, because I know your natures to be such as though you love to hear the best, yet afterwards when things fall not out accordingly you will call in question them that write it, I thought best to write the truth for my own safety's sake.

15. "And now think thus: that though we have carried ourselves, both captains and soldiers, in that for which we came at first hither, unblameably, yet since all Sicily is united against us and another army expected out of Peloponnesus, you must resolve (for those we have here are not enough for the enemy's present forces) either to send for these away, or to send hither

another army, both of land and sea soldiers, no less than the former, and money not a little; and also a general to succeed me, who am able no longer to stay here, being troubled with the stone [in the kidneys]. I must crave your pardon. I have done you many good services in the conducts of your armies when I had my health. What you will do, do in the very beginning of spring, and delay it not. For the enemy will soon have furnished himself of his Sicilian aids; and though those from Peloponnesus will be later, yet if you look not to it, they will get hither partly unseen, as before, and partly by preventing you with speed."

16. These were the contents of the letter of Nicias. The Athenians, when they had heard it read, though they released not Nicias of his charge, yet for the present, till such time as others chosen to be in commission might arrive, they joined with him two of those that were already in the army, Menander and Euthydemon, to the end that he might not sustain the whole burthen alone in his sickness. They concluded likewise to send another army, as well for the sea as the land, both of Athenians enrolled and of their confederates. And for fellow-generals with Nicias, they elected Demosthenes, the son of Alcisthenes, and Eurymedon, the son of Thucles. Eurymedon they sent away presently for Sicily, about the time of the winter solstice, with ten galleys and twenty talents of silver, to tell them there that aid was coming and that there was care taken of them.

17. But Demosthenes, staying, made preparation for the voyage to set out early the next spring; and sent unto the confederates, appointing what forces they should provide, and to furnish himself amongst them with money and galleys and men of arms.

The Athenians sent also twenty galleys about Peloponnesus, to watch that none should go over into Sicily from Corinth or Peloponnesus. For the Corinthians, after the ambassadors were come to them and had brought news of the amendment of the affairs in Sicily, thought it was well that they had sent thither those other galleys before; but now they were encouraged a great deal more, and prepared men of arms to be transported into Sicily in ships; and the Lacedaemonians did the like for the rest of Peloponnesus. The Corinthians manned five-and-twenty galleys to present battle to the fleet that kept watch at Naupactus, that the ships with the men of arms, whilst the Athenians attended these galleys so embattled against them, might pass by unhindered.

18. The Lacedaemonians, as they intended before, and being also instigated to it by the Syracusians and Corinthians, upon advertisement now of the Athenians' new supply for Sicily, prepared likewise to invade Attica, thereby to divert them. And Alcibiades also importunately urged the fortifying of Deceleia, and by no means to war remissly. But the Lacedaemonians were heartened thereunto principally because they thought the Athenians having in hand a double war, one against them and another against the Sicilians, would be the easier pulled down, and because they conceived the breach of the last peace was in themselves. For in the former war, the injury proceeded from their own side, in that the Thebans had entered Plataea in time of peace; and because also, whereas it was inserted in the former articles that arms should not be carried against such as would stand to trial of judgment, they had refused such trial when the Athenians offered it. And they thought all their misfortunes had deservedly befallen them for that cause, remembering amongst others, the calamity at Pylus. But when the Athenians with a fleet of thirty sail had spoiled part of the territory of Epidaurus and of Prasiae and other places, and their soldiers that lay in garrison in Pylus had taken booty in the country about, and seeing that as often as there arose any controversy touching any doubtful point of the articles, the Lacedaemonians offering trial by judgment, they refused it, then indeed, the Lacedaemonians, conceiving the Athenians to be in the same fault that themselves had been in before, betook themselves earnestly to the war. And this winter, they sent about unto their confederates to make ready iron, and all instruments of fortification. And for the aid they were to transport in ships to the Sicilians, they both made provision amongst themselves and compelled the rest of Peloponnesus to do the like. So ended this winter, and the eighteenth year of the war written by Thucydides.

19. The next spring, in the very beginning, earlier than ever

before, the Lacedaemonians and their confederates entered with
their army into Attica, under the command of Agis, the son of
Archidamus, their king. And first they wasted the champagne
country, and then went in hand with the wall at Deceleia, dividing the work amongst the army, according to their cities. This
Deceleia is from the city of Athens at the most but one hundred
and twenty furlongs, and about as much or a little more from
Boeotia. This fort they made in the plain, and in the most opportune place that could be to annoy the Athenians, and in
sight of the city. Now the Peloponnesians and their confederates in Attica went on with their fortification. They in Peloponnesus sent away their ships with the men of arms about
the same time into Sicily, of which the Lacedaemonians, out
of the best of their Helotes and men made newly free, sent in
the whole six hundred, and Eccritus, a Spartan, for commander;
and the Boeotians three hundred, under the conduct of Xenon
and Nicon, Thebans, and Hegesander, a Thespian. And these
set forth first, and put to sea at Taenarus in Laconia. After
them a little, the Corinthians sent away five hundred more,
part from the city itself of Corinth and part mercenary Arcadians, and Alexarchus, a Corinthian, for captain. The Sicyonians also sent two hundred with them that went from Corinth,
and Sargeus, a Sicyonian, for captain. Now the twenty-five
Corinthian galleys that were manned in winter lay opposite
to the twenty galleys of Athens which were at Naupactus till
such time as the men of arms in the ships from Peloponnesus
might get away; for which purpose they were also set out at
first, that the Athenians might not have their minds upon these
ships so much as upon the galleys.

20. In the meantime also the Athenians, whilst Deceleia was
fortifying, in the beginning of the spring, sent twenty galleys
about Peloponnesus under the command of Charicles, the son
of Apollodorus, with order when he came to Argos to take
aboard the men of arms which the Argives were to send them,
according to league; and sent away Demosthenes (as they intended before) into Sicily, with threescore galleys of Athens
and five of Chios, and one thousand two hundred men of arms
of the roll of Athens, and as many of the islanders as they could
get, provided by their subject confederates of all other neces-

saries for the war. But he had order to join first with Charicles and help him to make war first upon Laconia. So Demosthenes went to Aegina and stayed there both for the remnant of his own army, if any were left behind, and for Charicles till he had taken aboard the Argives.

21. In Sicily, about the same time of the spring, Gylippus also returned to Syracuse, bringing with him from the cities he had dealt withal as great forces as severally he could get from them. And having assembled the Syracusians, he told them that they ought to man as many galleys as they could and make trial of a battle by sea; and that he hoped thereby to perform somewhat to the benefit of the war which should be worthy the danger. Hermocrates also was none of the least means of getting them to undertake the Athenians with their navy, who told them that neither the Athenians had this skill by sea hereditary or from everlasting, but were more inland men than the Syracusians, and forced to become seamen by the Medes, and that to daring men, such as the Athenians are, they are most formidable that are as daring against them; for wherewith they terrify their neighbours, which is not always the advantage of power, but boldness of enterprizing, with the same shall they in like manner be terrified by their enemies. He knew it, he said, certainly, that the Syracusians, by their unexpected daring to encounter the Athenian navy, would get more advantage in respect of the fear it would cause than the Athenians should endamage them by their odds of skill. He bade them therefore to make trial of their navy and to be afraid no longer. The Syracusians, on these persuasions of Gylippus and Hermocrates, and others if any were, became now extremely desirous to fight by sea, and presently manned their galleys.

22. Gylippus, when the navy was ready, drew out his whole power of land soldiers in the beginning of night, meaning to go himself and assault the fortifications in Plemmyrium; withal the galleys of the Syracusians, by appointment, thirty-five of them came up towards it out of the great haven; and forty-five more came about out of the little haven, where also was their arsenal, with purpose to join with those within and to go together to Plemmyrium that the Athenians might be troubled on both sides. But the Athenians having quickly manned sixty galleys

to oppose them, with twenty-five of them they fought with the thirty-five of the Syracusians in the great haven, and with the rest went to meet those that came about from the little haven. And these fought presently before the mouth of the great haven and held each other to it for a long time, one side endeavouring to force, the other to defend the entrance.

23. In the meantime, Gylippus (the Athenians in Plemmyrium being now come down to the water side, and having their minds busied upon the fight of the galleys) betimes in the morning and on a sudden assaulted the fortifications before they could come back again to defend them, and possessed first the greatest and afterwards the two lesser; for they that watched in these, when they saw the greatest so easily taken, durst stay no longer. They that fled upon the losing of the first wall and put themselves into boats and into a certain ship got hardly into the camp; for whilst the Syracusians in the great haven had yet the better in the fight upon the water, they gave them chase with one nimble galley. But by that time that the other two walls were taken, the Syracusians upon the water were overcome; and the Athenians which fled from those two walls got to their camp with more ease. For those Syracusian galleys that fought before the haven's mouth, having beaten back the Athenians, entered in disorder, and falling foul one on another, gave away the victory unto the Athenians, who put to flight not only them, but also those other by whom they had before been overcome within the haven, and sunk eleven galleys of the Syracusians and slew most of the men aboard them, save only the men of three galleys, whom they took alive. Of their own galleys they lost only three. When they had drawn to land the wreck of the Syracusian galleys and erected a trophy in the little island over against Plemmyrium, they returned to their camp.

24. The Syracusians, though such were their success in the battle by sea, yet they won the fortification in Plemmyrium, and set up three trophies, for every wall one. One of the two walls last taken they demolished; but two they repaired and kept with a garrison. At the taking of these walls, many men were slain and many taken alive; and their goods, which altogether was a great matter, were all taken. For the Athenians

using these works for their storehouse, there was in them much
wealth and victual belonging unto merchants and much unto
captains of galleys. For there were sails within it for forty
galleys, besides other furniture, and three galleys drawn to
land. And this loss of Plemmyrium was it that most and principally impaired the Athenians' army. For the entrance of their
provision was now no longer safe; for the Syracusians lying
against them there with their galleys kept them out, and nothing could be brought in unto them but by fight; and the army
besides was thereby otherwise terrified and dejected.

25. After this the Syracusians sent out twelve galleys under
the command of Agatharchus, a Syracusian. Of which one
carried ambassadors into Peloponnesus to declare what hope
they had now of their business and to instigate them to a sharper
war in Attica. The other eleven went into Italy, upon intelligence of certain vessels laden with commodities coming to the
Athenian army, which also they met with and destroyed most
of them; and the timber, which for building of galleys the Athenians had ready framed, they burned in the territory of Caulonia.
After this they went to Locri; and riding here, there came unto
them one of the ships that carried the men of arms of the
Thespians, whom the Syracusians took aboard and went homeward by the coast. The Athenians that watched for them with
twenty galleys at Megara took one of them and the men that
were in her, but could not take the rest, so that they escaped
through to Syracuse. There was also a light skirmish in the
haven of Syracuse, about the piles which the Syracusians had
driven down before their old harbour, to the end that the
galleys might ride within and the Athenians not annoy them
by assault. The Athenians, having brought to the place a ship
of huge greatness, fortified with wooden turrets and covered
against fire, caused certain men with [little] boats to go and
fasten cords unto the piles, and so broke them up with cran-
ing. Some also the divers did cut up with saws. In the meantime
the Syracusians from the harbour and they from the great ship
shot at each other, till in the end the greatest part of the piles
were by the Athenians gotten up. But the greatest difficulty
was to get up those piles which lay hidden. For some of them
they had so driven in as that they came not above the water,

so that he that should come near was in danger to be thrown upon them as upon a rock. But these also, for reward, the divers went down and sawed asunder. But the Syracusians continually drave down other in their stead. Other devices they had against each other, as was not unlikely between armies so near opposed; and many light skirmishes passed, and attempts of all kinds were put in execution. The Syracusians moreover sent ambassadors, some Corinthians, some Ambraciotes, and some Lacedaemonians, unto the cities about them to let them know that they had won Plemmyrium and that in the battle by sea they were not overcome by the strength of the enemy, but by their own disorder; and also to show what hope they were in in other respects, and to entreat their aid both of sea and land forces; forsomuch as the Athenians expecting another army, if they would send aid before it came whereby to overthrow that which they had now there, the war would be at an end. Thus stood the affairs of Sicily.

26. Demosthenes, as soon as his forces which he was to carry to the succour of those in Sicily were gotten together, put to sea from Aegina, and sailing into Peloponnesus, joined with Charicles and the thirty galleys that were with him. And having taken aboard some men of arms of the Argives, came to Laconia, and first wasted part of the territory of Epidaurus Limera. From thence going to that part of Laconia which is over against the island Cythera, where there is a temple of Apollo, they wasted a part of the country and fortified an isthmus there, both that the Helotes might have a refuge in it running away from the Lacedaemonians and that freebooters from thence, as from Pylus, might fetch in prizes from the territory adjoining. As soon as the place was taken in, Demosthenes himself went on to Corcyra, to take up the confederates there, with intent to go thence speedily into Sicily. And Charicles, having stayed to finish and put a garrison into the fortification, went afterwards with his thirty galleys to Athens; and the Argives also went home.

27. The same winter also came to Athens a thousand and three hundred targetiers, of those called Machaerophori of the race of them that are called Dii, and were to have gone with Demosthenes into Sicily. But coming too late, the Athenians

resolved to send them back again into Thrace, as being too chargeable a matter to entertain them only for the war in Deceleia; for their pay was to have been a drachma a man by the day. For Deceleia, being this summer fortified first by the whole army and then by the several cities maintained with a garrison by turns, much endamaged the Athenians and weakened their estate, both by destroying their commodities and consuming of their men, so as nothing more. For the former invasions, having been short, hindered them not from reaping the benefit of the earth for the rest of the time. But now, the enemy continually lying upon them, and sometimes with greater forces, sometimes of necessity with the ordinary garrison making incursions and fetching in booty, Agis, the king of Lacedaemon, being always there in person and diligently prosecuting the war, the Athenians were thereby very grievously afflicted. For they were not only deprived of the fruit of the land, but also above twenty thousand of their slaves fled over to the enemy, whereof the greatest part were artificers; besides they lost all their sheep and oxen. And by the continual going out of the Athenian horsemen, making excursions to Deceleia and defending the country, their horses became partly lamed through incessant labour in rugged grounds and partly wounded by the enemy.

28. And their provision, which formerly they used to bring in from Euboea by Oropus the shortest way, through Deceleia by land, they were now forced to fetch in by sea at great cost about the promontory of Sunium. And whatsoever the city was wont to be served withal from without, it now wanted, and instead of a city was become as it were a fort. And the Athenians, watching on the battlements of the wall, in the day time by turns, but in the night, both winter and summer, all at once (except the horsemen), part at the walls and part at the arms, were quite tired. But that which pressed them most was that they had two wars at once. And yet their obstinacy was so great as no man would have believed till now they saw it. For being besieged at home from the fortification of the Peloponnesians, no man would have imagined that they should not only not have recalled their army out of Sicily, but have also besieged Syracuse there, a city of itself no less than Athens;

and therein so much have exceeded the expectation of the rest of the Grecians both in power and courage (who in the beginning of this war conceived that if the Peloponnesians invaded their territory, some of them, that they might hold out two years, others three, no man more), as that in the seventeenth year after they were first invaded they should have undertaken an expedition into Sicily, and being every way weakened already by the former war, have undergone another, not inferior to that which they had before with the Peloponnesians. Now their treasure being by these wars and by the detriment sustained from Deceleia and other great expenses that came upon them at a very low ebb, about this time they imposed on such as were under their dominion a twentieth part of all goods passing by sea for a tribute, by this means to improve their comings in. For their expenses were not now as before, but so much greater by how much the war was greater, and their revenue besides cut off.

29. The Thracians, therefore, that came too late to go with Demosthenes, they presently sent back, as being unwilling to lay out money in such a scarcity, and gave the charge of carrying them back to Diitrephes, with command as he went along those coasts (for his way was through the Euripus), if occasion served, to do somewhat against the enemy. He accordingly landed them by Tanagra and hastily fetched in some small booty. Then going over the Euripus from Chalcis in Euboea, he disbarked again in Boeotia and led his soldiers towards Mycalessus, and lay all night at the temple of Mercury undiscovered, which is distant from Mycalessus about sixteen furlongs. The next day he cometh to the city, being a very great one,* and taketh it; for they kept no watch nor expected that any man would have come in and assaulted them so far from the sea. Their walls also were but weak, in some places fallen down, and in others low-built, and their gates open through security. The Thracians, entering into Mycalessus, spoiled both houses and temples, slew the people without mercy on old or young, but killed all they could light on, both women and children, yea, and the labouring cattle, and whatsoever other

* The better reading in the manuscript is the negative "being *no* great one."

living thing they saw. For the nation of the Thracians, where they dare, are extreme bloody, equal to any of the barbarians. Insomuch as there was put in practice at this time, besides other disorder, all forms of slaughter that could be imagined; they likewise fell upon the schoolhouse, which was in the city a great one, and the children newly entered into it; and killed them every one. And the calamity of the whole city, as it was as great as ever befell any, so also was it more unexpected and more bitter.

30. The Thebans, hearing of it, came out to help them, and overtaking the Thracians before they had gone far, both recovered the booty and chased them to the Euripus and to the sea, where the galleys lay that brought them. Some of them they killed; of those most in their going aboard, for swim they could not, and such as were in the [small] boats, when they saw how things went a-land, had thrust off their boats, and lay without the Euripus. In the rest of the retreat, the Thracians behaved themselves not unhandsomely against the Theban horsemen, by whom they were charged first; but running out, and again rallying themselves in a circle, according to the manner of their country, defended themselves well and lost but few men in that action. But some also they lost in the city itself, whilst they stayed behind for pillage. But in the whole of thirteen hundred there were slain [only] two hundred and fifty. Of the Thebans and others that came out to help the city, there were slain, horsemen and men of arms, one with another about twenty; and amongst them Scirphondas of Thebes, one of the governors of Boeotia: and of the Mycallesians there perished a part. Thus went the matter at Mycalessus, the loss which it received being, for the quantity of the city, no less to be lamented than any that happened in the whole war.

31. Demosthenes, going from Corcyra * after his fortifying in Laconia, found a ship lying in Pheia of Elis, and in her certain men of arms of Corinth, ready to go into Sicily. The ship he sunk; but the men escaped, and afterwards, getting another ship, went on in their voyage. After this, Demosthenes, being about Zacynthus and Cephallenia, took aboard their men of arms and sent to Naupactus for the Messenians. From thence he

* The Greek is *"in the direction of* Corcyra."

crossed over to the continent of Acarnania, to Alyzea and Anactorium, which belonged to the Athenians. Whilst he was in these parts, he met with Eurymedon out of Sicily, that had been sent in winter unto the army with commodities, who told him amongst other things how he had heard by the way after he was at sea that the Syracusians had won Plemmyrium. Conon also, the captain of Naupactus, came to them and related that the twenty-five galleys of Corinth that lay before Naupactus would not give over war and yet delayed to fight, and therefore desired to have some galleys sent him, as being unable with his eighteen to give battle to twenty-five of the enemy. Whereupon Demosthenes and Eurymedon sent ten galleys more to those at Naupactus, the nimblest of the whole fleet, by Conon himself, and went themselves about furnishing of what belonged to the army. Of whom Eurymedon went to Corcyra, and having appointed them there to man fifteen galleys, levied men of arms; for now giving over his course to Athens, he joined with Demosthenes, as having been elected with him in the charge of general; and Demosthenes took up slingers and darters in the parts about Acarnania.

32. The ambassadors of the Syracusians, which after the taking of Plemmyrium had been sent unto the cities about, having now obtained and levied an army amongst them, were conducting the same to Syracuse. But Nicias, upon intelligence thereof, sent unto such cities of the Siculi as had the passages and were their confederates, the Centoripines, Halicyaeans, and others, not to suffer the enemy to go by, but to unite themselves and stop them, for that they would not so much as offer to pass any other way, seeing the Agrigentines had already denied them. When the Sicilians were marching, the Siculi, as the Athenians had desired them, put themselves in ambush in three several places, and setting upon them unawares and on a sudden, slew about eight hundred of them, and all the ambassadors save only one, a Corinthian, which conducted the rest that escaped, being about fifteen hundred, to Syracuse.

33. About the same time came unto them also the aid of the Camarinaeans, five hundred men of arms, three hundred darters, and three hundred archers. Also the Geloans sent them men for five galleys, besides four hundred darters and two hundred

horsemen. For now all Sicily, except the Agrigentines, who were neutral, but all the rest, who before stood looking on, came in to the Syracusian side against the Athenians. [Nevertheless], the Syracusians, after this blow received amongst the Siculi, held their hands and assaulted not the Athenians for a while.

Demosthenes and Eurymedon, having their army now ready, crossed over from Corcyra and the continent with the whole army to the promontory of Iapygia. From thence they went to the Choerades, islands of Iapygia, and here took in certain Iapygian darters to the number of two hundred and fifty, of the Messapian nation. And having renewed a certain ancient alliance with Artas, who reigned there and granted them those darters, they went thence to Metapontum, a city of Italy. There, by virtue of a league, they got two galleys and three hundred darters, which taken aboard, they kept along the shore till they came to the territory of Thurii. Here they found the adverse faction to the Athenians to have been lately driven out in a sedition. And because they desired to muster their army here, that they might see if any were left behind, and persuade the Thurians to join with them freely in the war, and, as things stood, to have for friends and enemies the same that were so to the Athenians; they stayed about that in the territory of the Thurians.

34. The Peloponnesians and the rest, who were at the same time in the twenty-five galleys that for safeguard of the ships lay opposite to the galleys before Naupactus, having prepared themselves for battle, and with more galleys, so as they were little inferior in number to those of the Athenians, went to an anchor under Irineus of Achaia in Rhypica. The place where they rode was in form like a half moon; and their land forces they had ready on either side to assist them, both Corinthians and their other confederates of those parts, embattled upon the points of the promontory; and their galleys made up the space between, under the command of Polyanthes, a Corinthian. Against these the Athenians came up with thirty-three galleys from Naupactus, commanded by Diphilus. The Corinthians at first lay still; but afterwards when they saw their time, and the signal given, they charged the Athenians and the fight began.

They held each other to it long. The Athenians sank three
galleys of the Corinthians; and though none of their own were
sunk, yet seven were made unserviceable, which, having encountered the Corinthian galleys a-head, were torn on both
sides between the beaks and the oars by the beaks of the Corinthian galleys, made stronger for the same purpose. After they
had fought with equal fortune, and so as both sides challenged
the victory; though yet the Athenians were masters of the
wrecks, as driven by the wind into the main, and because the
Corinthians came not out to renew the fight, they at length
parted. There was no chasing of men that fled, nor a prisoner
taken on either side; because the Peloponnesians and Corinthians
fighting near the land easily escaped, nor was there any galley
of the Athenians sunk. But when the Athenians were gone back
to Naupactus, the Corinthians presently set up a trophy as
victors, in regard that more of the Athenian galleys were made
unserviceable than of theirs, and thought themselves not to
have had the worse for the same reason that the others thought
themselves not to have had the better. For the Corinthians
think they have the better when they have not much the worse;
and the Athenians think they have the worse when they have
not much the better. And when the Peloponnesians were gone
and their army by land dissolved, the Athenians also set up a
trophy in Achaia, as if the victory had been theirs, distant from
Erineus, where the Peloponnesians rode, about twenty furlongs.
This was the success of that battle by sea.

35. Demosthenes and Eurymedon, after the Thurians had put
in readiness to go with them seven hundred men of arms and
three hundred darters, commanded their galleys to go along
the coast to Croton, and conducted their land soldiers, having
first taken a muster of them all upon the side of the river
Sybaris, through the territory of the Thurians. But coming to
the river Hylias, upon word sent them from the men of Croton
that if the army went through their territory it should be against
their will, they marched down to the seaside and to the mouth
of the river Hylias, where they stayed all that night and were
met by their galleys. The next day embarking, they kept along
the shore and touched at every town saving Locri till they arrived at Petra in the territory of Rhegium.

36. The Syracusians in the meantime, upon intelligence of their coming on, resolved to try again what they could do with their navy and with their new supply of landmen, which they had gotten together on purpose to fight with the Athenians before Demosthenes and Eurymedon should arrive. And they furnished their navy, both otherwise and according to the advantages they had learnt in the last battle, and also made shorter the heads of their galleys, and thereby stronger, and made beaks to them of a great thickness, which they also strengthened with rafters fastened to the sides of the galleys, both within and without, of six cubits long, in such manner as the Corinthians had armed their galleys a-head to fight with those before Naupactus. For the Syracusians made account that against the Athenian galleys not so built, but weak before, as not using so much to meet the enemy a-head as upon the side by fetching a compass, they could not but have the better, and that to fight in the great haven, many galleys in not much room was an advantage to them; for that using the direct encounter, they should break with their firm and thick beaks the hollow and infirm foreparts of the galleys of their enemies; and that the Athenians, in that narrow room, would want means both to go about and to go through them, which was the point of art they most relied on. For as for their passing through, they would hinder it themselves as much as they could; and for fetching compass, the straitness of the place would not suffer it. And that fighting a-head, which seemed before to be want of skill in the masters [to do otherwise], was what they would now principally make use of; for in this would be their principal advantage. For the Athenians, if overcome, would have no retiring but to the land, which was but a little way off and little in compass, near their own camp; and of the rest of the haven themselves should be masters. And the enemy being pressed, could not choose, thronging together into a little room and all into one and the same place, but disorder one another, which was indeed the thing that in all their battles by sea did the Athenians the greatest hurt, having not, as the Syracusians had, the liberty of the whole haven to retire unto. And to go about into a place of more room, they having it in their power to set upon them from the main sea, and to retire again at

pleasure, they should never be able, especially having Plemmyrium for enemy, and the haven's mouth not being large.

37. The Syracusians, having devised thus much over and above their former skill and strength, and far more confident now since the former battle by sea, assaulted them both with their army and with their navy at once. The landmen from the city Gylippus drew sooner out a little and brought them to the wall of the Athenians' camp upon the side toward the city; and from Olympieium, the men of arms, all that were there, and the horsemen and light armed of the Syracusians came up to the wall on the other side. And by and by after, came sailing forth also the galleys of the Syracusians and their confederates. The Athenians, that thought at first they would have made the attempt only with their landmen, seeing also the galleys on a sudden coming towards them, were in confusion; and some of them put themselves in order upon and before the walls against those that came from the city; and others went out to meet the horsemen and darters that were coming in great numbers and with speed from Olympieium and the parts without; others again went aboard, and withal came to aid those ashore. But when the galleys were manned they put off, being seventy-five in number, and those of Syracuse about eighty.

38. Having spent much of the day in charging and retiring and trying each other, and performed nothing worth the mentioning, save that the Syracusians sank a galley or two of the Athenians, they parted again; and the land soldiers retired at the same time from the wall of the Athenian camp. The next day the Syracusians lay still without showing any sign of what they meant to do. Yet Nicias, seeing that the battle by sea was with equality and imagining that they would fight again, made the captains to repair their galleys, such as had been torn, and two great ships to be moored without those piles which he had driven into the sea before his galleys, to be instead of a haven enclosed. These ships he placed about two acres' breadth asunder, to the end, if any galley chanced to be pressed, it might safely run in and again go safely out at leisure. In performing of this the Athenians spent a whole day from morning until night.

39. The next day the Syracusians assaulted the Athenians

again with the same forces, both by sea and land, that they had done before, but begun earlier in the morning; and being opposed fleet against fleet, they drew out a great part of the day now again as before in attempting upon each other without effect. Till at last Ariston, the son of Pyrrhichus, a Corinthian, the most expert master that the Syracusians had in their fleet, persuaded the commanders in the navy to send to such in the city as it belonged to and command that the market should be speedily kept at the seaside, and to compel every man to bring thither whatsoever he had fit for meat and there to sell it, that the mariners, disbarking, might presently dine by the galleys' side, and quickly again, unlooked for, assault the Athenians afresh the same day.

40. This advice being liked, they sent a messenger and the market was furnished. And the Syracusians suddenly rowed astern towards the city, and disbarking, dined there right on the shore. The Athenians, supposing they had retired towards the city as vanquished, landed at leisure, and amongst other business went about the dressing of their dinner, as not expecting to have fought again the same day. But the Syracusians, suddenly going aboard, came towards them again; and the Athenians, in great tumult and for the most part undined, embarking disorderly, at length with much ado went out to meet them. For a while they held their hands on both sides and but observed each other. But anon after, the Athenians thought not fit by longer dallying to overcome themselves with their own labour, but rather to fight as soon as they could, and thereupon at once with a joint shout charged the enemy, and the fight began. The Syracusians received [and resisted] their charge, and fighting, as they had before determined, with their galleys head to head with those of the Athenians, and provided with beaks for the purpose, brake the galleys of the Athenians very much between the heads of the galleys and the oars. The Athenians were also annoyed much by the darters from the decks, but much more by those Syracusians who, going about in small boats, passed under the rows of the oars of the enemy's galleys, and coming close to their sides, threw their darts at the mariners from thence.

41. The Syracusians, having fought in this manner with the

utmost of their strength, in the end gat the victory; and the Athenians, between the [two] ships, escaped into their harbour. The Syracusian galleys chased them as far as to those ships; but the dolphins hanging from the masts over the entrance of the harbour forbade them to follow any further. Yet there were two galleys, which upon a jollity after victory approached them, but both were lost, of which one with her men and all was taken. The Syracusians, after they had sunk seven galleys of the Athenians and torn many more, and of the men had taken some alive and killed others, retired, and for both the battles erected trophies, and had already an assured hope of being far superior by sea, and also made account to subdue the army by land. And they prepared to assault them again in both kinds.

42. In the meantime Demosthenes and Eurymedon arrived with the Athenian supply, being about seventy-three galleys, and men of arms, of their own and of their confederates, about five thousand, besides darters, as well barbarians as Greeks, not a few, and slingers and archers, and all other provision sufficient. For the present it not a little daunted the Syracusians and their confederates to see no end of their danger, and that, notwithstanding the fortifying in Deceleia, another army should come now equal and like unto their former, and that their power should be so great in every kind. And on the other side, it was a kind of strengthening after weakness to the Athenian army that was there before. Demosthenes, when he saw how things stood, and thinking it unfit to loiter and fall into Nicias' case—for Nicias, who was formidable at his first coming, when he set not presently upon Syracuse but wintered at Catana, both grew into contempt and was prevented also by the coming of Gylippus thither with an army out of Peloponnesus; the which, if Nicias had gone against Syracuse at first, had never been so much as sent for; for supposing themselves to have been strong enough alone, they had at once both found themselves too weak and the city been enclosed with a wall; whereby, though they had sent for it, it could not have helped them as it did— Demosthenes, I say, considering this, and that he also even at the present and the same day was most terrible to the enemy, intended with all speed to make use of this present terribleness of the army. And having observed that the cross wall of the

Syracusians, wherewith they hindered the Athenians from enclosing the city, was but single, and that if they could be masters
of the ascent to Epipolae and again of the camp there, the same
might easily be taken (for none would have stood against them),
hasted to put it to trial, and thought it his shortest way to the
dispatching of the war. For either he should have success, he
thought, and so win Syracuse, or he would lead away the army
and no longer without purpose consume both the Athenians
there with him and the whole state. The Athenians therefore
went out and first wasted the territory of the Syracusians about
the river Anapus, and were the stronger, as at first, both by sea
and land. For the Syracusians durst neither way go out against
them, but only with their horsemen and darters from Olympieium.

43. After this, Demosthenes thought good to try the wall
which the Athenians had built to enclose the city withal with
engines. But seeing the engines were burnt by the defendants
fighting from the wall, and that having assaulted it in divers
parts with the rest of his army he was notwithstanding put
back, he resolved to spend the time no longer, but having gotten
the consent of Nicias and the rest in commission thereunto, to
put in execution his design for Epipolae, as was before intended. By day it was thought impossible not to be discovered,
either in their approach or in their ascent. Having therefore
first commanded to take five days' provision of victual, and all
the masons and workmen, as also store of casting weapons, and
whatsoever they might need, if they overcame, for fortification, he and Eurymedon and Menander, with the whole army,
marched about midnight to Epipolae, leaving Nicias in the
camp. Being come to Epipolae at Euryelus, where also the army
went up before, they were not only not discovered by the
Syracusians that kept the watch, but ascending took a certain
fortification of the Syracusians there and killed part of them
that kept it. But the greatest number, escaping, ran presently to
the camps, of which there were in Epipolae three walled about
without the city, one of Syracusians, one of other Sicilians, and
one of confederates, and carried the news of their coming in,
and told it to those six hundred Syracusians that kept this part
of Epipolae at the first, who presently went forth to meet them.

But Demosthenes and the Athenians lighting on them, though they fought valiantly, put them to flight, and presently marched on, making use of the present heat of the army to finish what he came for before it were too late; and others [going on] in their first course took the cross-wall of the Syracusians, they flying that kept it, and were throwing down the battlements thereof. The Syracusians and their confederates, and Gylippus and those with him, came out to meet them from their camps; but because the attempt was unexpected and in the night, they charged the Athenians timorously, and were even at first forced to retire. But as the Athenians advanced more out of order, [chiefly] as having already gotten the victory, but desiring also quickly to pass through all that remained yet unfoughten with, lest through their remissness in following they might again rally themselves, the Boeotians withstood them first, and charging, forced them to turn their backs.

44. And here the Athenians were mightily in disorder and perplexed, so that it hath been very hard to be informed of any side in what manner each thing passed. For if in the day time, when things are better seen, yet they that are present cannot tell how all things go, save only what every man with much ado seeth near unto himself, how then in a battle by night (the only one that happened between great armies in all this war) can a man know anything for certain? For though the moon shined bright, yet they saw one another no otherwise than as by the moonlight was likely, so as to see a body, but not be sure whether it were a friend or not. And the men of arms on both sides, being not a few in number, had but little ground to turn in. Of the Athenians, some were already overcome, others went on in their first way. Also a great part of the rest of the army was already part gotten up and part ascending, and knew not which way to march. For after the Athenians once turned their backs, all before them was in confusion; and it was hard to distinguish of anything for the noise. For the Syracusians and their confederates prevailing encouraged each other and received the assailants with exceeding great shouts (for they had no other means in the night to express themselves); and the Athenians sought each other and took for enemies all before them, though friends and of the number of those that fled, and

by often asking the word, there being no other means of distinction, all asking at once they both made a great deal of stir amongst themselves and revealed the word to the enemy. But they did not in like manner know the word of the Syracusians, because these, being victorious and undistracted, knew one another better; so that when they lighted on any number of the enemy, though they themselves were more, yet the enemy escaped as knowing the watchword; but they, when they could not answer, were slain. But that which hurt them most was the tune of the Paean, which being in both armies the same, drave them to their wits' end. For the Argives and Corcyraeans and all other of the Doric race on the Athenians' part, when they sounded the Paean, terrified the Athenians on one side; and the enemy terrified them with the like on the other side. Wherefore at the last, falling one upon another in divers parts of the army, friends against friends, and countrymen against countrymen, they not only terrified each other, but came to handstrokes and could hardly again be parted. As they fled before the enemy, the way of the descent from Epipolae by which they were to go back being but strait, many of them threw themselves down from the rocks, and died so. And of the rest that gat down safely into the plain, though the greatest part, and all that were of the old army by their knowledge of the country, escaped into the camp; yet of these that came last, some lost their way, and straying in the fields, when the day came on were cut off by the Syracusian horsemen that ranged the country about.

45. The next day the Syracusians erected two trophies, one in Epipolae at the ascent and another where the first check was given by the Boeotians. The Athenians received their dead under truce. And many there were that died, both of themselves and of their confederates; but the arms taken were more than for the number of the slain. For of such as were forced to quit their bucklers and leap down from the rocks, though some perished, yet some there also were that escaped.

46. After this, the Syracusians, having by such unlooked-for prosperity recovered their former courage, sent Sicanus with fifteen galleys to Agrigentum, being in sedition, to bring that city, if they could, to their obedience. And Gylippus went

again to the Sicilian cities by land to raise yet another army, as being in hope to take the camp of the Athenians by assault, considering how the matter had gone in Epipolae.

47. In the meantime the Athenian generals went to council upon their late overthrow and present general weakness of the army. For they saw not only that their designs prospered not, but that the soldiers also were weary of staying. For they were troubled with sickness, proceeding from a double cause, this being the time of the year most obnoxious to diseases, and the place where they lay moorish and noisome; and all things else appeared desperate. Demosthenes thought fit to stay no longer, and since the execution of his design at Epipolae had failed, delivered his opinion for going out of the haven whilst the seas were open and whilst, at least with this addition of galleys, they were stronger than the army of the enemy. For it was better, he said, for the city to make war upon those which fortify against them at home than against the Syracusians, seeing they cannot now be easily overcome; and there was no reason why they should spend much money in lying before the city. This was the opinion of Demosthenes.

48. Nicias, though he also thought their estate bad, yet was unwilling to have their weakness discovered, and, by decreeing of their departure openly with the votes of many, to make known the same to the enemy; for if at any time they had a mind to be gone, they should then be less able to do it secretly. Besides, the estate of the enemy, inasmuch as he understood it better than the rest, put him into some hope that it might yet grow worse than their own, in case they pressed the siege, especially being already masters of the sea, far and near, with their present fleet. There was moreover a party for the Athenians in Syracuse that desired to betray the state into their hands, and that sent messengers unto him and suffered him not to rise and be gone. All which he knowing, though he were in truth doubtful what opinion to be of, and did yet consider, nevertheless openly in his speech he was against the withdrawing of the army, and said that he was sure the people of Athens would take it ill if he went thence without their order; for that they were not to have such judges as should give sentence upon their own sight of things done rather than upon the report of

calumniators, but such as would believe whatsoever some fine speaker should accuse them of. That many, nay most of the soldiers here, who now cry out upon their misery, will there cry out on the contrary, and say the generals have betrayed the state and come away for a bribe. That he would not, therefore, knowing the nature of the Athenians so well, choose to be put to death unjustly and charged with a dishonourable crime by the Athenians rather than, if he must needs do one, to suffer the same at the hand of the enemy by his own adventure. And yet, he said, the state of the Syracusians was still inferior to their own. For paying much money to strangers and laying out much more on forts [without and about the city], having also had a great navy a year already in pay, they must needs want money at last, and all these things fail them. For they have spent already two thousand talents, and are much in debt besides. And whensoever they shall give over this course and make pay no longer, their strength is gone, as being auxiliary and not constrained to follow the war as the Athenians are. Therefore it was fit, he said, to stay close to the city and not to go away as if they were too weak in money, wherein they were much superior.

49. Nicias, when he spake this, assured them of it, as knowing the state of Syracuse precisely and their want of money, and that there were some that desired to betray the city to the Athenians and sent him word not to go. Withal he had now confidence in the fleet, which, as being before overcome, he had not. As for lying where they did, Demosthenes would by no means hear of it. But if the army might not be carried away without order from the Athenians but must needs stay in Sicily, then, he said, they might go to Thapsus or Catana, from whence by their landmen they might invade and turn much of the country to them and wasting the fields of the enemies, weaken the Syracusians; and be to fight with their galleys in the main sea, and not in a narrow (which is the advantage of the enemy), but in a wide place, where the benefit of skill should be theirs, and where they should not be forced, in charging and retiring, to come up and fall off in narrow and circumscribed limits. In sum, he said, he by no means liked to stay where they were, but with all speed, no longer delaying the matter, to arise and be

gone. Eurymedon also gave the like counsel. Nevertheless, upon the contradiction of Nicias, there grew a kind of sloth and procrastination in the business, and a suspicion withal that the asseveration of Nicias was grounded on somewhat that he knew above the rest.* And thereupon the Athenians deferred their going thence and stayed upon the place.

50. In the meantime Gylippus and Sicanus returned unto Syracuse. Sicanus without his purpose at Agrigentum, for whilst he was yet in Gela, the sedition which had been raised in the behalf of the Syracusians was turned into friendship; but Gylippus not without another great army out of Sicily, besides the men of arms, which having set forth from Peloponnesus in ships the spring before, were then lately arrived at Selinus from out of Afric. For having been driven into Afric, and the Cyrenaeans having given them two galleys with pilots, in passing by the shore they aided the Euesperitae besieged by the Africans; and having overcome the Africans, they went over to Neapolis, a town of traffic belonging to the Carthagenians, where the passage into Sicily is shortest, and but two days and a night's sail over; and from thence they crossed the sea to Selinus. As soon as they were come, the Syracusians again presently prepared to set upon the Athenians, both by sea and land. The Athenian generals, seeing them have another army, and their own not bettering but every day growing worse than other, but especially as being pressed to it by the sickness of the soldiers, repented now that they removed not before; and Nicias, being now no longer against it as he was but desirous only that it might not be concluded openly, gave order unto all as secretly as was possible to put forth of the harbour and

---

* Nicias had actually been in touch with a faction in Syracuse which wished to turn over the city to the Athenians (Chap. 86 of this book). He was very wealthy and had many connections all over Greece. What Thucydides means here is that the other generals feared to insist on this plan of going away because they thought that Nicias' private information was definitely that the city would be betrayed to them, and that naturally enough at this stage he declined to be more explicit as to his sources or their reliability. It was obviously very hard for them to gauge accurately the proportions of Nicias' timidity and irresolution on the one hand and his access to secret information on the other.

to be ready when the sign should be given. But when they were about it and everything was ready, the moon happened to be eclipsed; for it was full moon. And not only the greatest part of the Athenians called upon the generals to stay, but Nicias also (for he was addicted to superstition and observations of that kind somewhat too much) said that it should come no more into debate whether they should go or not till the three times nine days were past which the soothsayers appoint in that behalf. And the Athenians, though upon going, stayed still for this reason.

51. The Syracusians, also having intelligence of this, were encouraged unto the pressing of the Athenians much the more, for that they confessed themselves already too weak for them, both by sea and land; for else they would never have sought to have run away. Besides, they would not have them sit down in any other part of Sicily, and become the harder to be warred on; but had rather thereright, and in a place most for their own advantage, compel them to fight by sea. To which end they manned their galleys; and after they had rested as long as was sufficient, when they saw their time, the first day they assaulted the Athenians' camp. And some small number of men of arms and horsemen of the Athenians sallied out against them by certain gates; and the Syracusians intercepting some of the men of arms, beat them back into the camp. But the entrance being strait, there were seventy of the horsemen lost, and men of arms some, but not many.

52. The next day they came out with their galleys, seventy-six in number, and the Athenians set forth against them with eighty-six; and being come together, they fought. Eurymedon had charge of the right wing of the Athenians, and desiring to encompass the galleys of the enemies, drew forth his own galleys in length more towards the shore, and was cut off by the Syracusians, that had first overcome the middle battle of the Athenians, from the rest, in the bottom and inmost part of the haven, and both slain himself, and the galleys that were with him lost. And that done, the rest of the Athenian fleet was also chased and driven ashore.

53. Gylippus, when he saw the navy of the enemy vanquished and carried past the piles and their own harbour, came with a

part of his army to the pier to kill such as landed and to cause that the Syracusians might the easier pull the enemy's galleys from the shore, whereof themselves were masters. But the Tuscans, who kept guard in that part for the Athenians, seeing them coming that way in disorder, made head, and charging these first, forced them into the marsh called Lysimeleia. But when afterwards a greater number of the Syracusians and their confederates came to help them, then also the Athenians, to help the Tuscans and for fear to lose their galleys, fought with them; and having overcome them, pursued them, and not only slew many of their men of arms, but also saved the most of their galleys and brought them back into the harbour. Nevertheless the Syracusians took eighteen and slew the men taken in them. And amongst the rest they let drive before the wind (which blew right upon the Athenians) an old ship full of faggots and brands set on fire to burn them. The Athenians on the other side, fearing the loss of their navy, devised remedies for the fire, and having quenched the flame and kept the ship from coming near, escaped that danger.

54. After this the Syracusians set up a trophy, both for the battle by sea, and for the men of arms which they intercepted above before the camp, where also they took the horses. And the Athenians erected a trophy likewise, both for the flight of those footmen which the Tuscans drave into the marsh and for those which they themselves put to flight with the rest of the army.

55. When the Syracusians had now manifestly overcome their fleet (for they feared at first the supply of galleys that came with Demosthenes), the Athenians were in good earnest utterly out of heart. And as they were much deceived in the event, so they repented more of the voyage. For having come against these cities, the only ones that were for institution like unto their own and governed by the people as well as themselves, and which had a navy and horses and greatness, seeing they could create no dissension amongst them about change of government to win them that way, nor could subdue it with the greatness of their forces when they were far the stronger, but misprospered in most of their designs, they were then at their wits' end; but now, when they were also vanquished by sea

(which they would never have thought), they were much more dejected than ever.

56. The Syracusians went presently about the haven without fear and meditated how to shut up the same that the Athenians might not steal away without their knowledge, though they would. For now they studied not only how to save themselves, but how to hinder the safety of the Athenians. For the Syracusians conceived, not untruly, that their own strength was at this present the greater, and that if they could vanquish the Athenians and their confederates both by sea and land, it would be a mastery of great honour to them amongst the rest of the Grecians. For all the rest of Greece should be one part freed by it, and the other part out of fear of subjection hereafter; for it would be impossible for the Athenians, with the remainder of their strength, to sustain the war that would be made upon them afterwards. And they, being reputed the authors of it, should be had in admiration, not only with all men now living, but also with posterity. And to say truth, it was a worthy mastery, both for the causes shewn and also for that they became victors not of the Athenians only but many others, their confederates; nor again they themselves alone but their confederates also, having been in joint command with the Corinthians and Lacedaemonians, and both exposed their city to the first hazard, and of the business by sea performed the greatest part themselves. The greatest number of nations, except the general roll of those which in this war adhered to Athens and Lacedaemon, were together at this one city.

57. And this number on both sides, against Sicily and for it, some to help win and some to help save it, came to the war at Syracuse, not on any pretence of right nor as kindred to aid kindred, but as profit or necessity severally chanced to induce them. The Athenians, being Ionic, went against the Syracusians, that be Doric, voluntarily. With these, as being their colonies, went the Lemnians and Imbrians, and the Aeginetae that dwelt in Aegina then, all of the same language and institutions with themselves; also the Hestiaeans of Euboea. Of the rest, some went with them as their subjects and some as their free confederates and some also hired. Subjects and tributaries: as the Eretrians, Chalcideans, Styrians, and Carystians, from

Euboea; Ceians, Andrians, Tenians, from out of the islands; Milesians, Samians, and Chians, from Ionia. Of these the Chians followed them as free, not as tributaries of money, but of galleys. And these were almost all of them Ionians, descended from the Athenians, except only the Carystians, that are of the nation of the Dryopes. And though they were subjects and went upon constraint, yet they were Ionians against Dorians. Besides these there went with them Aeolians, namely, the Methymnaeans, subjects to Athens, not tributaries of money but of galleys; and the Tenedians and Aenians, tributaries. Now here, Aeolians were constrained to fight against Aeolians, namely, against their founders the Boeotians, that took part with the Syracusians. But the Plataeans, and only they, being Boeotians, fought against Boeotians upon just quarrel. The Rhodians and Cythereans, Doric both, by constraint bore arms; one of them, namely the Cythereans, a colony of the Lacedaemonians, with the Athenians against the Lacedaemonians that were with Gylippus; and the other, that is to say, the Rhodians, being by descent Argives, not only against the Syracusians, who were also Doric, but against their own colony, the Geloans, which took part with the Syracusians. Then of the islanders about Peloponnesus, there went with them the Cephallenians and Zacynthians, not but that they were free states, but because they were kept in awe as islanders by the Athenians, who were masters of the sea. And the Corcyraeans, being not only Doric but Corinthians, fought openly against both Corinthians and Syracusians, though a colony of the one and of kin to the other, which they did necessarily (to make the best of it), but indeed no less willingly, in respect of their hatred to the Corinthians. Also the Messenians, now so called, in Naupactus, were taken along to this war, and the Messenians at Pylus, then holden by the Athenians. Moreover the Megarean outlaws, though not many, by advantage taken of their misery, were fain to fight against the Selinuntians that were Megareans likewise. But now the rest of their army was rather voluntary. The Argives not so much for the league as for their enmity against the Lacedaemonians and their present particular spleen, followed the Athenians to the war, though Ionic, against Dorians. And the Mantineans and other Arcadian mercenaries went with them as men accustomed ever to invade the enemy shewed them; and now for gain had for enemies, as much as any, those other Arcadians which went thither with the Corinthians. The Cretans and Aetolians were all mercenary; and it fell out that the Cretans, who together with the Rhodians were founders of Gela, not only took not part with their colony, but fought against it willingly for their hire. And some Acarnanians also went with them for gain; but most of them went as confederates, in love to Demosthenes and for good will to the state of Athens. And thus many within the bound of the Ionian gulf. Then of Italians, fallen into the same necessity of seditious times, there went with them to this war the Thurians and Metapontians; of Greek Sicilians, the Naxians and Catanaeans. Of barbarian, the Egestaeans, who also drew with them the most of those Greek Sicilians. Without Sicily, there went with them some Tuscans, upon quarrels between them and the Syracusians, and some Iapygian mercenaries. These were the nations that followed the army of the Athenians.

58. On the other side, there opposed them on the part of the Syracusians, the Camarinaeans their borderers; and beyond them again the Geloans; and then (the Agrigentines not stirring) beyond them again the same way, the Selinuntians. These inhabit the part of Sicily that lieth opposite to Afric. Then the Himeraeans, on the side that lieth on the Tyrrhene sea, where they are the only Grecians inhabiting, and only aided them. These were their confederates of the Greek nation within Sicily, all Dorians and free states. Then of the barbarians there, they had the Siculi, all but what revolted to the Athenians. For Grecians without Sicily, the Lacedaemonians sent them a Spartan commander, with some Helotes and the rest freedmen. Then aided them both with galleys and with land men the Corinthians only; and for kindred's sake, the Leucadians and Ambraciotes; out of Arcadia, those mercenaries sent by the Corinthians; and Sicyonians on constraint; and from without Peloponnesus, the Boeotians. To the foreign aids the Sicilians themselves, as being great cities, added more in every kind than as much again; for they got together men of arms, galleys, and horses, great store, and other number in abundance. And to all these again the Syracusians themselves added, as I may

say, about as much more, in respect of the greatness both of their city and of their danger.

59. These were the succours assembled on either part, and which were then all there; and after them came no more, neither to the one side nor the other. No marvel then if the Syracusians thought it a noble mastery if to the victory by sea already gotten they could add the taking of the whole Athenian army, so great as it was, and hinder their escape both by sea and land. Presently therefore they fall in hand with stopping up the mouth of the great haven, being about eight furlongs wide, with galleys laid cross and lighters and boats upon their anchors; and withal prepared whatsoever else was necessary in case the Athenians would hazard another battle, meditating on no small matters in anything.

60. The Athenians, seeing the shutting up of the haven and the rest of the enemy's designs, thought good to go to council upon it. And the generals and commanders of regiments having met and considered their present want, both otherwise and in this, that they neither had provision for the present (for upon their resolution to be gone, they had sent before to Catana to forbid the sending in of any more), nor were likely to have for the future unless their navy got the upper hand, they resolved to abandon their camp above and to take in some place, no greater than needs they must, near unto their galleys, with a wall, and leaving some to keep it, to go aboard with the rest of the army, and to man every galley they had, serviceable and less serviceable; and having caused all sorts of men to go aboard and fight it out, if they gat the victory, to go to Catana; if not, to make their retreat in order of battle by land (having first set fire on their navy) the nearest way unto some amicable place, either barbarian or Grecian, that they should best be able to reach unto before the enemy.

As they had concluded, so they did. For they both came down to the shore from their camp above and also manned every galley they had and compelled to go aboard every man of age of any ability whatsoever. So the whole navy was manned to the number of one hundred and ten galleys, upon which they had many archers and darters, both Acarnanians and other strangers, and all things else provided according to their means and purpose. And Nicias, when almost everything was ready, perceiving the soldiers to be dejected for being so far overcome by sea, contrary to their custom, and yet in respect of the scarcity of victual desirous as soon as could be to fight, called them together and encouraged them then the first time with words to this effect: *

61. "Soldiers, Athenians, and other our confederates, [though] the trial at hand will be common to all alike and will concern the safety and country no less of each of us than of the enemy (for if our galleys get the victory, we may every one see his native city again), yet ought we not to be discouraged like men of no experience, who failing in their first adventures, ever after carry a fear suitable to their misfortunes. But you Athenians here present, having had experience already of many wars, and you our confederates, that have always gone along with our armies, remember how often the event falleth out otherwise in war than one would think; and in hope that fortune will once also be of our side, prepare yourselves to fight again in such manner as shall be worthy the number you see yourselves to be.

62. "What we thought would be helps in the narrowness of

* Nothing stands out clearer throughout Book vii than the necessity under which the Athenian generals stood of taking account of the morale of their men from moment to moment. Even if this is true of any army at any time, the present case is extreme and its extremity proves the nature of the Athenian forces. These are citizens first and soldiers after. There is no professional army with a tradition of obedience, discipline, and endurance to death for a flag or a regiment—all the code that was created in the three centuries before the war of 1914–18. Here these citizens-in-arms were far from home, frightened and bewildered by the unexpected success of an enemy they had thought to defeat with little trouble. Consequently, from first to last their commanders had to persuade them, like an election meeting, of the necessity of fighting bravely. Furthermore, the commanders have to bear in mind what will happen to themselves by the votes of these same soldiers when they get home, if they ever do. See in Chapter 48 the speech of Nicias "that many of the soldiers who now cry out upon their misery will then cry out on the contrary and say the generals have betrayed the state for a bribe." Admitting the indecisiveness of Nicias' character, a great deal of the negligence and procrastination with which this campaign was conducted is directly due to the generals' fear of their soldiers as potential voters and fear of the home government as voters actually registering their votes on them at the time of their military actions.

the haven, against such a multitude of galleys as will be there and against the provision of the enemy upon their decks, whereby we were formerly annoyed, we have with the masters now considered them all, and as well as our present means will permit, made them ready. For many archers and darters shall go aboard: and that multitude, which if we had been to fight in the main sea we would not have used, because by slugging the galleys it would take away the use of skill, will nevertheless be useful here, where we are forced to make a land-fight from our galleys. We have also devised, instead of what should have been provided for in the building of our galleys, against the thickness of the beaks of theirs, which did most hurt us, to lash their galleys unto ours with iron grapnels, whereby (if the men of arms do their part) we may keep the galleys which once come close up from falling back again. For we are brought to a necessity now of making it a land-fight upon the water; and it will be the best for us neither to fall back ourselves nor to suffer the enemy to do so, especially when, except what our men on land shall make good, the shore is altogether hostile.

63. "Which you remembering, must therefore fight it out to the utmost and not suffer yourselves to be beaten back unto the shore; but when galley to galley shall once be fallen close, never think any cause worthy to make you part unless you have first beaten off the men of arms of the enemy from their decks. And this I speak to you rather that are the men of arms than to the mariners, inasmuch as that part belongeth rather unto you that fight above; and in you it lieth even yet to achieve the victory for the most part with the landmen. Now for the mariners, I advise, and withal beseech them, not to be too much daunted with the losses past, having now both a greater number of galleys and greater forces upon the decks. Think it a pleasure worth preserving that being taken, by your knowledge of the language and imitation of our fashions, for Athenians (though you be not so),* you are not only admired for it through all Greece, but also partake of our dominion in matter

---

* This is addressed to the *metoicoi,* or aliens permanently resident in Athens. This class was subject to military service and all the obligations of citizens. They also shared in all of the privileges except that of voting.

of profit no less than ourselves, and for awfulness to the nations subject and protection from injury, more. You therefore that alone participate freely of our dominion cannot with any justice betray the same. In despite therefore of the Corinthians, whom you have often vanquished, and of the Sicilians, who as long as our fleet was at the best durst never so much as stand us, repel them; and make it appear that your knowledge, even with weakness and loss, is better than the strength of another with fortune.

64. "Again, to such of you as are Athenians, I must remember this: that you have no more such fleets in your harbours, nor such able men of arms, and that if aught happen to you but victory, your enemies here will presently be upon you at home; and those at home will be unable to defend themselves both against those that shall go hence and against the enemy that lieth there already. So one part of us shall fall into the mercy of the Syracusians, against whom you yourselves know with what intent you came hither; and the other part, which is at home, shall fall into the hands of the Lacedaemonians. Being therefore in this one battle to fight both for yourselves and them, be therefore valiant now if ever; and bear in mind every one of you that you that go now aboard are the land forces, the sea forces, the whole estate and great name of Athens. For which, if any man excel others in skill or courage, he can never shew it more opportunely than now, when he may both help himself with it and the whole."

65. Nicias, having thus encouraged them, commanded presently to go aboard. Gylippus and the Syracusians might easily discern that the Athenians meant to fight by seeing their preparation. Besides, they had advertisement of their purpose to cast iron grapnels into their galleys; and as for everything else, so also for that they had made provision. For they covered the fore-part of their galleys and also the decks for a great way, with hides, that the grapnels cast in might slip and not be able to take hold. When all was ready, Gylippus likewise and the other commanders used unto their soldiers this hortative:

66. "That not only our former acts have been honourable, but that we are to fight now also for further honour, men of

Syracuse and confederates, the most of you seem to know already; for else you never would so valiantly have undergone it; and if there be any man that is not so sensible of it as he ought, we will make it appear unto him better. For whereas the Athenians came into this country with design first to enslave Sicily and then, if that succeeded, Peloponnesus and the rest of Greece, and whereas already they had the greatest dominion of any Grecians whatsoever, either present or past, you, the first that ever withstood their navy, wherewith they were everywhere masters, have in the former battles overcome them, and shall in likelihood overcome them again in this. For men that are cut short where they thought themselves to exceed become afterwards further out of opinion with themselves than they would have been if they had never thought so; and when they come short of their hope in things they glory in, they come short also in courage of the true strength of their forces. And this is likely now to be the case of the Athenians.

67. "Whereas with us it falleth out that our former courage, wherewith though unexperienced we durst stand them, being now confirmed, and an opinion added of being the stronger, giveth to every one of us a double hope. And in all enterprises the greatest hope conferreth for the most part the greatest courage. As for their imitation of our provisions, they are things we are acquainted withal, and we shall not in any kind be unprovided for them. But they, when they shall have many men of arms upon their decks, being not used to it, and many, as I may term them, land-darters, both Acarnanians and others, who would not be able to direct their darts though they should sit, how can they choose but put the galleys into danger and be all in confusion amongst themselves, moving in a fashion not their own? As for the number of their galleys, it will help them nothing, if any of you fear also that, as being to fight against odds in number. For many in little room are so much the slower to do what they desire, and easiest to be annoyed by our munition. But the very truth you shall now understand by these things, whereof we suppose we have most certain intelligence. Overwhelmed with calamities and forced by the difficulties which they are in at this present, they are grown desperate, not trusting to their forces, but willing to put them-

selves upon the decision of fortune, as well as they may, that so they may either go out by force or else make their retreat afterward by land, as men whose estates cannot change into the worse.

68. "Against such confusion, therefore, and against the fortune of our greatest enemies now betraying itself into our hands,* let us fight with anger, and with an opinion not only that it is most lawful to fulfil our hearts' desire upon those our enemies that justified their coming hither as a righting of themselves against an assailant, but also that to be revenged on an enemy is both most natural and, as is most commonly said, the sweetest thing in the world. And that they are our enemies, and our greatest enemies, you all well enough know, seeing them come hither into our dominion to bring us into servitude. Wherein if they had sped, they had put the men to the greatest tortures, the women and children to the greatest dishonesty, and the whole city to the most ignominious name in the world. In regard whereof, it is not fit that any of you should be so tender as to think it gain if they go away without putting you to further danger; for so they mean to do, though they get the victory; but effecting (as it is likely we shall) what we intend, both to be revenged of these and to deliver unto all Sicily their liberty, which they enjoyed before but now is more assured. Honourable is that combat and rare are those hazards wherein the failing bringeth little loss and the success a great deal of profit."

69. When Gylippus and the commanders of the Syracusians had in this manner encouraged their soldiers, they presently put their men on board, perceiving the Athenians to do the same. Nicias, perplexed with this present estate, and seeing how great and how near the danger was, being now on the point to put forth from the harbour, and doubting, as in great battles it falleth out that somewhat in every kind was still wanting, and

* More correctly it is "against the fortune of our greatest enemies that has already succumbed." The *Tyche,* or fortune, of the Athenians is thought of as something separate from them, in a certain sense. It is all the chances which by a throw of the dice might turn in their favor. What Gylippus implies is that fortune, personified in Tyche, has decisively deserted the Athenians.

that he had not yet sufficiently spoken his mind, called unto
him again all the captains of galleys and spake unto them every
one by their fathers, their tribes, and their proper names, and
entreated every one of them that had reputation in any kind
not to betray the same, and those whose ancestors were eminent
not to deface their hereditary virtues, remembering them of
their country's liberty and the uncontrolled power of all men
to live as they pleased; and saying whatsoever else in such a
pinch men are accustomed, not out of their store, to utter things
stale, and in all occasions the same, touching their wives, children, and patrial gods, but such things as being thought by
them available in the present discouragement, they use to cry
into their ears.* And when he thought he had admonished them,
not enough, but as much as the time would permit him, he went
his way and drew out those forces that were to serve on land
on the seaside and embattled them so as they might take up
the greatest length of ground they were able, thereby so much
the more to confirm the courage of them that were aboard.
And Demosthenes, Menander, and Eudemus (for those of the
Athenian commanders went aboard), putting forth of the
harbour, went immediately to the lock of the haven and to
the passage that was left open with intention to force their
way out.

70. But the Syracusians and their confederates, being out already with the same number of galleys they had before, disposed part of them to the guard of the open passage and the
rest in circle about the haven, to the end they might fall upon
the Athenians from all parts at once, and that their land forces
might withal be near to aid them wheresoever the galleys
touched. In the Syracusian navy commanded Sicanus and
Agatharchus, each of them over a wing; and Pythen, with
the Corinthians, had the middle battle. After the Athenians
were come to the lock of the haven, at the first charge they

---

* A more literal modern rendering is something like this: "Saying
other things, too, such as men are used to say at such a moment of
crisis, without seeming to anyone to guard against uttering platitudes,
things brought forward on behalf of every occasion about women
and children and gods of your country; yet in the immediacy of their
confusion, judging them useful, they have recourse to them."

overcame the galleys placed there to guard it, and endeavoured to break open the bars thereof. But when afterwards the Syracusians and confederates came upon them from every side, they fought not at the lock only but also in the haven itself; and the battle was sharp, and such as there had never before been the like. For the courage wherewith the mariners on both sides brought up their galleys to any part they were bidden was very great, and great was the plotting and counterplotting and contention one against another of the masters; also the soldiers, when the galleys boarded each other, did their utmost to excel each other in all points of skill that could be used upon the decks; and every man, in the place assigned him, put himself forth to appear the foremost. But many galleys falling close together in a narrow compass (for they were the most galleys that in any battle they had used, and fought in the least room, being little fewer on the one side and the other than two hundred), they ran against each other but seldom, because there was no means of retiring nor of passing by, but made assaults upon each other oftener, as galley with galley, either flying or pursuing, chanced to fall foul. And as long as a galley was making up, they that stood on the decks used their darts and arrows and stones in abundance; but being once come close, the soldiers at hand-strokes attempted to board each other. And in many places it so fell out, through want of room, that they which ran upon a galley on one side were run upon themselves on the other; and that two galleys, or sometimes more, were forced to lie aboard of one; and that the masters were at once to have a care, not in one place only but in many together, how to defend on the one side and how to offend on the other; and the great noise of many galleys fallen foul of one another both amazed them and took away their hearing of what their directors directed. For they directed thick and loud on both sides, not only as art required but out of their present eagerness; the Athenians crying out to theirs to force the passage, and now if ever valiantly to lay hold upon their safe return to their country; and the Syracusians and their confederates to theirs, how honourable a thing to every one of them it would be to hinder their escape and by this victory to improve every man the honour of his own country. Moreover, the commanders of either side, where they saw any man without necessity to row a-stern, would call unto the captain of the galley by his name and ask him, the Athenians, whether he retired because he thought the most hostile land to be more their friend than the sea, which they had so long been masters of; the Syracusians theirs, whether when they knew that the Athenians desired earnestly by any means to fly, they would nevertheless fly from the flyers.

71. Whilst the conflict was upon the water, the land men had a conflict and sided with them in their affections, they of the place contending for increase of the honours they had already gotten, and the invaders fearing a worse estate than they were already in. For the Athenians, who had their whole fortune at stake in their galleys, were in such a fear of the event as they had never been in the like, and were thereby of necessity to behold the fight upon the water with very different passions. For the sight being near, and not looking all of them upon one and the same part, he that saw their own side prevail took heart and fell to calling upon the gods that they would not deprive them of their safety, and they that saw them have the worse not only lamented but shrieked outright, and had their minds more subdued by the sight of what was done than they that were present in the battle itself. Others that looked on some part where the fight was equal, because the contention continued so as they could make no judgment on it, with gesture of body on every occasion agreeable to their expectation, passed the time in a miserable perplexity. For they were ever within a little either of escaping or of perishing. And one might hear in one and the same army, as long as the fight upon the water was indifferent, at one and the same time lamentations, shouts that they won, that they lost, and whatsoever else a great army in great danger is forced differently to utter. They also that were aboard suffered the same, till at last the Syracusians and their confederates, after long resistance on the other side, put them to flight, and manifestly pressing, chased them with great clamour and encouragement of their own to the shore. And the sea forces, making to the shore, some one way and some another, except only such as were lost by being far from it, escaped into the harbour. And the army that was upon the land,

no longer now of different passions, with one and the same vehemence, all with shrieks and sighs unable to sustain what befel, ran part to save the galleys, part to the defence of the camp, and the residue, who were far the greatest number, fell presently to consider every one of the best way to save himself. And this was the time wherein of all other they stood in greatest fear, and they suffered now the like to what they had made others to suffer before at Pylus. For the Lacedaemonians then, besides the loss of their fleet, lost the men which they had set over into the island; and the Athenians now, without some accident not to be expected, were out of all hope to save themselves by land.

72. After this cruel battle, and many galleys and men on either side consumed, the Syracusians and their confederates, having the victory, took up the wreck and the bodies of their dead, and returning into the city, erected a trophy. But the Athenians, in respect of the greatness of their present loss, never thought upon asking leave to take up their dead or wreck, but fell immediately to consultation how to be gone the same night. And Demosthenes, coming unto Nicias, delivered his opinion for going once again aboard and forcing the passage, if it were possible, betimes the next morning, saying that their galleys which were yet remaining and serviceable were more than those of the enemy; for the Athenians had yet left them about sixty, and the Syracusians under fifty. But when Nicias approved the advice and would have manned out the galleys, the mariners refused to go aboard, as being not only dejected with their defeat, but also without opinion of ever having the upperhand any more. Whereupon they now resolved all to make their retreat by land.

73. But Hermocrates of Syracuse, suspecting their purpose, and apprehending it as a matter dangerous that so great an army, going away by land and sitting down in some part or other of Sicily, should there renew the war, repaired unto the magistrates and admonished them that it was not fit, through negligence, to suffer the enemy in the night time to go their ways (alleging what he thought best to the purpose), but that all the Syracusians and their confederates should go out and fortify in their way and prepossess all the narrow passages with

a guard. Now they were all of them of the same opinion no less than himself and thought it fit to be done; but they conceived withal that the soldier now joyful and taking his ease after a sore battle, being also holiday (for it was their day of sacrifice to Hercules), would not easily be brought to obey. For through excess of joy for the victory, they would most of them, being holiday, be drinking, and look for anything rather than to be persuaded at this time to take up arms again and go out. But seeing the magistrates upon this consideration thought it hard to be done, Hermocrates, not prevailing, of his own head contrived this. Fearing lest the Athenians should pass the worst of their way in the night and so at ease out-go them, as soon as it grew dark he sent certain of his friends, and with them certain horsemen, to the Athenian camp; who, approaching so near as to be heard speak, called to some of them to come forth, as if they had been friends of the Athenians (for Nicias had some within that used to give him intelligence) and bade them to advise Nicias not to dislodge that night for that the Syracusians had beset the ways; but that the next day, having had the leisure to furnish their army, they might march away.

74. Upon this advertisement they abode that night, supposing it had been without fraud. And afterwards, because they went not presently, they thought good to stay there that day also, to the end that the soldiers might pack up their necessaries as commodiously as they could, and begone, leaving all things else behind them save what was necessary for their bodies. But Gylippus and the Syracusians, with their land forces, went out before them, and not only stopped up the ways in the country about by which the Athenians were likely to pass and kept a guard at the fords of brooks and rivers, but also stood embattled to receive and stop their army in such places as they thought convenient. And with their galleys they rowed to the harbour of the Athenians and towed their galleys away from the shore. Some few whereof they burnt, as the Athenians themselves meant to have done, but the rest at their leisure, as any of them chanced in any place to drive ashore, they afterwards hauled into the city.

75. After this, when everything seemed unto Nicias and Demosthenes sufficiently prepared, they dislodged, being now

the third day from their fight by sea. It was a lamentable departure, not only for the particulars, as that they marched away
with the loss of their whole fleet, and that instead of their great
hopes they had endangered both themselves and the state, but
also for the dolorous objects which were presented both to the
eye and mind of every of them in particular in the leaving of
their camp. For their dead lying unburied, when any one saw
his friend on the ground, it struck him at once both with fear
and grief. But the living that were sick or wounded both grieved
them more than the dead, and were more miserable. For with
entreaties and lamentations they put them to a stand, pleading
to be taken along by whomsoever they saw of their fellows or
familiars, and hanging on the necks of their comrades, and
following as far as they were able; and when the strength of
their bodies failed, that they could go no further, with ah-mes!
and imprecations were there left. Insomuch as the whole army,
filled with tears and irresolute, could hardly get away, though
the place were hostile and they had suffered already, and feared
to suffer in the future, more than with tears could be expressed;
but hung down their heads and generally blamed themselves.
For they seemed nothing else but even the people of some great
city expugned by siege and making their escape. For the whole
number that marched were no less one with another than forty
thousand men. Of which not only the ordinary sort carried
every one what he thought he should have occasion to use,
but also the men of arms and horsemen, contrary to their custom, carried their victuals under their arms, partly for want and
partly for distrust of their servants, who from time to time ran
over to the enemy; but at this time went the greatest number.
And yet what they carried was not enough to serve the turn,
for not a jot more provision was left remaining in the camp.
Neither were the sufferings of others and that equal division
of misery, which nevertheless is wont to lighten it in that we
suffer with many, at this time so much as thought light in itself. And the rather because they considered from what splendour and glory which they enjoyed before into how low an
estate they were now fallen. For never Grecian army so differed
from itself. For whereas they came with a purpose to enslave
others, they departed in greater fear of being made slaves them-

selves; and instead of prayers and hymns with which they put to sea, they went back again with the contrary maledictions; and whereas they came out seamen, they departed landmen, and relied not upon their naval forces but upon their men of arms. Nevertheless, in respect of the great danger yet hanging over them, these miseries seemed all [but] tolerable.

76. Nicias, perceiving the army to be dejected, and the great change that was in it, came up to the ranks and encouraged and comforted them as far as for the present means he was able. And as he went from part to part he exalted his voice more than ever before, both as being earnest in his exhortation and because also he desired that the benefit of his words might reach as far as might be.

77. "Athenians and confederates, we must hope still, even in our present estate. Men have been saved ere now from greater dangers than these are. Nor ought you too much to accuse yourselves, either for your losses past, or the undeserved miseries we are now in. Even I myself, that have the advantage of none of you in strength of body (you see how I am in my sickness), nor am I thought inferior to any of you for prosperity past, either in respect of mine own private person or otherwise, am nevertheless now in as much danger as the meanest of you. And yet I have worshipped the gods frequently according to the law and lived justly and unblameably towards men. For which cause my hope is still confident of the future, though these calamities, as being not according to the measure of our desert, do indeed make me fear. But they may perhaps cease. For both the enemies have already had sufficient fortune, and the gods, if any of them have been displeased with our voyage, have already sufficiently punished us. Others have invaded their neighbours as well as we; and as their offence, which proceeded of human infirmity, so their punishment also hath been tolerable. And we have reason now both to hope for more favour from the gods (for our case deserveth their pity rather than their hatred) and also not to despair of ourselves, seeing how good and how many men of arms you are, marching together in order of battle. Make account of this, that wheresoever you please to sit down, there presently of yourselves you are a city, such as not any other in Sicily can either easily sustain if you assault

or remove if you be once seated. Now for your march, that
it may be safe and orderly, look to it yourselves, making no
other account, any of you, but what place soever he shall be
forced to fight in, the same, if he win it, must be his country
and his walls. March you must with diligence, both night and
day alike, for our victual is short; and if we can but reach some
amicable territory of the Siculi (for these are still firm to us
for fear of the Syracusians), then you may think yourselves
secure. Let us therefore send before to them and bid them meet
us and bring us forth some supplies of victual. In sum, soldiers,
let me tell you it is necessary that you be valiant; for there
is no place near where, being cowards, you can possibly be
saved; whereas if you escape through the enemies at this time,
you may every one see again whatsoever anywhere he most
desires; and the Athenians may re-erect the great power of their
city, how low soever fallen. For the men, not the walls nor the
empty galleys, are the city."

78. Nicias, as he used this hortative, went withal about the
army, and where he saw any man straggle and not march in
his rank, he brought him about and set him in his place. Demosthenes, having spoken to the same or like purpose, did as
much to those soldiers under him. And they marched forward,
those with Nicias in a square battalion, and then those with
Demosthenes in the rear. And the men of arms received those
that carried the baggage and the other multitude within them.
When they were come to the ford of the river Anapus, they
there found certain of the Syracusians and their confederates
embattled against them on the bank; but these they put to flight,
and having won the passage marched forward. But the Syracusian horsemen lay still upon them, and their light-armed plied
them with their darts in the flank. This day the Athenians
marched forty furlongs, and lodged that night at the foot of
a certain hill. The next day, as soon as it was light, they marched
forwards about twenty furlongs, and descending into a certain
champaign ground, encamped there, with intent both to get
victual at the houses (for the place was inhabited) and to carry
water with them thence; for before them, in the way they were
to pass, for many furlongs together there was but little to be
had. But the Syracusians in the meantime got before them and

cut off their passage with a wall. This was at a steep hill, on either side whereof was the channel of a torrent with steep and rocky banks; and it is called Acraeum Lepas. The next day the Athenians went on; and the horsemen and darters of the Syracusians and their confederates, being a great number of both, pressed them so with their horses and darts that the Athenians after long fight were compelled to retire again into the same camp, but now with less victual than before, because the horsemen would suffer them no more to straggle abroad.

79. In the morning betimes they dislodged and put themselves on their march again, and forced their way to the hill which the enemy had fortified, where they found before them the Syracusian foot embattled in great length above the fortification [on the hill's side]; for the place itself was but narrow. The Athenians coming up assaulted the wall; but the shot of the enemy, who were many, and the steepness of the hill (for they could easily cast home from above) making them unable to take it, they retired again and rested. There happened withal some claps of thunder and a shower of rain, as usually falleth out at this time of the year, being now near autumn, which further disheartened the Athenians, who thought that also this did tend to their destruction. Whilst they lay still, Gylippus and the Syracusians sent part of their army to raise a wall at their backs, in the way they had come; but this the Athenians hindered by sending against them part of theirs. After this, the Athenians retiring with their whole army into a more champaign ground, lodged there that night, and the next day went forward again. And the Syracusians with their darts, from every part round about, wounded many of them; and when the Athenians charged, they retired, and when they retired, the Syracusians charged, and that especially upon the hindmost, that by putting to flight a few they might terrify the whole army. And for a good while the Athenians in this manner withstood them; and afterwards, being gotten five or six furlongs forward, they rested in the plain; and the Syracusians went from them to their own camp.

80. This night it was concluded by Nicias and Demosthenes, seeing the miserable estate of their army, and the want already of all necessaries, and that many of their men in many assaults

of the enemy were wounded, to lead away the army as far as they possibly could; not the way they purposed before, but toward the sea, which was the contrary way to that which the Syracusians guarded. Now this whole journey of the army lay not towards Catana, but towards the other side of Sicily, Camarina and Gela, and the cities, as well Grecian as barbarian, that way. When they had made many fires accordingly, they marched in the night; and (as usually it falleth out in all armies, and most of all in the greatest, to be subject to affright and terror, especially marching by night and in hostile ground, and the enemy near) were in confusion. The army of Nicias, leading the way, kept together and got far afore; but that of Demosthenes, which was the greater half, was both severed from the rest and marched more disorderly. Nevertheless, by the morning betimes they got to the seaside, and entering into the Helorine way they went on towards the river Cacyparis, to the end when they came thither to march upwards along the river's side through the heart of the country. For they hoped that this way the Siculi, to whom they had sent, would meet them. When they came to the river, here also they found a certain guard of the Syracusians stopping their passage with a wall and with piles. When they had quickly forced this guard, they passed the river and again marched on to another river, called Erineus; for that was the way which the guides directed them.

81. In the meantime the Syracusians and their confederates, as soon as day appeared and that they knew the Athenians were gone, most of them accusing Gylippus as if he had let them go with his consent, followed them with speed the same way, which they easily understood they were gone, and about dinner time overtook them. When they were come up to those with Demosthenes, who were the hindmost and had marched more slowly and disorderly than the other part had done, as having been put into disorder in the night, they fell upon them and fought. And the Syracusian horsemen hemmed them in and forced them up into a narrow compass, the more easily now because they were divided from the rest. Now the army of Nicias was gone by this time one hundred and fifty furlongs further on. For he led away the faster because he thought not

that their safety consisted in staying and fighting voluntarily, but rather in a speedy retreat, and then only fighting when they could not choose. But Demosthenes was both in greater and more continual toil, in respect that he marched in the rear and consequently was pressed by the enemy; and seeing the Syracusians pursuing him, he went not on but put his men in order to fight, till by his stay he was encompassed and reduced, he and the Athenians with him, into great disorder. For being shut up within a place enclosed round with a wall, and which on either side had a way [open] amongst abundance of olive trees, they were charged from all sides at once with the enemy's shot. For the Syracusians assaulted them in this kind, and not in close battle, upon very good reason. For to hazard battle against men desperate was not so much for theirs as for the Athenians' advantage. Besides, after so manifest successes, they spared themselves somewhat, because they were loth to wear themselves out before the end of the business, and thought by this kind of fight to subdue and take them alive.

82. Whereupon, after they had plied the Athenians and their confederates all day long from every side with shot and saw that with their wounds and other annoyance they were already tired, Gylippus and the Syracusians and their confederates first made proclamation that if any of the islanders would come over to them, they should be at liberty. And the men of some few cities went over. And by and by after, they made agreement with all the rest that were with Demosthenes that they should deliver up their arms, and none of them be put to death, neither violently, nor by bonds, nor by want of the necessities of life. And they all yielded, to the number of six thousand men; and the silver they had, they laid it all down, casting it into the hollow of targets, and filled with the same four targets. And these men they carried presently into the city.

Nicias, and those that were with him, attained the same day to the river Erineus, which passing, he caused his army to sit down upon a certain ground more elevate than the rest.

83. Where the Syracusians the next day overtook and told him, that those with Demosthenes had yielded themselves, and willed him to do the like. But he, not believing it, took truce

for a horseman to enquire the truth. Upon return of the horseman and word that they had yielded, he sent a herald to Gylippus and the Syracusians, saying that he was content to compound on the part of the Athenians to repay whatsoever money
the Syracusians had laid out, so that his army might be suffered to depart, and that till payment of the money were made,
he would deliver them hostages, Athenians, every hostage rated
as a talent. But Gylippus and the Syracusians, refusing the
condition, charged them, and having hemmed them in, plied
them with shot, as they had done the other army, from every
side till evening. This part of the army was also pinched with
the want both of victual and other necessaries. Nevertheless,
observing the quiet of the night, they were about to march.
But no sooner took they their arms up than the Syracusians
perceiving it gave the alarm. Whereupon the Athenians, finding
themselves discovered, sat down again, all but three hundred,
who breaking by force through the guards, marched as far as
they could that night.

84. And Nicias, when it was day, led his army forward, the
Syracusians and their confederates still pressing them in the
same manner, shooting and darting at them from every side.
The Athenians hasted to get the river Asinarus, not only because they were urged on every side by the assault of the many
horsemen and other multitude and thought to be more at ease
when they were over the river, but out of weariness also and
desire to drink. When they were come unto the river, they
rushed in without any order, every man striving who should
first get over. But the pressing of the enemy made the passage
now more difficult. For being forced to take the river in heaps,
they fell upon and trampled one another under their feet; and
falling amongst the spears and utensils of the army, some
perished presently; and others, catching hold one of another,
were carried away together down the stream. And [not only]
the Syracusians standing along the farther bank, being a steep
one, killed the Athenians with their shot from above as they
were many of them greedily drinking and troubling one another in the hollow of the river; but the Peloponnesians came
also down and slew them with their swords, and those especially

that were in the river. And suddenly the water was corrupted; nevertheless they drunk it, foul as it was with blood and mire; and many also fought for it.

85. In the end, when many dead lay heaped in the river, and the army was utterly defeated, part at the river, and part (if any gat away) by the horsemen, Nicias yielded himself unto Gylippus (having more confidence in him than in the Syracusians) to be for his own person at the discretion of him and the Lacedaemonians, and no further slaughter to be made of the soldiers. Gylippus from thenceforth commanded to take prisoners. So the residue, except such as were hidden from them (which were many), they carried alive into the city. They sent also to pursue the three hundred which brake through their guards in the night, and took them. That which was left together of this army to the public was not much; but they that were conveyed away by stealth were very many; and all Sicily was filled with them, because they were not taken, as those with Demosthenes were, by composition. Besides, a great part [of these] were slain; for the slaughter [at this time] was exceeding great, none greater in all the Sicilian war.* They were also not a few that died in those other assaults in their march. Nevertheless, many also escaped, some then presently and some by running away after servitude; the rendezvous of whom was Catana.

86. The Syracusians and their confederates, being come together, returned with their prisoners, all they could get, and with the spoil into the city. As for all the other prisoners of the Athenians and their confederates, they put them into the quarries as the safest custody. But Nicias and Demosthenes they killed, against Gylippus' will. For Gylippus thought the victory would be very honourable if, over and above all his other success, he could carry home both the generals of the enemy to Lacedaemon. And it fell out that one of them, Demosthenes, was their greatest enemy for the things he had done in the

---

* The word *Sicilian* is certainly a false insertion. What Thucydides means is unquestionably that the slaughter was greater than in any other battle in the whole Peloponnesian war, as anyone can see by looking at the figures.

island and at Pylus; and the other, upon the same occasion, their greatest friend. For Nicias had earnestly laboured to have those prisoners which were taken in the island to be set at liberty by persuading the Athenians to the peace. For which cause the Lacedaemonians were inclined to love him; and it was principally in confidence of that that he rendered himself to Gylippus. But certain Syracusians, as it is reported, some of them for fear (because they had been tampering with him) lest being put to the torture he might bring them into trouble, whereas now they were well enough; and others, especially the Corinthians, fearing he might get away by corruption of one or other, being wealthy, and work them some mischief afresh, having persuaded their confederates to the same, killed him. For these, or for causes near unto these, was he put to death; being the man that, of all the Grecians of my time, had least deserved to be brought to so great a degree of misery.*

87. As for those in the quarries, the Syracusians handled them at first but ungently. For in this hollow place, first the sun and suffocating air (being without roof) annoyed them one way; and on the other side, the nights coming upon that heat, autumnal and cold, put them, by reason of the alteration, into strange diseases; especially doing all things, for want of room, in one and the same place, and the carcasses of such as died of their wounds or change [of air] or other like accident lying together there on heaps. Also the smell was intolerable; besides that they were afflicted with hunger and thirst. For for eight months together, they allowed no more but to every man a cotyle of water by the day and two cotyles of corn. And whatsoever misery is probable that men in such a place may suffer, they suffered. Some seventy days they lived thus thronged. Afterwards, retaining the Athenians, and such Sicilians and Italians as were of the army with them, they sold the rest. How many were taken in all it is hard to say exactly; but they were seven thousand at the fewest. And this was the greatest action that happened in all this war, or at all, that we have

* Here is one of Hobbes' inexplicable omissions. The Greek reads "having least deserved to fall into such misfortune, *having regulated all his life in accordance with what has been considered virtue.*"

heard of amongst the Grecians, being to the victors most glorious and most calamitous to the vanquished. For being wholly overcome in every kind and receiving small loss in nothing, their army and fleet and all [that ever they had] perished (as they use to say) with an universal destruction. Few of many returned home. And thus passed the business concerning Sicily.

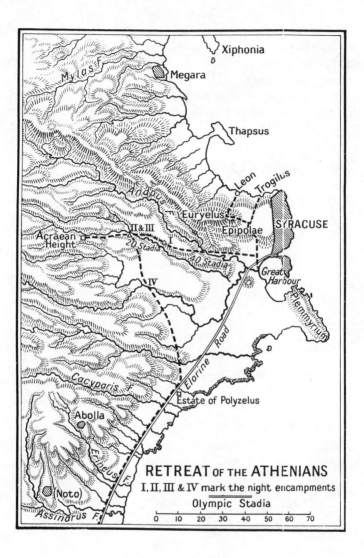

Xiphonia

Megara

Mylas F

Thapsus

Anapus

Leon

Trogilus

Euryelus

Epipolae

SYRACUSE

Acraean
Height

II & III

20 Stadia

I

40 Stadia

IV

Great
Harbour

Plemmyrium

Cacyparis F.

Elorine Road

Abolla

Estate of Polyzelus

Erineus F.

(Noto)

Assinarus F.

RETREAT OF THE ATHENIANS

I, II, III & IV mark the night encampments

Olympic Stadia

0   10   20   30   40   50   60   70

THE EIGHTH BOOK

1. When the news was told at Athens, they believed not a
long time, though it were plainly related and by those very
soldiers that escaped from the defeat itself that all was so utterly lost as it was. When they knew it, they were mightily
offended with the orators that furthered the voyage, as if they
themselves had never decreed it. They were angry also with
those that gave out prophecies and with the soothsayers and
with whosoever else had at first by any divination put them
into hope that Sicily should be subdued. Every thing, from
every place, grieved them; and fear and astonishment, the

greatest that ever they were in, beset them round. For they were not only grieved for the loss which both every man in particular and the whole city sustained of so many men of arms, horsemen, and serviceable men, the like whereof they saw was not left, but seeing they had neither galleys in their haven nor money in their treasury nor furniture in their galleys, were even desperate at that present of their safety; and thought the enemy out of Sicily would come forthwith with their fleet into Peiraeus, especially after the vanquishing of so great a navy, and that the enemy here would surely now, with double preparation in every kind, press them to the utmost both by sea and land and be aided therein by their revolting confederates. Nevertheless, as far as their means would stretch, it was thought best to stand it out and, getting materials and money where they could have it, to make ready a navy and to make sure of their confederates, especially those of Euboea; and to introduce a greater frugality in the city, and to erect a magistracy of the elder sort, as occasion should be offered to preconsult of the business that passed. And they were ready, in respect of their present fear (as is the people's fashion), to order every thing aright. And as they resolved this, so they did it. And the summer ended.

2. The winter following, upon the great overthrow of the Athenians in Sicily, all the Grecians were presently up against them. Those who before were confederates of neither side thought fit no longer, though uncalled, to abstain from the war, but to go against the Athenians of their own accord, as having not only every one severally this thought, that had the Athenians prospered in Sicily they would afterwards have come upon them also, but imagined withal that the rest of the war would be but short, whereof it would be an honour to participate. And such of them as were confederates of the Lacedaemonians longed now more than ever to be freed as soon as might be of their great toil. But above all, the cities subject to the Athenians were ready, even beyond their ability, to revolt; as they that judged according to their passion, without admitting reason in the matter, that the next summer they were to remain with victory. But the Lacedaemonians themselves took heart, not only from all this, but also principally from that,

that their confederates in Sicily with great power, having another navy now necessarily added to their own, would in all likelihood be with them in the beginning of the spring. And being every way full of hopes, they purposed without delay to fall close to the war, making account, if this were well ended, both to be free hereafter from any more such dangers as the Athenians, if they had gotten Sicily, would have put them into, and also, having pulled them down, to have the principality of all Greece now secure unto themselves.

3. Whereupon Agis, their king, went out with a part of his army the same winter from Deceleia and levied money amongst the confederates for the building of a navy; and turning into the Melian gulf, upon an old grudge took a great booty from the Oetaeans, which he made money of, and forced those of Pthiotis, being Achaians, and others in those parts subjects to the Thessalians (the Thessalians complaining and unwilling) to give them hostages and money. The hostages he put into Corinth, and endeavoured to draw them into the league. And the Lacedaemonians imposed upon the states confederate, the charge of building one hundred galleys; that is to say, on their own state and on the Boeotians, each twenty-five; on the Phoceans and Locrians, fifteen; on the Corinthians, fifteen; on the Arcadians, Sicyonians, and Pellenians, ten; and on the Megareans, Troezenians, and Hermionians, ten. And put all things else in readiness presently with the spring to begin the war.

4. The Athenians also made their preparations as they had designed, having gotten timber and built their navy this same winter, and fortified the promontory of Sunium that their corn-boats might come about in safety. Also they abandoned the fort in Laconia, which they had built as they went by for Sicily. And generally where there appeared expense upon anything unuseful, they contracted their charge.

5. Whilst they were on both sides doing thus, there came unto Agis about their revolt from the Athenians, first the ambassadors of the Euboeans. Accepting the motion, he sent for Alcamenes, the son of Sthenelaidas, and for Melanthus from Lacedaemon to go commanders into Euboea. Whom, when he was come to him with about three hundred freedmen, he was now about to send over. But in the meantime came the Lesbians,

they also desiring to revolt; and by the means of the Boeotians
Agis changed his former resolution and prepared for the revolt
of Lesbos, deferring that of Euboea, and assigned them Alcamenes, the same that should have gone into Euboea, for their
governor; and the Boeotians promised them ten galleys and Agis
other ten. Now this was done without acquainting therewith
the state of Lacedaemon. For Agis, as long as he was about
Deceleia with the power he had, had the law in his own hands
to send what army and whither he listed and to levy men and
money at his pleasure. And at this time, the confederates of
him (as I may call them) did better obey him than the confederates of the Lacedaemonians did them at home; for having
the power in his hands, he was terrible wheresoever he came.
And he was now for the Lesbians. But the Chians and Erythraeans, they also desiring to revolt, went not to Agis, but to
the Lacedaemonians in the city; and with them went also an
ambassador from Tissaphernes, lieutenant to king Darius in the
low countries of Asia.* For Tissaphernes also instigated the
Peloponnesians and promised to pay their fleet. For he had
lately begged of the king the tribute accruing in his own
province; for which he was in arrearage, because he could
receive nothing out of any of the Greek cities by reason of
the Athenians. And therefore he thought by weakening the
Athenians to receive his tribute the better, and withal to draw
the Lacedaemonians into a league with the king; and thereby,
as the king had commanded, to kill or take alive Amorges,
Pissuthnes' bastard son, who was in rebellion against him about

---

* The Persian king had divided Asia Minor into a number of satrapies
or governorships. Pharnabazus held one, comprising, among other
states, a number of the northern Greek cities, e.g., those in the Hellespont and in Phrygia and Bithynia. Tissaphernes held the southern
satrapy with Ionia, Caria, Lycia, etc. The policy of both of the
governors was, as far as the Peloponnesian War was concerned, only
to secure what could be secured for the Persians. To this end they
would use one of the Greek combatants to weaken the other. It is
only in the last five years of the war, after the period of which
Thucydides wrote, that the king sent down his son Prince Cyrus to
the coast with authority superior to that of the satraps. Cyrus took
the part of the Lacedaemonians with decision and his support was
one of the most potent factors against Athens in the end of the war.
See Book ii, Chapter 65.

Caria. The Chians, therefore, and Tissaphernes followed this business jointly.

6. Calligeitus, the son of Laophon, a Magarean, and Timagoras the son of Athenagoras, a Cyzicene, both banished their own cities and abiding with Pharnabazus, the son of Pharnaces, came also about the same time to Lacedaemon, sent by Pharnabazus to procure a fleet for the Hellespont, that he also, if he could, might cause the Athenian cities in his province to revolt for his tribute's sake, and be the first to draw the Lacedaemonians into league with the king, just the same things that were desired before by Tissaphernes. Now Pharnabazus and Tissaphernes treating apart, there was great canvassing at Lacedaemon between the one side that persuaded to send to Ionia and Chios and the other that would have the army and fleet go first into the Hellespont. But the Lacedaemonians indeed approved best by much of the business of the Chians and of Tissaphernes. For with these co-operated Alcibiades, hereditary guest and friend of Endius, the ephore of that year, in the highest degree; insomuch as in respect of that guesthood, Alcibiades' family received a Laconic name. For Endius was called Endius Alcibiadis. Nevertheless the Lacedaemonians sent first one Phrynis, a man of those parts, to Chios to see if the galleys they had were so many as they reported and whether the city were otherwise so sufficient as it was said to be. And when the messenger brought back word that all that had been said was true, they received both the Chians and the Erythraeans presently into their league and decreed to send them forty galleys, there being at Chios, from such places as the Chians named, no less than sixty already. And of these at first they were about to send out ten, with Melancridas for admiral; but afterwards, upon occasion of an earthquake, for Melancridas they sent Chalcideus, and instead of ten galleys they went about the making ready of five only in Laconia. So the winter ended, and nineteenth year of this war written by Thucydides.

7. In the beginning of the next summer, because the Chians pressed to have the galley sent away and feared lest the Athenians should get notice what they were doing (for all their ambassadors went out by stealth), the Lacedaemonians send

away to Corinth three Spartans to will them with all speed to transport their galleys over the isthmus to the other sea towards Athens, and to go all to Chios, as well those which Agis had made ready to go to Lesbos as the rest; the number of the galleys of the league which were then there being forty wanting one.

8. But Calligeitus and Timagoras, who came from Pharnabazus, would have no part in this fleet that went for Chios, nor would deliver the money, twenty-five talents, which they had brought with them to pay for their setting forth, but made account to go out with another fleet afterwards by themselves. When Agis saw that the Lacedaemonians meant to send first to Chios, he resolved not of any other course himself; but the confederates assembling at Corinth went to council upon the matter and concluded thus: that they should go first to Chios under the command of Chalcideus, who was making ready the five galleys at Laconia; and then to Lesbos under the charge of Alcamenes, intended also to be sent thither by Agis; and lastly into Hellespont, in which voyage they ordained that Clearchus, the son of Rhamphias, should have the command; and concluded to carry over the isthmus first the one half of their galleys, and that those should presently put to sea, that the Athenians might have their minds more upon those than on the other half to be transported afterwards. For they determined to pass that sea openly, contemning the weakness of the Athenians in respect they had not any navy of importance yet appearing. As they resolved, so presently they carried over one-and-twenty galleys.

9. But when the rest urged to put to sea, the Corinthians were unwilling to go along before they should have ended the celebration of the Isthmian holidays, then come. Hereupon Agis was content that they for their parts should observe the Isthmian truce, and he, therefore, to take the fleet upon himself as his own. But the Corinthians not agreeing to that, and the time passing away, the Athenians got intelligence the easier of the practice of the Chians and sent thither Aristocrates, one of their generals, to accuse them of it. The Chians denying the matter, he commanded them for their better credit to send along with him some galleys for their aid due by the league; and they

sent seven. The cause why they sent these galleys was the many not acquainted with the practice, and the few and conscious not willing to undergo the enmity of the multitude without having strength first, and their not expecting any longer the coming of the Lacedaemonians, because they had so long delayed them.

10. In the meantime the Isthmian games were celebrating, and the Athenians (for they had word sent them of it) came and saw; and the business of the Chians grew more apparent. After they went thence, they took order presently that the fleet might not pass from Cenchreiae undiscovered. And after the holidays were over, the Corinthians put to sea for Chios under the conduct of Alcamenes. And the Athenians at first with equal number came up to them and endeavoured to draw them out into the main sea; but seeing the Peloponnesians followed not far, but turned another way, the Athenians went also from them. For the seven galleys of Chios, which were part of this number, they durst not trust. But afterwards having manned thirty-seven others, they gave chase to the enemy by the shore and drave them into Peiraeus in the territory of Corinth (this Peiraeus is a desert haven, and the utmost upon the confines of Epidauria). One galley that was far from land the Peloponnesians lost; the rest they brought together into the haven. But the Athenians charging them by sea with their galleys, and withal setting their men a-land, mightily troubled and disordered them, brake their galleys upon the shore, and slew Alcamenes, their commander. And some they lost of their own.

11. The fight being ended, they assigned a sufficient number of galleys to lie opposite to those of the enemy and the rest to lie under a little island not far off, in which also they encamped, and sent to Athens for a supply. For the Peloponnesians had with them for aid of their galleys the Corinthians the next day, and not long after, divers others of the inhabitants thereabouts. But when they considered that the guarding of them in a desert place would be painful, they knew not what course to take; and once they thought to have set the galleys on fire; but it was concluded afterwards to draw them to the land and guard them with their landmen till some good occasion should be

offered for their escape. And Agis also, when he heard the news, sent unto them Thermon, a Spartan. The Lacedaemonians, having been advertised of the departure of these galleys from the isthmus (for the ephores had commanded Alcamenes when he put to sea to send them word by a horseman), were minded presently to have sent away also the five galleys also that were in Laconia, and Chalcideus the commander of them, and with him Alcibiades. But afterwards, as they were ready to go out, came the news of the galleys chased into Peiraeus, which so much discouraged them, in respect they stumbled in the very entrance of the Ionic war, that they purposed now not only not to send away those galleys of their own but also to call back again some of those that were already at sea.

12. When Alcibiades saw this, he dealt with Endius and the rest of the ephores again not to fear the voyage, alleging that they would [make haste, and] be there before the Chians should have heard of the misfortune of the fleet, and that as soon as he should arrive in Ionia himself, he could easily make the cities there to revolt by declaring unto them the weakness of the Athenians and the diligence of the Lacedaemonians, wherein he should be thought more worthy to be believed than any other. Moreover to Endius he said that it would be an honour in particular to him that Ionia should revolt and the king be made confederate to the Lacedaemonians by his own means, and not to have it the mastery of Agis; for he was at difference with Agis. So having prevailed with Endius and the other ephores, he took sea with five galleys, together with Chalcideus of Lacedaemon, and made haste.

13. About the same time came back from Sicily those sixteen galleys of the Peloponnesians, which, having aided Gylippus in that war, were intercepted by the way about Leucadia and evil entreated by twenty-seven galleys of Athens, that watched thereabouts under the command of Hippocles, the son of Menippus, for such galleys as should return out of Sicily. For all the rest, saving one, avoiding the Athenians, were arrived in Corinth before.

14. Chalcideus and Alcibiades, as they sailed, kept prisoner every man they met with by the way, to the end that notice might not be given of their passage. And touching first at

Corycus in the continent, where also they dismissed those whom they had apprehended, after conference there with some of the conspirators of the Chians, that advised them to go to the city without sending them word before, they came upon the Chians suddenly and unexpected. It put the commons into much wonder and astonishment; but the few had so ordered the matter beforehand that an assembly chanced to be holden at the same time. And when Chalcideus and Alcibiades had spoken in the same and told them that many galleys were coming to them, but not that those other galleys were besieged in Peiraeus, the Chians first and afterwards the Erythraeans revolted from the Athenians. After this they went with three galleys to Clazomenae and made that city to revolt also. And the Clazomenians presently crossed over to the continent and there fortified Polichna, lest they should need a retiring place from the little island wherein they dwelt. The rest also, all that had revolted, fell to fortifying and making of preparation for the war.

15. This news of Chios was quickly brought to the Athenians, who, conceiving themselves to be now beset with great and evident danger, and that the rest of the confederates, seeing so great a city to revolt, would be no longer quiet, in this their present fear decreed that those thousand talents, which through all this war they had affected to keep untouched, forthwith abrogating the punishment ordained for such as spake or gave their suffrages to stir it, should now be used, and therewith galleys not a few manned. They decreed also to send thither out of hand, under the command of Strombichides, the son of Diotimus, eight galleys of the number of those that besieged the enemy at Peiraeus; the which, having forsaken their charge to give chase to the galleys that went with Chalcideus, and not able to overtake them, were now returned; and shortly after also to send Thrasycles to help them with twelve galleys more, which also had departed from the same guard upon the enemy. And those seven galleys of Chios, which likewise kept watch at Peiraeus with the rest, they fetched from thence, and gave the bondmen that served in them their liberty, and the chains to those that were free. And instead of all those galleys that kept guard upon the galleys of the Peloponnesians, they

made ready other with all speed in their places, besides thirty more, which they intended to furnish out afterwards. Great was their diligence; and nothing was of light importance that they went about for the recovery of Chios.

16. Strombichides in the meantime arrived at Samos, and taking into his company one Samian galley, went thence to Teos and entreated them not to stir. But towards Teos was Chalcideus also coming with twenty-three galleys from Chios, and with him also the land forces of the Clazomenians and Erythraeans. Whereof Strombichides having been advertised, he put forth again before his arrival, and standing off at sea, when he saw the many galleys that came from Chios, he fled towards Samos, they following him. The land forces the Teians would not at first admit; but after this flight of the Athenians, they brought them in. And these for the most part held their hands for a while, expecting the return of Chalcideus from the chase; but when he stayed somewhat long, they fell of themselves to the demolishing of the wall built about the city of Teos by the Athenians towards the continent, wherein they were also helped by some few barbarians that came down thither under the leading of Tages, deputy lieutenant of Tissaphernes.

17. Chalcideus and Alcibiades, when they had chased Strombichides into Samos, armed the mariners that were in the galleys of Peloponnesus and left them in Chios, instead of whom they manned with mariners of Chios both those and twenty galleys more; and with this fleet they went to Miletus with intent to cause it to revolt. For the intention of Alcibiades, that was acquainted with the principal Milesians, was to prevent the fleet which was to come from Peloponnesus and to turn these cities first, that the honour of it might be ascribed to the Chians, to himself, to Chalcideus, and (as he had promised) to Endius that set them out, as having brought most of the cities to revolt with the forces of the Chians only and of those galleys that came with Chalcideus. So these, for the greatest part of their way undiscovered, and arriving not much sooner than Strombichides and Thrasycles (who now, chancing to be present with [those] twelve galleys from Athens, followed them with Strombichides), caused the Milesians to revolt. The Athenians following them at

the heels with nineteen galleys, being shut out by the Milesians, lay at anchor at Lada, an island over against the city.

Presently upon the revolt of Miletus was made the first league between the king and the Lacedaemonians by Tissaphernes and Chalcideus, as followeth:

18. "The Lacedaemonians and their confederates have made a league with the king and Tissaphernes on these articles:

"Whatsoever territory or cities the king possesseth and his ancestors have possessed, the same are to remain the king's.

"Whatsoever money or other profit redounded to the Athenians from their cities, the king and the Lacedaemonians are jointly to hinder, so as the Athenians may receive nothing from thence, neither money nor other thing.

"The king and the Lacedaemonians and their confederates are to make joint war against the Athenians. And without consent of both parts it shall not be lawful to lay down the war against the Athenians, neither for the king nor for the Lacedaemonians and their confederates.

"If any shall revolt from the king, they shall be enemies to the Lacedaemonians and their confederates; and if any shall revolt from the Lacedaemonians and their confederates, they shall in like manner be enemies to the king."

19. This was the league. Presently after this the Chians set out ten galleys more and went to Anaea, both to hearken what became of the business at Miletus and also to cause the cities thereabouts to revolt. But word being sent them from Chalcideus to go back, and that Amorges was at hand with his army, they went thence to the temple of Jupiter. [Being there] they descried sixteen galleys more, which had been sent out by the Athenians under the charge of Diomedon after the putting to sea of those with Thrasycles, upon sight of whom they fled, one galley to Ephesus, the rest towards Teos. Four of them the Athenians took, but empty, the men having gotten on shore; the rest escaped into the city of Teos. And the Athenians went away again towards Samos. The Chians, putting to sea again with the remainder of their fleet and with the land forces, caused first Lebedos to revolt and then Erae; and afterwards returned, both with their fleet and landmen, every one to his own.

20. About the same time, the twenty galleys of Peloponnesus, which the Athenians had formerly chased into Peiraeus, and against whom they now lay with a like number, suddenly forced their passage, and having the victory in fight, took four of the Athenian galleys, and going to Cenchreiae, prepared afresh for their voyage to Chios and Ionia. At which time there came also unto them from Lacedaemon for commander, Astyochus, who was now admiral of the whole navy. When the landmen were gone from Teos, Tissaphernes himself came thither with his forces; and he also demolished the wall, as much as was left standing, and went his way again. Not long after the going away of him, came thither Diomedon with ten galleys of Athens. And having made a truce with the Teians, that he also might be received, he put to sea again and kept the shore to Erae and assaulted it, but failing to take it, departed.

21. It fell out about the same time that the commons of Samos, together with the Athenians who were there with three galleys, made an insurrection against the great men and slew of them in all about two hundred. And having banished four hundred more and distributed amongst themselves their lands and houses (the Athenians having now, as assured of their fidelity, decreed them their liberty), they administered the affairs of the city from that time forward by themselves, no more communicating with the Geomori nor permitting any of the common people to marry with them.

22. After this, the same summer, the Chians, as they had begun, persevering in their earnestness to bring the cities to revolt, even without the Lacedaemonians, [with their single forces], and desiring to make as many fellows of their danger as they were able, made war by themselves with thirteen galleys against Lesbos; which was according to what was concluded by the Lacedaemonians, namely, to go thither in the second place, and thence into the Hellespont. And withal the land forces, both of such Peloponnesians as were present and of their confederates thereabouts, went along by them to Clazomenae and Cyme, these under the command of Eualas a Spartan, and the galleys, of Deiniades, a man of the parts thereabouts. The galleys putting in at Methymna, caused that city to revolt first.

23. Now Astyochus, the Lacedaemonian admiral, having set forth as he intended from Cenchreiae, arrived at Chios. The third day after his coming thither came Leon and Diomedon into Lesbos with twenty-five galleys of Athens; for Leon came with a supply of ten galleys more from Athens afterwards. Astyochus, in the evening of the same day, taking with him one galley more of Chios, took his way toward Lesbos to help it what he could, and put in at Pyrrha, and the next day at Eressos. Here he heard that Mytilene was taken by the Athenians, even with the shout of their voices. For the Athenians, coming unexpected, entered the haven, and having beaten the galleys of the Chians, disbarked and overcame those that made head against them and won the city. When Astyochus heard this, both from the Eressians and from those Chian galleys that came from Methymna with Eubulus, which having been left there before, as soon as Mytilene was lost fled, and three of them chanced to meet with him (for one was taken by the Athenians), he continued his course for Mytilene no longer; but having caused Eressos to revolt, and armed the soldiers he had aboard, made them to march toward Antissa and Methymna by land, under the conduct of Eteonicus; and he himself, with his own galleys and those three of Chios, rowed thither along the shore, hoping that the Methymnaeans, upon sight of his forces, would take heart and continue in their revolt. But when in Lesbos all things went against him, he re-embarked his army and returned to Chios. And the landmen that were aboard, and should have gone into Hellespont, went again into their cities. After this came to them six galleys to Chios, of those of the confederate fleet at Cenchreiae. The Athenians, when they had reestablished the state of Lesbos, went thence and took Polichna, which the Clazomenians had fortified in the continent, and brought them all back again into the city which is in the island, save only the authors of the revolt; for these got away to Daphnus. And Clazomenae returned to the obedience of the Athenians.

24. The same summer, those Athenians that with twenty galleys lay in the isle of Lada before Miletus, landing in the territory of Miletus at Panormus, slew Chalcideus, the Lacedaemonian commander, that came out against them but with a

few, and set up a trophy, and the third day after departed. But the Milesians pulled down the trophy, as erected where the Athenians were not masters.

Leon and Diomedon, with the Athenian galleys that were at Lesbos, made war upon the Chians by sea from the isles called Oenussae, which lie before Chios, and from Sidussa and Pteleum (forts they held in Erythraea), and from Lesbos. They that were aboard were men of arms of the roll, compelled to serve in the fleet. With these they landed at Cardamyle; and having overthrown the Chians that made head in a battle at Bolissus, and slain many of them, they recovered from the enemy all the places of that quarter. And again they overcame them in another battle at Phanae, and in a third at Leuconium. After this, the Chians went out no more to fight; by which means the Athenians made spoil of their territory, excellently well furnished. For except it were the Lacedaemonians, the Chians were the only men that I have heard of that had joined advisedness to prosperity, and the more their city increased, had carried the more respect in the administration thereof to assure it. Nor ventured they now to revolt (lest any man should think that, in this act at least, they regarded not what was the safest) till they had many and strong confederates with whose help to try their fortune, nor till such time as they perceived the people of Athens (as they themselves could not deny) to have their estate after the defeat in Sicily reduced to extreme weakness. And if through human misreckoning they miscarried in aught, they erred with many others, who in like manner had an opinion that the state of the Athenians would quickly have been overthrown.

Being therefore shut up by sea, and having their lands spoiled, some within undertook to make the city return unto the Athenians. Which though the magistrates perceived, yet they themselves stirred not; but having received Astyochus into the city with four galleys that were with him from Erythraea, they took advice together, how by taking hostages, or some other gentle way, to make them give over the conspiracy. Thus stood the business with the Chians.

25. In the end of this summer a thousand five hundred men of arms of Athens, and a thousand of Argos (for the Athenians

had put armour upon five hundred light-armed of the Argives),
and of other confederates a thousand more, with forty-eight
galleys, reckoning those which were for transportation of
soldiers, under the conduct of Phrynicus, Onomacles, and
Scironides, came in to Samos, and crossing over to Miletus encamped before it. And the Milesians issued forth with eight
hundred men of arms of their own, besides the Peloponnesians
that came with Chalcideus and some auxiliar strangers with
Tissaphernes (Tissaphernes himself being also there with his
cavalry) and fought with the Athenians and their confederates.
The Argives, who made one wing of themselves, advancing before the rest and in some disorder, in contempt of the enemy
as being Ionians and not likely to sustain their charge, were by
the Milesians overcome, and lost no less than three hundred of
their men. But the Athenians, when they had first overthrown
the Peloponnesians and then beaten back the barbarians and
other multitude and not fought with the Milesians at all (for
they, after they were come from the chase of the Argives and
saw their other wing defeated, went into the town), sat down
with their arms, as being now masters of the field, close under
the wall of the city. It fell out in this battle that on both sides
the Ionics had the better of the Dorics. For the Athenians overcame the opposite Peloponnesians, and the Milesians the Argives.
The Athenians, after they had erected their trophy, the place
being an isthmus, prepared to take in the town with a wall, supposing if they got Miletus, the other cities would easily come
in.

26. In the meantime it was told them about twilight that
the five-and-fifty galleys from Peloponnesus and Sicily were
hard by and only not already come. For there came into
Peloponnesus out of Sicily, by the instigation of Hermocrates
to help to consummate the subversion of the Athenian state,
twenty galleys of Syracuse and two of Selinus; and the galleys
that had been preparing in Peloponnesus being then also ready,
they were, both these and the other, committed to the charge
of Theramenes, to be conducted by him to Astyochus, the
admiral; and they put in first at Eleus, an island over against
Miletus. And being advertised there that the Athenians lay
before the town, they went from thence into the gulf of Iasus

to learn how the affairs of the Milesians stood. Alcibiades coming a horseback to Teichiussa of the territory of Miletus, in which part of the gulf the Peloponnesian galleys lay at anchor, they were informed by him of the battle; for Alcibiades was, with the Milesians and with Tissaphernes, present in it. And he exhorted them, unless they meant to lose what they had in Ionia and the whole business, to succour Miletus with all speed and not to suffer it to be taken in with a wall.

27. According to this, they concluded to go the next morning and relieve it. Phrynichus, when he had certain word from Derus of the arrival of those galleys, his colleagues advising to stay and fight it out with their fleet, said that he would neither do it himself nor suffer them to do it, or any other, as long as he could hinder it. For seeing he might fight with them hereafter, when they should know against how many galleys of the enemy and with what additions to their own, sufficiently and at leisure made ready, they might do it, he would never, he said, for fear of being upbraided with baseness (for it was no baseness for the Athenians to let their navy give way upon occasion; but by what means soever it should fall out, it would be a great baseness to be beaten), be swayed to hazard battle against reason and not only to dishonour the state but also to cast it into extreme danger, seeing that since their late losses it hath scarce been fit with their strongest preparation, willingly, no nor urged by precedent necessity, to undertake, how then without constraint to seek out voluntary, dangers? Therefore he commanded them with all speed to take aboard those that were wounded and their landmen and whatsoever utensils they brought with them; but to leave behind whatsoever they had taken in the territory of the enemy to the end that their galleys might be the lighter; and to put off for Samos, and thence, when they had all their fleet together, to make out against the enemy as occasion should be offered. As Phrynichus advised this, so he put it in execution, and was esteemed a wise man, not then only, but afterwards, nor in this only, but in whatsoever else he had the ordering of. Thus the Athenians presently in the evening, with their victory unperfect, dislodged from before Miletus. From Samos the Argives, in haste and in anger for their overthrow, went home.

28. The Peloponnesians, setting forth betimes in the morning
from Teichiussa, put in at Miletus and stayed there one day.
The next day they took with them those galleys of Chios which
had formerly been chased together with Chalcideus, and meant
to have returned to Teichiussa to take aboard such necessaries
as they had left ashore. But as they were going, Tissaphernes
came to them with his landmen and persuaded them to set
upon Iasus, where Amorges, the king's enemy, then lay. Whereupon they assaulted Iasus upon a sudden; and they within not
thinking but they had been the fleet of the Athenians, took it.
The greatest praise in this action was given to the Syracusians.
Having taken Amorges, the bastard son of Pissuthnes, but a
rebel to the king, the Peloponnesians delivered him to Tissaphernes to carry him if he would to the king, as he had
order to do. The city they pillaged, wherein, as being a place
of ancient riches, the army got a very great quantity of money.
The auxiliary soldiers of Amorges they received, without doing
them hurt, into their own army, being for the most part
Peloponnesians. The town itself they delivered to Tissaphernes,
with all the prisoners, as well free as bond, upon composition
with him, at a Daric stater by the poll.* And so they returned
to Miletus. And from hence they sent Pedaritus, the son of
Leon, whom the Lacedaemonians had sent hither to be governor
of Chios, to Erythrae, and with him the bands that had aided
Amorges by land, and made Philip governor there in Miletus.
And so this summer ended.

29. The next winter, Tissaphernes, after he had put a garrison
into Iasus, came to Miletus; and for one month's pay, which was
promised on his part at Lacedaemon, he gave unto the soldiers
through the whole fleet after an Attic drachma a man by the
day. But for the rest of the time he would pay but three oboles
till he had asked the king's pleasure; and if the king commanded
it, then he said he would pay them the full drachma. Nevertheless upon the contradiction of Hermocrates, general of the
Syracusians (for Theramenes was but slack in exacting pay, as
not being general, but only to deliver the galleys that came with
him to Astyochus), it was agreed that but for the five galleys
that were over and above, they should have more than three

* I.e., at a price the equivalent of twenty Attic drachmae apiece.

oboles a man. For to fifty-five galleys he allowed three talents
a month, and to as many as should be more than that number,
after the same proportion.

30. The same winter the Athenians that were at Samos (for
there were now come in thirty-five galleys more from home,
with Charminus, Strombichides, and Euctemon, their commanders), having gathered together their galleys, as well those
that had been at Chios as all the rest, concluded, distributing to
every one his charge by lot, to go lie before Miletus with a fleet,
but against Chios to send out both a fleet and an army of
landmen. And they did so. For Strombichides, Onomacles,
and Euctemon, with thirty galleys and part of those thousand
men of arms that went to Miletus, which they carried along
with them in vessels for transportation of soldiers, according
to their lot went to Chios; and the rest, remaining at Samos
with seventy-four galleys, were masters of the sea, and went to
Miletus.

31. Astyochus, who was now in Chios requiring hostages in
respect of the treason, after he heard of the fleet that was come
with Theramenes and that the articles of the league with Tissaphernes were mended, gave over that business, and with ten galleys of Peloponnesus and ten of Chios, went thence and assaulted
Pteleum; but not being able to take it, he kept by the shore to
Clazomenae. There he summoned those within to yield, with
offer to such of them as favoured the Athenians that they
might go up and dwell at Daphnus. And Tamos, the deputy
lieutenant of Ionia, offered them the same. But they not hearken-
ing thereunto, he made an assault upon the city, being unwalled;
but when he could not take it, he put to sea again, and with a
mighty wind was himself carried to Phocaea and Cume; but
the rest of the fleet put in at Marathusa, Pele, and Drimyssa,
islands that lie over against Clazomenae. After they had stayed
there eight days in regard of the winds, spoiling and destroying,
and partly taking aboard whatsoever goods of the Clazomenians
lay without, they went afterwards to Phocaea and Cume to
Astyochus.

32. While Astyochus was there, the ambassadors of the Lesbians came unto him, desiring to revolt from the Athenians. And
as for him, they prevailed with him; but seeing the Corinthians

and the other confederates were unwilling in respect of their former ill success there, he put to sea for Chios. Whither, after a great tempest, his galleys, some from one place and some from another, at length arrived all. After this, Pedaritus, who was now at Erythrae, whither he was come from Miletus by land, came over with his forces into Chios. Besides those forces he brought over with him, he had the soldiers which were of the five galleys that came thither with Chalcideus and were left there, to the number of five hundred, and armour to arm them.

Now some of the Lesbians having promised to revolt, Astyochus communicated the matter with Pedaritus and the Chians, alleging how meet it would be to go with a fleet and make Lesbos to revolt, for that they should either get more confederates, or failing, they should at least weaken the Athenians. But they gave him no ear; and for the Chian galleys, Pedaritus told him [plainly] he should have none of them.

33. Whereupon Astyochus, taking with him five galleys of Corinth, a sixth of Megara, one of Hermione, and those of Laconia which he brought with him, went towards Miletus to his charge, mightily threatening the Chians, in case they should need him, not to help them.

When he was come to Corycus in Erythraea, he stayed there. And the Athenians from Samos lay on the other side of the point, the one not knowing that the other was so near. Astyochus, upon a letter sent him from Pedaritus, signifying that there were come certain Erythraean captives dismissed from Samos with design to betray Erythrae, went presently back to Erythrae; so little he missed of falling into the hands of the Athenians. Pedaritus also went over to him; and having narrowly enquired touching these seeming traitors, and found that the whole matter was but a pretence which the men had used for their escape from Samos, they acquitted them, and departed one to Chios, the other, as he was going before, towards Miletus.

34. In the meantime, the army of the Athenians, being come about by sea from Corycus to Arginum, lighted on three long-boats of the Chians, which when they saw they presently chased. But there arose a great tempest; and the long-boats of Chios with much ado recovered the harbour. But of the

Athenian galleys, especially such as followed them furthest, there perished three, driven ashore at the city of Chios; and the men that were aboard them were part taken and part slain. The rest of the fleet escaped into a haven called Phoenicus, under the hill Mimas, from whence they got afterwards to Lesbos and there fortified.

35. The same winter, Hippocrates, setting out from Peloponnesus with ten galleys of Thurium, commanded by Dorieus, the son of Diogoras, with two others, and with one galley of Laconia and one of Syracuse, went to Cnidus. This city was now revolted from Tissaphernes; and the Peloponnesians that lay at Miletus, hearing of it, commanded that, the one half of their galleys remaining for the guard of Cnidus, the other half should go about Triopium and help to bring in the ships which were to come from Egypt. This Triopium is a promontory of the territory of Cnidus, lying out in the sea and consecrated to Apollo. The Athenians, upon advertisement hereof, setting forth from Samos, took those galleys that kept guard at Triopium; but the men that were in them escaped to land. After this they went to Cnidus, which they assaulted and had almost taken, being without wall. And the next day they assaulted it again; but being less able to hurt it now than before, because they had fenced it better this night, and the men also were gotten into it that fled from their galleys under Triopium, they invaded and wasted the Cnidian territory, and so went back to Samos.

36. About the same time, Astyochus being come to the navy at Miletus, the Peloponnesians had plenty of all things for the army. For they had not only sufficient pay, but the soldiers also had store of money yet remaining of the pillage of Iasus. And the Milesians underwent the war with a good will. Nevertheless, the former articles of the league made by Chalcideus with Tissaphernes seemed defective and not so advantageous to them as to him. Whereupon they agreed to new ones, in the presence of Tissaphernes, which were these:

37. "The agreement of the Lacedaemonians and their confederates with king Darius and his children and with Tissaphernes for league and amity according to the articles following:

"Whatsoever territories and cities do belong unto king Darius, or were his father's or his ancestors', against these shall neither the Lacedaemonians go to make war nor any way to annoy them; neither shall the Lacedaemonians nor their confederates exact tribute of any of those cities. Neither shall king Darius, nor any under his dominion, make war upon or any way annoy the Lacedaemonians or any of the Lacedaemonian confederates.

"If the Lacedaemonians or their confederates shall need anything of the king, or the king of the Lacedaemonians or their confederates, what they shall persuade each other to do, if they do it, shall be good.

"They shall both of them make war jointly against the Athenians and their confederates; and when they shall give over the war, they shall also do it jointly.

"Whatsoever army shall be in the king's country, sent for by the king, the king shall defray.

"If any of the cities comprehended in the league made with the king shall invade the king's territories, the rest shall oppose them and defend the king to the utmost of their power. If any city of the king's, or under his dominion, shall invade the Lacedaemonians or their confederates, the king shall make opposition and defend them to the utmost of his power."

38. After this accord made, Theramenes delivered his galleys into the hands of Astyochus and, putting to sea in a light-horseman, is no more seen.

The Athenians that were now come with their army from Lesbos to Chios, and were masters of the field and of the sea, fortified Delphinium, a place both strong to the landward, and that had also a harbour for shipping, and was not far from the city itself of Chios. And the Chians, as having been disheartened in divers former battles, and otherwise not only not mutually well affected but jealous one of another (for Tydeus and his accomplices had been put to death by Pedaritus for Atticism, and the rest of the city was kept in awe, but by force, and for a time), stirred not against them. And for the causes mentioned, not conceiving themselves, neither with their own strength nor with the help of those that Pedaritus had with him, sufficient to give them battle, they sent to Miletus to require aid from Astyochus. Which when he denied them,

Pedaritus sent letters to Lacedaemon complaining of the wrong. Thus proceeded the affairs of the Athenians at Chios. Also their fleet at Samos went often out against the fleet of the enemy at Miletus; but when theirs would never come out of the harbour to encounter them, they returned to Samos and lay still.

39. The same winter, about the solstice, went out from Peloponnesus towards Ionia those twenty-seven galleys which at the procurement of Calligeitus of Megara and Timagoras of Cyzicus were made ready by the Lacedaemonians for Pharnabazus. The commander of them was Antisthenes, a Spartan, with whom the Lacedaemonians sent eleven Spartans more to be of council with Astyochus, whereof Lichas, the son of Arcesilaus, was one. These had commission that when they should be arrived at Miletus, besides their general care to order everything to the best, they should send away these galleys, either the same or more or fewer, into the Hellespont to Pharnabazus if they so thought fit, and to appoint Clearchus, the son of Rhamphias, that went along in them, for commander; and that the same eleven, if they thought it meet, should put Astyochus from his charge and ordain Antisthenes in his place; for they had him in suspicion for the letters of Pedaritus. These galleys, holding their course from Malea through the main sea and arriving at Melos, lighted on ten galleys of the Athenians, whereof three they took, but without the men, and fired them. After this, because they feared lest those Athenian galleys that escaped from Melos should give notice of their coming to those in Samos (as also it fell out), they changed their course and went towards Crete; and having made their voyage the longer that it might be the safer, they put in at Caunus in Asia. Now from thence, as being in a place of safety, they sent a messenger to the fleet at Miletus for a convoy.

40. The Chians and Pedaritus about the same time, notwithstanding [their former repulse, and] that Astyochus was still backward, sent messengers to him, desiring him to come with his whole fleet to help them, being besieged, and not to suffer the greatest of their confederate cities in all Ionia to be thus shut up by sea and ravaged by land, as it was. For the Chians having many slaves, more than any one state except that of the

Lacedaemonians, whom for their offences they the more ungently punished because of their number, many of them, as
soon as the Athenians appeared to be settled in their fortifications, ran over presently to them; and were they, that knowing
the territory so well, did it the greatest spoil. Therefore the
Chians said he must help them whilst there was hope and possibility to do it, Delphinium being still in fortifying and unfurnished, and greater fences being in making both about their
camp and fleet. Astyochus, though he meant it not before, because he would have made good his threats, yet when he saw
the confederates were willing, he was bent to have relieved
them.

41. But in the meantime came the messenger from the twenty-
seven galleys and from the Lacedaemonian counsellors that
were come to Caunus. Astyochus, therefore, esteeming the waft-
ing in of these galleys, whereby they might the more freely
command the sea, and the safe coming in of those Lacedaemonians, who were to look into his actions, a business that
ought to be preferred above all other, presently gave over his
journey for Chios and went towards Caunus. As he went by
the coast, he landed at Cos Meropidis, being unwalled and
thrown down by an earthquake which had happened there,
the greatest verily in man's memory, and rifled it, the inhabitants being fled into the mountains; and overrunning the country, made booty of all that came in his way, saving of freemen, and those he dismissed. From Cos he went by night to
Cnidus, but found it necessary, by the advice of the Cnidians,
not to land his men there, but to follow as he was after those
twenty galleys of Athens, wherewith Charminus, one of the
Athenian generals gone out from Samos, stood watching for
those twenty-seven galleys that were come from Peloponnesus,
the same that Astyochus himself was going to convoy in. For
they at Samos had had intelligence from Miletus of their coming; and Charminus was lying for them about Syme, Chalce,
Rhodes, and the coast of Lycia; for by this time he knew that
they were at Caunus.

42. Astyochus, therefore, desiring to outgo the report of his
coming, went as he was to Syme, hoping to find those galleys

out from the shore. But [a shower of] rain, together with the cloudiness of the sky, made his galleys to miss their course in the dark and disordered them.

The next morning, the fleet being scattered, the left wing was manifestly descried by the Athenians, whilst the rest wandered yet about the island. And thereupon Charminus and the Athenians put forth against them with twenty galleys, supposing they had been the same galleys they were watching for from Caunus; and presently charging, sunk three of them and hurt others, and were superior in the fight till such time as, contrary to their expectation, the greater part of the fleet came in sight and enclosed them about. They then betook themselves to flight; and with the loss of six galleys the rest escaped into the island of Teuglussa, and from thence to Halicarnassus. After this the Peloponnesians, putting in at Cnidus and joining with those seven-and-twenty galleys that came from Caunus, went all together to Syme, and having there erected a trophy, returned again and lay at Cnidus.

43. The Athenians, when they understood what had passed in this battle, went from Samos with their whole navy to Syme. But neither went they out against the navy in Cnidus, nor the navy there against them. Whereupon they took up the furniture of their galleys at Syme, and assaulted Loryma, a town in the continent, and so returned to Samos.

The whole navy of the Peloponnesians, being at Cnidus, was [now] in repairing and refurnishing with such things as it wanted; and withal those eleven Lacedaemonians conferred with Tissaphernes (for he also was present) touching such things as they disliked in the articles before agreed on, and concerning the war, how it might be carried for the future in the best and most advantageous manner for them both. But Lichas was he that considered the business more nearly, and said that neither the first league nor yet the later by Theramenes was made as it ought to have been; and that it would be a very hard condition that whatsoever territories the king and his ancestors possessed before he should possess the same now; for so he might bring again into subjection all the islands, and the sea, and the Locrians, and all as far as Boeotia; and the Lacedaemonians, instead of restoring the Grecians into liberty, should put them into subjection to the rule of the Medes. Therefore he required other and better articles to be drawn, and not to stand to these; as for pay, in the new articles they would require none. But Tissaphernes, chafing at this, went his way in choler, and nothing was done.

44. The Peloponnesians, solicited by messengers from the great men of Rhodes, resolved to go thither, because they hoped it would not prove impossible with their number of seamen and army of land soldiers to bring that island into their power; and withal supposed themselves able, with their present confederates, to maintain their fleet without asking money any more of Tissaphernes. Presently therefore, the same winter, they put forth from Cnidus, and arriving in the territory of Rhodes at Cameirus, first frighted the commons out of it, that knew not of the business, and they fled. Then the Lacedaemonians called together both these and the Rhodians of the two cities Lindus and Iëlysus and persuaded them to revolt from the Athenians. And Rhodes turned to the Peloponnesians. The Athenians at the same time, hearing of their design, put forth with their fleet from Samos, desiring to have arrived before them, and were seen in the main sea, too late, though not much. For the present they went away to Chalce, and thence back to Samos; but afterwards they came forth with their galleys divers times, and made war against Rhodes from Chalce, Cos, and Samos. Now the Peloponnesians did no more to the Rhodians but levy money amongst them to the sum of thirty-two talents; and otherwise for fourscore days that they lay there, having their galleys hauled ashore, they meddled not.

45. In this time, as also before the going of the Peloponnesians to Rhodes, came to pass the things that follow. Alcibiades, after the death of Chalcideus in battle at Miletus, being suspected by the Peloponnesians, and Astyochus having received letters from them from Lacedaemon to put him to death (for he was an enemy to Agis, and also otherwise not well trusted), retired to Tissaphernes first, for fear, and afterwards to his power hindered the affairs of the Peloponnesians. And being in everything his instructor, he not only cut shorter their pay, insomuch as from a drachma he brought it to three oboles, and those also not continually paid, advising Tissaphernes to tell them

how that the Athenians, men of a long continued skill in naval affairs, allowed but three oboles to their own, not so much for want of money, but lest the mariners, some of them growing insolent by superfluity, should disable their bodies by spending their money on such things as would weaken them, and others should quit the galleys with the arrear of their pay in their captains' hands for a pawn; but also gave counsel to Tissaphernes to give money to the captains of the galleys and to the generals of the several cities, save only those of Syracuse, to give way unto it. For Hermocrates, [the general of the Syracusians,] was the only man, that in the name of the whole league stood against it. And for the cities that came to require money, he would put them back himself and answer them in Tissaphernes' name, and say, namely to the Chians, that they were impudent men, being the richest of the Grecian states and preserved by strangers, to expect nevertheless that others, for their liberty, should not only venture their persons but maintain them with their purses; and to other states, that they did unjustly, having laid out their money before they revolted that they might serve the Athenians, not to bestow as much or more now upon themselves; and told them that Tissaphernes, now he made war at his own charges, had reason to be sparing; but when money should come down from the king he would give them their full pay and assist the cities as should be fit.

46. Moreover, he advised Tissaphernes not to be too hasty to make an end of the war, nor to fetch in the Phoenician fleet which was making ready, nor take more men into pay, whereby to put the whole power both by sea and land into the hands of one, but to let the dominion remain divided into two, that the king, when one side troubled him, might set upon it with the other; whereas the dominion both by sea and land being in one, he will want by whom to pull down those that hold it unless with great danger and cost he should come and try it out himself; but thus the danger would be less chargeable, he being but at a small part of the cost; and he should wear out the Grecians one against another and himself in the meantime remain in safety. He said further that the Athenians were fitter to partake dominion with him than the other for that they were less ambitious of power by land and that their speeches and actions

tended more to the king's purpose; for that they would join
with him to subdue the Grecians, that is to say, for themselves
as touching the dominion by sea, and for the king as touching
the Grecians in the king's territories; whereas the Lacedaemonians, on the contrary, were come to set them free; and it
was not likely but that they that were come to deliver the
Grecians from the Grecians will, if they overcome the Athenians, deliver them also from the barbarians. He gave counsel
therefore, first to wear them out both and then, when he had
clipped, as near as he could, the wings of the Athenians, to dismiss the Peloponnesians out of his country.

And Tissaphernes had a purpose to do accordingly, as far
as by his actions can be conjectured. For hereupon he gave himself to believe Alcibiades as his best counsellor in these affairs,
and neither paid the Peloponnesians their wages nor would
suffer them to fight by sea; but pretending the coming of the
Phoenician fleet, whereby they might afterwards fight with
odds, he overthrew their proceedings and abated the vigour of
their navy, before very puissant, and was in all things else
more backward than he could possibly dissemble.

47. Now Alcibiades advised the king and Tissaphernes to this
whilst he was with them, partly because he thought the same to
be indeed the best course, but partly also to make way for his
own return into his country, knowing that if he destroyed
it not, the time would one day come that he might persuade
the Athenians to recall him. And the best way to persuade them
to it, he thought, was this: to make it appear unto them that he
was powerful with Tissaphernes. Which also came to pass. For
after the Athenian soldiers at Samos saw what power he had
with him, the captains of galleys and principal men there,
partly upon Alcibiades' own motion, who had sent to the
greatest amongst them that they should remember him to the
best sort and say that he desired to come home so the government might be in the hands of a few, not of evil persons nor yet
of the multitude that cast him out, and that he would bring
Tissaphernes to be their friend, [and to war on their side], but
chiefly of their own accords had their minds inclined to the
deposing of the popular government.

48. This business was set on foot first in the camp and from

thence proceeded afterwards into the city. And certain persons went over to Alcibiades out of Samos and had conference with him. And when he had undertaken to bring to their friendship first Tissaphernes and then the king, in case the government were taken from the people, for then, he said, the king might the better rely upon them, they that were of most power in the city, who also were the most toiled out, entered into great hope both to have the ordering of the state at home themselves and victory also over the enemy. And when they came back to Samos, they drew all such as were for their purpose into an oath of conspiracy with themselves, and to the multitude gave it out openly that if Alcibiades might be recalled and the people put from the government, the king would turn their friend and furnish them with money.

Though the multitude were grieved with this proceeding for the present, yet for the great hope they had of the king's pay they stirred not. But they that were setting up the oligarchy, when they had communicated thus much to the multitude, fell to consideration anew and with more of their complices of the things spoken by Alcibiades. And the rest thought the matter easy and worthy to be believed; but Phrynichus, who yet was general of the army, liked it not, but thought, as the truth was, that Alcibiades cared no more for the oligarchy than the democracy, nor had any other aim in it but only by altering the government that then was to be called home by his associates; and said they were especially to look to this, that they did not mutiny for the king, who could not very easily be induced (the Peloponnesians being now as much masters at sea as themselves, and having no small cities within his dominions) to join with the Athenians, whom he trusted not, and to trouble himself, when he might have the friendship of the Peloponnesians, that never did him hurt; as for the confederate cities to whom they promise oligarchy, in that they themselves do put down the democracy, he said, he knew full well that neither those which were already revolted would the sooner return to, nor those that remained be ever the more confirmed in their obedience thereby; for they would never be so willing to be in subjection either to the few or to the people, as they would be to have their liberty, which side soever it were that should give it them, but would think that even those which are termed the good men, if they had the government, would give them as much to do as the people, being contrivers and authors to the people of doing those mischiefs against them, out of which they make most profit unto themselves; and that if the few had the rule, then they should be put to death unheard and more violently than by the former; whereas the people is their refuge and moderator of the others' insolence. This, he said, he was certain that the cities thought; in that they had learned the same by the actions themselves; and that therefore what was yet propounded by Alcibiades, he by no means approved.

49. But those of the conspiracy there assembled, not only approved the present proposition, but also made preparation to send Pisander and others ambassadors to Athens to negotiate concerning the reduction of Alcibiades,* the dissolution of the democracy, and the procuring unto the Athenians the friendship of Tissaphernes.

50. Now Phrynichus, knowing that an overture was to be made at Athens for the restoring of Alcibiades and that the Athenians would embrace it, and fearing lest being recalled he should do him a mischief (in regard he had spoken against it) as one that would have hindered the same, betook himself to this course: He sends secret letters to Astyochus, the Lacedaemonian general, who was yet about Miletus, and advertised him that Alcibiades undid their affairs and was procuring the friendship of Tissaphernes for the Athenians, writing in plain terms the whole business and desiring to be excused if he rendered evil to his enemy with some disadvantage to his country. Astyochus had before this laid by the purpose of revenge against Alcibiades, especially when he was not in his own hands. And going to him to Magnesia and to Tissaphernes, related unto them what advertisement he had received from Samos, and made himself the appeacher. For he adhered, as was said, to Tissaphernes for his private lucre, both in this and in divers other matters; which was also the cause that concerning the pay, when the abatement was made, he was not so stout in op-

* This is Hobbes' seventeenth-century English for "the bringing back home of Alcibiades."

posing it as he ought to have been. Hereupon Alcibiades sendeth letters presently to those that were in office at Samos, accusing Phrynichus of what he had done and requiring to have
him put to death. Phrynichus, perplexed with this discovery
and brought into danger indeed, sends again to Astyochus,
blaming what was past as not well concealed, and promised
now to be ready to deliver unto him the whole army at Samos
to be destroyed; writing from point to point (Samos being
unwalled) in what manner he would do it, and saying that
since his life was brought in danger, they could not blame
him though he did this or any other thing rather than be destroyed by his most deadly enemies. This also Astyochus revealed unto Alcibiades.

51. But Phrynichus having had notice betimes how he abused
him, and that letters of this from Alcibiades were in a manner
come, he anticipates the news himself, and tells the army that
whereas Samos was unwalled and the galleys rid not all within,
the enemy meant to come and assault the harbour; that he had
sure intelligence hereof, and that they ought therefore with
all speed to raise a wall about the city and to put garrisons into
other places thereabouts. Now Phrynichus was general himself, and it was in his own power to see it done. They then
fell to walling, whereby Samos (which they meant to have
done howsoever) was so much the sooner walled in. Not long
after came letters from Alcibiades that the army was betrayed
by Phrynichus, and that the enemy purposed to invade the
harbour where they lay. But now they thought not Alcibiades
worthy to be believed, but rather that having foreseen the
design of the enemy, he went about, out of malice, to fasten it
upon Phrynichus as conscious of it likewise. So that he did
him no hurt by telling it, but bare witness rather of that
which Phrynichus had told them of before.

52. After this Alcibiades endeavoured to incline and persuade Tissaphernes to the friendship of the Athenians. For
though Tissaphernes feared the Peloponnesians, because their
fleet was greater than that of the Athenians, yet if he had been
able, he had a good will to have been persuaded by him, especially in his anger against the Peloponnesians after the dissension at Cnidus about the league made by Theramenes (for

they were already fallen out, the Peloponnesians being about this time in Rhodes). Wherein that which had been before spoken by Alcibiades, how that the coming of the Lacedaemonians was to restore all the cities to their liberty, was now verified by Lichas, in that he said it was an article not to be suffered that the king should hold those cities which he and his ancestors then or before had holden. Alcibiades, therefore, as one that laboured for no trifle, with all his might applied himself to Tissaphernes.

53. The Athenian ambassadors sent from Samos with Pisander, being arrived at Athens, were making their propositions to the people, and related unto them summarily the points of their business, and principally this, that if they would call home Alcibiades, and not suffer the government to remain in the hands of the people in such manner as it did, they might have the king for their confederate, and get the victory of the Peloponnesians. Now when many opposed that point touching the democracy, and the enemies of Alcibiades clamoured withal that it would be a horrible thing he should return by forcing the government, when the Eumolpidae and Ceryces bare witness against him concerning the mysteries for which he fled and prohibited his return under their curse, Pisander, at this great opposition and querimony, stood out, and going amongst them took out one by one those that were against it, and asked them whether, now that the Peloponnesians had as many galleys at sea to oppose them as they themselves had, and confederate cities more than they, and were furnished with money by the king and Tissaphernes, the Athenians being without, they had any other hope to save their state but by persuading the king to come about to their side. And they that were asked having nothing to answer, then in plain terms he said unto them: "This you cannot now obtain, except we administer the state with more moderation and bring the power into the hands of a few that the king may rely upon us. And we deliberate at this time, not so much about the form as about the preservation of the state; for if you mislike the form, you may change it again hereafter. And let us recall Alcibiades, who is the only man that can bring this to pass."

54. The people, hearing of the oligarchy, took it very heinously

at first; but when Pisander had proved evidently that there was no other way of safety, in the end, partly for fear and partly because they hoped again to change the government, they yielded thereunto. So they ordered that Pisander and ten others should go and treat both with Tissaphernes and Alcibiades as to them should seem best. Withal, upon the accusation of Pisander against Phrynichus, they discharged both Phrynichus and Scironides, his fellow-commissioner, of their command, and made Diomedon and Leon generals of the fleet in their places. Now the cause why Pisander accused Phrynichus and said he had betrayed Iasus and Amorges was only this: he thought him a man unfit for the business now in hand with Alcibiades.

Pisander, after he had gone about to all those combinations * (which were in the city before for obtaining of places of judicature and of command), exhorting them to stand together and advise about deposing the democracy, and when he had dispatched the rest of his business so as there should be no more cause for him to stay there, took sea with those other ten to go to Tissaphernes.

55. Leon and Diomedon, arriving the same winter at the Athenian fleet, made a voyage against Rhodes, and finding there the Peloponnesian galleys drawn up to land, disbarked and overcame in battle such of the Rhodians as made head, and then put to sea again and went to Chalce. After this they made sharper war upon them from Cos. For from thence they could better observe the Peloponnesian navy when it should put off from the land.

In this while there arrived at Rhodes Xenophontidas, a Laconian, sent out of Chios from Pedaritus, to advertise them that the fortification of the Athenians there was now finished and that unless they came and relieved them with their whole

* What is referred to here is the institution of the political clubs. These were private aristocratic associations, professedly existent to support their members in relation to offices, etc. Actually they were small, tightly organized power units with the continuous aim of destroying the democracy. They had existed for a very long time, thirty years or more, apparently, but became really politically important only in the last decade of the Peloponnesian War.

fleet, the state of Chios must utterly be lost. And it was resolved to relieve them. But Pedaritus in the meantime, with the whole power both of his own auxiliary forces and of the Chians, made an assault upon the fortification which the Athenians had made about their navy, part whereof he won, and had gotten some galleys that were drawn a-land. But the Athenians, issuing out upon them, first put to flight the Chians, and then overcame also the rest of the army about Pedaritus, and slew Pedaritus himself, and took many of the Chians prisoners and much armour.

56. After this the Chians were besieged both by sea and land more narrowly, and great famine was in the city.

Pisander, and the other Athenian ambassadors that went with him, when they came to Tissaphernes, began to confer about the agreement. But Alcibiades (for he was not sure of Tissaphernes, because he stood in fear too much of the Peloponnesians, and had a purpose besides, as Alcibiades himself had taught him, to weaken both sides [yet more]), betook himself to this shift: that Tissaphernes should break off the treaty by making to the Athenians exorbitant demands. And it seemed that Tissaphernes and he aimed at the same thing, Tissaphernes for fear, and Alcibiades for that when he saw Tissaphernes not desirous to agree, [though the offers were never so great], he was unwilling to have the Athenians think he could not persuade him to it, but rather that he was already persuaded and willing, and that the Athenians came not to him with sufficient offers. For Alcibiades being the man that spake for Tissaphernes, though he were also present, made unto them such excessive demands that though the Athenians should have yielded to the greatest part of them, yet it must have been attributed to them that the treaty went not on. For they demanded, first, that all Ionia should be rendered; then again, the adjacent islands and other things; which the Athenians stood not against. In fine, at the third meeting, when he feared now plainly to be found unable to make good his word, he required that they should suffer the king to build a navy and sail up and down by their coast wheresoever and with what number soever of galleys he himself should think good. Upon this the Athenians would treat no longer, esteeming the conditions intolerable and that Alcibiades had abused them, and so went away in a chafe to Samos.

57. Presently after this, the same winter, Tissaphernes went to Caunus with intent both to bring the Peloponnesians back to Miletus and also (as soon as he should have agreed unto new articles, such as he could get) to give the fleet their pay, and not to fall directly out with them for fear lest so many galleys, wanting maintenance, should either be forced by the Athenians to fight and so be overcome, or, emptied of men, the business might succeed with the Athenians according to their own desire without him. Besides, he was afraid lest looking for maintenance they should make spoil in the continent. In consideration and foresight of all which things he desired to counterpoise the Grecians. And sending for the Peloponnesians, he gave them their pay, and now made the third league, as followeth:

58. "In the thirteenth year of the reign of Darius, Alexippidas being ephor in Lacedaemon, agreement was made in the plain of Maeander between the Lacedaemonians and their confederates on one part and Tissaphernes and Hieramenes and the sons of Pharnaces on the other part concerning the affairs of the king and of the Lacedaemonians and their confederates.

"That whatsoever country in Asia belongeth to the king shall be the king's still; and that concerning his own countries, it shall be lawful for the king to do whatsoever he shall think meet.

"That the Lacedaemonians and their confederates shall not invade any the territories of the king to harm them; nor the king, the territories of the Lacedaemonians or their confederates.

"If any of the Lacedaemonians or their confederates shall invade the king's country to do it hurt, the Lacedaemonians and their confederates shall oppose it; and if any of the king's country shall invade the Lacedaemonians or their confederates to do them hurt, the king shall oppose it.

"That Tissaphernes shall, according to the rates agreed on, maintain the present fleet till the king's fleet arrive.

"That when the king's navy shall be come, the Lacedaemonians and their confederates shall maintain their own navy themselves, if they please; or if they will have Tissaphernes to maintain it, he shall do it; and that the Lacedaemonians and their confederates, at the end of the war, repay Tissaphernes whatsoever money they shall have received of him.

"When the king's galleys shall be arrived, both they and the galleys of the Lacedaemonians and their confederates shall make the war jointly, according as to Tissaphernes and the Lacedaemonians and their confederates shall seem good; and if they will give over the war against the Athenians, they shall give it over in the same manner."

59. Such were the articles. After this Tissaphernes prepared for the fetching in of the Phoenician fleet, according to the agreement, and to do whatsoever else he had undertaken, desiring to have it seen, at least, that he went about it.

60. In the end of this winter, the Boeotians took Oropus by treason. It had in it a garrison of Athenians. They that plotted it were certain Eretrians and some of Oropus itself, who were then contriving the revolt of Euboea. For the place being built to keep Eretria in subjection, it was impossible, as long as the Athenians held it, but that it would much annoy both Eretria and the rest of Euboea. Having Oropus in their hands already, they came to Rhodes to call the Peloponnesians into Euboea. But the Peloponnesians had a greater inclination to relieve Chios now distressed, and putting to sea, departed out of Rhodes with their whole fleet. When they were come about Triopium, they descried the Athenian fleet in the main sea going from Chalce. And neither side assaulting other, they put in, the one fleet at Samos, the other at Miletus; for the Peloponnesians saw they could not pass to relieve Chios without a battle. Thus ended this winter, and the twentieth year of this war written by Thucydides.

61. The next summer, in the beginning of the spring, Dercylidas, a Spartan, was sent by land into Hellespont with a small army to work the revolt of Abydos, a colony of the Milesians. And the Chians at the same time, whilst Astyochus was at a stand how to help them, were compelled by the pressure of the siege to hazard a battle by sea. Now whilst Astyochus lay at Rhodes, they had received into the city of Chios, after the death of Pedaritus, one Leon, a Spartan, that came along with Antisthenes as a private soldier, and with him twelve

galleys that lay at the guard of Miletus, whereof five were Thurians, four Syracusians, one of Anaea, one of Miletus, and one of Leon's own. Whereupon the Chians, issuing forth with the whole force of the city, seized a certain place of strength and put forth thirty-six galleys against thirty-two of the Athenians and fought. After a sharp fight, wherein the Chians and their associates had not the worst, and when it began to be dark, they retired again into the city.

62. Presently after this, Dercylidas being arrived now in Hellespont from Miletus by land, Abydos revolted to him and to Pharnabazus; and two days after revolted Lampsacus. Strombichides, having intelligence of this, made haste thither from Chios with four-and-twenty sail of Athenians, those being also of that number which transported his men of arms. And when he had overcome the Lampsacenes that came out against him, and taken Lampsacus, being an open town, at the first shout of their voices, and made prize of all the goods they found and of the slaves, he placed the freemen there again and went against Abydos. But when that city neither yielded nor could be taken by assault, he crossed over from Abydos to the opposite shore; and in Sestos, a city of Chersonesus, possessed heretofore by the Medes, he placed a garrison for the custody of the whole Hellespont.

63. In the meantime not only the Chians had the sea at more command, but Astyochus also and the army at Miletus, having been advertised of what passed in the fight by sea, and that Strombichides and those galleys with him were gone away, took heart. And Astyochus, going to Chios with two galleys, fetched away the galleys that were there, and with the whole fleet now together went against Samos. But seeing they of Samos, by reason of their jealousy one towards another, came not against him, he went back again to Miletus. For it was about this time that the democracy was put down at Athens.

For after that Pisander and his fellow-ambassadors that had been with Tissaphernes were come to Samos, they both assured their affairs yet better in the army and also provoked the principal men of the Samians to attempt with them the erecting of the oligarchy, though there were then an insurrection amongst them against the oligarchy. And withal the Athenians at Samos, in a conference amongst themselves, deliberated how, since Alcibiades would not, to let him alone; for indeed they thought him no fit man to come into an oligarchy; but for themselves, seeing they were already engaged in the danger, to take care both to keep the business from a relapse and withal to sustain the war and to contribute money and whatsoever else was needful with alacrity out of their private estates, and no more to toil for other than themselves.

64. Having thus advised, they sent Pisander with half the ambassadors presently home, to follow the business there, with command to set up the oligarchy in all the cities they were to touch at by the way; the other half they sent about, some to one part [of the state] and some to another. And they sent away Diotrephes to his charge, who was now about Chios, chosen to go governor of the cities upon Thrace.

He, when he came to Thasos, deposed the people. And within two months at most after he was gone, the Thasians fortified their city, as needing no longer an aristocracy with the Athenians but expecting liberty every day by the help of the Lacedaemonians. For there were also certain of them with the Peloponnesians driven out by the Athenians; and these practised with such in the city as were for their purpose to receive galleys into it and to cause it to revolt. So that it fell out for them just as they would have it, and that estate of theirs was set up without their danger and that the people was deposed that would have withstood it. Insomuch as at Thasos it fell out contrary to what those Athenians thought which erected the oligarchy; and so, in my opinion, it did in many other places of their dominion. For the cities, now grown wise and withal resolute in their proceedings, sought a direct liberty and preferred not before it that outside of a well-ordered government introduced by the Athenians.

65. They with Pisander, according to the order given them, entering into the cities as they went by, dissolved the democracies; and having in some places obtained also an aid of men of arms, they came to Athens, and found the business, for the greatest part, dispatched to their hands by their accomplices before their coming. For certain young men, combining themselves, had not only murdered Androcles privily, a principal

patron of the popular government and one that had his hand the farthest in the banishment of Alcibiades (whom they slew for two causes: for the sway he bare amongst the people, and to gratify Alcibiades, who they thought would return and get them the friendship of Tissaphernes), but had also made away divers men unfit for their design in the same manner. They had withal an oration ready made, which they delivered in public, wherein they said that there ought none to receive wages but such as served in the wars, nor to participate of the government more than five thousand, and those, such as by their purses and persons were best able to serve the commonwealth.

66. And this with the most carried a good shew, because they that would set forward the alteration of the state were to have the managing of the same. Yet the people and the Council of the Bean met still, but debated nothing, save what the conspirators thought fit; nay, all that spake were of that number, and had considered before what they were to say. Nor would any of the rest speak against them, for fear, because they saw the combination was great; and if any man did, he was quickly made away by one convenient means or other, and no inquiry made after the deed-doers, nor justice prosecuted against any that was suspected. But the people were so quiet and so afraid that every man thought it gain to escape violence though he said never a word. Their hearts failed them because they thought the conspirators more indeed than they were; and to learn their number, in respect of the greatness of the city and for that they knew not one another, they were unable. For the same cause also was it impossible for any man that was angry at it to bemoan himself, whereby to be revenged on them that conspired; for he must have told his mind either to one he knew not or to one he knew and trusted not. For the populars approached each other, every one with jealousy, as if they thought him of the plot. For indeed there were such amongst them as no man would have thought would ever have turned to the oligarchy; and those were they that caused in the many that diffidence, and by strengthening the jealousy of the populars one against another, conferred most to the security of the few.

67. During this opportunity, Pisander and they that were

with him, coming in, fell in hand presently with the remainder of the business. And first they assembled the people and delivered their opinion for ten men to be chosen with power absolute to make a draught of laws, and having drawn them, to deliver their opinion at a day appointed before the people, touching the best form of government for the city. Afterwards, when that day came, they summoned the assembly to Colonus, which is a place consecrated to Neptune without the city, about two furlongs off. And they that were appointed to write the laws, presented this, and only this: That it should be lawful for any Athenian to deliver whatsoever opinion he pleased; imposing of great punishments upon whosoever should either accuse any that so spake of violating the laws or otherwise do him hurt. Now here indeed it was in plain terms propounded that not any magistracy of the form before used might any longer be in force, nor any fee belong unto it; but that five Prytanes might be elected, and these five choose a hundred, and every one of this hundred take unto him three others; and these four hundred, entering into the council-house, might have absolute authority to govern the state as they thought best and to summon the five thousand as oft as to them it should seem good.

68. He that delivered this opinion was Pisander, who was also otherwise openly the forewardest to put down the democracy. But he that contrived the whole business, how to bring it to this pass, and had long thought upon it, was Antiphon, a man for virtue not inferior to any Athenian of his time, and the ablest of any man both to devise well and also to express well what he had devised; and though he came not into the assemblies of the people nor willingly to any other debatings, because the multitude had him in jealousy for the opinion they had of the power of his eloquence, yet when any man that had occasion of suit, either in the courts of justice or in the assembly of the people, came to him for his counsel, this one man was able to help him most. The same man, when afterwards the government of The Four Hundred went down and was vexed of the people, was heard plead for himself, when his life was in question for that business, the best of any man to this day. Phrynichus also shewed himself an earnest

man for the oligarchy, and that more earnestly than any other, because he feared Alcibiades and knew him to be acquainted with all his practices at Samos with Astyochus, and thought in all probability that he would never return to live under the government of the few. And this man, in any matter of weight, appeared the most sufficient to be relied on. Also Theramenes, the son of Agnon, an able man both for elocution and understanding, was another of the principal of those that overthrew the democracy.

So that it is no marvel if the business took effect, being by many and wise men conducted, though it were a hard one. For it went sore with the Athenian people, almost a hundred years after the expulsion of the tyrants, to be now deprived of their liberty, having not only not been subject to any, but also for the half of this time been inured to dominion over others.

69. When the assembly, after it had passed these things, no man contradicting, was dissolved, then afterwards they brought The Four Hundred into the council-house in this manner. The Athenians were evermore partly on the walls and partly at their arms in the camp in regard of the enemy that lay at Deceleia. Therefore, on the day appointed, they suffered such as knew not their intent to go forth as they were wont. But to such as were of the conspiracy they quietly gave order not to go to the camp itself but to lag behind at a certain distance, and if any man should oppose what was in doing, to take arms and keep them back. They to whom this charge was given were [the] Andrians, Tenians, three hundred Carystians, and such of the colony of Aegina which the Athenians had sent thither to inhabit, as came on purpose to this action with their own arms. These things thus ordered, The Four Hundred, with every man a secret dagger, accompanied with one hundred and twenty young men of Greece, whom they used for occasions of shedding of blood, came in upon the Counsellers of the Bean as they sat in the council-house and commanded them to take their salary and be gone, which also they brought ready with them, for the whole time they were behind, and paid it to them as they went out.

70. And the rest of the citizens mutinied not, but rested quiet.

The Four Hundred, being now entered into the council-house, created Prytanes amongst themselves by lot, and made their prayers and sacrifices to the gods, all that were before usual at the entrance upon the government. And afterwards receding far from that course which in the administration of the state was used by the people, saving that for Alcibiades' sake they recalled not the outlaws, in other things they governed the commonwealth imperiously, and not only slew some, though not many, such as they thought fit to be made away, and imprisoned some, and confined others to places abroad, but also sent heralds to Agis, king of the Lacedaemonians, who was then at Deceleia, signifying that they would come to composition with him, and that now he might better treat with them than he might before with the unconstant people.

71. But he, not imagining that the city was yet in quiet nor willing so soon to deliver up their ancient liberty, but rather that if they saw him approach with great forces they would be in tumult, not yet believing fully but that some stir or other would arise amongst them, gave no answer at all to those that came from The Four Hundred touching the composition, but having sent for new and great forces out of Peloponnesus, came down himself not long after, both with the army at Deceleia and those new comers, to the Athenian walls, hoping that they would fall into his hands according to his desire, at least the more easily for their confusion, or perhaps at the very first shout of their voices, in respect of the tumult that in all likelihood was to happen both within and without the city. For, as for the long walls, in regard of the few defendants likely to be found upon them, he thought he could not fail to take them. But when he came near, and the Athenians were without any the least alteration within, and had with their horsemen which they sent out, and a part of their men of arms and of their light-armed and of their archers, overthrown some of his men that approached too near and gotten some arms and bodies of the slain, rectified thus, he withdrew his army again. And himself, and such as were with him before, stayed in their places at Deceleia; but as for those that came last, after they had stayed awhile in the country, he sent them home again. After this The Four Hundred, notwithstanding their former repulse, sent ambassadors unto Agis

anew; and he now receiving them better, by his advice they sent ambassadors also to Lacedaemon about an agreement, being desirous of peace.

72. They likewise sent ten men to Samos, to satisfy the army and to tell them that the oligarchy was not set up to any prejudice of the city or citizens, but for the safety of the whole state; and that they which had their hands in it were five thousand and not four hundred only; notwithstanding that the Athenians, by reason of warfare and employment abroad, never assembled, of how great consequence soever was the matter to be handled, so frequent as to be five thousand there at once. And having in other things instructed them how to make the best of the matter, they sent them away immediately after the government was changed, fearing, as also it fell out, lest the seafaring multitude would not only not continue in this oligarchical form themselves, but the mischief beginning there would depose them also.

73. For in Samos there was a commotion about the oligarchy already; and this that followeth happened about the same time that The Four Hundred were set up in Athens. Those Samians that had risen against the nobility and were of the people's side, turning when Pisander came thither at the persuasion of him and of those Athenians in Samos that were his accomplices, conspired together to the number of three hundred and were to have assaulted the rest as populars. And one Hyperbolus, a lewd fellow, who, not for any fear of his power or for any dignity, but for wickedness of life and dishonour he did the city, had been banished by ostracism, they slew, abetted therein both by Charminus, one of the commanders, and by other Athenians that were amongst them, who had given them their faith. And together with these, they committed other facts of the same kind, and were fully bent to have assaulted the popular side. But they, having gotten notice thereof, made known the design both to the generals, Leon and Diomedon (for these, being honoured by the people, endured the oligarchy unwillingly), and also to Thrasybulus and Thrasyllus, whereof one was captain of a galley and the other captain of a band of men of arms, and to such others continually as they thought stood in greatest opposition to the conspirators; and required of them

that they would not see them destroyed and Samos alienated
from the Athenians by the only means of which their dominion
had till this time kept itself in the state it is in. They, hearing
it, went to the soldiers and exhorted them one by one not to
suffer it, especially to the Paralians, who were all Athenians and
freemen, come thither in the galley called Paralus, and had
always before been enemies to the oligarchy. And Leon and
Diomedon, whensoever they went forth any whither, left them
certain galleys for their guard, so that when the three hundred
assaulted them, the commons of the Samians, with the help of
all these, and especially of the Paralians, had the upperhand,
and of the three hundred slew thirty. Three of the chief authors they banished, and burying in oblivion the fault of the
rest, governed the state from that time forward as a democracy.

74. The Paralus, and in it Chaereas, the son of Archestratus,
a man of Athens, one that had been forward in the making of
this change, the Samians and the soldiers dispatched presently
away to Athens, to advertise them of what was done; for they
knew not yet that the government was in the hands of The
Four Hundred. When they arrived, The Four Hundred cast
some two or three of these of the Paralus into prison; the rest,
after they had taken the galley from them and put them aboard
another military galley, they commanded to keep guard about
Euboea. But Chaereas, by some means or other getting presently
away, seeing how things went, came back to Samos and related to the army all that the Athenians had done, aggravating
it to the utmost, as that they punished every man with stripes
to the end that none should contradict the doings of those that
bore rule; and that their wives and children at home were
abused; and that they had an intention further to take and im-
prison all that were of kin to any of the army which was not
of their faction, to the intent to kill them if they of Samos
would not submit to their authority. And many other things
he told them, adding lies of his own.

75. When they heard this, they were ready at first to have
fallen upon the chief authors of the oligarchy and upon such
of the rest as were partakers of it. Yet afterwards, being hindered by such as came between and advised them not to overthrow the state, the enemy lying so near with their galleys to

assault them, they gave it over. After this, Thrasybulus, the son of Lycus, and Thrasyllus (for these were the principal authors of the change), determining now openly to reduce the state at Samos to a democracy, took oaths of all the soldiers, especially of the oligarchicals, the greatest they could devise, both that they should be subject to the democracy and agree together and also that they should zealously prosecute the war against the Peloponnesians, and withal be enemies to The Four Hundred and not to have to do with them by ambassadors. The same oath was taken by all the Samians that were of age; and the Athenian soldiers communicated with them their whole affairs, together with whatsoever should succeed of their dangers; for whom and for themselves, they made account there was no refuge of safety; but that if either The Four Hundred or the enemy at Miletus overcame them, they must needs perish.

76. So there was a contention at this time, one side compelling the city to a democracy, the other, the army to an oligarchy. And presently there was an assembly of the soldiers called, wherein they deprived the former commanders, and such captains of galleys as they had in suspicion, of their charge, and chose others, both captains of galleys and commanders, in their places, of which Thrasybulus and Thrasyllus were two. And they stood up and encouraged one another, both otherwise and with this: that they had no cause to be dejected for the city's revolting from them; for they at Athens, being the lesser part, had forsaken them, who were not only the greater part, but also every way the better provided. For they, having the whole navy, could compel the rest of the cities subject unto them to pay in their money as well now as if they were to set out from Athens itself. And that they also had a city, namely Samos, no weak one, but even such a one as, when they were enemies, wanted little of taking the dominion of the sea from the Athenians. That the seat of the war was the same it was before; and that they should be better able to provide themselves of things necessary, having the navy, than they should be that were at home in the city. And that they at Athens were masters of the entrance of Peiraeus, both formerly by the favour of them at Samos; and that now also, unless they restore them the government, they shall again be brought to that pass that those at

Samos shall be better able to bar them the use of the sea than they shall be to bar it them of Samos. That it was a trifle and worth nothing, which was conferred to the overcoming of the enemy by the city, and a small matter it would be to lose it, seeing they had neither any more silver to send them (for the soldiers shifted for themselves), nor yet good direction, which is the thing for which the city hath the command of the armies. Nay, that in this point they erred which were at Athens, in that they had abrogated the laws of their country; whereas they at Samos did both observe the same themselves and endeavour to constrain the other to do so likewise. So that such of them in the camp as should give good council were as good as they in the city. And that Alcibiades, if they would decree his security and his return, would with all his heart procure the king to be their confederate. And that which is the main thing, if they failed of all other helps, yet with so great a fleet they could not fail of many places to retire to, in which they might find both city and territory.

77. When they had thus debated the matter in the assembly and encouraged one another, they made ready, as at other times, whatsoever was necessary for the war. And the ten ambassadors which were sent to Samos from The Four Hundred, hearing of this by the way at Delos, whither they were come already, stayed still there.

78. About the same time also, the soldiers of the Peloponnesian fleet at Miletus murmured amongst themselves that Astyochus and Tissaphernes overthrew the state of their affairs. Astyochus in refusing to fight, both before, when their own fleet was stronger and that of the Athenians but small, and also now, whilst they were said to be in sedition and their fleet divided; and in expecting the Phoenician fleet, in fame, not in fact to come from Tissaphernes; and Tissaphernes, in that he not only brought not in that fleet of his but also impaired theirs by not giving them their pay, neither fully nor continually; and that they therefore ought no longer to delay time, but to hazard battle. This was urged principally by the Syracusians.

79. Astyochus and the confederates, when they heard of the murmur and had in council resolved to fight, especially after

they were informed that Samos was in a tumult, putting forth with their whole fleet to the number of one hundred and twelve sail, with order given to the Milesians to march by land to the same place, went to Mycale. But the Athenians, being come out from Samos with their fleet of eighty-two galleys, and riding now at Glauce of the territory of Mycale ([for] in this part [toward Mycale] Samos is but a little way from the continent), when they descried the Peloponnesian fleet coming against them, put in again to Samos, as not esteeming themselves a sufficient number to hazard their whole fortune on the battle. Besides, they stayed for the coming of Strombichides from Hellespont to their aid (for they saw that they of Miletus had a desire to fight) with those galleys that went from Chios against Abydos; for they had sent unto him before. So these retired into Samos. And the Peloponnesians, putting in at Mycale, there encamped, as also did the land-forces of the Milesians and others of the country thereabouts. The next day, when they meant to have gone against Samos, they received news that Strombichides with his galleys was arrived out of Hellespont, and thereupon returned presently to Miletus. Then the Athenians on the other side, with the addition of these galleys, went to Miletus, being now one hundred and eight sail, intending to fight; but when nobody came out against them, they likewise went back to Samos.

80. Immediately after this, the same summer, the Peloponnesians, who refused to come out against the enemy, as holding themselves with their whole fleet too weak to give them battle, and were now at a stand how to get money for the maintenance of so great a number of galleys, sent Clearchus, the son of Rhamphias, with forty galleys, according to the order at first from Peloponnesus, to Pharnabazus. For not only Pharnabazus himself had sent for and promised to pay them, but they were advertised besides by ambassadors that Byzantium had a purpose to revolt. Hereupon, these Peloponnesian galleys, having put out into the main sea to the end that they might not be seen as they passed by, and tossed with tempests, part of them, which were the greatest number, and Clearchus with them, got into Delos, and came afterwards to Miletus again; but Clearchus went thence again into the Hellespont by land and had the

command there; and part under the charge of Helixus, a Mega-rean, which were ten sail, went safely through into the Helles-pont and caused Byzantium to revolt. And after this, when they of Samos heard of it, they sent certain galleys into Hellespont to oppose them and to be a guard to the cities thereabouts; and there followed a small fight between them of eight galleys to eight, before Byzantium.

81. In the meantime, they that were in authority at Samos, and especially Thrasybulus, who after the form of government changed was still of the mind to have Alcibiades recalled, at length in an assembly persuaded the soldiers to the same. And when they had decreed for Alcibiades both his return and his security, he went to Tissaphernes and fetched Alcibiades to Samos, accounting it their only means of safety to win Tis-saphernes from the Peloponnesians to themselves. An assembly being called, Alcibiades complained of and lamented the calam-ity of his own exile, and speaking much of the business of the state gave them no small hopes of the future time, hyperbolically magnifying his own power with Tissaphernes to the end that both they which held the oligarchy at home might the more fear him, and so the conspiracies dissolve, and also those at Samos the more honour him and take better heart unto them-selves; and withal, that the enemy might object the same to the utmost to Tissaphernes and fall from their present hopes. Alcibiades therefore, with the greatest boast that could be, affirmed that Tissaphernes had undertaken to him that as long as he had anything left, if he might but trust the Athenians they should never want for maintenance; no, though he should be constrained to make money of his own bed; and that he would fetch the Phoenician fleet, now at Aspendus, not to the Pelo-ponnesians but to the Athenians; and that then only he would rely upon the Athenians when Alcibiades called home should undertake for them.

82. Hearing this and much more, they chose him presently for general together with those that were before, and com-mitted unto them the whole government of their affairs. And now there was not a man that would have sold his present hopes, both of subsisting themselves and being revenged of The Four Hundred, for any good in the world, and were ready even

then, upon those words of his, contemning the enemy there present, to set sail for Peiraeus. But he, though many pressed it, by all means forbade their going against Peiraeus, being to leave their enemies so near; but since they had chosen him general, he was, he said, to go to Tissaphernes first and to dispatch such business with him as concerned the war. And as soon as the assembly brake up, he took his journey accordingly, to the end that he might seem to communicate everything with him, and for that he desired also to be in more honour with him, and to show that he was general and a man capable to do him good or hurt. And it happened to Alcibiades that he awed the Athenians with Tissaphernes and Tissaphernes with the Athenians.

83. When the Peloponnesians that were at Miletus heard that Alcibiades was gone home, whereas they mistrusted Tissaphernes before, now they much more accused him. For it fell out that when at the coming of the Athenians with their fleet before Miletus they refused to give them battle, Tissaphernes became thereby a great deal slacker in his payment; and besides that he was hated by them before this for Alcibiades' sake, the soldiers now, meeting in companies apart, reckoned up one to another the same matters which they had noted before, and some also, men of value and not the common soldier alone, recounted this withal, how they had never had their full stipend; that the allowance was but small, and yet not continually paid; and that unless they either fought or went to some other place where they might have maintenance, their men would abandon the fleet; and that the cause of all this was in Astyochus, who for private lucre gave way to the humour of Tissaphernes.

84. Whilst these were upon this consideration, there happened also a certain tumult about Astyochus. For the mariners of the Syracusians and Thurians, by how much they were a multitude that had greater liberty than the rest, with so much the stouter importunity they demanded their pay. And he not only gave them somewhat an insolent answer but also threatened Dorieus, that amongst the rest spake for the soldiers under himself, and lift up his staff against him. When the soldiers saw that, they took up a cry like seamen indeed, all at once, and were running upon Astyochus to have stricken him. But

foreseeing it, he fled to an altar, and was not stricken, but they were parted again. The Milesians also took in a certain fort in Miletus, built by Tissaphernes, having privily assaulted it, and cast out the garrison that was within it. These things were by the rest of the confederates, and especially by the Syracusians, well approved of; but Lichas liked them not, saying it behoved the Milesians and the rest dwelling within the king's dominion to have obeyed Tissaphernes in all moderate things, and till such time as the war should have been well dispatched to have courted him. And the Milesians, for this and other things of this kind, were offended with Lichas, and afterwards when he died of sickness, would not permit him to be buried in that place where the Lacedaemonians then present would have had him.

85. Whilst they were quarrelling about their business with Astyochus and Tissaphernes, Mindarus cometh in from Lacedaemon to succeed Astyochus in his charge of the fleet; and as soon as he had taken the command upon him, Astyochus departed. But with him Tissaphernes sent a Carian named Gauleites, one that spake both the languages, both to accuse the Milesians about the fort and also to make an apology for himself, knowing that the Milesians went principally to exclaim upon him, and that Hermocrates went with them and would bewray how Tissaphernes undid the business of the Peloponnesians with Alcibiades, and dealt on both hands. For he was continually at enmity with him about the payment of the soldiers' wages; and in the end, when Hermocrates was banished from Syracuse, and other commanders of the Syracusian fleet, namely, Potamis, Myscon, and Demarchus, were arrived at Miletus, Tissaphernes lay more heavy upon him, being an outlaw, than before, and accused him, amongst other things, that he had asked him money, and because he could not have it became his enemy. So Astyochus and Hermocrates and the Milesians went their way to Lacedaemon.

Alcibiades by this time was come back from Tissaphernes to Samos.

86. And those ambassadors of The Four Hundred, which had been sent out before to mollify and to inform those of Samos, came from Delos now whilst Alcibiades was present.

An assembly being called, they were offering to speak. But the
soldiers at first would not hear them, but cried out to have them
put to death for that they had deposed the people; yet afterwards with much ado they were calmed and gave them hearing. They declared that the change had been made for the
preservation of the city, not to destroy it nor to deliver it to
the enemy; for they could have done that before now when
the enemy during their government assaulted it, that every one
of The Five Thousand was to participate of the government
in their turns; and their friends were not, as Chaereas had laid
to their charge, abused, nor had any wrong at all, but remained
every one quietly upon his own. Though they delivered this
and much more, yet the soldiers believed them not, but raged
still and declared their opinions, some in one sort some in another, most agreeing in this to go against Peiraeus. And now
Alcibiades appeared to be the first and principal man in doing
service to the commonwealth. For when the Athenians at Samos
were carried headlong to invade themselves, in which case most
manifestly the enemy had presently possessed himself of Ionia
and Hellespont, [it was thought that] he was the man that
kept them from it. Nor was there any man at that time able
to have held in the multitude but himself. He both made them
to desist from the voyage and rated off from the ambassadors
those that were in their own particular incensed against them.
Whom also he sent away, giving them their answer himself:
That he opposed not the government of The Five Thousand,
but willed them to remove The Four Hundred and to establish
the council that was before of five hundred; that if they had
frugally cut off any expense so that such as were employed
in the wars might be the better maintained, he did much commend them for it. And withal he exhorted them to stand out
and give no ground to their enemies, for that as long as the city
held out, there was great hope for them to compound; but if
either part miscarry once, either this at Samos or the other
at Athens, there would none be left for the enemy to compound
withal.

There chanced to be present also the ambassadors of the
Argives, sent unto the popular faction of the Athenians in
Samos to assist them. These Alcibiades commended and ap-

pointed to be ready when they should be called for and so dismissed them. These Argives came in with those of the Paralus, that had been bestowed formerly in the military galley by The Four Hundred to go about Euboea and to convoy Laespodias, Aristophon, and Melesias, ambassadors from The Four Hundred, to Lacedaemon. These, as they sailed by Argos, seized on the ambassadors and delivered them as principal men in deposing of the people to the Argives, and returned no more to Athens, but came with the galley they then were in to Samos and brought with them these ambassadors from the Argives.

87. The same summer, Tissaphernes, at the time that the Peloponnesians were offended with him most, both for the going home of Alcibiades and divers other things, as now manifestly Atticizing, with purpose, as indeed it seemed, to clear himself to them concerning his accusations, made ready for his journey to Aspendus for the Phoenician fleet, and willed Lichas to go along with him, saying that he would substitute Tamos, his deputy lieutenant over the army, to pay the fleet whilst himself was absent.

This matter is diversly reported, and it is hard to know with what purpose he went to Aspendus and yet brought not the fleet away with him. For it is known that one hundred and forty-seven sail of Phoenicians were come forward as far as Aspendus; but why they came not through, the conjectures are various. Some think it was upon design (as he formerly intended) to wear out the Peloponnesian forces; for which cause also Tamos, who had that charge, made no better but rather worse payment than himself. Others, that having brought the Phoenicians as far as Aspendus, he might dismiss them for money, for he never meant to use their service. Some again said it was because they exclaimed so against it at Lacedaemon, and that it might not be said he abused them, but that he went openly to a fleet really set out.

For my own part, I think it most clear that it was to the end to consume and to balance the Grecians that he brought not those galleys in; consuming them, in that he went thither and delayed the time; and equalizing them, in that bringing them to neither he made neither party the stronger. For if he had had a mind to end the war, it is manifest he might have been sure to have done it. For if he had brought them to the Lacedaemonians, in all reason he had given them the victory, who had a navy already rather equal than inferior to that of their enemies. But that which hurt them most was the pretence he alleged for not bringing the fleet in. For he said they were not so many sail as the king had ordained to be gotten together. But sure he might have ingratiated himself more in this business by dispatching it with less of the king's money than by spending more. But whatsoever was his purpose, Tissaphernes went to Aspendus and was with the Phoenicians; and by his own appointment the Peloponnesians sent Philip, a Lacedaemonian, with him with two galleys as to take charge of the fleet.

88. Alcibiades, when he heard that Tissaphernes was gone to Aspendus, goes after him with thirteen galleys, promising to those at Samos a safe and great benefit, which was that he would either bring those Phoenician galleys to the service of the Athenians, or at least hinder their coming to the Peloponnesians; knowing, as is likely, the mind of Tissaphernes by long acquaintance, that he meant not to bring them on, and desiring, as much as he could, to procure him the ill will of the Peloponnesians for the friendship shown to himself and to the Athenians that he might thereby the better engage him to take their part. So he presently put to sea, holding his course for Phaselis and Caunus upwards.

89. The ambassadors of The Four Hundred being returned from Samos to Athens and having related what they had in charge from Alcibiades, how that he exhorted them to hold out and not give ground to the enemy, and that he had great hopes to reconcile them to the army and to overcome the Peloponnesians, whereas many of the sharers in the oligarchy were formerly discontented and would gladly, if they could have done it safely, have quitted the business, they were now a great deal more confirmed in that mind. And already they had their meetings apart and did cast aspersions on the government, and had for their ringleaders some of the heads of the oligarchicals and such as bare office amongst them, as Theramenes, the son of Agnon, and Aristocrates, the son of Scellius, and others, who though they were partakers with the foremost in the affairs of state, yet feared, as they said, Alcibiades and the army at Samos;

and joined in the sending of ambassadors to Lacedaemon, because they were loth, by singling themselves from the greater number, to hurt the state, not that they dismissed the state into the hands of a very few, but said that The Five Thousand ought in fact to be assigned, and not in voice only, and the government to be reduced to a greater equality. And this was indeed the form pretended in words by The Four Hundred. But the most of them, through private ambition, fell upon that by which an oligarchy made out of a democracy is chiefly overthrown. For at once they claimed every one not to be equal but to be far the chief. Whereas in a democracy, when election is made, because a man is not overcome by his equals, he can better brook it. But the great power of Alcibiades at Samos and the opinion they had that the oligarchy was not like to last was it that most evidently encouraged them; and thereupon they every one contended who should most eminently become the patron of the people.

90. But those of The Four Hundred that were most opposite to such a form of government, and the principal of them, both Phrynichus, who had been general at Samos and was ever since at difference with Alcibiades, and Aristarchus, a man that had been an adversary to the people both in the greatest manner and for the longest time, and Pisander and Antiphon, and others of the greatest power, not only formerly, as soon as they entered into authority and afterwards when the state at Samos revolted to the people, sent ambassadors to Lacedaemon and bestirred themselves for the oligarchy, and built a wall in the place called Eetioneia; but much more afterwards, when their ambassadors were come from Samos and that they saw not only the populars but also some others of their own party, thought trusty before, to be now changed. And to Lacedaemon they sent Antiphon and Phrynichus with ten others with all possible speed, as fearing their adversaries both at home and at Samos, with commission to make a peace with the Lacedaemonians on any tolerable conditions whatsoever or howsoever; and in this time went on with the building of the wall in Eetioneia with greater diligence than before. The scope they had in this wall, as it was given out by Theramenes, [the son of Agnon], was not so much to keep out those of Samos in case they should

attempt by force to enter into Peiraeus as at their pleasure to be able to let in both the galleys and the land forces of the enemies. For this Eetioneia is the pier of the Peiraeus, close unto which is the mouth of the haven. And therefore they built this wall so to another wall that was built before to the continent that a few men lying within it might command the entrance. For the end of each wall was brought to the tower upon the [very] mouth of the haven, as well of the old wall towards the continent as of the new which was built within it to the water. They built also an open ground-gallery, an exceeding great one and close to their new wall within Peiraeus, and were masters of it, and constrained all men as well to bring thither their corn which they had already come in, as to unload there whatsoever should come in afterward, and to take and sell it from thence.

91. These things Theramenes murmured at long before; and when the ambassadors returned from Lacedaemon without compounding for them all in general, he gave out that this wall would endanger the undoing of the city. For at this very instant there happened to be riding on the coast of Laconia forty-two galleys, amongst which were some of Tarentum, some of Locri, some Italians, and some Sicilians, set out from Peloponnesus at the instance of the Euboeans, bound for Euboea and commanded by Hegesandridas, the son of Hegesander, a Spartan. And these Theramenes said were coming not so much towards Euboea as towards those that fortified in Eetioneia, and that if they were not looked to, they would surprise the city. Now some matter might indeed be gathered also from those that were accused, so that it was not a mere slander. For their principal design was to retain the oligarchy with dominion over their confederates; but if they failed of that, yet being masters of the galleys and of the fortification, to have subsisted free themselves; if barred of that, then rather than to be the only men to suffer death under the restored democracy, to let in the enemy; and without either navy or fortification to have let what would have become of the city and to have compounded for the safety of their own persons.

92. Therefore they went diligently on with the fortification, wherein were wickets and entries and backways for the enemy,

and desired to have it finished in time. And though these things were spoken but amongst a few before and in secret, yet when Phrynichus, after his return from his Lacedaemonian ambassage, was by a certain watchman wounded treacherously in the market place when it was full, as he went from the councilhouse, and not far from it fell instantly dead, and the murtherer gone, and that one of his complices, an Argive, taken by The Four Hundred and put to the torture, would confess no man of those named to him nor anything else saving this, that many men used to assemble at the house of the captain of the watch and at other houses; then at length, because this accident bred no alteration, Theramenes and Aristocrates, and as many other either of The Four Hundred or out of that number as were of the same faction proceeded more boldly to assault the government. For now also the fleet, being come about from Laconia and lying upon the coast of Epidaurus, had made incursions upon Aegina. And Theramenes thereupon alleged that it was improbable that those galleys holding their course for Euboea would have put in at Aegina and then have gone back again to lie at Epidaurus, unless they had been sent for by such men as he had ever accused of the same; and that therefore there was no reason any longer to sit still. And in the end, after many seditious and suspicious speeches, they fell upon the state in good earnest. For the soldiers that were in Peiraeus employed in fortifying Eetioneia (amongst whom was also Aristocrates, captain of a band of men, and his band with him) seized on Alexicles, principal commander of the soldiers under The Four Hundred, an eminent man of the other side, and carrying him into a house, kept him in hold. As soon as the news hereof was brought unto The Four Hundred, who chanced at the same time to be sitting in the council-house, they were ready all of them presently to have taken arms, threatening Theramenes and his faction. He to purge himself was ready to go with them and to help to rescue Alexicles, and taking with him one of the commanders who was also of his faction, went down into Peiraeus. To help him went also Aristarchus and certain horsemen of the younger sort. Great and terrible was the tumult. For in the city they thought Peiraeus was already taken and him that was laid in hold slain; and in Peiraeus they expected

every hour the power of the city to come upon them. At last
the ancient men, stopping them that ran up and down the city
to arm themselves, and Thucydides of Pharsalus, the city's host,
being then there, going boldly and close up to every one he
met and crying out unto them not to destroy their country
when the enemy lay so near waiting for an advantage, with
much ado quieted them and held their hands from spilling their
own blood. Theramenes, coming into Peiraeus (for he also had
command over the soldiers), made a shew by his exclaiming of
being angry with them; but Aristarchus and those that were
of the contrary side were extremely angry in good earnest.
Nevertheless the soldiers went on with their business and repented not a jot of what they had done. Then they asked
Theramenes if he thought this fortification were made to any
good end and whether it were not better to have it demolished.
And he answered that if they thought good to demolish it, he
also thought the same. At which word they presently got up,
both the soldiers and also many others of Peiraeus, and fell a
digging down of the wall. Now the provocation that they used
to the multitude was in these words, that whosoever desired
that the sovereignty should be in The Five Thousand instead
of The Four Hundred ought also to set himself to the work
in hand. For notwithstanding all this, they thought fit as yet
to veil the democracy with the name of The Five Thousand
and not to say plainly whosoever will have the sovereignty
in the people, lest The Five Thousand should have been extant
indeed, and so a man by speaking to some or other of them
might do hurt to the business through ignorance. And for this
cause it was that The Four Hundred would neither let The
Five Thousand be extant nor yet let it be known that they were
not. For to make so many participant of the affairs of state they
thought was a direct democracy, but to have it doubtful would
make them afraid of one another.

93. The next day, The Four Hundred, though out of order,
yet met together in the council-house, and the soldiers in
Peiraeus, having enlarged Alexicles whom they had before imprisoned, and quite razed the fortification, came into the theatre
of Bacchus near to Munychia and there sat down with their
arms; and presently, according as they had resolved in an as-

sembly then holden, marched into the city and there sat down again in the temple of Castor and Pollux. To this place came unto them certain men elected by The Four Hundred, and man to man reasoned and persuaded with such as they saw to be of the mildest temper both to be quiet themselves and to restrain the rest, saying that not only The Five Thousand should be made known who they were, but that out of these such should be chosen in turns to be of The Four Hundred as The Five Thousand should think good, and entreating them by all means that they would not in the meantime overthrow the city and force it into the hand of the enemy. Hereupon the whole number of the men of arms, after many reasons alleged to many men, grew calmer and feared most the loss of the whole city. And it was agreed betwixt them that an assembly should be held for making of accord in the temple of Bacchus at a day assigned.

94. When they came to the temple of Bacchus and wanted but a little of a full assembly, came news that Hegesandridas with his forty-two galleys came from Megara along the coast towards Salamis. And now there was not a soldier but thought it the very same thing that Theramenes and his party had before told them, that those galleys were to come to the fortification, and that it was now demolished to good purpose. But Hegesandridas, perhaps upon appointment, hovered upon the coast of Epidaurus and thereabouts; but it is likely that in respect of the sedition of the Athenians he stayed in those parts with hope to take hold of some good advantage. Howsoever it was, the Athenians, as soon as it was told them, ran presently with all the power of the city down to Peiraeus, less esteeming their domestic war than that of the common enemy, which was not now far off but even in the haven. And some went aboard the galleys that were then ready, some launched the rest, and others ran to defend the walls and mouth of the haven.

95. But the Peloponnesian galleys, being now gone by and gotten about the promontory of Sunium, cast anchor between Thoricus and Prasiae and put in afterwards at Oropus. The Athenians with all speed, constrained to make use of tumultuary forces, such as a city in time of sedition might afford, and de-

sirous with all haste to make good their greatest stake (for
Euboea, since they were shut out of Attica, was all they had),
sent a fleet under the command of Timocharis to Eretria. Which
arriving, with those galleys that were in Euboea before, made
up the number of six-and-thirty sail. And they were presently
constrained to hazard battle; for Hegesandridas brought out
his galleys from Oropus when he had first there dined. Now
Oropus is from Eretria about threescore furlongs of sea. Whereupon the Athenians also, as the enemy came towards them, began to embark, supposing that their soldiers had been somewhere near unto the galleys. But it fell out that they were
gone abroad to get their dinner, not in the market (for by set
purpose of the Eretrians, to the end that the enemy might fall
upon the Athenians that embarked slowly before they were
ready and force them to come out and fight, nothing was there
to be sold), but in the utmost houses of the city. There was
besides a sign set up at Eretria to give them notice at Oropus
at what time to set forward. The Athenians, drawn out by this
device and fighting before the haven of Eretria, made resistance
nevertheless for a while; but afterwards they turned their backs
and were chased ashore. Such as fled to the city of the Eretrians,
taking it for their friend, were handled most cruelly and
slaughtered by them of the town; but such as got to the fort
in Eretria, holden by the Athenians, saved themselves; and so
did so many of their galleys as got to Chalcis.

The Peloponnesians, after they had taken twenty-two Athenian galleys with the men, whereof some they slew and some
they took prisoners, erected a trophy; and not long after, having caused all Euboea to revolt save only Oreus, which the
Athenians held with their own forces, they settled the rest of
their business there.

96. When the news of that which had happened in Euboea
was brought to Athens, it put the Athenians into the greatest
astonishment that ever they had been in before. For neither
did their loss in Sicily, though then thought great, nor any
other at any time so much affright them as this. For now when
the army at Samos was in rebellion, when they had no more
galleys nor men to put aboard, when they were in sedition

amongst themselves and in continual expectation of falling together by the ears, then in the neck of all arrived this great calamity, wherein they not only lost their galleys, but also, which was worst of all, Euboea, by which they [had] received more commodity than by Attica. How then could they choose but be dejected? But most of all they were troubled, and that for the nearness, with a fear lest upon this victory the enemy should take courage and come immediately into Peiraeus, now empty of shipping, of which they thought nothing wanting, but that they were not there already. And had they been anything adventurous, they might easily have done it; and then, had they stayed there and besieged them, they had not only increased the sedition but also compelled the fleet to come away from Ionia to the aid of their kindred and of the whole city, though enemies to the oligarchy, and in the meantime gotten the Hellespont, Ionia, the Islands, and all places even to Euboea, and, as one may say, the whole Athenian empire into their power. But the Lacedaemonians, not only in this but in many other things, were most commodious enemies to the Athenians to war withal. For being of most different humours, the one swift, the other slow; the one adventurous, the other timorous; the Lacedaemonians gave them great advantage, especially when their greatness was by sea. This was evident in the Syracusians, who, being in condition like unto them, warred best against them.

97. The Athenians upon this news made ready, notwithstanding, twenty galleys, and called an assembly, one then presently in the place called Pnyx, where they were wont to assemble at other times, in which having deposed The Four Hundred, they decreed the sovereignty to The Five Thousand, of which number were all such to be as were charged with arms; and from that time forward to salariate no man for magistracy, with a penalty on the magistrate receiving the salary to be held for an execrable person. There were also divers other assemblies held afterwards, wherein they elected law-makers, and enacted other things concerning the government. And now first (at least in my time) the Athenians seem to have ordered their state aright; which consisted now of a moderate temper, both

of the few and of the many. And this was the first thing that after so many misfortunes past made the city again to raise her head.

They decreed also the recalling of Alcibiades and those that were in exile with him, and sending to him and to the army at Samos, willed them to fall in hand with their business.

98. In this change Pisander and Alexicles, and such as were with them, and they that had been principal in the oligarchy, immediately withdrew themselves to Deceleia. Only Aristarchus (for it chanced that he had charge of the soldiers) took with him certain archers of the most barbarous and went with all speed to Oenoe. This was a fort of the Athenians in the confines of Boeotia; and (for the loss that the Corinthians had received by the garrison of Oenoe) was by voluntary Corinthians and by some Boeotians by them called in to aid them now besieged. Aristarchus, therefore, having treated with these, deceived those in Oenoe and told them that the city of Athens had compounded with the Lacedaemonians and that they were to render up the place to the Boeotians, for that it was so conditioned in the agreement. Whereupon, believing him as one that had authority over the soldiery and knowing nothing because besieged, upon security for their pass they gave up the fort. So the Boeotians receive Oenoe; and the oligarchy and sedition at Athens cease.

99. About the same time of this summer, when none of those whom Tissaphernes at his going to Aspendus had substituted to pay the Peloponnesian navy at Miletus did it, and seeing neither the Phoenician fleet nor Tissaphernes came to them, and seeing Philip, that was sent along with him, and also another, one Hippocrates, a Spartan, that was lying in Phaselis, had written to Mindarus, the general, that the fleet was not to come at all and in every thing Tissaphernes abused them; seeing also that Pharnabazus had sent for them and was willing, upon the coming to him of their fleet, for his own part also as well as Tissaphernes, to cause the rest of the cities within his own province to revolt from the Athenians; then at length, Mindarus, hoping for benefit by him, with good order and sudden warning that the Athenians at Samos might not be aware of their setting forth, went into the Hellespont with seventy-

three galleys, besides sixteen which the same summer were gone into the Hellespont before and had overrun part of Chersonnesus. But tossed with the wind she was forced to put in at Icarus; and after he had stayed there through ill weather some five or six days, he arrived at Chios.

100. Thrasyllus having been advertised of his departure from Miletus, he also puts to sea from Samos with five-and-fifty sail, hasting to be in the Hellespont before him. But hearing that he was in Chios and conceiving that he would stay there, he appointed spies to lie in Lesbos and in the continent over against it, that the fleet of the enemy might not remove without his knowledge; and he himself, going to Methymna, commanded provision to be made of meal and other necessaries, intending, if they stayed there long, to go from Lesbos and invade them in Chios. Withal, because Eressos was revolted from Lesbos, he purposed to go thither with his fleet; if he could, to take it in. For the most potent of the Methymnaean exiles had gotten into their society about fifty men of arms out of Cume and hired others out of the continent, and with their whole number in all three hundred, having for their leader Anaxarchus, a Theban, chosen in respect of their descent from the Thebans, first assaulted Methymna. But beaten in the attempt by the Athenian garrison that came against them from Mytilene and again in a skirmish without the city driven quite away, they passed by the way of the mountain to Eressos, and caused it to revolt. Thrasyllus therefore intended to go thither with his galleys and to assault it. At his coming he found Thrasybulus there also before him with five galleys from Samos, for he had been advertised of the outlaws coming over; but being too late to prevent them, he went to Eressos and lay before it at anchor. Hither also came two galleys of Methymna that were going home from the Hellespont; so that they were in all threescore and seven sail, out of which they made an army, intending with engines, or any other way they could, to take Eressos by assault.

101. In the meantime, Mindarus and the Peloponnesian fleet that was at Chios, when they had spent two days in victualling their galleys and had received of the Chians three Chian tessaracostes a man, on the third day put speedily off from Chios

and kept far from the shore, that they might not fall amongst the galleys at Eressos. And leaving Lesbos on the left hand, went to the continent side, and putting in at a haven in Craterei, belonging to the territory of Phocaea, and there dining, passed along the territory of Cume, and came to Arginusae in the continent over against Mytilene, where they supped. From thence they put forth late in the night and came to Harmatus, a place in the continent over against Methymna; and after dinner going a great pace by Lectus, Larissa, Hamaxitus, and other the towns in those parts, came before midnight to Rhoeteium; this now is in Hellespont. But some of his galleys put in at Sigeium and other places thereabouts.

102. The Athenians that lay with eighteen galleys at Sestos knew that the Peloponnesians were entering into the Hellespont by the fires, both those which their own watchmen put up and by the many which appeared on the enemies' shore; and therefore the same night in all haste as they were, kept the shore of Chersonnesus towards Elaeus, desiring to get out into the wide sea and to decline the fleet of the enemy, and went out unseen of those sixteen galleys that lay at Abydos, though these had warning before from the fleet of their friends that came on to watch them narrowly that they went not out. But in the morning, being in sight of the fleet with Mindarus and chased by him, they could not all escape, but the most of them got to the continent and into Lemnos; only four of the hindmost were taken near Elaeus, whereof the Peloponnesians took one with the men in her that had run herself aground at the temple of Protesilaus, and two other without the men, and set fire on a fourth, abandoned upon the shore of Imbros.

103. After this they besieged Elaeus the same day with those galleys of Abydos which were with them, and with the rest, being now altogether fourscore and six sail. But seeing it would not yield, they went away to Abydos.

The Athenians, who had been deceived by their spies, and not imagining that the enemy's fleet could have gone by without their knowledge, and attended at leisure the assault of Eressos, when now they knew they were gone, immediately left Eressos and hasted to the defence of Hellespont. By the way they took two galleys of the Peloponnesians that, having ventured into the main more boldly in following the enemy than the rest had done, chanced to light upon the fleet of the Athenians. The next day they came to Elaeus and stayed; and thither from Imbros came unto them those other galleys that had escaped from the enemy. Here they spent five days in preparation for a battle.

104. After this, they fought in this manner: The Athenians went by the shore, ordering their galleys one by one, towards Sestos. The Peloponnesians also, when they saw this, brought out their fleet against them from Abydos.

Being sure to fight, they drew out their fleets in length, the Athenians along the shore of Chersonnesus, beginning at Idacus and reaching as far as Arrhiana, threescore and six galleys; and the Peloponnesians, from Abydos to Dardanum, fourscore and six galleys. In the right wing of the Peloponnesians were the Syracusians; in the other, Mindarus himself and those galleys that were nimblest. Amongst the Athenians, Thrasyllus had the left wing and Thrasybulus the right; and the rest of the commanders, every one the place assigned him.

Now the Peloponnesians laboured to give the first onset and with their left wing to over-reach the right wing of the Athenians and keep them from going out, and to drive those in the middle to the shore which was near. The Athenians, who perceived it, where the enemy went about to cut off their way out, put forth the same way that they did and outwent them; the left wing of the Athenians was also gone forward by this time beyond the point called Cynos-sema. By means whereof that part of the fleet which was in the midst became both weak and divided, especially when theirs was the less fleet; and the sharp and angular figure of the place about Cynos-sema took away the sight of what passed there from those that were on the other side.

105. The Peloponnesians, therefore, charging this middle part, both drave their galleys to the dry land, and being far superior in fight, went out after them and assaulted them upon the shore. And to help them neither was Thrasybulus able, who was in the right wing, for the multitude of the enemies that pressed him; nor Thrasyllus in the left wing, both because he could not see what was done for the promontory of Cynos-sema and be-

cause also he was kept from it by the Syracusians and others, lying upon his hands no fewer in number than themselves. Till at last the Peloponnesians, bold upon their victory, chasing some one galley some another, fell into some disorder in a part of their army. And then those about Thrasybulus, having observed that the opposite galleys sought now no more to go beyond them, turned upon them, and fighting put them presently to flight; and having also cut off from the rest of the fleet such galleys of the Peloponnesians, of that part that had the victory, as were scattered abroad, some they assaulted, but the greatest number they put into affright unfoughten. The Syracusians also, whom those about Thrasyllus had already caused to shrink, when they saw the rest fly fled outright.

106. This defeat being given and the Peloponnesians having for the most part escaped first to the river Pydius and afterwards to Abydos, though the Athenians took but few of their galleys (for the narrowness of the Hellespont afforded to the enemy a short retreat), yet the victory was the most seasonable to them that could be. For having till this day stood in fear of the Peloponnesian navy, both for the loss which they had received by little and little and also for their great loss in Sicily, they now ceased either to accuse themselves or to think highly any longer of the naval power of their enemies. The galleys they took were these: eight of Chios, five of Corinth, of Ambracia two, of Leucas, Laconia, Syracuse, and Pellene, one apiece. Of their own they lost fifteen.

When they had set up a trophy in the promontory of Cynossema and taken up the wrecks and given truce to the enemies to fetch away the bodies of their dead, they presently sent away a galley with a messenger to carry news of the victory to Athens. The Athenians, upon the coming in of this galley hearing of their unexpected good fortune, were encouraged much after their loss in Euboea and after their sedition, and conceived that their estate might yet keep up if they plied the business courageously.

107. The fourth day after this battle, the Athenians that were in Sestos, having hastily prepared their fleet, went to Cyzicus, which was revolted; and espying, as they passed by, the eight galleys come from Byzantium riding under Harpagium and

Priapus, set upon them, and having also overcome those that came to their aid from the land, took them. Then coming to Cyzicus, being an open town, they brought it again into their own power and levied a sum of money amongst them.

The Peloponnesians in the meantime, going from Abydos to Elaeus, recovered as many of their galleys [formerly] taken as remained whole; the rest the Elaeusians [had] burnt. They also sent Hippocrates and Epicles into Euboea to fetch away the fleet that was there.

108. About the same time also returned Alcibiades to Samos with his thirteen galleys from Caunus and Phaselis, reporting that he had diverted the Phoenician fleet from coming to the Peloponnesians and that he had inclined Tissaphernes to the friendship of the Athenians more than he was before. Thence manning out nine galleys more, he exacted a great sum of money of the Hallicarnasseans, and fortified Cos. Being now almost autumn, he returned to Samos.

The Peloponnesians being now in Hellespont, the Antandrians (who are Aeolians) received into the city men of arms from Abydos by land through mount Ida, upon injury that had been done them by Arsaces, a deputy lieutenant of Tissaphernes. This Arsaces, having feigned a certain war, not declared against whom, had formerly called out the chiefest of the Delians (the which in hallowing of Delos by the Athenians were turned out and had planted themselves in Adramyttium) to go with him to this war; and when under colour of amity and confederacy he had drawn them out, he observed a time when they were at dinner, and having hemmed them in with his own soldiers, murdered them with darts. And therefore, for this act's sake fearing lest he might do some unlawful prank against them also, and for that he had otherwise done them injury, they cast his garrison out of their citadel.

109. Tissaphernes, hearing of this, being the act of the Peleponnesians as well as that at Miletus or that at Cnidus (for in those cities his garrisons had also been cast out in the same manner), and conceiving that he was deeply charged to them, and fearing lest they should do him some other hurt, and withal not enduring that Pharnabazus should receive them and with less time and cost speed better against the Athenians than he

had done, resolved to make a journey to them in the Hellespont, both to complain of what was done at Antandros and to clear himself of his accusations the best he could, as well concerning the Phoenician fleet as other matters. And first he put in at Ephesus and offered sacrifices to Diana.

When the winter following this summer shall be ended, the one-and-twentieth year [of this war] shall be complete.

ON THE LIFE AND
HISTORY OF THUCYDIDES

We read of divers men that bear the name of Thucydides. There is
Thucydides a Pharsalian, mentioned in the eighth book of this
history; who was public host of the Athenians in Pharsalus, and
chancing to be at Athens at the time that the government of THE
FOUR HUNDRED began to go down, by his interposition and persuasion kept asunder the factions then arming themselves, that they
fought not in the city to the ruin of the commonwealth. There is
Thucydides the son of Milesias, an Athenian, of the town of Alope,
of whom Plutarch speaketh in the life of Pericles; and the same, in
all probability, that in the first book of this history is said to have
had the charge of forty galleys sent against Samos, about twenty-
four years before the beginning of this war. Another Thucydides
the son of Ariston, an Athenian also, of the town of Acherdus,
was a poet; though of his verses there be nothing extant. But
Thucydides the writer of this history, an Athenian, of the town
of Halimus, was the son of Olorus (or Orolus) and Hegesypele.
His father's name is commonly written Olorus, though in the inscription on his tomb it was Orolus. Howsoever it be written,
it is the same that was borne by divers of the kings of Thrace; and
imposed on him with respect unto his descent from them. So that
though our author (as Cicero saith of him, lib. ii. De Oratore,) had
never written an history, yet had not his name not been extant, in
regard of his honour and nobility. And not only Plutarch, in the
life of Cimon, but also almost all others that have touched this
point, affirm directly that he was descended from the Thracian
kings: adducing this for proof, that he was of the house of
Miltiades, that famous general of the Athenians against the Persians

at Marathon; which they also prove by this, that his tomb was a long time extant amongst the monuments of that family. For near unto the gates of Athens, called Melitides, there was a place named Coela; and in it the monuments called *Cimoniana*, belonging to the family of Miltiades, in which none but such as were of that family might be buried. And amongst those was the monument of Thucydides; with this inscription, THUCYDIDES OROLI HALIMUSIUS. Now Miltiades is confessed by all, to have descended from Olorus king of Thrace; whose daughter another Miltiades, grandfather to this, married and had children by. And Miltiades, that won the memorable victory at Marathon, was heir to goodly possessions and cities in the Chersonnesus of Thrace; over which also he reigned. In Thrace lay also the possessions of Thucydides, and his wealthy mines of gold: as he himself professeth in his fourth book. And although those riches might come to him by a wife (as is also by some affirmed) which he married in Scapte-Hyle, a city of Thrace; yet even by that marriage it appeareth, that his affairs had a relation to that country, and that his nobility was not there unknown. But in what degree of kindred Miltiades and he approached each other, is not anywhere made manifest. Some also have conjectured that he was of the house of the Peisistratides: the ground of whose conjecture hath been only this, that he maketh honourable mention of the government of Peisistratus and his sons, and extenuateth the glory of Harmodius and Aristogeiton; proving that the freeing of the state of Athens from the tyranny of the Peisistratides was falsely ascribed to their fact, (which proceeded from private revenge in a quarrel of love), by which the tyranny ceased not, but grew heavier to the state, till it was at last put down by the Lacedæmonians. But this opinion, as it is not so well-grounded, so neither is it so well received as the former.

Agreeable to his nobility, was his institution in the study of eloquence and philosophy. For in philosophy, he was the scholar (as also was Pericles and Socrates) of Anaxagoras; whose opinions, being of a strain above the apprehension of the vulgar, procured him the estimation of an atheist: which name they bestowed upon all men that thought not as they did of their ridiculous religion, and in the end cost him his life. And Socrates after him for the like causes underwent the like fortune. It is not therefore much to be regarded, if this other disciple of his were by some reputed an atheist too. For though he were none, yet it is not improbable, but by the light of natural reason he might see enough in the religion of these heathen, to make him think it vain and superstitious; which was enough to make him an atheist in the opinion of the people. In some places of his history he noteth the equivocation of the oracles; and yet he confirmeth an assertion of his own, touching the time this war lasted, by the oracle's prediction. He taxeth Nicias for being too punctual in the observation of the ceremonies of their religion, when he overthrew himself and his army, and indeed the whole dominion and liberty of his country, by it. Yet he commendeth him in another place for his worshipping of the gods, and saith in that respect, he least of all men deserved to come to so great a degree of calamity as he did. So that in his writings our author appeareth to be, on the one side not superstitious, on the other side not an atheist.

In rhetoric, he was the disciple of Antiphon; one (by his description in the eighth book of this history) for power of speech almost a miracle, and feared by the people for his eloquence. Insomuch as in his latter days he lived retired, but so as he gave counsel to, and writ orations for other men that resorted to him to that purpose. It was he that contrived the deposing of the people, and the setting up of the government of THE FOUR HUNDRED. For which also he was put to death, when the people again recovered their authority, notwithstanding that he pleaded his own cause the best of any man to that day.

It need not be doubted, but from such a master Thucydides was sufficiently qualified to have become a great demagogue, and of great authority with the people. But it seemeth he had no desire at all to meddle in the government: because in those days it was impossible for any man to give good and profitable counsel for the commonwealth, and not incur the displeasure of the people. For their opinion was such of their own power, and of the facility of achieving whatsoever action they undertook, that such men only swayed the assemblies, and were esteemed wise and good commonwealth's men, as did put them upon the most dangerous and desperate enterprizes. Whereas he that gave them temperate and discreet advice, was thought a coward, or not to understand, or else to malign their power. And no marvel: for much prosperity (to which they had now for many years been accustomed) maketh men in love with themselves; and it is hard for any man to love that counsel which maketh him love himself the less. And it holdeth much more in a multitude, than in one man. For a man that reasoneth with himself, will not be ashamed to admit of timorous suggestions in his business, that he may the stronglier provide; but in public deliberations before a multitude, fear (which for the most part adviseth well, though it execute not so) seldom or never sheweth itself or is admitted. By this means it came to pass amongst the Athenians, who thought they were able to do anything, that wicked men and flatterers drave them headlong into those actions that were to ruin them; and the good men either durst not oppose, or if they did, undid themselves. Thucydides therefore, that he might not be either of them that committed or of them that suffered the evil, forbore to come into the assemblies; and propounded to himself a private life, as far as the eminency of so wealthy a person, and the writing of the history he had undertaken, would permit.

For his opinion touching the government of the state, it is manifest that he least of all liked the democracy. And upon divers occasions he noteth the emulation and contention of the demagogues for reputation and glory of wit; with their crossing of each other's counsels, to the damage of the public; the inconsistency of resolutions, caused by the diversity of ends and power of rhetoric in the orators; and the desperate actions undertaken upon the flattering advice of such as desired to attain, or to hold what they had attained, of authority and sway amongst the common people. Nor doth it appear that he magnifieth anywhere the authority of *the few:* amongst whom, he saith, every one desireth to be the chief; and they that are undervalued, bear it with less patience than in a democracy; whereupon sedition followeth, and dissolution of the government. He praiseth the government of Athens, when it was mixed of *the few* and *the many;* but more he commendeth it, both when Peisistratus reigned, (saving that it was an usurped power), and when in the beginning of this war it was democratical in name, but in effect monarchical under Pericles. So that it seemeth, that as he was of regal descent, so he best approved of the regal government. It is therefore no marvel, if he meddled as little as he could in the business of the commonwealth; but gave himself rather to the observation and recording of what was done by those that had the managing thereof. Which also he was no less prompt, diligent, and faithful by the disposition of his mind, than by his fortune, dignity, and wisdom able, to accomplish. How he was disposed to a work of this nature, may be understood by this: that when being a young man he heard Herodotus the historiographer reciting his history in public, (for such was the fashion both of that, and many ages after), he felt so great a sting of emulation, that it drew tears from him: insomuch as Herodotus himself took notice how violently his mind was set on letters, and told his father Olorus. When the Peloponnesian war began to break out, he conjectured truly that it would prove an argument worthy of his labour: and no sooner it began, than he began his history; pursuing the same not in that perfect manner in which we see it now, but by way of commentary or plain register of the actions and passages thereof, as from time to time they fell out and came to his knowledge. But such a commentary it was, as might perhaps deserve to be preferred before a history written by another. For it is very probable that the eighth book is left the same as it was when he first writ it: neither beautified with orations, nor so well cemented at the transitions, as the former seven books are. And though he began to write as soon as ever the war was on foot; yet began he not to perfect and polish his history, till after he was banished.

For notwithstanding his retired life upon the coast of Thrace, where his own possessions lay, he could not avoid a service to the state which proved to him afterwards very unfortunate. For whilst he resided in the isle Thasos, it fell out that Brasidas, the Lacedæmonian besieged Amphipolis; a city belonging to the Athenians, on the confines of Thrace and Macedonia, distant from Thasos about half a day's sail. To relieve which, the captain thereof for the Athenians sent to Thucydides, to levy a power and make haste unto him: for Thucydides was one of the Strategi, that is, had authority to raise forces in those parts for the service of the commonwealth. And he did accordingly; but he came thither one night too late, and found the city already yielded up. And for this he was afterwards banished; as if he had let slip his time through negligence, or purposely put it off upon fear of the enemy. Nevertheless he put himself into the city of Eion, and preserved it to the Athenians with the repulse of Brasidas; which came down from Amphipolis the next morning, and assaulted it. The author of his banishment is supposed to have been Cleon; a most violent sycophant in those times, and thereby also a most acceptable speaker amongst the people. For where affairs succeed amiss, though there want neither providence nor courage in the conduction; yet with those that judge only upon events, the way to calumny is always open and envy, in the likeness of zeal to the public good, easily findeth credit for an accusation.

After his banishment he lived in Scapte-Hyle, a city of Thrace before mentioned, as Plutarch writeth; but yet so, as he went abroad, and was present at the actions of the rest of the war; as appeareth by his own words in his fifth book, where he saith, that he was present at the actions of both parts, and no less at those of the Peloponnesians, by reason of his exile, than those of the Athenians. During this time also he perfected his history, so far as is now to be seen; nor doth it appear that after his exile he ever again enjoyed his country. It is not clear in any author, where, or when, or in what year of his own age he died. Most agree that he died in banishment: yet there be that have written, that after the defeat in Sicily the Athenians decreed a general revocation of all banished persons, except those of the family of Peisistratus; and that he then returned, and was afterwards put to death at Athens. But this is very unlikely to be true, unless by *after* the defeat in Sicily, be meant *so long after*, that it was also after the end of the Peloponnesian war; because Thucydides himself maketh no mention of such return, though he outlived the whole war, as is manifest by his words in the fifth book. For he saith he lived in banishment twenty years after his charge at Amphipolis; which happened in the eighth year of this war: which, in the whole, lasted but twenty-seven years complete. And in another place he maketh mention of the razing of the long walls between Peiræus and the city; which was the last stroke of this war. They that say he died at Athens, take their conjecture from his monument which was there. But this is not a sufficient argument; for he might be buried there secretly, (as some have written he was), though he died abroad: or his monument might be there, and (as others have affirmed) he not buried in it. In this variety of conjecture, there is nothing more probable than that which is written by Pausanias, where he describeth the monuments of the Athenian city; and saith thus: "The worthy act of Œnobius in the behalf of Thucydides, is not without honour": meaning that he had a statue. "For Œnobius obtained to have a decree passed for his return; who returning was slain by treachery; and his sepulchre is near the gates called Melitides." He died, as saith Marcellinus, after the seven and fiftieth year of his age. And if it be true that is written by A. Gellius, of the ages of Hellanicus, Herodotus, and Thucydides, then died he not before the sixty-eighth year. For if he were forty when the war began, and lived (as he did certainly) to see it ended, he might be more when he died, but not less than sixty-eight years of age. What children he left, is not manifest. Plato in Menone, maketh mention of Milesias and Stephanus, sons of a Thucydides of a very noble family; but it is clear they were of Thucydides the rival of Pericles, both by the name Milesias, and because this Thucydides also was of the family of Miltiades, as Plutarch testifieth in the life of Cimon. That he had a son, is affirmed by Marcellinus out of the authority of Polemon; but of his name there is no mention, save that a learned man readeth there in the place of θοε . . . . (which is in the imperfect copy), Timotheus. Thus much of the person of Thucydides.

Now for his writings, two things are to be considered in them: *truth* and *elocution*. For in *truth* consisteth the *soul*, and in *elocution* the *body* of history. The latter without the former, is but a picture of history; and the former without the latter, unapt to instruct. But let us see how our author hath acquitted himself in both. For the faith of this history, I shall have the less to say: in respect that no man hath ever yet called it into question. Nor indeed could any man justly doubt of the truth of that writer, in whom they had nothing at all to suspect of those things that could have caused him either voluntarily to lie, or ignorantly to deliver an untruth. He overtasked not himself by undertaking an history of things done long before his time, and of which he was not able to inform himself. He was a man that had as much means, in regard both of his dignity and wealth, to find the truth of what he relateth, as was needful for a man to have. He used as much diligence in search of the truth, (noting every thing whilst it was fresh in memory, and laying out his wealth upon intelligence), as was possible for a man to use. He affected least of any man the acclamations of popular auditories, and wrote not his history to win present applause, as was the use of that age: but for a monument to instruct the ages to come; which he professeth himself, and entitleth his book ΚΤΗΜΑ ΕΣ ΑΕΙ, *a possession for everlasting.* He was far from the necessity of servile writers, either to fear or flatter. And whereas he may peradventure be thought to have been malevolent towards his country, because they deserved to have him so; yet hath he not written any thing that discovereth such passion. Nor is there any thing written of them that tendeth to their dishonour as Athenians, but only as *people;* and that by the necessity of the narration, not by any sought digression. So that no word of his, but their own actions do sometimes reproach them. In sum, if the truth of a history did ever appear by the manner of relating, it doth so in this history: so coherent, perspicuous and persuasive is the whole narration, and every part thereof.

In the *elocution* also, two things are considerable: *disposition* or *method*, and *style.* Of the *disposition* here used by Thucydides, it will be sufficient in this place briefly to observe only this: that in his first book, first he hath, by way of exordium, derived the state of Greece from the cradle to the vigorous stature it then was at when he began to write: and next, declared the causes, both real and pretended, of the war he was to write of. In the rest, in which he handleth the war itself, he followeth distinctly and purely the order of time throughout; relating that came to pass from year to year, and subdividing each year into a summer and winter. The grounds and motives of every action he setteth down before the action itself, either narratively, or else contriveth them into the form of *deliberative orations* in the persons of such as from time to time bare sway in the commonwealth. After the actions, when there is just occasion, he giveth his judgment of them; shewing by what means the success came either to be furthered or hindered. Digressions for instruction's cause, and other such open conveyances of precepts, (which is the philosopher's part), he never useth; as having so clearly set before men's eyes the ways and events of good and evil counsels, that the narration itself doth secretly instruct the reader, and more effectually than can possibly be done by precept.

For his *style*, I refer it to the judgment of divers ancient and competent judges. Plutarch in his book, *De gloria Atheniensium*, saith of him thus: "Thucydides aimeth always at this; to make his auditor a spectator, and to cast his reader into the same passions that they were in that were beholders. The manner how Demosthenes arranged the Athenians on the rugged shore before Pylus; how Brasidas urged the steersman to run his galley aground; how he went to the ladder or place in the galley for descent; how he was hurt, and swooned, and fell down on the ledges of the galley; how the Spartans fought after the manner of a land-fight upon the sea, and the Athenians of a sea-fight upon land: again, in the Sicilian war, how a battle was fought by sea and land with equal fortune: these things, I say, are so described and so evidently set before our eyes, that the mind of the reader is no less affected therewith than if he had been present in the actions." There is for his perspicuity. Cicero in his book entitled *Orator*, speaking of the affection of divers Greek rhetoricians, saith thus: "And therefore Herodotus and Thucydides are the more admirable. For though they lived in the same age with those I have before named," (meaning Thrasymachus, Gorgias, and Theodorus), "yet were they far from this kind of delicacy, or rather indeed foolery. For the one without rub, gently glideth like a still river; and the other" (meaning Thucydides) "runs stronglier, and in matter of war, as it were, bloweth a trumpet of war. And in these two (as saith Theophrastus) history hath roused herself, and adventured to speak, but more copiously, and with more ornament than in those that were before them." This commends the gravity and the dignity of his language. Again in his second book, *De Oratore*, thus: "Thucydides, in the art of speaking, hath in my opinion far exceeded them all. For he is so full of matter, that the number of his sentences doth almost reach to the number of his words; and in his words he is so apt and so close, that it is hard to say whether his words do more illustrate his sentences, or his sentences his words." There is for the pithiness and strength of his style. Lastly, for the purity and propriety, I cite Dionysius Halicarnassius: whose testimony is the stronger in this point, because he was a Greek rhetorician for his faculty, and for his affection, one that would no further commend him than of necessity he must. His words are these: "There is one virtue in eloquence, the chiefest of all the rest, and without which there is no other goodness in speech. What is that? That the language be pure, and retain the propriety of the Greek tongue. This they both observe diligently. For Herodotus is the best rule of the Ionic, and Thucydides of the Attic dialect." These testimonies are not needful to him that hath read the history itself; nor at all, but that this same Dionysius hath taken so much pains, and applied so much of his faculty in rhetoric, to the extenuating of the worth thereof. Moreover, I have thought it necessary to take out the principal objections he maketh against him; and without many words of mine own to leave them to the consideration of the reader. And first, Dionysius saith thus: "The principal and most necessary office of any man that intendeth to write a history, is to choose a noble argument, and grateful to such as shall read it. And this Herodotus, in my opinion, hath done better than Thucydides. For Herodotus hath written the joint history both of the Greeks and barbarians, to save from oblivion, &c. But Thucydides writeth one only war, and that neither honourable nor fortunate; which principally were to be wished never to have been; and next, never to have been remembered nor known to posterity. And that he took an evil argument in hand, he maketh it manifest in his proeme, saying: *that many cities were in that war made desolate and utterly destroyed, partly by barbarians, partly by the Greeks themselves: so many banishments, and so much slaughter of men, as never was the like before,* &c.: so that the hearers will abhor it at the first propounding. Now by how much it is better to write of the wonderful acts both of the barbarians and Grecians, than of the pitiful and horrible calamities of the Grecians; so much wiser is Herodotus in the choice of his argument than Thucydides."

Now let any man consider whether it be not more reasonable to say: That the principal and most necessary office of him that will write a history, is to take such an argument as is both within his power well to handle, and profitable to posterity that shall read it, which Thucydides, in the opinion of all men, hath done better than Herodotus: for Herodotus undertook to write of those things, of which it was impossible for him to know the truth; and which delight more the ear with fabulous narrations, than satisfy the mind with truth: but Thucydides writeth one war; which, how it was carried from the beginning to the end, he was able certainly to inform himself: and by propounding in his proeme the miseries that happened in the same, he sheweth that it was a great war, and worthy to be known; and not to be concealed from posterity, for the calamities that then fell upon the Grecians; but the rather to be truly delivered unto them, for that men profit more by looking on adverse events, than on prosperity: therefore by how much men's miseries do better instruct, than their good success; by so much was Thucydides more happy in taking his argument, than Herodotus was wise in choosing his.

Dionysius again saith thus: "The next office of him that will write a history, is to know where to begin, and where to end. And in this point Herodotus seemeth to be far more discreet than Thucydides. For in the first place he layeth down the cause for which the barbarians began to injure the Grecians; and going on, maketh an end at the punishment and the revenge taken on the barbarians. But Thucydides begins at the good estate of the Grecians; which, being a Grecian and an Athenian, he ought not to have done: nor ought he, being of that dignity amongst the Athenians, so evidently to have laid the fault of the war upon his own city, when there were other occasions enough to which he might have imputed it. Nor ought he to have begun with the business of the Corcyræans, but at the more noble acts of his country, which they did immediately after the Persian war: which afterward in convenient place he mentioneth, but it is but cursorily, and not as he ought. And when he had declared those with much affection, as a lover of his country, then he should have brought in, how that the Lacedæmonians, through envy and fear, but pretending other causes, began the war: and so have descended to the Corcyræan business, and the decree against the Megareans, or whatsoever else he had to put in. Then in the ending of his history, there be many errors committed. For though he profess he was present in the whole war, and that he would write it all: yet he ends with the naval battle at Cynos-sema, which was fought in the twenty-first year of the war. Whereas it had been better to have gone through with it, and ended his history with that admirable and grateful return of the banished Athenians from Phile; at which time the city recovered her liberty."

To this I say, that it was the duty of him that had undertaken to write the history of the Peloponnesian war, to begin his narration no further off than at the causes of the same, whether the Grecians were then in good or in evil estate. And if the injury, upon which the war arose, proceeded from the Athenians; then the writer, though an Athenian and honoured in his country, ought to declare the same; and not to seek nor take, though at hand, any other occasion to transfer the fault. And that the acts done before the time comprehended in the war he writ of, ought to have been touched but cursorily, and no more than may serve for the en-lightening of the history to follow, how noble soever those acts have been. Which when he had thus touched, without affection to either side, and not as a lover of his country but of truth; then to have proceeded to the rest with the like indifferency. And to have made an end of writing, where the war ended, which he undertook to write; not producing his history beyond that period, though that which followed were never so admirable and acceptable. All this Thucydides hath observed.

These two criminations I have therefore set down at large, translated almost verbatim, that the judgment of Dionysius Halicarnassius may the better appear concerning the main and principal virtues of a history. I think there was never written so much absurdity in so few lines. He is contrary to the opinion of all men that ever spake of this subject besides himself, and to common sense. For he makes the scope of history, not profit by writing truth, but delight of the hearer, as if it were a song. And the argument of history, he would not by any means have to contain the calamities and misery of his country; these he could have buried in silence: but only their glorious and splendid actions. Amongst the virtues of an historiographer, he reckons affection to his country; study to please the hearer; to write of more than his argument leads him to; and to conceal all actions that were not to the honour of his country. Most manifest vices. He was a rhetorician; and it seemeth he would have nothing written, but that which was most capable of rhetorical ornament. Yet Lucian, a rhetorician also, in a treatise entitled, *How a history ought to be written*, saith thus: "that a writer of history ought, in his writings, to be a foreigner, without country, living under his own law only, subject to no king, nor caring what any man will like or dislike, but laying out the matter as it is."

The third fault he finds is this: that the method of his history is governed by the time, rather than the periods of several actions: for he declares in order what came to pass each summer and winter, and is thereby forced sometimes to leave the narration of a siege, or sedition, or a war, or other action in the middest, and enter into a relation of somewhat else done at the same time, in another place, and to come to the former again when the time requires it. This, saith he, causes confusion in the mind of his hearer, so that he cannot comprehend distinctly the several parts of the history.

Dionysius aimeth still at the delight of the *present* hearer; though Thucydides himself profess that his scope is not that, but to leave his work for a *perpetual possession for posterity:* and then have men leisure enough to comprehend him thoroughly. But indeed, whosoever shall read him once attentively, shall more distinctly conceive of every action this way than the other. And the method is more natural; forasmuch as his purpose being to write of one Peloponnesian war, this way he has incorporated all the parts thereof into one body; so that there is unity in the whole, and the several narrations are conceived only as parts of that. Whereas the other way, he had sewed together many little histories, and left the Peloponnesian war, which he took for his subject, in a manner unwritten: for neither any part nor the whole could justly have carried such a title.

Fourthly, he accuseth him for the method of his first book: in that he deriveth Greece from the infancy thereof to his own time: and in that he setteth down the narration of the quarrels about Corcyra and Potidæa, before he entreateth of the true cause of the war; which was the greatness of the Athenian dominion, feared and envied by the Lacedæmonians.

For answer to this, I say thus. For the mentioning of the ancient state of Greece, he doth it briefly, insisting no longer upon it than is necessary for the well understanding of the following history. For without some general notions of these first times, many places of the history are the less easy to be understood; as depending upon the knowledge of the original of several cities and customs, which could not be at all inserted into the history itself, but must be either supposed to be foreknown by the reader, or else be delivered to him in the beginning as a necessary preface. And for his putting first the narration of the public and avowed cause of this war, and after that the true and inward motive of the same; the reprehension is absurd. For it is plain, that a cause of war divulged and avowed, how slight soever it be, comes within the task of the historiographer, no less than the war itself. For without a pretext, no war follows. This pretext is always an injury received, or pretended to be received. Whereas the inward motive to hostility is but conjectural; and not of that evidence, that a historiographer should be always bound to take notice of it: as envy to the greatness of another state, or fear of an injury to come. Now let any man judge, whether a good writer of history ought to handle, as the principal cause of war, proclaimed injury or concealed envy. In a word, the image of the method used by Thucydides in this point, is this: "The quarrel about Corcyra passed on this manner; and the quarrel about Potidæa on this manner": relating both at large: "and in both the Athenians were accused to have done the injury. Nevertheless, the Lacedæmonians had not upon this injury entered into a war against them, but that they envied the greatness of their power, and feared the consequence of their ambition." I think a more clear and natural order cannot possibly be devised.

Again he says, that he maketh a funeral oration (which was solemnly done on all occasions through the war) for fifteen horsemen only, that were slain at the brooks called Rheiti: and that for this reason only, that he might make it in the person of Pericles, who was then living, but before another the like occasion happened was dead.

The manner of the Athenians was, that they that were slain the first in any war, should have a solemn funeral in the suburbs of the city. During this war, they had many occasions to put this custom in practice. Seeing therefore it was fit to have that custom and the form of it known, and that once for all, the manner being ever the same; it was the fittest to relate it on the first occasion, what number soever they were that were then buried: which nevertheless is not likely to have been so few as Dionysius saith. For the funeral was not celebrated till the winter after they were slain: so that many more were slain before this solemnity, and may all be accounted amongst the first. And that Pericles performed the office of making their funeral oration, there is no reason alledged by him why it should be doubted.

Another fault he finds, is this: that he introduceth the Athenian generals, in a dialogue with the inhabitants of the Isle of Melos, pretending openly for the cause of their invasion of that isle, the power and will of the state of Athens; and rejecting utterly to enter into any disputation with them concerning the equity of their cause, which, he saith, was contrary to the dignity of the state.

To this may be answered, that the proceeding of these generals was not unlike to divers other actions, that the people of Athens openly took upon them: and therefore it is very likely they were allowed so to proceed. Howsoever, if the Athenian people gave in charge to these their captains, to take in the island by all means whatsoever, without power to report back unto them first the equity of the islanders' cause; as is most likely to be true; I see then no reason the generals had to enter into disputation with them, whether they should perform their charge or not, but only whether they should do it by fair or foul means; which is the point treated of in this dialogue. Other cavils he hath touching the matter and order of this history, but not needful to be answered.

Then for his phrase, he carpeth at it in infinite places, both for obscure and licentious. He that will see the particular places he reprehendeth, let him read Dionysius himself, if he will: for the matter is too tedious for this place. It is true, that there be some sentences in him somewhat long: not obscure to one that is attentive: and besides that, they are but few. Yet is this the most important fault he findeth. For the rest, the obscurity that is, proceedeth from the profoundness of the sentences; containing contemplations of those human passions, which either dissembled or not commonly discoursed of, do yet carry the greatest sway with men in their public conversation. If then one cannot penetrate into them without much meditation, we are not to expect a man should understand them at the first speaking. Marcellinus saith, he was obscure on purpose; that the common people might not understand him. And not unlikely: for a wise man should so write, (though in words understood by all men), that wise men only should be able to commend him. But this obscurity is not to be in the narrations of things done, nor in the descriptions of places or of battles, in all which Thucydides is most perspicuous: as Plutarch in the words before cited hath testified of him. But in the characters of men's humours and manners, and applying them to affairs of consequence: it is impossible not to be obscure to ordinary capacities, in what words soever a man deliver his mind. If therefore Thucydides in his orations, or in the description of a sedition, or other thing of that kind, be not easily understood; it is of those only that cannot penetrate into the nature of such things, and proceedeth not from any intricacy of expression. Dionysius further findeth fault with his using to set word against word: which the rhetoricians call *antitheta*. Which, as it is in some kind of speech a very great vice, so is it not improper in characters: and of comparative discourses, it is almost the only style.

And whereas he further taxeth him for licentiousness in turning nouns into verbs, and verbs into nouns, and altering of genders, cases, and numbers; as he doth sometimes for the more efficacy of his style, and without solœcism; I leave him to the answer of Marcellinus: who says, "That Dionysius findeth fault with this, as being ignorant" (yet he was a professed rhetorician) "that this was the most excellent and perfect kind of speaking."

Some man may peradventure desire to know, what motive Dionysius might have to extenuate the worth of him, whom he himself acknowledgeth to have been esteemed by all men for the best by far of all historians that ever wrote, and to have been taken by all the ancient orators and philosophers for the measure and rule of writing history. What motive he had to it, I know not: but what glory he might expect by it, is easily known. For having first preferred Herodotus, his countryman, a Halicarnassian, before Thucydides, who was accounted the best; and then conceiving that his own history might perhaps be thought not inferior to that of Herodotus: by this computation he saw the honour of the best historiographer falling on himself. Wherein, in the opinion of all men, he hath misreckoned. And thus much for the objections of Denis of Halicarnasse.

It is written of Demosthenes, the famous orator, that he wrote over the history of Thucydides with his own hand eight times. So much was this work esteemed, even for the eloquence. But yet was this his eloquence not at all fit for the bar; but proper for history, and rather to be read than heard. For words that pass away (as in public orations they must) without pause, ought to be understood with ease, and are lost else: though words that remain in writing for the reader to meditate on, ought rather to be pithy and full. Cicero therefore doth justly set him apart from the rank of pleaders; but withal, he continually giveth him his due for history, (lib. ii. De Oratore): "What great rhetorician ever borrowed any thing of Thucydides? Yet all men praise him, I confess it, as a wise, severe, grave relator of things done: not for a pleader of causes at the bar, but a reporter of war in history. So that he was never reckoned an orator: nor if he had never written a history, had his name therefore not been extant, being a man of honour and nobility. Yet none of them imitate the gravity of his words and sentences; but when they have uttered a kind of lame and disjointed stuff, they presently think themselves brothers of Thucydides." Again, in his book *De Optimo Oratore*, he saith thus: "But here will stand up Thucydides: for his eloquence is by some admired; and justly. But this is nothing to the orator we seek: for it is one thing to unfold a matter by way of narration; another thing to accuse a man, or clear him by arguments. And in narrations, one thing to stay the hearer, another to stir him." Lucian, in his book entitled *How a history ought to be written*, doth continually exemplify the virtues which he requires in an historiographer by Thucydides. And if a man consider well that whole discourse of his, he shall plainly perceive that the image of this present history, preconceived in Lucian's mind, suggested unto him all the precepts he there delivereth. Lastly, hear the most true and proper commendation of him from Justus Lipsius, in his notes to his book *De Doctrina Civili* in these words: "Thucydides, who hath written not many nor very great matters, hath perhaps yet won the garland from all that have written of matters both many and great. Everywhere for elocution grave; short, and thick with sense; sound in his judgments; everywhere secretly instructing and directing a man's life and actions. In his orations and excursions, almost divine. Whom the oftener you read, the more you shall carry away; yet never be dismissed without appetite. Next to him is Polybius, &c."

And thus much concerning the life and history of Thucydides.

INDEX